Frommer's
San Diego 2004

Sea lions are among the aquatic animals competing for attention at SeaWorld. See chapter 7. © James Lemass/Folio, Inc.

Koalas are among the most famous residents of the San Diego Zoo. See chapter 7.
© Kelly/Mooney Photography.

The Wild Animal Park's "Heart of Africa" offers the opportunity to see cheetahs, giraffes, and other exotic animals up close rather than behind bars. See chapter 7.
© San Diego Wild Animal Park.

The cliffs at Point Loma are a great place to watch the sunset. For more unforgettable San Diego experiences, see chapter 1. © Richard Cummins/The Viesti Collection.

The 18th-century Mission Basilica San Diego de Alcala was the first in the chain of 21 missions established by Spanish missionary Junípero Serra. See chapter 7. *Photo above © David Olsen/Getty Images; photo below © Robert Landau Photography.*

The Old Town section of San Diego is a reminder of the 19th-century days when the city was a Mexican outpost. See the walking tour in chapter 8. © Kelly/Mooney Photography.

Seaport Village is a waterfront shopping and dining complex designed to look like a small Cape Cod community. See chapter 9. © James Lemass/Folio, Inc.

The bullfights of Tijuana and the cantinas found in every town throughout Baja California are two reasons to explore south of the border. See chapter 11. *Photos above and below © Nik Wheeler Photography.*

After the spring rains, thousands of wildflowers burst into bloom in Anza-Borrego Desert State Park, 90 miles northeast of San Diego. See chapter 11. © Christopher Talbot Frank Photography.

Frommer's

San Diego

2004

by David Swanson

Here's what the critics say about Frommer's:

"Amazingly easy to use. Very portable, very complete."
—*Booklist*

"Detailed, accurate, and easy-to-read information for all price ranges."
—*Glamour Magazine*

"Hotel information is close to encyclopedic."
—*Des Moines Sunday Register*

"Frommer's Guides have a way of giving you a real feel for a place."
—*Knight Ridder Newspapers*

WILEY

Wiley Publishing, Inc.

Published by:

Wiley Publishing, Inc.

111 River St.
Hoboken, NJ 07030

ISBN 0-7645-3870-5
ISSN 1047-787X

Editor: Myka Carroll
Production Editor: Donna Wright
Cartographer: John Decamillis
Photo Editor: Richard Fox
Production by Wiley Indianapolis Composition Services

Front cover photo: Balboa Park
Back cover photo: The Embarcadero marina

For information on our other products and services or to obtain technical support, please contact our Customer Care Department within the U.S. at 800-762-2974, outside the U.S. at 317-572-3993 or fax 317-572-4002.

Wiley also publishes its books in a variety of electronic formats. Some content that appears in print may not be available in electronic formats.

Manufactured in the United States of America

5 4 3 2 1

Contents

List of Maps vi

What's New in San Diego 1

1 The Best of San Diego 3

1 Frommer's Favorite San Diego
Experiences 3
2 Best Hotel Bets 6

The Best of San Diego Online . . .7
3 Best Dining Bets 8

2 Planning Your Trip to San Diego 10

1 Visitor Information 10
2 Money 10
What Things Cost in
San Diego 12
3 When to Go 12
San Diego Calendar
of Events 13
Packing for Your Trip 18
4 Travel Insurance 19
5 Health & Safety 19
6 Specialized Travel Resources 20
7 Planning Your Trip Online 25

Frommers.com: The Complete
Travel Resource 26
8 The 21st-Century Traveler 26
Your Link to Home:
Internet Cafes 27
Online Traveler's Toolbox 29
9 Getting There 29
10 Package Deals for the
Independent Traveler 32
11 Escorted Tours 33
12 Recommended Reading 34

3 For International Visitors 36

1 Preparing for Your Trip 36
2 Getting to the United States . . .42
3 Getting Around the
United States 42

Fast Facts: For the
International Traveler 43

4 Getting to Know San Diego 48

1 Orientation 49
The Neighborhoods in Brief 54
Off the Beaten Path:
Golden Hill 55

2 Getting Around 57
Fast Facts: San Diego 62

5 Where to Stay   65

1 Downtown 67   **5** La Jolla 85

2 Hillcrest/Uptown 74   **6** Coronado 92

3 Old Town & Mission Valley 77   *A Century of Intrigue: Scenes*
                                                    from the Hotel del Coronado . . .94
   Family-Friendly
   Accommodations 80   **7** Near the Airport 97

4 Mission Bay & the Beaches 80

6 Where to Dine   98

1 Restaurants by Cuisine 99   *Baja Fish Tacos* 116

2 Downtown & Little Italy 102   **6** La Jolla 120

3 Hillcrest & Uptown 107   *To See . . . Perchance to Eat* . . .125

   Wood-Fired Pizza 110   **7** Coronado 126

4 Old Town & Mission Valley . . .112   *Picnic Fare* 128

   Family-Friendly Restaurants . . .115   **8** Off the Beaten Path 129

5 Mission Bay & the Beaches . . .115

7 What to See & Do   130

   Suggested Itineraries 130   **4** More Attractions 151

1 The Three Major   **5** Free of Charge &
   Animal Parks 132   Full of Fun 161

   Panda-monium 135   **6** Especially for Kids 163

2 San Diego's Beaches 138   **7** Special-Interest Sightseeing . . .165

   Beach Snack Staples: Quick   **8** Organized Tours 167
   (& Cheap) Taco Stands 140
                                                  9 Outdoor Pursuits 170
3 Attractions in Balboa Park 144
                                                  10 Spectator Sports 181
   Balboa Park Guided Tours 149

8 City Strolls   184

   Walking Tour 1:   *Walking Tour 3:*
   The Gaslamp Quarter 184   *Old Town* 193

   Walking Tour 2:   *Walking Tour 4:*
   The Embarcadero 190   *Balboa Park* 197

9 Shopping 203

1 The Shopping Scene 203
2 The Top Shopping
Neighborhoods 203
3 Shopping A to Z 211

10 San Diego After Dark 216

1 The Performing Arts 217
2 The Club & Music Scene 219
3 The Bar & Coffeehouse
Scene 222
Late-Night Bites 224
4 Gay & Lesbian Nightlife 225
5 More Entertainment 226
Running with the Grunion 227
6 Only in San Diego 228

11 Side Trips from San Diego 229

1 North County Beach Towns:
Spots to Surf & Sun 229
2 North County Inland: From
Rancho Santa Fe to
Palomar Mountain 243
Touring Temecula's Wineries . . .246
3 The Disneyland Resort &
Knott's Berry Farm 247
*The Art of the
(Package) Deal* 251
4 Julian: Apple Pies & More 262
5 Anza-Borrego Desert
State Park 268
6 Tijuana: Going South of
the Border 272
Exploring Beyond Tijuana 280

Appendix: San Diego in Depth 285

1 The Arrival of Spanish Mission
"Style" 285
Dateline 285
2 The Missions Give
Way to Gold 287
3 Location, Location, Location . . .288
4 The Navy Builds a Home 289
5 An Identity Beyond the Navy &
Beaches 290

Index 292

General Index 292
Accommodations Index 301
Restaurant Index 302

List of Maps

San Diego Area at a Glance   5

San Diego Neighborhoods   52

Downtown San Diego
  Accommodations   69

Hillcrest/Uptown
  Accommodations   75

Accommodations in
  Old Town & Mission Valley   79

Accommodations in
  Mission Bay & the Beaches   81

La Jolla Accommodations   87

Coronado Accommodations   93

Downtown San Diego Dining   103

Hillcrest/Uptown Dining   109

Old Town Dining   113

Dining in Mission Bay &
  the Beaches   117

La Jolla Dining   121

Coronado Dining   127

San Diego Area Attractions   131

San Diego Beaches   139

Balboa Park   145

Downtown San Diego
  Attractions   153

Old Town & Mission Valley
  Attractions   155

La Jolla Attractions   159

Outdoor Pursuits in
  the San Diego Area   171

Walking Tour:
  The Gaslamp Quarter   185

Walking Tour:
  The Embarcadero   191

Walking Tour: Old Town   195

Walking Tour: Balboa Park   199

Downtown San Diego
  Shopping   205

Hillcrest/Uptown Shopping   207

Shopping in Mission Bay &
  the Beaches   208

La Jolla Shopping   210

Northern San Diego County   231

Getting Around the
  Disneyland Resort   249

Eastern San Diego County   263

Tijuana   273

About the Author

A third-generation San Diego native, **David Swanson** was "researching" the zoo, beaches, and museums of his hometown long before he carried a notepad to do it. Since 1995, his writing and photography has appeared in more than 45 North American newspapers, including the *Los Angeles Times, Chicago Tribune, Boston Globe, Miami Herald,* and *The Globe and Mail.* His work also regularly appears in *National Geographic Traveler, Bride's,* and *TravelAge West,* and he is a contributing editor at *Caribbean Travel & Life.* Swanson spends his downtime bicycling, hiking, tending the garden, enjoying obscure movies, and occasionally pondering his former career in movie marketing and publicity.

Acknowledgments

Many individuals contributed to the content and accuracy of this book, but a special thank you is due for the support of the San Diego Convention and Visitors Bureau—especially Joe Timko and Rick Prickett, who make my glamorous career of hotel inspections and fact-chasing a lot more pleasant.

An Invitation to the Reader

In researching this book, we discovered many wonderful places—hotels, restaurants, shops, and more. We're sure you'll find others. Please tell us about them, so we can share the information with your fellow travelers in upcoming editions. If you were disappointed with a recommendation, we'd love to know that, too. Please write to:

Frommer's San Diego 2004
Wiley Publishing, Inc. • 111 River St. • Hoboken, NJ 07030

An Additional Note

Please be advised that travel information is subject to change at any time—and this is especially true of prices. We therefore suggest that you write or call ahead for confirmation when making your travel plans. The authors, editors, and publisher cannot be held responsible for the experiences of readers while traveling. Your safety is important to us, however, so we encourage you to stay alert and be aware of your surroundings. Keep a close eye on cameras, purses, and wallets, all favorite targets of thieves and pickpockets.

Frommer's Star Ratings, Icons & Abbreviations

Every hotel, restaurant, and attraction listing in this guide has been ranked for quality, value, service, amenities, and special features using a **star-rating system.** In country, state, and regional guides, we also rate towns and regions to help you narrow down your choices and budget your time accordingly. Hotels and restaurants are rated on a scale of zero (recommended) to three stars (exceptional). Attractions, shopping, nightlife, towns, and regions are rated according to the following scale: zero stars (recommended), one star (highly recommended), two stars (very highly recommended), and three stars (must-see).

In addition to the star-rating system, we also use **seven feature icons** that point you to the great deals, in-the-know advice, and unique experiences that separate travelers from tourists. Throughout the book, look for:

Finds	Special finds—those places only insiders know about
Fun Fact	Fun facts—details that make travelers more informed and their trips more fun
Kids	Best bets for kids, and advice for the whole family
Moments	Special moments—those experiences that memories are made of
Overrated	Places or experiences not worth your time or money
Tips	Insider tips—great ways to save time and money
Value	Great values—where to get the best deals

The following **abbreviations** are used for credit cards:

AE	American Express	DISC	Discover	V	Visa
DC	Diners Club	MC	MasterCard		

Frommers.com

Now that you have the guidebook to a great trip, visit our website at **www.frommers.com** for travel information on more than 3,000 destinations. With features updated regularly, we give you instant access to the most current trip-planning information available. At Frommers.com, you'll also find the best prices on airfares, accommodations, and car rentals—and you can even book travel online through our travel booking partners. At Frommers.com, you'll also find the following:

- Online updates to our most popular guidebooks
- Vacation sweepstakes and contest giveaways
- Newsletter highlighting the hottest travel trends
- Online travel message boards with featured travel discussions

What's New in San Diego

Whether you've never been to San Diego or your last visit was more than a few years ago, this relaxed and scenic city will hold some surprises for you. It's growing up. San Diego is no longer just a laid-back beach-and-navy town: Avant-garde architecture, sophisticated dining options, and a booming tourism industry all point to its coming-of-age.

Although San Diegans generally prefer to keep things as they are—eagerly passing "no growth" legislation and vocalizing fears about the "Los Angeles-ization" of our metropolis—we are also quick to brag about our latest hot eateries and up-to-date attractions. Here is a sampling of recent changes and additions.

PLANNING YOUR TRIP JetBlue Airways (© 800/JET-BLUE; www.jet blue.com) debuted two daily nonstop flights between its JFK hub and San Diego in June 2003. For underserved San Diego, the added service is a boon—particularly since it reinstates a red-eye flight to the East Coast that both United and American dropped in the cutbacks following the September 11, 2001, terrorist attacks.

In summer 2004, the San Diego Museum of Art in Balboa Park will host the touring exhibit *St. Peter and the Vatican: The Legacy of the Popes.* The collection features a number of works that have never been seen outside Vatican City. Highlights of the show include pieces by Michelangelo, Giotto, and Bernini, as well as more contemporary works such as a Buddhist *Thangka* created by the Dalai Lama as a gift to

Pope John Paul II. Call © 619/232-7931 for more details.

WHERE TO STAY Hot on the heels of the expansion of downtown's Manchester Grand Hyatt and the debut of the trendy W Hotel, the once-dowdy **Westgate Hotel** (© 619/238-1818) received a $5.5 million facelift that brings those 18th-century style furnishings to life again. $25,000 was spent gutting and primping each room, and the hotel's Fontainebleau dining room continues to earn local accolades.

A new **Omni San Diego Hotel,** 675 L St. (© 619/231-6664), arrives in spring 2004 and will be connected via skybridge to the San Diego Padres' new ballpark. The 511-room hotel is located directly across from the recently expanded Convention Center and a few blocks from the Gaslamp Quarter, and the rooftop terrace and many rooms will offer ballpark views.

WHERE TO DINE The turn of the century saw a revitalized dining scene and new attention being devoted to San Diego's restaurants. This year there are a few big-name arrivals, as well as a couple of makeovers that are drawing attention. La Jolla never quite got the point of the *nuevo latino* Tamarindo, so its owners went back to the drawing board and created **Fresh,** 1044 Wall St. (© 858/551-7575). Chef Matthew Zappoli oversees a seafood-festooned menu with delicate coriander-crusted mahimahi and a mouthwatering lobster Napoleon. The prices are surprisingly moderate (particularly for La Jolla) and the room got an eye-catching redesign as well.

Meanwhile, downtown culture vultures and urban hipsters that never quite latched on to Royale Brasserie have taken a shine to **Lou & Mickey's,** 224 Fifth Ave., across the street from the Convention Center (© **619/237-4900**). The good news: The owners kept the gorgeous room as is—it's still filled with exquisite hard woods and mosaic tiles to create a 1940s brasserie ambience. The better news: The chophouse menu is more successful and varied than you might expect, ranging from bone-in steaks and prime seafood to an oyster bar and scrumptiously good gulf shrimp served curry-like "Manales" style. Throw in unpretentious ambience and service that isn't predatory (like some steakhouses in the Gaslamp) and you have all the makings of a winner.

EXPLORING SAN DIEGO San Diego's biggest debut for 2004 is surely the new Padres ballpark called—wait for it—**Petco Park.** Located across the street from the Convention Center downtown, the ballpark's construction has been mired in political squabbles and legal delays, but don't expect city denizens not to rally around in support when it opens in April (see **www.padres.com** for more details). It is also pushing the redevelopment of downtown a few blocks eastward, a side effect that pleases everyone. The venue is said to combine great sight lines and downtown skyline views, and will be most easily accessed via the San Diego Trolley.

Speaking of which, the **San Diego Trolley** system is set for an important extension, when a 6-mile section of the Blue Line track heads east from Qualcomm Stadium to San Diego State University, connecting with the Orange Line in La Mesa. The project won't be finished until 2005, but if you head east on I-8 you'll surely note the impressive spans crossing and paralleling the freeway. More info is available at **www.sandiegotrolley.com**.

No one visits San Diego without experiencing one of the city's fantastic animal parks, and the news this year is at Balboa Park's **San Diego Zoo,** 2920 Zoo Dr. (© **619/234-3153;** www.sandiegozoo.org), where a $26 million **Heart of the Zoo** project is designed to transform the outdated "monkey yard," one of the zoo's original enclosures, into the bioclimatically correct (and multispecies) exhibits. New homes for the flamingoes, and a shared domicile for the Borneo and Sumatran orangutans opened in 2003, and other improvements by 2005 should improve traffic flow in the busiest part of the zoo.

AFTER DARK Opening its doors just as we go to press, the **Yard House**—part of a mini-chain of beer joints spreading across America—has arrived in San Diego. Located across the street from Horton Plaza, at Fourth Avenue and Broadway (© **619/233-YARD**), the bar doesn't brew its own suds but has a bar lined with tap after tap, 130 in all. You'll find everything from little-known Hollywood Blonde to Hemp Ale and other oddities—just don't you dare order a Coors Light! There's also a full menu.

SIDE TRIPS Families planning a Disneyland excursion will find the charming **Many Adventures of Winnie the Pooh** replacing the hoary Country Bear Jamboree in Critter Country. If you're headed to Disney's California Adventure theme park, watch for the arrival of the terrific **Twilight Zone Tower of Terror** (a spinoff from Disney's Orlando parks), scheduled to open in mid-2004. If you're headed to Anaheim, make sure to budget 2 days to see the two parks and other new features of the renamed **Disneyland Resort** (© **714/781-4565;** www.disneyland.com).

The Best of San Diego

Best known for its benign climate and fabulous beaches, San Diego is one big outdoor playground. With 70 miles of sandy coastline—plus pretty, sheltered Mission Bay—you can choose from swimming, snorkeling, windsurfing, kayaking, bicycling, skating, and tons of other fun in or near the water. The city is also home to top-notch attractions, including three world-famous animal parks and splendid Balboa Park, a cultural and recreational jewel that's one of the finest urban parks in the country. And of course San Diego also reflects its Spanish-Mexican heritage in every corner—in fact, bustling Tijuana is just across the border, 40 minutes away.

Once dismissed as a slow-growth, politically conservative navy town, San Diego has been expanding steadily during the past 2 decades, and now boasts an almost Los Angeles–like diversity of neighborhoods and residents. Approximately 1.3 million people live here, making it the seventh-largest city in the United States. At this writing, the city's biotech/tourism/telecom-based economy fires on all burners, and San Diego also boasts one of the fastest-rising housing markets in the country; fortunately, a heightened sensitivity to historical preservation means formerly seedy downtown areas and architecturally rich suburbs are being carefully restored. These often charming districts lure yuppies to invest in the future of these neighborhoods, and also help to update the face of San Diego's dining, shopping, and entertainment.

So pack a laid-back attitude along with your sandals and swimsuit, and welcome to California's grown-up beach town.

1 Frommer's Favorite San Diego Experiences

- **Driving Over the Bridge to Coronado:** The first time or the fiftieth, there's always an adrenaline rush as you follow this engineering marvel's dramatic curves and catch a glimpse of the panoramic view to either side. Driving west, you can easily pick out the distinctive Hotel Del in the distance long before you reach the "island." See "Orientation" in chapter 4 for more about the city's neighborhoods.
- **Riding on the San Diego Trolley to Mexico:** The trip from downtown costs a mere $2.50, takes only 40 minutes, and the clean, quick, bright red trolleys are fun

in their own right. See "Getting Around" in chapter 4.

- **Taking the Ferry to Coronado:** The 15-minute ride gets you out into San Diego Harbor and provides some of the best views of the city. The ferry runs every hour from the Broadway Pier, so you can tour Coronado on foot, by bike, or by trolley, and return whenever you please. See "Getting Around" in chapter 4.
- **Escaping to Torrey Pines State Reserve:** This state park is set aside for the rarest pine tree in North America. But the bluff-side reserve has short trails that immerse hikers

into a delicate and beautiful coastal environment that is rapidly disappearing. See p. 160.

- **Drinking Coffee at Sidewalk Cafe:** San Diego offers a plethora of places beyond the ubiquitous Starbucks to enjoy lattes, espressos, and cappuccinos, many of them have outdoor seating areas. Some of my favorites include **Peet's,** 350 University Ave., Hillcrest (© **619/ 296-5995**), **Gargoyle Gallery and Café,** 1845 India St., Little Italy (© **619/234-1344**), the **Pannikin,** 7467 Girard Ave., La Jolla (© **858/454-5453**), and the various branches of **Living Room Coffeehouse** (p. 114).

- **Watching the Sun Set Over the Ocean:** It's a free and memorable experience. Excellent sunset-watching spots include the Mission Beach and Pacific Beach boardwalks, as well as the beach in Coronado in front of the Hotel del Coronado. At La Jolla's Windansea Beach, wandering down to the water at dusk, wineglass in hand, is a nightly neighborhood event. See "San Diego's Beaches" in chapter 7.

- **Watching the Seals at the Children's Pool:** This tiny La Jolla cove was originally named for the toddlers who could safely frolic behind a man-made seawall. These days, the sand is mostly off-limits to humans, who congregate along the seawall railing or onshore to admire the protected pinnipeds that sun themselves on the beach or on semisubmerged rocks. You can get surprisingly close, and it's a truly mesmerizing sight. See "San Diego's Beaches" in chapter 7.

- **Renting Bikes, Skates, or Kayaks in Mission Bay:** Landscaped shores, calm waters, paved paths, and friendly neighbors make Mission Bay an aquatic playground like no other. Explore on land or water, depending on your energy

level, then grab a bite at funky Mission Cafe. See "Outdoor Pursuits" in chapter 7.

- **Strolling Through the Gaslamp Quarter:** Victorian commercial buildings that fill a 16½-block area will make you think you've stepped back in time. The beautifully restored buildings, in the heart of downtown, house some of the city's most popular shops, restaurants, and nightspots. See "Walking Tour 1: The Gaslamp Quarter" in chapter 8.

- **Walking Along the Water:** One of my favorite places to stroll in the city is along the waterfront from the Convention Center to the Maritime Museum, with views of aircraft carriers, tuna seiners, and sailboats. See "Walking Tour 2: The Embarcadero" in chapter 8.

- **Listening to Free Sunday Organ Recitals in Balboa Park:** Even if you usually don't like organ music, you might enjoy these outdoor concerts and the crowds they draw— San Diegans with their parents, their children, and their dogs. The music, enhanced by the organist's commentary, runs the gamut from classical to contemporary. Concerts start at 2pm. See "Walking Tour 4: Balboa Park" in chapter 8.

- **Purchasing Just-Picked Produce at a Farmers' Market or Farm-Fresh Stand:** Markets throughout the area sell the bountiful harvest of San Diego County, and organic farms like Chino's are nationally famous for their delicious produce. For directions, see "Shopping A to Z" in chapter 9.

- **Listening to Live Music Outdoors at Humphrey's:** An intimate, palm-fringed venue located on the water at Shelter Island, Humphrey's has name acts from mid-May to October and puts those impersonal summer concert "sheds" found in other cities to

San Diego Area at a Glance

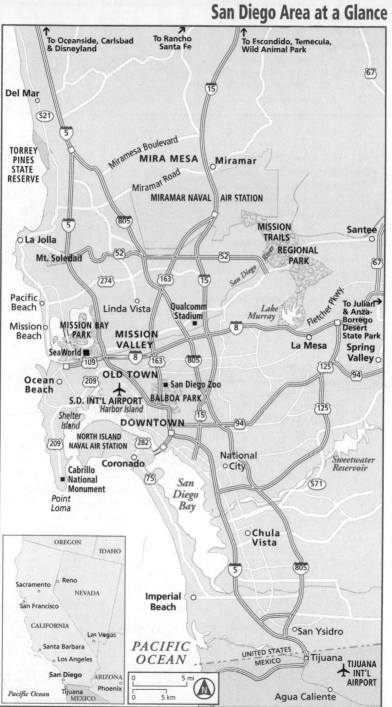

Impressions

Thanks be to God, I have arrived at this Port of San Diego. It is beautiful to behold and does not belie its reputation.

—Father Junípero Serra, 1769

I thought San Diego must be a Heaven on Earth . . . It seemed to me the best spot for building a city I ever saw.

—Alonzo Horton, who developed San Diego's first downtown

shame. See "The Club & Music Scene" in chapter 10.

- **Running with the Grunion:** These tiny fish spawn on San Diego beaches between April and June, and the locals love to be there. To find the date of the next run, pick up a free tide chart at a surf shop or consult the daily newspaper. See the "Running with the Grunion" box on p. 227.

- **Floating Up, Up, and Away Over North County:** Hot-air balloons carry passengers over the golf courses and luxury homes north of the city. These rides are especially enjoyable at sunset. For details, see "North County Beach Towns: Spots to Surf & Sun" in chapter 11.

- **Visiting the "Lobster Village" in Puerto Nuevo:** South of the border, a few miles south of tacky TJ, Puerto Nuevo's time-honored seaside restaurants serve lobster with rice, beans, tortillas, and freshly made salsa. It's an affordable and deliciously filling meal. See "Exploring Beyond Tijuana" on p. 280.

2 Best Hotel Bets

- **Best Historic Hotel:** The **Hotel del Coronado,** 1500 Orange Ave. (*©* **800/HOTEL-DEL** or 619/435-8000), positively reeks of history. Opened in 1888, this Victorian masterpiece had some of the first electric lights in existence, and legend has it that the course of history was changed when the Prince of Wales met Wallis Simpson here at a ball. Meticulous restoration has enhanced this glorious landmark, whose early days are well chronicled in displays throughout the hotel. See p. 92.

- **Best for Business Travelers:** The **Marriott San Diego Hotel & Marina,** 333 W. Harbor Dr. (*©* **800/228-9290** or 619/234-1500), screams "business traveler," with a full-service business center offering plenty of amenities for suits on the go, but there's still room for a tropical pool and harbor views. Its prime location offers excellent access to downtown. See p. 68.

- **Best for a Romantic Getaway:** You don't need to know much about Craftsman-style architecture to appreciate the taste and keen craftsmanship that went into creating **The Lodge at Torrey Pines,** 11480 North Torrey Pines Rd. (*©* **858/777-6690**). The lodge—the city's only AAA Five Diamond hotel—sits next to the Torrey Pines Golf Course, San Diego's top links, and you can enjoy a fireplace in your room, sunset ocean views from your balcony, and superb meals at the hotel's A.R. Valentine restaurant. See p. 88.

- **Best for Families:** The **Paradise Point Resort & Spa,** 1404 W. Vacation Rd. (*©* **800/344-2626** or 858/274-4630), is a tropical playground offering enough activities to keep family members of all ages happy. In addition to a virtual Disneyland of on-site options, the aquatic playground of Mission Bay surrounds the hotel's private peninsula. See p. 82.

- **Best Moderately Priced Hotel:** The **Gaslamp Plaza Suites,** 520 E St. (© **619/232-9500**), is an elegant landmark full of creature comforts that belie its super-friendly rates. You'll also be smack-dab in the heart of the trendy Gaslamp Quarter. See p. 74.

- **Best Budget Hotel:** In San Diego's Little Italy, **La Pensione Hotel,** 606 W. Date St. (© **800/232-4683** or 619/236-8000), feels like a small European hotel and offers tidy lodgings at bargain prices. There's an abundance of great dining in the surrounding blocks, and you'll be perfectly situated to explore the rest of town by car. See p. 74.

- **Best Unusual Lodgings:** Fulfill the fantasies of your inner yachtsman with the **Harbor Vacations Club,** 1880 Harbor Island Dr., G-Dock (© **800/YACHT-DO** or 619/297-9484). It provides powerboats, sailboats, and houseboats docked in a Harbor Island marina. You can sleep on board, lulled by the gentle rocking of the

---

ⓒ The Best of San Diego Online

You can find lots of information on San Diego on the Internet; here are a few of my favorite helpful planning and general information sites.

- **www.sandiegoartandsol.com** is the link for cultural tourism, also overseen by the Convention and Visitors Bureau. You'll find a list of art shows and music events, plus intriguing touring itineraries that delve into the city's culture.

- **www.sandiego-online.com**, the *San Diego* magazine website, features abbreviated stories from the current month's issue, plus dining and events listings.

- **www.sdreader.com**, the site of the free weekly *San Diego Reader,* is a great source for club and show listings, plus edgy topical journalism. It has printable dining and other coupons you can really use, plus opinionated arts, eats, and entertainment critiques.

- **www.signonsandiego.com** is where CitySearch teams up with the *San Diego Union-Tribune,* catering as much to locals as to visitors. It offers plenty of helpful links, plus reviews of restaurants, music, movies, performing arts, museums, outdoor recreation, beaches, and sports.

- **ww.digitalcity.com/sandiego** is a lifestyle guide targeted at locals, and therefore yields occasional off-the-beaten-tourist-path recommendations. You'll find everything from personal ads to constantly changing restaurant spotlights and daily "Top Clicks."

- **www.sandiegoinsider.com** is a well-rounded online guide containing bar, club, and movie reviews. The dining guide includes lengthy descriptions but few assertive critiques. Suggestions abound for beach-going, hiking, and other outdoor excursions. Searching this site can be tedious, but the articles are generally rewarding.

hull, and then have breakfast ashore; complete the adventure with a skippered cruise later in the day. See p. 72.

- **Best Bed & Breakfast:** The picture-perfect **Heritage Park Bed & Breakfast Inn,** 2470 Heritage Park Row (© **800/995-2470** or 619/299-6832), has it all—an exquisitely maintained Victorian house, lively and gracious hosts who delight in creating a pampering and romantic ambience, and an Old Town location equally close to downtown, Hillcrest, and Mission Bay. See p. 78.

- **Best Boutique Inn:** Smartly located in the center of La Jolla, the 20-room **Hotel Parisi,** 1111 Prospect St. (© **877/4-PARISI** or 858/454-1511), has the composed, quiet feel of a Zen garden, with feng shui–inspired suites, modern furnishings, and subdued color schemes. See p. 86.

- **Best Place to Stay on the Beach:** Although the Hotel Del operation takes the cake, a more moderate landing is found at La Jolla's **The Sea Lodge,** 8110 Camino del Oro

(© **800/237-5211** or 858/459-8271), where you can walk right onto the wide beach and frolic amid great waves. Lifeguards and the lack of undertow make this a popular choice for families. Though the rooms are plain, the staff is all-pro. See p. 90.

- **Best Hotel for Travelers with Disabilities:** While many of San Diego's hotels make minimal concessions to wheelchair-accessibility codes, downtown's **Manchester Grand Hyatt San Diego,** 1 Market Place (© **800/233-1234** or 619/232-1234), goes the distance. There are 23 rooms with roll-in showers and lowered closet racks and peepholes. Ramps are an integral part of all the public spaces, rather than an afterthought. The hotel's Braille labeling is also thorough. See p. 68.

- **Best Hotel Pool:** The genteel pool at **La Valencia,** 1132 Prospect St. (© **800/451-0772** or 858/454-0771), is oh-so-special, with its spectacular setting overlooking Scripps Park and the Pacific. See p. 86.

3 Best Dining Bets

- **Best Spot for a Business Lunch: Dakota Grill & Spirits,** 901 Fifth Ave., in the Gaslamp Quarter (© **619/234-5554**), has the three most important ingredients of a business lunch locale—great location, appropriate atmosphere, and excellent food—but without prices that scream "power lunch." See p. 104.

- **Best View:** Many restaurants overlook the ocean, but only from **Brockton Villa,** 1235 Coast Blvd., La Jolla (© **858/454-7393**), can you see sublime La Jolla Cove. Diners with a window seat will feel as if they're looking out on a gigantic picture postcard. See p. 124.

- **Best Value:** The word "huge" barely begins to describe the portions at **Filippi's Pizza Grotto,** 1747 India St. (© **619/232-5095**), where a salad for one is enough for three, and an order of lasagna must weigh a pound. There's a kids' menu, and Filippi's has locations all over, including Pacific Beach, Mission Valley, and Escondido. See p. 106.

- **Best for Kids:** At the **Old Spaghetti Factory,** 275 Fifth Ave., in the Gaslamp Quarter (© **619/233-4323**), family dining is the name of the game—so if your kids are noisy, nobody will notice. See p. 107.

- **Best Chinese Cuisine: Emerald Restaurant,** 3709 Convoy St., Kearny Mesa (© **858/565-6888**), is in the most unromantic of locations, yet the culinary wizardry that transpires in the kitchen draws the Chinese community citywide for Hong Kong–style seafood, much of it plucked from live fish tanks. See p. 129.

- **Best Class Act:** The polished service and elegant setting at **Laurel,** 505 Laurel St., next to Balboa Park (© **619/239-2222**), are urbane and discriminating, like the best New York restaurants. But the food is prepared with inventive flair and the Rhône-heavy wine list soars, making Laurel a rewarding splurge for a special occasion. See p. 107.

- **Best Seafood:** At **Star of the Sea,** 1380 N. Harbor Dr. (© **619/232-7408**), you'll find the city's best package of fresh seafood, graceful presentation, and memorable views from the edge of San Diego Bay. See p. 102.

- **Best New-American Cuisine:** Chef Deborah Scott's menu at **Indigo Grill,** 1536 India St., in Little Italy (© **619/234-6802**), cleverly fuses the flavors of the Pacific Coast from Mexico to Alaska. The results create the city's most adventurous menu, and one of its most delicious. See p. 104.

- **Best Mexican Cuisine:** Rather than the "combination plate" fare that's common on this side of the border, **El Agave Tequileria,** 2304 San Diego Ave., Old Town (© **619/220-0692**), offers a memorable combination of freshly prepared recipes from Veracruz, Chiapas, Puebla, and Mexico City—along with an impressive selection of boutique and artisan tequilas. See p. 113.

- **Best Pizza:** For gourmet pizza from a wood-fired oven, head for **Sammy's California Woodfired Pizza,** a local institution with several locations, including 770 Fourth Ave., in the Gaslamp Quarter (© **619/230-8888.** For the traditional Sicilian variety, line up for **Filippi's Pizza Grotto** (see "Best Value," above, or p. 106).

- **Best Desserts:** You'll forget your diet at **Extraordinary Desserts,** 2929 Fifth Ave., Hillcrest (© **619/294-7001**). Heck, it's so good you might forget your name! Proprietor Karen Krasne has a *Certificate de Patisserie* from Le Cordon Bleu in Paris, and makes everything fresh on the premises daily. See p. 110.

- **Best Late-Night Dining:** Open later than anyplace else downtown, **Café Lulu,** 419 F St. (© **619/238-0114**), serves eclectic meat-free fare and inventive espresso drinks until 1am during the week, 3am on weekends. See p. 106.

- **Best Fast Food:** Fish tacos from the burgeoning local chain **Rubio's,** 4504 E. Mission Bay Dr. (© **619/272-2801**), and other locations, are legendary in San Diego. Sounds strange? Taste one and you'll know why there's a line. See "Baja Fish Tacos" on p. 116.

- **Best Picnic Fare:** Pack a superb sandwich from the **Bread & Cie.,** 350 University Ave. (© **619/683-9322**), where the hearty breads are the toast of the city; see p. 111. Or head to one of several locations of **Whole Foods,** where the deli houses a smashing selection of delicious hot and cold items, the city's best cheese collection and a crisp salad bar; you'll find them in Hillcrest at 711 University Ave. (© **619/294-2800**), and in La Jolla at 8825 Villa La Jolla Dr. (© 858/642-6700).

2

Planning Your Trip to San Diego

This chapter contains all the practical information and logistical advice you need to make your travel arrangements a snap, from deciding when to go to finding the best airfare.

1 Visitor Information

You can do your homework by contacting the **International Visitor Information Center,** 11 Horton Plaza, San Diego, CA 92101 (*©* **619/236-1212;** www.sandiego.org). Ask for the *San Diego Vacation Planning Kit* which includes the *Visitors Planning Guide,* featuring information on accommodations, activities, and attractions, and excellent maps. The *San Diego Travel Values* insert is full of discount coupons for hotels at all price levels, restaurants, attractions, cultural and recreational activities, and tours.

You can also find information in advance of your trip online at the following websites: **www.infosandiego. com,** for general information; **www.gas lamp.org,** for information about the Gaslamp's history and revival; **www. coronadohistory.org,** for details about Coronado; and **www.sandiegonorth. com,** for information on excursion

areas in northern San Diego County, including Del Mar, Carlsbad, Escondido, Julian, and Anza-Borrego Desert State Park. For more helpful websites, see "The Best of San Diego Online" on p. 7.

If you're thinking of attending the theater while you're in town, contact the **San Diego Performing Arts League** (*©* **619/238-0700;** www.sandiego performs.com) for a copy of *What's Playing?,* which contains information on upcoming shows. **San Diego Art + Sol** (*©* **619/236-1212;** www.sandiego artandsol.com) is a cultural marketing campaign guided by the San Diego Convention and Visitors Bureau. The website lists performances and exhibits scheduled for any specific date and you may also request a free copy of the biannual magazine, which contains a 6-month calendar of events and cultural itineraries.

2 Money

San Diego is a moderately priced destination compared to New York, Boston, or San Francisco. If you're visiting from outside the United States, you can find more information on American currency in "Preparing for Your Trip" in chapter 3.

ATMS

The easiest and best way to get cash away from home is from an ATM. The

Cirrus (*©* **800/424-7787;** www. mastercard.com) and **PLUS** (*©* **800/ 843-7587;** www.visa.com) networks span the globe; look at the back of your bank card to see which network you're on, then call or check online for ATM locations at your destination. Be sure you know your personal identification number (PIN) before you leave home and be sure to find out your daily withdrawal limit before you depart. Also keep in mind that many banks impose a fee every time a card is used at a different bank's ATM. To compare banks' ATM fees within the U.S., use www.bankrate.com.

One of California's most popular banks is Wells Fargo, a member of the Star, PLUS, Cirrus, and Global Access systems. It has hundreds of ATMs at branches and stores (including most Vons supermarkets) throughout San Diego County. Other statewide banks include Bank of America (which accepts PLUS, Star, and Interlink cards), and First Interstate Bank (Cirrus).

TRAVELER'S CHECKS

Traveler's checks are something of an anachronism from pre-ATM era. They used to be the only sound alternative to traveling with dangerously large amounts of cash. They were as reliable as currency, but, unlike cash, could be replaced if lost or stolen.

These days, traveler's checks are less essential because 24-hour ATMs are found throughout cities like San Diego, allowing you to withdraw small amounts of cash as needed. But since you will likely be charged an ATM withdrawal fee if the bank is not your own, you might be better off with traveler's checks—provided that you don't mind showing identification every time you want to cash one.

You can get traveler's checks in denominations as small as $20, and at almost any bank. **American Express** adds a service charge ranging from 1% to 4%. You can also get American Express traveler's checks over the phone by calling ℭ **800/221-7282;** Amex gold and platinum cardholders who use this number are exempt from the service fee. **Visa** offers traveler's checks at Citibank and several other banks. The service fee ranges between 1.5% and 2%. Call ℭ **800/732-1322** for information. AAA members can obtain Visa checks without a surcharge

at most AAA offices or by calling ℭ **866/339-3378. MasterCard** also offers traveler's checks. Call ℭ **800/ 223-9920** for a location near you.

If you choose to carry traveler's checks, be sure to keep a record of their serial numbers separate from your checks in the event that they are stolen or lost. You'll get a refund faster if you know the numbers.

CREDIT CARDS

Credit cards are safe way to carry money, they provide a convenient record of all your expenses, and they generally offer good exchange rates. San Diego's hotels, restaurants, and attractions accept most major credit cards; the most common are **Visa, MasterCard, American Express,** and **Discover.** A small handful of stores and restaurants accept only cash, however, so be sure to ask if you're not sure.

You can also withdraw cash advances from your credit cards at banks or ATMs, provided you know your PIN. If you've forgotten yours, or didn't even know you had one, call the number on the back of your credit card and ask the bank to send it to you. It usually takes 5 to 7 business days.

WHAT TO DO IF YOUR WALLET IS LOST OR STOLEN

Be sure to tell all of your credit-card companies the minute you discover your wallet has been lost or stolen and file a report at the nearest police precinct. Your credit-card company or insurer may require a police report number or record of the loss. Most credit-card companies have an emergency toll-free number to call if your card is lost or stolen; they may be able to wire you a cash advance immediately or deliver an emergency credit card in a day or two. Visa's U.S. emergency number is ℭ **800/847-2911** or 410/581-9994. American Express cardholders and traveler's check holders should call ℭ **800/221-7282.** MasterCard holders

What Things Cost in San Diego	U.S.$	U.K.£
Taxi from the airport to downtown	10.00	6.20
Bus from the airport to downtown	2.25	1.40
Local telephone call	.35–.50	.22–.31
Double at the Hotel del Coronado (very expensive)	260.00	161.00
Double at the Catamaran Resort Hotel (expensive)	209.00	130.00
Double at the Sommerset Suites Hotel (moderate)	139.00	86.00
Double at La Pensione Hotel (inexpensive)	75.00	47.00
Two-course lunch for one at Casa de Guadalajara (moderate)	17.00	10.75
Two-course lunch for one at the Mission (inexpensive)	13.00	8.25
Three-course dinner for one at Dakota Grill (expensive)	40.00	25.00
Three-course dinner for one at Fifth & Hawthorne (moderate)	28.00	18.00
Three-course dinner for one at the Old Spaghetti Factory (inexpensive)	11.00	7.00
Pint of beer at Karl Strauss Brewery	4.25	2.75
Cup of coffee	2.00	1.35
San Diego Zoo adult admission	19.50	12.00
San Diego Zoo children's admission	11.75	7.50
Best seat at the Globe Theater	50.00	31.00

should call ℂ 800/307-7309 or 636/722-7111. For other credit cards, call the toll-free number directory at ℂ 800/555-1212.

If you need emergency cash over the weekend when all banks and American Express offices are closed, you can have money wired to you via Western Union (ℂ 800/325-6000; www.westernunion.com).

Identity theft or fraud are potential complications of losing your wallet, especially if you've lost your driver's license along with your cash and credit cards. Notify the major credit-reporting bureaus immediately; placing a fraud alert on your records may protect you against liability for criminal activity. The three major U.S. credit-reporting agencies are Equifax (ℂ 800/766-0008; www.equifax.com), Experian (ℂ 888/397-3742; www.experian.com), and TransUnion (ℂ 800/680-7289; www.transunion.com). Finally, if you've lost all forms of photo ID call your airline and explain the situation; they might allow you to board the plane if you have a copy of your passport or birth certificate and a copy of the police report you've filed.

3 When to Go

San Diego is blessed with a mild climate, low humidity, good air quality, and welcoming blue skies through much of the year. In fact, *Pleasant*

Weather Rankings, published by Consumer Travel, ranked San Diego's weather number two in the world (behind Las Palmas, in the Canary Islands). Indeed, could there be any better advertisement for visiting San Diego than when the Super Bowl commentators for the January 2003 game in San Diego noted that the afternoon high was 82°F (28°C)?

Although the temperature can change 20° to 30° between day and evening, it rarely reaches a point of extreme heat or cold—daytime highs above 100°F (38°C) are usually limited to two or three a year, and the mercury dropping below freezing can be counted in mere hours once or twice each year. San Diego receives very little precipitation (9½ in. of rainfall in an average year); what rain does fall comes primarily between November and April, and by July our hillsides start to look brown and parched. It's not unusual for the city to go without measurable precipitation for as long as 6 months in the summer and fall.

My favorite weather in San Diego is in the fall. October and November are usually ideal months to visit—daytime temperatures are warm, the skies are clearest and water temps are still comfortable for swimming. February and March are often beautiful periods when the landscapes are greenest and flowers at their peak, but most of us find it's still too cold for ocean swimming. Beach bunnies should note that late spring and early summer tanning sessions are often compromised by a local phenomenon called June Gloom—a layer of low-lying clouds or fog along the coast that sometimes doesn't burn off till noon or later and returns before sunset. Use days like these to explore inland San Diego, where places like the Wild Animal Park are probably warm and clear.

San Diego is most crowded between Memorial Day and Labor Day. The kids are out of school and *everyone* wants to be by the seashore; if you visit in summer, expect fully booked hotels, crowded family attractions, and full parking lots at the beach. Along the beaches the week of the July 4th holiday is a zoo—you'll love it or hate it. But San Diego's popularity as a convention destination and its year-round weather keep the tourism business steady the rest of the year, as well. The only slow season is from Thanksgiving to early February. Hotels are less full, and the beaches are peaceful and uncrowded; the big family attractions are still busy on weekends, though, with residents taking advantage of holiday breaks.

Average Monthly Temperatures & Rainfall (in.)

	Jan	Feb	Mar	Apr	May	June	July	Aug	Sept	Oct	Nov	Dec
High (°F)	65	66	66	68	70	71	75	77	76	74	70	66
(°C)	18	19	19	20	21	21	24	25	25	23	21	19
Low (°F)	46	47	50	54	57	60	64	66	63	58	52	47
(°C)	7	9	10	12	14	15	17	19	17	15	10	8
Rainfall	1.88	1.48	1.55	0.81	0.15	0.05	0.01	0.07	0.13	0.34	1.25	1.73

SAN DIEGO CALENDAR OF EVENTS

You might want to plan your trip around one of these annual events in the San Diego area (including the destinations covered in chapter 11, "Side Trips from San Diego"). For even more up-to-date planning information, contact the **International Visitor** Information Center (© 619/236-1212; www.sandiego.org).

January

Whale-Watching. From mid-December to mid-March is the eagerly anticipated whale-watching season. Scores of graceful yet gargantuan California gray whales make their annual migration to warm breeding lagoons in Baja, then return with their calves to springtime feeding grounds in Alaska. For information on vantage points and excursions that bring you closer to the largest mammals, see "Whale-Watching" in "Organized Tours" in chapter 7.

San Diego Marathon. The course begins in Carlsbad and stretches 26¼ miles, mainly along the coast. It's a gorgeous run, and spectators don't need tickets. For more information, call ℂ **858/792-2900.** For an entry application, send a self-addressed stamped envelope to In Motion, 511 S. Cedros, Suite B, Solana Beach, CA 92075. Third Sunday in January.

Nations of San Diego International Dance Festival. Founded in 1993, this festival is Southern California's largest ethnic dance showcase, featuring over 200 dancers from different cultures and dance groups and companies. Performances are at the Mandeville Auditorium at the UCSD Campus. Call ℂ **619/220-TIXS.** Mid-January.

February
Wildflowers bloom in the desert, usually February through April at Anza-Borrego Desert State Park. The peak of blooming last for a few weeks and varies from year to year, depending on the winter rainfall (see "Anza-Borrego Desert State Park" in chapter 11). For details, call ℂ **760/767-4684** or 760/767-4205 (park information).

Buick Invitational, Torrey Pines Golf Course, La Jolla. This PGA Tour men's tournament, an annual event since 1952, draws more than 100,000 spectators each year. It features 150 of the finest professionals in the world. For information, call ℂ **800/888-BUICK** or 619/281-4653; or write Buick Invitational,

3333 Camino Del Rio S., Suite 100, San Diego, CA 92108. Early to mid-February.

March
Kiwanis Ocean Beach Kite Festival. The late-winter skies over the Ocean Beach Recreational Center get a brilliant shot of color. Learn to make and decorate a kite of your own, participate in an all-ages flying contest, take part in all types of food and entertainment, and finish up with the grand finale—a parade down to the beach. For more information, call ℂ **619/531-1527.** First weekend in March.

St. Patrick's Day Parade. A tradition since 1980, the parade starts at Sixth and Juniper and ends at Sixth and Laurel. An **Irish Festival** follows in Balboa Park. For details, call ℂ **858/268-9111.** Sunday before March 17.

Flower Fields in Bloom at Carlsbad Ranch. One of the most spectacular sights in North County is the yearly blossoming of a gigantic sea of bright ranunculuses during March and April, creating a striped blanket that's visible from the freeway. Visitors are welcome to view and tour the fields, which are off Interstate 5 at the Palomar Airport Road exit (adults $7). For more information, call ℂ **760/431-0352.**

April
Rosarito-Ensenada 50-Mile Fun Bicycle Ride, Mexico. About 8,000 participants cycle from the Rosarito Beach Hotel along the two-lane free road to Ensenada and the Finish Line Fiesta. There's another ride in September. For information, call ℂ **619/424-6084** or visit www.rosaritoensenada.com. Early to mid-April.

San Diego Crew Classic, Crown Point Shores, Mission Bay. Since 1973, it has drawn more than

3,000 athletes from collegiate teams in the United States and Canada. Call ✆ **619/488-0700** or check out www.crewclassic.org. First or second weekend in April.

Del Mar National Horse Show, Del Mar Fairgrounds. The first event in the Del Mar racing season takes place from late April into early May at the famous Del Mar Fairgrounds. The field at this show includes Olympic-caliber and national championship horse-and-rider teams; there are also Western fashion boutiques and artist displays and demonstrations. For more information, call ✆ **858/792-4288,** or visit www.sdfair.com.

Adams Avenue Roots Festival, Normal Heights. Vintage blues, folk, bluegrass and international music held on six stages at 35th and Adams, and free to the public. Food, beer garden, and arts and crafts vendors. Check it out by calling ✆ **619/282-7329** or stop by www.gothere.com/adamsave. Late April.

Day at the Docks, Harbor Drive and Scott Street, Point Loma. This sportfishing tournament and festival features food, entertainment, and free boat rides. Call ✆ **800/994-FISH,** or see www.sportfishing.org. Usually the last weekend of April or the first weekend in May.

May

Cinco de Mayo Celebration, Old Town. Uniformed troops march and guns blast to mark the 1862 triumph of Mexican soldiers over the French. Festivities include a battle reenactment with costumed actors, mariachi music, and margaritas galore. Free admission. For further details, call ✆ **619/296-3236,** or visit www.fiestacincodemayo.com. Weekend closest to May 5.

June

Temecula Valley Balloon & Wine Festival. Colorful hot-air balloons dominate the sky over Lake Skinner during the 2½-day festival, which also features wine tastings, good food, jazz music, and other entertainment. General admission is $15 to $17, and reservations for balloon rides ($145) should be made in advance by calling ✆ **800/965-2122.** The lake is about 10 miles northeast of Temecula. To find out about this year's festival or purchase advance tickets, call the event organizers at ✆ **909/676-6713,** or visit www.tvbwf.com. Early June.

Indian Fair, Museum of Man, Balboa Park. Native Americans from the southwestern United States gather to demonstrate tribal dances and sell arts, crafts, and ethnic food. Call ✆ **619/239-2001.** Mid-June.

Twilight in the Park Concerts, Spreckels Organ Pavilion, Balboa Park. These free concerts held on Tuesday, Wednesday and Thursday evenings have been held since 1979 and run from mid-June to August. For information, call ✆ **619/235-1105.** The Spreckels Organ Society also holds free organ concerts on Mondays at 7:30pm in summer (✆ **619/702-8138;** www.serve.com/sosorgan).

San Diego County Fair. Referred to as the Del Mar Fair by everyone locally, this is the *other* happening (besides horse racing) at the Del Mar Fairgrounds. All of the county participates in this annual fair. Livestock competitions, thrill rides, flower and garden shows, gem and mineral exhibits, food and crafts booths, carnival games, and home arts exhibits dominate the event, and concerts by name performers are free with admission. The fair usually lasts 3 weeks, from mid-June to early July. For details, call ✆ **858/793-5555,** or check www.sdfair.com.

San Diego Symphony Summer Pops. The symphony's summer pops series features lighter classical, jazz and other vocalists, opera, Broadway, and show tunes, all performed under the stars and sometimes capped by fireworks. Held most weekends, from late June to August, at the Navy Pier, Broadway and Harbor Drive. For details, call ✆ **619/235-0804** or www.sandiegosymphony.com.

July

World Championship Over-the-Line Tournament, Mission Bay. This popular tournament is a San Diego original. The beach softball event dates from 1953 and is renowned for boisterous, beer-soaked, anything-goes behavior—a total of 1,150, three-person teams compete, and upwards of 50,000 attend. It's a heap of fun for the open-minded, but a bit much for small kids. It takes place on two consecutive weekends in mid-July, on Fiesta Island in Mission Bay, and the admission is free. For more details, call ✆ **619/688-0817,** or visit www.ombac.org.

Festival of the Bells, Mission San Diego de Alcala. This fiesta commemorates the founding of California's first church. Music, dancing, food, and the blessing of the animals are included. The 2004 event honors the 235th anniversary. For details, call ✆ **619/283-7319.** Mid-July.

San Diego Lesbian and Gay Pride Parade, Rally, and Festival. This parade is one of San Diego's biggest draws. It begins at Friday night with a rally at the Organ Pavilion in Balboa Park, reconvenes at noon on Saturday for the parade through Hillcrest, followed by a massive festival—held south of Sixth and Laurel in the park—that continues Sunday. The parade route is along University Avenue from Normal Street to Sixth Avenue. For more information, call ✆ **619/297-7683,** or visit www.sdpride.org. Third or fourth weekend in July.

Thoroughbred Racing Season. The "turf meets the surf" in Del Mar from mid-July to mid-September during the Thoroughbred racing season at the Del Mar Race Track. Post time is 2pm most days; the track is dark on Tuesdays. Hollywood stars continue to flock here, in the grand tradition begun by Bing Crosby, Betty Grable, and Jimmy Durante. For this year's schedule of events, call ✆ **858/792-4242** or 858/755-1141.

U.S. Open Sandcastle Competition, Imperial Beach Pier. Here's the quintessential beach event: There's a parade and children's sand castle contest on Saturday, followed by the main competition Sunday. Past years have seen creations of astounding complexity, but note that the castles are usually plundered right after the award ceremony. Late July. For further details, call ✆ **619/424-6663.**

August

Hillcrest Cityfest Street Fair, Fifth Avenue, between Ivy Lane and University Avenue. Held since 1983, the street fair features arts and crafts, food booths, a beer garden, and live entertainment. Call ✆ **619/299-3330.** The 1-day fair takes place early August.

Julian Weed & Craft Show, Julian. This is one event that's better than its name. Artwork and arrangements culled from the area's myriad woods, rocks, wildflowers and indigenous plants (okay, weeds) are displayed and sold. The Julian Chamber of Commerce (✆ **760/765-1857**) has further details. Second half of August.

Surfing Competitions. Oceanside's world-famous surfing spots attract numerous competitions, including the **World Bodysurfing Championships** and **Longboard Surf Club Competition.** The Longboard Competition takes place in mid-August at the Oceanside pier, and includes a trade show and gala awards presentation with music and dancers. For further details, call the Oceanside Visitors Bureau at ✆ **800/350-7873** or 760/722-1534 or visit www.oceansidelongboard surfingclub.org.

September

Street Scene, Gaslamp Quarter. This 3-day, 25-block extravaganza fills the historic streets of downtown's Gaslamp Quarter and East Village with music, food, dance, and international character. Twelve separate stages are erected to showcase jazz, blues, reggae, rock, and soul music all weekend. Attendees must be 21 or over for Friday and Saturday events—Sunday is all-ages day. For ticket and show information, call ✆ **800/260-9985,** or visit www.street-scene.com. Weekend after Labor Day.

La Jolla Rough Water Swim, La Jolla Cove. The country's largest rough-water swimming competition began in 1916 and features masters, men's and women's swims, a junior swim, and an amateur swim. All are 1-mile events except the junior swim and gator-man 3-mile championship. Spectators don't need tickets. For recorded information, call ✆ **858/456-2100.** For an entry form, send a self-addressed stamped envelope to Entries Chairman, La Jolla Sports Group, P.O. Box 46, La Jolla, CA 92038. Sunday after Labor Day.

Julian Fall Apple Harvest, Julian. The phenomenally popular apple harvest season runs from mid-September to mid-November, and

every weekend local artisans display their wares; there's also plenty of cider and apple pie, plus entertainment and brilliant fall foliage. For more information, contact the chamber of commerce at ✆ **760/765-1857.**

Rosarito-Ensenada 50-Mile Fun Bicycle Ride, Mexico. This race is held twice yearly; see the April entry, above.

October

Underwater Pumpkin Carving Contest, La Jolla. This event might never make it to the Olympics, but plenty of divers have turned out each year since 1981. The rules are relaxed, the panel of judges is serendipitous (one year it was the staff of a local dive shop, the next year five kids off the beach), and it's always a fun party. Spectators can hang out and wait for triumphant artists to break the surface with their creations. For details, call ✆ **858/565-6054.** Weekend before Halloween.

November

Carlsbad Fall Village Faire. Billed as the largest 1-day street fair in the California, this festival features more than 800 vendors on 24 city blocks. Items for sale include ceramics, jewelry, clothing, glassware, and plants. Mexican, Italian, Japanese, Korean, Indonesian, and other edible fare is sold at booths along the way. The epicenter is the intersection of Grand Avenue and Jefferson Street. Call ✆ **760/945-9288** or visit www.carlsbad.org. First Sunday in November.

Fall Flower Tour and the **Poinsettia Festival Street Fair,** Encinitas. Like its close neighbor Carlsbad, Encinitas is a flower-growing center—90% of the world's poinsettia plants get their start here. These two events celebrate the quintessential holiday

---

Tips Packing for Your Trip

Yes, bring a **sweater** or **light jacket,** even in summer. Because the ocean is close by, cold, damp breezes are common after the sun sets. But otherwise you can leave behind your heavy coats and cold-weather gear, no matter when you're coming. Pack **casual clothes.** Shorts, jeans, and T-shirts are common at all attractions and many restaurants, year-round. Men who plan to try one of San Diego's nicer restaurants may want to bring a sports jacket, but this is really an informal town. Bring **good, comfortable walking shoes;** you can cover a lot of ground on foot in this pleasant, outdoorsy city.

Don't forget **sunglasses,** an essential accessory (especially if you'll be on or near the water, which reflects and amplifies the sun's rays). If you have **binoculars,** bring them—they'll come in handy during whale-watching season. Regardless of the time of year, it's wise to pack a **bathing suit.** Most hotels have heated pools and whirlpools, and you might be surprised by a day warm enough for the beach.

---

plant and other late-flowering blooms. The 1-day Street Festival takes place in late November. For the Flower Tour, make reservations by early October; the nursery tours take place early December. For information, call the Encinitas Visitors Center at © **800/953-6041** or 760/753-6041.

December

Coronado Christmas Open House and Parade. Santa's arrival by ferry is followed by a small-town parade along Orange Avenue, followed by fireworks. Call © **619/437-8788,** or visit www.coronadohistory.org. First Friday of December.

Balboa Park December Nights, Balboa Park. San Diego's fine urban park is decked out in holiday splendor for a weekend of evening events. A candlelight procession, traditional caroling, and baroque music ensembles are just part of the entertainment. There are crafts displays, ethnic food, traditional hot cider, and a grand Christmas tree and nativity scene in Spreckels Pavilion.

The event is free and lasts from 5 to 9pm both days; the park's museums are free during those hours. For more information, call © **619/239-0512,** or check www.balboapark. org. First weekend in December.

Whale-Watching. The season starts in mid-December; see the January listing earlier in this section.

Mission Bay Boat Parade of Lights, from Quivira Basin in Mission Bay. Held on a Saturday, the best viewing is around Crown Point, on the east side of Vacation Island, or the west side of Fiesta Island; it concludes with the lighting of a 320-foot tower of Christmas lights at SeaWorld. Call © **858/488-0501.** For more vessels dressed up like Christmas trees, the **San Diego Boat Parade of Lights** is held in San Diego Bay on a Sunday, with a route starting at Shelter Island and running past Seaport Village and the Coronado Ferry Landing Marketplace. Visit www.sdparadeof lights.org for more information. Mid-December.

4 Travel Insurance

Check your existing insurance policies and credit-card coverage before you buy travel insurance. You may already be covered for lost luggage, canceled tickets, or medical expenses. The cost of travel insurance varies widely, depending on the cost and length of your trip, your age, health, and the type of trip you're taking.

TRIP-CANCELLATION INSURANCE Trip-cancellation insurance helps you get your money back if you have to back out of a trip, if you have to go home early, or if your travel supplier goes bankrupt. Allowed reasons for cancellation can range from sickness to natural disasters to the State Department declaring your destination unsafe for travel. (Insurers usually won't cover vague fears, though, as many travelers discovered who tried to cancel their trips in October 2001 because they were wary of flying.) In this unstable world, trip-cancellation insurance is a good buy if you're getting tickets well in advance—who knows what the state of the world, or of your airline, will be in nine months? Insurance policy details vary, so read the fine print—and especially make sure that your airline or cruise line is on the list of carriers covered in case of bankruptcy. For information, contact one of the following insurers: **Access America** (© 866/807-3982; www.access america.com); **Travel Guard International** (© 800/826-4919; www.travel guard.com); **Travel Insured International** (© 800/243-3174; www.travel insured.com); and **Travelex Insurance**

Services (© 888/457-4602; www. travelex-insurance.com).

MEDICAL INSURANCE Most health insurance policies cover you if you get sick away from home—but check, particularly if you're insured by an HMO. If you require additional medical insurance, try **MEDEX International** (© 800/527-0218 or 410/453-6300; www.medexassist.com) or **Travel Assistance International** (© 800/821-2828; www.travel assistance.com; for general information on services, call the company's Worldwide Assistance Services, Inc., at © 800/777-8710).

LOST-LUGGAGE INSURANCE On domestic flights, checked baggage is covered up to $2,500 per ticketed passenger. If you plan to check items more valuable than the standard liability, see if your valuables are covered by your homeowner's policy, get baggage insurance as part of your comprehensive travel-insurance package or buy Travel Guard's "BagTrak" product. Don't buy insurance at the airport, as it's usually overpriced. Be sure to take any valuables or irreplaceable items with you in your carry-on luggage, as many valuables (including books, money, and electronics) aren't covered by airline policies.

If your luggage is lost, immediately file a lost-luggage claim at the airport, detailing the luggage contents. For most airlines, you must report delayed, damaged, or lost baggage within 4 hours of arrival. The airlines are required to deliver luggage, once found, directly to your house or destination free of charge.

5 Health & Safety

STAYING HEALTHY

In most cases, your existing health plan will provide the coverage you need. But double-check; you may want to buy **travel medical insurance**

instead (see the section on insurance above). Bring your insurance ID card with you when you travel.

If you suffer from a chronic illness, consult your doctor before your departure. For conditions like epilepsy, diabetes, or heart problems, wear a **Medic Alert Identification Tag** (© 800/825-3785; www.medicalert. org), which will immediately alert doctors to your condition and give them access to your records through Medic Alert's 24-hour hot line.

Pack **prescription medications** in your carry-on luggage, and carry prescription medications in their original containers, with pharmacy labels— otherwise they won't make it through airport security. Also bring along copies of your prescriptions in case you lose your pills or run out. Don't forget an extra pair of contact lenses or prescription glasses.

STAYING SAFE

Fortunately, San Diego is a relatively safe destination, by big-city standards. Of the 10 largest cities in the United States, it historically has had the lowest incidence of violent crime, per capita. Still, it never hurts to take some precautions.

Virtually all areas of the city are safe during the day. Caution is advised in Balboa Park, in areas not frequented by regular foot traffic (particularly off the walkways on the Sixth Ave. side of the park). Homeless transients are common in San Diego—especially downtown, in Hillcrest, and in the beach area. They are rarely a problem, but can be unpredictable when inebriated. Downtown areas to the east of Petco Park are sparsely populated after dusk, and poorly lighted. Historically the areas with the highest rate of crime have been National City and Chula Vista.

Parts of the city that are usually safe on foot at night include the Gaslamp Quarter, Hillcrest, Old Town, Mission Valley, La Jolla, and Coronado.

6 Specialized Travel Resources

TRAVELERS WITH DISABILITIES

Most disabilities shouldn't stop anyone from traveling. There are more options and resources out there than ever before, and San Diego is one of the most accessible cities in the country. Most of the city's major attractions are wheelchair friendly, including the walkways and museums of Balboa Park, the zoo (which has bus tours to navigate the steep canyons), and downtown's Gaslamp Quarter. Old Town and the beaches require a little more effort, but are generally accessible.

Obtain more specific information from **Accessible San Diego** (© 858/ 279-0704; www.accessandiego.com), the nation's oldest center for information for travelers with disabilities. The center has an info line that helps travelers find accessible hotels, tours, attractions, and transportation. If you call long distance and get the answering machine, leave a message, and the staff will call you back collect. Ask for the annual *Access in San Diego* pamphlet, a citywide guide with specifics on which establishments are accessible for those with visual, mobility, or hearing disabilities (a nominal donation is requested). Another organization providing info and referrals is **Access Center of San Diego** (© 619/293-3500). In the San Diego Convention & Visitors Bureau's *Dining and Accommodations* guide, a wheelchair symbol designates places that are accessible to persons with disabilities.

On buses and trolleys, riders with disabilities pay a fixed fare of $1. Because discounted fares are subsidized, *technically* you must obtain a Transit Travel ID from the **Transit Store** (© 619/234-1060); the ID card certifies that a rider is eligible for the discount, but most drivers use visual qualifications to establish criteria. All MTS buses and trolleys are equipped with wheelchair lifts; priority seating is available on buses and trolleys. People with visual impairments benefit from the white reflecting ring that circles the bottom of the trolley door to increase its visibility. Airport transportation for travelers with disabilities is available in vans holding one or two wheelchairs from **Cloud 9 Shuttle** (*©* **800/9-SHUTTLE** or 858/9-SHUTTLE; www.cloud9shuttle.com).

Many of the major car-rental companies offer hand-controlled cars. **Avis** can provide a vehicle at any of its locations in the United States with 48-hour advance notice; **Hertz** requires 24 to 72 hours of advance reservation at most of its locations. **Wheelchair Getaways** (*©* **800/642-2402**; www. wheelchair-getaways.com) rents specialized vans with wheelchair lifts and other features for travelers with disabilities in more than 100 cities across the United States.

Many travel agencies offer customized tours and itineraries for travelers with disabilities. **Flying Wheels Travel** (*©* **507/451-5005**; www.flying wheelstravel.com) offers escorted tours and cruises that emphasize sports and private tours in minivans with lifts. **Accessible Journeys** (*©* **800/846-4537** or 610/521-0339; www.disabilitytravel. com) caters specifically to slow walkers and wheelchair travelers and their families and friends.

Organizations that offer assistance to travelers with disabilities include the **Moss Rehab Hospital** www.moss resourcenet.org), which provides a library of accessible-travel resources online; the **Society for Accessible Travel and Hospitality** (*©* 12/447-7284; www.sath.org; annual membership fees: $45 adults, $30 seniors and students), which offers a wealth of travel resources for all types of disabilities and informed recommendations on destinations, access guides, travel agents, tour operators, vehicle rentals, and companion services; and the **American Foundation for the Blind** (*©* **800/232-5463**; www.afb.org), which provides information on traveling with Seeing Eye dogs.

For more information specifically targeted to travelers with disabilities, the community website **iCan** (www. icanonline.net/channels/travel/index.cf m) has destination guides and several regular columns on accessible travel. Also check out the quarterly magazine *Emerging Horizons* ($14.95 per year, $19.95 outside the U.S.; www. emerginghorizons.com); **Twin Peaks Press** (*©* **360/694-2462**), offering travel-related books for travelers with special needs; and *Open World Magazine,* published by the Society for Accessible Travel and Hospitality (see above; subscription: $18/year, $35 outside the U.S.).

GAY & LESBIAN TRAVELERS

Despite the sometimes conservative local politics, San Diego is one of America's gay-friendliest destinations, boasting the country's first openly gay District Attorney in the U.S., Bonnie Dumanis. Gay and lesbian visitors might already know about Hillcrest, the trendy part of town near Balboa Park that's the city's most prominent "out" community. Many gay-owned restaurants, boutiques, and nightspots cater to a gay and straight clientele, and the scene is lively most nights of the week. In the 1990s the community's residential embrace has spread west to Mission Hills, and east along Adams Avenue to Kensington.

The **Lesbian and Gay Men's Community Center** is located at 3909 Centre St. in Hillcrest (*©* **619/692-2077**; www.thecentersd.org). It's open Monday through Friday from 9am to 10pm and Saturday from 9am to 7pm. Community outreach and counseling are offered.

The **Annual San Diego Lesbian and Gay Pride Parade, Rally, and Festival** is held on the third or fourth weekend in July. The parade begins at noon on Saturday at University Avenue and Normal Street, and proceeds west on University to Sixth Avenue, ending in Balboa Park. A festival follows on Saturday from 2 to 10pm and Sunday from noon to 10pm. For more information, call © 619/297-7683, or check www.sdpride.org).

The free *San Diego Gay and Lesbian Times,* published every Thursday, is available at the gay and lesbian **Obelisk** bookstore, 1029 University Ave., Hillcrest (© 619/297-4171), along with other gay-friendly businesses in Hillcrest and neighboring communities. And check out the **San Diego Gay & Lesbian Chamber of Commerce** online at www.gsdba.org, where you can search the 650-member business directory and find a variety restaurants, cafes, hotels, and other establishments that welcome gay and lesbian clients.

The **International Gay & Lesbian Travel Association (IGLTA)** (© 800/448-8550 or 954/776-2626; www.iglta.org) is a national trade association for the gay and lesbian travel industry, and offers an online directory of gay and lesbian-friendly travel businesses; go to their website and click on "Members."

The following travel guides are available at most travel bookstores and gay and lesbian bookstores, or you can order them from **Giovanni's Room** bookstore, 1145 Pine St., Philadelphia, PA 19107 (© 215/923-2960; www.giovannisroom.com). *Out and About* (© 800/929-2268 or 415/644-8044; www.outandabout.com) is a newsletter published 10 times a year and filled with information on the global gay and lesbian scene; *Spartacus International Gay Guide* and *Odysseus,* both good, annual English-language guidebooks focused on gay men; and the *Damron* guides, with separate, annual books for gay men and lesbians.

SENIOR TRAVEL

Nearly every attraction in San Diego offers a senior discount; age requirements vary, and prices are discussed in chapter 7 with each individual listing. Public transportation and movie theaters also have reduced rates. Don't be shy about asking for discounts, but always carry identification, such as a driver's license, that shows your date of birth. San Diego's special seniors referral and information line is © 619/560-2500.

Mention the fact that you're a senior when you make your travel reservations. Although all of the major U.S. airlines except America West have canceled their senior discount and coupon book programs, many hotels still offer discounts for seniors. In most cities, people over the age of 60 qualify for reduced admission to theaters, museums, and other attractions, as well as discounted fares on public transportation.

Members of **AARP** (formerly known as the American Association of Retired Persons), 601 E St. NW, Washington, DC 20049 (© 800/424-3410 or 202/434-2277; www.aarp.org), get discounts on hotels, airfares, and car rentals. AARP offers members a wide range of benefits, including *AARP The Magazine* and a monthly newsletter. Anyone over 50 can join.

Many reliable agencies and organizations target the 50-plus market. **Elderhostel** (© 877/426-8056; www.elderhostel.org) arranges study programs for those age 55 and over (and a spouse or companion of any age) in the U.S. and in more than 80 countries around the world. Most courses last 5 to 7 days in the U.S., and many include airfare, accommodations in university dormitories or modest inns, meals, and tuition; there is an Elderhostel program in the San Diego area, at the Point Loma Youth Hostel.

Recommended publications offering travel resources and discounts for seniors include: the quarterly magazine *Travel 50 & Beyond* (www.travel50andbeyond.com); *Travel Unlimited:*

Uncommon Adventures for the Mature Traveler (Avalon); *101 Tips for Mature Travelers,* available from Grand Circle Travel (© 800/221-2610 or 617/350-7500; www.gct.com); and *Unbelievably Good Deals & Great Adventures That You Absolutely Can't Get Unless You're Over 50* (McGraw-Hill).

FAMILY TRAVEL

If you have enough trouble getting your kids out of the house in the morning, dragging them thousands of miles away may seem like an insurmountable challenge. But family travel can be immensely rewarding, giving you new ways of seeing the world through smaller pairs of eyes, and San Diego is an ideal family-friendly destination.

You can find good family-oriented vacation advice on the Internet from sites like the **Family Travel Network** (www.familytravelnetwork.com) and **Family Travel Files** (www.thefamily travelfiles.com), which offers an online magazine and a directory of off-the-beaten-path tours and tour operators for families. Other resources include *The Unofficial Guide to California with Kids* (Wiley Publishing, Inc.), and *How to Take Great Trips with Your Kids* (The Harvard Common Press), which is full of good general advice that can apply to travel anywhere.

Family Travel Times is published six times a year (© 888/822-4388 or 212/477-5524; www.familytravel times.com), and includes a weekly call-in service for subscribers. Subscriptions are $39 a year, $49 for 2 years.

Be sure to check out the "Family-Friendly" boxes in the hotel and restaurant chapters; they will point you to the most accommodating and fun establishments. The "Especially for Kids" section in chapter 7 offers tips about which San Diego sights and attractions have the most appeal for the little ones.

MULTICULTURAL TRAVELERS

Although San Diego has a reputation as a predominantly white, middle-class, conservative-leaning metropolis, a closer look reveals a more diverse picture: 24% of the city's inhabitants are Hispanic, 9% are Asian, and 6% are African American. The **San Diego Art + Sol** website (www.sandiegoartandsol. com) is an excellent place to begin researching the city's contemporary cultural attractions; it also features interesting touring itineraries. The **San Diego Museum of Man** covers 4 million years of human history, with a particular focus on the native heritage of the Americas (p. 150).

San Diego's original residents were Native Americans, and their history is related at **Mission Trails Regional Park,** the **Junípero Serra Museum,** and at the new **American Indian Cultural Center & Museum** (© 619/819-7809; www.aiccm.org).

With the Mexican border just 16 miles from downtown San Diego, Mexico's influence is unmistakable, and Spanish street and place names are prevalent (La Jolla, for starters). The **Mission Basilica San Diego de Alcala, Junípero Serra Museum,** and **Old Town** showcase Mexican history, while contemporary culture is reflected in the murals of **Chicano Park** (under the San Diego–Coronado Bridge). **Cinco de Mayo (May 5)** is a huge celebration in Old Town, but any day is great for shopping for Central American handcrafts in **Bazaar del Mundo.** Americanized Mexican food is ubiquitous, but for a taste of the real Mexico try **El Agave Tequilaria** (p. 113), or head south of the border.

People of African descent are thought to have been a part of the convoy when Spanish explorer Cortez made his journey along the California coast in 1519, and their presence has been felt in small but important ways during San Diego's history. The Clermont Hotel, 501 Seventh Ave., was built in 1887 and was one of the city's first black-owned businesses, a segregated hotel "for colored people" until 1956; it may be the oldest surviving historically black hotel in the nation and was designated an African-American landmark in 2001. The **Gaslamp Black Historical Society** (© 619/685-7215; www.harlemofthe west.com) offers 45-minute tours of downtown San Diego's black history on Saturdays at 10:30am and 1pm; the cost is $5.

Soul of America (www.soulof america.com) is a comprehensive website offering travel tips, event and family reunion postings, and sections on historically black beach resorts and active vacations. The section on San Diego is fairly detailed and has a calendar of events.

STUDENT TRAVEL

The **International Student Identity Card (ISIC)** offers a few puny discounts on lodging and attractions in San Diego—not nearly the number of breaks you'll get in Europe. But the card also offers savings on rail passes and plane tickets and it provides you with *very* basic health and life insurance and a 24-hour help line, so it can prove worthwhile. The card is available for $22 from **STA Travel** (© 800/781-4040; www.statravel.com), the biggest student travel agency in the world. If you're no longer a student but are still under 26, you can get a **International Youth Travel Card (IYTC)** for the same price from the same people, which entitles you to some discounts (but not on museum admissions). (*Note:* In 2002, STA Travel bought competitors **Council Travel** after they went bankrupt. It's still operating some offices under the Council name, but it's owned by STA.)

Travel CUTS (© 800/667-2887 or 416/614-2887; www.travelcuts.com) offers similar services for both Canadians and US residents. Irish students should turn to **USIT** (© 01/602-1600; www.usitnow.ie).

TRAVELING WITH PETS

Many of us wouldn't dream of going on vacation without our pets. And these days, more and more lodgings and restaurants are going the pet-friendly route. In chapter 5, I've noted which hotels accept pets; the **Loews Coronado Bay Resort** (p. 93), in particular, goes out of its way to welcome pets. Many San Diegans congregate with their canine friends at **Dog Beach,** a strand located at the north end of Ocean Beach, where dogs can go for a swim, play, and socialize. After your pooch is thoroughly coated in seawater and sand, take him to the do-it-yourself **Dog Beach Dog Wash,** 2 blocks away at 4933 Voltaire St. (© 619/523-1700). For $9 you get the tub, shampoo, and all the towels you need to render him clean-smelling again.

An excellent resource is **www.pets welcome.com**, which dispenses medical tips, names of animal-friendly lodgings and campgrounds, and lists of kennels and veterinarians. Also check out *The Portable Petswelcome.com: The Complete Guide to Traveling with Your Pet* (Howell Book House), which features the best selection of pet travel information anywhere. Another resource is *Pets-R-Permitted Hotel, Motel & Kennel Directory: The Travel Resource for Pet Owners Who Travel* (Annenberg Communications).

If you plan to fly with your pet, a list of requirements for transporting live animals is available at **http://air consumer.ost.dot.gov/publications/ animals.htm**. You may be able to carry your pet on board a plane if it's small enough to put inside a carrier that can slip under the seat. Pets usually count as one piece of carry-on luggage. The ASPCA discourages travelers from checking pets as luggage at any time, as storage conditions on planes are loosely monitored, and fatal accidents are not unprecedented. Your other option is to ship your pet with a professional carrier, which can be expensive. Ask your veterinarian whether you should sedate your pet on a plane ride or give it anti-nausea medication. Never give your pet sedatives used by humans.

7 Planning Your Trip Online

SURFING FOR AIRFARES

The "big three" online travel agencies, **Expedia.com**, **Travelocity.com**, and **Orbitz.com** sell most of the air tickets bought on the Internet. (Canadian travelers should try Expedia.ca and Travelocity.ca; U.K. residents can go for Expedia.co.uk and Opodo.co.uk.) Each has different business deals with the airlines and may offer different fares on the same flights, so it's wise to shop around. Expedia and Travelocity will also send you **e-mail notification** when a cheap fare becomes available to your favorite destination. Of the smaller travel agency websites, **Side-Step** (www.sidestep.com) has gotten the best reviews from Frommer's authors. It's a browser add-on that purports to "search 140 sites at once," but in reality only beats competitors' fares as often as other sites do.

Also remember to check **airline websites,** especially those for low-fare carriers such as Southwest (the dominant carrier into San Diego) and whose fares are often misreported or simply missing from travel agency websites. Even with major airlines, you can often shave a few bucks from a fare by booking directly through the airline and avoiding a travel agency's transaction fee. But you'll get these discounts only by **booking online:** Most airlines now offer online-only fares that even their phone agents know nothing about. For the websites of airlines that fly to and from your destination, go to "Getting There," below.

Great **last-minute deals** are available through free weekly e-mail services provided directly by the airlines. Most of these are announced on Tuesday or Wednesday and must be purchased online. Most are only valid for travel that weekend, but some (such as Southwest's) can be booked weeks or months in advance. Sign up for weekly e-mail alerts at airline websites or check mega-sites that compile comprehensive lists of last-minute specials, such as **Smarter Living** (www.smarter living.com). For last-minute trips, **Site59.com** in the U.S. and **LastMinute.com** in Europe often have better deals than the major-label sites.

If you're willing to give up some control over your flight details, use an **opaque fare service** like **Priceline** (www.priceline.com; www.priceline. co.uk for Europeans) or **Hotwire** (www.hotwire.com). Both offer rock-bottom prices in exchange for travel on a "mystery airline" at a mysterious time of day, often with a mysterious change of planes enroute. The mystery airlines are all major, well-known carriers, and the airlines' routing computers have gotten a lot better than they used to be, but your chances of getting a 6am or 11pm flight are pretty high. Hotwire tells you flight prices before you buy; Priceline usually has better deals than Hotwire, but you have to play their "name our price" game. If you're new at this, the helpful folks at **BiddingForTravel** (www.biddingfor travel.com) do a good job of demystifying Priceline's prices. Priceline and Hotwire are great for flights within North America and between the U.S. and Europe. But for flights to other parts of the world, consolidators will almost always beat their fares.

For much more about airfares and savvy air-travel tips and advice, pick up a copy of *Frommer's Fly Safe, Fly Smart* (Wiley Publishing, Inc.).

SURFING FOR HOTELS

Shopping online for hotels is much easier in the U.S., Canada, and certain

> ### ⓒ Frommers.com: The Complete Travel Resource
>
> For an excellent travel-planning resource, we highly recommend Frommers.com (www.frommers.com). We're a little biased, of course, but we guarantee that you'll find the travel tips, reviews, monthly vacation giveaways, and online-booking capabilities indispensable. Among the special features are our popular **Message Boards,** where Frommer's readers post queries and share advice (sometimes we authors even show up to answer questions); **Frommers.com Newsletter,** for the latest travel bargains and insider travel secrets; and **Frommer's Destinations Section,** where you'll get expert travel tips, hotel and dining recommendations, and advice on the sights to see for more than 3,000 destinations around the globe. When your research is done, the **Online Reservations System** (www.frommers.com/book_a_trip) takes you to Frommer's preferred online partners for booking your vacation at affordable prices.

parts of Europe than it is in the rest of the world. Also, many smaller hotels and B&Bs don't show up on websites at all. Of the "big three" sites, **Expedia** may be the best choice, thanks to its long list of special deals. **Travelocity** runs a close second. Hotel specialist sites **Hotels.com** and **HotelDiscounts. com** are also reliable. An excellent free program, **TravelAxe** (www.travelaxe. net), can help you search multiple hotel sites at once, even ones you may never have heard of.

Priceline and Hotwire are even better for hotels than for airfares; with both, you're allowed to pick the neighborhood and quality level of your hotel before offering up your money. Priceline's hotel product even covers Europe and Asia, though it's much better at getting luxury lodging at discount prices than at finding anything at the bottom of the scale.

SURFING FOR RENTAL CARS

For booking rental cars online, the best deals are usually found at rental-car company websites, although all the major online travel agencies also offer rental-car reservations services. Priceline and Hotwire work well for rental cars, too; the only "mystery" is which major rental company you get, and for most travelers the difference between Hertz, Avis, and Budget is negligible.

8 The 21st-Century Traveler

INTERNET ACCESS AWAY FROM HOME

Travelers have any number of ways to check their e-mail and access the Internet on the road. Of course, using your own laptop—or even a PDA or electronic organizer with a modem—gives you the most flexibility. But even if you don't have a computer, you can still access your e-mail and even your office computer from cybercafes.

WITHOUT YOUR OWN COMPUTER

It's hard nowadays to find a city that *doesn't* have a few cybercafes. Although there's no definitive directory for cybercafes—these are independent businesses, after all—three places to start looking are at **www.cybercaptive.com**, **www.netcafeguide.com**, and **www. cybercafe.com**. See also "Your Link to Home: Internet Cafes," in this section, for my recommendations.

Aside from formal cybercafes, **public libraries** in San Diego offer free Internet access. The downtown main library (820 E St.; © **619/236-5800**) and the more modern Mission Valley branch (2123 Fenton Pkwy.; © **800/573-5007**) have the largest quantity of computers, but the waits are sometimes shorter at other branch libraries. **Hotels** that cater to business travelers often have in-room dataports and business centers, but the charges can be exorbitant. Also, most **youth hostels** nowadays have at least one computer where you can get online.

Most major airports now have **Internet kiosks** scattered throughout their gates. These kiosks, which you'll also see in shopping malls, hotel lobbies, and tourist information offices around the world, give you basic Web access for a per-minute fee that's usually higher than cybercafe prices. The kiosks' clunkiness and high price means they should be avoided whenever possible.

To retrieve your e-mail, ask your **Internet Service Provider (ISP)** if it has a Web-based interface tied to your existing e-mail account. If your ISP doesn't have such an interface, you can use the free **mail2web** service (www.mail2web.com) to view and reply to your home e-mail. For more flexibility, you may want to open a free, Web-based e-mail account with **Yahoo! Mail** (http://mail.yahoo.com) or **Fastmail** (www.fastmail.fm). (Microsoft's Hotmail is another popular option, but Hotmail has severe spam problems.) Your home ISP may be able to forward your e-mail to the Web-based account.

If you need to access files on your office computer, look into a service called **GoToMyPC** (www.gotomypc.com). The service provides a Web-based interface for you to access and

---

⎛Tips Your Link to Home: Internet Cafes

If you're looking to send e-mail or surf the Web, it's easy to do. In Hillcrest, the popular coffeehouse and study hall the Living Room, 1417 University, just west of Park Blvd. (© **619/295-7911**; www.livingroomcafe.com), has an Internet terminal. Resembling a video game screen, it takes dollar bills ($1 per 10 min.) and is open daily from 7am to 12 midnight. Other Living Room locations with terminals include 1018 Rosecrans St. in Point Loma (© 619/222-6852); 5900 El Cajon Blvd., near San Diego State University (© 619/286-8434); and 1010 Prospect St. in La Jolla (© 858/459-1187). Be aware that the terminals are prone to freeze up when performing functions more radical than e-mail.

In La Jolla's Golden Triangle, next to Von's supermarket, you'll find **Espresso Net**, 7770 Regents Rd., at Arriba Street (© **858/453-5896**; www.espressonet.com). It's a comfy, welcoming hangout with tempting desserts. The state-of-the-art computer terminals have ergonomic keyboards; online time is $6 an hour, or $1.50 for 15 minutes. It's open weekdays from 7am to 9pm, weekends from 8am to 8pm.

Near the Gaslamp Quarter, **Internet Café**, 800 Broadway, at Eighth Avenue (© **619/702-2233**), has an institutional feel and isn't much on atmosphere, but you can sip an espresso while you surf, and the relatively up-to-date computer stations will do the job. Internet access is priced $8 per hour. Open daily from 11am to 11pm.

manipulate a distant PC from any-where—even a cybercafe—provided your "target" PC is on and has an always-on connection to the Internet (such as with Road Runner cable). The service offers top-quality security, but if you're worried about hackers, use your own laptop rather than a cybercafe to access the GoToMyPC system.

WITH YOUR OWN COMPUTER

Major Internet Service Providers (ISP) have **local access numbers** around the world, allowing you to go online by simply placing a local call. Check your ISP's website or call its toll-free number and ask how you can use your current account away from home, and how much it will cost.

If you're traveling outside the reach of your ISP, the **iPass** network has dial-up numbers in most of the world's countries. You'll have to sign up with an iPass provider, who will then tell you how to set up your computer for your destination(s). For a list of iPass providers, go to www.ipass.com and click on "Individuals." One solid provider is **i2roam** (✆ **866/811-6209** or 920/235-0475; www.i2roam.com).

Wherever you go, bring a **connection kit** of the right power and phone adapters, a spare phone cord, and a spare Ethernet network cable. Almost all electrical outlets in San Diego are three-prong. Most business-class hotels offer dataports for laptop modems, and a number of hotels now offer high-speed Internet access using an Ethernet network cable. You'll have to bring your own cables either way, so call your hotel in advance to find out what the options are.

If you have an 802.11b/**Wi-fi** card for your computer, several commercial companies have made wireless service available in airports, hotel lobbies and coffee shops. **T-Mobile Hotspot** (www.t-mobile.com/hotspot) serves up wireless connections at more than 1,000 Starbucks coffee shops nation-wide. **Boingo** (www.boingo.com) and **Wayport** (www.wayport.com) have set up networks in airports and high-class hotel lobbies. IPass providers (see above) also give you access to a few hundred wireless hotel lobby setups. Best of all, you don't need to be staying at the Four Seasons to use the hotel's network; just set yourself up on a nice couch in the lobby. Unfortunately, the companies' pricing policies are byzantine, with a variety of monthly, per-connection, and per-minute plans.

Community-minded individuals have also set up **free wireless networks** in major cities around the U.S., Europe, and Australia. These networks are spotty, but you get what you (don't) pay for. Each network has a home page explaining how to set up your computer for their particular system; start your explorations at www.personal telco.net/index.cgi/Wireless Communities.

USING A CELLPHONE

Just because your cellphone works at home doesn't mean it'll work elsewhere in the country (thanks to our nation's fragmented cellphone system). It's a good bet that your phone will work in major cities. But take a look at your wireless company's coverage map on its website before heading out—T-Mobile, Sprint, and Nextel are particularly weak in rural areas.

If you're not from the U.S., you'll be appalled at the poor reach of our **GSM (Global System for Mobiles) wireless network.** Your phone will probably work in most major U.S. cities; it definitely won't work in many rural areas. And you may or may not be able to send SMS (text messaging) home—something Americans tend not to do anyway, for various cultural and technological reasons. Assume nothing—call your wireless provider and get the full scoop. In a worst-case

Online Traveler's Toolbox

Veteran travelers usually carry some essential items to make their trips easier. Following is a selection of online tools to bookmark and use.

- **Visa ATM Locator** (www.visa.com), for locations of Plus ATMs worldwide, or **MasterCard ATM Locator** (www.mastercard.com), for locations of Cirrus ATMs worldwide.
- **Intellicast** (www.intellicast.com) and **Weather.com** (www.weather.com). Gives weather forecasts for all 50 states and for cities around the world.
- **Mapquest** (www.mapquest.com). This best of the mapping sites lets you choose a specific address or destination, and in seconds, it will return a map and detailed directions.

scenario, you can always rent a phone; in San Diego, **Four Points Communications,** 3856 First Ave., Hillcrest (© 619/234-6182; www.fourpoints com.com) and **BearCom,** 4506 Federal Blvd. (© 619/263-2159; www.bearcom.com) deliver to hotels within the metro area.

9 Getting There

BY PLANE

Flights arrive at San Diego International Airport/Lindbergh Field (airport code: SAN), named after aviation hero Charles Lindbergh. It's located close to downtown San Diego and is served by most national and regional air carriers as well as Aeroméxico. Although no airline uses San Diego as a hub for connections, Southwest Airlines controls 47% of the airlift into the city.

Airlines flying into San Diego include: **Aeroméxico** (© 800/237-6639; www.aeromexico.com), **Alaska Airlines** (© 800/252-7522; www.alaskaair.com), **America West** (© 800/235-9292; www.americawest.com), **American Airlines** (© 800/433-7300; www.aa.com), **Continental Airlines** (© 800/525-0280; www.continental.com), **Delta Airlines** (© 800/221-1212; www.delta.com), **Frontier Airlines** (© 800/432-1359; www.frontierairlines.com), **Hawaiian**

Airlines (© 800/367-5320; www.hawaiianair.com), **JetBlue** (© 800/538-2583; www.jetblue.com), **Northwest Airlines** (© 800/225-2525; www.nwa.com), **Southwest Airlines** (© 800/435-9792; www.southwest.com), **United Airlines** (© 800/241-6522; www.united.com), and **US Airways** (© 800/428-4322; www.usairways.com). The Commuter Terminal, located a half-mile from the main terminals, is used by regional carriers **American Eagle** and **United Express** (for flight info contact the parent carriers listed above).

If you are staying at a hotel in Carlsbad, Encinitas, or Rancho Santa Fe, the McClellan-Palomar Airport in Carlsbad (CLD) may be a more convenient point of entry. The airport is located 42 miles north of downtown San Diego and is served by **America West Express** from Phoenix and **United Express** from Los Angeles.

GETTING THROUGH THE AIRPORT

With the federalization of airport security, security procedures at U.S. airports are more stable and consistent than ever. Generally, you'll be fine if you arrive at the airport **1 hour** before a domestic flight and **2 hours** before an international flight; if you show up late, tell an airline employee and she'll probably whisk you to the front of the line.

Bring a **current, government-issued photo ID** such as a driver's license or passport, and if you've got an E-ticket, print out the **official confirmation page;** you'll need to show your confirmation at the security checkpoint, and your ID at the ticket counter or the gate. (Children under 18 do not need photo IDs for domestic flights, but the adults checking in with them need them.)

Security lines are getting shorter, but some doozies remain. If you have trouble standing for long periods of time, tell an airline employee; the airline will provide a wheelchair. Speed up security by **not wearing metal objects** such as big belt buckles or clanky earrings. If you've got metallic body parts, a note from your doctor can prevent a long chat with the security screeners. Keep in mind that only **ticketed passengers** are allowed past security, except for folks escorting passengers with disabilities or children.

Federalization has stabilized **what you can carry on** and **what you can't.** The general rule is that sharp things are out, nail clippers are okay, and food and beverages must be passed through the X-ray machine—but that security screeners can't make you drink from your coffee cup. Bring food in your carry-on rather than checking it, as explosive-detection machines used on checked luggage have been known to mistake food (especially chocolate, for some reason) for bombs. Travelers in the U.S. are allowed one carry-on bag, plus a "personal item" such as a purse, briefcase, or laptop bag. Carry-on hoarders can stuff all sorts of things into a laptop bag; as long as it has a laptop in it, it's still considered a personal item. The Transportation Security Administration (TSA) has issued a list of restricted items; check its website (www.tsa.gov) for details.

In 2003 the TSA phased out **gate check-in** at all U.S. airports. Passengers with E-tickets and without checked bags can still beat the ticket-counter lines by using **electronic kiosks** or even **online check-in.** Ask your airline which alternatives are available, and if you're using a kiosk, bring the credit card you used to book the ticket. If you're checking bags, you will still be able to use most airlines' kiosks; again call your airline for up-to-date information. **Curbside check-in** is also a good way to avoid lines, although a few airlines still ban curbside check-in entirely; call before you go.

FLYING FOR LESS: TIPS FOR GETTING THE BEST AIRFARE

Passengers sharing the same airplane cabin rarely pay the same fare. Travelers who need to purchase tickets at the last minute, change their itinerary at a moment's notice, or fly one-way often get stuck paying the premium rate. Here are some ways to keep your airfare costs down.

- Passengers who can book their ticket **long in advance,** who can **stay over Saturday night,** or who **fly midweek** or **at less-trafficked hours** will pay a fraction of the full fare. If your schedule is flexible, say so, and ask if you can secure a cheaper fare by changing your flight plans.

- You can also save on airfares by keeping an eye out in local newspapers for **promotional specials** or **fare wars,** when airlines lower prices on their most popular routes. You rarely see fare wars offered for peak travel times, but if you can travel in the off-months, you may snag a bargain.
- Search **the Internet** for cheap fares (see "Planning Your Trip Online," earlier in this chapter).
- **Consolidators,** also known as bucket shops, are great sources for international tickets, although they usually can't beat the Internet on fares within North America. Start by looking in Sunday newspaper travel sections; U.S. travelers should focus on the *New York Times, Los Angeles Times,* and *Miami Herald. Beware:* Bucket shop tickets are usually nonrefundable or rigged with stiff cancellation penalties, often as high as 50% to 75% of the ticket price, and some put you on charter airlines with questionable safety records. Several reliable consolidators are worldwide and available on the Net. **STA Travel** is now the world's leader in student travel, thanks to its purchase of Council Travel. It also offers good fares for travelers of all ages. **Flights.com** (© 800/TRAV-800;** www.flights.com) started in Europe and has excellent fares worldwide, but particularly to that continent. It also has "local" websites in 12 countries. **FlyCheap** (© 800/FLY-CHEAP;** www.1800flycheap.com) is owned by package-holiday megalith MyTravel and so has especially good access to fares for sunny destinations.
- Join **frequent-flier clubs.** Accrue enough miles, and you'll be rewarded with free flights. Fly 25,000 miles in a calendar year and most airlines will bump you "elite" status, which affords other benefits. But you don't need to fly to build frequent-flier miles— **credit cards** tied to frequent flier programs can provide 1 mile or more per $1 charged for doing everyday shopping like groceries and gas purchases.

BY CAR

If you're planning a road trip, being a member of the **American Automobile Association (AAA)** offers helpful perks. Members who carry their cards with them not only receive free roadside assistance, but also have access to a wealth of free travel information (detailed maps and guidebooks). Also, many hotels and attractions throughout California offer discounts to AAA members—always inquire. Call © 800/922-8228 or your local branch for membership information.

Travel in the Age of Bankruptcy

At press time, two major U.S. airlines were struggling in bankruptcy court and most of the rest weren't doing very well either. To protect yourself, **buy your tickets with a credit card,** as the Fair Credit Billing Act guarantees that you can get your money back from the credit-card company if a travel supplier goes under (and if you request the refund within 60 days of the bankruptcy.) **Travel insurance** can also help, but make sure it covers against "carrier default" for your specific travel provider. And be aware that if a U.S. airline goes bust mid-trip, a 2001 federal law requires other carriers to take you to your destination (albeit on a space-available basis) for a fee of no more than $25, provided you rebook within 60 days of the cancellation.

Visitors driving to San Diego from Los Angeles and points north do so via coastal route I-5. From points northeast, take I-15 and link up with Highway 163 South as you enter Miramar (use I-8 West for the beaches). From the east, use I-8 into the city, connecting to Highway 163 South for Hillcrest and downtown. Entering the downtown area, Highway 163 turns into 10th Avenue. Try to avoid arriving during weekday rush hours, between 7 and 9am and 3 and 6pm. If you are heading to Coronado, take the San Diego–Coronado Bay Bridge from I-5. Maximum speed in the San Diego area is 65 mph, and many areas are limited to 55 mph.

San Diego is 130 miles (2–3 hr.) from **Los Angeles;** 149 miles from **Palm Springs,** a 2½-hour trip; 532 miles, or 8 to 9 hours, from **San Francisco.**

BY TRAIN

Trains from all points in the United States and Canada will take you to Los Angeles, where you'll need to change trains for the 2-hour, 40-minute journey to San Diego. You'll arrive at San Diego's striking, mission-style Santa Fe Station, built in 1914 and located downtown at Broadway and Kettner Boulevard. A few hotels are found within walking distance. The San Diego Trolley station is across the street. For price and schedule information, call **Amtrak** (© **800/USA-RAIL;** www.amtrak.com).

BY BUS

Greyhound buses serve San Diego from downtown Los Angeles, Phoenix, Las Vegas, and other southwestern cities, arriving at the downtown terminal, located at 120 W. Broadway (© **800/231-2222** or 619/239-8082; www.greyhound.com). Several hotels, Horton Plaza, and the Gaslamp Quarter are within walking distance. Buses from Los Angeles are as frequent as every 30 minutes, take about 2½ hours for the journey, and round-trip fare is $25 (one-way is $15).

10 Package Deals for the Independent Traveler

Before you start your search for the lowest airfare, you may want to consider booking your flight as part of a travel package. Packages are not the same thing as escorted tours. Packages are simply a way to buy the airfare, accommodations, and other elements of your trip (such as car rentals, airport transfers, and sometimes even activities) at the same time and often at discounted prices—kind of like one-stop shopping. Packages are sold in bulk to tour operators—who resell them to the public at a cost that usually undercuts standard rates.

Package deals can vary by leaps and bounds. Some offer a better class of hotels than others. Some offer flights on scheduled airlines, while others book charters. Some limit your choice of accommodations and travel days. You are often required to make a large payment up front. On the plus side, packages can save you money, offering group prices but allowing for independent travel. Some even let you to add on a few guided excursions or escorted day trips (also at prices lower than if you booked them yourself) without booking an entirely escorted tour.

Before you invest in a package tour, get some answers. Ask about the **accommodation choices** and prices for each. If you need a certain type of room, ask for it; don't take whatever is thrown your way. Finally, look for **hidden expenses.** Ask whether airport departure fees and taxes, for example, are included in the total cost.

One good source of package deals is the airlines themselves. Most major airlines offer air/land packages, including **American Airlines Vacations**

(© 800/321-2121; www.aavacations.com), **Continental Airlines Vacations** (© 800/301-3800; www.coolvacations.com), **Delta Vacations** (© 800/221-6666; www.deltavacations.com), **Southwest Airlines Vacations** (© 800/423-5683; www.southwest.com and www.swavacations.com), and **United Vacations** (© 888/854-3899; www.unitedvacations.com). The **San Diego Convention and Visitors Bureau** (© 800/350-6205; www.sandiego.org) has its own booking engine for packages incorporating air, hotel and activities, and the **Walt Disney Travel Company** (© 714/520-5047; www.disney.com) is the largest tour operator featuring San Diego.

Several big **online travel agencies**— Expedia, Travelocity, Orbitz, Site59, and LastMinute—also do a brisk business in packages. If you're unsure about the pedigree of a smaller packager, check with the Better Business Bureau in the city where the company is based, or go online at www.bbb.org. If a packager won't tell you where it's based, don't fly with them.

Travel packages are also listed in the travel section of your local Sunday newspaper. Or check ads in the national travel magazines such as *Arthur Frommer's Budget Travel Magazine*, *Travel & Leisure*, *National Geographic Traveler*, and *Condé Nast Traveler*.

11 Escorted Tours

Escorted tours are structured group tours, with a group leader. The price usually includes everything from airfare to hotels, meals, tours, admission costs, and local transportation.

Many people derive a certain ease and security from escorted trips. Escorted tours—whether by bus, motor coach, train, or boat—let travelers sit back and enjoy their trip without having to spend lots of time behind the wheel. All the little details are taken care of; you know your costs up front; and there are few surprises. Escorted tours can take you to the maximum number of sights in the minimum amount of time with the least amount of hassle—you don't have to sweat over the plotting and planning of a vacation schedule. Escorted tours are particularly convenient for people with limited mobility.

On the downside, an escorted tour often requires a big deposit up front, and lodging and dining choices are predetermined. As part of a cloud of tourists, you'll get little opportunity for serendipitous interactions with locals. The tours can be jam-packed with activities, leaving little room for individual sightseeing, whim, or adventure—plus they also often focus only on the heavily touristed sites, so you miss out on the lesser-known gems.

Before you invest in an escorted tour, ask about the **cancellation policy;** consider purchasing trip-cancellation insurance, especially if the tour operator asks you to pay up front. (See the section on "Travel Insurance," earlier in this chapter.) You'll also want to get a complete **schedule** of the trip to find out how much sightseeing is planned each day and whether enough time has been allotted for relaxing or wandering solo.

The **size** of the group is also important to know up front, as well as the **demographics** of the group. Be sure to discuss what is included in the **price,** and ask about the **accommodation choices.** Finally, if you plan to travel alone, you'll need to know if a **single supplement** will be charged and if the company can match you up with a roommate.

Companies that specialize in escorted trips to San Diego include **Collette Tours** (© 800/340-5158; www.collettevacations.com), **MayflowerTours** (© 630/435-8207; www.mayflowertours.com), and **Tauck World Discovery** (© 203/226-6911; www.tauck.com).

12 Recommended Reading

While New York and San Francisco may be more well known for their cosmopolitan literary mentions, San Diego is no slouch when it comes to colorful characters, bigger-than-life biographies, hard-core history, and famous fiction.

Philip Marlowe, Raymond Chandler's classic detective, spent most of his time in the literary Los Angeles of the 1940s. But the last Marlowe mystery, *Playback* (Vintage Books, 1988), includes a beautiful woman who hides out in "Esmeralda," a coastal town north of downtown San Diego that's actually La Jolla, where Chandler spent the last 13 years of his life.

The 1980 film starring Christopher Reeve and Jane Seymour may have moved the story from the Hotel del Coronado to a turn-of-the-20th-century hotel in Mackinac Island, Michigan, but *Somewhere in Time* (St. Martin's Press, 1999), penned by master thriller novelist Richard Matheson—also known for *A Stir of Echoes* (Tor Books, 1999) and *What Dreams May Come* (Tor Books, 1998)—is one of the most famous stories set in San Diego to date. Originally published in 1975 under the title *Bid Time Return* (Buccaneer Books, 1995), this science fiction slanted romantic fantasy works not only as a love story but a vivid travelogue of Southern California and the Coronado.

Coronado also figures largely in L. Frank Baum's *Oz* books, including *The Wizard of Oz* (Tor Books, 1995). The author, who lived in Coronado, based his description of the Emerald City on it. Another San Diego local, Theodor Geisel (aka Dr. Seuss), wrote many of his much-loved fantasy books while living in La Jolla.

Best-selling cop novelist Joseph Wambaugh has also placed two of his recent novels in his adopted hometown. *Finnegan's Week* (Bantam Books, 1996) depicts a week in the life of an aging detective juggling his midlife crisis with citywide crimes and hijinks. And *Floaters* (Bantam Books, 1997) is a mystery revolving around an impending America's Cup sailing race.

The Pump House Gang (Bantam Doubleday Dell, 1999), a psychedelic collection of 1960s essays by Tom Wolfe, is named for the often-crazy coterie of expert surfers that hung out at La Jolla's Windansea beach; the eponymous short story vividly captures a sense of place and of an entire generation.

Generally recognized as the most accurate depiction of sea life at the time, Richard Henry Dana's *Two Years Before the Mast* (Signet, 2000) is an autobiographical account of Dana's voyage along the coast of California in the 1840s. Much of the book features Dana's experiences in ports in San Diego and Orange County.

Thomas S. Hines's gorgeous coffee-table book, *Irving Gill and the Architecture of Reform: A Study in Modernist Architectural Culture* (Monacelli, 2000), features photographs and text that showcases the artist's early-20th-century modern style. Architectural buffs will enjoy Gill's designs that, while lesser known than those of his contemporaries like Wright, Frey, Neutra, and Schindler, are local landmarks. Much of Gill's work is in La Jolla. The city's distinctive style is also highlighted in the guidebook *San Diego Architecture* (San Diego Architectural Foundation, 2002), by Dirk Sutro.

Mission San Luis Rey in northern San Diego County inspired the setting in Helen Hunt Jackson's 1884 novel, *Ramona: A Story* (New American Library, 1988). A love story that holds up even with today's jaded audiences, Jackson's tale incorporates a changing California (the fading Spanish order, the decline of Native American tribes, the arrival of white settlers) into its enduring drama. The Estudillo House in Old Town is sometimes called "Ramona's House" because it so closely resembles the vivid description in the book.

Local sports hero Greg Louganis (a San Diego native) is best known for his gold medal–winning diving performances at the 1984 and 1988 Olympics, but *Breaking the Surface* (Plume, 1996), his emotional and inspiring autobiography, paints a portrait not just of physical accomplishment, but of a sensitive athlete who struggled with self-doubt before coming out as an HIV-positive gay man. An avid animal lover and breeder, Louganis is also the author of *For the Life of Your Dog: A Complete Guide to Having a Dog in Your Life* (Pocket Books, 1999).

Published by the San Diego Historical Society, Elizabeth C. MacPhail's *The Story of New San Diego and of its Founder, Alonzo E. Horton* (San Diego Historical Society, 1989) is packed with facts about Horton's tireless belief that San Diego could be a major port city, and reasons why his "New" San Diego—the genesis of today's bustling downtown—succeeded where two previous attempts to relocate from "Old Town" had failed. Even just flipping through the many archival photos is eye-opening.

The brother-and-sister team of E. W. and Ellen Browning were responsible for, among other things, the establishment of the Scripps Institute of Oceanography, early funding of the San Diego Zoo, creating Torrey Pines State Park, and leaving a permanent imprint on the community of La Jolla. In *Edward Willis and Ellen Browning Scripps: An Unmatched Pair* (Image Books, 1990), Charles Preece offers the best biography of these two pillars of San Diego's philanthropic Scripps family.

Another local luminary, Dr. Harry M. Wegeforth, was the energetic founder of the San Diego Zoo and is the subject of *It Began With a Roar* (Zoological Society of San Diego, 1990), written by Wegeforth and San Diego newspaperman Neil Morgan. This thin, fun volume relates the adventures of the zoo's early days from Wegeforth's own memoirs.

3

For International Visitors

Whether it's your first visit or your tenth, a trip to the United States may require an additional degree of planning. This chapter will provide you with essential information, helpful tips, and advice for the more common problems that some visitors encounter.

1 Preparing for Your Trip

ENTRY REQUIREMENTS

Check at any U.S. embassy or consulate for current information and requirements. You can also obtain a visa application and other information online from the **U.S. State Department** website at **http://travel.state.gov**.

VISAS The U.S. State Department has a **Visa Waiver Program** allowing citizens of certain countries to enter the United States without a visa for stays of up to 90 days. At press time these included Andorra, Australia, Austria, Belgium, Brunei, Denmark, Finland, France, Germany, Iceland, Ireland, Italy, Japan, Liechtenstein, Luxembourg, Monaco, the Netherlands, New Zealand, Norway, Portugal, San Marino, Singapore, Slovenia, Spain, Sweden, Switzerland, and the United Kingdom. Citizens of these countries need only a valid passport and a round-trip air or cruise ticket in their possession upon arrival. If they first enter the United States, they may also visit Mexico, Canada, Bermuda, and/or the Caribbean islands and return to the United States without a visa. Further information is available from any U.S. embassy or consulate. Canadian citizens may enter the United States without visas; they need only proof of residence.

Citizens of all other countries must have (1) a valid passport that expires at least 6 months later than the scheduled end of their visit to the United States, and (2) a tourist visa, which may be obtained without charge from any U.S. consulate.

British subjects can obtain up-to-date visa information by calling the **U.S. Embassy Visa Information Line** (✆ **0891/200-290**) or by visiting the "Consular Services" section of the American Embassy London's website at www.usembassy.org.uk.

Irish citizens can obtain up-to-date visa information through the **Embassy of USA Dublin** at ✆ **353/1-668-8777** or by checking the "Consular Services" section of the website at www.usembassy.ie.

Australian citizens can obtain up-to-date visa information by contacting the **U.S. Embassy Canberra** at ✆ **02/6214-5600**, or by checking the U.S. Diplomatic Mission's website at http://usembassy-australia.state.gov/consular.

Citizens of **New Zealand** can obtain up-to-date visa information by calling the **U.S. Embassy New Zealand** at ✆ **644/472-2068**, or get the information directly from the "Services to New Zealanders" section of the website at http://usembassy.org.nz.

MEDICAL REQUIREMENTS

Unless you're arriving from an area known to be suffering from an **epidemic** (particularly cholera or yellow fever), inoculations or vaccinations are not required for entry into the United States. If you have a medical condition that requires **syringe-administered medications,** carry a valid signed prescription from your physician—the Federal Aviation Administration (FAA) no longer allows airline passengers to pack syringes in their carry-on baggage without documented proof of medical need. If you have a disease that requires treatment with **narcotics,** you should also carry documented proof with you—smuggling narcotics aboard a plane is a serious offense that carries severe penalties in the United States.

For **HIV-positive visitors,** requirements for entering the United States are somewhat vague and change frequently. According to the latest publication of *HIV and Immigrants: A Manual for AIDS Service Providers,* the Immigration and Naturalization Service (INS) doesn't require a medical exam for entry into the United States, but INS officials may stop individuals because they look sick or because they are carrying AIDS/HIV medicine.

If an HIV-positive noncitizen applies for a nonimmigrant visa, the question on the application regarding communicable diseases is tricky no matter which way it's answered. If the applicant checks "no," INS may deny the visa on the grounds that the applicant committed fraud. If the applicant checks "yes" or if INS suspects the person is HIV-positive, it will deny the visa unless the applicant asks for a special waiver for visitors. This waiver is for people visiting the United States for a short time, to attend a conference, for instance, to visit close relatives, or to receive medical treatment. It can be a confusing situation. For up-to-the-minute information, contact the **AIDSinfo** (✆ **800/448-0440**

or 301/519-6616; www.aidsinfo.nih. gov) or the **Gay Men's Health Crisis** (✆ **212/367-1000;** www.gmhc.org).

DRIVER'S LICENSES Foreign driver's licenses are mostly recognized in the United States, although you may want to get an international driver's license if your home license is not written in English.

PASSPORT INFORMATION

Safeguard your passport in an inconspicuous, inaccessible place like a money belt. Make a copy of the critical pages, including the passport number, and store it in a safe place, separate from the passport itself. If you lose your passport, visit the nearest consulate of your native country as soon as possible for a replacement. Passport applications are downloadable from the websites listed below.

Note: Many countries are now requiring that children must be issued their own passport to travel internationally, where before those under 16 or so may have been allowed to travel on a parent or guardian's passport.

IN CANADA You can pick up a passport application at one of 28 regional passport offices or most travel agencies. Canadian children who travel must have their own passport. However, if you hold a valid Canadian passport issued before December 11, 2001, that bears the name of your child, the passport remains valid for you and your child until it expires. Passports cost C$85 for those 16 years and older (valid 5 years), C$35 children 3 to 15 (valid 5 years), and C$20, children under 3 (valid for 3 years). Applications are available at travel agencies throughout Canada or from the central **Passport Office,** Department of Foreign Affairs and International Trade, Ottawa K1A 0G3 (✆ **800/567-6868;** www.dfait-maeci. gc.ca/passport). Processing takes 5 to 10 days if you apply in person, or about 3 weeks by mail.

IN THE UNITED KINGDOM

To pick up an application for a standard 10-year passport (5-year passport for children under 16), visit the nearest Passport Office, major post office, or travel agency. You can also contact the **United Kingdom Passport Service** at ℂ **0870/571-0410** or visit its website at www.passport.gov.uk. Passports are £33 for adults and £19 for children under 16, with an additional £30 fee if you apply in person at a Passport Office. Processing takes about 2 weeks (1 week if you apply at the Passport Office).

IN IRELAND

You can apply for a 10-year passport, costing €57, at the main **Passport Office,** Setanta Centre, Molesworth Street, Dublin 2 (ℂ **01/ 671-1633;** www.irlgov.ie/iveagh). You can also apply at 1A South Mall, Cork (ℂ 021/272-525), or over the counter at most main post offices. Travelers under 18 and over 65 must apply for a 3-year passport, which costs €12.

IN AUSTRALIA

You can pick up an application from your local post office or any **Australian State Passport Office,** but you must schedule an interview at a passport office to present your application materials. Call the passport office information service at ℂ **131-232** or visit the government website at www.passports.gov.au for complete details. Passports for adults are A$144 and for those under 18 A$72.

IN NEW ZEALAND

You can pick up a passport application at any New Zealand Passports Office or download it from their website. Contact the **Passport Office** at ℂ **0800/225-050** in New Zealand or 04/474-8100, or log on to www.passports.govt.nz. Passports for adults are NZ$80 and for children under 16 NZ$40.

CUSTOMS

WHAT YOU CAN BRING IN

Every visitor more than 21 years of age may bring in, free of duty, the following: (1) 1 liter of wine or hard liquor; (2) 200 cigarettes, 100 cigars (but not from Cuba), or 3 pounds of smoking tobacco; and (3) $100 worth of gifts. These exemptions are offered to travelers who spend at least 72 hours in the United States and who have not claimed them within the preceding 6 months. It is altogether forbidden to bring into the country foodstuffs (particularly fruit, cooked meats, and canned goods) and plants (vegetables, seeds, tropical plants, and the like). Foreign tourists may bring in or take out up to $10,000 in U.S. or foreign currency with no formalities; larger sums must be declared to U.S. Customs on entering or leaving, which includes filing form CM 4790. For more specific information regarding U.S. Customs, call your nearest U.S. embassy or consulate, or the **U.S. Customs** office at ℂ **202/927-1770** or www.customs.gov.

WHAT YOU CAN TAKE HOME

FOR CANADIAN CITIZENS   If you've been out of the country for over 48 hours, you may bring back C$200 worth of goods, and if you've been gone for 7 consecutive days or more, not counting your departure, the limit is C$750. The limit for alcohol is up to 1.5 liters of wine or 1.14 liters of liquor, or 24 12-ounce cans or bottles of beer; and up to 200 cigarettes, 50 cigars, or 200 grams of tobacco. You may not ship tobacco or alcohol, and you must be of legal age for your province to bring these items through Customs. For the helpful booklet *I Declare,* call the **Canada Customs and Review Agency** at ℂ **800/461-9999** in Canada, or 204/983-3500, or visit its website at www.ccra-adrc.gc.ca.

FOR U.K. CITIZENS   U.K. citizens returning from a non-EU country have an allowance of 200 cigarettes; 50 cigars; 250 grams of smoking tobacco; 2 liters of still table wine; 1 liter of spirits or strong liqueurs (over 22% volume); 2 liters of fortified wine, sparkling wine or other liqueurs; 60cc (ml) perfume; 250cc (ml) of toilet water; and £145 worth of all other goods, including gifts and souvenirs. People under 17 cannot have the tobacco or alcohol allowance. For more information, call the **HM Customs & Excise** at (✆ **0845/ 010-9000,** or log on to www.hmce. gov.uk.

FOR AUSTRALIAN CITIZENS

The duty-free allowance in Australia is A$400 or, for those under 18, A$200. Citizens over 18 can bring in 250 cigarettes or 250 grams of loose tobacco, and 1,125 milliliters of alcohol. If you're returning with valuables you already own, such as foreign-made cameras, you should file form B263. A helpful brochure available from Australian consulates or Customs offices is *Know Before You Go.* For more information, call the **Australian Customs Service** at (✆ **1300/363-263,** or log on to www.customs.gov.au.

FOR NEW ZEALAND CITIZENS

The duty-free allowance for New Zealand is NZ$700. Citizens over 17 can bring in 200 cigarettes, 50 cigars, or 250 grams of tobacco (or a mixture of all three if their combined weight doesn't exceed 250g); plus 4.5 liters of wine and beer, or 1.125 liters of liquor. New Zealand currency does not carry import or export restrictions. Fill out a certificate of export, listing the valuables you are taking out of the country; that way, you can bring them back without paying duty. Most questions are answered in a free pamphlet available at New Zealand consulates and Customs offices: *New Zealand Customs Guide for Travellers, Notice no. 4.* For more information, contact **New Zealand Customs,** The Customhouse, 17–21 Whitmore St., Box 2218, Wellington (✆ **0800/ 428-786** or 04/473-6099; www. customs.govt.nz).

HEALTH INSURANCE

Although it's not required of travelers, health insurance is highly recommended. Unlike many European countries, the United States does not usually offer free or low-cost medical care to its citizens or visitors. Doctors and hospitals are expensive, and in most cases will require advance payment or proof of coverage before they render their services. Policies can cover everything from the loss or theft of your baggage and trip cancellation to the guarantee of bail in case you're arrested. Good policies will also cover the costs of an accident, repatriation, or death. See "Travel Insurance" in chapter 2 for more information. Packages such as **Europ Assistance's "Worldwide Healthcare Plan"** are sold by European automobile clubs and travel agencies at attractive rates. **Worldwide Assistance Services, Inc.** (✆ **800/821-2828;** www.worldwide assistance.com) is the agent for Europ Assistance in the United States.

Though lack of health insurance may prevent you from being admitted to a hospital in nonemergencies, don't worry about being left on a street corner to die: The American way is to fix you now and bill the heck out of you later.

INSURANCE FOR BRITISH TRAVELERS Most big travel agents offer their own insurance, and will probably try to sell you their package when you book a holiday. Think before you sign. **Britain's Consumers' Association** recommends that you insist on seeing the policy and reading the fine print before buying travel insurance. **The Association of British Insurers** (✆ **020/7600-3333;** www.abi.org.uk) gives advice by phone and publishes *Holiday Insurance,* a free guide to policy provisions and prices. You might also shop around for better deals: Try **Columbus Direct** at (✆ **020/7375-0011** or www.columbusdirect.net.

INSURANCE FOR CANADIAN TRAVELERS Canadians should check with their provincial health plan offices or call **Health Canada** (© **613/ 957-2991**; www.hc-sc.gc.ca) to find out the extent of their coverage and what documentation and receipts they must take home in case they are treated in the United States.

MONEY

CURRENCY The U.S. monetary system is very simple: The most common **bills** are the $1 (colloquially, a "buck"), $5, $10, and $20 denominations. There are also $2 bills (seldom encountered), $50 bills, and $100 bills (the last two are usually not welcome as payment for small purchases). All the paper money was recently redesigned, making the famous faces adorning them disproportionately large. The old-style bills are still legal tender.

There are seven denominations of coins: 1¢ (1 cent, or a penny); 5¢ (5 cents, or a nickel); 10¢ (10 cents, or a dime); 25¢ (25 cents, or a quarter); 50¢ (50 cents, or a half dollar); the newer gold "Sacagawea" coin worth $1; and, prized by collectors, the rare, older silver dollar.

Note: The "foreign-exchange bureaus" so common in Europe are rare even at airports in the United States, and nonexistent outside major cities. It's best not to change foreign money (or traveler's checks denominated in a currency other than U.S. dollars) at a small-town bank, or even a branch in a big city; in fact, leave any currency other than U.S. dollars at home—it may prove a greater nuisance to you than it's worth.

TRAVELER'S CHECKS Though traveler's checks are widely accepted, make sure that they're denominated in U.S. dollars, as foreign-currency checks are often difficult to exchange. The three traveler's checks that are most widely recognized—and least likely to be denied—are **Visa, American Express,** and **Thomas Cook.** Be sure to record the numbers of the checks, and keep that information in a separate place in case they get lost or stolen. Most businesses are pretty good about taking traveler's checks, but you're better off cashing them in at a bank (in small amounts, of course) and paying in cash. *Remember:* You'll need identification, such as a driver's license or passport, to change a traveler's check.

CREDIT CARDS & ATMs Credit cards are the most widely used form of payment in the United States: **Visa** (BarclayCard in Britain), **MasterCard** (EuroCard in Europe, Access in Britain, Chargex in Canada), **American Express, Diners Club,** and **Discover.** There are, however, a few stores and restaurants that do not take credit cards, so be sure to ask in advance. Most businesses display a sticker near their entrance to let you know which cards they accept.

It is strongly recommended that you bring at least one major credit card. You must have a credit or charge card to rent a car. Hotels and airlines usually require a credit-card imprint as a deposit against expenses, and in an emergency a credit card can be priceless.

You'll find **automated teller machines (ATMs)** on just about every block—at least in areas where there are shops and businesses—across the country. Some ATMs will allow you to draw U.S. currency against your bank and credit cards. Check with your bank before leaving home, and remember that you will need your personal identification number (PIN) to do so. Most accept Visa, MasterCard, and American Express, as well as ATM cards from other U.S. banks. Expect to be charged up to $3 per transaction, however, if you're not using your own bank's ATM.

One way around these fees is to ask for cash back at grocery stores that accept ATM cards and don't charge

---

Travel Tip

Be sure to keep a copy of all your travel papers separate from your wallet or purse, and leave a copy with someone at home should you need it faxed in an emergency.

---

usage fees. Of course, you'll have to purchase something first.

SAFETY

GENERAL SAFETY SUGGESTIONS Although San Diego's tourist areas are generally safe, urban areas in the United States tend to be less safe than those in Europe or Japan. You should always stay alert, although San Diego's crime rate is low compared to other American cities. If you're in doubt about which neighborhoods are safe, don't hesitate to make inquiries with the hotel front desk staff or the local tourist office.

Avoid deserted areas at night, and don't go into public parks after dark unless there's a concert or similar occasion that will attract a crowd. In Balboa Park, stay on designated walkways and away from secluded areas, day and night. In downtown, don't stray east of Petco Park at night. Homeless individuals are found in many pockets of the city—they are rarely looking for trouble but you should avoid groups of vagrants or those who may be inebriated.

Avoid carrying valuables with you on the street, and keep expensive cameras or electronic equipment bagged up or covered when not in use. If you're using a map, try to consult it inconspicuously—or better yet, study it before you leave your room. Hold onto your pocketbook, and place your billfold in an inside pocket. In theaters, restaurants, and other public places, keep your possessions in sight.

Always lock your room door—don't assume that once you're inside the hotel you are automatically safe and no longer need to be aware of your surroundings. Hotels are open to the public, and in a large hotel, security may not be able to screen everyone who enters.

DRIVING SAFETY Driving safety is important too, and carjacking is not unprecedented. Question your rental agency about personal safety and ask for a traveler-safety brochure when you pick up your car. Obtain written directions—or a map with the route clearly marked—from the agency showing how to get to your destination. (Many agencies now offer the option of renting a cellphone for the duration of your car rental; check with the rental agent when you pick up the car. Otherwise, contact **InTouch USA** at © **800/872-7626** or www.intouchusa.com for short-term cellphone rental.) And, if possible, arrive and depart during daylight hours.

If you drive off a highway and end up in a dodgy-looking neighborhood, leave the area as quickly as possible. If you have an accident, even on the highway, stay in your car with the doors locked until you assess the situation or until the police arrive. If you're bumped from behind on the street or are involved in a minor accident with no injuries, and the situation appears to be suspicious, motion to the other driver to follow you. Never get out of your car in such situations. Go directly to the nearest police precinct, well-lit service station, or 24-hour store.

Whenever possible, always park in well-lit and well-traveled areas. Always keep your car doors locked, whether the vehicle is attended or unattended. Never leave any packages or valuables in sight. If someone attempts to rob you or steal your car, don't try to resist the thief/carjacker. Report the incident to the police department immediately by calling © **911.**

2 Getting to the United States

The only direct international flights to San Diego are from Mexico. Other overseas travelers bound for San Diego will need to change planes at another U.S. gateway. If your port of entry is Los Angeles, you can fly to San Diego or take a train or bus. Unfortunately, the Los Angeles train and bus stations are a long way from Los Angeles International Airport (LAX), so it isn't convenient to use these modes of transportation to get to San Diego. However, if you're flying into Los Angeles and staying there a few days, taking the train or bus to San Diego makes a lot of sense, particularly as a round-trip Los Angeles–San Diego plane ticket can cost well over $100 (purchasing it in conjunction with your international ticket usually costs less).

As mentioned in chapter 2, **Aeroméxico** (℗ **01800/021-4010** in Mexico, or 800/237-6639 in the U.S.; www.aeromexico.com) serves San Diego International Airport. International carriers that serve LAX and other U.S. gateways include **Aer Lingus** (℗ **01/705-3333** in Dublin, or 800/IRISH-AIR in the U.S.; www.aerlingus.ie); **Air New Zealand** (℗**0800/737-000** in Auckland, or 800/262-1234 in the U.S.; www.airnz.com); **Japan Airlines** (℗ **0354/89-1111** in Tokyo, or 800/JAL-FONE in the U.S.; www.jal.co.jp); and **Qantas** (℗ **13-13-13** in Australia, or 800/227-4500 in the U.S.; www.qantas.com.au).

AIRLINE DISCOUNTS You can find numerable ways to reduce the price of a plane ticket simply by taking time to shop around. For example, overseas visitors can take advantage of the APEX (Advance Purchase Excursion) reductions offered by all major U.S. and European carriers. For more money-saving airline advice, see "Getting There," in chapter 2. For the best rates, compare fares and be flexible with the dates and times of travel.

IMMIGRATION & CUSTOMS CLEARANCE Visitors arriving by air, no matter what the port of entry, should cultivate patience and resignation before setting foot on U.S. soil. Getting through immigration control can take as long as 2 hours on some days, especially on summer weekends, so be sure to carry this guidebook or something else to read.

3 Getting Around the United States

BY PLANE
Some large airlines (for example, Northwest and Delta) offer travelers on their transatlantic or transpacific flights special discount tickets under the name **Visit USA**, allowing mostly one-way travel from one U.S. destination to another at very low prices. These discount tickets are not on sale in the United States and must be purchased abroad in conjunction with your international ticket. This system is the best, easiest, and fastest way to see the United States at low cost. You should obtain information well in advance from your travel agent or the office of the airline concerned, since the conditions attached to these discount tickets can be changed without advance notice.

BY TRAIN
Although train service between San Diego and Los Angeles is frequent and easy, rail travel from points outside of Southern California is limited and can

be time-consuming. Still, exploring America by train can be pleasurable, if you have the time. International visitors (excluding Canada) can buy a **USA Railpass,** good for 15 or 30 days of unlimited travel on Amtrak (© **800/ USA-RAIL;** www.amtrak.com). The pass is available through many foreign travel agents. If your exploring will be limited to the West Coast, you can buy a 30-day **Coastal Rail Pass** covering routes within California, Oregon, and Washington; a **California Rail Pass** is also available. With a foreign passport, you can also buy passes at some Amtrak offices in the United States, including locations in San Francisco, Los Angeles, Chicago, New York, Miami, Boston, and Washington, D.C. Reservations are generally required and should be made for each part of your trip as early as possible.

BY BUS

Although bus travel is often the most economical form of public transit for short hops between U.S. cities, it can also be slow and uncomfortable—

certainly not an option for everyone (particularly when Amtrak, which is more luxurious, offers similar rates). **Greyhound/Trailways** (©**800/231-2222;** www.greyhound.com), the sole nationwide bus line, offers an **International Ameripass** that must be purchased before coming to the United States, or by phone through the Greyhound International Office at the Port Authority Bus Terminal in New York City (© **212/971-0492**). The pass can be obtained from foreign travel agents and costs less than the domestic version. You can get more info on the pass at by calling © **402/ 330-8552** or visiting Greyhound's website. In addition, special rates are available for seniors and students.

BY CAR

The most cost-effective, convenient, and comfortable way to travel around the United States—especially California—is by car. For detailed information on automobile rentals in San Diego, see "Getting Around: By Car," in chapter 4.

FAST FACTS: For the International Traveler

Automobile Organizations Auto clubs will supply maps, suggested routes, guidebooks, accident and bail-bond insurance, and emergency road service. The **American Automobile Association (AAA)** is the major auto club in the United States. If you belong to an auto club in your home country, inquire about AAA reciprocity before you leave. You may be able to join AAA even if you're not a member of a reciprocal club; to inquire, call AAA at © **800/222-4357,** or visit www.aaa-calif.com.

Business Hours Banks and offices are usually open weekdays from 9am to 5pm. Stores, especially in shopping complexes, tend to stay open until about 9pm on weekdays and 6pm on weekends.

Electricity Like Canada, the United States uses 110 to 120 volts AC (60 cycles), compared to 220 to 240 volts AC (50 cycles) in most of Europe, Australia, and New Zealand. If your small appliances use 220 to 240 volts, you'll need a 110-volt transformer and a plug adapter with two flat parallel pins to operate them here. Downward converters that change 220–240 volts to 110–120 volts are difficult to find in the United States, so bring one with you.

Embassies & Consulates All embassies are located in the nation's capital, Washington, D.C.; some consulates are located in major U.S. cities. If your country isn't listed below, call for directory information in Washington, D.C. (© **202/555-1212**) or log on to www.embassy.org/embassies.

The embassy of **Australia** is at 1601 Massachusetts Ave. NW, Washington, DC 20036 (© **202/797-3000;** www.austemb.org).

The embassy of **Canada** is at 501 Pennsylvania Ave. NW, Washington, DC 20001 (© **202/682-1740;** www.canadianembassy.org).

The embassy of **Ireland** is at 2234 Massachusetts Ave. NW, Washington, DC 20008 (© **202/462-3939;** www.irelandemb.org).

The embassy of **New Zealand** is at 37 Observatory Circle NW, Washington, DC 20008 (© **202/328-4800;** www.nzemb.org). A consular office is located in San Diego at 4365 Executive Dr., Suite 1100 (© **858/677-1485**).

The embassy of the **United Kingdom** is at 3100 Massachusetts Ave. NW, Washington, DC 20008 (© **202/462-1340;** www.britainusa.com). There is a consular office in San Diego at 7825 Fay Ave. (© **858/459-8232**).

Emergencies Call © **911** to report a fire, call the police, or get an ambulance anywhere in the United States. This is a toll-free call (meaning that no coins are required at public telephones).

If you encounter serious problems, contact the San Diego chapter of **Traveler's Aid International** at © **619/231-7361,** or log on to www.travelers aid.org to help direct you to a local branch. This nationwide, nonprofit, social-service organization geared to helping travelers in difficult straits offers services that might include reuniting families separated while traveling, providing food and/or shelter to people stranded without cash, or even emotional counseling. If you're in trouble, seek them out.

Gasoline (Petrol) Petrol is known as gasoline (or simply "gas") in the United States, and petrol stations are known as both gas stations and service stations. Gasoline costs about half as much here as it does in Europe (about $1.90 per gal. at press time), and taxes are already included in the printed price. One U.S. gallon equals 3.8 liters or .85 imperial gallons. Most gas stations accept credit cards.

Holidays Banks, government offices, post offices, and many stores, restaurants, and museums are closed on the following legal national holidays: January 1 (New Year's Day), the third Monday in January (Martin Luther King, Jr., Day), the third Monday in February (Presidents' Day), the last Monday in May (Memorial Day), July 4 (Independence Day), the first Monday in September (Labor Day), the second Monday in October (Columbus Day), November 11 (Veterans' Day/Armistice Day), the fourth Thursday in November (Thanksgiving Day), and December 25 (Christmas). Also, the Tuesday following the first Monday in November is Election Day and is a federal government holiday in presidential-election years (held every 4 years, and next in 2004).

Legal Aid If you are "pulled over" for a minor infraction (such as speeding), never attempt to pay the fine directly to a police officer; this could be construed as attempted bribery, a much more serious crime. Pay fines by mail, or directly into the hands of the clerk of the court. If accused of a more serious offense, say and do nothing before consulting a lawyer.

Here the burden is on the state to prove a person's guilt beyond a reasonable doubt, and everyone has the right to remain silent, whether he or she is suspected of a crime or actually arrested. Once arrested, a person can make one telephone call to a party of his or her choice. Call your embassy or consulate.

Liquor Laws The legal age for purchase and consumption of alcoholic beverages is 21; proof of age is required and often requested at bars, nightclubs, and restaurants, so it's always a good idea to bring ID when you go out. Beer and wine can be purchased in California supermarkets, but liquor laws vary in other states.

Do not carry open containers of alcohol in your car or any public area that isn't zoned for alcohol consumption—the police can fine you on the spot. Beer in a can, *not* a bottle, is allowed at San Diego beaches—check signs at beach entrances for exact rules. Nothing will ruin your trip faster than getting a citation for DUI ("driving under the influence"), so don't even think about driving while intoxicated.

Mail If you aren't sure what your address will be in the United States, mail can be sent to you, in your name, c/o General Delivery, San Diego Post Office, 2535 Midway Dr., San Diego, CA 92138 U.S.A. (Call © **800/ 275-8777** for more information, or log on to **www.usps.gov**.) The addressee must pick up mail in person and must produce proof of identity (driver's license, passport, and so on). Most post offices will hold your mail for up to 1 month, and are open Monday through Friday from 8am to 5pm, and Saturday from 9am to 12noon.

At press time, domestic postage rates were 23¢ for a postcard and 37¢ for a letter. For international mail, a first-class letter of up to a half-ounce costs 60¢ (46¢ to Canada and 40¢ to Mexico); a first-class postcard costs 50¢ (including to Canada and Mexico); and a preprinted postal aerogramme costs 50¢.

Measurements See the chart on the inside front cover of this book for details on converting metric measurements to U.S. equivalents.

Taxes The United States has no value-added tax (VAT) or other indirect tax at the national level. Every state, county, and city has the right to levy its own local tax on all purchases, including hotel and restaurant checks, airline tickets, and so on. These taxes are not included in the price you'll see on merchandise, and are not refundable for foreign visitors. Sales tax in San Diego is 7.75%; tax on hotel rooms is 10.5%.

Telephone & Fax The telephone system in the United States is run by private corporations, so rates, especially for long-distance service and operator-assisted calls, can vary widely. Generally, hotel surcharges on long-distance and local calls are astronomical, so you're usually better off using a **public pay telephone,** which you'll find clearly marked in most public buildings and private establishments as well as on the street. Convenience grocery stores and gas stations always have them. Many convenience groceries and packaging services sell **prepaid calling cards** in denominations up to $50; these can be the least expensive way to call home. Many public phones at airports now accept American Express, MasterCard, and Visa credit cards. **Local calls** made from public pay phones in most locales cost either 25¢ or 35¢. Pay phones do not accept pennies, and few will take anything larger than a quarter.

Most long-distance and international calls can be dialed directly from any phone. **For calls within the United States, to Canada and to some Caribbean islands,** dial 1 followed by the three-digit area code and the seven-digit local number. **For other international calls, including Mexico,** dial 011 followed by the country code, city code, and the telephone number of the person you are calling.

Calls to area codes **800, 888, 877,** and **866** are toll-free. However, calls to numbers in area codes **700** and **900** (chat lines, bulletin boards, "dating" services, and so on) can be very expensive—usually a charge of 95¢ to $3 or more per minute, and they sometimes have minimum charges that can run as high as $15 or more.

For **reversed-charge or collect calls,** and for person-to-person calls, dial 0 (zero, not the letter O) followed by the area code and number you want; an operator will then come on the line, and you should specify that you are calling collect, or person-to-person, or both. If your operator-assisted call is international, ask for the overseas operator.

For **directory assistance** ("information"), dial 411 for both local and long distance numbers.

Most hotels have **fax machines** available for guest use (be sure to ask about the charge to use it). Many hotel rooms are even wired for guests' fax machines. A less expensive way to send and receive faxes may be at stores such as The UPS Store (formerly known as Mail Boxes Etc.), a national chain of packing service shops. (Look in the Yellow Pages directory under "Packing Services.")

Time The continental United States is divided into **four time zones:** Eastern Standard Time (EST), Central Standard Time (CST), Mountain Standard Time (MST), and Pacific Standard Time (PST). Alaska and Hawaii have their own zones. For example, noon in New York City (EST) is 11am in Chicago (CST), 10am in Denver (MST), 9am in San Diego (PST), 8am in Anchorage (AST), and 7am in Honolulu (HST).

Daylight savings time is in effect from 1am on the first Sunday in April to 1am on the last Sunday in October, except in Arizona. Daylight savings time moves the clock 1 hour ahead of standard time.

Tipping Tips are a very important part of certain workers' salaries, so it's necessary to leave appropriate gratuities. In hotels, tip **bellhops** at least $1 per bag ($2–$3 if you have a lot of luggage) and tip the **chamber staff** $1 to $2 per day (more if you've left a disaster area for him or her to clean up). Tip the **doorman** or **concierge** only if he or she has provided you with some specific service (for example, calling a cab for you or obtaining difficult-to-get theater tickets). Tip the **valet-parking attendant** $1 every time you get your car.

In restaurants, bars, and nightclubs, tip **service staff** 15% to 20% of the check, tip **bartenders** 10% to 15%, tip **checkroom attendants** $1 per garment, and tip **valet-parking attendants** $1 per vehicle.

As for other service personnel, tip **cab drivers** 15% of the fare; tip **skycaps** at airports at least $1 per bag ($2–$3 if you have a lot of luggage); and tip **hairdressers** and **barbers** 15% to 20%.

Toilets You won't find public toilets or "restrooms" on the streets in most U.S. cities, but they can be found in hotel lobbies, bars, restaurants, museums, department stores, railway and bus stations, and service stations. Large hotels, shopping malls, and fast-food restaurants are probably the best bet for good, clean facilities. If possible, avoid the toilets at parks and beaches, which tend to be dirty; some may be unsafe. Restaurants and bars may reserve their restrooms for patrons. Some establishments display a notice indicating this. You can ignore this sign or, better yet, avoid arguments by paying for a cup of coffee or a soft drink, which will qualify you as a patron.

4

Getting to Know San Diego

Tucked into the sunny and parched southwest corner of the United States, San Diego is situated in one of the country's most naturally beautiful metropolitan settings. Learning the lay of the land is neither confusing nor daunting, but it helps to understand a few geographical features. I think two characteristics give San Diego its top-ographical personality: a superb and varied coastline, and a series of mesas bisected by (mostly) undeveloped canyons inland.

Located 16 miles north of the Mex-ico border, San Diego's downtown sits at the edge of a large natural harbor, the San Diego Bay. The harbor is almost enclosed by two fingers of land: flat Coronado Island on one side, and peninsular Point Loma on the other. Both of these areas hold important military bases, bordered by classic neighborhoods dating to the 1890s and 1920s, respectively. Coron-ado isn't really an island—a ribbon of sand called the Silver Strand connects it to Imperial Beach, just north of the border.

Heading north from Point Loma is Mission Bay, a lagoon that was carved out of tidal estuary in the 1940s, and now a watersports playground. A series of communities are found along the beach-lined coast: Ocean Beach, Mission Beach, Pacific Beach, La Jolla, and, just outside San Diego's city lim-its, Del Mar. To the south of down-town you'll find National City, which is distinguished by shipyards on its bay side, then Chula Vista, and San Ysidro, which ends abruptly at the

border (and where the huge city of Tijuana begins, equally abruptly). Chula Vista and south has been an area of intense housing development in the last decade.

That's the coast. Inland areas, where most of us live, are perhaps best defined by Mission Valley, a mile-wide canyon that runs east-west, 2 miles north of downtown. Half a century ago, the valley held little beyond a few dairy farms, California's first mission, and the San Diego River (which is more like a creek for about 51 weeks a year). Then Interstate 8 was built through the valley, followed by a shop-ping center, a sports stadium, another shopping center, and lots of condos; today, Mission Valley is perhaps the most congested part of the city (and one of the least charming). In spite of this, we all use the valley and many of us live along its perimeter: On the southern rim are desirable older neighborhoods like Mission Hills, Hillcrest, Normal Heights, and Kens-ington; and to the north lies Linda Vista and Kearny Mesa—bedroom communities that emerged in the 1950s—and Miramar Naval Air Sta-tion. Just outside the city limits is Rancho Bernardo, one of the wealthi-est communities in the country.

The city of San Diego possesses one other vital (if man-made) ingredient: Balboa Park. Nestled in a 1,200-acre square between downtown and Mis-sion Valley, the park contains the San Diego Zoo, many of our best muse-ums, wonderful gardens, and splendid architecture.

1 Orientation
ARRIVING
BY PLANE

We have a love-hate relationship with our **San Diego International Airport** (© **619/231-2100;** www.san.org), also known as Lindbergh Field. The facility is conveniently located just 2 miles northwest of downtown, and the landing approach is right at the edge of the central business district. Pilots thread a passage between high-rise buildings and Balboa Park on their final descent to the runway—you'll get a great view on either side of the plane.

But Lindbergh Field is a surprisingly small facility for a city the size of San Diego, and so flight options are limited, particularly because of airline schedule cutbacks. Of course, we don't need a large airport: Because San Diego lies in one corner of the United States, we're not a connecting hub for domestic airlines, and most international travel arrives via Los Angeles or points east. Still, in 1998 the Port of San Diego completed a sorely needed expansion of Lindbergh Field. It's not the podunk little airport it once was. Besides adding much-needed gate space to an airport that's grown awkwardly since the 1920s, the renovation brought dramatic pieces of local artwork, which are displayed in public spaces and described in a slick, colorful brochure, available at information desks.

Planes land at Terminal 1 or 2, though most flights to and from Southern California airports use the Commuter Terminal, a half-mile away; the "red bus" provides free service from the main airport to the Commuter Terminal, or there's a footpath. General **information desks** with visitor materials, maps, and other services are located near the baggage claim areas of both Terminal 1 and 2. You can exchange foreign currency at **Travelex America** (© **619/295-1501;** www. travelexusa.com), in Terminal 1 across from the United Airlines ticket counter, or in Terminal 2 on the second level (*inside* the security area, near the gates). **Hotel reservation** and **car-rental courtesy phones** are located in the baggage-claim areas of Terminals 1 and 2.

Getting into Town from the Airport

BY BUS   The **Metropolitan Transit System (MTS)** (© **619/233-3004;** www. sdcommute.com) operates the San Diego Transit Flyer—bus route no. 992—providing service between the airport and downtown San Diego, running along

---

Tips **Need a Lift into Town?**

When you're thinking about transportation from Lindbergh Field, remember to ask your hotel whether it has an **airport shuttle.** It's common for hotels to offer this service—usually free, sometimes for a nominal charge—and some also offer complimentary shuttles from the hotel to popular shopping and dining areas around town. Make sure the hotel knows when you're arriving, and get precise directions on where it'll pick you up.

Web surfers who'd like to investigate airport transportation options beforehand should visit **QuickAid's Guide to the San Diego Airport** (www. quickaid.com/airports/san), a low-tech site with excellent resources including ground transportation options, terminal maps, airline lists, and nearby hotels.

Broadway. Bus stops are located at each of Lindbergh Field's three terminals. The one-way fare is $2.25, and exact change is required. Request a transfer if you're connecting to another bus or San Diego Trolley route downtown. The ride takes about 15 minutes and buses come at 10- to 15-minute intervals.

At the **Transit Store,** 102 Broadway, at First Avenue (© **619/234-1060**), you can get information about greater San Diego's mass transit system (bus, rail, and ferry) and pick up free brochures, route maps, and timetables.

BY TAXI   Taxis line up outside both terminals and the trip to a downtown location, usually a 10-minute ride, is about $10 (plus tip); budget $20 to $22 for Coronado or Mission Beach, and about $30 to $35 for La Jolla.

BY SHUTTLE   Several airport shuttles run regularly from the airport to points around the city; you'll see designated pick-up areas outside each terminal. The shuttles are a good deal for single travelers; two or more people traveling together might as well take a taxi. The fare is about $5 per person to downtown hotels; Mission Valley and Mission Beach are $8 to $10; La Jolla and Coronado are around $12. One company that serves all of San Diego county is **Cloud 9 Shuttle** (© **800/9-SHUTTLE** or 858/9-SHUTTLE; www.cloud9shuttle.com).

BY CAR   If you're driving to downtown from the airport, take Harbor Drive south to Broadway, the main east-west thoroughfare, and turn left. To reach Hillcrest or Balboa Park, exit the airport toward I-5, and follow the signs for Laurel Street. To reach Mission Bay, take I-5 north to I-8 west. To reach La Jolla, take I-5 north to the La Jolla Parkway exit, bearing left onto Torrey Pines Road. For complete information on rental cars in San Diego, see "Getting Around," later in this chapter.

BY CAR

Three main interstates lead into San Diego. **I-5** is the primary route from San Francisco, central California and Los Angeles; it runs straight through downtown to the Tijuana border crossing. **I-8** cuts across California from points east like Phoenix, terminating just west of I-5 at Mission Bay. **I-15** leads from the deserts to the north through inland San Diego; as you enter Miramar, take **Highway 163** south to reach the central parts of the city.

BY TRAIN

San Diego's **Santa Fe Station** is located at the west end of Broadway, between Front Street and First Avenue, within a half-mile of most downtown hotels and the Embarcadero. Taxis line up outside the main door, the trolley station is across the street, and a dozen local bus routes stop on Broadway or Pacific Highway, 1 block away.

BY BUS

Greyhound buses from Los Angeles, Phoenix, Las Vegas, and other points in the southwest U.S. arrive at the station in downtown San Diego at 120 W. Broadway. Local buses stop in front and the San Diego Trolley line is nearby.

VISITOR INFORMATION

There are staffed information booths at airport terminals, the train station, and the cruise-ship terminal.

In downtown San Diego, the Convention & Visitors Bureau's **International Visitor Information Center** (© **619/236-1212;** www.sandiego.org) is downtown at 11 Horton Plaza, at First Avenue and F Street. The glossy *Official Visitors*

Pocket Guide includes information on accommodations, dining, activities, attractions, tours, and transportation, and be sure to ask for the *San Diego Travel Values* pamphlet, which is full of money-saving coupons for hotels, restaurants, and attractions. The center is open Monday through Saturday from 8:30am to 5pm year-round and Sunday from 11am to 5pm, June through August; it is closed major holidays. There is also a walk-up only facility at the **La Jolla Visitor Center**, 7966 Herschel Ave., near the corner of Prospect St. This office is open daily in summer, from 10am to 7pm; from mid-September to mid-June the center is open daily except Wednesday, from 10am to 5pm.

If you're driving into town, the **Mission Bay Visitor Information Center,** 2688 Mission Bay Dr. (© 619/276-8200; www.infosandiego.com), is conveniently located next to the I-5, at the Clairemont Drive exit. This private facility books hotels and sells discounted admission tickets to a variety of attractions. There's plenty of parking; stop in between 9am and dusk.

The **Coronado Visitors Center,** 1100 Orange Ave. (© 619/437-8788; www. coronadovisitors.com), dispenses maps, newsletters, and information-packed brochures. Located inside the Coronado Museum, they're open Monday through Friday from 9am to 5pm, Saturday from 10am to 5pm, and Sunday from 11am to 4pm.

San Diego has two major print publications. The daily *San Diego Union-Tribune* is a rah-rah booster of all things local, especially when it involves spectator sports or pouring cement for the local teams. The leading "alternative" publication, the *San Diego Weekly Reader,* is alternative only in the sense that it rains on most any parade, especially if it involves the *Union-Tribune*. But for local nightlife and entertainment, comprehensive listings are found in the *Reader,* free and published on Thursdays and available all over the city at bookstores, cafes, liquor stores, and other outlets. The *Union-Tribune* publishes a weekly entertainment supplement called "Night and Day," also on Thursdays.

For websites with up-to-the-minute information, see "The Best of San Diego Online" in chapter 1.

CITY LAYOUT
MAIN ARTERIES & STREETS

It's not hard to find your way around downtown San Diego. Most streets run one-way, in a grid pattern. First through Twelfth avenues run north and south—odd-number avenues are northbound, even numbers run south (Fifth Ave. is two-way south of Market only); A through K streets alternate running east and west. Broadway (the equivalent of D St.) runs both directions, as do Market Street and Harbor Drive. North of A Street the east-west streets bear the names of trees, in alphabetical order: Ash, Beech, Cedar, Date, and so on. Harbor Drive runs past the airport and along the waterfront, which is known as the Embarcadero. Ash Street and Broadway are the downtown arteries that connect with Harbor Drive.

The Coronado Bay Bridge leading to Coronado is accessible from I-5 south of downtown, and I-5 north leads to Old Town, Mission Bay, La Jolla, and North County coastal areas. Balboa Park (home of the San Diego Zoo), Hillcrest, and uptown areas lie north of downtown San Diego. The park and zoo are easily reached by way of Twelfth Avenue, which turns into Park Boulevard and leads to the parking lots. Fifth Avenue leads to Hillcrest. Highway 163, which heads north from Eleventh Avenue, leads into Mission Valley.

San Diego Neighborhoods

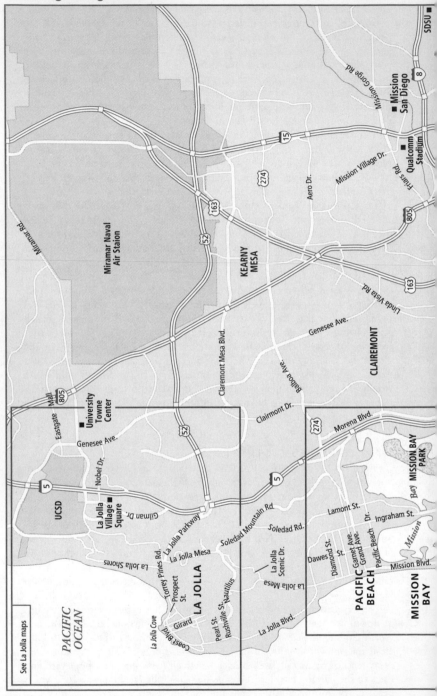

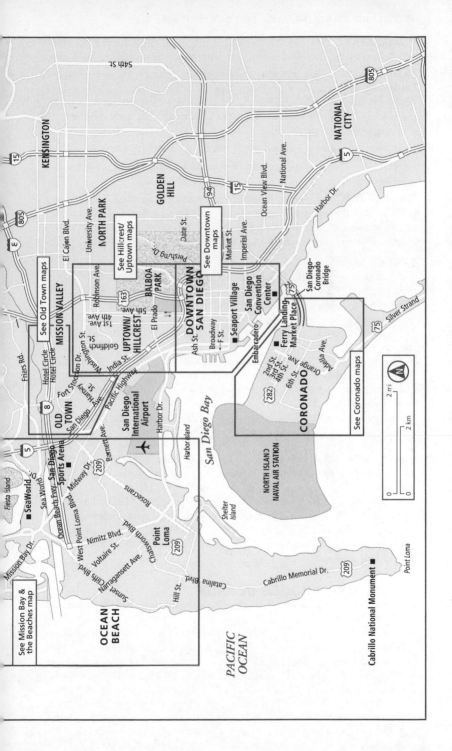

CORONADO   The main streets are Orange Avenue, where most of the hotels and restaurants are clustered, and Ocean Drive, which follows Coronado Beach.

DOWNTOWN   The major thoroughfares are Broadway (a major bus artery), Fourth and Fifth avenues (which run south and north, respectively), C Street (the trolley line), and Harbor Drive, which curls along the waterfront and passes the Maritime Museum, Seaport Village, the Convention Center, and Petco Park.

HILLCREST   The main streets are University Avenue and Washington Street (both two-way, running east and west), and Fourth and Fifth avenues.

LA JOLLA   The main avenues are Prospect and Girard, which are perpendicular to each other.

PACIFIC BEACH   Mission Boulevard is the main drag, parallel to and one block in from the beach, and perpendicular to it are Grand and Garnet avenues and Pacific Beach Drive. East and West Mission Bay drives encircle most of the bay and Ingraham Street cuts through the middle of it.

STREET MAPS

The **International Visitor Information Center,** at First Avenue and F Street (© 619/236-1212), provides an illustrated pocket map, as well as the *San Diego Visitors Pocket Guide,* which includes map inserts. Also available are maps of the 59-mile scenic drive around San Diego, the Gaslamp Quarter, Tijuana, San Diego's public transportation, and a "Campgrounds and Recreation" map for the county.

The **Automobile Club of Southern California** has 10 San Diego offices (© 619/233-1000). It distributes great maps, which are free to AAA members and to members of many international auto clubs, and sells auto insurance for those driving within Mexico.

Car-rental outfits usually offer maps of the city that show the freeways and major streets, and hotels often provide complimentary maps of the downtown area. You can buy maps of the city and vicinity at **Le Travel Store** at 745 Fourth Ave., downtown (© 619/544-0005). The **Transit Store,** 102 Broadway, at First Avenue (© 619/233-3004), is a storehouse of bus and trolley maps, with a friendly staff on duty to answer specific questions.

If you're moving to San Diego or plan to spend an extended period here, I recommend the ***Thomas Bros. Guide,*** available at bookstores, drugstores, and large supermarkets for $27, or by calling (© 800/899-6277). This all-encompassing book of maps deciphers San Diego County street by street, and includes a CD-ROM version.

THE NEIGHBORHOODS IN BRIEF

In this guidebook, San Diego is divided into six main areas, where most visitors spend the bulk of their visit.

Downtown The business, shopping, dining, and entertainment heart of the city, the downtown area encompasses Horton Plaza, the Gaslamp Quarter, the Embarcadero (waterfront), and the Convention Center, sprawling over eight individual "neighborhoods." The Maritime Museum and the downtown branch of the Museum of Contemporary Art are also here. Visitors with business in the city center would be wise to stay downtown. This is also the best area for those attending meetings at the Convention Center. The **Gaslamp Quarter** is the center of a massive redevelopment kicked off in the mid-1980s

C Off the Beaten Path: Golden Hill

You don't think the trendy Gaslamp Quarter will be the last San Diego neighborhood to be rediscovered and gentrified, do you? If you like to explore, check out another old neighborhood that's quietly attracting history-minded fans . . . will it be the preservationists' next stop?

When the downtown area we now call the Gaslamp Quarter was enjoying its turn-of-the-20th-century heyday as the city's commercial center, the most convenient suburb was Golden Hill. Directly east of downtown, Golden Hill had the added advantage of being next to Balboa Park—it "wraps" around the southeast corner of the park. Homes here also enjoyed a sweeping view south to the bay, now mostly blocked by development. For a drive-by look at some oldies but goodies, visit Broadway, where finely preserved Victorians now serve as legal and medical offices; 28th Street along the park; and any other side street that catches your eye.

Some of the neighborhood's best Victorians and bungalows already show the caring touch of deep-pocketed architecture buffs, though plenty have fallen victim to the wrecking ball. Sandwiched between a natural arroyo (now the pathway of the 94 freeway) and vast Balboa Park, Golden Hill is an area where you're likely to see coyotes, opossums, and even red foxes trotting down quiet streets. You'll find (tie-) dyed-in-the-wool hippies shacking up in unrestored shanties and hanging out at Santos Coffeehouse, whose bohemian style is reminiscent of San Francisco's Haight-Ashbury.

Small stretches of retail interest lie at the intersection of Beech and 30th streets (Santos Coffeehouse, grass-roots art galleries, and funky antiques stores), and along 25th Street north of Broadway, home to several Mexican restaurants and the retro grill-your-own Turf Supper Club (p. 223).

with the opening of the Horton Plaza shopping complex; now, the once-seedy area is jam-packed with trendy boutiques, restaurants, and nightspots. Immediately southeast of the Gaslamp is the brand new **Petco Park,** home of the San Diego Padres. Also undergoing a renaissance is **Little Italy,** a small neighborhood along India Street between Cedar and Fir at the northern edge of downtown, and a great place to find gelato, espresso, pizza, and pasta.

Hillcrest & Uptown At the turn of the 20th century, the "uptown" neighborhoods north of downtown were home to San Diego's white-collar elite (hence such sobriquets as "Bankers Hill" and "Pill Hill," named for the area's many doctors). Hillcrest was the city's first self-contained suburb in the 1920s. Despite the cachet of being close to Balboa Park (home of the San Diego Zoo and numerous museums), the area fell into neglect in the 1960s. However, starting in the late 1970s, legions of preservation-minded residents—particularly its lively gay community—restored Hillcrest's charms, making it the local equivalent of a West Hollywood or SoHo.

Centrally located and brimming with popular restaurants and avant-garde boutiques, Hillcrest also offers less expensive and more personalized accommodations than any other area in the city. Other Uptown neighborhoods of interest are **Mission Hills** to the west of Hillcrest, and **University Heights, Normal Heights, North Park,** and **Kensington** to the east.

Old Town & Mission Valley These two busy areas wrap around the neighborhood of Mission Hills. On one end is the Old Town State Historic Park (where California "began"), Presidio Park, Heritage Park, and numerous museums that recall the turn of the 20th century and the city's beginnings. There's shopping and dining here, too, aimed largely at tourists. Not far from Old Town lies the vast suburban sprawl of Mission Valley, home to gigantic shopping centers. Hotel Circle is an elongated loop road paralleling the I-8, where a string of moderately priced and budget hotels offer an alternative to the ritzier neighborhoods. In recent years several major hotel and convention complexes have opened in Mission Valley, and 1990s condo developments have made the valley a residential area.

Mission Bay & the Beaches Here's where they took the picture on the postcard you'll send home. Mission Bay is a watery playground perfect for water-skiing, sailing, and windsurfing. The adjacent communities of **Ocean Beach, Mission Beach,** and **Pacific Beach** are known for their wide stretches of sand, active nightlife, and casual dining. Many single San Diegans live here, and once you've visited you'll understand why. The boardwalk, which runs from South Mission Beach to Pacific Beach, is a popular place for in-line skating,

bike riding, people-watching, and sunsets. This is the place to stay if you are traveling with beach-loving children or want to walk barefoot on the sand.

La Jolla With an atmosphere that's somewhere between Rodeo Drive and a Mediterranean village, this seaside community is home to an inordinate number of wealthy folks who could live anywhere. They choose La Jolla, surrounded by the beach, the **University of California, San Diego,** outstanding restaurants, both pricey and traditional shops, and some of the world's best medical facilities. Tourists who bed down here can take advantage of the community's attributes without having to buy its high-priced real estate, though all share in La Jolla's problematic parking and traffic snarls. There are really two La Jollas: the so-called "village" is the original seaside community, while residential and business areas that have sprouted along La Jolla Village Drive east of I-8 are of less interest to visitors. Incidentally, the name is a compromise between Spanish and American Indian, as is the pronunciation (la *hoy*-ya); it has come to mean "the jewel."

Coronado You may be tempted to think of Coronado as an island, as San Diegans once called it. Coronado does have an isolated, resort ambience and is most easily accessed by ferry or sweeping bridge, but the city of Coronado is actually on a bulbous peninsula connected to the mainland by a narrow sand spit, the **Silver Strand.** The northern portion of the peninsula is home to the **U.S. Naval Air Station,** in use since World War I. The southern sector has a history as an elite playground for snowbirds and represents a charming suburban community. Quaint shops line the main street, Orange Avenue, and you'll find several ritzy resorts, including the landmark **Hotel del Coronado** (p. 92). Coronado has a lovely duned beach (one of the area's finest), fine restaurants, and a "downtown" reminiscent of a small Midwestern town; it's also home to more retired admirals than any other community in the country.

2 Getting Around

San Diego has many walkable neighborhoods, from the historic downtown area, to Hillcrest and nearby Balboa Park, to the Embarcadero, to Mission Bay Park. You get there by car, bus, or trolley, and your feet do the rest. For inspiration, turn to chapter 8, "City Strolls."

BY CAR

We complain of increasing traffic, but San Diego is still easy to navigate by car. Most downtown streets run one-way, in a grid pattern. However, outside downtown, canyons and bays often make streets indirect. Finding a parking space can be tricky in the Gaslamp, Old Town, Mission Beach, and La Jolla, but parking lots are often centrally located. Rush hour on the freeways is generally concentrated from 7 to 9am and 4:30 to 6:30pm. Be aware that San Diego's gas prices are often the highest in the country.

RENTALS

I'd love to tell you that public transportation is a good way to get around, as in New York City or San Francisco, but the distances between attractions and indirect bus routings usually make it inefficient. Those staying for a short time downtown will find plenty to see and do within close reach (including Balboa Park and Old Town), but otherwise, if you don't drive to San Diego with your own car, you'll want to rent one. You *can* reach virtually all sights of interest using public transportation, but having your own wheels is a big advantage.

All the major car-rental firms have an office at the airport and several in larger hotels. Some of the national companies include **Alamo** (© 800/462-5266; www.alamo.com), **Avis** (© 800/230-4898; www.avis.com), **Budget** (© 800/527-0700; www.budget.com), **Dollar** (© 800/800-3665; www.dollar.com), **Enterprise** (© 800/736-8222; www.enterprise.com), **Hertz** (© 800/654-3131; www.hertz.com), **National** (© 800/227-7368; www.nationalcar.com), and **Thrifty** (© 800/847-4389; www.thrifty.com). Avis and several other companies will allow their cars into Mexico as far as Ensenada, but other rental outfits won't allow you to drive south of the border.

Demystifying Renter's Insurance

Before you drive off in a rental car, be sure you're insured. Hasty assumptions about your personal auto insurance or a rental agency's additional coverage could end up costing you tens of thousands of dollars, even if you are involved in an accident that was clearly the fault of another driver.

If you already hold a **private auto insurance** policy, you are most likely covered in the United States for loss of or damage to a rental car and liability in case of injury to any other party involved in an accident. Be sure to find out whether you are covered in the area you are visiting, whether your policy extends to everyone who will be driving the car, how much liability is covered in case an outside party is injured in an accident, and whether the type of vehicle you are renting is included under your contract. (Rental trucks, sport-utility vehicles, and luxury vehicles or sports cars may not be covered.)

Most **major credit cards** (especially gold and platinum cards) provide some degree of coverage as well, provided they're used to pay for the rental. Terms vary widely, however, so be sure to call your credit card company directly before you rent.

If you are **uninsured,** your credit card will probably provide primary coverage as long as you decline the rental agency's insurance and as long as you rent with that card. This means that the credit card will cover damage or theft of a rental car for the full cost of the vehicle. (In a few states, however, theft is not covered; ask specifically about state law where you will be renting and driving.) If you already have insurance, your credit card will provide secondary coverage, which basically covers your deductible.

Note: Though they may cover damage to your rental car, *credit cards will not cover liability,* or the cost of injury to an outside party, damage to an outside party's vehicle, or both. If you do not hold an insurance policy, you may seriously want to consider purchasing additional liability insurance from your rental company, even if you decline collision coverage. Be sure to check the terms, however. Some rental agencies cover liability only if the renter is not at fault; even then, the rental company's obligation varies from state to state.

The basic insurance coverage offered by most car-rental companies, known as the **Loss/Damage Waiver (LDW)** or **Collision Damage Waiver (CDW),** can cost as much as $20 a day. It usually covers the full value of the vehicle with no deductible if an outside party causes an accident or other damage to the rental car. Liability coverage varies according to the company policy and state law, but the minimum is usually at least $15,000. If you are at fault in an accident, you will be covered for the full replacement value of the car, but not for liability. Some states allow you to buy additional liability coverage for such cases. Most rental companies will require a police report to process any claims you file, but your private insurer will not be notified of the accident.

Saving Money on a Rental Car

Car-rental rates vary even more than airline fares. Prices depend on the size of the car, where and when you pick it up and drop it off, the length of the rental period, where and how far you drive it, whether you buy insurance, and a host of other factors. A few key questions could save you hundreds of dollars:

- Are weekend rates lower than weekday rates? Ask if the rate is the same for pickup Friday morning, for instance, as it is for Thursday night.
- Does the agency assess a drop-off charge if you don't return the car to the same location where you picked it up?
- Are special promotional rates available? If you see an advertised price in your local newspaper, be sure to ask for that specific rate; otherwise you may be charged the standard cost.
- Are discounts available for members of AARP, AAA, frequent-flyer programs, or trade unions?
- How much tax will be added to the rental bill? Local tax? State use tax?
- How much does the rental company charge to refill your gas tank if you return with the tank less than full? Though most rental companies claim these prices are competitive, fuel is almost always cheaper in town.

PARKING

Metered parking spaces are found in downtown, Hillcrest, and the beach communities, but demand outpaces supply. Posted signs indicate operating hours—generally from 8am to 6pm, even on Saturdays. Be prepared with several dollars in quarters—some meters take no other coin, and 25¢ usually buys only 15 minutes, even on a 2-hour meter. Most unmetered areas have signs restricting street parking to 1 or 2 hours; count on vigilant chalking and ticketing during the regulated hours. Three-hour meters line Harbor Drive opposite the ticket offices for harbor tours; even on weekends, you have to feed them. If you can't find a metered space, there are plenty of hourly lots downtown. Parking in Mission Valley is usually within large parking structures and free, though congested on weekends and particularly leading up to Christmas.

The first pitch has yet to be thrown, but I predict downtown parking will be tougher on evenings when Padres games are scheduled with the opening of Petco Park in April 2004.

DRIVING RULES

San Diegans are relatively respectful drivers, although admittedly we often speed and sometimes we lose patience with those who don't know their way around. California has a seat-belt law for both drivers and passengers, so buckle up before you venture out. You may turn right at a red light after stopping unless a sign says otherwise. Likewise, you can turn left on a red light from a one-way street onto another one-way street after coming to a full stop. Keep in mind when driving in San Diego that pedestrians have the right of way at all times, not just in cross walks, so stop for pedestrians who have stepped off the curb. Penalties in California for drunk driving are among the toughest in the country. Speed limits on freeways, particularly Highway 8 through Mission Valley, are aggressively enforced after dark, partly as a pretext for nabbing drivers who might have imbibed.

BY PUBLIC TRANSPORTATION
BY BUS

San Diego has an adequate bus system that will get you to where you're going—eventually. Most drivers are friendly and helpful. The system encompasses more than 100 routes in the greater San Diego area. Bus stops are marked by rectangular blue signs every other block or so on local routes, farther apart on express routes. More than 20 bus routes pass through the downtown area. Most **bus fares** are $2.25; a few express routes are $2.50. Buses accept dollar bills, but the driver can't give change. You can request a free transfer as long as you continue on a bus with an equal or lower fare (if it's higher, you pay the difference). Transfers must be used within 90 minutes, and you can return to where you started.

The **Transit Store,** 102 Broadway, at First Avenue (© **619/234-1060**), dispenses passes, tokens, timetables, maps, brochures, and lost-and-found information. It issues ID cards for seniors 60 and older, and for travelers with disabilities, all of whom pay $1 per ride. Request a copy of the useful brochure

---

⟨Tips⟩ Money-Saving Bus & Trolley Passes

The **Day Tripper pass** allows unlimited rides on MTS (bus) and trolley routes. Passes are good for 1, 2, 3, and 4 consecutive days, and cost $5, $9, $12, and $15, respectively. Day Trippers are for sale at the Transit Store and all trolley station automatic ticket vending machines; call © **619/685-4900** for more information.

Way to Go to See the Sights, which details the city's most popular tourist attractions and the buses that will take you to them. The office is open Monday through Friday from 9am to 5pm. There is also a small **kiosk** staffed during the day located at the northwest corner of Fifth Avenue and University Avenue in Hillcrest—they have maps and schedules and can sell bus and trolley passes. If you know your route and just need schedule information—or automated answers to FAQs—call **Info Express** (© **619/685-4900**) from any touch-tone phone, 24 hours a day.

Some of the most popular tourist attractions served by bus and rail routes are Balboa Park (Rte. 1, 3, 7, 7A, 7B, and 25); the San Diego Zoo (Rte. 7, 7A, and 7B); the Convention Center and Gaslamp Quarter (San Diego Trolley's Orange Line); Coronado (Rte. 901); Horton Plaza (most downtown bus routes and the San Diego Trolley's Blue and Orange Lines); Old Town (San Diego Trolley's Blue Line); Cabrillo National Monument (Rte. 26 from Old Town Transit Center); Seaport Village (Rte. 7 and the San Diego Trolley's Orange Line); SeaWorld (Rte. 9 from the Old Town Transit Center); Qualcomm Stadium (San Diego Trolley's Blue Line); and, Tijuana (San Diego Trolley's Blue Line to San Ysidro).

The Coronado Shuttle, bus Route 904, runs between the Marriott Coronado Island Resort and the Old Ferry Landing, and then continues along Orange Avenue to the Hotel del Coronado, Glorietta Bay, Loews, and back again. It costs $1 per person. Route 901 goes all the way to Coronado from San Diego and costs $2 for adults. Call © **619/233-3004** for more information about this and other bus routes. You can also view timetables, maps, and fares online—and learn how the public transit system accommodates travelers with disabilities—at **www.sdcommute.com**.

When planning your route, note that schedules vary and most buses do not run all night. Some stop at 6pm, while other lines continue to 9pm, midnight, and 2am—ask your bus driver for more specific information. On Saturdays some routes run all night.

BY TROLLEY

Although the system is too limited for most San Diegans to utilize for work commutes, the San Diego Trolley is great for visitors, particularly if you're staying downtown or plan to visit Tijuana. There are two routes which intersect downtown: The Blue Line travels from the Mexican border north through downtown, Old Town, and then east through Mission Valley to Qualcomm Stadium; the Orange Line runs from downtown east through Lemon Grove and El Cajon to the city of Santee. In the central business district, both lines run along C Street (1 block north of Broadway). Trolleys also circle around downtown's Bayside (parallel to Harbor Dr.), with stops serving the Gaslamp Quarter, the Convention Center, Seaport Village, and the Santa Fe Depot. The trip to the border takes 40 minutes from downtown. For a route map, see the inside back cover of this guide.

Trolleys operate on a self-service fare-collection system; riders buy tickets from machines in stations before boarding. The machines list fares for each destination ($1.25–$3) and dispense change. Tickets are valid for 2 hours from the time of purchase, in any direction. Fare inspectors board trains at random to check tickets. A round-trip ticket is double the price, but is valid all day between the origination and destination points.

Both lines run every 15 minutes during the day and every 30 minutes at night; during peak weekday rush hours the Blue Line runs every 10 minutes.

Trolleys stop at each station for only 30 seconds. To open the door for boarding, push the lighted green button; to open the door to exit the trolley, push the lighted white button.

For recorded transit information, call © **619/685-4900.** To speak with a customer service representative, call © **619/233-3004** (TTY/TDD 619/234-5005) daily from 5:30am to 8:30pm. For wheelchair lift info call © **619/595-4960.** The trolley generally operates daily from 5am to about 12 midnight; the Blue Line runs 24 hours Saturday night/Sunday morning.

BY TAXI

Half a dozen taxi companies serve the area. Rates are based on mileage, and can add up quickly in sprawling San Diego—a trip from downtown to La Jolla for example will cost $30 to $35. Other than in the Gaslamp Quarter after dark, taxis don't cruise the streets as they do in other cities, so you have to call ahead for quick pickup. If you are at a hotel or restaurant, the front-desk attendant or concierge will call one for you. Among the local companies are **Orange Cab** (© 619/291-3333), **San Diego Cab** (© 619/226-TAXI), and **Yellow Cab** (© 619/234-6161). The **Coronado Cab Company** (© 935/435-6211) serves Coronado. In La Jolla, use **La Jolla Cab** (© 858/453-4222).

BY TRAIN

San Diego's express rail commuter service, the **Coaster,** travels between the downtown Santa Fe Depot station and the Oceanside Transit Center, with stops at Old Town, Sorrento Valley, Solana Beach, Encinitas, and Carlsbad. Fares range from $3.50 to $4.75 each way, depending on how far you go, and can be paid by credit card at vending machines at each station. Eligible seniors and riders with disabilities pay half price. The scenic trip between downtown San Diego and Oceanside takes just under an hour. Trains run Monday through Friday about once an hour, with four trains each direction on Saturday; call © **800/ COASTER** for the current schedule, or log onto **www.sdcommute.com**.

Amtrak (© **800/USA-RAIL;** www.amtrakwest.com) trains run between San Diego and downtown Los Angeles, about 11 times daily each way. Trains to Los Angeles depart from the Santa Fe Depot and stop at Solana Beach, Oceanside, San Juan Capistrano, and Anaheim (Disneyland). The travel time from San Diego to Los Angeles is about 2 hours, 45 minutes (for comparison, driving time can be as little as 2 hr., or as much as 4 hr. during rush hour). A one-way ticket to Los Angeles is $24 ($48 round-trip), or $36 each way in business class. One-way to Solana Beach is $7, to Oceanside $9.50, to San Juan Capistrano $12, and to Anaheim $17.

BY WATER

BY FERRY   There's regularly scheduled ferry service between San Diego and Coronado (© **619/234-4111** for information). Ferries leave from the Broadway Pier (1050 N. Harbor Dr., at the intersection of Broadway) on the hour from 9am to 9pm Sunday through Thursday, and until 10pm Friday and Saturday. They return from the Old Ferry Landing in Coronado to the Broadway Pier every hour on the half-hour from 9:30am to 9:30pm Sunday through Thursday and until 10:30pm Friday and Saturday. The ride takes 15 minutes. The fare is $2 each way (50¢ extra if you bring your bike). Buy tickets at the Harbor Excursion kiosk on Broadway Pier or at the Old Ferry Landing in Coronado.

BY WATER TAXI   Water taxis (✆ **619/235-TAXI**) will pick you up from any dock around San Diego Bay, and operate daily between noon and 10pm, with extended hours in summer. If you're staying in a downtown hotel, this is a great way to reach the beach fronting the Hotel del Coronado. Boats are sometimes available spur of the moment, but reservations are advised. Fares are just $5 per person to most locations.

BY BICYCLE

San Diego is ideal for exploration by bicycle, and many roads have designated bike lanes. Bikes are available for rent in most areas; see "Outdoor Pursuits" in chapter 7 for suggestions.

The San Diego Ridelink publishes a comprehensive map of the county detailing bike *paths* (separate rights-of-way for bicyclists), bike *lanes* (alongside motor vehicle ways), and bike *routes* (shared ways designated only by bike-symbol signs). The **San Diego Region Bike Map** is available at visitor centers; to receive a copy in advance, call ✆ **619/231-BIKE.**

If you want to take your two-wheeler on a city bus, look for bike-route signs at the bus stop. The signs mean that the buses that stop here have bike racks. Let the driver know you want to stow your bike on the front of the bus, then board and pay the regular fare. With this service, you can bus the bike to an area you'd like to explore, do your biking there, then return by bus. Not all routes are served by buses with bike racks; call ✆ **619/233-3004** for information.

The San Diego Trolley has a **Bike-N-Ride** program that lets you bring your bike on the trolley for free. Bikers must board at the back of each trolley car, where the bike-storage area is located; cars carry two bikes except during weekday rush hours, when the limit is one bike per car. Several trolley stops connect with routes for buses with bike racks. For more information, call the **Transit Information Line** (✆ **619/233-3004**).

Bikes are permitted on the ferry connecting San Diego and Coronado, which has 15 miles of dedicated bike paths.

Ⓒ *FAST FACTS:* San Diego

American Express   A full-service travel office is located in La Jolla at 1020 Prospect St. (✆ **858/459-4161**).

Area Codes   San Diego's main area code is **619**, used primarily by downtown, uptown, Mission Valley, Point Loma, Coronado, La Mesa, and El Cajon. The area code **858** is used for northern and coastal areas, including Mission Beach, Pacific Beach, La Jolla, Del Mar, Rancho Sante Fe, and Rancho Bernardo. Use **760** to reach the remainder of San Diego County, including Encinitas, Carlsbad, Oceanside, Escondido, Ramona, Julian, and Anza-Borrego.

Babysitters   **Marion's Childcare** (✆ **619/582-5029**) has bonded babysitters available to come to your hotel room. **Panda Services** (✆ **858/292-5503**) is also available.

Business Hours   Banks are open weekdays from 9am to 4pm or later, and sometimes Saturday morning. Shops in shopping malls tend to stay open until about 9pm weekdays and until 6pm weekends, and are open on secondary holidays.

Camera Repair For major repair contact **Kurt's Camera Repair** at 7811 Mission Gorge Rd., in Allied Gardens (© **619/286-1810**), or **Professional Photographic Repair,** 7910 Raytheon Rd. (© **619/277-3700**). Simple repairs and photographic supplies are available at **George's Camera & Video** in North Park at 3827 30th St. (© **619/297-3544**), **Bob Davis' Camera Shop** in La Jolla at 7720 Fay St. (© **858/459-7355**), **Nelson Photo Supply** in Little Italy at 1909 India St., at Fir Street (© **619/234-6621**), and **Point Loma Camera Store,** 1310 Rosecrans St. (© **619/224-2719**).

Dentists For dental referrals, contact the **San Diego County Dental Society** at © **800/201-0244,** or call © 800/DENTIST.

Doctors **Hotel Docs** (© **800/468-3537**) is a 24-hour network of physicians, dentists, and chiropractors. They accept credit cards, and their services are covered by most insurance policies. In a life-threatening situation, dial © **911.**

Drugstores Long's, Rite-Aid, and Sav-On sell pharmaceuticals and non-prescription products. Look in the phone book to find the one nearest you. If you need a pharmacy after normal business hours, the following branches are open 24 hours: **Sav-On Drugs,** 8831 Villa La Jolla Dr., La Jolla (© **858/457-4390**), and 313 E. Washington St., Hillcrest (© **619/291-7170**); and **Rite-Aid,** 535 Robinson Ave., Hillcrest (© **619/291-3703**). Local hospitals also sell prescription drugs.

Emergencies Call © **911** for fire, police, and ambulance. The main police station is at 1401 Broadway, at 14th Street (© **619/531-2000,** or 619/531-2065 for the hearing impaired).

Eyeglass Repair **Optometric Expressions,** 55 Horton Plaza (© **619/544-9000**), is at street level near the Westin Hotel; it's open Monday through Saturday from 9:30am to 6pm. **Optometry on the Plaza,** on the second level of Horton Plaza (© **619/239-1716**), is open Monday through Saturday from 10am to 6pm. Both can fill eyeglass prescriptions, repair glasses, and replace contact lenses. The major shopping centers in Mission Valley also have eyeglass stores that can fill prescriptions and handle most repairs.

Hospitals Near downtown San Diego, **UCSD Medical Center–Hillcrest,** 200 W. Arbor Dr. (© **619/543-6400**), has the most convenient emergency room. In La Jolla, **Thornton Hospital,** 9300 Campus Point Dr. (© **858/657-7600**), has a good emergency room, and you'll find another in Coronado, at **Coronado Hospital,** 250 Prospect Place, opposite the Marriott Resort (© **619/435-6251**).

Hot Lines HIV Hot Line © **619/236-2352.** Alcoholics Anonymous © **619/265-8762.** Debtors Anonymous © **619/525-3065.** Mental Health Access and Crisis Line © **800/479-3339.** Traveler's Aid Society © **619/231-7361.**

Liquor Laws The drinking age in California is 21. Beer, wine, and hard liquor are sold daily from 6am to 2am and are available in grocery stores.

Newspapers & Magazines The *San Diego Union-Tribune* is published daily, and its entertainment section, "Night & Day," is in the Thursday edition. The free *San Diego Weekly Reader* is published Thursdays and is available at many shops, restaurants, theaters, and public hot spots; it's the best source for up-to-the-minute club and show listings. *San Diego* magazine is filled with dining listings for an elite audience (which explains all the ads for face-lifts and tummy tucks). *San Diego Home-Garden Lifestyles* magazine highlights the city's homes and gardens, and includes a monthly calendar of events and some savvy articles about the restaurant scene. Both magazines are published monthly and sold at newsstands.

Police The downtown police station is at 1401 Broadway (© **619/531-2000**). Call © **911** in an emergency.

Post Office San Diego's main post office is located at 2535 Midway Drive, just west of Old Town; it is open Monday through Friday from 8am to 5pm, and Saturdays from 8am to 4pm. Post offices are located downtown, at 815 E St. and at 51 Horton Plaza, next to the Westin Hotel. There is a post office in the Mission Valley Shopping Center, next to Macy's. These branch offices are generally open Monday through Friday during regular business hours, plus Saturday morning; for specific branch information, call © **800/ASK-USPS** or log on to **www.usps.gov**.

Restrooms Horton Plaza and Seaport Village downtown, Balboa Park, Old Town State Historic Park in Old Town, and the Ferry Landing Marketplace in Coronado all have well-marked public restrooms. In general, you won't have a problem finding one. The restrooms in most fast-food restaurants are usually clean and accessible.

Smoking Smoking is prohibited in nearly all indoor public places, including theaters, hotel lobbies, and enclosed shopping malls. In 1998, California enacted legislation prohibiting smoking in all restaurants and bars, except those with outdoor seating.

Taxes Sales tax in restaurants and shops is 7.75%. Hotel tax is 10.5%.

Time Zone San Diego, like the rest of the West Coast, is in the Pacific Standard Time zone, which is 8 hours behind Greenwich (mean) time. Daylight savings time is observed. To check the time, call © **619/853-1212**.

Transit Information Call © **619/233-3004** (TTY/TDD 619/234-5005). If you know your route and just need schedule information, call © **619/685-4900**.

Useful Telephone Numbers For the latest San Diego arts and entertainment information, call © **619/238-0700**; for half-price day-of-performance tickets, call © **619/497-5000**; for a beach and surf report, call © **619/221-8824**.

Weather Call © **619/289-1212**.

Where to Stay

Where would you prefer to sleep? Over the water or right next to the sand? In Victorian surroundings or in hip, modern digs adjacent to downtown nightlife? Facing the bay or ocean or overlooking carefully landscaped gardens? San Diego offers a variety of places to stay that range from pricey high-rise hostelries to spa- and golf-blessed resorts; from inexpensive cookie-cutter motels to out-of-the-ordinary B&Bs.

In this chapter I'll take you through all the options within the city proper. Lodging recommendations for Del Mar, Encinitas, and Carlsbad (all beautifully situated along the coast and within 40 min. of the city) are found in chapter 11, as are hotels for the Disneyland area, south of the border, and inland regions. For a list of my favorites in various categories, see "Best Hotel Bets" in chapter 1.

High season is vaguely defined as the summer period between Memorial Day and Labor Day—some hotels inch rates higher still in July and August. However, as San Diego has grown into a convention destination, you'll find rates for the larger downtown hotels and a few of the Mission Valley hotels are largely determined by the ebb and flow of conventions in town—weekend and holiday rates can offer good bargains. On the other hand, leisure-oriented hotels along the coast and in Mission Valley are generally busier on weekends, especially in summer, so mid-week deals are easier to snag. (Here's an idea to maximize your discounts: Spend the weekend at a downtown high-rise and duck into a beach bungalow on Monday.)

Keep in mind that you should use the star ratings in this chapter to compare accommodations within a certain type. In other words, a two-star bed-and-breakfast is not comparable to a two-star beach resort in terms of service, amenities, and facilities.

Note: Unless you have a particular sensitivity to even mild heat, air-conditioning is more a convenience than a necessity. In San Diego's temperate climate, ocean breezes cool the air year-round, particularly along the coast.

SAVING ON YOUR HOTEL ROOM

A hotel's "rack rate" is the official published rate—I use these prices to help you make an apples-and-apples comparison. The truth is, hardly anybody pays rack rates, and you can nearly always do better. Here's how I've organized the price categories: **Very Expensive** means the least expensive room costs $250 and up in the high season, with no discounts applied; **Expensive,** $190 to $249; **Moderate,** $120 to $189; and **Inexpensive,** under $120. But *always* peruse the category above your target price—you might just find the perfect match, especially if you follow the advice below.

- **Ask about special rates or other discounts.** Ask whether a room less expensive than the first one quoted is available, or whether any special rates apply to you. You may qualify for corporate, student, military, senior, or other discounts. Mention membership in AAA, AARP, frequent-flier programs, or trade unions, which may entitle you to special deals as well. Find out the hotel policy on children—do kids stay free in the room or is there a special rate?

- **Dial direct.** When booking a room in a chain hotel, you'll often get a better deal by calling the individual hotel's reservation desk than at the chain's main number.

- **Book online.** Many hotels offer Internet-only discounts, or supply rooms to Priceline, Hotwire, or Expedia at rates much lower than the ones you can get through the hotel itself.

- **Remember the law of supply and demand.** Resort hotels are most crowded and therefore most expensive on weekends, so discounts are usually available for midweek stays. Business hotels in downtown locations are busiest during the week, so you can expect big discounts over the weekend. Many hotels have high-season and low-season prices, and booking the day after high season ends (sometime in Sept or Oct for beachfront beds) can mean big discounts.

- **Look into group or long-stay discounts.** If you come as part of a large group, you should be able to negotiate a bargain rate, since the hotel can then guarantee occupancy in a number of rooms. Likewise, if you're planning a long stay (at least 5 days), you might qualify for a discount. As a general rule, expect 1 night free after a 7-night stay.

- **Avoid excess charges and hidden costs.** When you book a room, confirm whether the hotel charges for parking. Use your own cellphone, pay phones, or prepaid phone cards instead of dialing direct from hotel phones, which usually have exorbitant rates. And don't be tempted by the room's minibar offerings: Most hotels charge through the nose for water, soda, and snacks. Finally, ask about local taxes and service charges, which can increase the cost of a room by 15% or more. California had a notorious energy crisis in 2001, but the rate hikes were largely erased by 2002. Yet while researching this book, I still found a few hotels adding an "energy surcharge" of $3 or so to their nightly room rates. Shame, shame.

- **Book an efficiency.** A room with a kitchenette allows you to shop for groceries and cook your own meals. This is a big money saver, especially for families on long stays.

- **Investigate reservation services.** These outfits usually work as consolidators, buying up or reserving rooms in bulk, and then dealing them out to customers at a profit. They do garner deals that range from 10% to 50% off, but remember, the discounts apply to rack rates—inflated prices that people rarely end up paying. You're probably better off dealing directly with a hotel, but if you don't like bargaining, this is certainly a viable option. Most of them offer online reservation services as well. Here are a few of the more reputable providers: **San Diego Hotel Reservations** (© **800/SAVE-CASH;** www.sandiegohotelres.com); **Hotel Locators** (© **800/423-7846;** www.hotellocators.com); **Accommodations Express** (© **800/950-4685;** www.accommodationsexpress.com); **Hotel Discounts** (© **800/715-7666;** www.hoteldiscount.com); and **Quikbook** (© **800/789-9887,** includes fax-on-demand service; www.quikbook.com).

Note: Rates given in this chapter do not include the hotel tax, which is an additional 10.5% (at press time, an increase was being debated). Also, many San

---

Tips **"What's Your Best Rate for Tonight?"**

Trying to score the lowest rate for a downtown hotel can be an amusing exercise, providing a convention hasn't sucked up the availability. As an experiment, I called all the major downtown hotels on a Tuesday morning to see what their best rate on a room for that night would be. In all instances the rate I was quoted was 25% to 40% lower than the lowest rack rate. When I called the Grand Hyatt, I was quoted $240 for a city view. The price fell to $220 when I mentioned my AAA membership. I said, "Thanks, I'll get back to you." The very helpful reservations agent countered, "Let me check to see if there are any packages available." Within a few seconds she found a rate of $139 that included breakfast for two, free parking (a $15 savings), and a 15% discount off dinner at the hotel. I started to end the call again, and she cut me off to say, "Oh, here's a $99 promotional rate you might want to consider . . ."

Diego hotels provide a free shuttle to and from the airport, so before you pony up for a taxi, check to see what your hotel offers.

BED & BREAKFASTS

Travelers who seek bed-and-breakfast accommodations will be pleasantly surprised by the variety and affordability of San Diego B&Bs (especially compared to the rest of California). The trend was late in coming to San Diego, but some have become well established. Many B&Bs are traditional, strongly reflecting the personality of an on-site innkeeper and offering as few as two guest rooms; others accommodate more guests in a slickly professional way. Ten B&Bs are part of the close-knit **San Diego Bed & Breakfast Guild** (© 619/523-1300; www.bandbguildsandiego.org), whose members work actively at keeping prices reasonable; many good B&Bs average $100 to $125 a night.

HOSTELS

Those in search of less expensive accommodations should check in to San Diego's small collection of hostels. Downtown, you'll find **USAHostels** (© 800/438-8622 or 619/232-3100; www.usahostels.com), located in the heart of the Gaslamp Quarter at 726 Fifth Avenue, in a historic building; double rooms cost $50 and dorm rooms run $21 per person. Also in the Gaslamp is **HI Downtown Hostel** (© 800/909-4776, ext. 43, or 619/525-1531; www.sandiegohostels.com), 521 Market St.; doubles cost $44 to $55 and dorm rooms run $18 to $25. Hostelling International (formerly American Youth Hostels) also has a 60-bed location in **Point Loma** (© 800/909-4776, ext. 44, or 619/223-4778), which is about 2 miles inland from Ocean Beach; rates run $15 to $18 per person.

1 Downtown

Visitors with business in the city center—including the Convention Center—will find the downtown area convenient. Keep in mind that the area I refer to as "downtown" includes hotels in the stylish Gaslamp Quarter, as well as properties conveniently located near the harbor and other attractions. *Remember:* On weekends and holidays you'll find lower prices than the rack rates shown below—half-off or more—and prices drop even midweek when big conventions aren't tying up rooms.

VERY EXPENSIVE

Embassy Suites Hotel San Diego Bay–Downtown 🕸🕸 What might seem like an impersonal business hotel can actually work out to a good deal for families, if you can snag a room when a big convention isn't hogging downtown hotels. This spot provides modern accommodations with lots of room for families or claustrophobes. Built in 1988, the neoclassical high-rise is topped with a distinctive neon bull's-eye that's visible from far away. Every room is a suite, with a king or two doubles in the bedroom, plus a sofa bed in the living/dining area; each has convenient features like a kitchenette and a dining table that converts into a work area. All rooms open onto a 12-story atrium filled with palm trees, koi ponds, and a bubbling fountain; each also has a city or bay view. Located 1 block from Seaport Village and 8 blocks from the Gaslamp Quarter, the Embassy Suites may be a second-tier choice of convention groups (after the pricier Grand Hyatt and Marriott), but it provides solid extras like a full breakfast and complimentary evening cocktail hour that make it a fine pick for groups of three or more.

601 Pacific Hwy. (at N. Harbor Dr.), San Diego, CA 92101. © **800/EMBASSY** or 619/239-2400. Fax 619/239-1520. www.embassysuites.com. 337 suites. $279–$329 suite. Rates include full breakfast and afternoon cocktail. Children under 18 stay free in parent's room. AE, DC, DISC, MC, V. Valet parking $18; indoor self-parking $15. Bus: 7. Trolley: Seaport Village. Amtrak Station 3 blocks away. **Amenities:** 2 restaurants; indoor pool; tennis court; exercise room; Jacuzzi; concierge; car-rental desk; babysitting; laundry service; self-service laundry. *In room:* A/C, TV w/pay movies, dataport, kitchenette, fridge, coffeemaker, hair dryer, iron.

Manchester Grand Hyatt San Diego 🕸🕸 As we went to press, the Hyatt was putting the finishing touches on a second tower that substantially increases the facility's meeting space and guest rooms. While a behemoth with 1,625 rooms can't offer very personalized service, you'll definitely enjoy all the amenities those with expense accounts are used to, including a 40th-floor lounge that offers stunning views over the city and San Diego Bay. In fact, the Hyatt is the tallest waterfront lodging on the West Coast. All the public spaces are light and airy, sporting a limestone-and-marble neoclassical theme; guest rooms are quiet and furnished with high-quality but standard Hyatt-issue furnishings. Bathrooms have ample counter space, and the facility gets kudos for superior service for travelers with disabilities. The city's largest hotel is generally the first choice of convention groups, so the rack rates can be deceptively high. Don't let them scare you off if you want to stay in downtown's best modern high-rise—weekend rates in particular can be a great deal.

1 Market Place (at Harbor Dr.), San Diego, CA 92101. © **800/233-1234** or 619/232-1234. Fax 619/239-5678. www.hyatt.com. 1,625 units. $350 double; from $600 suite. Extra person $25. Children under 12 stay free in parent's room. Packages and weekend rates available. AE, DC, DISC, MC, V. Valet parking $21; self-parking $15. Bus: 4 or 7. Trolley: Seaport Village. **Amenities:** 3 restaurants; 2 bars; 2 outdoor pools; 6 outdoor tennis courts (4 lit for night play); health club and spa; Jacuzzi; watersports equipment rental; bike rental; concierge; business center; salon; 24-hr. room service; laundry service; dry cleaning. *In room:* A/C, TV w/pay movies, dataport, minibar, coffeemaker, hair dryer, iron.

Marriott San Diego Hotel & Marina 🕸🕸 In the prosperous late 1980s, well before San Diego's Convention Center was even a blueprint, this stylish mirrored tower arose. By the time a second tower took shape, adding more rooms and multiple banquet and ballrooms, the Marriott *was* a convention center. Today it merely stands next door, garnering a large share of convention attendees. They're drawn by the scenic 446-slip marina, lush grounds, waterfall pool, and breathtaking bay-and-beyond views. The Marriott competes with the newer Grand Hyatt next door, and guests benefit from constantly improved facilities and decor.

Downtown San Diego Accommodations

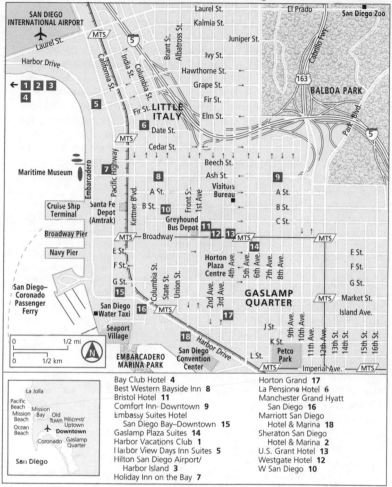

Bay Club Hotel **4**		Horton Grand **17**
Best Western Bayside Inn **8**		La Pensione Hotel **6**
Bristol Hotel **11**		Manchester Grand Hyatt
Comfort Inn- Downtown **9**		San Diego **16**
Embassy Suites Hotel		Marriott San Diego
San Diego Bay–Downtown **15**		Hotel & Marina **18**
Gaslamp Plaza Suites **14**		Sheraton San Diego
Harbor Vacations Club **1**		Hotel & Marina **2**
Harbor View Days Inn Suites **5**		U.S. Grant Hotel **13**
Hilton San Diego Airport/		Westgate Hotel **12**
Harbor Island **3**		W San Diego **10**
Holiday Inn on the Bay **7**		

Leisure travelers can also take advantage of greatly reduced weekend rates and enjoy a free-form tropical pool area (at the edge of downtown!). Note that rooms in the north tower have a (small) balcony; only the suites in the south tower do. Because the Marriott tends to focus on public features and business services, guest quarters are well maintained but plain, and standard rooms are on the small side. Hallway noise can sometimes be disturbing.

333 W. Harbor Dr. (at Front St.), San Diego, CA 92101-7700. © **800/228-9290** or 619/234-1500. Fax 619/234-8678. 1,408 units. $380–$400 double; from $750 suite. Children under 18 stay free in parent's room. AE, DC, DISC, MC, V. Valet parking $22; self-parking $16. Bus: 4. Trolley: Convention Center. Pets accepted. **Amenities:** 3 restaurants; bar; 2 lagoonlike outdoor pools; 6 night-lit tennis courts; fitness center; 2 Jacuzzis; sauna; boat rental; bike rental; game room; concierge, tour desk; car-rental desk; business center with secretarial services; salon; 24-hr. room service; coin-op laundry and laundry service; dry cleaning. *In room:* A/C, TV w/pay movies, dataport, minibar, coffeemaker, hair dryer, iron.

U.S. Grant Hotel ⚐⚐   In 1910, Ulysses S. Grant Jr. opened this stately hotel, now on the National Register of Historic Places, in honor of his famous father.

Since then, guests have included Albert Einstein, Charles Lindbergh, and a dozen U.S. presidents. The hotel was purchased by the Wyndham folks in 2001—they did a full technological overhaul (including high-speed Internet) to bring the facilities up to today's basic business travelers' needs. An elegant style more often found on the East Coast prevails, with age-smoothed marble, wood paneling, crystal chandeliers, and formal decor. Guest rooms range in size, and feature upgraded linens and nicely framed botanical prints and historical photos, but the standard bathrooms are disappointing. Extras in the suites make them worth the splurge; each has a fireplace and Jacuzzi tub, and suite rates include continental breakfast and afternoon cocktails and hors d'oeuvres. Afternoon tea is served in the lobby Friday and Saturday. While the hotel has preserved a nostalgic air, the surrounding neighborhood is a hodgepodge of chic bistros, wandering panhandlers, and the visually loud Horton Plaza shopping center (which looms large right across the street).

326 Broadway (between Third and Fourth aves.), San Diego, CA 92101. © 800/237-5029 or 619/232-3121. Fax 619/232-3626. www.wyndham.com. 340 units. $289–$329 double; from $425 suite. Extra person $20. Children under 18 stay free in parent's room. AE, DC, MC, V. Parking $20. Bus: All Broadway routes. Trolley: Civic Center. **Amenities:** Restaurant; jazz bar; fitness center; concierge; business center; room service; babysitting; laundry and dry-cleaning service. In room: A/C, TV w/pay movies, dataport, minibar, hair dryer.

W San Diego 𝒜𝒜   This W is hands-down San Diego's newest scene to beat. Opening just weeks ahead of the 2003 Super Bowl, the brand's 17th hotel quickly took the city by storm for its swanky nightlife, which on Friday and Saturday evenings means there's a line to get in to the packed lobby. But if you hold a reservation, go to the front of the line and let one of the many black-clad *Friends* castoffs that work here lead you past the velvet rope to the front desk, where check-in can be accomplished by shouting above the din. Fortunately, your room is bright and cheery—like a mod beach cabana beamed into downtown, replete with sexy shower. *Nouveau nautique* is the theme, with elegant aqua and sand tones accenting the whites, a window seat (great idea) for gazing down on this languid corner of downtown, and a beach ball–shaped pillow, which should be the only exclamation point needed to remind you that this hotel is supposed to be fun.

So, go downstairs and sample the restaurant, Rice (the food earns mixed reviews), and enjoy its adjoining bar, where cocktail waitresses clad in leather hot pants and fishnets serve blue-tinged cotton-candy treats that float through the room like tiny psychedelic clouds. This is also one of the hotel's three bars, so a DJ spins here while another mixes in the Living Room—i.e., the lobby. Here, the path leading to the bathrooms is a catwalk with see-through plexi portholes underfoot. Then there's the Beach, up on the third floor, where the developers got really creative: The open-air bar has a sand floor (heated at night), a fire pit, and cabanas; drinks are served in plastic, allowing you to safely roam the terrace barefoot. Shoe check, please.

The cacophony mostly dies down by Sunday, when the contingent of mostly Los Angelenos departs, and for a few days the W is the very model of a proper business hotel—albeit one with a (tiny) pool, a 24-hour open-air gym, and a bank of 18 video screens glowing with an idealized landscape of bubbles floating heavenward. Look closely and you'll notice that each bubble has a floating W logo within it. Self-absorbed? To the max. Fun? Check me in.

421 West B St. (at State St.), San Diego, CA 92101. © 888/625-5144 or 619/231-8220. Fax 619/231-5779. www.whotels.com/sandiego. 261 units. $389–$439 double; $700 suite. AE, DC, DISC, MC, V. Valet parking $23. Bus: All Broadway routes. Trolley: American Plaza or Civic Center. **Amenities:** Restaurant; 3 bars; 24-hr.

concierge; 24-hr. room service; laundry service; dry cleaning. *In room:* A/C, TV/VCR/DVD, CD player, dataport, minibar, coffeemaker, hair dryer, iron.

EXPENSIVE

Holiday Inn on the Bay ★★ *(Kids)*   Renovated in 2001, this better-than-average Holiday Inn is reliable and nearly always offers great deals. The three-building high-rise complex is located on the Embarcadero across from the harbor and the Maritime Museum; this scenic spot is only 1½ miles from the airport (you can watch planes landing and taking off), and 2 blocks from the train station and trolley. Rooms, while basic, always seem to sport clean new furnishings and plenty of thoughtful comforts. Although rooms are identical inside, choose carefully; the bay views are astounding, while city views can be depressing (you're looking at utilitarian older office buildings). In either case, request the highest floor possible.

1355 N. Harbor Dr. (at Ash St.), San Diego, CA 92101-3385. ℭ 800/HOLIDAY or 619/232-3861. Fax 619/232-4924. 600 units. $199–$219 double; from $400 suite. Children under 18 stay free in parent's room. AE, DC, MC, V. Self-parking $15. Bus: All Pacific Hwy. routes. Trolley: American Plaza. Pets accepted with $25 fee and $100 deposit. **Amenities:** 4 restaurants; bar; outdoor heated pool; exercise room; concierge; business center; limited room service (6–11am and 5–11pm); babysitting; laundry service; self-service laundry. *In room:* A/C, TV w/pay movies, dataport, coffeemaker, hair dryer, iron.

The Westgate Hotel ★★★   Before downtown's 1990s resurgence, the lavish Westgate and its elegant neighbor, the U.S. Grant, were the only hotels of note in the business district. But whereas the latter came by its formality during an era when royal treatment was expected, the Westgate was considered nouveau riche when it opened in 1970. Legend has it that President Eisenhower, during an early 1960s visit to San Diego, asked local banker C. Arnholt Smith (of an unnamed hotel), "Is this the best you have?" Smith took Eisenhower up on the challenge and built the Westgate; when it opened, it was downtown's first new hotel in 35 years. Smith's wife toured Europe collecting pieces to furnish the public spaces, including Louis XVI–period antiques and Baccarat crystal chandeliers. But ultimately, the Westgate became a money pit, leading to its sale to the Holding family in 1975; they in turn spent years nurturing a profile for the white elephant, eventually establishing a standard of luxury—including fruit baskets and deferential, European-style service—that today holds great appeal to visiting celebrities and dignitaries.

Despite the plain, modern exterior of this high-rise, the lobby appears straight out of 18th-century France; it's a recreation of an anteroom from the Palace of Versailles, featuring brocade upholstery, tapestries, crystal chandeliers, parquet floors, and Persian rugs. Afternoon tea is conducted daily here with great aplomb. The once-dowdy rooms were gutted and upgraded in 2003—old-world decadence remains, but now they feature high-speed Internet connections, DVD players, Italian armoires, and new marble finishings. At 400 square feet, standard rooms are the largest of any downtown hotel, and the harbor and city views are splendid. The Westgate has a fine jewel-box restaurant, Le Fontainebleau, noted for its French-California-Asian fusion cuisine, live piano, silver place settings, and Saturday night dinner dancing. Yes, it's more formal than the convention-centric Marriott or Hyatt down the street, but the Westgate is actually a bit cheaper, and you get a bigger room—a good bet for anyone thinking of packing fancy duds.

1055 Second Ave. (between Broadway and C St.), San Diego, CA 92101. ℭ 800/221-3802 or 619/238-1818. Fax 619/557-3604. www.westgatehotel.com. 223 units. $239–$349 double; from $490 suite. Children 18 and under stay free in parent's room. AE, DC, DISC, MC, V. Underground valet parking $18. Bus: All Broadway routes. Trolley: Civic Center. **Amenities:** 3 restaurants; bar; fitness center; concierge; business center; barber-shop; 24-hr. room service; laundry service; dry cleaning. *In room:* A/C, TV/DVD w/pay movies, dataport, mini-bar, hair dryer, safe.

MODERATE

Best Western Bayside Inn 🎿   This corner of downtown is just starting to become developed, but this high-rise, representative of reliable Best Western, offers quiet lodgings. Although calling it "bayview" would be more accurate than "bayside," rooms in the 14-story hotel reveal nice city and harbor views. Rooms and bathrooms are basic chain-hotel issue, but are well maintained and feature brand-new bedding, towels, and draperies; all have balconies overlooking the bay or downtown (ask for the higher floors). The accommodating staff makes this a mecca for budget-minded business travelers, and this Best Western is also close to downtown's tourist sites. It's an easy walk to the Embarcadero, a bit farther to Horton Plaza, and just 5 blocks to the train station. Best of all, there's no charge for parking—almost unheard of among downtown hotels.

555 W. Ash St. (at Columbia St.), San Diego, CA 92101. ℂ 800/341-1818 or 619/233-7500. Fax 619/239-8060. www.baysideinn.com. 122 units. $189 double. Extra person $10. Children under 12 stay free in parent's room. Rates include continental breakfast. AE, DC, DISC, MC, V. Free covered parking. Bus: 5 or 16. Trolley: Little Italy. **Amenities:** Restaurant (lunch daily, dinner Mon–Fri only); outdoor pool; Jacuzzi; laundry service; dry cleaning. *In room:* A/C, TV w/pay movies, dataport, fridge, microwave, coffeemaker, hair dryer, iron.

Bristol Hotel 🎿 *Value*   If you're looking for a basic business hotel with a sunny splash of style, you can do no better than the economical Bristol, which boasts a boxy, IKEA-esque geometric decor accented by energetic primary colors and an admirable collection of late-20th-century pop art from Warhol, Kandinsky, Lichtenstein, and Haring. Everything still feels crisply new from the 2001 makeover that rendered this formerly baroque boutique property almost unrecognizable. Though it doesn't offer many on-site amenities to keep you around during the day, and the staff could be warmer, these brightly modern rooms are fun to come home to. Each morning a nice breakfast spread is laid out in the downstairs Daisies Bistro, which offers all-day dining and a cozy, after-work bar.

1055 First Ave. (between Broadway and C St.), San Diego, CA 92101. ℂ 800/662-4477 or 619/232-6141. Fax 619/232-1948. www.thebristolsandiego.com. 102 units. $179–$199 double. Children under 18 stay free in parent's room. AE, DC, DISC, MC, V. Valet parking $18. Bus: All Broadway routes. Trolley: Civic Center. **Amenities:** Restaurant; bar; concierge; laundry service; dry cleaning. *In room:* A/C, TV w/pay movies, Web TV, CD player, dataport, minibar, coffeemaker, hair dryer, iron.

Harbor Vacations Club 🎿 *Finds*   Here's an unusual opportunity to sleep on the water in your own power yacht, sailboat, or "floating villa" (also known as a houseboat). You fall asleep to the gentle lapping of waves and awaken to the call of seagulls. The vessels are docked in a recreational marina on Harbor Island, near the airport and close to downtown; for an additional charge you can even charter a private cruise aboard your "room" ($125–$495 for a 3- to 4-hr. cruise, plus $45/hr. for a skipper).

The 32- to 55-foot floating villas average 650 square feet and feel like modern condos, with their own laundry facilities, comfortable furnishings, multiple TVs and VCR, a stereo, and many other comforts, including a balcony and sun deck. The well-kept power yachts have two staterooms, two heads, a full galley, and stereo system. Serious sailors may prefer to sleep on one of three sailboats. They range in length from 22 feet to 30 feet and accommodate two to four people, but are best suited for one couple. If showering on board any of the boats is too cramped for you, guests have the use of full restrooms at the marina headquarters, as well as the swimming pool there. Formerly known as San Diego Yacht and Breakfast, the company is now tied in with a time-share operation.

Marina Cortez, 1880 Harbor Island Dr., G-Dock, San Diego, CA 92101. (© **800/YACHT-DO** or 619/297-9484. Fax 619/298-6625. www.yachtdo.com. 11 vessels. $189–$300 double. AE, DISC, MC, V. Free parking. **Amenities:** Deli. *In room:* TV/VCR, kitchen, coffeemaker, hair dryer, iron.

Horton Grand ⭐ A cross between an elegant hotel and a charming inn, the Horton Grand combines two hotels that date from 1886—the Horton Grand (once an infamous red-light establishment) and the Brooklyn Hotel (which for a time was the Kahle Saddlery Shop). Both were saved from demolition, moved to this spot, and connected by an airy atrium lobby filled with white wicker. The facade, with its graceful bay windows, is original.

Each room is utterly unique—all were renovated in 2000 with vintage furnishings, gas fireplaces, and business-savvy features—and bathrooms are lush with reproduction floor tiles, fine brass fixtures, and genteel appointments. Rooms overlook either the city or the fig tree–filled courtyard; they're divided between the clubby and darker "saddlery" side and the pastel-toned and Victorian "brothel" side. The suites (really just large studio-style rooms) are located in a newer wing; choosing one means sacrificing historic character for a sitting area/sofa bed and minibar with microwave. With all these offerings, there's a room that's right for everyone, so query your reservationist on the different features. The Palace Bar serves afternoon tea Saturdays from 2:30 to 5pm. My only qualm about this property is a lackadaisical staff that doesn't live up to the potential of this place.

311 Island Ave. (at Fourth Ave.), San Diego, CA 92101. (© **800/542-1886** or 619/544-1886. Fax 619/239-3823. www.hortongrand.com. 132 units. $169–$189 double; $279 suite. Extra person $20. Children under 18 stay free in parent's room. AE, DC, MC, V. Valet parking $20. Bus: 1, 4, 5, 16, or 25. Trolley: Convention Center. **Amenities:** Restaurant (Fri–Sat dinner and Sun brunch only); bar. *In room:* A/C, TV, dataport, hair dryer.

INEXPENSIVE

Inexpensive motels line Pacific Highway between the airport and downtown. The **Harbor View Days Inn Suites,** 1919 Pacific Hwy. at Grape Street (© **800/ 325-2525** or 619/232-1077), is within walking distance of the Embarcadero, the Maritime Museum, and the Harbor Excursion. Rates range from $79 to $89. Also see "Hostels," earlier in this chapter.

Comfort Inn–Downtown In the northern corner of downtown, this place is popular with business travelers without expense accounts, and vacationers who just need reliable, safe accommodations. This humble chain motel must be surprised to find itself in a quickly regentrifying part of town: The landmark El Cortez Hotel across the street has been transformed into upscale condos and shops, and new residential construction is winding down on the surrounding blocks. The Comfort Inn is smartly designed so rooms open onto exterior walkways surrounding the drive-in entry courtyard, lending an insular feel in this once-dicey corner of town. There are few frills here, but coffee is always brewing in the lobby. The hotel operates a free shuttle to the airport and the train and bus stations. **Note:** The hilltop location gives thighs a workout on the walk to and from the Gaslamp Quarter.

719 Ash St. (at Seventh Ave.), San Diego, CA 92101. (© **619/232-2525.** Fax 619/687-3024. www.comfortinn sandiego.com. 67 units. $89–$139 double. Extra person $15. Children under 18 stay free in parent's room. Rates include continental breakfast. AE, DISC, MC, V. Free parking. Bus: 1, 3, 25, or 992. **Amenities:** Jacuzzi; laundry service. *In room:* A/C, TV, dataport, coffeemaker.

Gaslamp Plaza Suites ☆☆ *Value* You can't get closer to the center of the vibrant Gaslamp Quarter than this impeccably restored late Victorian. At 11 stories, it was San Diego's first skyscraper, built in 1913. Crafted (at great expense) of Australian gumwood, marble, brass, and exquisite etched glass, this splendid building originally housed San Diego Trust & Savings. Various other businesses (jewelers, lawyers, doctors, photographers) set up shop here until 1988, when the elegant structure was placed on the National Register of Historic Places and reopened as a boutique hotel.

You'll be surprised at the timeless elegance, from the dramatic lobby and wide corridors to guest rooms furnished with European flair. Each bears the name of a writer (Emerson, Swift, Zola, Shelley, Fitzgerald, and so on). Most rooms are spacious and offer luxuries rare in this price range, like pillow-top mattresses and premium toiletries; microwaves and dinnerware; and impressive luxury bathrooms. Beware of the cheapest rooms on the back side—they are uncomfortably small (although they do have regular-size bathrooms) and have no view. The higher floors boast splendid city and bay views, as do the rooftop patio, Jacuzzi, and breakfast room. Despite the welcome addition of noise-muffling windows, don't be surprised to hear a hum from the street below, especially when the Quarter gets rockin' on the weekends.

520 E St. (corner of Fifth Ave.), San Diego, CA 92101. © 800/874-8770 or 619/232-9500. Fax 619/238-9945. www.gaslampplaza.com. 64 units. $95–$189 double; from $199 suite. Rates include continental breakfast. AE, DC, DISC, MC, V. Valet parking $18. Bus: 1, 3, or 25. Trolley: Fifth Ave. **Amenities:** Rooftop Jacuzzi; limited room service (lunch and dinner). *In room:* A/C, TV/VCR, dataport, fridge, microwave, coffeemaker, hair dryer, iron, safe.

La Pensione Hotel ☆ *Value* This place has a lot going for it: modern amenities, remarkable value, a convenient location within walking distance of the central business district, a friendly staff, and free parking (a premium for small hotels in San Diego). The four-story Pensione is built around a courtyard and feels like a small European hotel. The decor throughout is modern and streamlined, with plenty of sleek black and metallic surfaces, crisp white walls, and modern wood furnishings. Guest rooms, while not overly large, make the most of their space and leave you with room to move around. Each room offers a ceiling fan and minifridge; some have a small balcony. Try for a bay or city view rather than the concrete courtyard view. La Pensione is in San Diego's Little Italy and within walking distance of eateries (mostly Italian) and nightspots; there are two restaurants directly downstairs.

606 W. Date St. (at India St.), San Diego, CA 92101. © 800/232-4683 or 619/236-8000. Fax 619/236-8088. www.lapensionehotel.com. 80 units. $75 double. AE, DC, DISC, MC, V. Limited free underground parking. Bus: 5 or 16. Trolley: Little Italy. **Amenities:** Self-service laundry. *In room:* TV, dataport, fridge.

2 Hillcrest/Uptown

Although they're certainly no longer a secret, the gentrified historic neighborhoods north of downtown are still something of a bargain. They're convenient to Balboa Park and offer easy access to the rest of town. Filled with casual and upscale restaurants, eclectic shops, and sizzling nightlife, the area is also easy to navigate. All of the following accommodations cater to the mainstream market but attract a gay and lesbian clientele, as well.

*A **note on driving directions:*** All of these accommodations are reached from I-5.

Hillcrest/Uptown Accommodations

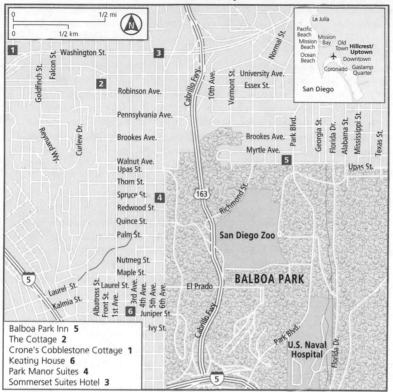

Balboa Park Inn **5**
The Cottage **2**
Crone's Cobblestone Cottage **1**
Keating House **6**
Park Manor Suites **4**
Sommerset Suites Hotel **3**

MODERATE

Crone's Cobblestone Cottage Bed & Breakfast ★ *Finds*   After just 1 night at this magnificently restored Craftsman bungalow, you'll feel like an honored guest rather than a paying customer. Artist Joan Crone lives in the architectural award-winning addition to her 1913 home, which is a designated historical landmark. Guests have the run of the entire house, including a book-filled, wood-paneled den and antique-filled living room. Both cozy guest rooms have antique beds, goose-down pillows and comforters, and eclectic bedside reading. They share a full bathroom; the Eaton Room also has a private half bathroom. You can rent the entire house (2 bedrooms plus the den) to sleep five or six, for $285. Bookmaker Crone lends a calm and craftsman aesthetic to the surroundings, aided by a pair of cats, who peer in from their side of the house. Mission Hills, the neighborhood a half-mile west of Hillcrest, is one of San Diego's treasures, and lots of other historic homes can be explored along quiet streets.

1302 Washington Place (4 blocks west of Goldfinch St. at Ingalls St.), San Diego, CA 92103. © 619/295-4765. www.cobblestonebandb.com. 2 units. $125 double. Rates include continental breakfast. Minimum 2 nights. No credit cards (checks accepted). Bus: 3. From I-5, take Washington St. exit east uphill. Make a U-turn at Goldfinch, then keep right at Y intersection onto Washington Place. *In room:* No phone.

Sommerset Suites Hotel ★★   This all-suite hotel on a busy street was originally built as apartment housing for interns at the hospital nearby. It retains a residential ambience and unexpected amenities such as huge closets, medicine cabinets, and fully equipped kitchens in all rooms (executive suites even have dishwashers). Poolside barbecue facilities encourage warm-weather mingling. The hotel has a personal, welcoming feel, from the friendly, helpful staff to the snacks, soda, beer, and wine served each afternoon. You'll even get a welcome basket with cookies and microwave popcorn. Rooms are comfortably furnished, and each has a private balcony. Be prepared for noise from the busy thoroughfare below, though. Several blocks worth of restaurants and shops start just across the street, plus a multiplex cinema. Guest services include a courtesy van to the airport, SeaWorld, the zoo, and other attractions within a 5-mile radius.

606 Washington St. (at Fifth Ave.), San Diego, CA 92103. ℂ **800/962-9665** or 619/692-5200. Fax 619/692-5299. www.sommersetsuites.com. 80 units. $139–$329 double. Children under 12 stay free in parent's room. Rates include continental breakfast and afternoon refreshments. AE, DC, DISC, MC, V. Free covered parking. Bus: 1, 3, 7, 11, or 25. Take Washington St. exit off I-5. **Amenities:** Outdoor pool; Jacuzzi; coin-op laundry. *In room:* A/C, TV, dataport, kitchen, coffeemaker, hair dryer, iron.

INEXPENSIVE

Balboa Park Inn ⨀   Insiders looking for unusual accommodations head straight for this small pink inn at the northern edge of Balboa Park. It's a cluster of four Spanish colonial–style former apartment buildings in a mostly residential neighborhood a half-mile east of Hillcrest proper. The hotel is popular with gay travelers drawn to Hillcrest's hip restaurants and clubs, but note that all of these are at least 4 blocks away. All the rooms and suites are tastefully decorated; the specialty suites, however, are over-the-top. There's the "Tara Suite," as in *Gone With the Wind;* the "Nouveau Ritz," which employs every Art Deco cliché, including mirrors and Hollywood lighting; and the "Greystoke" suite, a jumble of jungle, safari, and tropical themes with a completely mirrored bathroom and Jacuzzi tub. From here, you're close enough to walk to the San Diego Zoo and other Balboa Park attractions. ℂ

3402 Park Blvd. (at Upas St.), San Diego, CA 92103. ℂ **800/938-8181** or 619/298-0823. Fax 619/294-8070. www.balboaparkinn.com. 26 units. $99 double; $119–$199 suites. Extra person $10. Children under 12 stay free in parent's room. Rates include continental breakfast. AE, DC, DISC, MC, V. Parking available on street. Bus: 7 or 7A/B. From I-5, take Washington St. east, follow signs to University Ave. E. Turn right at Park Blvd. *In room:* TV, fridge, coffeemaker.

The Cottage   Built in 1913, this B&B at the end of a residential cul-de-sac is surrounded by a secret garden, and features a private hideaway—"the cottage"— tucked behind a homestead-style house. There's an herb garden in front, birdbaths, and a walkway lined with climbing roses. The cottage has a king-size bed, a living room with a wood-burning stove and a queen-size sofa bed, and a charming kitchen with a coffeemaker. The guest room in the main house features a king-size bed. Both accommodations are filled with fresh flowers and antiques put to clever uses, and each has a private entrance. Owner Carol Emerick (she used to run an antiques store—and it shows!) serves a scrumptious breakfast, complete with the morning paper. Guests are welcome to use the dining room and parlor in the main house, where they sometimes light a fire and rev up the 19th-century player piano. The Cottage is located 5 blocks from the cafes of Mission Hills and Hillcrest, and a short drive from Balboa Park.

3829 Albatross St. (off Robinson Ave.), San Diego, CA 92103. ℂ **619/299-1564.** Fax 619/299-6213. www. sandiegobandb.com/cottage.htm. 2 units. $75 double; $99 cottage. Extra person in cottage $10. 2-night minimum stay. Rates include continental breakfast. AE, DISC, MC, V. Bus: 3 or 11. Take Washington St. exit off I-5, take University Ave. exit.; right on First Ave., right on Robinson Ave. *In room:* TV, fridge, hair dryer.

Keating House ⨀⨀ *Finds*   This grand 1880s Bankers Hill mansion, located between downtown and Hillcrest and 4 blocks from Balboa Park, has been meticulously restored by two energetic innkeepers with a solid background in architectural preservation. Doug Scott and Ben Baltic not only know old houses, but are also neighborhood devotees filled with historical knowledge. Authentic period design is celebrated throughout, even in the overflowing gardens that bloom on four sides of this local landmark. The house contains a comfortable hodgepodge of antique furnishings and appointments; three additional rooms are in the restored carriage house opening onto an exotic garden patio. The downstairs entry, parlor, and dining room all have cozy fireplaces; bathrooms—all private—are gorgeously restored with updated period fixtures. Breakfast is served in a sunny, friendly setting; special dietary needs are cheerfully considered. In contrast to many B&Bs in Victorian-era homes, this one eschews dollhouse frills for a classy, sophisticated approach. The inn draws guests ranging from Europeans to business travelers avoiding the cookie-cutter ambience of chain hotels.

2331 Second Ave. (between Juniper and Kalmia sts.), San Diego, CA 92101. © **800/995-8644** or 619/239-8585. Fax 619/239-5774. www.keatinghouse.com. 9 units. $95–$155 double. Rates include full breakfast. AE, DISC, MC, V. Bus: 1, 3, 11, or 25. From the airport, take Harbor Dr. toward downtown; turn left on Laurel St., then right on Second Ave. *In room:* Hair dryer, no phone.

Park Manor Suites *Value*   Popular with actors appearing at the Old Globe Theatre in neighboring Balboa Park, this eight-story was built as a full-service luxury hotel in 1926 on a prime corner overlooking the park. One of the original investors was the family of child actor Jackie Coogan. The Hollywood connection continued—the hotel became a popular stopping-off point for celebrities headed for Mexican vacations in the 1920s and 1930s. Although dated, guest rooms are huge and very comfortable, featuring full kitchens, dining rooms, living rooms, and bedrooms with a separate dressing area. A few have glassed-in terraces; request one when you book. The overall feeling is that of a prewar East Coast apartment building, complete with steam heat and lavish moldings. Park Manor Suites does have its weaknesses, particularly bathrooms that have mostly original fixtures and could use some renovation. But prices are quite reasonable for Hillcrest; there's a darkly old-world restaurant on the ground floor, laundry service is also available, and a simple continental breakfast buffet is served in the penthouse banquet room (the view is spectacular). In fact, the penthouse bar becomes a bustling social scene on Friday evenings, drawing a horde—the single elevator gets a real workout that night.

525 Spruce St. (between Fifth and Sixth aves.), San Diego, CA 92103. © **800/874-2649** or 619/291-0999. Fax 619/291-8844. www.parkmanorsuites.com. 74 units. $99–$129 studio; $139–$179 1-bedroom suite; $199–$229 2-bedroom suite. Extra person $15. Children under 12 stay free in parent's room. Rates include continental breakfast. AE, DC, DISC, MC, V. Free parking. Bus: 1, 3, or 25. Take Washington St. exit off I-5, right on Fourth Ave., left on Spruce. **Amenities:** Restaurant/bar; access to nearby health club ($5); laundry service; dry cleaning; self-service laundry. *In room:* TV, dataport, kitchen, coffeemaker, hair dryer, iron.

3 Old Town & Mission Valley

Old Town is a popular area for families because of its proximity to Old Town State Historic Park and other attractions that are within walking distance—SeaWorld and the San Diego Zoo are within a 10-minute drive. Around the corner is Mission Valley, where you'll find the city's largest collection of hotels offering rooms under $100 a night. Mission Valley lacks much homegrown personality—this is the spot for chain restaurants and shopping malls, not gardens or water views. But it caters to convention groups, families visiting the University of San Diego or San Diego State University, and leisure travelers drawn by the lower prices and competitive facilities.

A note on driving directions: All Old Town and Mission Valley hotels are reached from either I-5 or I-8.

MODERATE

Heritage Park Bed & Breakfast Inn 🌟🌟 This exquisite 1889 Queen Anne mansion is set in a Victorian park—an artfully arranged cobblestone cul-de-sac lined with historic buildings saved from the wrecking ball and assembled here, in Old Town, as a tourist attraction. Most of the Inn's rooms are in the main house, with a handful of equally appealing choices in an adjacent 1887 Italianate companion. Owner Nancy Helsper is an amiable and energetic innkeeper with an eye for every necessary detail; she's always eager to share tales of these homes' fascinating history and how they crossed paths with Nancy and her husband, Charles. A stay here is about surrendering to the pampering of afternoon tea, candlelight breakfast, and a number of romantic extras (champagne and chocolates, dear?) available for special celebrations. Like the gracious parlors and porches, each room is outfitted with meticulous period antiques and luxurious fabrics; the small staff provides turndown service and virtually anything else you might require. Although the fireplaces are all ornamental, some rooms have whirlpool baths. In the evenings, vintage films are shown in the Victorian parlor.

2470 Heritage Park Row, San Diego, CA 92110. ℭ **800/995-2470** or 619/299-6832. Fax 619/299-9465. www.heritageparkinn.com. 12 units. $120–$250 double. Extra person $20. Rates include full breakfast and afternoon tea. AE, DC, DISC, MC, V. Free parking. Bus: 5. Trolley: Old Town. Take I-5 to Old Town Ave., turn left onto San Diego Ave., then turn right onto Harney St. *In room:* A/C, hair dryer, iron.

Holiday Inn Express–Old Town 🌟 Just a couple of easy walking blocks from the heart of Old Town, this Holiday Inn has a Spanish colonial exterior that suits the neighborhood's theme. Inside you'll find better-than-they-have-to-be contemporary furnishings and surprising small touches that make this hotel an affordable option favored by business travelers and families alike. There's nothing spectacular about the adjacent streets, so the hotel is smartly oriented toward the inside; request a room whose patio or balcony opens onto the pleasant courtyard. Rooms are thoughtfully and practically appointed, with extras like microwaves and writing tables. The lobby, surrounded by French doors, features a large fireplace, several sitting areas, and a TV. The hotel entrance, on Jefferson Street, is hard to find but definitely worth the search.

3900 Old Town Ave., San Diego, CA 92110. ℭ **800/451-9846** or 619/299-7400. Fax 619/299-1619. www. hiexpress.com/ex-oldtown. 125 units. $139–$169 double. Extra person $10. Children under 18 stay free in parent's room. Rates include continental breakfast. AE, DC, DISC, MC, V. Free parking. Bus: 5. Take I-5 to Old Town Ave. exit. **Amenities:** Outdoor pool; Jacuzzi; laundry service; dry cleaning. *In room:* A/C, TV, fridge, microwave, coffeemaker.

Red Lion Hanalei Hotel 🌟 My favorite hotel along Mission Valley's Hotel Circle has a Polynesian theme and comfort-conscious sophistication that sets it apart from the rest of the pack. Most rooms are split between two eight-story towers, set back from the freeway and cleverly positioned so that the balconies open onto the tropically landscaped pool courtyard or the attractive links of a golf club. A few more rooms are found in the Presidio Building, which is too close to the freeway for my comfort. The heated outdoor pool is large enough for any luau, as is the oversize Jacuzzi beside it. The hotel boasts an unmistakable 1960s vibe and Hawaiian ambience; the restaurant and bar have over-the-top kitschy decor, with waterfalls, outrigger canoes, and more. But guest rooms are outfitted with contemporary furnishings and conveniences; some have microwaves and

Accommodations in Old Town & Mission Valley

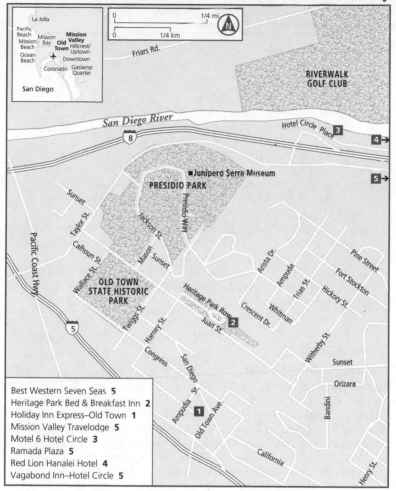

Best Western Seven Seas **5**
Heritage Park Bed & Breakfast Inn **2**
Holiday Inn Express–Old Town **1**
Mission Valley Travelodge **5**
Motel 6 Hotel Circle **3**
Ramada Plaza **5**
Red Lion Hanalei Hotel **4**
Vagabond Inn–Hotel Circle **5**

fridges. Services include a free shuttle to Old Town and the Fashion Valley Shopping Center, plus meeting facilities; golf packages are available.

2270 Hotel Circle N., San Diego, CA 92108. © **800/RED-LION** or 619/297-1101. Fax 619/297-6049. www. redlion.com. 416 units. $159 double; $275–$375 suite. Extra person $10. AE, DISC, MC, V. Parking $8. Bus: 6. From I-8, take Hotel Circle exit, follow signs for Hotel Circle N. Pets accepted with $50 deposit. **Amenities:** 2 restaurants; bar; outdoor pool; nearby golf course; fitness center; Jacuzzi; game room; activities desk; 24-hr. business center; limited room service (6am–10pm); coin-op laundry and laundry service; dry cleaning. *In room:* A/C, TV w/pay movies, dataport, coffeemaker, hair dryer, iron.

INEXPENSIVE

Room rates at properties on Hotel Circle are significantly cheaper than those in many other parts of the city. You'll find a cluster of inexpensive chain hotels and motels, including **Best Western Seven Seas** (© **800/421-6662** or 619/291-1300), **Mission Valley Travelodge** (© **800/255-3050** or

Kids   Family-Friendly Accommodations

Catamaran Resort Hotel (p. 83)   Numerous sports facilities and a safe swimming beach make this resort an ideal place for families. Accommodations are comfortable, but not so posh that Mom and Dad need to worry.

Holiday Inn on the Bay (p. 71)   Of the downtown options, this is the most kid-centric one and is well priced for strained family budgets; it even offers babysitting services for strained parents.

Loews Coronado Bay Resort (p. 93)   In the summer, the Commodore Kids Club, for children ages 4 to 12, provides supervised indoor and outdoor activities during the day and some evenings, too. Programs for older kids keep them out of harm's way without making them feel babysat.

Paradise Point Resort & Spa (p. 82)   This self-contained property in the middle of Mission Bay has plenty of space for kids to safely explore, and is just up the street from SeaWorld.

The Sea Lodge (p. 90)   Right smack on the La Jolla Shores beach, kids can choose between the pool and the ocean. They can even eat in their swimsuits on the patio.

619/297-2271), **Ramada Plaza** (© 800/532-4241 or 619/291-6500), and **Vagabond Inn–Hotel Circle** (© 800/522-1555 or 619/297-1691).

Motel 6 Hotel Circle   Yes, it's a Motel 6, so you know the drill: No mint on the pillow and you have to trundle down to the front desk to retrieve a cup of coffee in the morning. On the other hand, these budget hotels—now part of the mammoth Accor chain, the world's third-largest hotel company—know how to provide a consistent product at dependably inexpensive rates, and this one is very central to San Diego's sightseeing. The modern, four-story motel sits at the western end of Hotel Circle. Rooms are sparingly but adequately outfitted, with standard motel furnishings; bathrooms are perfunctory. Stay away from the loud freeway side—rooms in the four-story structure in back overlook a scenic 18-hole golf course and river. The hotel doesn't have a restaurant, but a fair steakhouse is across the street.

2424 Hotel Circle N., San Diego, CA 92108. © 800/4-MOTEL6 or 619/296-1612. Fax 619/543-9305. www. motel6.com. 204 units. $66–$80 double. Extra person $3. Children under 18 stay free in parent's room. AE, DC, DISC, MC, V. Free parking. Bus: 6. From I-8, take Taylor St. exit. **Amenities:** Outdoor pool; coin-op laundry. *In room:* A/C, TV.

4 Mission Bay & the Beaches

If the beach and aquatic activities are front-and-center in your San Diego agenda, this part of town may be just the ticket. Some hotels are right on Mission Bay, San Diego's water playground; they're usually good choices for families. Ocean Beach is more neighborhood oriented and easygoing, while Mission Beach and Pacific Beach provide a taste of the transient beach-bum lifestyle—they can be a bit raucous at times, especially on summer weekends, and dining

Booked aisle seat.

Reserved room with a view.

With a queen – no, make that a king-size bed.

With Travelocity, you can book your flights and hotels together, so you can get even better deals than if you booked them separately. You'll save time and money without compromising the quality of your trip. Choose your airline seat, search for alternate airports, pick your hotel room type, even choose the neighborhood you'd like to stay in.

Travelocity

Visit www.travelocity.com or call 1-888-TRAVELOCITY

Accommodations in Mission Bay & the Beaches

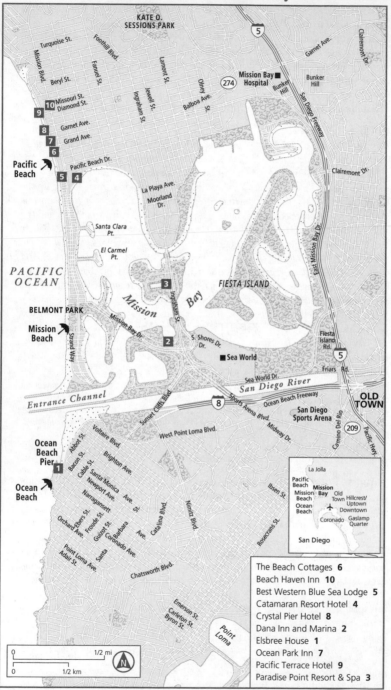

The Beach Cottages **6**
Beach Haven Inn **10**
Best Western Blue Sea Lodge **5**
Catamaran Resort Hotel **4**
Crystal Pier Hotel **8**
Dana Inn and Marina **2**
Elsbree House **1**
Ocean Park Inn **7**
Pacific Terrace Hotel **9**
Paradise Point Resort & Spa **3**

options are largely limited to chain eateries. If you're looking for a more refined landing, head to La Jolla or Coronado.

Accommodations here tend to book up solid on summer weekends and even weekdays, but discounts can be had, especially for those who try walk-up bookings on the afternoon of arrival. Even though the beach communities are far removed in atmosphere, downtown and Balboa Park are only a 15-minute drive away.

A note on driving directions: All directions are provided from I-5.

VERY EXPENSIVE

Pacific Terrace Hotel 😿😿   The best modern hotel on the boardwalk swaggers with a heavy-handed South Seas–meets–Spanish colonial ambience. Rattan fans circulate in the lobby and hint at the sunny Indonesian-inspired decor in guest rooms, which are named after Caribbean islands. Hands-on owners kicked up the luxury factor (and prices) following a renovation, resulting in a more upscale atmosphere than most of the casual beach pads nearby are able to muster, and the staff is friendly and accommodating. Located at the north end of the Pacific Beach boardwalk, the surfer contingent tends to stay a few blocks south.

Large, comfortable guest rooms each come with balconies or terraces and fancy wall safes; bathrooms, designed with warm-toned marble and natural woods, have a separate sink/vanity area. About half the rooms have kitchenettes, and top-floor rooms in this three-story hotel enjoy particularly nice views—you'll find yourself mesmerized by the rhythmic waves and determined surfers below. Management keeps cookies, coffee, and iced tea at the ready throughout the day; the lushly landscaped pool and hot tub overlook a relatively quiet stretch of beach. Five nearby restaurants allow meals to be billed to the hotel, but there's no restaurant on the premises.

610 Diamond St., San Diego, CA 92109. © 800/344-3370 or 858/581-3500. Fax 858/274-3341. www.pacific terrace.com. 75 units. $260–$385 double; from $435 suite. Rates include continental breakfast. AE, DC, DISC, MC, V. Parking $8; limited free parking in off-street lot. Bus: 30 or 34. Take I-5 to Grand/Garnet exit and follow Grand or Garnet west to Mission Blvd., turn right (north), then left (west) onto Diamond. **Amenities:** Pool; access to nearby health club ($5); Jacuzzi; bike rental nearby; activities desk; limited room service (11am–10:30pm); in-room massage; coin-op laundry and laundry service; dry cleaning. *In room:* A/C, TV w/pay movies, dataport, minibar, coffeemaker, hair dryer, iron.

Paradise Point Resort & Spa 😿😿 *Kids*   Smack dab in the middle of Mission Bay, this hotel complex is almost as much a theme park as its closest neighbor, SeaWorld (a 3-min. drive). Single-story accommodations are spread across 44 tropically-landscaped acres of duck-filled lagoons, lush gardens, and swim-friendly beaches; all have private lanais and plenty of thoughtful conveniences. The resort was recently updated to keep its low-tech 1960s charm but lose tacky holdovers—rooms now have a refreshingly colorful beach cottage decor. And despite daunting high-season rack rates, there's usually a deal to be had here. There's an upscale waterfront restaurant, Baleen (fine dining in a contemporary, fun space), and a stunning Indonesian-inspired spa that offers cool serenity and aroma-tinged Asian treatments—this spa is a vacation in itself!

1404 Vacation Rd. (off Ingraham St.), San Diego, CA 92109. © 800/344-2626 or 858/274-4630. Fax 858/581-5924. www.paradisepoint.com. 457 units. $279–$479 double; from $499 suite. Extra person $20. Children 17 and under stay free in parent's room. AE, DC, DISC, MC, V. Parking $14. Bus: 9. Follow I-8 west to Mission Bay Dr. exit; take Ingraham St. north to Vacation Rd. **Amenities:** 3 restaurants; bar; pool bar; 6 outdoor pools; 18-hole putting course; tennis courts; fitness center; full-service spa; Jacuzzi; bike rental; shuttle to Fashion Valley; limited room service (6am–midnight); laundry service; dry cleaning. *In room:* A/C, TV w/pay movies, dataport, fridge, coffeemaker, hair dryer, iron.

EXPENSIVE

Best Western Blue Sea Lodge   The three-story Blue Sea Lodge is a reliable choice in a prime location. While I'd like to see more meticulous maintenance and decor upgrades, Best Western keeps up with the other bargain properties in the chain. And, despite the rates listed, this can be a bargain. There are many ways to get a discount—including just asking. Aesthetically, the original rooms are a dreary snore, but nevertheless boast a balcony or patio and a handful of necessary comforts. Rooms with full ocean views overlook the sand and have more privacy than those on the street, but the Pacific Beach boardwalk has never been known for quiet or solitude. If an ocean view is not important, save a few bucks and check into one of the units in an expansion building that opened in 2003; the decor is brighter, more enticing. Casual beach cafes and grills are nearby, along with several rambunctious Pacific Beach bars. The lobby offers a cafe for guests in the morning, and its heated pool and Jacuzzi are steps from the beach.

707 Pacific Beach Dr., San Diego, CA 92109-5094. (℃ **800/BLUE-SEA** or 858/488-4700. Fax 858/488-7276. www.bestwestern-bluesea.com. 128 units. $209–$299 double; up to $309 suite. Children under 18 stay free in parent's room. AE, DC, DISC, MC, V. Underground and outdoor parking $7. Bus: 27 or 34. Take I-5 to Grand/Garnet exit, follow Grand Ave. to Mission Blvd. and turn left, then turn right onto Pacific Beach Dr. **Amenities:** Outdoor pool; Jacuzzi; coin-op laundry. *In room:* A/C, TV w/pay movies, dataport, microwave, coffeemaker, hair dryer, iron, safe.

Catamaran Resort Hotel ⭑⭑ *Kids*   Ideally situated right on Mission Bay, the Catamaran has its own bay and ocean beaches, complete with watersports facilities. Built in the 1950s, the hotel has been fully renovated to modern standards without losing its trademark Polynesian theme; the atrium lobby holds a 15-foot waterfall and full-size dugout canoe, and koi-filled lagoons meander through the property. After dark, torches blaze throughout the grounds, with numerous varieties of bamboo and palm sprouting; during the day, the resident tropical birds chirp away. Guest rooms—in a 13-story building or one of the six two-story buildings—have subdued South Pacific decor, and each has a balcony or patio. High floors of tower rooms have commanding views of the bay, the San Diego skyline, La Jolla, and Point Loma. Studios and suites have the added convenience of kitchenettes. The Catamaran is within walking distance of Pacific Beach's restaurant and nightlife. It's also steps away from the bay's exceptional jogging and biking path; runners with tots-in-tow can rent jogging strollers at the hotel. The resort's Mississippi-style sternwheeler, the *Bahia Belle*, cruises the bay Friday and Saturday evenings (nightly in summer) and is free to hotel guests.

3999 Mission Blvd. (4 blocks south of Grand Ave.), San Diego, CA 92109. (℃ **800/422-8386** or 858/488-1081. Fax 858/488-1387. www.catamaranresort.com. 313 units. $209–$349 double; from $299 suite. Children under 12 stay free in parent's room. AE, DC, DISC, MC, V. Valet parking $10; self-parking $8. Bus: 27 or 34. Take Grand/Garnet exit off I-5 and go west on Grand Ave., then south on Mission Blvd. **Amenities:** Restaurant; 2 bars; outdoor pool; fitness room; Jacuzzi; watersports equipment rental; bike rental; children's programs; concierge; limited room service (5am–11pm); in-room massage; laundry service; dry cleaning. *In room:* A/C, TV w/pay movies, dataport, fridge in most units, coffeemaker, hair dryer, iron.

Crystal Pier Hotel ⭑⭑ *Finds*   When historic charm is higher on your wish list than hotel-style service, head to this utterly unique cluster of cottages sitting literally over the surf on the vintage Crystal Pier at Pacific Beach. Like renting your own self-contained hideaway, you'll get a separate living room and bedroom, fully equipped kitchen, and private patio with breathtaking ocean views—all within the whitewashed walls of sweet, blue-shuttered cottages that date from 1936 but have been meticulously renovated. Each of the Cape Cod–style cottage has a deck—the more expensive units farthest out have a more privacy.

There are six units not actually on the pier, but still offering sunset-facing sea views; these accommodations are cheaper. The sound of waves is soothing, yet the boardwalk action is only a few steps (and worlds) away, and the pier is a great place for watching sunsets and surfers. Guests drive right out and park beside their cottages, a real boon on crowded weekends. But this operation is strictly BYOBT (beach towels), and the office is only open from 8am to 8pm. The accommodations book up fast, especially with long-term repeat guests, so reserve for summer and holiday weekends a couple months in advance.

4500 Ocean Blvd. (at Garnet Ave.), San Diego, CA 92109. © 800/748-5894 or 858/483-6983. Fax 858/483-6811. www.crystalpier.com. 29 units. $195–$320 double; $270–$400 for larger units sleeping 4 to 6. 3-night minimum in summer. DISC, MC, V. Free parking. Bus: 27, 30, or 34. Take I-5 to Grand/Garnet exit; follow Garnet to the pier. **Amenities:** Beach equipment rental. *In room:* TV, kitchen.

Ocean Park Inn ✿   This modern oceanfront motor hotel offers attractive, spacious rooms with well-coordinated contemporary furnishings. Although the inn has a level of sophistication uncommon in this casual, surfer-populated area, you won't find much solitude and quiet. The cool marble lobby and plushly carpeted hallways will help you feel a little insulated from the boisterous scene outside, though. You can't beat the location (directly on the beach) and the view (ditto). Rates vary according to view, but most rooms have at least a partial ocean view; all have a private balcony or patio. Units in front are most desirable, but it can get noisy directly above the boardwalk; try for the second or third floor, or pick one of the three junior suites, which have huge bathrooms and pool views. The Ocean Park Inn doesn't have its own restaurant, but the casual High Tide Cafe (p. 119) is outside the front door.

710 Grand Ave., San Diego, CA 92109. © 800/231-7735 or 858/483-5858. Fax 858/274-0823. www.oceanparkinn.com. 73 units. $199–$249 double; $239–$269 suite. Rates include continental breakfast. AE, DC, DISC, MC, V. Free indoor parking. Bus: 34 or 34A/B. Take Grand/Garnet exit off I-5; follow Grand Ave. to ocean. **Amenities:** Outdoor pool; Jacuzzi; laundry service; dry cleaning. *In room:* A/C, TV, dataport, fridge, coffeemaker, hair dryer.

MODERATE

Dana Inn and Marina   The closest lodging to SeaWorld, with a complimentary shuttle to and from the park, this friendly, low-tech hotel features several low-rise buildings, next to Mission Bay. Some overlook bobbing sailboats in the recreational marina, others face onto the sunny kidney-shaped pool whose surrounding tiki torch–lit gardens offer shuffleboard and Ping-Pong. You'll pay a little extra for bay and marina views; if the view doesn't matter, save your money—every room is the same size, with plain but well-maintained furnishings. Beaches or SeaWorld are a 15-minute walk away. Meals and room service (including poolside food and cocktail ministrations) are available through the casual Red Hen Country Kitchen next door. An expansion is planned that will add rooms to the west of the current accommodations.

1710 W. Mission Bay Dr., San Diego, CA 92109. © 800/345-9995 or 619/222-6440. Fax 619/222-5916. www.danainn.com. 196 units. $133–$191 double (sleeps up to 4). AE, DC, DISC, MC, V. Free parking. Bus: 27 or 34. Follow I-8 west to Mission Bay Dr. exit; take W. Mission Bay Dr. **Amenities:** Outdoor heated pool and Jacuzzi; tennis court; bike rental; watersports equipment rental; limited room service (7am–8:30pm); coin-op laundry and laundry service; dry cleaning. *In room:* A/C, TV, dataport, fridge, coffeemaker, hair dryer, iron.

INEXPENSIVE

The Beach Cottages   This family-owned operation has been around since 1948 and offers a variety of guest quarters, most of them geared to the long-term visitor. It's the 17 cute little detached cottages just steps from the sand that give it real appeal, though some of them lack a view (of anything!); each has a patio

with tables and chairs. Adjoining apartments are perfectly adequate, especially for budget-minded families who want to log major hours on the beach—all cottages and apartments sleep four or more and have full kitchens. There are also standard motel rooms that are worn but cheap (most of these sleep two). The property is within walking distance of shops and restaurants—look both ways for speeding cyclists before crossing the boardwalk—and enjoy shared barbecue grills, shuffleboard courts, and table tennis. The cottages themselves aren't pristine, but have a rustic charm that makes them popular with young honeymooners and those nostalgic for the golden age of laid-back California beach culture. Reserve the beachfront cottages well in advance.

4255 Ocean Blvd. (1 block south of Grand Ave.), San Diego, CA 92109-3995. (C) **858/483-7440.** Fax 858/273-9365. www.beachcottages.com. 61 units, 17 cottages. $110–$200 double; $210–$240 cottages for 4 to 6. Monthly rates available mid-Sept to Apr. AE, DC, DISC, MC, V. Free parking. Bus: 27, 30, or 34. Take I-5 to Grand/Garnet exit, go west on Grand Ave. and left on Mission Blvd. **Amenities:** Self-service laundry. *In room:* TV, fridge, microwave, coffeemaker.

Beach Haven Inn A great spot in for beach lovers who can't quite afford to be on the beach, this motel lies 1 block from the sand. Rooms face an inner courtyard, where guests enjoy a secluded ambience for relaxing by the pool. On the street side it looks kind of marginal, but once on the property you'll find all quarters well maintained and sporting clean, up-to-date furnishings; nearly all units have eat-in kitchens. The friendly staff provides free coffee in the lobby and rents VCRs and movies.

4740 Mission Blvd. (at Missouri St.), San Diego, CA 92109. (C) **800/831-6323** or 858/272-3812. Fax 858/272-3532. www.beachhaveninn.com. 23 units. $120–$170 double; 2-night minimum on weekends. Extra person $5. Children under 12 stay free in parent's room. Rates include continental breakfast. AE, DC, DISC, MC, V. Free parking. Bus: 30 or 34. Take I-5 to Grand/Garnet exit, follow Grand Ave. to Mission Blvd. and turn right. **Amenities:** Outdoor pool; Jacuzzi. *In room:* A/C, TV, kitchenette in most units.

Elsbree House 🛪 Katie and Phil Elsbree have turned this modern Cape Cod–style building into an immaculate, exceedingly comfortable B&B, half a block from the water's edge in Ocean Beach. One condo unit with a private entrance rents only by the week; the Elsbrees occupy another. Each of the six guest rooms has a patio or balcony. Guests share the cozy living room (with a fireplace and TV), breakfast room, and kitchen. Although other buildings on this tightly packed street block the ocean view, sounds of the surf and fresh sea breezes waft in open windows, and a charming garden—complete with trickling fountain—runs the length of the house. This Ocean Beach neighborhood is eclectic, occupied by ocean-loving couples, dedicated surf bums, and the occasional contingent of punk skater kids who congregate near the pier. Its strengths are proximity to the beach, a limited but pleasing selection of eateries that attract mostly locals, and San Diego's best antiquing (along Newport Ave.).

5054 Narragansett Ave., San Diego, CA 92107. (C) **800/607-4133** or 619/226-4133. www.bbinob.com. 7 units. $110–$135 double; $1,600 per week 3-bedroom condo (lower rates if only 1 or 2 rooms used). Room rates include continental breakfast. MC, V. Bus: 23 or 35. From airport, take Harbor Dr. west to Nimitz Blvd. to Lowell St., which becomes Narragansett Ave. *In room:* Hair dryer, iron, no phone.

5 La Jolla

The name "La Jolla" is often translated from the Spanish as "the jewel," a fitting comparison for this section of the city with a beautiful coastline, as well as a compact downtown village that makes for delightful strolling. You'll have a hard time finding bargain accommodations in this upscale, conservative community.

But remember, most hotels—even those in the "Very Expensive" category—have occupancy-driven rates, meaning you can score surprising discounts during the off-season or when the beds go begging. Here at Frommer's, we can't say it often enough: It always pays to ask.

Most of my choices are in the "village," with two below the bluffs right on the beach. Chain hotels farther afield include the **Hyatt Regency,** 3777 La Jolla Village Dr. (© **800/233-1234** or 858/552-1234). It's a glitzy, business-oriented place with several acclaimed restaurants next door. The **Marriott Residence Inn,** 8901 Gilman Dr. (© **800/331-3131** or 858/587-1770), is a good choice for those who want a fully equipped kitchen and more space. Both are near the University of California, San Diego.

A note on driving directions: To reach the places listed here, use the La Jolla Parkway exit from **I-5 north** or the La Jolla Village Drive west exit from **I-5 south,** both of which merge with Torrey Pines Road, then follow individual directions.

VERY EXPENSIVE

Hotel Parisi *ᕮᕮᕮ* *Finds* Nestled within the "Village's" fashionable clothing boutiques, and across the street from the vaunted pink lady, La Valencia, the sleek boutique Hotel Parisi caters to the traveler seeking inner peace for both entertainment and relaxation. The hotel is on the second floor overlooking one of La Jolla's main intersections (street-facing rooms are well insulated from the modest din). Parisi's nurturing, wellness-inspired intimacy first becomes evident in the lobby, where elements of earth, wind, fire, water, and metal are blended according to classic feng shui principles. The Italy-meets-Zen composition is carried into the 20 rooms, where custom furnishings are modern yet comfy. Parisi calls the spacious rooms "suites" (some are more like junior suites) and each has an ergonomic desk, dimmable lighting, goose-down superluxe bedding, and creamy neutral decor to further that calming effect—10-foot ceilings and original art throughout allow your head to wander. Each darkly cool marble bathroom boasts a shower (some with dual shower heads), separate tub with contoured backrest, and smoothly sculpted fixtures. Less expensive rooms are smaller and have little or no view. Though primped and elegant, Parisi is not stuffy, yet the personal service stops at nothing—there's a menu of 24-hour in-room holistic health services (from individual yoga to Thai massage, psychotherapy, and obscure Asian treatments). If the W Hotel downtown is too swinging, but chic design is your style, the Parisi may be just right.

1111 Prospect St. (at Herschel Ave.), La Jolla, CA 92037. © **877/4-PARISI** or 858/454-1511. Fax 858/454-1531. www.hotelparisi.com. 20 units. $295–$475 double. Rates include continental breakfast. AE, DC, DISC, MC, V. Free covered parking. Bus: 30 or 34. Take Torrey Pines Rd. to Prospect Place and turn right; Prospect Place becomes Prospect St., turn left on Herschel. **Amenities:** 24-hr. in-room spa treatments; limited room service (11:30am–2:30pm and 5:30pm–10pm) from Tapenade Restaurant; laundry service; dry cleaning. *In room:* A/C, TV/VCR, dataport, minibar with complimentary beverages, coffeemaker, hair dryer, iron, safe.

La Valencia Hotel *ᕮᕮᕮ* Within its bougainvillea-draped walls and wrought-iron garden gates, this gracious bastion of gentility does a fine job of resurrecting golden-age elegance, when celebrities like Greta Garbo and Charlie Chaplin vacationed here alongside the world's moneyed elite. The blufftop hotel, which looks much like a Mediterranean villa, has been the centerpiece of La Jolla since opening in 1926, and a $10 million renovation in 2000 refined some of the details and added 15 villas and an enlarged pool, without breaking with its historical glamour. Brides still pose in front of the lobby's picture window (against a backdrop of the Cove and Pacific Ocean), well-coiffed ladies

La Jolla Accommodations

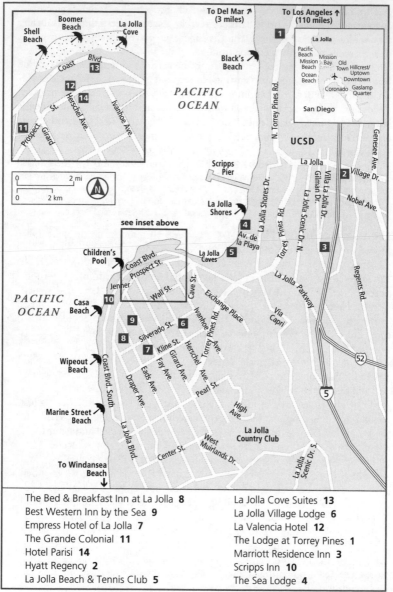

The Bed & Breakfast Inn at La Jolla **8**
Best Western Inn by the Sea **9**
Empress Hotel of La Jolla **7**
The Grande Colonial **11**
Hotel Parisi **14**
Hyatt Regency **2**
La Jolla Beach & Tennis Club **5**

La Jolla Cove Suites **13**
La Jolla Village Lodge **6**
La Valencia Hotel **12**
The Lodge at Torrey Pines **1**
Marriott Residence Inn **3**
Scripps Inn **10**
The Sea Lodge **4**

lunch in the dappled shade of the garden patio, and neighborhood cronies quaff libations in the clubby Whaling Bar (La Jolla's version of the power lunch). The latter was once a western Algonquin for literary inebriates as well as a watering hole for Hollywood royalty, who performed at the Playhouse at the urging of La Jollan resident Gregory Peck. One chooses La Valencia for its history and unbeatably scenic location, but you won't be disappointed by the old-world standards of service and style.

All rooms are comfortably and traditionally furnished, each boasting lavish appointments, and all-marble bathrooms with signature toiletries. Because rates vary wildly according to view (from sweeping to *nada*), my advice is to get a cheaper room and enjoy the scene from one of the many lounges, serene garden terraces, or the amazing pool, which fronts the Pacific and nearby Scripps Park. Room decor, layouts, and size (starting at a relatively snug 246 sq. ft.) are all over the map, too—a few extra minutes spent with the reservationist will ensure a custom match for you. If you've got the bucks, spring for one of the newer villas, which feature fireplaces and butler service. The hotel's 12-table Sky Room is one of the city's most celebrated dining rooms.

1132 Prospect St. (at Herschel Ave.), La Jolla, CA 92037. ℂ 800/451-0772 or 858/454-0771. Fax 858/456-3921. www.lavalencia.com. 117 units. $300–$550 double; from $775 suites and villas. 2-night minimum summer weekends AF, DC, DISC, MC, V. Valet parking $15. Bus: 30 or 34. Take Torrey Pines Rd. to Prospect Place and turn right. Prospect Place becomes Prospect St. **Amenities:** 3 restaurants; bar; outdoor pool; exercise room with spa treatments; Jacuzzi; sauna; concierge; secretarial services; 24-hr. room service; babysitting; laundry service; dry cleaning. *In room:* A/C, TV/VCR, dataport, minibar, coffeemaker, hair dryer, iron, safe.

The Lodge at Torrey Pines ★★★
Located 10 minutes north of La Jolla proper, this triumphant *trompe l'oeil* creation at the edge of the Torrey Pines Golf Course is the fantasy of local hotelier Bill Evans (of the Catamaran), who took his appreciation for Craftsman-style homes and amplified it into a 175-room upscale hotel. Patterned largely after the 1908 Greene and Greene-designed Gamble House of Pasadena, the Lodge brims with perfectly assembled nuances of the era: clinker-brick masonry, art glass windows and doors, Stickley furniture, and exquisite pottery. Interior designers often can be found with plans unrolled in the lobby as they seek to duplicate this gentle period of design. Most guest rooms fall into two main categories. The least expensive rooms are an unstinting 520 square feet and lavished with Tiffany-style lamps, period wallpaper, and framed Hiroshige prints, and lots of wood accents; views face a courtyard carefully landscaped to mimic the rare coastal environment that exists just beyond the hotel grounds. More expensive rooms overlook the golf course and the sea in the distance; most of these have balconies, fireplaces, and giant bathrooms with separate tub and shower. Sumptuous suites are also available.

The 9,500-square-foot spa specializes in treatments utilizing coastal sage and other local plants. An excellent restaurant named after painter A. R. Valentien features superb seasonal vegetables served with most entrees; Valentien's wildflower watercolors line the walls and his personal effects and medals are found in glass bookcases. As a San Diegan, I find the embrace of local artists and the native natural environment to be absolutely inspired. My only (small) caveat is that in polishing and augmenting Arts and Crafts style for the masses, something is lost: the soul and warmth of a true family home. But the Lodge is unsurpassed as San Diego's ultimate luxury destination, with every whim catered to by a mindful staff.

11480 N. Torrey Pines Rd., La Jolla, CA 92037. ℂ 800/656-0087 or 858/453-4420. Fax 858/453-7464. www.lodgetorreypines.com. 175 units. $450–$625 double; from $900 suite. Children under 18 stay free in parent's room. AE, DC, DISC, MC, V. $14 self-parking; $17 valet parking. Bus: 301. From I-8 take La Jolla Village Dr. West, bear right (north) onto N. Torrey Pines Rd. **Amenities:** 2 restaurants; outdoor pool; Jacuzzi; fitness center; spa; preferential tee times at the golf course; concierge; 24-hr. room service; laundry service; dry cleaning. *In room:* A/C, TV, dataport in many units, minibar, coffeemaker, hair dryer, safe.

EXPENSIVE
The Grande Colonial ★★ (Finds)
Possessed of an old-world European flair that's more London or Georgetown than seaside La Jolla, the Grande Colonial

earned accolades for the complete restoration in 2001 of its polished mahogany paneling, brass fittings, and genteel library and lounge. During the original heyday of the La Jolla Playhouse, it was the temporary home for everyone from Groucho Marx to Jane Wyatt. Today, a large spray of fresh flowers is the focal point in the lounge, where guests gather in front of the fireplace for drinks—often before enjoying dinner at the hotel's superb Nine-Ten restaurant (p. 122). Guest rooms are quiet and elegantly appointed, with beautiful draperies and traditional furnishings. The hotel is 1 block from the ocean, but many of the rooms have sea views. The guest rooms have newly installed air-conditioning and thoughtful amenities; terry robes are available on request. Relics from the early days include oversize closets, meticulously tiled bathrooms, and heavy fireproof doors suspended in the corridors. Numerous historic photos on the walls illustrate the hotel's fascinating story; the reception desk has a printed sheet with more details of its beginnings as a full-service apartment hotel in 1913. Among La Jolla's mini-horde of deluxe properties, the Grande Colonial is sometimes overlooked. In fact, the centrally located hotel is a sleeper that provides comparatively good value.

910 Prospect St. (between Fay and Girard), La Jolla, CA 92037. © **800/826-1278** or 858/454-2181. Fax 858/54-5679. www.thegrandecolonial.com. 75 units. $249–$379 double; from $319 suite. AE, DC, DISC, MC, V. Valet parking $14. Bus: 30 or 34. Take Torrey Pines Rd. to Prospect Place and turn right. Prospect Place becomes Prospect St. **Amenities:** Restaurant; outdoor pool; access to nearby health club; limited room service (6:30am–10:30pm); laundry service; dry cleaning. *In room:* A/C, TV w/pay movies, dataport, hair dryer, iron, safe.

La Jolla Beach & Tennis Club *Overrated*

You're supposed to pack your best tennis whites for a stint at La Jolla's private "B&T" (as it's locally known), where CEOs and MDs come to relax and recreate. The location is unbeatable—right on the beach—and the physical property is attractive, in a Spanish hacienda sort of way. However, standard guest rooms are unbelievably plain and outmoded (think late-1970s Holiday-Inn styling); most have full kitchens that are appropriate for families or longer stays. Beachfront rooms are tiny—the showers are tight enough to give anyone with broad shoulders claustrophobia—but they're brighter, and the wide ocean panorama at the foot of your bed is undeniably splendid (if totally un-private). A variety of suites are available. The beach is popular and staff stays busy shooing away non-guests, in between primping the comfy sand chairs and umbrellas, and keeping guests stocked with fluffy towels, beverages, and snacks. Kayaks and watersports equipment can be rented; there's even a sand croquet court. There's no room service, but the hotel's distinctive Marine Room restaurant (p. 122) is one of San Diego's very best, and waves literally smash against its broad windows, inches away from diners.

This historic property was founded in the 1920s, when original plans included constructing a yacht harbor (egad!); today it's known primarily for tennis, and for the $40,000 down payment it takes to become a member. You get better room value for your money at the club's sister hotel next door, the Sea Lodge (see below), but you don't stay here for the quality—B&T guests are chasing exclusive, old-money atmosphere and fawning service.

2000 Spindrift Dr., La Jolla, CA 92037. © **800/624-CLUB** or 858/454-7126. Fax 858/456-3805. www.ljbtc.com. 90 units. $209–$439 double; from $329 suite. Extra person $20. Children under 12 stay free in parent's room. AE, DC, MC, V. Free parking. Bus: 34. Take La Jolla Shores Dr., turn left on Paseo Dorado, and follow to Spindrift Dr. **Amenities:** 2 restaurants; seasonal beach snack bar; 75-ft. pool; 12 championship tennis courts; 9-hole pitch-and-putt course; fitness room; watersports equipment rental; massage; babysitting; coin-op laundry and laundry service; dry cleaning. *In room:* TV w/pay movies, dataport, coffeemaker, hair dryer, iron.

Scripps Inn *(★★)*   This meticulously maintained inn is tucked away behind the Museum of Contemporary Art, and you'll be rewarded with seclusion even though the attractions of La Jolla are just a short walk away. Only a small, grassy park comes between the inn and the beach, cliffs, and tide pools; the view from the second-story deck can hypnotize guests, who gaze out to sea indefinitely. Rates vary depending on ocean view (all have one, but some are better than others); rooms have a pleasant pale cream/sand palette, and are furnished in "early American comfortable," with new bathroom fixtures and appointments. All rooms have sofa beds; two have wood-burning fireplaces, and four have kitchenettes. The inn supplies beach towels, firewood, and French pastries each morning. Repeat guests keep their favorite rooms for up to a month each year, so book ahead for the best choice.

555 Coast Blvd. S. (at Cuvier), La Jolla, CA 92037. ℂ **858/454-3391.** Fax 858/456-0389. 14 units. $225–$255 double; from $295 suite. Extra person $10. Children under 5 stay free in parent's room. Rates include continental breakfast. AE, DC, DISC, MC, V. Free parking. Bus: 30 or 34. Take Torrey Pines Rd., turn right on Prospect Place; past the museum, turn right onto Cuvier. *In room:* TV, fridge, coffeemaker, hair dryer, iron, safe.

The Sea Lodge *(★ (Kids)*   This three-story 1960s hotel in a mainly residential enclave is under the same management as the La Jolla Beach & Tennis Club next door. It has an identical on-the-sand location, minus the country club ambience—there are no reciprocal privileges. About half the rooms have some view of the ocean, and the rest look out on the pool or a tiled courtyard. The rooms are pretty basic, with perfunctory, outdated furnishings, priced by view and size. Bathrooms feature separate dressing areas with large closets; balconies or patios are standard, and some rooms have fully equipped kitchenettes. From the Sea Lodge's beach you can gaze toward the top of the cliffs, where La Jolla's village hums with activity (and relentless traffic). Like the "B&T," the Sea Lodge is popular with families but also attracts business travelers looking to balance meetings with time on the beach or the tennis court.

8110 Camino del Oro (at Avenida de la Playa), La Jolla, CA 92037. ℂ **800/237-5211** or 858/459-8271. Fax 858/456-9346. 128 units. $249–$559 double; $739 suite. Extra person $20. Children under 12 stay free in parent's room. AE, DC, DISC, MC, V. Free covered parking. Bus: 34. Take La Jolla Shores Dr., turn left onto Avenida de la Playa, turn right on Camino del Oro. **Amenities:** Restaurant; 2 pools (including a wading pool for kids); 2 tennis courts; fitness room; Jacuzzi; babysitting; laundry service; dry cleaning. *In room:* A/C, TV, dataport, fridge, coffeemaker, hair dryer, iron.

MODERATE
The Bed & Breakfast Inn at La Jolla *(★★)*   A 1913 Cubist house designed by San Diego's first important architect, Irving Gill—and occupied in the 1920s by John Philip Sousa and his family—is the setting for this cultured and elegant B&B. Reconfigured as lodging, the house has lost none of its charm, and its appropriately unfrilly period furnishings add to the sense of history. The inn also features lovely enclosed gardens and a cozy library and sitting room. Sherry and fresh-cut flowers await in every room, some of which feature a fireplace or ocean view. Each room has a private bathroom, most of which are on the compact size. The furnishings are tasteful and cottage-style, with plenty of historic photos of La Jolla. Gourmet breakfast is served wherever you desire—dining room, patio, sun deck, or in your room. Picnic baskets (extra charge) are available with a day's notice. The gardens surrounding the inn were originally planned by Kate Sessions, who went on to create much of the landscaping for Balboa Park.

7753 Draper Ave. (near Prospect), La Jolla, CA 92037. ℂ **800/582-2466** or 858/456-2066. Fax 858/456-1510. www.InnLaJolla.com. 15 units. $179–$359 double; $399 suite. 2-night minimum on weekends. Rates

include full breakfast and afternoon wine and cheese. AE, DISC, MC, V. Bus: 30 or 34. Take Torrey Pines Rd. to Prospect Place and turn right. Prospect Place becomes Prospect St.; proceed to Draper Ave. and turn left. *In room:* A/C, hair dryer, iron.

Best Western Inn by the Sea

Occupying an enviable location at the heart of La Jolla's charming village, this independently managed property puts guests just a short walk from the cliffs and beach. The low-rise tops out at five stories, with the upper floors enjoying ocean views (and the highest room rates). The Best Western (and the more formal Empress, a block away), offer a terrific alternative to pricier digs nearby. Rooms here are Best Western standard issue— freshly maintained, but nothing special. All rooms do have balconies, though, and refrigerators are available at no extra charge; the hotel offers plenty of welcome amenities.

7830 Fay Ave. (between Prospect and Silverado sts.), La Jolla, CA 92037. © **800/526-4545** or 858/459-461. Fax 858/456-2578. www.bestwestern.com/innbythesea. 132 units. $139–$209 double; from $399 suite. Rates include continental breakfast. AE, DC, DISC, MC, V. Parking $9. Bus 30 or 34. Take Torrey Pines Rd. to Prospect Place and turn right. Prospect Place becomes Prospect St.; proceed to Fay Ave. and turn left. **Amenities:** Outdoor heated pool; car-rental desk; limited room service from adjacent IHOP (7am–10pm); coin-op laundry and laundry service; dry cleaning. *In room:* A/C, TV w/pay movies, dataport, coffeemaker, hair dryer, iron.

Empress Hotel of La Jolla

The Empress Hotel offers spacious quarters with traditional furnishings a block or two from La Jolla's main drag and the ocean. It's quieter here than at the premium clifftop properties, and you'll sacrifice little other than direct ocean views (many rooms on the top floors afford a partial view.) If you're planning to explore La Jolla on foot, the Empress is a good base, and it exudes a classiness many comparably priced chains lack, with warm service to boot. Rooms are tastefully decorated (and regularly renovated), and well equipped. Bathrooms are of average size but well appointed, and four "Empress" rooms have sitting areas with full-size sleeper sofas. Breakfast is set up next to a serene sun deck.

7766 Fay Ave. (at Silverado), La Jolla, CA 92037. © **888/369-9900** or 858/454-3001. Fax 858/454-6387. www.empress-hotel.com. 73 units. $179–$189 double; $299 suite. Rates include continental breakfast. AE, DC, DISC, MC, V. Valet parking $8. Bus: 30 or 34. Take Torrey Pines Rd. to Girard Ave., turn right, then left on Silverado St. **Amenities:** Fitness room and spa; limited room service (lunch and dinner hours). *In room:* A/C, TV, dataport, fridge, coffeemaker, hair dryer, iron.

La Jolla Cove Suites *Value*

Tucked in beside prime ocean view condos across from Ellen Browning Scripps Park, this family-run 1950s-era catbird seat actually sits closer to the ocean than its pricey uphill neighbor La Valencia. The to-die-for ocean view is completely unobstructed, and La Jolla Cove—one of California's prettiest swimming spots—is steps away from the hotel. The six-story property is peaceful at night, but Village dining and shopping are only a short walk away. You'll pay more depending on the quality of your view; about 80% of guest quarters gaze upon the ocean. On the plus side, most rooms are wonderfully spacious, each featuring a fully equipped kitchen, plus private balcony or patio. On the minus side, their functional but almost institutional furnishings could use a touch of Martha Stewart. An oceanview rooftop deck offers lounge chairs and cafe tables; breakfast is served up here each morning, indoors or outdoors depending on the weather.

1155 Coast Blvd. (across from the cove), La Jolla, CA 92037. © **888/LA-JOLLA** or 858/459-2621. Fax 858/ 551-3405. www.lajollacove.com. 90 units. $164–$269 double; from $324 suite. Rates include continental breakfast. AE, DC, DISC, MC, V. Parking $8. Bus: 30 or 34. Take Torrey Pines Rd. to Prospect Place and turn right. When the road forks, veer right (downhill) onto Coast Blvd. **Amenities:** Outdoor (nonview) pool; Jacuzzi; car-rental desk; coin-op laundry. *In room:* TV, kitchen, safe.

INEXPENSIVE

Wealthy, image-conscious La Jolla is *really* not the best place for deep bargains, but if you're determined to stay here as cheaply as possible, you won't do better than the **La Jolla Village Lodge,** 1141 Silverado St., at Herschel Avenue (© **858/551-2001;** www.lajollavillagelodge.com). This 30-room motel is standard Americana, arranged around a small parking lot with cinder-block construction and small, basic rooms. Rates reach $110 in July and August, including breakfast, but are under $100 the rest of the year.

6 Coronado

The "island" (really a peninsula) of Coronado is a great escape. It offers quiet, architecturally rich streets, a small-town, navy-oriented atmosphere, and laid-back vacationing on one of the state's most beautiful and welcoming beaches. Coronado's resorts are especially popular with Southern California and Arizona families for weekend escapes. Although downtown San Diego is just a 10-minute drive or 20-minute ferry ride away, you may feel pleasantly isolated in Coronado, so it isn't your best choice if you're planning to spend lots of time in more central parts of the city.

A note on driving directions: To reach the places listed here, take I-5 to the Coronado Bridge, then follow individual directions.

VERY EXPENSIVE

Hotel del Coronado ★★★   Opened in 1888 and designated a National Historic Landmark in 1977, the "Hotel Del," as it's affectionately known, is the last of California's grand old seaside hotels. This monument to Victorian grandeur boasts tall cupolas, red turrets, and gingerbread trim, all spread out over 31 acres. Rooms—almost no two alike—run the gamut from compact to extravagant, and all are packed with antique charm; most have custom-made furnishings. The least expensive rooms are snug and have views of a roof or parking lot. The best are junior suites with large windows and balconies fronting the one of the state's finest white-sand beaches, but note that even here, bathrooms are modest in size. Or there are nine cottages lining the sand that are more private (Marilyn Monroe stayed in the first one). Note that almost half the hotel's rooms are in the seven-story contemporary tower and offer more living space, but none of the historical ambience; personally, I can't imagine staying here in anything but the Victorian structure, but you pay a premium for the privilege (especially for an ocean view), and 2-night minimums often apply.

In 2001, the hotel completed a painstaking, $55 million, 3-year restoration. Purists will rejoice to hear that historical accuracy was paramount, resulting in this priceless grande dame being returned to its turn-of-the-20th-century splendor. Much of the renovation was behind-the-scenes: $21 million alone was spent shoring up the structural integrity of this delicate building. Even if you don't stay here, don't miss a stroll through the grand, wood-paneled lobby or along the pristine wide beach. Accolades have been awarded to the Prince of Wales, remodeled from a dark, clubby room to an airy, elegant salon with oceanfront dining; cocktails and afternoon tea are served in the wood-paneled lobby and adjoining Palm Court, and Sunday Brunch in the Crown Room is a San Diego tradition.

1500 Orange Ave., Coronado, CA 92118. © **800/468-3533** or 619/435-6611. Fax 619/522-8238. www.hotel del.com. 688 rooms. $260–$800 double; from $625 cottages and suites. Children under 18 stay free in parent's room. Additional person $25. Minimum stay requirements apply most weekends. AE, DC, DISC, MC, V. Valet parking $20; self-parking $15. Bus: 901 or 902. From Coronado Bridge, turn left onto Orange Ave.

Coronado Accommodations

Coronado Inn **6**
El Cordova Hotel **5**
Glorietta Bay Inn **3**
Hotel del Coronado **2**
Loews Coronado
  Bay Resort **1**
Marriott Coronado
  Island Resort **7**
The Village Inn **4**

Amenities: 5 restaurants; 4 bars; 2 outdoor pools; 3 tennis courts; health club and spa; 2 Jacuzzis; bike rental; children's activities; concierge; shopping arcade; 24-hr. room service; babysitting; laundry service; dry cleaning. *In room:* A/C, TV w/pay movies, dataport, minibar, hair dryer, iron, safe.

Loews Coronado Bay Resort ⭐⭐ *Kids* This luxury resort on the Silver Strand opened in 1991, situated on a secluded 15-acre peninsula, well removed from San Diego and even downtown Coronado, 5 miles away. It's perfect for those who prefer a self-contained resort in a get-away-from-it-all location, and is surprisingly successful in appealing to business travelers, convention groups, vacationing families, and couples. Rooms offer terraces that look either onto the hotel's private 80-slip marina, or the San Diego–Coronado Bridge and San Diego Bay. A private pedestrian underpass leads to nearby Silver Strand Beach. Rooms boast generous, well-appointed marble bathrooms with deep tubs; VCRs come standard in suites, and are available free upon request to any room (video rentals are also available). A new spa is set to open in early 2004. A highlight here is the Gondola Company (☎ **619/429-6317**), which offers romantic and fun gondola cruises through the canals of tony Coronado Cays. The seasonal Commodore Kids Club, for children ages 4 to 12, offers supervised half-day, full-day, and evening programs with meals, and pets are encouraged, at no additional charge.

4000 Coronado Bay Rd., Coronado, CA 92118. ☎ **800/81-LOEWS** or 619/424-4000. Fax 619/424-4400. www.loewshotels.com. 438 units. $295–$345 double; from $525 suite. Children under 18 stay free in parent's room. AE, DC, DISC, MC, V. Valet parking $18; covered self-parking $13. Bus: 904. From Coronado Bridge, go

Fun Fact **A Century of Intrigue: Scenes from the Hotel del Coronado**

San Diego's romantic Hotel del Coronado is an unmistakable land-mark, filled with enchanting and colorful memories.

Several familiar names helped shape the hotel. When it opened in 1888, it was among the first buildings with Thomas Edison's new inven-tion, electric light; the Hotel Del had its own electrical power plant, which supplied the entire city of Coronado until 1922. Author L. Frank Baum, a frequent guest, designed the Crown Room's frumpy crown-shaped chandeliers. Baum wrote several of the books in his beloved *Wizard of Oz* series in Coronado, and some believe he modeled the Emerald City's geometric spires after the Del's conical turrets.

The hotel has played host to royalty and celebrities as well. The first visiting monarch was Kalakaua, Hawaii's last king, who spent Christ-mas here in 1890. But the best-known royal guest was Edward, Prince of Wales (later Edward VIII, then duke of Windsor). He came to the hotel in April 1920, the first British royal to visit California. Of the many lavish social affairs held during his stay, at least two were attended by Wallis Simpson (then navy wife Wallis Warfield), 15 years before her official introduction to the prince in London. Speculation continues about whether their love affair, which culminated in his abdication of the throne, might have begun right here.

America's own "royalty" often visited the Hotel Del. In 1927, San Diego's beloved son Charles Lindbergh was honored here following his historic 33½-hour solo flight across the Atlantic. Hollywood stars including Mary Pickford, Greta Garbo, Charlie Chaplin, and Esther Williams have flocked to the Del. Henry James wrote in 1905 of "the charming sweetness and comfort of this spot," and the "languid lisp of the Pacific, which my windows overhang." The hotel has also hosted 10 U.S. presidents. Perhaps most famously, director Billy Wilder filmed *Some Like It Hot* at the hotel; longtime staffers remember stars Mari-lyn Monroe, Tony Curtis, and Jack Lemmon romping on the beach. The *Stuntman,* starring Peter O'Toole, was also filmed here, in 1980. And some guests have never left: The ghost of Kate Morgan, whose body was found in 1892 where the tennis courts are today, supposedly still roams the halls—room 3327 has a reputation for being haunted.

Visitors and guests intrigued by the Hotel Del's past can stroll through the lower-level History Gallery, a minimuseum of hotel memorabilia.

left onto Orange Ave, continue 6 miles down Silver Strand Hwy. Turn left at Coronado Bay Rd. Pets welcome. **Amenities:** 3 restaurants (including acclaimed Azzura Point); bar; 3 outdoor pools; tennis courts; fitness cen-ter; spa; Jacuzzi; watersports equipment rental; bike and skate rental; children's programs; concierge; car-rental desk; business center; salon; 24-hr. room service; babysitting; laundry service; dry cleaning. *In room:* A/C, TV, dataport, minibar, coffeemaker, hair dryer, iron.

EXPENSIVE

Marriott Coronado Island Resort ★★   Once expected to give competitor Loews a run for its money in the leisure market, this high-end Marriott seems

content with the substantial group business it gets from the convention center across the bay. Elegance and luxury here are understated. Although the physical property is generic, with impersonal architecture, the staff goes out of its way to provide upbeat attention: Guests just seem to get whatever they need, be it a lift downtown (by water taxi from the private dock), a tee time at the neighboring golf course, or a prime appointment at the spa.

Despite its mostly business clientele, this hotel offers many enticements for the leisure traveler: a prime waterfront setting offering a sweeping view of the San Diego skyline; a location within a mile of Coronado shopping and dining, and walking distance from the ferry landing; casual, airy architecture; lushly planted grounds filled with preening exotic birds; and a wealth of sporting and recreational activities. Guest rooms are generously sized and attractively furnished—actually decorated—in colorful French country style, and all feature balconies or patios. The superbly designed bathrooms hold an array of fine toiletries. In terms of room size and amenities, your dollar goes a lot farther here than at the Hotel Del.

2000 Second St. (at Glorietta Blvd.), Coronado, CA 92118. ℂ **800/228-9290** or 619/435-3000. Fax 619/435-3032. http://marriotthotels.com/sanci. 300 units. $209–$399 double; from $449 suites and villas. Children under 12 stay free in parent's room. AE, DC, MC, V. Valet parking $20; self-parking $15. Bus: 901 or 902. Ferry: From Broadway Pier. From Coronado Bridge, turn right onto Glorietta Blvd., take first right to hotel. **Amenities:** 2 restaurants; bar; 3 outdoor pools; 6 night-lit tennis courts; fitness center; spa; 2 Jacuzzis; watersports equipment rental; bike rental; concierge; courtesy shuttle to Horton Plaza; water taxi to convention center $5; business center; salon; 24-hr. room service; babysitting; laundry service; dry cleaning. *In room:* A/C, TV w/pay movies, dataport, minibar, coffeemaker, hair dryer, iron, safe.

MODERATE

Coronado Inn 𝆮   Well located and terrifically priced, this renovated 1940s courtyard motel has such a friendly ambience, it's like staying with old friends. Iced tea, lemonade, and fresh fruit are even provided poolside on summer days. It's still a motel, though—albeit with brand-new paint and fresh tropical floral decor—so rooms are pretty basic. The six rooms with bathtubs also have small kitchens; microwaves are available for the rest, along with hair dryers and irons (just ask upfront). Rooms close to the street are noisiest, so ask for one toward the back. The Coronado shuttle stops a block away; it serves the shopping areas and Hotel Del.

266 Orange Ave. (corner of 3rd St.), Coronado, CA 92118. ℂ **800/598-6624** or 619/435-4121. www.coronadoinn.com. 30 units (most with shower only). $125–$195 double (sleeps up to 4). Rates include continental breakfast. AE, DISC, MC, V. Free parking. Bus: 901 or 902. From Coronado Bridge, stay on 3rd St. Pets accepted with $10 nightly fee. **Amenities:** Outdoor pool; coin-op laundry. *In room:* A/C, TV, fridge.

Glorietta Bay Inn 𝆮𝆮   Right across the street and somewhat in the (figurative) shadow of the Hotel Del, this pretty white hotel consists of the charmingly historic John D. Spreckels mansion (1908) and several younger, motel-style buildings. Only 11 rooms are in the mansion, which boasts original fixtures, a grand staircase, and old-fashioned wicker furniture; the guest rooms are also decked out in antiques, and have a romantic and nostalgic ambience.

Rooms and suites in the 1950s annexes are much less expensive but were upgraded from motel-plain to better match the main house's classy ambience (though lacking the mansion's superluxe featherbeds); some have kitchenettes and marina views. The least expensive units are small and have parking-lot views. Wherever your room is, you'll enjoy the inn's trademark personalized service, including extra-helpful staffers who remember your name and happily offer dining and sightseeing recommendations or arrange tee times; special

attention to return guests and families with toddlers; and a friendly continental breakfast. In addition to offering bikes and boat rentals on Glorietta Bay across the street, the hotel is within easy walking distance of the beach, golf, tennis, watersports, shopping, and dining. Rooms in the mansion get booked early, but are worth the extra effort and expense.

1630 Glorietta Blvd. (near Orange Ave.), Coronado, CA 92118. © **800/283-9383** or 619/435-3101. Fax 619/435-6182. www.gloriettabayinn.com. 100 units. Double $150–$215 annex, $275–$415 mansion. Suites from $275 annex, penthouse suite $650 mansion. Extra person $10. Children under 18 stay free in parent's room. Rates include continental breakfast and afternoon refreshment. AE, DC, DISC, MC, V. Self-parking $7. Bus: 901 or 902. From Coronado Bridge, turn left on Orange Ave. After 2 miles, turn left onto Glorietta Blvd.; the inn is across the street from the Hotel del Coronado. **Amenities:** Outdoor pool; Jacuzzi; in-room massage; baby-sitting; coin-op laundry and laundry service; dry cleaning. *In room:* A/C, TV w/pay movies, dataport, fridge, coffeemaker, hair dryer.

INEXPENSIVE

El Cordova Hotel *ℛ*   This Spanish hacienda across the street from the Hotel del Coronado began life as a private mansion in 1902. By the 1930s it had become a hotel; the original building was augmented by a series of attachments housing retail shops along the ground-floor arcade. Shaped like a baseball diamond and surrounding a courtyard with meandering tiled pathways, flowering shrubs, a swimming pool, and patio seating for Miguel's Cocina Mexican restaurant, El Cordova hums pleasantly with activity.

Each room is a little different from the next—some sport a Mexican colonial ambience, while others evoke a comfy beach cottage. All feature ceiling fans and brightly tiled bathrooms, but lack the frills that would command exorbitant rates. El Cordova has a particularly inviting aura, and its prime location makes it a popular option; reserving several months in advance is advised for summer month. Facilities include a barbecue area with picnic table.

1351 Orange Ave. (at Adella Ave.), Coronado, CA 92118. © **800/229-2032** or 619/435-4131. Fax 619/435-0632. www.elcordovahotel.com. 40 units. $119–$189 double; from $229 suite. Children under 12 stay free in parent's room. Weekly and monthly rates available in winter. AE, DC, DISC, MC, V. Parking in neighboring structure $6/day. Bus: 901 or 902. From Coronado Bridge, turn left onto Orange Ave. **Amenities:** Restaurant; outdoor pool; shopping arcade; coin-op laundry. *In room:* A/C, TV.

The Village Inn *Value*   Its location a block or two from Coronado's main sights—the Hotel Del, the beach, shopping, and cafes—is this inn's most appealing feature. Historic charm runs a close second; a plaque outside identifies the three-story brick-and-stucco hotel as the once-chic Blue Lantern Inn, built in 1928. The charming vintage lobby sets the mood in this European-style hostelry; each simple but well-maintained room holds antique dressers and armoires, plus lovely Battenberg lace bedcovers and shams. Front rooms enjoy the best view, and coffee and tea are available all day in the kitchen where breakfast is served. The appealing inn's only Achilles' heel is tiny, tiny bathrooms, so cramped that you almost have to stand on the toilet to use the small-scale sinks. Surprisingly, some bathrooms have been updated with Jacuzzi tubs.

1017 Park Place (at Orange Ave.), Coronado, CA 92118. © **619/435-9318.** www.coronadovillageinn.com. 15 units. $85–$95 double summer. Winter and weekly rates available. Rates include continental breakfast. AE, MC, V. Parking available on street. Bus: 901 or 902. From Coronado Bridge, turn left onto Orange Ave., then right on Park Place.

7 Near the Airport

San Diego's airport has the unusual distinction of being virtually in downtown. While immediate neighbors grouse about the noise and decreased property values, it's good news for travelers: The accommodations reviewed in the downtown, Hillcrest, and Old Town/Mission Valley sections are only 5 to 10 minutes from the airport.

For those who wish to stay even closer, there are two good airport hotels—these bay-side properties won't remind you of the dives found next to most airports. The 1,045-room **Sheraton San Diego Hotel & Marina,** 1380 Harbor Island Dr. (© **800/325-3535** or 619/291-2900), offers rooms from $369. At the 208-room **Hilton San Diego Airport/Harbor Island,** 1960 Harbor Island Dr. (© **800/774-1500** or 619/291-6700), rooms start at $249. Both hotels offer a marina view, a pool, and proximity to downtown San Diego—as always, hefty discounts are usually available. I also recommend the nearby **Bay Club Hotel,** 2131 Shelter Island Dr. (© **800/672-0800** or 619/224-8888; www.bay clubhotel.com), a pretty marina-front low-rise offering a vacation ambience even for business travelers; rates start at $145, including breakfast.

6

Where to Dine

San Diego's dining scene, once a culinary backwater, has come into its own during the past decade. The spark for this new spirit of experimentation and style has been an explosion in the transplant population and cultural diversification. But other factors are at play. A bustling economy helps, motivating folks to step out and exercise their palates. These new foodies have been taught to respect the seasonality of vegetables, allowing chefs to revel in the bounteous agriculture of San Diego County by focusing on vegetables when flavors are at their peak at specialized North County growers like Chino Farms and Be Wise Ranch.

Top young cooks are increasingly lured by San Diego's agreeable lifestyle and the chance to make a fast impression in the region's dining scene. How many chefs have been seduced by the idea that you can surf in the ocean each morning, then hand-select fresh produce at the farm where it was grown for preparation that afternoon? And although we import chefs from around the world, we've even started exporting them—Marine Room wizard Bernard Guillas represents America at illustrious events like the Masters of Food and Wine.

But don't just take my word for it. In 2003, *Gourmet* magazine announced: "Perhaps for the first time ever, San Diego has a buzzing restaurant scene as engaging as the area's other tourist attractions." Finally, we can be known for something on the table beyond tacos and frijoles.

As you can imagine, San Diego offers terrific seafood: Whether at unembellished market-style restaurants that let the fresh catch take center stage or at upscale restaurants that feature extravagant presentations, the ocean's bounty is everywhere. Those traditional mainstays, American and Continental cuisine, still carry their share of the weight in San Diego. But, with increasing regularity, they're mating with lighter, more contemporary, often ethnic styles. The movement is akin to the eclectic fusion cuisine that burst onto the scene in the early 1990s. That's not to say traditionalists will be disappointed: San Diego still has plenty of clubby steak-and-potatoes stalwarts, and we're loaded with the chain restaurants you'll probably recognize from home.

Number one on most every visitor's list of priorities is Mexican food—a logical choice given the city's history and location. You'll find lots of highly Americanized interpretations of Mexican fare along with a few hidden gems, like El Agave and Berta's, that serve true south-of-the-border cuisine. The most authentic Mexican import may be the humble fish taco, perhaps the city's favorite fast food.

If you love Italian food, you're also in luck. Not only does San Diego boast a strong contingent of old-fashioned Sicilian-style choices, but you almost can't turn a corner without running into a trattoria. The Gaslamp Quarter corners the market with upscale northern Italian bistros on virtually every block. Hillcrest, La Jolla, and other neighborhoods also boast their fair share. They cater mostly to locals (usually a good thing) and their menus

almost always include gourmet pizzas baked in wood-fired ovens, a trend that shows no signs of slowing down.

San Diego's multicultural fabric ensures that ethnic foods are a good option when you want something more exotic than Mexican or Italian fare. While Chinese restaurants have long had a place at the table, Asian cuisine today also means Japanese, Thai, Vietnamese, and Cambodian restaurants. A drive through the heart of Kearny Mesa reveals a panoply of Asian eateries at all prices, along with vast grocery stores brimming with quirky delicacies. But also note that many intrepid "mainstream" chefs fuse Asian ingredients and preparations with more familiar Mediterranean or French menus.

In this chapter, restaurants in San Diego proper are indexed by location and price category. However, note that some of San Diego's finest dining venues lie 30 to 40 minutes to the north, in the communities of Rancho Bernardo, Del Mar, and Carlsbad. These are found in chapter 11, as are dining options for the Disneyland area and south of the border. For a list of my favorites in all kinds of categories, see "Best Dining Bets" in chapter 1.

For diners on a budget, the more expensive San Diego restaurants are usually accommodating if you want to order a few appetizers instead of a main course, and many offer more reasonably priced lunch menus. Worthwhile discount coupons are found in the *San Diego Weekly Reader,* available free on Thursdays (and known as *The Weekly* in an edited version distributed at local hotels). In keeping with our beach culture, even in the more pricey places, dress tends to be casual; some notable exceptions are downtown and La Jolla's more expensive restaurants and the hotels on Coronado, where jeans are a no-no and gentlemen will feel most comfortable in a dinner jacket.

Restaurants are categorized by the average cost of one entree, an appetizer (if the entree does not come with a side dish or appetizer), one *non*-alcoholic drink, tax, and tip: **Very Expensive** means a meal averages $50 per person and up; **Expensive,** $30 to $50; **Moderate,** $15 to $30; and **Inexpensive,** under $15.

A note on parking: Unless a listing specifies otherwise, drivers can expect to park within 2 or 3 blocks of the restaurants listed here. If you can't find a free or metered space on the street, you can seek out a garage or lot; most Gaslamp Quarter and La Jolla venues offer valet parking.

1 Restaurants by Cuisine

AMERICAN

Bay Beach Cafe (Coronado, $$, p. 128)

Chive 🐾🐾🐾 (Downtown, $$$, p. 103)

Clayton's Coffee Shop (Coronado, $, p. 129)

Corvette Diner (Hillcrest/Uptown, $, p. 111)

Crest Cafe (Hillcrest/Uptown, $, p. 112)

Dakota Grill & Spirits 🐾🐾 (Downtown, $$$, p. 104)

Fat City (Little Italy, $$, p. 105)

Fifth & Hawthorn 🐾 (Hillcrest/Uptown, $$, p. 111)

The Green Flash (Pacific Beach, $$, p. 119)

Hash House a Go Go (Hillcrest/Uptown, $$, p. 107)

High Tide Cafe (Pacific Beach, $, p. 119)

Indigo Grill 🐾🐾 (Little Italy, $$$, p. 104)

Kansas City Barbecue (Downtown, $, p. 107)

Key to Abbreviations: $$$$ = Very Expensive; $$$ = Expensive; $$ = Moderate; $ = Inexpensive

Karl Strauss Brewery & Grill ⍟
(Downtown, La Jolla,
$$, p. 106)
Rhinoceros Cafe & Grill ⍟
(Coronado, $$, p. 128)

BREAKFAST

Bread & Cie. ⍟⍟
(Hillcrest/Uptown, $, p. 111)
Brockton Villa ⍟⍟
(La Jolla, $$, p. 124)
Café Lulu ⍟ (Downtown,
$, p. 106)
Clayton's Coffee Shop
(Coronado, $, p. 129)
The Cottage ⍟ (La Jolla,
$, p. 126)
Crest Cafe (Hillcrest/Uptown,
$, p. 112)
Hash House a Go Go
(Hillcrest/Uptown, $$, p. 107)
The Mission (Mission Beach,
$, p. 120)
Primavera Pastry Caffe ⍟ (Coron-
ado, $, p. 129)

CALIFORNIAN

Azzura Point (Coronado,
$$$$, p. 126)
Baleen ⍟⍟⍟ (Mission Bay,
$$$$, p. 116)
Brockton Villa ⍟⍟ (La Jolla,
$$, p. 124)
Cafe Pacifica ⍟⍟ (Old Town,
$$$, p. 112)
California Cuisine ⍟⍟ (Hill-
crest/Uptown, $$$, p. 108)
The Cottage ⍟ (La Jolla,
$, p. 126)
George's at the Cove ⍟⍟⍟ (La
Jolla, $$$$, p. 120)
Marine Room ⍟⍟⍟ (La Jolla,
$$$$, p. 122)
Mixx ⍟⍟ (Hillcrest/Uptown,
$$$, p. 108)
Nine-Ten ⍟⍟⍟ (La Jolla,
$$$$, p. 122)
Ocean Terrace and George's Bar
⍟⍟ (La Jolla, $$, p. 125)
Prince of Wales ⍟⍟ (Coronado,
$$$$, p. 126)

Qwiig's ⍟ (Ocean Beach,
$$$, p. 118)

CHINESE

Emerald Restaurant ⍟⍟ (Kearny
Mesa, $$, p. 129)
Jasmine ⍟ (Kearny Mesa,
$$, p. 129)

COFFEE & TEA

Brockton Villa ⍟⍟ (La Jolla,
$$, p. 124)
Café Lulu (Downtown, $, p. 106)
Living Room Coffeehouse (Old
Town, $, p. 114)
The Mission (Mission Beach,
$, p. 120)
Mrs. Burton's Tea Parlor (Old
Town, $$, p. 112)

CONTINENTAL

Thee Bungalow ⍟⍟ (Ocean
Beach, $$$, p. 118)
Top of the Cove ⍟⍟⍟ (La Jolla,
$$$$, p. 122)

DESSERTS

Extraordinary Desserts ⍟⍟ (Hill-
crest/Uptown, $$, p. 110)

ECLECTIC

Cafe W ⍟ (Hillcrest, $$, p. 107)
Chive ⍟⍟⍟ (Downtown,
$$$, p. 103)
Indigo Grill ⍟⍟ (Little Italy,
$$$, p. 104)
Kensington Grill ⍟⍟ (Kensington,
$$$, p. 129)
Parallel 33 ⍟⍟ (Hillcrest/Uptown,
$$$, p. 109)
Roppongi ⍟ (La Jolla,
$$$, p. 123)

FRENCH

Bertrand at Mr. A's ⍟⍟ (Hillcrest,
$$$, p. 125)
Chez Loma ⍟⍟ (Coronado,
$$$, p. 127)
Laurel ⍟⍟⍟ (Hillcrest/Uptown,
$$$$, p. 107)
Marine Room ⍟⍟⍟ (La Jolla,
$$$$, p. 122)

Thee Bungalow 𝕲𝕲 (Ocean Beach, $$$, p. 118)

INTERNATIONAL

Mixx 𝕲𝕲 (Hillcrest/Uptown, $$$, p. 108)

Parallel 33 𝕲𝕲 (Hillcrest/Uptown, $$$, p. 109)

ITALIAN

Caffe Bella Italia 𝕲𝕲 (Pacific Beach, $$, p. 118)

Filippi's Pizza Grotto (Downtown, Pacific Beach, and other locations, $, p. 106)

Old Spaghetti Factory (Downtown, $, p. 107)

Pizza Nova 𝕲 (Hillcrest, Pt. Loma, $$, p. 110)

Sammy's California Woodfired Pizza 𝕲 (Downtown, Mission Valley, and other locations, $$, p. 110)

Trattoria Acqua 𝕲𝕲 (La Jolla, $$$, p. 124)

JAPANESE/SUSHI

Cafe Japengo 𝕲𝕲 (La Jolla, $$$, p. 123)

Sushi Ota 𝕲𝕲 (Mission Bay, $$, p. 119)

LATIN AMERICAN

Berta's Latin American Restaurant 𝕲 (Old Town, $$, p. 114)

LIGHT FARE

Bread & Cie. 𝕲𝕲 (Hillcrest/Uptown, $, p. 111)

Living Room Coffeehouse (Old Town, $, p. 114)

Primavera Pastry Caffe 𝕲 (Coronado, $, p. 129)

MEDITERRANEAN

Azzura Point (Coronado, $$$$, p. 126)

Bread & Cie. 𝕲𝕲 (Hillcrest/Uptown, $, p. 111)

Laurel 𝕲𝕲𝕲 (Hillcrest/Uptown, $$$$, p. 107)

Nine-Ten 𝕲𝕲𝕲 (La Jolla, $$$$, p. 122)

Trattoria Acqua 𝕲𝕲 (La Jolla, $$$, p. 124)

MEXICAN

Casa Guadalajara 𝕲 (Old Town, $$, p. 114)

El Agave Tequileria 𝕲𝕲 (Old Town, $$$, p. 113)

Miguel's Cocina (Coronado, $$, p. 126)

Old Town Mexican Café (Old Town, $, p. 115)

Rubio's Baja Grill (throughout the city, $, p. 116)

PACIFIC RIM/ASIAN FUSION

Cafe Japengo 𝕲𝕲 (La Jolla, $$$, p. 123)

Peohe's (Coronado, $$$, p. 125)

Roppongi 𝕲 (La Jolla, $$$, p. 123)

SEAFOOD

Baleen 𝕲𝕲𝕲 (Mission Bay, $$$$, p. 116)

The Brigantine 𝕲 (Coronado, $$$, p. 126)

Cafe Pacifica 𝕲𝕲 (Old Town, $$$, p. 112)

Emerald Restaurant 𝕲𝕲 (Kearny Mesa, $$, p. 129)

The Fish Market/Top of the Market 𝕲 (Downtown, $$, p. 105)

Peohe's (Coronado, $$$, p. 125)

Star of the Sea 𝕲𝕲𝕲 (Downtown, $$$$ p. 102)

SOUTHWESTERN

Dakota Grill & Spirits 𝕲𝕲 (Downtown, $$$, p. 104)

THAI

Spice & Rice Thai Kitchen 𝕲 (La Jolla, $$, p. 125)

VEGETARIAN

Indigo Grill 𝕲𝕲 (Little Italy, $$$, p. 104)

Jyoti Bihanga (Normal Heights, $, p. 129)

2 Downtown & Little Italy

Only a decade or so ago, downtown was the domain of a few high-priced and highfalutin Continental and American restaurants and little else. But the area was turned on its ear when Horton Plaza was redeveloped. Swank spots began moving in to the Gaslamp Quarter's restored Victorian buildings in the late 1980s. Although the initial trend—no doubt designed to cater to the meeting-and-convention crowd—leaned to thick steaks and heaping plates of pasta, we're starting to notice a change toward the less heavy and the more ethnic. Today, the Gaslamp positively percolates with its concentration of dining options, at all price levels and showcasing a variety of cuisines. As half-million-dollar downtown condos continue to be bought up before they're even built, watch for the number and variety of restaurants here to swell even further.

Our downtown section is hardly limited to the 16½-block Gaslamp Quarter (although that's where you'll find the nightlife after 9pm). The **Embarcadero,** a stretch of waterfront along the bay, is also home to several great eating spots, all of which capitalize on their bay views. And **Little Italy**—home to stalwart Filippi's Pizza Grotto—has benefited from the arrival of Indigo Grill, where the fusion of cuisines seems to include almost everything *but* Italian. There are several excellent restaurants just north of the "border" created by the I-5—these are described in the Hillcrest/Uptown section that follows.

Fridays and Saturdays can be very busy, and when a convention has filled the streets with visitors you may have to compete for parking (fortunately, pedicabs—three-wheeled bikes that carry two passengers—are easy to hire). Downtown dining tends to be more formal than elsewhere, because of the business clientele and evening theater- and operagoers, but no one posts a jacket policy anymore. If you stroll down Fifth Avenue between E and Market streets, you'll find a month's worth of restaurants, all packed with a fashionable, mainly local crowd.

VERY EXPENSIVE

Star of the Sea ✸✸✸ SEAFOOD   An Embarcadero fine-dining bastion since 1966, the former Anthony's Star of the Sea Room slumbered through the 1990s, the subject of mournful disdain by the city's emerging foodies. But, a millennium makeover banished its stuffy, outmoded aura to the past, and the restaurant reopened with a new look, new chef, and new name (to better differentiate it from the unexceptional waterfront fish houses next door, also in the Anthony's restaurant family). Gone is that dated dress code and off-putting formality, replaced by a comfortable ambience and modern decor matched to the still-glorious harbor view.

The focus here is on the fine dining, though: Executive chef Brian Johnston imbues the menu with sophisticated touches that show he's in touch with today's gourmands. The menu is seasonally composed; representative dishes include grilled baquetta (sea bass) with wild mushrooms and white truffle risotto, and New Zealand John Dory with fennel pollen, lemon caper brown butter, and parsnip purée. There are always a few offerings for carnivores like a Black Angus rib-eye or boneless beef short ribs, but otherwise, smart diners stick to the always-fresh seafood delights. There's a reasonably priced wine list and a welcoming bar with its own abbreviated menu.

1360 N. Harbor Dr. (at Ash St.) ☏ **619/232-7408.** www.staroftthe sea.com. Reservations recommended. Main courses $26–$29. AE, DC, DISC, MC, V. Daily 5:30–10:30pm. Valet parking $4. Bus: All Harbor Dr. routes. Trolley: America Plaza.

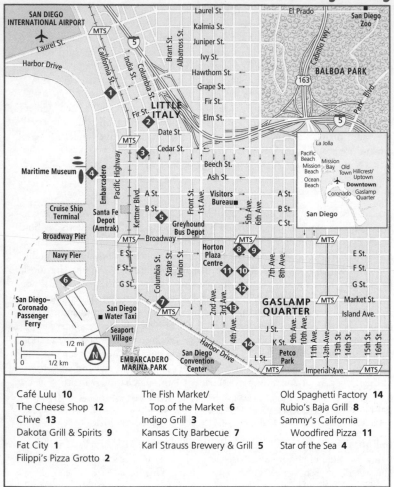

Downtown San Diego Dining

Café Lulu **10**
The Cheese Shop **12**
Chive **13**
Dakota Grill & Spirits **9**
Fat City **1**
Filippi's Pizza Grotto **2**

The Fish Market/
 Top of the Market **6**
Indigo Grill **3**
Kansas City Barbecue **7**
Karl Strauss Brewery & Grill **5**

Old Spaghetti Factory **14**
Rubio's Baja Grill **8**
Sammy's California
 Woodfired Pizza **11**
Star of the Sea **4**

EXPENSIVE

Chive 🍴🍴🍴 AMERICAN/ECLECTIC   This big city–style Gaslamp venue introduced San Diego to sleek and chic dining rooms of the East Coast, and to daring kitchen inventions. Chef A. J. Voytko bailed from a restaurant in traditionalist La Jolla for a place where he could take his diners on a culinary adventure. Start with a fashionable cocktail, of course: The local martini is embellished with Gorgonzola-stuffed olives, and Chive's twist on the *mojito* adds a gingery splash to the Cuban trademark. An ambient jazz soundtrack permeates the background while a legion of practiced servers help decipher such unfamiliar menu ingredients as *picholine* (a tiny French olive), *endigia* (a hybrid of endive and radicchio from France), or *edamame* (the fresh soybeans served in place of bread).

Voytko's menu changes every 6 to 8 weeks, but popular dishes found more often than not include spice-crusted lamb loin, a roasted baby beet salad, a nightly "noodle" (pasta) of the chef's whim, and salads that balance crispy greens with pungent, creamy cheeses and sweet fruit accents. But don't be surprised to encounter culinary curiosities like foie gras with banana bread and caramelized bananas—diners who take a chance on such eccentricities are usually richly rewarded. An international wine list offers many intriguing selections by "cork" or "stem," and includes post-meal sipping tequilas, ports, and Scotch. Chive balances its angular, wide space with cozy lighting, warm fabrics, and a pervasive sense of relaxed fun. One lament: In pursuit of elegant modernity, the cement floors and other hard surfaces amplify the noise level.

558 Fourth Ave. (at Market St.). (℃ **619/232-4483**. www.chiverestaurant.com. Reservations recommended. Main courses $17–$28. AE, DC, DISC, MC, V. Daily 5pm–11pm. Live jazz Sat. Valet parking $7. Bus: 1, 3, 4, 5, 16, or 25. Trolley: Convention Center.

Dakota Grill & Spirits ⋩⋩ AMERICAN/SOUTHWESTERN

This downtown business-lunch favorite is always busy and noisy; the Southwestern cowboy kitsch matches the cuisine in a beautiful room on the ground floor of San Diego's first high-rise. An open, copper-accented kitchen bustles smoothly, most easily enjoyed from the second-level terrace that circles the room. Among the most popular items are the spit-roasted chicken with orange chipotle glaze or Dakota barbecue sauce, the mixed grill served with roasted garlic and grilled red potatoes, and the pan-seared halibut accompanied by tequila cream potatoes and roasted pepper-chipotle coulis. There's also a short list of New Mexican–style pasta and pizzas (made with chipotle-spiced dough) that can keep the dinner bill at a moderate level. When the kitchen is on, Dakota's innovation makes it one of the Gaslamp's best, and the atmosphere is the right mix of informal and smooth to fit the lively cuisine. A pianist plays Wednesday through Saturday nights.

901 Fifth Ave. (at E St.). (℃ **619/234-5554**. Reservations recommended. Main courses $9–$12 lunch, $11–$27 dinner. AE, DC, DISC, MC, V. Mon–Fri 11:30am–2:30pm; Mon–Thurs 5–10pm; Fri–Sat 5–11pm; Sun 5–9pm. Valet parking (after 5pm) $7–$9. Bus: 1, 3, 5, 16, or 25. Trolley: Gaslamp Quarter.

Indigo Grill ⋩⋩ AMERICAN/ECLECTIC/VEGETARIAN

Bracing "aboriginal" cuisine of the Pacific coast—from Mexico to Alaska—is showcased at Chef Deborah Scott's new Little Italy venture. This dance of diverse cooking ingredients and styles is as perilous as a tango, but memorable for its quantity of shrewd moves. Root veggies, game, and fruit are integral to the menu, and unusual spices are used liberally. Yes, occasionally the reach is too far, but no matter: This place is a treat for the palates of foodies yearning for something original. Start with the Oaxaca Fire, a tequila-based cocktail with a salt-and-pepper rim (lotsa kick there), and move on to a lush salad of spinach, spaghetti squash, and strawberries. The alderwood plank salmon, served with a tangle of squid-ink pasta spotted with smoky Oaxacan cheese is a wonderful entree, or go for the rack of lamb, lacquered in wild blueberries—all are extravagantly garnished. Although the menu is primarily meat- and fish-oriented, there are always several noteworthy vegetarian entrees, plus a throng of delicious meatless appetizers (many of the starters are big enough that two will make a meal).

The room is filled with native iconography, rippling water, and glass dividers that mimic sheets of ice; sharp angles, masks, and varied textures of wood, stone, metal, and leather invoke elements of the geographical territory encompassed by the menu. Scott made her name in the mid-1990s at Kemo Sabe (where Pacific Rim meets Southwestern), and now juggles helming duties there and at this new venture. If you enjoy one, it's worth checking out the other; Kemo Sabe is located at 3958 Fifth Ave., between University Avenue and Washington Street, Hillcrest (© 619/220-6802).

1536 India St. (at Cedar St.). © **619/234-6802.** Reservations recommended. Main courses $9–$13 lunch, $18–$28 dinner. AE, DC, DISC, MC, V. Mon–Fri 11:30am–2pm; Sun–Wed 5–9pm; Thurs 5–10pm; Fri–Sat 5–11pm. Bus: 5 or 16. Trolley: Little Italy.

MODERATE

Fat City *Value* AMERICAN   If you need a steak but don't want to get caught up with the Gaslamp's roster of pricey chophouses and also don't want to settle for one of those chain eateries, Fat City is a your place. Overlook the vaguely scary name (the owner's name is Tom Fat) and the overly vivid hot-pink paint job (the building is vintage Art Deco), and settle in to one of the cushy booths, with Tiffany lamps hovering overhead. You can skip the skimpy list of appetizers since the entrees come with a potato side, and specials on the blackboard throw in a salad for a couple bucks more. The steaks are USDA Choice, aged 21 days and grilled to order over mesquite charcoal. Better yet, aim for the USDA Prime top sirloin: A hunky 12-ounce cut is just $14, and miles ahead in flavor of what you get at a Black Angus–type joint. For those who haven't signed on to the Atkins regimen, you'll also find teriyaki salmon, brandy-marinated chicken, and a couple pasta dishes. I haven't tried those—I come here for the steaks and haven't found a reason to look farther down the menu.

2137 Pacific Hwy. (at Hawthorn). © **619/232-9303.** Main courses $10–$19. AE, MC, V. Daily 5–10pm. Free parking. Bus: 34.

The Fish Market *Value* SEAFOOD   Ask any San Diegan where to go for the biggest selection of the freshest fish, and they'll send you to the bustling Fish Market on the end of the G Street Pier on the Embarcadero. Chalkboards announce the day's catches—be it Mississippi catfish, Maine lobster, Canadian salmon, or Mexican yellowtail—which are sold by the pound or available in a number of classic, simple preparations in the casual, always-packed restaurant. Upstairs, the fancy offshoot **Top of the Market** offers sea fare with souped-up presentations (and jacked-up prices). Either way, the fish comes from the same trough, so I recommend having a cocktail in Top's posh, clubby atmosphere to enjoy the stupendous panoramic bay views, and then head downstairs for solid affordable fare or treats from the sushi and oyster bars.

There's another Fish Market in Del Mar at 640 Via de la Valle (© 858/755-2277), and a counter outlet in Mission Valley at 2401 Fenton Pkwy. (© 619/280-2277).

750 N. Harbor Dr. © **619/232-FISH.** www.thefishmarket.com. Reservations not accepted. Main courses $12–$27 (Top of the Market main courses $17–$43). AE, DC, DISC, MC, V. Daily 11am–10pm. Valet parking $5. Bus: 7/7B. Trolley: Seaport Village.

Karl Strauss Brewery & Grill ✦ AMERICAN   Brew master Karl Strauss put San Diego on the microbrewery map with this unpretentious factory setting, now all but engulfed by the city's new W Hotel. The smell of hops and malt wafts throughout, and the stainless-steel tanks are visible from the bar. Brews, all on tap, range from pale ale to amber lager. Five-ounce samplers are $1 each; if you like what you taste, 12-ounce glasses, pints, and hefty schooners stand chilled and ready. There's also nonalcoholic beer and wine by the glass. It used to be that the Cajun fries, hamburgers, German sausage (sans sauerkraut), and other greasy bar foods were secondary to the stylin' suds, but they've dressed up the lunch and dinner menu with items like Southwestern salmon linguini and filet mignon. Beer-related memorabilia and brewery tours are available. There's another location in La Jolla at 1044 Wall St. (© 858/551-2739).

1157 Columbia St. (at B St.). © **619/234-BREW**. Main courses $8–$15 lunch, $8–$23 dinner. AE, MC, V. Opens Mon–Fri 11am, Sat–Sun 11:30am; Sun–Thurs kitchen serves till 10pm (bar serves till 11pm); Fri kitchen till 11pm (bar till midnight); Sat kitchen till midnight (bar till 1am). Bus: 5 or 16. Trolley: America Plaza.

INEXPENSIVE

Café Lulu BREAKFAST/COFFEE & TEA   Smack-dab in the heart of the Gaslamp Quarter, Café Lulu aims for a hip, bohemian mood despite little clues to the contrary (like the *Wall Street Journal* hanging on racks for browsing). Ostensibly a coffee bar, the cafe also makes a good choice for casual dining; if the stylishly dark interior is too harsh for you, watch the street action from a sidewalk table. The food is health conscious, largely prepared with organic ingredients. Soups, salads, cheese melts, and veggie lasagna are on the list; breads come from the incomparable Bread & Cie. uptown (p. 111). Eggs, granola, and waffles are served in the morning, but anytime is the right time to try one of the inventive coffee drinks, like cafe Bohème (mocha with almond syrup) or cafe L'amour (iced latte with a hazelnut tinge). Beer and wine are also served, and if you're staying downtown they offer free delivery in the Gaslamp Quarter.

419 F St. (near Fourth Ave.). © **619/238-0114**. Main courses $6–$9. No credit cards. Sun–Thurs 10am–1am; Fri–Sat 10am–3am. Bus: 1, 3, 5, 16, or 25. Trolley: Convention Center.

Filippi's Pizza Grotto (Kids) (Value) ITALIAN   For longtime locals, when we think "Little Italy," Filippi's comes to mind—it was a childhood fixture for many of us. To get to the dining area, decorated with Chianti bottles and red-checked table-cloths, you walk through a "cash and carry" Italian grocery store and deli strewn with cheeses, pastas, wines, bottles of olive oil, and salamis. You might even end up eating behind shelves of canned olives, but don't feel bad—this has been a tradition since 1950. The intoxicating smell of pizza wafts into the street; Filippi's has more than 15 varieties (including vegetarian), plus old-world spaghetti, lasagna, and other pasta. Children's portions are available, and kids will feel right at home under the sweeping mural of the Bay of Naples. The Friday and Saturday night lines to get in can look intimidating, but they move quickly.

The original of a dozen branches throughout the county, this Filippi's has free parking. Other locations include 962 Garnet Ave. in Pacific Beach (© 858/483-6222).

1747 India St. (between Date and Fir sts.), Little Italy. © **619/232-5095**. Reservations not accepted on weekends. Main courses $5–$13. AE, DC, DISC, MC, V. Sun–Mon 9am–10pm; Tues–Thurs 9am–10:30pm; Fri–Sat 9am–11:30pm. Free parking. Bus: 5. Trolley: Little Italy.

Kansas City Barbecue AMERICAN Kansas City Barbecue's honky-tonk mystique was fueled by its appearance as the fly-boy hangout in the movie *Top Gun* ("one of our better business decisions," reflects the understated owner). Posters from the film share wall space with county-fair memorabilia, old Kansas car tags, and a photograph of official "bar wench" Carry Nation. This homey dive is right next to the railroad tracks and across from the tony Hyatt Regency. The spicy barbecue ribs, chicken, and hot links are slow-cooked over an open fire and served with sliced white bread and your choice of coleslaw, beans, fries, onion rings, potato salad, or corn on the cob. The food is okay, but the atmosphere is the real draw.

610 W. Market St. (C) **619/231-9680.** Reservations not accepted. Main courses $7–$12. MC, V. Daily 11am–1am. Trolley: Seaport Village.

Old Spaghetti Factory *Kids* ITALIAN It's lively, it's family friendly, and it's a great deal—no wonder folks are always waiting for tables. The menu is basic spaghetti-and-meatball fare; for the price of a main course, you also get salad, sourdough bread, ice cream, and coffee or tea (with refills). I've been wolfing down the spaghetti with browned butter and Greek mizithra cheese since I was a kid. Table wines are available by the glass or decanter. Part of a chain that always has creative settings, the restaurant is in a former printing factory, with some tables enclosed in a 1917 trolley car. The decor is lavish early bordello—fun for adults and stimulating for kids.

275 Fifth Ave. (at K St.). (C) **619/233-4323.** Reservations not accepted. Main courses $4–$7 lunch, $6–$10 dinner. AE, DISC, MC, V. Mon–Fri 11:30am–2pm and 5–10pm (Fri till 11pm); Sat 11:30am–11pm; Sun 11:30am–10pm. Trolley: Gaslamp Quarter.

3 Hillcrest & Uptown

Hillcrest and the other gentrified uptown neighborhoods to its west and east are jam-packed with great food for any palate (and any wallet). Some are old standbys filled nightly with loyal regulars; others are cutting-edge experiments that might be gone next year. Whether it's ethnic food, French food, health-conscious bistro fare, retro comfort food, specialty cafes and bakeries, and California cuisine, they're often mastered with the innovative panache you'd expect in the most nonconformist part of town.

Cafe W ✿, 3680 Sixth Ave. ((C) **619/291-0200**), is the latest venture of Chris Walsh, formerly of California Cuisine. This time he does flavorful international tapas-style small plates in a revived Hillcrest cottage with chic decor. Nearby, **Hash House a Go Go,** 3628 Fifth Ave. ((C) **619/298-4646**), is another reconverted building with an equally eclectic pun-filled menu. They serve three meals a day, but breakfast is the locals' choice; you'd better be hungry, because portions are mountainous. Also note that the popular **Whole Foods** supermarket, 711 University Ave. ((C) **619/294-2800**), has a mouthwatering deli and a robust salad bar—you can pack for a picnic or eat at the tables up front.

VERY EXPENSIVE

Laurel ✿✿✿ FRENCH/MEDITERRANEAN Laurel is one of my favorite spots for a special meal. The Bankers Hill location is close to downtown and Hillcrest, the decor is sophisticated yet understated, and the crowd is reliably elegant. Throw in a wine list with the city's best selection of French Rhône and extravagant Napa cabernets, and a well-composed menu of southern French country dishes with the occasional Moroccan accent, and it's no wonder this restaurant continues to be at the top of its game; when Jason Shaeffer took over

for founding chef Doug Organ in 2001, the transition went without a hiccup. Live piano music adds to the panache of this graceful room, located on the ground floor of an amorphous office building, a block west of the Laurel Street entrance to Balboa Park. Start by choosing from an extensive selection of tantalizing appetizers, including saffron-tinged red pepper-and-shellfish soup, veal sweetbreads with salsify and truffle, and warm caramelized onion-and-Roquefort tart. Main courses include mouthwatering crisp duck confit with Toulouse sausage, or the seafood specials like sautéed monkfish cheek with braised baby fennel and lemony couscous. If you're overwhelmed by the choices, succumb to the five-course tasting menu ($59 with three wine pairings).

One of the most reliable choices outside downtown and La Jolla for fine dining, Laurel has New York–style ambience coupled with San Diego's slightly more temperate prices. The restaurant is also popular with theatergoers, who are offered shuttle service to the Globe Theaters.

505 Laurel St. (at Fifth Ave.). © **619/239-2222.** www.laurelrestaurant.com. Reservations recommended. Main courses $21–$32. AE, DC, DISC, MC, V. Daily 5–10pm; lunch Fri only 11:30am–1:30pm. Valet parking $6. Bus: 1, 3, or 25.

EXPENSIVE

California Cuisine ★★ CALIFORNIAN   This popular restaurant encountered a rocky patch, when its identity as a place for light, cutting-edge food was in jeopardy. But Justin Hoehn took over the kitchen in early 2003 and reworked and slimmed down the menu to bring back the qualities that put this restaurant on the map when it originally opened in 1982. Since these trademarks are now well established at many serious restaurants across town, it's not as easy to stand out from the crowd, but the menu here is once again fresh and contemporary. The spare, understated dining room and delightfully romantic patio set the stage as a smoothly professional and respectful staff proffers fine dining at fair prices to a casual crowd.

The menu changes daily but often contains mouthwatering appetizers like sesame-seared ahi with hot-and-sour raspberry sauce and a jicama papaya slaw, or New Zealand green lip mussels in a white-wine tomato garlic broth. Main courses are composed with equal care and might include maple-glazed pork loin with yam spaetzle and grilled radicchio; a spinach-asparagus risotto; or chanterelle-dusted lamb loin, topped with whole grain mustard-sherry sauce and accompanied by crispy polenta. And don't miss desserts by pastry chef Laurel Hufnagle, who tries inventive twists on old standards, like the jasmine-and–green tea crème brûlée. Allow time to find parking, which can be scarce along this busy stretch of University Avenue.

1027 University Ave. (east of 10th St.). © **619/543-0790.** www.californiacuisine.cc. Reservations recommended for dinner. Main courses $7–$16 lunch, $17–$27 dinner. AE, DISC, MC, V. Tues–Fri 11am–10pm; Sat–Sun 5–10pm. Bus: 908.

Mixx ★★ CALIFORNIAN/INTERNATIONAL   Aptly named for its subtle global fusion fare, Mixx embodies everything good about Hillcrest dining: an attractive, relaxing room; a worldly crowd of regulars; thoughtfully composed dinners; and polished, friendly service. It's easy to see why locals gravitate to Mixx's wood-paneled, street-level cocktail lounge and the often jovial dining room above. Menu standouts include a starter of crispy Indonesian shrimp or the eggplant Sumatra (spiced eggplant and crispy tofu in chile sauce). The pan-roasted whitefish with a lemon-garlic confit served with roasted fennel and rosemary spiked potatoes, and the balsamic-basted flat iron steak are favored entrees. Prepared and presented

Bertrand at Mr. A's **13**
Bread & Cie. **2**
Cafe W **9**
California Cuisine **6**
Corvette Diner **3**
Crest Cafe **8**
Extraordinary Desserts **12**
Fifth & Hawthorn **15**
Hash House a Go Go **11**
Laurel **14**
Living Room Coffeehouse **7**
Mixx **10**
Parallel 33 **1**
Pizza Nova **4**
Whole Foods **5**

with finesse by chef Zhee Zhee Charisma Aguirre—no, she's not a drag queen!—one meal here will quickly convince you that Mixx cares about substance *and* value.

3671 Fifth Ave. (at Pennsylvania Ave.). (C) **619/299-6499.** Reservations recommended, especially on weekends. Main courses $15–$24. AE, DC, DISC, MC, V. Sun–Thurs 5–10pm; Fri–Sat 5–11pm. Bus: 1, 3, or 25.

Parallel 33 🎯🎯 *Finds* ECLECTIC/INTERNATIONAL   Inspired by a theory that all locales along the 33rd parallel (San Diego's latitude) of the globe might share the rich culinary traditions of the Tigris-Euphrates Valley (birthplace of civilization), chef Amiko Gubbins presents a cuisine that beautifully combines flavors from Morocco, Lebanon, India, China, and Japan. Even if the globe-girdling concept doesn't quite make sense, sit back and savor the creativity displayed in a menu that leaps enthusiastically from fragrant Moroccan chicken *b'stilla* to soft shell crab crusted with *panko* (wispy Japanese bread crumbs) and black sesame seeds; from scallops pan-seared in garam masala and served over couscous to oven-roasted *za'atar* chicken with basmati rice, English peas, and *harissa*. The *ahi poke* (raw tuna) appetizer fuses a Hawaiian mainstay with Asian pear and mango and Japanese wasabi—it's a winner! The restaurant is nice but not fancy, just an upscale neighborhood joint that's easily overlooked by visitors. The Indian/African/Asian decor throws soft shadows throughout, inviting conversation and leisurely dining. The intimate dining room was instantly popular after opening, and the number of devout fans shows no signs of waning—you'll want to reserve a table in advance.

741 W. Washington St. (at Falcon), Mission Hills. ℂ 619/260-0033. Reservations recommended. Main courses $18–$27. AE, DISC, MC, V. Mon–Thurs 5:30–10pm; Fri–Sat 5:30–11pm. Bus: 3, 16, or 908.

MODERATE

Extraordinary Desserts ⭐⭐ DESSERTS   If you're a lover of sweets—heck, if you've ever eaten a dessert at all—you owe it to yourself to visit this unique cafe. Chef and proprietor Karen Krasne's name features prominently on the sign, as well it should: Krasne's talent surpasses the promise of her impressive pedigree, which includes a *Certificate de Patisserie* from Le Cordon Bleu in Paris. Dozens of divine creations are available daily, and even the humble carrot cake is savory enough to wow naysayers. Others—mostly garnished with edible gold or flowers—include a passion fruit ricotta torte bursting with kiwis, strawberries, and bananas; a *gianduia* of chocolate cake lathered with hazelnut butter cream, chocolate mousse, and boysenberry preserves, and sprinkled with shards of praline; or the new bête noir, which is a dark chocolate cake layered with vanilla crème brûlée, chocolate mousse, and chocolate truffle cream. Originally educated in Hawaii, Krasne likes to incorporate island touches like macadamia nuts, fresh coconut, fruit, and pure Kona coffee. Her Parisian experience is also

---

✐ Wood-Fired Pizza

It all started with Wolfgang Puck, that crafty Austrian chef who dazzled Hollywood diners at Spago and went on to build a dynasty of California cuisine. By now, everyone is familiar with the building block of that empire; you can even get it in the frozen-food section. We're talking about pizza, of course. Not the marinara-and-pepperoni variety found in other pizza meccas like New York and Chicago—for a whole generation of Californians, pizza will always mean barbecued chicken, tomato-basil, or goat cheese and sun-dried tomato. Gourmet pizzas appear to have overtaken the traditional variety in popularity, and kitchens all over San Diego stoke their wood-fired ovens to keep up with the demand.

Most of the Italian restaurants in this chapter feature at least a handful of individual-size pizzas. Always tops in San Diego polls is **Sammy's California Woodfired Pizza** ⭐ at 770 Fourth Ave., at F Street, in the Gaslamp Quarter (ℂ **619/230-8888**); 1620 Camino de la Reina in Mission Valley (ℂ 619/298-8222); 702 Pearl St., at Draper Street, La Jolla (ℂ 858/456-8018); and 12925 El Camino Real, at Del Mar Heights Road, Del Mar (ℂ 858/259-6600). Often crowded, Sammy's serves creations like duck sausage, potato garlic, or Jamaican jerk shrimp atop 10-inch rounds. It also excels at enormous salads, making it easy to share a meal and save a bundle.

A similar menu is available at **Pizza Nova** ⭐, a similarly stylish mini-chain with a similarly vibrant atmosphere. Despite being alike, each chain thrives by covering the neighborhoods the other doesn't. You'll find Pizza Nova at 3955 Fifth Ave., north of University Avenue in Hillcrest (ℂ **619/296-6682**); 5120 N. Harbor Dr., west of Nimitz Boulevard in Point Loma (ℂ 619/226-0268); and 8650 Genesee Ave., at Nobel Drive in La Jolla's Golden Triangle (ℂ 858/458-9525).

represented; the shop sells tea and accouterments from the fine salon Mariage Frères, as well as boutique items like candles and bath products.

2929 Fifth Ave. (between Palm and Quince sts.). © **619/294-7001**. www.extraordinarydesserts.com. Desserts $2–$9. MC, V. Opens Mon–Fri 8:30am, Sat–Sun 11am; closes Sun–Thurs 11pm, Fri–Sat midnight. Street parking usually available. Bus: 1, 3, or 25.

Fifth & Hawthorn ✮ *Value* AMERICAN   You won't find a sign in front of this neighborhood hideaway—just look for the street-sign marking the intersection of Fifth and Hawthorn, a few blocks north of downtown, and aim for the red neon "open" sign. Inhabited by a slew of regulars, the comfortable room is somewhat dark, vaguely romantic—just enough, anyway, to take your mind off the planes coming in for a landing overhead. The menu has pretty much stayed the same for 16 years: You won't find anything daring, but you will find lots of well-executed basics, like a filet mignon in green peppercorn sauce and linguini with clams, white wine, and garlic. There are a few dishes Fifth & Hawthorn excels at: The mustard-crusted catfish is simple and delicious, and the calamari, sautéed "abalone-style," are rendered tender and sweet. The restaurant also offers a terrific four-course meal: appetizer, soup or salad, one of six entrees, and dessert for $50 per couple, *including* a bottle of wine to share.

515 Hawthorn St. (at Fifth Ave.). © **619/544-0940**. Main courses $15–$25. AE, MC, V. Mon–Thurs 5pm–9pm; Fri–Sat 5–10:15pm; Sun 4:30–8:30pm. Street parking usually available. Bus: 1, 3, or 25.

INEXPENSIVE

Bread & Cie. ✮✮ BREAKFAST/LIGHT FARE/MEDITERRANEAN   Delicious aromas permeate this cavernous Hillcrest bakery, where the city's most treasured breads are baked before your eyes all day long. The traditions of European artisan bread-making and attention to the fine points of texture and crust quickly catapulted Bread & Cie. to local stardom—they now supply bread to more than 75 local restaurants. Among my favorites available daily are anise and fig, black olive, jalapeño and cheese—even the relatively plain sourdough *batard* is tart, chewy perfection. Others are available just 1 or 2 days a week, like the *panella dell'uva* (grape bread; weekends), or the hunky walnut and scallion (Wed and Sat). Ask for a free sample, or order one of the many Mediterranean-inspired sandwiches. Try tuna niçoise with walnuts and capers; the mozzarella, roasted peppers, and olive tapenade on focaccia; or, roast turkey with hot pepper cheese on rosemary/olive oil bread. Specialty coffee drinks delivered in bowl-like mugs are perfect accompaniment to a light breakfast of fresh scones, muffins, and homemade granola with yogurt. Seating is at bistro-style tables in full view of the busy ovens and tattoo-embraced staff.

350 University Ave. (between Third and Fourth sts.). © **619/683-9322**. Sandwiches and light meals $4–$8. MC, V. Mon–Fri 7am–7pm; Sat 7am–6pm; Sun 8am–6pm. Bus: 1, 3, 16, 25, or 908.

Corvette Diner *Kids* AMERICAN   Travel back in time to the rockin' 1950s at this theme diner, where the jukebox is loud, the gum-snapping waitresses slide into your booth to take your order, and the decor is neon and vintage Corvette to the highest power. Equal parts *Happy Days* hangout and Jackrabbit Slim's (as in *Pulp Fiction*), the Corvette Diner is a comfy, family-friendly time warp in the midst of Hillcrest, and the diner-esque eats ain't bad for the price, either. Burgers, sandwiches, appetizer munchies, blue-plate specials, and salads share the menu with a *very* full page of fountain favorites. Beer and wine are served, and there's a large bar in the center of the cavernous dining room. The party jumps a notch at night, with a DJ providing more entertainment (on top of the already

captivating atmosphere)—the decibel level is always high. A reliable favorite for pre-teen birthdays.

3946 Fifth Ave. (between Washington St. and University Ave.). © **619/542-1001.** Reservations not accepted. Main courses $5–$11. AE, DC, DISC, MC, V. Sun–Thurs 11am–10pm; Fri–Sat 11am–midnight. Valet parking $4. Bus: 1, 3, 16, 25, or 908.

Crest Cafe AMERICAN/BREAKFAST   This long-popular Hillcrest diner is a great refuge from sleek designer food and swank settings. The cheery pink interior announces 1940s style, and the room bubbles with upbeat waiters and comfort food doled out on Fiestaware. The church pew–like booths are comfortable enough, but the small stucco room doesn't do much to mask the near constant clang of plates. No matter: Burger-lovers will fall in love with the spicy, rich "butter burger"—a dollop of herb butter is buried in the patty before cooking (it's even better than it sounds). And the East Texas fried chicken breast crusted with hunks of jalapeño peppers is none too subtle, either, but it's tasty. A variety of sandwiches and salads, the popular steamed vegetable basket, and broiled chicken dishes are healthier options. During the early evening, the joint brims with neighborhood bohemians in search of a cholesterol fix, while later the club contingent swoops in; the breakfast of omelets or hot cakes is a happy eye-opener.

425 Robinson Ave. (between Fourth and Fifth aves.). © **619/295-2510.** www.crestcafe.com. Reservations not accepted. Main courses $5–$12. AE, MC, V. Daily 7am–midnight. Bus: 1, 3, 25, or 908.

4 Old Town & Mission Valley

Visitors usually have at least one meal in Old Town, and although this area showcases San Diego at its most touristy, I can't argue with the appeal of dining in California's charming and oldest settlement. Mexican food and bathtub-size margaritas are the big draws, as are mariachi music and colorful decor. For a change of pace, stop by **Mrs. Burton's Tea Parlor** in Heritage Park (© **619/ 294-4600**), where afternoon tea is served with an assortment of sandwiches, scones, tarts, and fresh fruit for $18 ($15 for children 12 and under); reservations are requested, and it's closed on Mondays.

Old Town is also the gateway to the decidedly less historic Mission Valley. Here you'll find plenty of chain eateries, both good and bad, and not discussed in depth below. In the very busy Fashion Valley Shopping Center complex lies Cheesecake Factory, California Pizza Kitchen, and P.F. Chang's—expect long waits for a table at each. In or near the Mission Valley Shopping Center is an Outback Steakhouse, Hooters, and Mimi's Cafe.

EXPENSIVE

Cafe Pacifica ⭐⭐ CALIFORNIAN/SEAFOOD   You can't tell a book by its cover: Inside this cozy Old Town casita, the decor is cleanly contemporary (but still romantic) and the food anything but Mexican. Established in 1980, Cafe Pacifica serves upscale, imaginative seafood at decent prices and produces kitchen alumni who go on to enjoy local fame. Among the temptations are crab-stuffed portobello mushrooms topped with grilled asparagus, anise-scented bouillabaisse, and daily fresh fish selections served grilled with your choice of five sauces. Signature items include Hawaiian ahi with shiitake mushrooms and ginger butter, griddled mustard catfish, and the "Pomerita," a pomegranate margarita. To avoid the crush, arrive before 6:30—you'll also get to take advantage of the early-bird special, entree with soup or salad for $21. On Tuesdays the corkage fee is waived for bottles you bring in yourself (though the wine list is hardly a slouch).

Old Town Dining

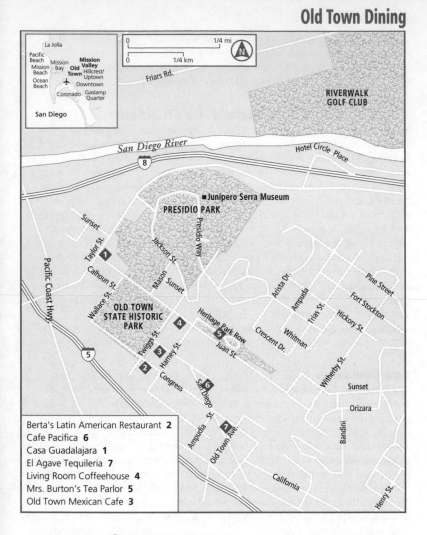

Berta's Latin American Restaurant **2**
Cafe Pacifica **6**
Casa Guadalajara **1**
El Agave Tequileria **7**
Living Room Coffeehouse **4**
Mrs. Burton's Tea Parlor **5**
Old Town Mexican Cafe **3**

2414 San Diego Ave. ✆ **619/291-6666.** www.cafepacifica.com. Reservations recommended. Main courses $17–$28. AE, DC, DISC, MC, V. Daily 5–10pm. Valet parking $4. Bus: 5/5A. Trolley: Old Town.

El Agave Tequileria ★★ MEXICAN   Don't be misled by this restaurant's less than impressive location above a liquor store on the outskirts of Old Town. This warm, bustling eatery continues to draw local gourmands for the regional Mexican cuisine and rustic elegance that leave the touristy fajitas-and-cerveza joints of Old Town far behind. El Agave is named for the agave plant from which tequilas are derived, and they boast more than 850 boutique and artisan tequilas from throughout the Latin world—bottles of every size, shape, and jewel-like hue fill shelves and cases throughout the dining room. But even tee-totalers will enjoy the restaurant's authentically flavored *mole* sauces (from Chiapas, rich with peanuts; tangy tomatillo from Oaxaca; and the more familiar dark mole flavored with chocolate and sesame), along with giant shrimp and sea bass prepared in a dozen variations, or El Agave's signature beef filet with goat cheese and dark tequila sauce. On the other hand, I could almost make a meal

out of the warm watercress salad dressed with onions and bacon, folded into tortillas. Lunches are simpler affairs without the exotic sauces, and inexpensive.

2304 San Diego Ave. ✆ 619/220-0692. www.elagave.com. Reservations recommended. Main courses $7–$10 lunch, $16–$32 dinner. AE, MC, V. Daily 11am–10pm. Street parking. Bus: 5. Trolley: Old Town.

MODERATE

Berta's Latin American Restaurant 🌟 *Finds* LATIN AMERICAN   Berta's is a welcome change from the nacho-and-fajita joints that dominate Old Town dining, though the small room can attract as large a crowd on weekends. Housed in a charming, basic cottage tucked away on a side street, Berta's faithfully recreates the sunny flavors of Central and South America, where slow cooking mellows the heat of chiles and other spices. Everyone starts with a basket of fresh flour tortillas and mild salsa verde, which usually vanishes before you're done contemplating such mouthwatering dishes as Guatemalan *chilimal,* a rich pork-and-vegetable casserole with chiles, tomatoes, cornmeal *masa,* cilantro, and cloves. Try the Salvadoran *pupusas* (at lunch only)—dense corn-mash turnovers with melted cheese and black beans, their texture perfectly offset with crunchy cabbage salad and one of Berta's special salsas. Or opt for a table full of Spanish-style tapas, grazing alternately on crispy *empanadas* (filled turnovers), strong Spanish olives, or *Pincho Moruno,* skewered lamb and onion redolent of spices and red saffron.

3928 Twiggs St. (at Congress St.). ✆ 619/295-2343. www.bertasinoldtown.com. Main courses $6–$9 lunch, $11–$16 dinner. AE, MC, V. Tues–Sun 11am–10pm (lunch menu till 3pm). Free parking. Bus: 5/5A. Trolley: Old Town.

Casa Guadalajara 🌟 *Kids* MEXICAN   The best of the mini-chain of restaurants operated by Bazaar del Mundo, Casa Guadalajara is actually located a block away from the shops, which provides another advantage: It's often less crowded than its counterparts (though waits of 30 min. or more are not unusual here Fri and Sat). Mariachi tunes played by strolling musicians enliven the room nightly, and you can also dine alfresco, in a picturesque courtyard occupied by a 200-year-old pepper tree. Birdbath-size margaritas start most meals, while dining ranges from gourmet Mexican to simpler south-of-the-border fare. My favorite is the *tacos de cochinita*—2 soft corn tacos bulging with achiote-seasoned pork and marinated red onions—but the extensive menu features all the fajita and combo plates most people expect. This place (like the Bazaar) is touristy, but it's where I bring out-of-towners for old California ambience and reliable Mexican food.

4105 Taylor St. (at Juan St. in Old Town). ✆ 619/295-5111. www.casaguadalajara.com. Reservations recommended. Main courses $8–$16. AE, DC, DISC, MC, V. Sun–Thurs 11am–10pm; Fri–Sat 11am–11pm. Free parking. Bus: 5/5A. Trolley: Old Town.

INEXPENSIVE

Living Room Coffeehouse COFFEE & TEA/LIGHT FARE   You're liable to hear the whir of laptops from college students, who use this spot as a sort of off-campus study hall. Grab a sidewalk table and enjoy some splendid people-watching any time of day; indoors you'll find faux antiques, appropriately weathered for a lived-in feel. I think the pastries and coffee fall a bit short, but this local mini-chain is also known for surprisingly good light meals that make it a good choice for early risers and insomniacs alike. Breakfast includes omelets and waffles, while the rest of the day's fare is posted on a chalkboard menu; try the turkey lasagna, chicken Dijon, tuna melt, or one of several hearty entree salads. Plus

---

(Kids) Family-Friendly Restaurants

Casa Guadalajara (p. 114) With the ambient noise of fountains and mariachis, fidgety children won't feel like they have to be on best behavior at this pleasant Mexican eatery—there's also plenty for them to see.

Corvette Diner (p. 111) Resembling a 1950s diner, this place appeals to teens and preteens. Parents will have fun reminiscing, and kids will enjoy the burgers and fries or other short-order fare, served in sock-hop surroundings.

Filippi's Pizza Grotto (p. 106) Children's portions are available, and kids will feel right at home at this red-checked-vinyl-tablecloth joint. The pizzas are among the best in town.

Old Spaghetti Factory (p. 107) Kids get special attention here, and even their own toys. There's a play area, too.

---

you'll find exotic iced and hot coffee drinks, like the Emerald Isle (espresso, white chocolate, and mint). Other locations are in La Jolla at 1010 Prospect St. (© 858/459-1187), in Hillcrest at 1417 University Ave. (© 619/295-7911), the Sports Arena area at 1018 Rosecrans (© 619/222-6852), and in the College area near San Diego State University, at 5900 El Cajon Blvd. (© 619/286-8434).

2541 San Diego Ave. © **619/523-4445.** www.livingroomcafe.com. Menu items $3–$8. AE, MC, V. Sun–Thurs 7am–10pm; Fri–Sat 7am–midnight. Bus: 5. Trolley: Old Town.

Old Town Mexican Cafe *(Overrated* MEXICAN This place is so popular that it's become an Old Town tourist attraction in its own right. You, on the other hand, might proceed with caution. The original structure is wonderfully funky and frayed, but the restaurant long ago expanded into additional, less appealing dining rooms and outdoor patios—still, the wait for a table is often 30 to 60 minutes. You can pass the time by gazing in from the sidewalk as tortillas are hand-patted the old-fashioned way, soon to be a hot-off-the-grill treat accompanying every meal, or by watching the chickens spinning around the barbecue. But the place is loud and crowded, and the food usually fails to impress. When I come here it's for one of three things: the margarita, served neat, in a shaker for two; the delicious rotisserie chicken accompanied by tortillas, guacamole, sour cream, beans, and rice; and the cheap breakfasts, when the place is pleasantly sleepy and throng-free. Otherwise, the fried *carnitas*—reputedly a specialty—remind me of mystery meat that's been pitched into the deep-fat fryer.

2489 San Diego Ave. © **619/297-4330.** Reservations accepted only for parties of 10 or more. Main courses $6–$9 breakfast, $9–$15 lunch and dinner. AE, DISC, MC, V. Sun–Thurs 7am–11pm; Fri–Sat 7am–midnight (bar till 2am). Bus: 5. Trolley: Old Town.

5 Mission Bay & the Beaches

Generally speaking, restaurants at the beach exist primarily to provide an excuse for sitting and gazing at the water. Because this activity is most commonly accompanied by steady drinking, it stands to reason that the food isn't often remarkable. I've tried to balance the most scenic of these typical hangouts with places actually known for above-average food—with a little effort, they can be found.

Noteworthy beach spots include **Kono's Surf Club Cafe,** 704 Garnet Ave., Pacific Beach (© **858/483-1669**), a Hawaiian-themed boardwalk breakfast shack that's cheap and delicious. A plump Kono's breakfast burrito provides enough fuel for a day of surfing or sightseeing, while a side order of savory "Kono Potatoes" is a meal in itself.

VERY EXPENSIVE

Baleen ★★★ SEAFOOD/CALIFORNIAN   This fine waterfront eatery at the Paradise Point Resort in the middle of Mission Bay is exactly the touch of class the hotel owners hoped for when they lured celebrity restaurateur Robbin Haas (creator of two Baleens in Florida). With a spectacular bayfront view (and a dining deck that is sublime on warm evenings), it's easy to miss the design details indoors—from a monkey motif that includes simians hanging off chandeliers to specialized serving platters for many of Baleen's artistically arranged dishes.

Start with chilled lobster in a martini glass (avoid sticker shock by asking the price first), a warm salad of roasted mushrooms and asparagus, or fresh oysters delivered in a small cart and shucked table-side. Then savor a selection of seafood simply grilled, wood-roasted, or sautéed with hummus crust, honey wasabi glaze, or ginger sauce. Wood-roasted meats include Roquefort-crusted filet mignon and Sonoma Farms chicken with goat cheese dumplings and forest mushroom sauté.

✐ Baja Fish Tacos

One of San Diego's culinary ironies is that, although the city is conscious of its Hispanic roots—not to mention within visual range of the Mexican border—it's hard to find anything other than gringo-ized combo plates in most local Mexican restaurants.

Perhaps the most authentic recipes are those found inside humble **Rubio's Baja Grill.** Actually, it's not so humble anymore, since proprietor Ralph Rubio began branching out into every corner of Southern California with his enormously successful yet deceptively simple fare; you can now find Rubio's throughout California and the Southwest, and even edging out hot dogs in the stands at San Diego's Qualcomm Stadium. But, back in 1983, it was an achievement for local surfer Rubio to open a tiny walk-up taco stand on busy Mission Bay Drive. After years of scarfing down cheap beers and fish tacos in the Mexican fishing village of San Felipe, Rubio secured the "secret" recipe for this quintessentially Baja treat: batter-dipped, deep-fried fish filets folded in corn tortillas and garnished with shredded cabbage, salsa, and tangy *crema* sauce. You'll find them dispensed from thatched-roof shacks along Baja's beach roads, and in the past decade they've taken this side of the border by storm. Rubio's has since expanded its menu to include other Mexican specialties, all accented by the distinctively Baja flavors of fresh lime and tangy cilantro. And unlike your average McDrive-through, at Rubio's you can wash it all down with an icy-cold beer.

Because many of the two-dozen-or-so newer locations have a homogenous fast-food look to them, it's fun to stop by the original stand, at 4504 E. Mission Bay Dr., at Bunker Hill Street (© **858/272-2801**), if you're in the neighborhood.

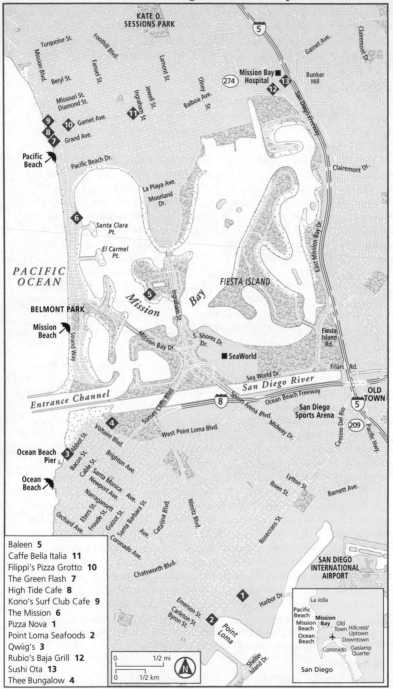

KATE O. SESSIONS PARK

Turquoise St.
Foothill Blvd.
Famosa St.
Lamont St.
Garnet Ave.
Clairemont Dr.

Mission Blvd.
Beryl St.
Missouri St.
Diamond St.
Jewell St.
Ingraham St.
Olney Ave.
Balboa St.

21

274 Mission Bay Hospital **12** **13**
Bunker Hill

9 **10** Garnet Ave.
8
7 Grand Ave.

Pacific Beach

Pacific Beach Dr.

Clairemont Dr.

La Playa Ave.
Moorland Dr.

6

Santa Clara Pt.

El Carmel Pt.

FIESTA ISLAND

PACIFIC OCEAN

Mission Bay

East Mission Bay Dr.

BELMONT PARK

Mission Beach

Strand Way

5

Ingraham St.

Mission Bay Dr.

S. Shores Dr.

Fiesta Island Rd.

■ SeaWorld

Friars Rd.

Entrance Channel

Sea World Dr.
San Diego River

OLD TOWN

8
Sports Arena Blvd.
Ocean Beach Freeway

5
209

4
Voltaire Blvd.
Sunset Cliffs Blvd.
West Point Loma Blvd.
Midway Dr.
San Diego Sports Arena
Camino Del Rio
Pacific Hwy.

Ocean Beach Pier **3**
Abbott St.
Bacon St.
Brighton Ave.

Ocean Beach

Cable St.
Santa Monica Ave.
Newport Ave.
Narragansett
Ebers St.
Froude St.
Guizot St.
Santa Barbara St.
Orchard Ave.
Coronado Ave.
Catalina Blvd.
Nimitz Blvd.
Rosecrans St.
Ibsen St.
Lytton St.
Barnett Ave.

SAN DIEGO INTERNATIONAL AIRPORT

Restaurant	No.
Baleen	**5**
Caffe Bella Italia	**11**
Filippi's Pizza Grotto	**10**
The Green Flash	**7**
High Tide Cafe	**8**
Kono's Surf Club Cafe	**9**
The Mission	**6**
Pizza Nova	**1**
Point Loma Seafoods	**2**
Qwiig's	**3**
Rubio's Baja Grill	**12**
Sushi Ota	**13**
Thee Bungalow	**4**

Chatsworth Blvd.

Emerson St.
Carleton St.
Byron St.
2
Point Loma

1
Harbor Dr.

La Jolla
Pacific Beach
Mission Beach
Ocean Beach
Mission Bay
Old Town
Hillcrest/Uptown
Downtown
Coronado
Gaslamp Quarter
San Diego

Shelter Island Dr.

0   1/2 mi
0   1/2 km

N

Should you have appetite—and credit—left over, indulge in an intricately rich dessert like chocolate fondue, or the quartet of fruit-infused custards.

1404 Vacation Rd., Mission Bay (Paradise Point Resort). © **858/490-6363.** www.paradisepoint.com. Reservations recommended. Main courses $19–$35. AE, DC, DISC, MC, V. Sun–Thurs 5–9pm; Fri–Sat 5–10pm. Free parking. Bus: 9.

EXPENSIVE

Qwiig's ✦ CALIFORNIAN   It's taken more than a sunset view overlooking the Ocean Beach Pier to keep this moderately upscale bar and grill going since 1985; the restaurant owes its consistent popularity to well-prepared food served without pretense. Every table faces the sea, but the best view is from slightly elevated crescent-shaped booths (ask for one when reserving). Even the after-work crowd that gathers at the bar to munch on fried calamari, artichokes, and oysters can see to the pier; only sushi bar patrons in the corner miss out on the view.

Large and welcoming, Qwiig's hums pleasantly with conversation and serves food that's better than any other view-oriented oceanfront spot in this area. The fresh-fish specials are most popular; choices often include rare ahi with braised spinach and soy-sesame sauce, and fettuccine with seafood. Meat and poultry dishes include a popular prime rib, an outstanding half-pound burger, and nightly specials that always shine. The dessert list stars a boysenberry-peach cobbler made by the on-site pastry chef. Wines are well matched to the cuisine, and there are imaginative, special cocktails each night. The restaurant got its strange name from a group of Ocean Beach surfers nicknamed "qwiigs."

5083 Santa Monica Ave. (at Abbott St.), Ocean Beach. © **619/222-1101.** Reservations recommended. Main courses $6–$14 lunch, $14–$25 dinner. AE, MC, V. Sun–Fri 11:30am–2pm; daily 5:30–9pm. Bus: 35 or 923.

Thee Bungalow ✦✦ FRENCH/CONTINENTAL   This small cottage stands alone at the edge of Robb Field near the Ocean Beach channel, a romantic hideaway beckoning diners for consistently rewarding Continental cuisine. By far the fanciest restaurant in laid-back Ocean Beach, Thee Bungalow endears itself to the local crowd with daily early-bird specials ($14–$16), but oenophiles will revel in a wine list that doesn't suffer snobs yet features a multitude of classy older wines at surprisingly reasonable prices. The house specialty is crispy roast duck, served with your choice of sauce (the best is black cherry), ideally followed by one of the decadent, made-to-order dessert soufflés for two (chocolate or Grand Marnier). Another menu standout is *osso buco*–style lamb shank adorned with shallot–red wine purée. Equally appealing first courses include brie and asparagus baked in puff pastry, and warm chicken salad (stuffed with sun-dried tomatoes and basil, and then presented with feta cheese and fruit, it also doubles as a light meal). There's always a sampler plate featuring house-made patés with Dijon, cornichons, capers, and little toasts.

Regular special events and noteworthy wine-tasting dinners are listed on the website. The appealing and newish restaurant **3rd Corner** (© 619/223-2700), just across the street, is owned by the same team and has more of a seafood focus.

4996 W. Point Loma Blvd. (at Bacon St.), Ocean Beach. © **619/224-2884.** www.theebungalow.com. Reservations recommended. Main courses $19–$29; early bird specials $14–$16. AE, MC, V. Mon–Thurs 5:30–9:30pm; Fri–Sat 5–10pm; Sun 5–9pm. Free parking. Bus: 35 or 923.

MODERATE

Caffe Bella Italia ✦✦ ITALIAN   If the odd-looking stucco exterior in a less-than-promising section of P.B. looks like a dry cleaner adorned with umbrellas, well, it once was a spot for 1-hour Martinizing. But in just a few short years, this charmer has found a niche in the community—many non-beach residents have

Plan your vacation

- flights, hotels, car rentals
- cruises & vacation packages
- destination guides
- fare alerts
- go to yahoo.com, click travel

DO YOU YAHOO!?

never heard of it. Although located well away from the surf, it's lovely inside, and the food can knock your socks off. It's the best spot in the area for shellfish-laden pasta, wood-fired pizzas, and management that welcomes guests like family. Romantic lighting, sheer draperies, and warmly earthy walls create a vaguely North African ambience, assisted by the lilting Milan accents of the staff (when the din of a few dozen happy diners doesn't drown them out, that is). Every item on the menu bears the unmistakable flavor of freshness and homemade care— even the simplest curled-edge ravioli stuffed with ricotta, spinach, and pine nuts is elevated to culinary perfection, while salmon is dealt with unusually firmly, endowed with olives, capers and thick hunks of tomato in wine and garlic. You may leave wishing you could be adopted by this gracious family.

1525 Garnet Ave. (between Ingraham and Haines), Pacific Beach. © 858/273-1224. www.caffebella italia.com. Reservations suggested for dinner. Main courses $7–$15 lunch, $9–$27 dinner. AE, MC, V. Tues–Thurs 11:30am–2:30pm and 5:30–10:30pm; Fri–Sat 11am–2:30pm and 5:30–11pm; Sun 5–10:30pm. Free (small) parking lot. Bus: 9 or 27.

The Green Flash AMERICAN   Known throughout Pacific Beach for its location and hip, local clientele, the Green Flash serves adequate (and typically beachy) food at decent prices. The menu includes plenty of grilled and deep-fried seafood, straightforward steaks, and giant main-course salads. You'll also find appetizer platters of shellfish (oysters, clams, shrimp) and jalapeno "poppers" (cheese-stuffed fried peppers). The glassed-in patio is probably P.B.'s best place for people-watching, and locals congregate at sunset to catch a glimpse of the optical phenomenon for which this boardwalk hangout is named. It has something to do with the color spectrum at the moment the sun disappears below the horizon, but the scientific explanation becomes less important—and the decibel level rises—with every round of drinks.

701 Thomas Ave. (at Mission Blvd.), Pacific Beach. © 858/270-7715. Reservations not accepted. Main courses $4–$8 breakfast, $8–$13 lunch, $10–$35 dinner. AE, DC, DISC, MC, V. Daily 8am–10pm (bar till 2am). Bus: 27 or 34.

Sushi Ota 🌟🌟 JAPANESE   Masterful chef-owner Yukito Ota creates San Diego's finest sushi. This sophisticated, traditional restaurant (no Asian fusion here) is a minimalist bento box with stark white walls and black furniture, softened by indirect lighting. The sushi menu is short, because discerning regulars look first to the daily specials posted behind the counter. The city's most experienced chefs, armed with nimble fingers and very sharp knives, turn the day's fresh catch into artful little bundles accented with mounds of wasabi and ginger. The rest of the varied menu features seafood, teriyaki-glazed meats, feather-light tempura, and a variety of small appetizers perfect to accompany a large sushi order.

This restaurant is difficult to find, mainly because it's hard to believe that such outstanding dining would hide behind a laundromat and convenience store in the rear of a mini-mall that's perpendicular to the street. It's also in a nondescript part of Pacific Beach, a stone's throw from the I-5, but none of that should discourage you from seeking it out.

4529 Mission Bay Dr. (at Bunker Hill), Pacific Beach. © 858/270-5670. Reservations strongly recommended on weekends. Main courses $6–$9 lunch, $8–$16 dinner; sushi $4–$10. AE, MC, V. Tues–Fri 11:30am–2pm; daily 5:30–10:30pm. Free parking (additional lot behind the mall). Bus: 27.

INEXPENSIVE

High Tide Cafe AMERICAN   This cheerful, comfortably crowded place offers pleasant rooftop dining with an ocean view if you're lucky enough to snag a seat. Just off the Pacific Beach boardwalk, the cafe sees a lot of foot traffic and socializing locals. Those in the know go for great breakfasts—till 2pm on weekends, when there's a make-your-own bloody mary bar. Choices include skillets of huevos rancheros (eggs Mexican style) and breakfast burritos, French toast, and omelets. During happy hour (Mon–Sat 4–7pm), you'll find bargain prices on drinks and finger-lickin' appetizers. The rest of the menu is adequate, running the gamut from fish tacos to tequila fajita chicken pasta to all-American burgers.

722 Grand Ave., Pacific Beach. (C) 858/272-1999. www.hightidecafe.com. Reservations recommended on weekends. Main courses $4–$10 breakfast, $6–$15 lunch and dinner. MC, V. Mon–Fri 9am–midnight; Sat–Sun 8am–1am. Limited free parking. Bus: 27 or 34.

The Mission (Value) BREAKFAST/COFFEE & TEA   Located alongside the funky surf shops, bikini boutiques, and alternative galleries of bohemian Mission Beach, the Mission is the neighborhood's central meeting place. But it's good enough to attract more than just locals, and now has an upscale sister location east of Hillcrest—at either spot expect waits of half an hour or more on weekends. The menu features all-day breakfasts (from traditional pancakes to nouvelle egg dishes to Latin-flavored burritos and quesadillas), plus light lunch sandwiches and salads. Standouts include tamales and eggs with tomatillo sauce, chicken-apple sausage with eggs and a mound of rosemary potatoes, and cinnamon French toast with blackberry purée. Seating is casual, comfy, and conducive to lingering (tons of students, writers, and diarists hang out here), if only with a soup bowl–size latte. The other location is at 2801 University Ave. in North Park ((C) 619/220-8992); it has a similar menu and hours.

3795 Mission Blvd. (at San Jose), Mission Beach. (C) 858/488-9060. Menu items $6–$10. AE, MC, V. Daily 7am–3pm. Bus: 27 or 34.

6 La Jolla

As befits an upscale community with time (and money) on its hands, La Jolla seems to have more than its fair share of good restaurants. Happily, they're not all expensive and are more ethnically diverse than you might expect in a community that still supports a haberdashery called The Ascot Shop. While many restaurants are clustered in the village, on Prospect Street and the few blocks directly east, you can also cruise down La Jolla Boulevard or up by the La Jolla Beach & Tennis Club for additional choices.

VERY EXPENSIVE

George's at the Cove 🏵🏵🏵 CALIFORNIAN   You'll find host and namesake George Hauer at his restaurant's door most nights; he greets loyal regulars by name, and his confidence assures newcomers that they'll leave impressed with this beloved La Jolla institution. Voted San Diego's most popular restaurant in the last *Zagat Survey,* George's wins consistent praise for impeccable service, gorgeous views of the cove, and outstanding California cuisine.

The menu, in typical San Diego fashion, presents many inventive seafood options, filtered through the myriad influences of chef Trey Foshee, selected as one of America's top 10 chefs by *Food & Wine.* Classical culinary training, Hawaiian ingenuity, and a stint at Robert Redford's Utah Sundance resort are among his many accomplishments. Foshee starts each day with a trek up to Chino Farms to select the evening's produce, which work their way into exquisite starters like the Jerusalem artichoke–and-leek soup. Mains combine divergent flavors with practiced artistry, ranging from the Neiman Ranch pork tasting (three variations of naturally raised pork) to roasted lamb loin and braised lamb shoulder with a spicy

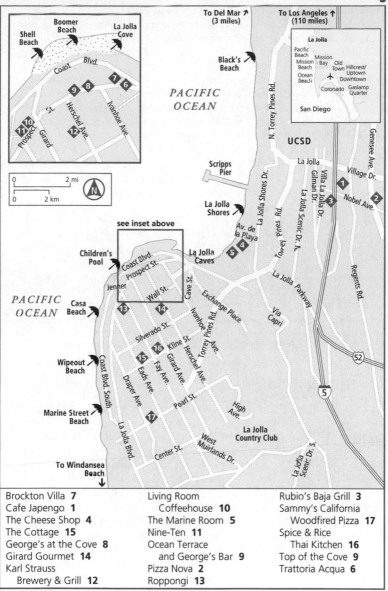

La Jolla Dining

To Del Mar ↗ (3 miles)
To Los Angeles ↑ (110 miles)

La Jolla
Pacific Beach
Mission Beach
Ocean Beach
Mission Bay
Old Town
Hillcrest/Uptown
Downtown
Coronado
Gaslamp Quarter
San Diego

Black's Beach

PACIFIC OCEAN

UCSD

Scripps Pier

La Jolla Shores

Children's Pool

La Jolla Caves

PACIFIC OCEAN

Casa Beach

Wipeout Beach

Marine Street Beach

To Windansea Beach ↓

La Jolla Country Club

see inset above

Shell Beach
Boomer Beach
La Jolla Cove

Coast Blvd.

Brockton Villa	**7**	Living Room		Rubio's Baja Grill	**3**
Cafe Japengo	**1**	Coffeehouse	**10**	Sammy's California	
The Cheese Shop	**4**	The Marine Room	**5**	Woodfired Pizza	**17**
The Cottage	**15**	Nine-Ten	**11**	Spice & Rice	
George's at the Cove	**8**	Ocean Terrace		Thai Kitchen	**16**
Girard Gourmet	**14**	and George's Bar	**9**	Top of the Cove	**9**
Karl Strauss		Pizza Nova	**2**	Trattoria Acqua	**6**
Brewery & Grill	**12**	Roppongi	**13**		

medjool date couscous and baby spinach. George's signature smoked chicken, broccoli, and black-bean soup is still a mainstay at lunch; they'll even give out the recipe for this local legend. As an alternative to dinner's pricey main courses, try the tasting menu, which offers a seasonally composed five-course sampling for $52 per person. The informal Ocean Terrace (see review below) is upstairs.

1250 Prospect St. ℭ **858/454-4244**. www.georgesatthecove.com. Reservations strongly recommended for dinner. Main courses $25–$36 dinner, $13–$17 lunch. AE, DC, DISC, MC, V. Daily 11:30am–2:30pm; Sun–Thurs 5:30–10:30pm; Fri–Sat 5–11pm. Valet parking $6. Bus: 34.

The Marine Room ★★★ *Moments* FRENCH/CALIFORNIAN   For more than 6 decades, San Diego's most celebrated dining room has been this shorefront institution, perched within kissing distance of the waves that snuggle up to La Jolla Shores. But it wasn't until the 1994 arrival of Executive Chef Bernard Guillas of Brittany that the food finally lived up to its glass-fronted room with a view. A 2001 spruce-up did away with most of the dated decor, and today the Marine Room is the city's top "special occasion" destination. Guillas and Chef de Cuisine Ron Oliver work with local produce, but never hesitate to pursue unusual flavors from other corners of the globe. So, a favored entree includes barramundi, a delicate white fish from Australia, encrusted with a hazelnut fennel pollen, garnished with flowering chive and a lacy crisp of fried lotus root. Then there's the ingot of foie gras sitting atop paper-thin slices of duck breast—the buttery concoction is smartly cut with a garnish of young tomatillo. The vigilant service is charmingly deferential, yet never condescending.

The Marine Room ranks as one of San Diego's most expensive venues, but usually is filled to the gills on weekends; weekdays it's much easier to score a table, and the four-course tasting menu available Monday through Wednesday for $49 ($65 paired with wines) is an excellent value. Ideally, schedule your reservation a half-hour or so before sunset—this will give you a chance to enjoy the scampering sandpipers and fishing pelicans while the sand takes on a honeyed aura at dusk. If you can't get in at that magic hour, experience sundown by the bar—you'll still get to enjoy the parade of illuminated rollers throughout dinner.

2000 Spindrift Dr. © 858/459-7222. www.marineroom.com. Reservations recommended, especially weekends. Main courses $15–$20 lunch, $26–$39 dinner. AE, DC, DISC, MC, V. Tues–Sat 11:30am–2pm; Sun brunch 11am–2pm; Sun–Thurs 5:30pm–9pm; Fri–Sat 5:30pm–10pm. Complimentary valet parking. Bus: 34.

Nine-Ten ★★★ CALIFORNIAN/MEDITERRANEAN   The anticipation was almost too much to bear as eager La Jollans awaited this overhaul of venerable Putnam's, and the arrival of pedigreed chef Michael Stebner (twice invited to cook at the James Beard House). But there's no overhype or spotlight jitters here; Stebner delivers on a superbly crafted and executed menu in a warmly stylish and understated space. Window-side and sidewalk tables enjoy a street scene of La Jolla's beautiful people, who in turn gaze in at mouthwatering seasonal presentations like chestnut agnolotti with fennel and sweet squash, rich veal tenderloin with rosemary and olives atop creamy polenta, and scallops braised in a rich mushroom broth. A favorite Stebner wouldn't dare take off the menu is the delicious porcini risotto topped with lobster and aromatic white truffle oil. All of the entrees are available in half portions, a boon to smaller appetites or creative types who want to compose their own multi-course "sampling" meal; there's also a five-course "Mercy of the Chef" menu for $49. It also helps leave room for never-too-heavy desserts like spicy carrot-parsnip cake, persimmon panna cotta, or refreshing honey-rosemary ice cream. When you're looking for a classy fine-dining experience—with none of the old guard "fancy" attitude—this hotel eatery stands alone on the culinary scene.

910 Prospect St. (between Fay and Girard) © 858/964-5400. www.nine-ten.com. Reservations recommended. Main courses $6–$13 breakfast, $9–$14 lunch, $24–$34 dinner. AE, DC, DISC, MC, V. Daily 6:30–11am, 11:30am–2:30pm, and 6–10:30pm. Bus: 34.

Top of the Cove ★★★ CONTINENTAL   Always vying with George's and the Marine Room for "most romantic" in local diner surveys, Top of the Cove is a mainstay for special occasions—first dates, marriage proposals, anniversaries. They're banking that its timeless elegance will enhance the evening's mood, and they're rarely disappointed. The finely proportioned historic cottage is one of the last remaining along Prospect Street, and it's shaded by 100-year-old Australian fig trees. Fireplaces glow on chilly evenings, and a gazebo and patio make the perfect setting for balmy summer dining or Sunday brunch.

The menu is peppered with French names and classic preparations with just a few welcome contemporary accents. Standouts include bacon-wrapped filet mignon in a syrah sauce, duck breast dressed with a balsamic-orange reduction, and a molasses seared elk with Swiss chard, grilled boniato and a blackberry shallot compote. Sorbet is served between courses. The dessert specialty is a bittersweet-chocolate box filled with cream and fruit in a raspberry sauce—try it with a liqueur-laced house coffee. Aficionados will thrill to the epic wine list, but its steep markup threatens to spoil the mood. Lunch is lighter—salads, sandwiches, and pastas along with a few cuts of meat and fish.

1216 Prospect St. ⒸⒸ 858/454-7779. www.topofthecove.com. Reservations recommended. Jackets suggested for men at dinner. Main courses $8–$22 lunch, $24–$38 dinner. AE, MC, V. Daily 11:30am–11:30pm. Valet parking $6. Bus: 34.

EXPENSIVE

Cafe Japengo ⓡⓡ JAPANESE/SUSHI/PACIFIC RIM/ASIAN FUSION Despite being contrived and self-conscious, Cafe Japengo is worth a trip for the food alone. With subdued lighting and a highly stylized Asian atmosphere, this restaurant is the best of several connected with La Jolla's behemoth Hyatt Regency Hotel. The beautiful people know they look even more so among the warm woods and leafy shadows here, so there's lots of posing and people-watching. It's always packed; patrons come from all over the county for Japengo's Pacific Rim fusion cuisine, which incorporates South American and even European touches.

Appetizers like duck pot stickers in coriander pesto, or the lemon grass–marinated swordfish, are superb; others, like the seared ahi "napoleon," suffer from extra ingredients that just make the dish fussy. Sushi here is the same way; Japengo features the finest and freshest fish, but churns out enormously popular specialty rolls (combinations wrapped in even more ingredients, often drenched in sauce and garnished even further). The dramatic, colorfully presented inventions are enormously popular, but sushi purists will be happiest sticking to the basics. Entrees will set you back, but choice picks include the roast duckling and crisp vegetables served moo-shu style with crepes and plum sauce, and the wok-cooked shrimp and scallops with a spicy peanut sauce.

8960 University Center Lane (opposite the Hyatt Regency La Jolla). Ⓒ 858/450-3355. www.cafejapengo.com. Reservations recommended. Main courses $12–$16 lunch, $16–$30 dinner. AE, DC, DISC, MC, V. Mon–Fri 11:30am–2:30pm; Sun–Wed 5:30–10pm; Thurs–Sat 6–11pm. Valet parking $4; validated self-parking free. Bus: 41.

Roppongi ⓡ PACIFIC RIM/ASIAN FUSION/ECLECTIC At Roppongi, the cuisines of Japan, Thailand, China, Vietnam, Korea, and India collide, sometimes gracefully, in a vibrant explosion of flavors. You might not get past the first menu page, a long list of small tapas dishes designed for sharing—each table is even preset with a tall stack of plates that quietly encourage a communal meal of successive appetizers. It takes an adventuresome palate to hip-hop from Thai satay to Chinese pot stickers to a Mongolian duck quesadilla then back to Indonesian spicy shrimp without missing a beat, but when you order right, it works (note that a number of the dishes are sweet, so ask your waiter for a good balance).

Highlights include the Polynesian crab stack, and the seared scallops on potato pancakes floating in a silky puddle of Thai basil hollandaise. Traditionally sized main courses feature seafood, meat, and game, all colorfully prepared, and the weekend brunch menu is also a real eye-opener. If your sweet tooth hasn't been sated, indulge in dessert—the caramelized Tahitian banana, framed by dollops of ice cream and a "lid" of candy glass, is scrumptious. Although the restaurant claims to utilize the Chinese discipline of feng shui to enhance contentment among diners, the bamboo-and-booth atmosphere feels a little like Denny's-meets-upscale Bangkok. That's all right, because day or night the outdoor patio is always preferable, anchored by a leaping fire pit and accented with ponds and torches.

875 Prospect St. (at Fay Ave.) ℂ 858/551-5252. www.roppongiusa.com. Reservations recommended. Main courses $16–$30; tapas $8–$24. AE, DISC, MC, V. Sun–Thurs 11:30am–10pm; Fri–Sat 11:30am–11pm.

Trattoria Acqua 𝒾𝒾 ITALIAN/MEDITERRANEAN Nestled on tiled terraces close enough to catch ocean breezes, this excellent northern Italian spot has a more relaxed ambience than similarly sophisticated Gaslamp Quarter trattorias. Rustic walls and outdoor seating shaded by flowering vines evoke a romantic Tuscan villa. A mixed crowd of suits and well-heeled couples gather to enjoy expertly prepared seasonal dishes; every table starts with bread served with an indescribably pungent Mediterranean spread. Acqua's pastas (all available as appetizers or main courses) are as good as it gets—rich, heady flavor combinations like spinach, chard, and four-cheese gnocchi, or veal-and-mortadella tortellini in fennel cream sauce. Other specialties include *osso buco alla pugliese* (veal shank braised with tomatoes, olives, capers and garlic and served over pappardelle pasta), *quaglie a beccafico* (roasted Sonoma quails with Italian bacon, spinach, raisins and pine nuts), and *salmone con lenticchie* (grilled Atlantic salmon served over Beluga lentils with a lemon-coriander vinaigrette). The well-chosen wine list has received *Wine Spectator* accolades several years in a row.

1298 Prospect St. (on Coast Walk). ℂ 858/454-0709. www.trattoriaacqua.com. Reservations recommended. Main courses $9–$19 lunch, $14–$30 dinner. AE, MC, V. Daily 11:30am–2:30pm; Sun–Thurs 5–9:30pm; Fri–Sat 5–10:30pm. Validated self-parking. Bus: 34.

MODERATE

Brockton Villa 𝒾𝒾 𝒻𝒾𝓃𝒹𝓈 BREAKFAST/CALIFORNIAN/COFFEE & TEA In a restored 1894 beach bungalow, this charming cafe has a history as intriguing as its varied, eclectic menu. Named for an early resident's hometown (Brockton, Massachusetts), the cottage is imbued with the spirit of artistic souls drawn to this breathtaking perch overlooking La Jolla Cove. Rescued by the trailblazing Pannikin Coffee Company in the 1960s, the restaurant is now independently run by a Pannikin alum.

The biggest buzz is at breakfast, when you can enjoy inventive dishes such as soufflélike "Coast Toast" (the house take on French toast) and Greek "steamers" (eggs scrambled with an espresso steamer, then mixed with feta cheese, tomato, and basil). The dozens of coffee drinks include the "Keith Richards"—four shots of espresso topped with Mexican hot chocolate (Mother's Little Helper indeed!). Lunch stars include homemade soups and salads, plus unusual sandwiches like turkey meat loaf on toasted sourdough bread with spicy tomato-mint chutney. The expanding supper menu includes Moroccan halibut with a spicy tomato relish, and villa paella (seafood and shellfish tumbled with artichoke hearts and a warm caper vinaigrette), plus pastas, stews, and grilled meats. Steep stairs from the street limit access for wheelchair users.

1235 Coast Blvd. (across from La Jolla Cove). ℂ 858/454-7393. www.brocktonvilla.com. Reservations recommended (call by Thurs for Sat–Sun brunch). Main courses $5–$9 breakfast, $7–$11 lunch, $15–$25 dinner. AE, DISC, MC, V. Mon 8am–3pm; Tues–Sun 8am–9pm.

(Moments To See . . . Perchance to Eat

Incredible ocean views, a sweeping skyline, and sailboats fluttering along the shore—it's the classic backdrop for a memorable meal. So where can you find the best views?

Downtown, the **Fish Market** and its pricier cousin **Top of the Market** overlook San Diego Bay, and the management even provides binoculars for getting a good look at aircraft carriers and other vessels. Not far is **Star of the Sea,** where an intimate room faces the elegant *Star of India* ship. Across the harbor in Coronado, the **Bay Beach Cafe** and **Peohe's,** 1201 1st St. (© 619/437-4474), offer panoramic views of the San Diego skyline, and the tony **Azzura Point** at Loews Coronado Bay Resort looks out across the bay.

In Ocean Beach, **Qwiig's** sits on a second-floor perch across the street from the sand, while in Pacific Beach, the **Green Flash** is just 5 feet from the sand (although the year-round parade of bodies may prove a distraction from the ocean). Nearby, the **Atoll** (© 619/539-8635), in the Catamaran Resort Hotel, has a romantic patio facing tranquil Mission Bay. In La Jolla, **George's at the Cove** and **Top of the Cove** are near the water (and offer panoramic elevated views), but **Brockton Villa** actually offers the La Jolla Cove outlook as advertised on every postcard stand in town.

My two favorite vistas to feast on give you a choice of city or sea view. **Bertrand at Mr. A's** (© 619/239-1377) sits on the 12th floor at Fifth and Laurel and the panorama here encompasses Balboa Park to the east, downtown to the south, and the San Diego Harbor to the west, and it's punctuated every few minutes by aircraft on their final approach. If you want to get up close and personal with the marine scene, grab your gold card and head to **The Marine Room,** where Sea-World technology (yes, SeaWorld) helped build the windows that withstand the crashing tide each day.

Ocean Terrace and George's Bar 🏖️ *Value* CALIFORNIAN   The legendary main dining room at George's at the Cove has won numerous awards for its haute cuisine. But George's also accommodates those seeking good food and a spectacular setting with a more reasonable price tag: The upstairs Ocean Terrace and George's Bar prepare similar dishes as well as new creations in the same kitchen as the high-priced fare. The two areas offer indoor and spectacular outdoor seating overlooking La Jolla Cove, and the same great service as the main dining room. For dinner, you can choose from several seafood or pasta dishes, or have something out of the ordinary like George's meatloaf served with mushroom-and-corn mashed potatoes. The award-winning smoked chicken, broccoli, and black-bean soup appears on both menus.

1250 Prospect St. © 858/454-4244. www.georgesatthecove.com. Reservations recommended. Main courses $9–$12 lunch, $12–$20 dinner. AE, DC, DISC, MC, V. Daily 11am–10pm (Fri–Sat till 10:30pm). Valet parking $6. Bus: 34.

Spice & Rice Thai Kitchen 🏖️ THAI   This attractive Thai restaurant is a couple of blocks from the village's tourist crush—far enough to ensure effortless parking.

The lunch crowd consists of shoppers and curious tourists, while dinner is quieter; all the local businesses have shut down. The food is excellent, with polished presentations and expert renditions of the classics like pad Thai, satay, curry, and glazed duck. The starters often sound as good as the entrees: Consider making a grazing meal of house specialties like "gold bags" (minced pork, vegetables, glass noodles, and herbs wrapped in crispy rice paper and served with earthy plum sauce) or prawns with yellow curry lobster sauce; crispy calamari is flavored with tamarind sauce and chile sauce. The romantically lit covered front patio has a secluded garden feel, and inside tables also have indirect lighting. Despite the passage of time, this all-around satisfier remains something of an insider's secret.

7734 Girard Ave. ⓒ 858/456-0466. Reservations recommended. Main courses $8–$13. AE, MC, V. Mon–Thurs 11am–3pm and 5–10pm; Fri–Sat 11am–3pm and 5–11pm; Sun 5–10pm. Bus: 34.

INEXPENSIVE

The Cottage ⋆ BREAKFAST/CALIFORNIAN   La Jolla's best—and friendliest—breakfast is served at this turn-of-the-20th-century bungalow on a sunny village corner. Newly modernized, the cottage is light and airy, but most diners opt for tables outside, where a charming white picket fence encloses the trellis-shaded brick patio. Omelets and egg dishes feature Mediterranean, Asian, or classic American touches; my favorite has creamy mashed potatoes, bacon, and melted cheese folded inside. The Cottage bakes its own muffins, breakfast breads, and—you can quote me on this—the best brownies in San Diego. While breakfast dishes are served all day, toward lunch the kitchen begins turning out freshly made, healthful soups, light meals, and sandwiches. Summer dinners (never heavy, always tasty) are a delight, particularly when you're seated before dark on a balmy seaside night.

7702 Fay Ave. (at Kline St.). ⓒ 858/454-8409. www.cottagelajolla.com. Reservations accepted for dinner only. Main courses $6–$9 breakfast, $7–$11 lunch, $9–$15 dinner. AE, DISC, MC, V. Daily 7:30am–3pm; dinner (June–Sept only) Tues–Sat 5–9:30pm. Bus: 34.

7 Coronado

Rather like the conservative, old-school navy aura that pervades the entire "island," Coronado's dining options are reliable and often quite good, but the restaurants aren't breaking new culinary ground.

Some notable exceptions are the resort dining rooms, which seem to be waging a little rivalry over who can attract the most prestigious, multiple-award-winning executive chef. If you're in the mood for a special-occasion meal that'll knock your socks off, consider **Azzura Point** (ⓒ 619/424-4000), in Loews Coronado Bay Resort (p. 93). With its plushly upholstered, gilded, and view-endowed setting, this stylish dining room wins continual raves from deep-pocketed San Diego foodies willing to cross the bay for inventive and artistic California-Mediterranean creations. The Hotel Del's fancy **Prince of Wales** (ⓒ 619/522-8496) is equally scenic, gazing at the beach across the hotel's regal Windsor Lawn; the eclectic California menu always showcases the best of seasonally fresh ingredients.

But if you seek ethnic or funky food, better head back across the bridge. Mexican fare (gringo-style, but well practiced) is served on the island at popular **Miguel's Cocina,** inside El Cordova Hotel (ⓒ 619/437-4237).

EXPENSIVE

The Brigantine ⋆ SEAFOOD   The Brigantine is best known for its oyster-bar happy hour from 3 to 6pm and 10 to 11pm daily (4:30pm–close on Sun).

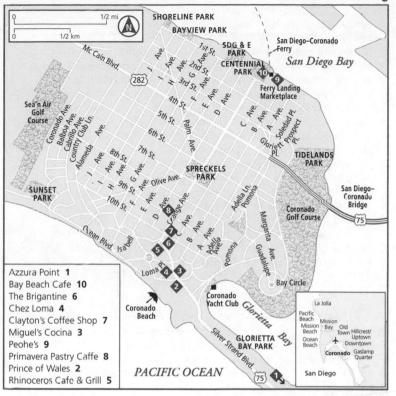

Azzura Point **1**
Bay Beach Cafe **10**
The Brigantine **6**
Chez Loma **4**
Clayton's Coffee Shop **7**
Miguel's Cocina **3**
Peohe's **9**
Primavera Pastry Caffe **8**
Prince of Wales **2**
Rhinoceros Cafe & Grill **5**

Beer, margaritas, and food are heavily discounted, and you can expect standing room only. Early-bird "sundowner" specials include a seafood, steak, or chicken entree served with soup or salad, a side of veggies, and bread for $16. The food is good, not great, but the congenial atmosphere is the certifiable draw. Inside, the decor is upscale and resolutely nautical; outside, there's a pleasant patio with a heaters to take the chill off the night air. At lunch, you can get everything from crab cakes or fish and chips to fresh fish or pasta. Lunch specials come with sourdough bread and two side dishes. The bar and oyster bar are open nightly until at least 11pm.

1333 Orange Ave. ✆ **619/435-4166.** www.brigantine.com. Reservations recommended on weekends. Main courses $7–$11 lunch, $16–$26 dinner. AE, DC, MC, V. Daily 11am–2:30pm (Sun opens at 10am); Mon–Thurs 5–10pm; Fri–Sat 5–10:30pm; Sun 4:30–9:30pm. Bus: 901, 902, or 904.

Chez Loma ✿✿ FRENCH You'd be hard-pressed to find a more romantic dining spot than this intimate Victorian cottage filled with antiques and subdued candlelight. The house dates from 1889, the French-Continental restaurant from 1975. Tables are scattered throughout the house and on the enclosed garden terrace; an upstairs wine salon, reminiscent of a Victorian parlor, is a cozy spot for coffee or conversation.

Among the creative entrees are salmon with smoked-tomato vinaigrette, and roast duckling with lingonberry, port, and burnt-orange sauce. All main courses are served with soup or salad, rice or potatoes, and fresh vegetables. California

---

ⓒ Picnic Fare

San Diego's benign climate lends itself to dining alfresco. An excellent spot to pick up sandwiches is **The Cheese Shop,** a gourmet deli with locations downtown at 627 4th Ave. (ⓒ 619/232-2303) and in La Jolla Shores at 2165 Avenida de la Playa (ⓒ 858/459-3921). Other places to buy picnic fare include **Girard Gourmet,** 7837 Girard Ave., La Jolla (ⓒ 858/454-3321); **Boudin Sourdough Bakery and Cafe** (ⓒ 619/234-1849) and the **Farmer's Market,** both in Horton Plaza; and **Old Town Liquor and Deli,** 2304 San Diego Ave. (ⓒ 619/291-4888).

Another spot that's very popular is **Point Loma Seafoods,** on the water's edge in front of the Municipal Sportfishing Pier, at 2805 Emerson near Scott Street, south of Rosecrans and west of Harbor Drive (ⓒ 619/223-1109). There's a fish market here, and you can pick up seafood sandwiches, fresh sushi, and salads to go. If you decide to make your own sandwiches, the best bread in the county comes from **Bread & Cie.,** 350 University Ave., Hillcrest (ⓒ 619/683-9322), and **Primavera Pastry Caffe,** 956 Orange Ave., Coronado (ⓒ 619/435-4191).

---

wines and American microbrews are available. Follow dinner with a silky crème caramel or Kahlúa crème brûlée. Chez Loma's service is attentive, the herb rolls are addictive, and early birds enjoy specially priced meals.

1132 Loma (off Orange Ave.). ⓒ **619/435-0661.** www.chezloma.com. Reservations recommended. Main courses $20–$30. AE, DC, MC, V. Daily 5–10pm; Sun brunch 10am–2pm. Bus: 901, 902, or 904.

MODERATE

Bay Beach Cafe AMERICAN   This loud, friendly gathering place isn't on a real beach, but enjoys a prime perch on San Diego Bay. Seated indoors or on a glassed-in patio, diners gaze endlessly at the city skyline, which is dramatic by day and breathtaking at night. The cafe is quite popular at happy hour, when the setting sun glimmers on downtown's mirrored high-rises. The ferry docks at a wooden pier a few steps away, discharging passengers into the complex of gift shops and restaurants with a New England fishing-village theme. Admittedly, the food takes a back seat to the view, but the lunchtime menu of burgers, sandwiches, salads, and appetizers is modestly priced and satisfying; dinner entrees—chops and pastas—aren't quite good enough for the price.

1201 First St. (Ferry Landing Marketplace). ⓒ **619/435-4900.** Reservations recommended for dinner on weekends. Main courses $9–$11 lunch, $14–$19 dinner. DISC, MC, V. Mon–Fri 11am–9pm; Sat–Sun 8am–11am. Free parking. Bus: 901, 903, or 904.

Rhinoceros Cafe & Grill ⓡ AMERICAN   With its quirky name and something-for-everyone menu, this light, bright bistro is a welcome addition to the Coronado dining scene. It's more casual than it looks from the street and offers large portions, though the kitchen can be a little heavy-handed with sauces and spices. At lunch, every other patron seems to be enjoying the popular penne à la vodka in creamy tomato sauce; favorite dinner specials are Italian cioppino, Southwestern-style meatloaf, and simple herb-roasted chicken. Plenty of crispy fresh salads balance out the menu. There's a good wine list, or you might decide to try Rhino Chaser's American Ale.

1166 Orange Ave. ℭ 619/435-2121. Main courses $10–$22. AE, DISC, MC, V. Daily 11am–2:45pm; Sun–Thurs 5–9pm; Fri–Sat 5–10pm. Street parking usually available. Bus: 901, 902, or 904.

INEXPENSIVE

Clayton's Coffee Shop AMERICAN/BREAKFAST   The Hotel Del isn't the only relic of a bygone era in Coronado—just wait until you see this humble neighborhood favorite. Clayton's has occupied this corner spot seemingly forever, at least since a time when *everyone's* menus were full of plain American good eatin' in the $1 to $5 range. Now their horseshoe counter, chrome barstools, and well-worn pleather-lined booths are "retro," but the burgers, fries, and chicken noodle soup just as good—plus you can still play three oldies for a quarter on the table-side jukebox. Behind the restaurant, Clayton's Mexican takeout kitchen does a brisk business in homemade tamales.

959 Orange Ave. ℭ 619/437-8811. Menu items under $10. No credit cards. Mon–Sat 6am–8pm; Sun 6am–2pm. Bus: 901, 902, or 904.

Primavera Pastry Caffe ⚘ *Value* BREAKFAST/LIGHT FARE   If the name sounds familiar, it's because this fantastic little cafe—the best of its kind on the island—is part of the family that includes Primavera Ristorante, up the street. In addition to fresh-roasted coffee and espresso drinks, it serves omelets and other breakfast treats (until 1:30pm), burgers and deli sandwiches on the delicious house bread, and a daily fresh soup. It's the kind of spot where half the customers are greeted by name. Locals rave about the "Yacht Club" sandwich, a croissant filled with yellowfin tuna, and the breakfast croissant, topped with scrambled ham and eggs and cheddar cheese. I can't resist Primavera's fat, gooey cinnamon buns.

956 Orange Ave. ℭ 619/435-4191. Main courses $4–$7. MC, V. Daily 6:30am–5pm (closes at 6pm in summer). Bus: 901, 902, or 904.

8 Off the Beaten Path

Don't limit your dining experience in San Diego to the main tourist zones outlined above. Five minutes north of Mission Valley is the mostly business neighborhood of Kearny Mesa, home to San Diego's best Asian venues. One to try is **Emerald Restaurant** ⚘⚘, 3709 Convoy St. (ℭ **858/565-6888**), which occupies a nondescript building sandwiched between the 805 and 163 freeways; the room is spare, but the kitchen exhibits finesse with southern Chinese delicacies and always has excellent (sometimes pricey) live fish specials. Nearby is **Jasmine** ⚘, 4609 Convoy St. (ℭ **858/268-0888**), which at lunch showcases Hong Kong–style dumplings that are wheeled around the room on carts; dinners are more elaborate, with Peking duck two ways a good choice.

Just east of Hillcrest (south and parallel to Mission Valley) is Adams Avenue, one of the city's streets of character, with antiques shops and bistros en route to Kensington. Here you'll find the **Kensington Grill** ⚘⚘, 4055 Adams Ave., next to the Ken Cinema (ℭ **619/281-4014**), owned by the same crew in charge of the Gaslamp's hip Chive restaurant and featuring contemporary American cuisine in a chic setting that draws lots of neighborhood types. In nearby Normal Heights, **Jyoti Bihanga,** 3351 Adams Ave. (ℭ **619/282-4116**), caters to followers of Sri Chinmoy and delivers a vegetarian menu of Indian-influenced salads, wraps, and curries; the "neatloaf" is a winner. All items are priced under $10.

7

What to See & Do

You won't run out of things to see and do, especially if outdoor activities are high on the agenda. The San Diego Zoo, SeaWorld, and the Wild Animal Park are the city's three top attractions, but leave room in the schedule for Balboa Park's museums, downtown's Gaslamp Quarter, the beaches, shopping in Old Town, and perhaps a performance at one of our prized live theatres.

Designing the perfect itinerary—particularly for a short stay—depends a lot on your personal interests. Here are a few suggestions for how to see the best of the city during a limited visit.

SUGGESTED ITINERARIES

If You Have 1 Day

With only 1 day in San Diego, you'll have to choose between two different kind of itineraries: the wildlife route versus a scenic tour of the city. If you go for the **animal agenda,** decide on the San Diego Zoo or Sea-World, both of which require at least a half-day to explore. Either way, get there when the gates open to maximize your touring. Plan to leave the animals by early afternoon for a late lunch; I recommend The Prado near the zoo, or Baleen near SeaWorld. If a late-afternoon shopping spree beckons, explore the classy boutiques of La Jolla or the international shops of Bazaar del Mundo in Old Town. Or, if shopping isn't your bag, breathe in the seaside ambience by walking along the Pacific Beach boardwalk (for the blond and bronzed) or the downtown Embarcadero (which bustles with fishing boats against a naval backdrop).

If you pick the **scenic agenda,** you don't need to worry about renting a car if you go with Old Town Trolley Tours, where a $24 ticket buys you all-day privileges along the trackless trolley's 30-mile route visiting many of the city's highlights, including Horton Plaza and the Gaslamp Quarter, the Hotel del Coronado, Balboa Park, Old Town, and more. You can get on and off the trolley through the day (one comes by every 30 min.), spending as little or as much time as you want at each stop.

Whichever agenda you choose, finish the day in the Gaslamp Quarter, which always promises a lively evening street scene. Pick from dozens of restaurants, and stick around for live music after dinner—if you have the energy!

If You Have 1 Night

If you're in town just briefly for a convention but on your own for the evening, you'll find plenty of nightlife options in the Gaslamp Quarter. But if the drink-and-dine scene is not your thing, there are alternatives, especially during summer or on Thursday through Saturday nights. In summer months the zoo and SeaWorld are open until 9pm or later. The San Diego Symphony's pops concerts are held on weekends from late June to August at the Embarcadero. Year-round, you'll find several museums open

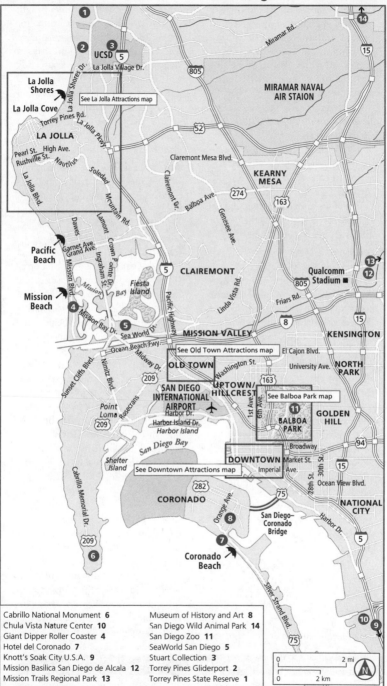

San Diego Area Attractions

See La Jolla Attractions map

See Old Town Attractions map

See Balboa Park map

See Downtown Attractions map

Cabrillo National Monument **6**
Chula Vista Nature Center **10**
Giant Dipper Roller Coaster **4**
Hotel del Coronado **7**
Knott's Soak City U.S.A. **9**
Mission Basilica San Diego de Alcala **12**
Mission Trails Regional Park **13**

Museum of History and Art **8**
San Diego Wild Animal Park **14**
San Diego Zoo **11**
SeaWorld San Diego **5**
Stuart Collection **3**
Torrey Pines Gliderport **2**
Torrey Pines State Reserve **1**

late on Thursdays, including the Museum of Contemporary Art in La Jolla and the Museum of Art and the Museum of Photographic Arts in Balboa Park. At the latter, the cinema features a repertory of classic films several nights a week.

Don't forget that the San Diego Trolley system offers an easy and cheap way to access Old Town, Mission Valley, and Tijuana from downtown, and you can take a water taxi or the ferry over to Coronado and stroll the Ferry Landing Marketplace. Or if you want to let someone else do all the work, board one of the harbor dinner cruises for an easy evening.

If You Have 2 Days

With 2 full days in the city, you can devote each one to the zoo and SeaWorld. After the zoo, allow several hours for strolling through the rest of Balboa Park, enjoying the great architecture and peeking into a couple of its fantastic museums. Some, such as the Automotive Museum, the Model Railroad Museum, the Mingei International Museum, the Museum of San Diego History, and the Timken, take less than an hour to visit. If the weather is too perfect to believe, after you've visited SeaWorld, rent your favorite recreational gear (bikes, inline skates, kayaks—they're all available), and spend a few hours at our splendid public aquatic park, Mission Bay.

If You Have 3 Days

Plan the first 2 days as above, and spend the third at Coronado for a tour of the majestic Hotel del Coronado and lunch on the island. Or, devote the day to La Jolla, where there's an excellent contemporary art museum and a bevy of outdoor dining venues. If it's summer or fall, be sure to allow a few hours for swimming or sunbathing at one of San Diego's beaches (don't miss a sunset walk along the coast any time of year). If it's winter, spend the afternoon on a whale-watching cruise. Take in an evening performance at the Globe Theatres, the La Jolla Playhouse, or with San Diego's symphony or opera.

If You Have 4 Days or More

With an extended stay comes the opportunity to indulge your personal passions. For example, you can play one of San Diego's 90-plus golf courses; take kayak lessons along La Jolla's coast; go ballooning in Del Mar; try hang gliding from Torrey Pines; or poke around a historic house museum (like the Marston House or Villa Montezuma). Other worthwhile highlights include the Cabrillo National Monument, Old Town State Historic Park, and the Birch Aquarium at Scripps. If you haven't tired of animal sightings, spend the day at the Wild Animal Park. Or, assemble a picnic in Hillcrest with sandwiches from Bread & Cie. or the bountiful deli at Whole Foods; Presidio Park and Torrey Pines State Park are among my favorite spots for a sack lunch.

Another option would be to explore beyond the city limits. Take the trolley to Tijuana and spend a day shopping and sampling south-of-the-border flavor. Or treat the kids to a day at LEGOLAND in Carlsbad (40 min. north of downtown), or the Disneyland Resort in Anaheim (a little more than 1½ hr. away); or enjoy the dynamic desert scenery of Anza-Borrego (1½ hr. away).

1 The Three Major Animal Parks

Looking for wild times? San Diego supplies them as no other city can. The world-famous **San Diego Zoo** is home to more than 800 animal species, many of them rare and exotic. A sister attraction, the **Wild Animal Park,** offers another 3,500 creatures representing 430 species in an *au naturel* setting. And, Shamu and his friends form a veritable chorus line at **SeaWorld San Diego**— waving their flippers, waddling across an ersatz Antarctica, and blowing killer-whale kisses—in more than a dozen shows a day.

In 1999, San Diego's "Big Three" family attractions were joined by the instantly popular **LEGOLAND California,** which is located about 30 miles away in the seaside community of Carlsbad. You'll find full information on visiting the park on p. 235.

San Diego Zoo *Kids*   More than 4,000 creatures reside at this celebrated and influential zoo, operated by the Zoological Society of San Diego. The Society was founded in 1916 with a handful of animals originally brought here for the Panama-California International Exposition (many of the buildings you see in surrounding Balboa Park were built for that fair). Legend has it that the zoo's founder, Dr. Harry Wegeforth, a local physician and lifelong animal lover, once braved the fury of an injured tiger to toss medicine into its roaring mouth.

In the early days of the zoo, "Dr. Harry" traveled around the world and bartered native Southwestern animals such as rattlesnakes and sea lions for more exotic species. The loan of two giant pandas from the People's Republic of China in 1996 was a twist on the long-standing tradition: Instead of exchanging exotic species, the San Diego Zoo agreed to pay $1 million annually for the pandas, to aid conservation efforts in China (see "Panda-monium" sidebar below). The 100-acre zoo is also an accredited botanical garden, lavished with more than 700,000 plants. Dr. Harry brought home plants from every location where animals were acquired, ensuring what would become the zoo's naturalistic and mature environment. The species of flora from a variety of climate zones are said to be worth more than the animal collection, and in many cases (such as the eucalyptus for the koalas) the plants also serve as the primary diet of the animals.

The giant pandas may be the marquee attraction, but the zoo has many other rare and wondrous species: Buerger's tree kangaroos of New Guinea, long-billed kiwis from New Zealand, wild Przewalski horses from Mongolia, lowland gorillas from Africa, and giant tortoises from the Galapagos. The Zoological Society is involved with animal preservation efforts around the world and has engineered many "firsts" in breeding: It was here that the Anegada iguana was successfully bred in captivity for the first time, and where a home for a captive-breeding group of the recently discovered Visayan warty pigs was created.

Of course, the zoo's traditional beasties—lions, elephants, giraffes, tigers, and bears—prowl around as well, and a diverse collection of tropical birds is experienced via sprawling walk-through aviaries. The zoo was a forerunner in creating bar-less, moated enclosures that allow animals to roam in sophisticated environments resembling their natural habitats. The most recent of these is **Absolutely Apes**, a habitat that opened in 2003 to showcase orangutans and siamangs of Indonesia; it marks the first time these primates of a single ecosystem will share an enclosure at the zoo. This exhibit's debut also marks the first stage in the ongoing $26 million "heart of the zoo" project, designed not only to enrich primate and other quarters but to improve human traffic flow in the most congested part of the zoo. In addition to the **Panda Discovery Center**, other highlights include **Ituri Forest**, which simulates a central African rainforest teeming with forest buffalos, otters, monkeys, and shy okapis; **Tiger River**, a steep gorge with lush enclosures for fishing cats, tapirs, and tigers; the **Polar Bear Plunge**, where you'll find a 2.2-acre summer tundra habitat inhabited by Siberian reindeer, yellow-throated martens, and diving ducks, along with the titular heroes; and the **Children's Zoo,** which features a nursery with baby animals and a petting area where kids can cuddle up to sheep, goats, and the like. There's also an entertaining **sea lion show** at the 3,000-seat amphitheater (though this is easy to skip if you're headed to SeaWorld).

My favorite way to experience the zoo is to spend the day on foot navigating the lush canyons and dry mesas that bisect the facility. But if a lot of walking—some of it on steep hills, some of it quite exposed to afternoon sun—isn't your passion, the zoo offers a 40-minute **guided bus tour** that provides a narrated overview and covers about 75% of the facility. It costs $10 for adults, $5.50 for children 3 to 11, and is included in the "Best Value" admission package. You get only brief glimpses of the enclosures, and animals won't always be visible, so you'll be enticed to revisit some of the areas. Included in the bus ticket is access to the un-narrated **Express Bus,** which allows you to get on and off at one of five different stops along the same route. You can also get an aerial perspective from the **Skyfari,** which costs $2.50 per person each way. The ride lasts about 5 minutes—but it's better for a bird's-eye view than it is for spotting creatures. I recommend taking the complete bus tour first thing in the morning, when the animals are more active (waits for the bus tour can top an hour by midday). Ideally, after the bus tour, take the Skyfari to the far side of the park and wend your way back on foot or by Express Bus to revisit animals that you want to see.

In addition to snack bars and fast-food options, the zoo has **Albert's** ⟨R⟩, a beautiful restaurant at the lip of a canyon and named after the zoo's most famous ape. It's located behind Gorilla Tropics, and although the food is unexceptional, Albert's is a lovely place in which to break up the middle of the day (when the animals are laziest).

2920 Zoo Dr., Balboa Park. ⟨C⟩ 619/234-3153 (recorded info) or 619/231-1515. www.sandiegozoo.org. Admission $20 adults, $12 children 3–11, free for military in uniform. "Best Value" package (admission, guided bus tour, round-trip Skyfari aerial tram) $32 adults, $29 seniors, $20 children. AE, DISC, MC, V. Mid-June to Aug 9am–9pm (grounds close at 10pm); rest of year daily 9am–4pm (grounds close at 5 or 6pm). Bus: 7 or 7A/B. Take I-5 to Pershing Dr., then follow the signs.

San Diego Wild Animal Park ⟨RRR⟩ ⟨Kids⟩   Located 34 miles north of San Diego, outside of Escondido, this terrific "zoo of the future" will transport you to the African plains and other faraway landscapes. Originally established as a breeding facility for the San Diego Zoo (the Zoological Society oversees both operations), the 1,800-acre Wild Animal Park now holds around 3,500 animals representing 430 different species—many of them endangered. Approximately 650 animals are born every year in the park. What makes the Wild Animal Park unique is that many of the animals roam freely in vast enclosures, allowing giraffes to interact with antelopes, much as they would in Africa. You'll find the largest crash of rhinos at any zoological facility in the world; a wonderful exhibit for the critically endangered California condor; and a mature landscape of exotic vegetation from many corners of the globe. You can stroll through an epiphyllum house, a bonsai pavilion and protea garden, and then purchase the unusual species to take home from the Plant Trader shop. Although the San Diego Zoo may be world famous, it is the Wild Animal Park that many visitors celebrate as their favorite. To me, they are both essential components of the San Diego experience; to maximize your enjoyment see the zoo first, then make the trek to the Wild Animal Park a few days later. If you have a good zoo at home and have only one day for animals in San Diego, go for the Wild Animal Park, an experience which is all but unduplicated anywhere else.

(*Fun Fact* **Panda-monium**

Giant pandas are among the rarest mammals in the world: It is estimated that only 1,000 remain in the wild, where they live in dense bamboo and coniferous forests at altitudes above 4,000 feet. Their numbers have dwindled due to the destruction of their natural habitat and poaching. Currently there are about 110 giant pandas in captivity, mostly in China; zoos in Atlanta, Washington, D.C., Mexico City, Japan, and Germany also have giant pandas. In 1996, following 3 years of intense negotiation by the U.S. Department of the Interior, the Wolong Giant Panda Conservation Centre in China, and the Chinese government, two giant pandas from China, Shi Shi (then a 13-year-old male born in the wild) and Bai Yun (a 3-year-old female born in captivity), arrived at the San Diego Zoo.

Successful breeding in captivity is an unusually delicate process: Female pandas are in estrus for only 2 or 3 days a year, and otherwise avoid interaction with other pandas. Shi Shi turned out to be a less-than-suitable suitor, although In 1999, through artificial insemination, Bai Yun gave birth to a healthy baby girl. She was named Hua Mei (pronounced "hwa may"), meaning "China USA," and was the first surviving panda cub born in the U.S. For his lack of mating interest, Shi Shi was returned to Wolong in January 2003. In the same month the zoo welcomed 13-year-old Gao Gao, a male who was born in the wild and taken to Wolong after he was found wounded at a young age—probably from a fight with another male panda. From the start, the more rambunctious, inquisitive, and alert Gao Gao gave zoo researchers hope that he would get along better with Bai Yun. Remarkably, the two mated right after their introduction and the zoo hopes to have a new panda baby by the time you read this. Alas, the news won't be known until after we go to press: Females don't show signs of pregnancy until only a few days before delivery.

Giant pandas are related to both bears and raccoons. They are bearlike in shape, with striking black-and-white markings, and have unique front paws that enable them to grasp stalks of bamboo. Bamboo makes up about 95% of their diet, and they eat as much as 84 pounds of food every day. This takes them 10 to 16 hours, so there's a pretty good chance that you'll see them eating. Fortunately, the efforts of panda specialists around the globe are starting to pay off: In the last few years, the pregnancy rate of females in captivity has risen, and infant survival has dramatically increased.

Because of the exhibit's enormous popularity and the fact that the pandas are not always on display, the zoo provides a panda-viewing hot line (© **888/MY-PANDA**). Call before you go.

The central focus of the park is the 5-mile **Wgasa Bush Line Railway** 🐾🐾, a 60-minute monorail ride that's included in the price of admission. Trains leave every 10 minutes or so from the station, and lines build up by late morning—make this your first or last attraction of the day (the animals are more active anyway), and for the best views, sit on the right-hand side. The monorail passes through areas designated as East Africa, South Africa, Asian Plains, and the

Asian Waterhole, through swaying grasses and along rocky outcrops. A pair of binoculars is handy to have along since many of the animals can be hundreds of feet away, but the monorail is meant to give you an experience of the open plains and wildlife diversity, not the up-close experience of a traditional zoo.

The monorail is the signature attraction of the park, but you'll find other rewarding exhibits. There are several excellent, self-guided walking tours: the 1¾-mile **Kilimanjaro Safari Walk** 𝆑𝆑, which visits the Australian rainforest and the fringe of East Africa; the **Heart of Africa** 𝆑𝆑, a ¾-mile trail that winds through a 32-acre wilderness with varied habitats (dense forest, flourishing wetlands, sprawling savannas, and open plains) to a cheetah overlook and a giraffe-feeding station; and the ¼-mile round-trip hike to **Condor Ridge** 𝆑, which ascends past 13 rare or endangered North American species, including the fabulously ugly California condor.

Nairobi Village is the commercial hub of the park, but even here are interesting animal exhibits, including the **nursery area,** where irresistible young 'uns can be seen frolicking, being bottle-fed, and sleeping; a **petting station;** the **lowland gorillas** 𝆑; and the **South American Aviary** 𝆑. There are amphitheaters for a bird show and another featuring elephants, scheduled two or three times daily. Within Nairobi Village are souvenir stores, and several spots for mediocre dining. Visitors should be prepared for sunny, often downright hot weather. It's not unusual for temperatures to be 5 to 10 degrees warmer here than in San Diego—sunscreen, a hat, and light clothing are always a good idea.

If you really want to get up close and personal with the animals, take one of the park's **Photo Caravans** 𝆑𝆑𝆑, which shuttles groups of eight in flatbed trucks out into the open areas that are not accessible to the general public. In my experience, the photos are secondary to the sheer enjoyment of crossing the fence to meet the rhinos, ostriches, zebras, and deer on their home turf, even getting nose-to-nose with giraffes along the way—it's not quite as dramatic as a real African safari, but it ranks pretty high. There are two different itineraries available, each 1¾ hours long, or you can take both trips with a 30-minute break in between—either way you'll want to make reservations in advance by calling ⓒ **619/718-3050.** The price is $99 per person for one caravan, or $145 for both

---

⸨Moments⸩ Things That Go Bump in the Night

The Wild Animal Park's **Roar & Snore program,** which runs every Friday, Saturday, and Sunday from April to October, lets you camp out next to the animal compound and observe the nocturnal movements of rhinos, lions, and other creatures. The park provides all the equipment, including a cookout dinner and a pancake breakfast. You'll check in at 4pm and go for a guided sunset hike; after dinner, sit around the campfire listening to tales of animal behavior punctuated by the extraordinary animal calls emanating from dark corners of the park. After breakfast in the morning (sorry, no showers), you'll take a dawn hike through the Heart of Africa, and then spend the day enjoying the rest of the park. The 1-night camp-overs are $126 for adults, $106 for kids 8 to 11; children under 8 are not permitted, and campers under 18 must accompanied by an adult. To request Roar & Snore information by mail or to make reservations, call ⓒ **619/718-3050.** Don't forget your sleeping bag!

(park admission included); children must be at least 8 years old, and ages 8 to 17 must be accompanied by an adult.

15500 San Pasqual Valley Rd., Escondido. ℂ 760/747-8702. www.wildanimalpark.org. Admission $27 adults, $24 seniors 60 and over, $20 children 3–11, free for children under 3 and military in uniform. AE, DISC, MC, V. Daily 9am–4pm (grounds close at 5pm); extended hours during summer and Festival of Lights (2 weekends in Dec). Parking $6. Take I-15 north from San Diego to Via Rancho Pkwy.; follow the signs for about 3 miles.

SeaWorld San Diego *Kids* One of the best-marketed attractions in California, SeaWorld is a main draw for many visitors coming to San Diego and celebrates its 40th year of operation in 2004. With each passing year the educational pretext increasingly takes a back seat to slick shows and rides, but the 165-acre aquatic theme park—owned by the Anheuser-Busch Corporation—is perhaps the country's premiere showplace for marine life, made politically correct with a nominally informative atmosphere. At its heart, SeaWorld is a shoreside family entertainment center where the performers are dolphins, otters, sea lions, walruses, and seals. The 20- to 30-minute shows run several times each throughout the day, while visitors can rotate through the various open-air amphitheaters.

Several successive 4-ton black-and-white killer whales have functioned as the park's mascot, and the **Shamu Adventure** is SeaWorld's most popular show. Performed in a 5,500-seat stadium, the stage is a 7-million-gallon pool lined with plexiglass walls that offer magnified views of the huge performers. But you won't want to sit in the seats down front—a highlight of the act is multiple drenchings in the first 12 or so rows of spectators. The slapstick **Sea Lion and Otter Show,** the fast-paced **Dolphin Show,** and the **Pet's Playhouse** are other performing animal routines, all in huge venues seating more than 1,000 guests. In 2003, a "4-D" movie, **R.L. Stine's Haunted Lighthouse,** opened starring Christopher Lloyd, Lea Thompson, and a roster of multisensory effects. There is also a small collection of rides, including **Shipwreck Rapids**, a wet adventure ride on raftlike inner tubes through caverns, waterfalls, and wild rivers, and **Wild Arctic,** a motion simulator helicopter trip to the frozen north.

Guests disembarking Wild Arctic (or those using the ride bypass) find themselves in the midst of one of SeaWorld's real specialties: carefully simulated marine environments. In this case it's an **arctic research station**, surrounded by beluga whales and polar bears. Other animal environments worth seeing are **Manatee Rescue, Shark Encounter,** and the **Penguin Encounter.** The 2-acre hands-on area called **Shamu's Happy Harbor** encourages kids to handle things—and features everything from a pretend pirate ship, with plenty of netted towers, to tube crawls, slides, and chances to get wet.

The **Dolphin Interaction Program** creates an opportunity for people to meet bottlenose dolphins. Although the program stops short of allowing you to swim with the dolphins, it does offer the opportunity to wade waist-deep, and plenty of time to stroke the mammals and to try giving training commands. This 1-hour program includes some classroom time before you wriggle into a wet suit and climb into the water for 20 minutes with the dolphins. It costs $140 per person (not including park admission); participants must be age 6 or older. One step further is the **Trainer for a Day** program, which is a 7-hour work shift with an animal trainer. Food preparation, feeding, a training session with a dolphin, and lunch is included; the price is $395 per person. This program is limited to three participants daily, and the minimum age is 13. Advance reservations are required for both programs (ℂ 877/436-5746).

Although SeaWorld is best known as the home to pirouetting dolphins and fluke flinging killer whales, the facility also plays a role in rescuing and rehabilitating

(*Value* Now That's What I Call a Deal!

Always aware of what side their tourism bread is buttered on, San Diego's three main animal attractions have joined forces with combo ticket deals that reward big savings to visitors with recreational stamina. Here's how it works: If you plan to visit both the zoo and Wild Animal Park, a two-park ticket (the "Best Value" zoo package, plus Wild Animal Park admission) is $53 adults, $36 children 3 to 11 (a $59/$39 value). You get one visit to each attraction, to be used within 5 days of purchase. If you throw in SeaWorld within the same 5 days, this combo works out to $89 adults, $63 children ages 3 to 9 (a $103/$75 value). If the museums of Balboa Park rate high with the zoo on your agenda, check out "Balboa Park Money-Savers" on p. 146.

beached animals found along the West Coast—including more than 200 seals, sea lions, marine birds, and dolphins in an average year, more than 65% of which are rehabilitated and returned to the wild.

500 Sea World Dr., Mission Bay. (*C*) **619/226-3901.** www.seaworld.com. Admission $45 adults, $35 children 3–9, free for children under 3. Guided 90-min. walking tours, $8 adults, $7 children. AE, DISC, MC, V. Open daily. Hours vary seasonally and by day, but always open 10am–5pm; most weekends and summer open at 9am, and stays open as late as 10pm during peak periods. Parking $7. Bus: 9 or 27. From I-5, take Sea World Dr. exit; from I-8, take W. Mission Bay Dr. exit to Sea World Dr.

2 San Diego's Beaches

The promo materials from the local Convention and Visitors Bureau say it all: San Diego County is blessed with 70 miles of sandy coastline and more than 30 individual beaches. Now, truth be told, you'll find whiter sand and warmer water in the Caribbean and much of Hawaii. Even Florida has dozens of picture-perfect shores—the only problem there is that you have to go to *Florida* to reach them. And although I love tropical islands, you'll spend a lot more time getting there as well as more money to enjoy them, and you'll have a lot less to do off the beach than in San Diego. On the other hand, if you want to spend your entire vacation cloaked in sunblock, on a beach riddled with jet skis, and surrounded by drunken 19-year-olds, go to Cancún.

But I'll stay in San Diego for the whole enchilada and enjoy beaches that cater equally to surfers, snorkelers, swimmers, sailors, divers, walkers, volleyballers, sunbathers . . . You get the drift. Even in winter and spring, when water temperatures drop to the high 50s, the beaches are great places to walk and jog, and surfers happily don wet suits to pursue their passion. In summer, the beaches teem with locals and visitors alike—the bikinis come out, the pecs are bared, and a spring-break atmosphere threatens to break loose. Fortunately, common sense and good taste usually prevail and a good time is had by all.

A word (rather, two) to the wise: **June Gloom.** It's a local phenomenon, probably brought about by devious weather gods hired by Caribbean despots and, from mid-May to mid-July, can be counted on to foil sunbathing more mornings than not. June Gloom is caused as inland deserts like Anza-Borrego heat up at the end of spring, and suck the marine layer—a thick bank of fog—inland for a few miles. It's why my roses sometimes suffer from mildew, and it's why you should be prepared for clammy mornings and evenings (and sometimes even afternoons) at our beaches for those 2 months of the year.

San Diego Beaches

Oceanside

Oceanside City Beach

S21

Carlsbad

Carlsbad State Beach

5

South Carlsbad State Beach

La Costa

Moonlight State Beach

Encinitas

San Elijo State Beach

S9

Rancho Santa Fe

Cardiff by the Sea

Cardiff State Beach

S8

South Cardiff State Beach

Solana Beach

S21

S6

Del Mar

Del Mar

Torrey Pines State Beach

Black's Beach

La Jolla Shores

La Jolla Cove

Children's Pool

La Jolla

805

52

Marine Street Beach

Windansea

Tourmaline Surfing Park

Pacific Beach

Mission Beach

Bonita Cove

Ocean Beach

5

MISSION BAY PARK

163

8

Sunset Cliffs

SAN DIEGO

15

94

Point Loma

Coronado

National City

Coronado Beach

Chula Vista

PACIFIC OCEAN

Silver Strand State Beach

805

5

Imperial Beach

Border Field State Beach

San Marcos

Escondido

15

75

Exploring **tide pools**—pot-holed, rocky shores that retain ponds of water after the tide has gone out, providing homes for a plethora of sea creatures—can be a lot of fun. You can get a tide chart free or for a nominal charge from many surf and diving shops, including **Emerald City Surf & Sport,** 1118 Orange Ave. in Coronado (© **619/435-6677),** and **San Diego Divers Supply,** 5701 La Jolla Blvd. in La Jolla (© **619/224-3439).** Among my favorite places for tide-pooling are Cabrillo National Monument, at the oceanside base of Point Loma; at Sunset Cliffs in Ocean Beach; and the rocky coast immediately south of the Cove in La Jolla.

✐ Beach Snack Staples: Quick (& Cheap) Taco Stands

Looking for some sustenance after a day of cavorting on San Diego's beautiful beaches? Someplace that's tasty, affordable—and doesn't enforce that pesky shirt-and-shoes policy? Then follow the example of serious surfers and beach bums, who always know where the nearest taco stand can be found. Tacos—and accompanying Mexican favorites like burritos and tamales—are ubiquitous in Southern California, as common as burger stands in the heartland (or hot dog carts in New York City). And like those other famously utensil-less foods, tacos are easy to eat out-of-hand—perfect for a quickie meal before heading back to catch some more waves or rays. Here are a few of my favorites in San Diego's beach communities (from south to north):

A block from the pier—and across the street from Belmont Park— **Roberto's Taco Shop,** 3202 Mission Blvd., Mission Beach (© **858/488-1610),** is an institution on this corner, feeding beach-goers and amusement park revelers alike, around the clock. Step inside the historic corner building for a full menu of family recipe Mexican favorites.

Paquito's Mexican Food, 3852 Mission Blvd., Mission Beach (© **858/488-9212),** sits in the heart of Mission Beach's best people-watching, and is a happy-hour favorite with locals who stop by in sandy flip-flops straight from the sand. Sit on their sidewalk patio to enjoy a bottle of Mexican beer and the daily special; Thursday is 99¢ fish taco day.

When time is of the essence, roll through the 24-hour drive-through window at **Ramiro's,** 4525 Mission Blvd., Pacific Beach (© **858/273-5227),** for some truly tasty burritos and tacos at rock-bottom prices. There's also a walk-up window and a few outdoor tables.

The name says it all at **Taco Surf,** 4657 Mission Blvd., Pacific Beach (© **858/272-3877),** the most "formal" of the bunch—for the laid-back surfing crowd, that means table service. They've got a fine selection of beers to accompany platters of Baja-style fish tacos, along with a full Mexican menu.

As you make your way toward La Jolla, join the throngs of beach-goers and lunch-breakers at tiny **Los Dos Pedros #1,** 723 Turquoise St., Pacific Beach (© **858/488-3102);** surfers from Windansea fuel their day at **Los Dos Pedros #2,** 6986 La Jolla Blvd., La Jolla (© **858/456-2692),** a welcome sight on a stretch lacking many fast-food options.

Here's a list of San Diego's most accessible beaches, each with its own personality and devotees. They are listed geographically from south to north. All California beaches are open to the public to the mean high-tide line, and you can check **www.sannet.gov/lifeguards/beaches** for descriptions and water quality.

Note: All beaches are good for swimming unless otherwise indicated.

IMPERIAL BEACH

A half-hour south of downtown San Diego by car or trolley, and only a few minutes from the Mexican border, lies Imperial Beach. It's popular with surfers and local youth, who can be somewhat territorial about "their" sands in summer. The beach boasts 3 miles of surf breaks plus a guarded "swimmers only" stretch; check with lifeguards before getting wet, though, since sewage runoff from nearby Mexico can sometimes foul the water. I.B. also plays host to the annual **U.S. Open Sandcastle Competition** in late July—the best reason to come here—with world-class sand creations ranging from sea scenes to dragons to dinosaurs.

CORONADO BEACH 🐾

Lovely, wide, and sparkling, this beach is conducive to strolling and lingering, especially in the late afternoon. At the north end, you can watch fighter jets in formation flying from the Naval Air Station, while just south is the pretty section fronting Ocean Boulevard and the Hotel del Coronado. Waves are gentle here, so the beach draws many Coronado families—and their dogs, which are allowed off-leash at the most northwesterly end. South of the Hotel Del, the beach becomes the beautiful, often deserted **Silver Strand.** The islands visible from here, Los Coronados, are 18 miles away and belong to Mexico.

OCEAN BEACH

The northern end of Ocean Beach Park is officially known as **Dog Beach,** and is one of only a few in the county where your pooch can roam freely on the sand (and frolic with several dozen other people's pets). Surfers generally congregate around the O.B. Pier, mostly in the water but often at the snack shack on the end. Rip currents can be strong here and discourage most swimmers from venturing beyond waist depth (check with the lifeguard stations). Facilities at the beach include restrooms, showers, picnic tables, volleyball courts, and plenty of metered parking lots. To reach the beach, take West Point Loma Boulevard all the way to the end.

MISSION BAY PARK

This inland, 4,600-acre aquatic playground contains 27 miles of bayfront, picnic areas, children's playgrounds, and paths for biking, in-line skating, and jogging. The bay lends itself to windsurfing, sailing, water-skiing, and fishing. There are dozens of access points; one of the most popular is off I-5 at Clairemont Drive (though this is not my favorite area for swimming). Also accessed from this spot is **Fiesta Island,** where the annual **Over the Line Tournament** is held to raucous enthusiasm in July.

BONITA COVE/MARINER'S POINT & MISSION POINT

Also enclosed in Mission Bay Park (facing the bay, not the ocean) this pretty and protected cove's calm waters, grassy picnic areas, and playground equipment make it perfect for families—or as a paddling destination if you've rented kayaks elsewhere in the bay. The water is cleaner for swimming than in the northeastern reaches of Mission Bay. Get there from Mission Boulevard in south Mission Beach.

MISSION BEACH

While Mission Bay Park is a body of saltwater surrounded by land and bridges, Mission Beach is actually a beach on the Pacific Ocean, anchored by the **Giant Dipper** roller coaster. Always popular, the sands and wide cement "boardwalk" sizzle with activity and great people-watching in summer; at the southern end there's always a volleyball game in play. The long beach and path extend from the jetty north to Belmont Park and Pacific Beach Drive. Parking is often tough, with your best bets being the public lots at Belmont Park or at the south end of West Mission Bay Drive. This busy street is the centerline of a 2-block-wide isthmus which leads a mile north to . . .

PACIFIC BEACH

There's always action here, particularly along **Ocean Front Walk,** a paved promenade featuring a human parade akin to that at L.A.'s Venice Beach boardwalk. It runs along Ocean Boulevard (just west of Mission Blvd.) to the pier. Surfing is popular year-round here, in marked sections, and the beach is well staffed with lifeguards. You're on your own to find street parking. Pacific Beach is also the home of **Tourmaline Surfing Park,** a half-mile north of the pier, where the sport's old guard gathers to surf waters where swimmers are prohibited.

WINDANSEA BEACH

The fabled locale of Tom Wolfe's *Pump House Gang,* Windansea is legendary to this day among California's surf elite and remains one of San Diego's prettiest strands. Reached by way of Bonair Street (at Neptune Place), Windansea has no facilities, and street parking is first-come, first-served. Not ideal for swimming, so come to surf, watch surfers, or soak in the camaraderie and party atmosphere.

CHILDREN'S POOL 🅖

Think clothing-optional Black's Beach is the city's most controversial sun-sea-sand situation? Think again—the Children's Pool is currently home to the biggest man-vs.-beast struggle since *Moby Dick.* A seawall protects this pocket of sand, originally intended as a calm swimming bay for children—many of us first learned to bob in the ocean here. It was also location of a battle sequence for the movie *The Stuntman.* But since 1994, when a rock outcrop off the shore was designated as a protected mammal reserve, the beach has also been cordoned off for the resident **harbor seal** population. On an average day you'll spot dozens lolling in the sun. Swimming is now prohibited, as is touching or disturbing the seals, but it's fun to watch them. A heated debate over the status of the beach has boiled over in the last couple years, and politicians have been flooded with petition drives, both pro- and anti-seal—alas, the day may come when the creatures are shooed away from the cove and this unusually natural California coastal scene may disappear in favor of diaper-clad bathing beauties. The beach is at Coast Boulevard and Jenner Street; there's limited free street parking.

LA JOLLA COVE 🅖🅖

The protected, calm waters—celebrated as the clearest along the coast—attract snorkelers and scuba divers, along with a fair share of families. The stunning setting offers a small sandy beach, as well as, on the cliffs above, the **Ellen Browning Scripps Park.** The cove's "look but don't touch" policy protects the colorful garibaldi, California's state fish, plus other marine life, including abalone, octopus, and lobster. The unique Underwater Park stretches from here to the northern end of Torrey Pines State Reserve and incorporates kelp forests, artificial reefs, two deep submarine canyons, and tidal pools. The Cove is terrific for swimming, cramped for sunbathing, and accessible from Coast Boulevard; parking nearby is free, if sparse.

LA JOLLA SHORES

The wide, flat mile of sand at La Jolla Shores is popular with joggers, swimmers, and beginning body- and board surfers, as well as families. It looks like a picture postcard, with fine sand under blue skies, kissed by gentle waves. In summer, you need to shuffle your feet entering the water so as not to step on occasional (harmless) jellyfish. Weekend crowds can be enormous, though, quickly occupying both the sand and the metered parking spaces in the lot. There are restrooms, showers, and picnic areas here, as well the grassy, palm-lined Kellogg Park across the street.

BLACK'S BEACH ✿

The area's unofficial (and illegal) nude beach, 2-mile-long Black's lies between La Jolla Shores and Torrey Pines State Beach, at the base of steep, 300-foot-high cliffs. The beach is out of the way and not easy to reach, but it draws scores with its secluded beauty and good swimming conditions—the graceful spectacle of hang gliders launching from the cliffs above adds to the show. To get here, take North Torrey Pines Road, park at the Gliderport, and clamber down the makeshift path, staying alert to avoid veering off to one of several false trails. To bypass the cliff descent, you can walk to Black's from beaches north (Torrey Pines) or south (La Jolla Shores). *Note:* There is no permanent lifeguard station, though lifeguards are usually present from spring break to October, and no restroom facilities. Citations for nude sunbathing, however, are rarely issued. The beach's notoriety came about when, from 1974 to 1977, swimsuits *were* optional—the only such beach in the U.S. to be so designated at the time. Rich neighbors on the cliffs above complained enough to the city about their view being denigrated that the clothing-optional status was reversed.

TORREY PINES BEACH ✿

The north end of Black's Beach, at the foot of the Torrey Pines State Park is this fabulous, underused strand, accessed by a pay parking lot at the entrance to the park. In fact, combining a visit to the park with a day at the beach is my concept of the quintessential San Diego insider's experience. It's rarely crowded, though you need to be aware of high tide (when most of the sand gets a bath). In almost any weather, it's a great beach for walking.

DEL MAR BEACH

After a visit to the Del Mar Thoroughbred Club, make tracks for this town beach, a long stretch of sand backed by grassy cliffs and a playground area. This area is not heavily trafficked, and you can get a wonderful meal on the beach at Jake's. Del Mar is about 15 miles from downtown San Diego; see "North County Beach Towns: Spots to Surf & Sun" in chapter 11.

NORTHERN SAN DIEGO COUNTY BEACHES

Those inclined to venture farther north in San Diego County won't be disappointed. Pacific Coast Highway leads to inviting beaches, such as these in Encinitas: peaceful **Boneyards Beach, Swami's Beach** for surfing, and **Moonlight Beach,** popular with families and volleyball buffs. Farthest north is Oceanside, which has one of the West Coast's longest wooden piers, wide sandy beaches, and several popular surfing areas. See "North County Beach Towns: Spots to Surf & Sun" in chapter 11 for more information.

3 Attractions in Balboa Park

New York has Central Park, San Francisco has Golden Gate Park. San Diego's crown jewel is Balboa Park, a 1,174-acre city-owned playground and the largest urban cultural park in the nation. The park was established in 1868 in the heart of the city, bordered by downtown to the southwest and fringed by the early communities of Hillcrest and Golden Hill to the north and east. Originally called City Park, the name was eventually changed to commemorate the Spanish explorer Balboa. Tree plantings started in the late 19th century, while the initial buildings were created to host the 1915–16 Panama-California Exposition; another expo in 1935–36 brought additional developments.

The park's most distinctive features are its mature landscaping, the architectural beauty of the Spanish-Moorish buildings lining **El Prado** (the park's east-west thoroughfare), and the outstanding and diverse museums contained within it. You'll also find eight different gardens, walkways, 4½ miles of hiking trails in Florida Canyon, historic buildings, several restaurants, an ornate pavilion with the world's largest outdoor organ, a high-spouting fountain, an IMAX domed theater, the acclaimed **Globe Theatres** (p. 164), and the world-famous **San Diego Zoo** (p. 133).

If you really want to visit the zoo and a few of the park's museums, don't try to tackle them both the same day. Allow at least 5 hours to tour the zoo; the amount of time you spend in the 13 major museums will vary depending on your personal interests. There are informal restaurants serving sandwiches and snacks throughout the park, and the **Prado Restaurant** (p. 202) is a San Diego favorite.

The park is divided by Highway 163 into two distinct sections. The narrow western wing of the park is largely grassy open areas that parallel Sixth Avenue; there are no museums in this section, but it's a good place for picnics, strolling, sunning, and dog walking. The main portion of the park, east of 163, contains the zoo and all of the museums, and is bordered by Park Boulevard; just east is largely undeveloped Florida Canyon. There are two primary entrances to the park. The most distinctive is from Sixth Avenue and Laurel Street: Laurel enters the park via the beautiful **Cabrillo Bridge** ⍟ across Highway 163 and turns into El Prado. You can also enter via Presidents Way from Park Boulevard, just north of downtown. Major parking areas are at Inspiration Point on the east side of Park Boulevard at Presidents Way, in front of the zoo, and along Presidents Way between the Aerospace Museum and Spreckels Organ Pavilion. Other lots, though more centrally located, are small and in high demand, especially on weekends.

Public **bus routes** 7, 7A, and 7B run along Park Boulevard; for the west side of the park, routes 1, 3, and 25 run along Fourth/Fifth avenues (except for the Marston House, all museums are closer to Park Blvd.). Free **tram** transportation within the park runs daily from 8:30am to 6pm, with extended hours in summer months. The red trolley trams originate at the Inspiration Point parking lot to circuit the park, arriving every 8 to 10 minutes and stopping at designated pickup areas. Stop by the **Balboa Park Visitors Center,** located in the House of Hospitality (© **619/239-0512;** www.balboapark.org) to learn about free walking and museum **tours,** or to pick up a brochure about the **gardens** of the park. We've also mapped out a **walking tour** in chapter 8.

Botanical Building and Lily Pond ⍟ *Moments*   This is a serene park within the park where ivy, ferns, orchids, impatiens, begonias, and other plants—about 2,100 tropical and flowering varieties, plus rotating exhibits—are sheltered

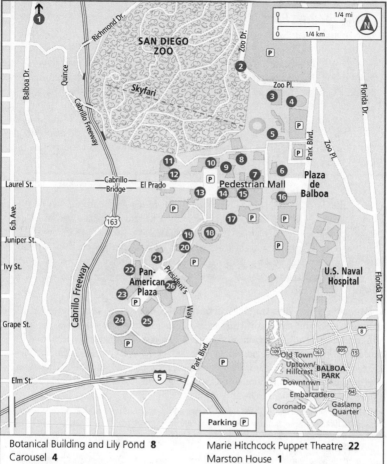

SAN DIEGO ZOO

Skyfari

Pedestrian Mall

Plaza de Balboa

Pan-American Plaza

President's Way

U.S. Naval Hospital

Richmond Dr.

Zoo Dr.

Zoo Pl.

Park Blvd.

Zoo Pl.

Florida Dr.

Florida Dr.

Balboa Dr.

Quince

Cabrillo Freeway

Cabrillo Bridge

El Prado

6th Ave.

Cabrillo Freeway

Park Blvd.

Laurel St.

Juniper St.

Ivy St.

Grape St.

Elm St.

163

5

Old Town

Uptown/Hillcrest

Downtown

Coronado

BALBOA PARK

Embarcadero

Gaslamp Quarter

109

163

805

15

8

94

1/4 mi

1/4 km

Parking P

Botanical Building and Lily Pond **8**
Carousel **4**
Casa de Balboa **15**
  Model Railroad Museum
  Museum of Photographic Arts
  San Diego Historical Society Museum
Casa del Prado **7**
The Globe Theatres **11**
Hall of Nations **19**
House of Charm **13**
  Mingei International Museum
  SDAI Museum of the Living Artist
House of Hospitality **14**
  Balboa Park Visitors Center
  Prado Restaurant
House of Pacific Relations
  International Cottages **21**
Japanese Friendship Garden **17**

Marie Hitchcock Puppet Theatre **22**
Marston House **1**
Reuben H. Fleet Science Center **16**
San Diego Aerospace Museum **24**
San Diego Automotive Museum **23**
San Diego Hall of Champions
  Sports Museum **26**
San Diego Miniature Railroad **3**
San Diego Museum of Art **10**
San Diego Museum of Man **12**
San Diego Museum
  of Natural History **6**
San Diego Zoo entrance **2**
Spanish Village Art Center **5**
Spreckels Organ Pavilion **18**
Starlight Bowl **25**
Timken Museum of Art **9**
United Nations Building **20**

beneath the domed lath house. The striking 250-foot-long building, part of the 1915 Panama-California Exposition, and is one of the world's largest wood lath structures, and emerged from a complete renovation in 2002. Kids love the "touch and smell" garden and the smelly bog of carnivorous plants; the lily pond out front attracts sun worshipers, painters, and street entertainers.

El Prado. (℃ **619/235-1100.** Free admission. Fri–Wed 10am–4pm; closed Thurs and major holidays. Bus: 7 or 7A/B.

House of Pacific Relations International Cottages   This cluster of 17 charming one- and two-room cottages disseminates information about the culture, traditions, and history of 28 countries. Light refreshments are served, and outdoor lawn programs are presented on Sundays, March through October. The adjacent **United Nations Building** houses an international gift shop where you can buy jewelry, toys and books, and UNICEF greeting cards (℃ **619/233-5044**); it's open daily from 10am to 4pm.

Adjacent to Pan American Plaza. (℃ **619/234-0739.** Free admission (donations welcome). Sun noon–4pm; 2nd and 4th Tues of each month 11am–3pm. Bus: 7 or 7A/B.

Japanese Friendship Garden *(Finds*   Of the 11½ acres designated for the garden, only 1 acre—a beautiful, peaceful one—has been developed. The garden's Information Center shows a model of the future installation, San-Kei-En (Three-Scenery Garden). A self-guided tour is available at the main gate. From the gate, a crooked path (to confound evil spirits, who move only in a straight line) threads its way to the information center in a Zen-style house; here you can view the most ancient kind of garden, the *sekitei,* made only of sand and stone. Refreshments are served on a Japanese-style deck to the left of the entrance. Japanese holidays are celebrated here, and the public is invited.

2125 Park Blvd., adjacent to the Organ Pavilion. (℃ **619/232-2721.** www.niwa.org. Admission $3 adults, $2 students and military, free for children 6 and under. Free 3rd Tues of each month. Tues–Sun 10am–4pm. Bus: 7 or 7A/B.

Marston House *(*   Noted San Diego architect Irving Gill designed this house in 1905 for George Marston, a local businessman and philanthropist. Listed on the National Register of Historic Places and now managed by the San Diego Historical Society, the house is a classic example of Craftsman-style architecture, reminiscent of the work of Frank Lloyd Wright. Some of its interesting features are wide hallways, brick fireplaces, and redwood paneling. Opened to the public in 1991, it contains few original pieces, but does exhibit Roycroft, Stickley, and Lampert furniture and is slowly being furnished with Craftsman-era pieces or copies as funds become available. Tours take about 45 minutes.

3525 Seventh Ave. (northwest corner of Balboa Park at Balboa Dr. and Upas St.). (℗ **619/298-3142.** Guided tour $5 adults, $4 seniors and students, free for children 5 and under. Fri–Sun 10am–4:30pm (last tour at 3:45pm). Bus: 1, 3, or 25.

Mingei International Museum *α̂α̂*   This captivating museum (pronounced "*min*-gay," meaning "art of the people" in Japanese), offers changing exhibitions generally describable as folk art. The rotating exhibits—usually four at a time—feature artists from countries across the globe; displays include textiles, costumes, jewelry, toys, pottery, paintings, and sculpture. The small permanent collection includes whimsical contemporary sculptures by the late French artist Niki de Saint Phalle, who made San Diego her home in 1993. Martha Longenecker, a potter and professor emeritus of art at San Diego State University, founded the museum in 1977. It is one of only two major museums in the United States devoted to folk crafts on a worldwide scale (the other is in Santa Fe, New Mexico) and well worth a look. Allow half an hour to an hour to view the collection.

1439 El Prado, in the House of Charm. (℗ **619/239 0003.** www.mingei.org. Admission $5 adults, $2 children 6–17 and students with ID, free for children under 6. Free 3rd Tues of each month. AE, MC, V. Tues–Sun 10am–4pm. Bus: 7 or 7A/B.

Museum of Photographic Arts *α̂α̂*   If names like Ansel Adams and Edward Weston stimulate your fingers to do the shutterbug, then don't miss the a taste of the 7,000-plus collection of images housed by this museum—one of few in the United States devoted exclusively to the photographic arts (which, at MOPA, encompasses cinema, video, and digital photography). A 1999 expansion allowed the museum to display even more of the permanent collection, while leaving room for provocative traveling exhibits that change every few months. Photos by Alfred Stieglitz, Margaret Bourke-White, Imogen Cunningham, Paul Strand, and Manuel Alvarez Bravo are all in the permanent collection, and the plush cinema illuminates classic films Friday, Saturday, and some weeknights. Allow 30 to 60 minutes to see the collection.

1649 El Prado. (℗ **619/238-7559.** www.mopa.org. Admission $6 adults, $4 seniors and students, free for children under 12 with adult; cinema admission $5 adults, $4.50 seniors and students. Free 2nd Tues of each month. Daily 10am–5pm (Thurs until 9pm). Bus: 7 or 7A/B.

Reuben H. Fleet Science Center *α̂* *Kids*   A must-see for kids of any age is this tantalizing collection of interactive exhibits and rides designed to provoke the imagination and teach scientific principles. The Virtual Zone includes SciTours, a motion simulator ride that lurches you into virtual deep sea, plus two different virtual reality attractions with a scientific bent. The Fleet also houses a 76-foot-high IMAX Dome Theater that shows films so realistic that ocean footage can actually give you motion sickness! And in 2001, the Fleet unveiled a spiffy new planetarium simulator powered by computer graphics. Planetarium shows are the first Wednesday of each month ($6.75 adults, $5.50 kids age 3–12, $6 seniors). The gift shop features an inspired collection of toys, gadgets, and clever souvenirs.

Tips **Activities Farther Afield**

To find information on attractions in nearby Del Mar, Carlsbad, Encinitas, and Oceanside—only 20 to 40 minutes from downtown San Diego—turn to "North County Beach Towns: Spots to Surf & Sun," in chapter 11.

1875 El Prado. ℭ **619/238-1233.** www.rhfleet.org. Fleet Experience admission includes 1 IMAX film and exhibit galleries $12 adults, $10 seniors 65 and over, $8.50 children 3–12 (exhibit gallery can be purchased individually). Free 1st Tues of each month (exhibit galleries only). AE, DISC, MC, V. Open daily 9:30am; closing times vary, but always until at least 5pm. Bus: 7 or 7A/B.

San Diego Aerospace Museum ℜℜ ℜids
The other big kid-pleaser of the museums (along with the Fleet Science Center, above), this popular facility provides an overview of the nation's air-and-space history, from the days of hot-air balloons to the space age, with plenty of biplanes and military fighters in between. It emphasizes local aviation history, particularly the construction here of the *Spirit of St. Louis*. Highlights include the only GPS Satellite on display in a museum, and a World War I–era Spad. The museum is housed in a stunning cylindrical hall built by the Ford Motor Company in 1935 (for the park's 2nd international expo), and has an imaginative gift shop with items like old-fashioned leather flight hoods and new-fashioned freeze-dried astronaut ice cream. Allow at least an hour for your visit.

2001 Pan American Plaza. ℭ **619/234-8291.** www.aerospacemuseum.org. Admission $8 adults, $6 seniors, $3 juniors 6–17, free for active military with ID and children under 6. Free 4th Tues of each month. Sept–May daily 10am–4:30pm; June–Aug daily 10am–5:30pm. Bus: 7 or 7A/B.

San Diego Automotive Museum ℜ
Even if you don't know a distributor from a dipstick, you're bound to ooh-and-aah over the classic, antique, and exotic cars here. Every one is so pristine you'd swear it just rolled off the line, from an 1886 Benz to a 1931 Rolls-Royce Phaeton to the 1981 DeLorean. Most of the time, temporary shows take over the facility, so check ahead to see if it's one you're interested in. Some days you can take a peek at the ongoing restoration program, and the museum sponsors many outdoor car rallies and other events. Allow 30 to 45 minutes for your visit.

2080 Pan American Plaza. ℭ **619/231-2886.** www.sdautomuseum.org. Admission $7 adults, $6 seniors and active military, $3 children 6–15, free for children under 6. Free 4th Tues of each month. MC, V. Daily 10am–5pm (last admission 4:30pm). Bus: 7 or 7A/B.

San Diego Hall of Champions Sports Museum
One of the country's few multisport museums, the slick Hall of Champions has been a destination for sports fans since 1961. The museum highlights more than 40 professional and amateur sports. More than 25 exhibits surround a centerpiece statue, the *Discus Thrower*. One particularly interesting exhibit is devoted to athletes with disabilities. You can see it all in under an hour.

2131 Pan American Plaza. ℭ **619/234-2544.** www.sandiegosports.org. Admission $6 adults, $4 seniors 65 and older and military, $3 children 6–17, free for children under 6. Free 4th Tues of each month. Daily 10am–4:30pm. Bus: 7 or 7A/B.

San Diego Historical Society Museum
A good place to start if you are a newcomer to San Diego, the recently remodeled museum offers permanent and changing exhibits on topics related to the history of the region, from pioneer outposts in the 1800s to the present day. Many of the museum's photographs depict Balboa Park and the growth of the city. Plan to spend about 30 to 45 minutes here. Docent tours are available; call ℭ **619/232-6203,** ext. 117, for information and reservations. Books about San Diego's history are available in the gift shop, and the research library downstairs is open Thursday through Saturday.

1649 El Prado, in Casa del Balboa. ℭ **619/232-6203.** www.sandiegohistory.org. Admission $5 adults, $4 students, seniors and military with ID, $2 children 6–12, free for children 5 and under. Free 2nd Tues of each month. Tues–Sun 10am–4:30pm. Bus: 7 or 7A/B.

Tips **Balboa Park Guided Tours**

In addition to the walking tour we've mapped out in chapter 8, there are rewarding guided tours of the park that cater to a wide variety of interests. The visitor center conducts free rotating tours on Saturdays at 10am that highlight either the palm trees and vegetation or park history; they meet at the visitor center (© **619/235-1122**). The park rangers lead free 1-hour tours focusing on the park's history, architecture, and botanical resources Tuesday and Sunday at 1pm, also meeting in front of the visitor center. The author of *Discover Balboa Park* conducts free walking tours of the park on Fridays at 11am and 1pm, meeting at the visitor center; call © **619/239-0512** for more information.

The Committee of 100 (© **619/223-6566**), an organization dedicated to preserving the park's Spanish colonial architecture, offers a free exploration of the Prado's structures on the first Wednesday of the month at 9:30am, starting from the visitor center. The Globe Theatres Tour visits the three performance venues on Saturdays and Sundays at 10:30am; the tour costs $3 for adults, $1 for seniors and students (© **619/231-1941**). Plant Day at the San Diego Zoo is held the third Friday of each month from 10am to 2pm, and features self and guided horticultural tours and functions; the orchid house is open to the public on this day (zoo admission required; call © **619/234-3153** for more details).

San Diego Model Railroad Museum *Kids* Okay, so it's not high culture as we know it, but this museum is cool and pleasing, and worth 30 to 60 minutes of your time, especially if you have kids in tow. Six permanent, scale-model railroads depict Southern California's transportation history and terrain with an astounding attention to miniature details—the exhibits occupy a 24,000-square-foot space. Children will enjoy the hands-on Lionel trains, and train buffs of all ages will appreciate the interactive multimedia displays. Allow a half-hour to an hour for your visit.

1649 El Prado (Casa de Balboa), under the Museum of Photographic Arts. © **619/696-0199**. www.sdmodel railroadm.com. Admission $4 adults, free for children under 15. Senior, student, and military discounts with ID. Free 1st Tues of each month. Tues–Fri 11am–4pm; Sat–Sun 11am–5pm. Bus: 7 or 7A/B.

San Diego Museum of Art With one of the grandest entrances along El Prado—the rotunda at the head of dramatic stairs features striking Spanish tile work—the museum is known in the art world for its outstanding collection of Spanish baroque painting, and possibly the largest horde of Indian paintings outside India. The American collection includes works by Georgia O'Keeffe and Thomas Eakins, and San Diegans like Maurice Braun and Dan Dickey are represented. Over 12,000 pieces are part of the permanent collection, only a small percentage of which is on display at any given time, in favor of varied, often prestigious touring shows. In 2004, *St. Peter and the Vatican: The Legacy of the Popes* should be blockbuster, an exhibit featuring the largest collection of objects from the Vatican ever to tour North America. The museum's high-tech touch is an interactive computer-image system that allows visitors to locate museum highlights and custom design a tour. Plan to spend at least an hour here.

1450 El Prado. ℂ **619/232-7931.** www.sdmart.org. Admission $8 adults 25 and older; $6 seniors, military, and youths 18–24; $3 children 6–17; free for children under 6. Admission to traveling exhibits varies. Free 3rd Tues of each month. Tues–Sun 10am–6pm (Thurs until 9pm). Bus: 7 or 7A/B.

San Diego Museum of Man   Located under the iconic, rococo, tiled **California building and bell tower** 𝍂𝍂 just inside the park entrance at the Cabrillo Bridge, this museum is devoted to anthropology, with an emphasis on the peoples of North and South America. Favorite exhibits include life-size replicas of a dozen varieties of Homo sapiens, from Cro-Magnon and Neanderthal to Peking Man, and a small room featuring Egyptian mummies and artifacts. Don't overlook the annex across the street, which houses more exhibits, and the lady making fresh tortillas and quesadillas Wednesday through Sunday. The museum's annual Indian Fair, held in June, features American Indians from the Southwest demonstrating tribal dances and selling food, arts, and crafts. Allow at least an hour for your visit.

1350 El Prado. ℂ **619/239-2001.** www.museumofman.org. Admission $6 adults, $5 seniors, $3 children 6–17, free for children under 6. Free 3rd Tues of the month. Daily 10am–4:30pm. Bus: 1, 3, 7, 7A/B, or 25.

San Diego Natural History Museum   This museum focuses on the flora, fauna, and mineralogy of the Southern and Baja California. Kids marvel at the animals they find here, including live snakes, tarantulas, and turtles. As a binational museum, research is done on both sides of the border and most exhibits are bilingual. You can see them all in about half an hour. Call or check the museum's website for a current schedule of special visiting exhibits. There's a 300-seat large-format movie theater and two films are included in the price of admission.

1788 El Prado. ℂ **619/232-3821.** www.sdnhm.org. Admission $8 adults, $6 seniors and active-duty military, $5 children 3–17, free for children under 3. Free 1st Tues of each month. Daily 9:30am–4:30pm; open till 5:30pm in summer. Bus: 7 or 7A/B.

SDAI Museum of the Living Artist   Around since 1941, the San Diego Art Institute now has a museum to house exhibits of new artworks by local artists. The 10,000-square-foot municipal gallery rotates juried shows in and out every 4 to 6 weeks, ensuring a variety of mediums and styles. It's a good place to see what the local art community is up to. Plan to spend about half an hour here.

1439 El Prado. ℂ **619/236-0011.** www.sandiego-art.org. Admission $3 adults, $2 seniors and students, free to children 12 and under. Free 3rd Tues of the month. Tues–Sat 10am–4pm; Sun 12–4pm. Bus: 7 or 7A/B.

Spreckels Organ Pavilion   Given to San Diego citizens in 1914 by brothers John D. and Adolph Spreckels, the ornate, curved pavilion houses a magnificent organ with over 4,500 individual pipes. They range in length from less than a half-inch to more than 32 feet. With only brief interruptions, the organ has been in continuous use in the park, and today visitors can enjoy free hour-long concerts on Sundays at 2pm. There's seating for 2,400.

South of El Prado. ℂ **619/702-8138.** Free 1-hr. organ concerts Sun 2pm year-round; free organ concerts July–Aug Mon 7:30pm; free Twilight in the Park concerts Tues–Thurs mid-June to Aug (call ℂ 619/235-1105 for schedule). Bus: 7 or 7A/B.

Timken Museum of Art 𝍂 *(Finds*   How many art museums invite you to see great works of art, free of charge? How many of them have smiling guards who welcome guests as graciously as the Timken's? This jewel-like repository houses the Putnam Foundation's collection of 19th-century American paintings and works by European old masters, as well as a worthy display of Russian icons. Yes, it's a small horde, but the marquee attractions include a Peter Paul Reubens, *Portrait of a Young Man in Armor;* San Diego's only Rembrandt, *St. Bartholomew;* and a masterpiece by Eastman Johnson, *The Cranberry Harvest.* You'll find a spot apiece for works by Bierstadt, Pissaro, Corot, and Cézanne. Since you can tour all of the museum in well under an hour, the Timken also makes for an easy introduction to fine art for younger travelers (pick up a copy of the *Children's Gallery Guide* for $2). Docents are available Tuesday from 10am to noon and 1 to 3pm; Wednesday and Thursday from 10 to noon; or by appointment.

1500 El Prado. © 619/239-5548. www.timkenmuseum.org. Free admission. Tues–Sat 10am–4:30pm; Sun 1:30–4:30pm. Closed Sept. Bus: 7 or 7A/B.

4 More Attractions
DOWNTOWN & BEYOND

Downtown San Diego is undergoing a huge construction project as we go to press: When the Padres' **Petco Park** opens in April 2004 downtown's revitalization will have a new icon. It will also extend the rebuilt downtown a few blocks farther east, and real estate developers in the "East Village" are stepping up to the plate in hope of cashing in on a home run.

In the meantime, you can wander from the turn-of-the-20th-century **Gaslamp Quarter** ** to the joyful, modern architecture of the **Horton Plaza** * shopping center (see "Walking Tour 1: The Gaslamp Quarter," in chapter 8). The Gaslamp consists of 16½ blocks of restored historic buildings. It gets its name from the old-fashioned street lamps that line the sidewalks. You'll find many of San Diego's best restaurants and our most vigorous nightlife scene here. At Horton Plaza, you can shop, stroll, snack or dine, enjoy free entertainment, see a movie, and people-watch—all within a unique and playful village framework (see p. 203 in chapter 9).

Seaport Village is a shopping and dining complex on the waterfront (see p. 204 in chapter 9). It was designed to look like a New England seaport community. If you find the views across the water alluring, another way to experience San Diego's waterfront is with one of several harbor tours (see "Organized Tours," later in this chapter).

Cabrillo National Monument ** Breathtaking views mingle with the early history of San Diego, which began when Juan Rodríguez Cabrillo arrived in 1542. His statue dominates the tip of Point Loma, which is also a vantage point for watching migrating Pacific gray whales en route from the Arctic Ocean to Baja California December through March. A tour of the restored lighthouse (1855) illuminates what life was like here more than a century ago. National Park Service rangers lead walks at the monument, and there are tide pools at the base of the peninsula that beg for exploration. Free 30-minute films on Cabrillo, tide pools, and the whales are shown on the hour daily from 10am to 4pm. The drive from downtown takes about a half-hour.

1800 Cabrillo Memorial Dr., Point Loma. © 619/557-5450. www.nps.gov/cabr. Admission $5 per vehicle, $3 for walk-ins. Daily 9am–5:15pm. Bus: 26. By car, take I-8 west to Rosecrans St., right on Canon St., left on Catalina and follow signs.

Firehouse Museum *Kids* Appropriately housed in San Diego's oldest firehouse, the museum features shiny fire engines, including hand-drawn and horse-drawn models, a 1903 steam pumper, and memorabilia such as antique alarms, fire hats, and foundry molds for fire hydrants. There's also a small gift shop. Allow about half an hour for your visit.

1572 Columbia St. (at Cedar St.). © 619/232-FIRE. Admission $2 adults, $1 seniors and military in uniform, $1 youths 13–17, free for children under 13. Thurs–Fri 10am–2pm; Sat–Sun 10am–4pm. Bus: 5 or 16. Trolley: America Plaza.

Maritime Museum ✺ (*Kids*)   This unique museum consists of a trio of fine ships: the full-rigged merchant vessel *Star of India* (1863), whose impressive masts are an integral part of the San Diego cityscape; the gleaming white San Francisco–Oakland steam-powered ferry *Berkeley* (1898), which worked round-the-clock to carry people to safety following the 1906 San Francisco earthquake; and the sleek *Medea* (1904), one of the world's few remaining large steam yachts. You can board and explore each vessel, and in July and August you can watch movies on deck (see "Only in San Diego" in chapter 10). Allow 45 minutes to an hour for your visit.

1306 N. Harbor Dr. ℂ 619/234-9153. www.sdmaritime.com. Admission $7 adults, $5 seniors over 62 and youths 13–17, $4 children 6–12, free for children under 6. Daily 9am–8pm. Bus: 2, 4, 20, 23, or 29. Trolley: America Plaza.

Museum of Contemporary Art San Diego Downtown   Opened in 1993, the downtown branch is the second location of the Museum of Contemporary Art (the original branch is in La Jolla). Two large and two smaller galleries present changing exhibitions of nationally and internationally distinguished contemporary artists; plan to spend about half an hour here. Lectures and tours for adults and children are also offered. The first Thursday evening of every month is "TNT" (Thursday Night Thing), with eclectic artist events and drawing the martini set. In 2005 MCA takes over the baggage building of the Santa Fe depot across the street, which will almost triple the exhibition space at this branch, making it the preeminent museum in downtown. Docent tours are available on request.

1001 Kettner Blvd. (at Broadway). ℂ 619/234-1001. www.mcasd.org. Free admission. Thurs–Tues 11am–5pm. Parking $2 with validation at America Plaza Complex. Bus: 2, 4, 7, 7A/B, 15, 20, 23, 34, or 115. Trolley: America Plaza.

Villa Montezuma ✺ (*Finds*)   This exquisite mansion just southeast of downtown was built in 1887 for internationally acclaimed musician and author Jesse Shepard. Lush with Victoriana, it features more stained glass than most churches are blessed with; windows depict Mozart, Beethoven, Sappho, Rubens, St. Cecilia (patron saint of musicians), and other notables. The striking ceilings are of Lincrusta Walton—pressed canvas coated with linseed oil, a forerunner of linoleum, which never looked this good. Shepard lived here with his life companion, Lawrence Tonner, for only 2 years, and died in obscurity in Los Angeles in 1927. The San Diego Historical Society painstakingly restored the house, which is on the National Register of Historic Places, and furnished it with period pieces. The neighborhood is not as fashionable as the building, but it's safe to park your car in the daytime. If you love Victorian houses, don't miss this one for its quirkiness. Join the 45-minute docent-led tour, which begins every hour on the hour (except the last tour, which starts at 3:45pm).

1925 K St. (at 20th St.). ℂ 619/239-2211. Admission $5 adults; $4 seniors, military, and students; $2 children 6–17; free for children 5 and under. Fri–Sun 10am–4:30pm. Bus: 3, 3A, 5, or 16. By car, follow Market St. east, turn right on 20th St. and follow it to K St.

William Heath Davis House Museum   Shipped by boat to San Diego in 1850 from Portland, Maine, this is the oldest structure in the Gaslamp Quarter. It is a well-preserved example of a prefabricated "saltbox" family home, and has remained structurally unchanged for more than 150 years. A museum, on the first and second floors, is open to the public, as is the small park adjacent to the house. The house is also home to the Gaslamp Quarter Historical Foundation, which sponsors walking tours of the quarter for $8 ($6 for seniors, students, and military), every Saturday at 11am.

410 Island Ave. (at Fourth Ave.). ℂ 619/233-4692. www.gaslampquarter.org. Suggested donation $3. Tues–Sun 11am–3pm. Bus: 1, 3, 5, 16, or 25. Trolley: Gaslamp Quarter or Convention Center.

Downtown San Diego Attractions

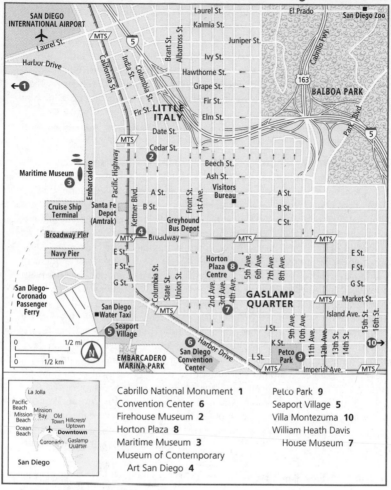

Cabrillo National Monument **1**
Convention Center **6**
Firehouse Museum **2**
Horton Plaza **8**
Maritime Museum **3**
Museum of Contemporary
 Art San Diego **4**
Petco Park **9**
Seaport Village **5**
Villa Montezuma **10**
William Heath Davis
 House Museum **7**

OLD TOWN & MISSION VALLEY

The birthplace of San Diego—indeed, of California—Old Town takes you back to the Mexican California, which existed here until the mid-1800s. **Bazaar del Mundo** 🐠 is a 1930s-era motel that was turned into a collection of shops selling well-chosen south-of-the-border wares. The complex suffers a tourist invasion daily, but who can blame them? The Bazaar is vivid, intimate, and anything but plastic (see p. 206 in chapter 9). It's also a popular for California-style Mexican meals and margaritas. "Walking Tour 3: Old Town" in chapter 8 covers Old Town's historic sights.

Mission Valley, which starts just north of Presidio Park and heads straight east, is decidedly more modern: Until I-8 was built in the 1950s, it was little more than cow pastures with a couple of dirt roads. Shopping malls, motels, a golf course, condos, car dealerships, and a massive sports stadium fill the expanse today, following the San Diego River upstream to the **Mission Basilica San Diego**, and just a few miles beyond, an outstanding park with walking trails.

Few visitors make it this far, but **Mission Trails Regional Park** reveals what San Diego looked like before the Spanish arrived.

Heritage Park This 8-acre county park, dedicated to preservation of Victorian architecture of the 1880s, contains seven original 19th-century houses moved here from other places and given new uses. Among them are a bed-and-breakfast, a doll shop, and a gift shop. The small charming synagogue at the entrance, Temple Beth Israel, was built in 1889 in Classic Revival style and relocated here in 1989. A glorious coral tree crowns the top of the hill.

2450 Heritage Park Row (corner of Juan and Harney sts.). ℂ **858/694-3049**. Free admission. Daily 9:30am–3pm. Bus: 5, 5A, or 6. Trolley: Old Town.

Junípero Serra Museum Perched on a hill above Old Town, this stately Spanish mission–style **building** 🐾🐾 built in 1929 overlooks the slopes where, in 1769, the first mission, first presidio, and first non-native settlement on the west coast of the United States and Canada were founded (the San Diego Mission was relocated 6 miles up Mission Valley in 1774; see below). The museum's exhibits introduce visitors to the Native American, Spanish, and Mexican people who first called this place home. On display are their belongings, from cannons to cookware; a Spanish furniture collection; and, one of the first paintings brought to California, which survived being damaged in an Indian attack. The settlement remained San Diego's only European village until the 1820s, when families began to move down the hill into what is now Old Town. An archaeological dig on the lower slopes is underway to uncover more of the items used by early settlers. From the 70-foot tower, visitors can compare the spectacular view with historic photos to see how this land has changed over time. Designed by William Templeton Johnson, the structure can be seen from miles around. **Presidio Park,** which was established around the museum, has a large cross, made of floor tile from the presidio ruins. Sculptor Arthur Putnam made the statues of Father Serra, founder of the missions in California. Climb up to **Inspiration Point,** as many have done for marriage ceremonies, for a sweeping view of the area.

2727 Presidio Dr., Presidio Park. ℂ **619/297-3258**. Admission $5 adults; $4 seniors, students, and military; $2 children 6–17; free for children under 6. Fri–Sun 10am–4:30pm. Bus: 5, 5A, or 6. Trolley: Old Town. Take I-8 to the Taylor St. exit. Turn right on Taylor, then left on Presidio Dr.

Mission Basilica San Diego de Alcala 🐾 Established in 1769 above Old Town, this was the first link in a chain of 21 missions founded by Spanish missionary Junípero Serra. In 1774, the mission was moved from Old Town to its present site for agricultural reasons, and to separate Native American converts from the fortress that included the original building. The mission was burned by Indians a year after it was built—Father Serra rebuilt the structure using 5- to 7-foot-thick adobe walls and clay tile roofs, rendering it harder to burn. In the process he inspired a bevy of 20th-century California architects. A few bricks belonging to the original mission can be seen in Presidio Park in Old Town. Mass is said daily in this active Catholic parish. Other missions in San Diego County include Mission San Luis Rey de Francia in Oceanside, Mission San Antonia de Pala near Mount Palomar, and Mission Santa Ysabel near Julian. Known as "the King of Missions," the San Luis Rey is the largest of California's missions and one of its most beautiful (see "North County Beach Towns: Spots to Surf & Sun" in chapter 11).

10818 San Diego Mission Rd., Mission Valley. ℂ **619/281-8449**. Admission $3 adults, $2 seniors and students, $1 children under 13. Free Sun and for daily Masses. Daily 9am–4:45pm; Mass daily 7am and 5:30pm. Bus: 13. Trolley: Mission San Diego. Take I-8 to Mission Gorge Rd. to Twain Ave., which turns into San Diego Mission Rd.

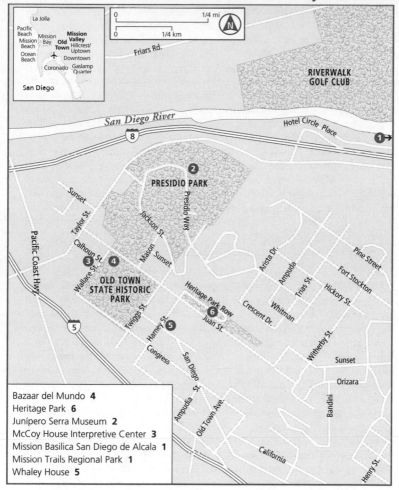

Old Town & Mission Valley Attractions

Bazaar del Mundo **4**
Heritage Park **6**
Junípero Serra Museum **2**
McCoy House Interpretive Center **3**
Mission Basilica San Diego de Alcala **1**
Mission Trails Regional Park **1**
Whaley House **5**

Mission Trails Regional Park ★ *Finds*   Located well off the beaten track for tourists, this is one of the nation's largest urban parks, a 5,800-acre spread that includes abundant birdlife, two lakes, a picturesque stretch of the San Diego River, the Old Mission Dam (probably the first irrigation project in the West), and 1,592-foot Cowles Mountain, the summit of which reveals outstanding views over much of the county. There are trails up to 4 miles in length, including a 1½-mile interpretive trail, some of which are designated for mountain bike use, and a 46-space campground (© **619/668-2748**). The park came about in 1974 when the area surrounding Cowles Mountain began to experience a housing boom; city and county representatives worked with Navajo community planners to make an initial purchase of land. In 1989 the first park ranger was hired, and in 1995 the visitor center opened, cementing a place for Mission Trails in the hearts of outdoor-loving San Diegans.

1 Father Junípero Serra Trail, Mission Gorge. © **619/582-7800**. www.mtrp.org. Free admission. Daily until 5pm Nov–Mar, until 7pm Apr–Oct. Take I-8 to Mission Gorge Rd.; follow for 4 miles to entrance.

Old Town State Historic Park 👁 Dedicated to re-creating the early life the city from 1821 to 1872, this is where San Diego's Mexican heritage shines brightest. The community was briefly Mexico's informal capital of the California territory; the Stars and Stripes were finally raised over Old Town in 1846. Seven of the park's 20 structures are original, including homes made of adobe; the rest are reconstructed. The park's headquarters is at the Robinson-Rose House, 4002 Wallace St., where you can pick up a map and peruse a model of Old Town, as it looked in 1872. Among the park's attractions are La Casa de Estudillo, which depicts the living conditions of a wealthy family in 1872; and Seeley Stables, named after A. L. Seeley, who ran the stagecoach and mail service in these parts from 1867 to 1871. The stables have two floors of wagons, carriages, stagecoaches, and other memorabilia, including washboards, slot machines, and hand-worked saddles. On Wednesday and Saturday, costumed park volunteers re-enact life in the 1800s with cooking and crafts demonstrations, a working blacksmith, and parlor singing. Free 1-hour walking tours leave daily at 11am and 2pm from the Robinson-Rose House. Note that on weekdays throughout the school year, Old Town buzzes with fourth-graders.

4002 Wallace St., Old Town. © 619/220-5422. Free admission (donations welcome). Daily 10am–5pm. Bus: 5, 5A, or 6. Trolley: Old Town.

Whaley House In 1856, this striking two-story brick house (the 1st one in these parts) was built for Thomas Whaley and his family. Whaley was a New Yorker who arrived via San Francisco, where he had been lured by the gold rush. It's probably an urban legend that Whaley's house is designated as "one of only two authenticated haunted houses in California," yet 10,000 schoolchildren visit each year to see for themselves. Besides, no one can really explain why photos taken inside the house often develop with foggy apparitions (apparently, 4 spirits haunt the structure). Exhibits include a life mask of Abraham Lincoln, one of only six made; the spinet piano used in the movie *Gone With the Wind;* and the concert piano that accompanied Swedish soprano Jenny Lind on her final U.S. tour in 1852. In back is the cottage that was San Diego's first drugstore (dating to 1867)—it now houses a shop selling attractive Native American art and jewelry. And the nice shop in front is run by the Save Our Heritage Organisation, which offers beautiful Arts & Crafts pottery, architecture-themed books, and crafts.

2482 San Diego Ave. © 619/297-7511. Admission $5 adults, $4 seniors over 60, $3 children 3–12. Wed–Mon 10am–4:30pm. Bus: 5, 5A, or 6. Trolley: Old Town.

MISSION BAY & THE BEACHES

Mission Bay is a manmade, 4,600-acre aquatic playground created in 1945 by dredging tidal mud flats and opening them to sea water. Today, you can this is a great area for walking, jogging, in-line skating, biking, and boating. The boardwalk connecting Mission Beach and Pacific Beach is almost always bustling and colorful. If you get fogged out by June Gloom, head for **The Plunge,** the 175-foot-long indoor pool at the foot of the Giant Dipper. For all of these activities, see the appropriate headings in "Outdoor Pursuits," later in this chapter. For **SeaWorld San Diego,** see p. 137.

Giant Dipper Roller Coaster A local landmark for almost 80 years, the Giant Dipper is one of two surviving fixtures from the original Belmont Amusement Park (the other is the Plunge swimming pool). After sitting dormant for 15 years, the vintage wooden roller coaster, with more than 2,600 feet of track and 13 hills, underwent extensive restoration and reopened in 1991. If you're in the neighborhood (especially with older kids), it's worth a stop, but adults may find the whole experience a bit too spine-rattling. You must be at least 50 inches tall to ride the roller coaster. You can also ride on the Giant Dipper's neighbor, the **Liberty Carousel** ($2), and other carny-style rides (unlimited ride wristband $14). Younger kids will appreciate **Pirate's Cove,** an indoor play center (children 12 and under $6.50).

3190 Mission Blvd., corner of W. Mission Bay Dr. ⓒ **858/488-1549.** www.giantdipper.com. Ride on the Giant Dipper $4. MC, V. Daily 11am–7 or 8pm (weekend and summer hours later). Bus: 34 or 34A. Take I-5 to the SeaWorld exit, and follow W. Mission Bay Dr. to Belmont Park.

LA JOLLA

One of San Diego's most scenic spots—the star of postcards for more than 100 years—is **La Jolla Cove** 𝒜𝒜 and the **Ellen Browning Scripps Park** 𝒜𝒜 on the bluff above it. The walk through the park, along Coast Boulevard (start from the north at Prospect St.), offers some of California's most resplendent coastal scenery. Offshore, the park is a boat-free zone, with protected undersea flora and fauna that draw scuba divers and snorkelers, many of them hoping for a glimpse of the state fish, the rare and brilliant orange garibaldi. Swimming, sunning, picnicking, barbecuing, reading, and strolling along the oceanfront walkway are all ongoing activities, and just south is the **Children's Pool** 𝒜, a beach where dozens of harbor seals can be spotted lazing in the sun (sorry, no swimming here). The unique 6,000-acre **San Diego–La Jolla Underwater Park** 𝒜𝒜 established in 1970, stretches for 10 miles from La Jolla Cove to the northern end of **Torrey Pines State Reserve,** and extends from the shoreline to a depth of 900 feet. It can be reached from La Jolla Cove or La Jolla Shores.

Highlights in town include **Mary Star of the Sea,** 7727 Girard (at Kline), a beautiful Roman Catholic church; and the **La Valencia Hotel,** 1132 Prospect St., a fine example of Spanish colonial structure. The **La Jolla Woman's Club,** 7791 Draper Ave.; the adjacent **Museum of Contemporary Art San Diego;** the **La Jolla Recreation Center;** and **The Bishop's School** are all examples of village buildings designed by architect Irving Gill.

At La Jolla's north end, you'll find the 1,200-acre, 22,000-student **University of California, San Diego** (UCSD), which was established in 1960 and represents the county's largest single employer. The campus features the **Geisel Library** 𝒜𝒜, a striking and distinguished contemporary structure, as well as the **Stuart Collection** of public sculpture and the **Birch Aquarium at Scripps** (see individual listings, below). Louis Kahn designed the **Salk Institute for Biological Studies** 𝒜𝒜,

---

Finds **Hidden Attractions**

While droves of folks stroll the sidewalks adjacent to the San Diego–La Jolla Underwater Park and La Jolla Cove, only a few know about **Coast Walk.** Starting behind the **Cave Store,** 1325 Coast Blvd. (ⓒ **858/459-0746**), it meanders along the wooded cliffs and affords a wonderful view of the beach and beyond. The shop also serves as entry for **Sunny Jim Cave,** an evocative natural sea cave reached by a precipitous constricted staircase through the rock. The tunnel was hand-carved in 1903—it lets out on a wood-plank observation deck from which you can gaze out at the sea. It's a cool treat, particularly on a hot summer day, and costs $3 per person ($2 for kids 16 and under). Hold the handrail and your little ones' hands tightly.

10010 N. Torrey Pines Rd. The research facility named for the creator of the polio vaccine is perhaps San Diego's most noted architectural work (for tours, see "For Architecture Buffs," below). Farther north is an ersatz jewel, **The Lodge at Torrey Pines** (p. 88), a modern re-creation of early-20th-century Craftsman style in the guise of a 175-room luxury resort; it overlooks the revered **Torrey Pines Golf Course** (p. 177).

For a fine scenic drive, follow La Jolla Boulevard to Nautilus Street and turn east to get to 800-foot-high **Mount Soledad** ✿, which offers a 360-degree view of the area. The cross on top, erected in 1954, is 43 feet high and 12 feet wide, and has been a recently been a subject of debate about its suitability in a public park.

Birch Aquarium at Scripps ✿✿   This beautiful facility is both an aquarium and a museum, operated as the interpretive arm of the world-famous Scripps Institution of Oceanography. To make the most of the experience, be sure to pick up a visitor guide from the information booth just inside the entrance, and take time to read the text on each of the exhibits. The aquarium affords close-up views of the Pacific Northwest, the California coast, Mexico's Sea of Cortez, and the tropical seas, all presented in 33 marine-life tanks. The giant kelp forest is particularly impressive; keep an eye out for a tiger shark or an eel swimming through. Be sure to check out the fanciful white anemones and the ethereal moon jellies, which look like parachutes. The sea horse propagation program here has met with excellent results—nine different species of sea horse are on display here. The rooftop demonstration tide pool not only shows visitors marine coastal life but also offers an amazing view of Scripps Pier, La Jolla Shores Beach, the village of La Jolla, and the ocean. Free tidepool talks are offered on weekends, which is also when the aquarium is most crowded, and off-site adventures are conducted year-round (call for more details).

The museum section has numerous interpretive exhibits on current and historic research at the Scripps Institution, which was established in 1903 and became part of the University of California system in 1912. You'll learn what fog is and why salt melts snow; the number of supermarket products with ingredients that come from the sea (including toothpaste and ice cream) might surprise you; and you can feel what an earthquake is like and experience a 12-minute simulated submarine ride. The bookstore is well stocked with textbooks, science books, educational toys, gifts, and T-shirts.

2300 Expedition Way. © **858/534-FISH.** www.aquarium.ucsd.edu. Admission $9.50 adults, $8 seniors, $6 children 3–17, free for children under 3. AE, MC, V. Daily 9am–5pm. Parking $3. Bus: 34. Take I-5 to La Jolla Village Dr. exit, go west 1 mile, and turn left at Expedition Way.

Museum of Contemporary Art San Diego La Jolla ✿✿   Focusing on work produced since 1950, this museum is known internationally for its permanent collection and thought-provoking exhibitions. The MCASD's collection of contemporary art comprises more than 3,000 works of painting, sculpture, drawings, prints, photography, video, and multimedia works. The holdings include every major art movement of the past half-century, with a strong representation by California artists. You'll see particularly noteworthy examples of minimalism, light and space work, conceptualism, installation, and site-specific art—the outside sculptures were designed specifically for this site.

The museum is perched on a cliff overlooking the Pacific Ocean, and the views from the galleries are gorgeous. The original building on the site was the residence of the legendary Ellen Browning Scripps, designed by Irving Gill in 1916. It became an art museum in 1941, and the original Gill building facade

Bus: 30, 34, or 34A. Take I-5 north to La Jolla Pkwy or take I-5 south to La Jolla Village Dr. west. Take Torrey Pines Rd. to Prospect Place and turn right; Prospect Place becomes Prospect St.

Stuart Collection ⚐   Consider the Stuart Collection a work in progress on a large scale. Through a 1982 agreement between the Stuart Foundation and UCSD, the still-growing collection consists of site-related sculptures by leading contemporary artists. Start by picking up a map from the information booth, and wend your way through the 1,200-acre campus to discover the 14 highly diverse artworks. Among them is Niki de Saint-Phalle's *Sun God,* a jubilant 14-foot-high fiberglass bird on a 15-foot concrete base. Nicknamed "Big Bird," it's been made an unofficial mascot by the students, who use it as the centerpiece of their annual celebration, the Sun God Festival. Also in the collection are Alexis Smith's *Snake Path,* a 560-foot-long slate-tile pathway that winds up the hill from the Engineering Mall to the east terrace of the spectacular Geisel Library (breathtaking architecture that's a fabulous sculpture itself); and Terry Allen's *Trees,* three eucalyptus trees encased in lead. One tree emits songs, and another poems and stories, while the third stands silent in a grove of trees the students call "The Enchanted Forest." Allow at least 2 hours to tour the entire collection.

University of California, San Diego. ⓒ 858/534-2117. http://stuartcollection.ucsd.edu. Free admission. Bus: 30, 34, 41, or 101. From La Jolla, take Torrey Pines Rd. to La Jolla Village Dr., turn right, go 2 blocks to Gilman Dr. and turn left into the campus; in about a block the information booth will be visible on the right.

Torrey Pines State Reserve ⚐⚐ *Moments*   The rare torrey pine tree grows only two places in the world: Santa Rosa Island, 175 miles northwest of San Diego, and here, at the north end of La Jolla. Even if the twisted shape of these awkwardly beautiful trees doesn't lure you to this spot, the equally scarce undeveloped coastal scenery should. The city first donated 369 acres as a public park, and the 1,750-acre reserve was established in 1921, from a gift by Ellen Browning Scripps. The reserve encompasses the beach below, as well as a lagoon immediately north, but the focus is the 300-foot-high, water-carved limestone bluffs, which provide a precarious footing for the trees. In spring, the wildflower show includes bush poppies, cleveland sage, agave, and yucca. A half-dozen trails (all under 1½ miles in length) travel from the road to the cliff edge or down to the beach, and there's a small visitor center, built in the traditional adobe style of the Hopi Indians and featuring a lovely 12-minute video about the park. Watch for migrating gray whales in winter, or dolphins who patrol these shores year-round. For a taste of what Southern California's coast looked like a couple hundred years ago, this delicate spot is one of San Diego's unique treasures. *Note:* There are no facilities for food or drinks inside the park—bring a picnic lunch.

Hwy. 101, La Jolla. ⓒ 858/755-2063. www.torreypine.org. Admission $4 per car, $3 seniors. Daily 8am–sunset. Bus: 101. From I-5, take Carmel Valley Rd. west; turn left at Hwy. 101.

CORONADO

It's hard to miss one of Coronado's most famous landmarks: the **San Diego–Coronado Bay Bridge** ⚐. Completed in 1969, this five-lane bridge rises 246 feet above the bay, spanning 2 miles and linking San Diego and the "island" of Coronado. When it opened, it put the delightful commuter ferries out of business; in 1986 passenger-only ferry service restarted, making Coronado a very pleasant day trip from downtown (see "Getting Around: By Water" in chapter 4). Crossing the bridge to Coronado by car or bus is a thrill because you can see Mexico and the shipyards of National City to the left, the San Diego skyline to the right, and Coronado, the naval station, and Point Loma in front

La Jolla Attractions

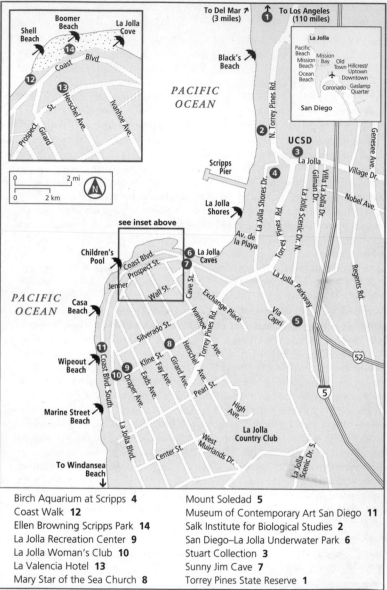

Birch Aquarium at Scripps **4**

Coast Walk **12**

Ellen Browning Scripps Park **14**

La Jolla Recreation Center **9**

La Jolla Woman's Club **10**

La Valencia Hotel **13**

Mary Star of the Sea Church **8**

Mount Soledad **5**

Museum of Contemporary Art San Diego **11**

Salk Institute for Biological Studies **2**

San Diego–La Jolla Underwater Park **6**

Stuart Collection **3**

Sunny Jim Cave **7**

Torrey Pines State Reserve **1**

was uncovered and restored in 1996. More than a dozen exhibitions are presented each year; in 2004 watch for "Chicano Visions," an exhibit curated by Cheech Marin, to take over much of the space here, and at the smaller downtown branch of MCASD. Guided docent tours available daily at 2pm, with a second tour Thursdays at 5:30pm. The bookstore is a great place for cutting-edge gifts, and the cafe is a pleasant stop before or after your visit.

700 Prospect St. ℰ 858/454-3541. www.mcasd.org. Admission $6 adults; $2 students, seniors, and military; free for children under 12. Free 1st Sun and 3rd Tues of each month. Fri–Tues 11am–5pm; Thurs 11am–7pm.

of you (designated drivers have to promise to keep their eyes on the road!). The bridge toll was abolished in 2002, so passage is free. Bus no. 901 from downtown will also take you across the bridge.

Hotel del Coronado 🖈🖈   Built in 1888, this turreted Victorian seaside resort remains an enduring, endearing national treasure. Whether you are lucky enough to stay, dine, or dance here, or simply to wander through to tour its grounds and photo gallery, prepare to be enchanted. See "A Century of Intrigue: Scenes from the Hotel del Coronado" on p. 94 for more details.

1500 Orange Ave., Coronado. ℂ 619/435-6611. Free admission. Parking $4 per hour. Bus: 901. Ferry: Broadway Pier, then ½-hr. walk, or take a bus or the Coronado trolley, or rent a bike.

Museum of History and Art   This museum's new facility offers archival materials about the development of Coronado, as well as tourist information. Exhibits range from photographs of the Hotel Del in its infancy; the old ferries; Tent City, a seaside campground for middle-income vacationers from 1900 to 1939; and notable residents and visitors. Other memorabilia include army uniforms, old postcards, and even recorded music. You'll also learn about the island's military aviation history during World Wars I and II. Plan to spend up to half an hour here. The museum has a self-guided walking tour of Coronado available.

1100 Orange Ave. ℂ 619/435-7242. www.coronadohistory.org. Suggested donation $4 adults, $3 seniors and military, $2 youths 9–18, free to children 8 and under. Mon-Fri 10am–5pm; Sat 11am–4pm. Bus: 901.

FARTHER AFIELD

Chula Vista Nature Center *(Kids*   Sweetwater Marsh is one of San Diego's top bird-watching spots, and the nature center provides walking trails and a facility for experiencing the bird life, as well as stingrays and small sharks in kid-level open tanks. There's a walk-through aviary of shore birds, and other aviaries feature raptors and burrowing owls. The parking lot is located away from the center and a shuttle bus ferries guests between the two points.

1000 Gunpowder Point Dr., Chula Vista. ℂ 619/409-5900. www.chulavistanaturecenter.org. $3.50 adults, $2.50 seniors and students, $1 children 6–17. Tues–Sun 10am–4pm. Free parking. Bus: 708. Trolley: E St. (must call to request shuttle pick-up). From I-5 south take the E St. exit.

Knott's Soak City U.S.A. *(Kids*   Themed to replicate San Diego's surfer towns around the 1950s and 1960s, this 32-acre water park is San Diego's only facility of its type. There are 22 slides of all shapes and sizes, a 500,000-gallon wave pool, a ¼-mile lazy river, and assorted snack facilities. The park is located about 25 minutes south of downtown, just north of the border line.

2052 Entertainment Circle, Chula Vista. ℂ 619/661-7373. www.knotts.com. Admission $23 adults, $17 children ages 3–11; reduced admission after 3pm. Late May to Aug daily 10am–6pm or later; open weekends late April to mid-May and Sept. Parking $6. Take I-5 or I-805 to Main St.; turn right on Entertainment Circle.

5 Free of Charge & Full of Fun

It's easy to get charged up on vacation—$10 here, $5 there, and pretty soon your credit-card balance looks like the national debt. To keep that from happening, here's a summary of free San Diego activities, most of which are described in detail earlier in this chapter. In addition, scan the lists of "Outdoor Pursuits," "Spectator Sports," and "Special-Interest Sightseeing," later in this chapter, and the "San Diego Calendar of Events" in chapter 2. Many events listed in these sections, such as the U.S. Open Sandcastle Competition, are no-charge affairs. And also note that the walking tours outlined in chapter 8 are free to anyone.

DOWNTOWN & BEYOND

It doesn't cost a penny to stroll around the **Gaslamp Quarter,** which brims with restaurants, shops, and historic buildings, or along the Embarcadero (waterfront), and around the shops at Seaport Village or Horton Plaza. And don't forget: **Walkabout International** offers free guided walking tours (described in "Organized Tours," later in this chapter), and Centre City Redevelopment Corporation's Downtown Information Center gives bus tours.

If you'd rather drive around, ask for the map of the **52-mile San Diego Scenic Drive** when you're at the International Visitor Information Center.

The downtown branch of the **Museum of Contemporary Art San Diego** is always free to the public. And you can fish free of charge from any municipal pier (that is, if you bring your own pole).

BALBOA PARK

All the **museums** in Balboa Park are open to the public without charge 1 day a month. Here's a list of the free days:

> **1st Tuesday of each month:** Natural History Museum, Reuben H. Fleet Science Center, Model Railroad Museum.
> **2nd Tuesday:** Museum of Photographic Arts, Historical Society Museum.
> **3rd Tuesday:** Museum of Art, Museum of Man, Mingei International Museum, Japanese Friendship Garden, Museum of the Living Artist.
> **4th Tuesday:** Aerospace Museum, Automotive Museum, Hall of Champions Sports Museum.

These Balboa Park attractions are always free: The Botanical Building and Lily Pond, House of Pacific Relations International Cottages, and Timken Museum of Art.

Free 1-hour Sunday afternoon organ concerts year-round, and free concerts Monday through Thursday evenings in summer are given at the **Spreckels Organ Pavilion.**

There are four free **tours** of the park available, leaving from in front of the visitor center. See "Balboa Park Guided Tours" on p. 149 for more information.

Although it's a local best-kept secret, the **San Diego Zoo** is free to all on the first Monday of October (Founders Day), and children under 12 enter free every day during October.

OLD TOWN & MISSION VALLEY

Explore **Heritage Park, Presidio Park,** or **Old Town State Historic Park.** A 1-hour walking tour of Old Town is conducted twice daily. There's free entertainment (mariachis and folk dancers) at the **Bazaar del Mundo,** 2754 Calhoun, on Saturdays and Sundays.

Mission Trails Regional Park, which offers hiking trails and an interpretive center, is reached by following Highway 8 east to Mission Gorge Road.

MISSION BAY, PACIFIC BEACH & BEYOND

Walk along the **beach** or around the bay—it's free, fun, and holding hands at sunset is a proven aphrodisiac. Bring a picnic lunch to enjoy on the **Ocean Beach Pier** or the **Crystal Pier** in Pacific Beach.

LA JOLLA

Enjoy free outdoor **concerts** at Scripps Park on Sundays from 2 to 4pm, from mid-June to mid-September (© **858/525-3160**).

The half-mile **Coast Walk** between the La Jolla Cove and Children's Pool is San Diego at its most beautiful—dabble in the tide pools along the way and enjoy the harbor seal colony at Seal Rock and the Children's Pool.

It's also fun to meander around the campus of the University of California, San Diego, and view the **Stuart Collection** (bring a pocket-full of quarters for the hungry parking meters). The main branch of the **Museum of Contemporary Art San Diego** is free the first Sunday and third Tuesday of each month. Watching the hang gliders and paragliders launching from the **Gliderport** near Torrey Pines is a blast.

For the **best vista,** follow the SCENIC DRIVE signs to Mount Soledad and a 360-degree view of the area.

CORONADO

Drive across the toll-free Coronado Bay Bridge and take a self-guided tour of the **Hotel del Coronado's** grounds and photo gallery. A walk on beautiful Coronado **beach** costs nothing—so does a lookie-loo tour of the neighborhood's restored Victorian and Craftsman homes.

FARTHER AFIELD

Free tours of the **ARCO Olympic Training Center** in Chula Vista are given year-round. This is the country's first warm-weather, year-round, multisport Olympic training complex. It's on the western shore of Lower Otay Reservoir in Chula Vista, and is one of three United States Olympic Committee training centers. (The others are in Colorado Springs, Colorado, and Lake Placid, New York.) Visitors see a 6-minute film about the Olympic movement, followed by a narrated tour (1½-mile walk) of the 150-acre campus. The hour-long tours are given every hour on the hour, Monday through Saturday from 10am to 3pm, Sunday from 11am to 3pm. Call © **619/482-6222** for more information.

To get here, take I-805 south to Telegraph Canyon Road, then go east about 7 miles until you reach a sign directing you to turn right; follow this road to the visitor center.

6 Especially for Kids

If you didn't know better, you would think that San Diego was designed by parents planning a long summer vacation. Activities abound for toddlers to teens. Dozens of public parks, 70 miles of beaches, and many museums are just part of what awaits kids and families. For up-to-the-minute information about activities for children, pick up a free copy of the monthly *San Diego Family Press;* its calendar of events is geared toward family activities and kids' interests. The **International Visitor Information Center,** at First Avenue and F Street (© **619/236-1212**), is always a great resource. The **Children's Museum of San Diego** (downtown on Island St.) is currently undergoing a construction project and will reopen in 2005.

THE TOP ATTRACTIONS

- **Balboa Park** (p. 144) has street entertainers and clowns that always rate high with kids. They can usually be found around El Prado on weekends. The **Natural History Museum,** the **Model Railroad Museum,** the **Aerospace Museum,** and the **Reuben H. Fleet Science Center**—with its hands-on exhibits and IMAX theater—draw kids like magnets.
- The **San Diego Zoo** (p. 133) appeals to children of all ages, and the double-decker bus tours bring all the animals into easy view of even the smallest visitors. There's a Children's Zoo within the zoo, and kids adore the performing sea lion show.

- **SeaWorld San Diego** (p. 137), on Mission Bay, entertains everyone with killer whales, pettable dolphins, and plenty of penguins—the park's penguin exhibit is home to more penguins than are in all other zoos combined. Try out the family adventure land, "Shamu's Happy Harbor," where everyone is encouraged to explore, crawl, climb, jump, and get wet in more than 20 interactive areas; or, brave a raging river in Shipwreck Rapids.
- The **San Diego Wild Animal Park** (p. 134) brings geography classes to life when kids find themselves gliding through the wilds of Africa and Asia in a monorail. For visitors age 8 and up, the Roar & Snore camping program— held April through October on weekends—is immensely popular.

OTHER ATTRACTIONS

- **Seaport Village** (p. 204) has an old-fashioned carousel for children to enjoy.
- **Old Town State Historic Park** (p. 156) has a one-room schoolhouse that rates high with kids. They'll also enjoy the freedom of running around the safe, park-like compound to "discover" their own fun.
- **Birch Aquarium at Scripps** (p. 158), in La Jolla, is an aquarium that lets kids explore the realms of the deep and learn about life in the sea.
- **Knott's Soak City U.S.A.** (p. 161) is a water park with slides, raft adventures, and a wave pool.
- **The Gliderport** will entertain kids as they watch aerial acrobats swoop through the skies. See "Outdoor Pursuits: Hang Gliding & Paragliding," later in this chapter for details.
- **Chula Vista Nature Center** (p. 177) is a small facility located near the bottom of San Diego Bay that has a walk-through aviary and tanks for getting up-close with stingrays and small sharks.
- **LEGOLAND California** (p. 235), in Carlsbad, features impressive models built entirely with LEGO blocks. There are also rides, refreshments, and LEGO and DUPLO building contests. The park advertises itself as a "country just for kids"—need I say more?

THAT'S ENTERTAINMENT

The Globe Theatres (© **619/239-2255;** www.theglobetheatres.org) showcases *Dr. Seuss' How the Grinch Stole Christmas* each year during the holidays—performances are scheduled mid-November through December. **San Diego Junior Theatre** (© **619/239-8355;** www.juniortheatre.com) is the oldest continuing children's theater program in the country, operating since 1948. The productions—shows like *Peter Pan* and *Little Women,* and staged at Balboa Park's Casa del Prado Theatre—are acted and managed by kids 8 to 18. Ticket prices are $7 to $10 for adults, $5 to $7 for children and seniors, and performances are held on Friday evenings and Saturday and Sunday afternoons.

Sunday afternoon is a great time for kids in **Balboa Park.** They can visit both the outdoor Spreckels Organ Pavilion for a free concert (the mix of music isn't too highbrow for a young audience) and the House of Pacific Relations to watch folk dancing on the lawn and taste food from many nations. Or, try the **Marie Hitch-cock Puppet Theatre,** in Balboa Park's Palisades Building (© **619/685-5990**). Individual shows might feature marionettes, hand puppets, or ventriloquism, and the stories range from classic *Grimm's Fairy Tales* and *Aesop's Fables* to more obscure yarns. Performances are Wednesday through Friday at 10 and 11:30am and Saturday and Sunday at 11am, 1, and 2:30pm. The shows cost $3 for adults, $2 for seniors and children over 2; they're free for children under 2.

7 Special-Interest Sightseeing

FOR ARCHITECTURE BUFFS

San Diego's historical architecture is most often defined by the abundance of Spanish mission structures, a style that was introduced to California by Father Junípero Serra at the **Mission Basilica San Diego.** Ostensibly, the adobe walls and tile roofs made it harder for Indians to burn down his churches. Spanish colonial style was revived gloriously for the 1915–16 **Panama-California Exposition** in Balboa Park by New York architect Bertram Goodhue, who oversaw a romantic fantasia abounding with Mediterranean flourishes.

But San Diego's first important architect was Irving Gill, who arrived in the city in 1893 and soon made his mark by designing buildings to integrate into the desert-like landscape. Gill's structures include numerous homes in Uptown and La Jolla. Following the Expo, prolific local architects like William Templeton Johnson and Richard Requa integrated the Spanish/Mediterranean concept into their structures around the city, most famously the **Serra Museum** at Presidio Park, downtown's **County Administration Center,** and the **Torrey Pines Visitors Center.**

Modernism swept through the city after World War II, championed by Lloyd Ruocco, and the city's steady growth after the war allowed many inspired architects to leave their handprint on San Diego. The fast development has led to more than a few blunders along the way, and *San Diego Union-Tribune* architecture critic Ann Jarmusch publishes an annual "Orchids and Onions" list of the city's best and worst debuts; my least favorite addition to the city is the recent expansion of the **San Diego Convention Center,** which proves most effective as a ludicrous barrier to any view of the waterfront from downtown.

Historic buildings of particular interest include houses like the Victorian **Villa Montezuma** (p. 152) and the Craftsman-style **Marston House** (p. 146). The **Gaslamp Quarter** walking tour (see chapter 8) will lead you past the area's restored Victorian commercial buildings. A stroll along the **Prado of Balboa Park** (also described in chapter 8) is a must, and turn-of-the-20th-century neighborhoods like **Bankers Hill** (just west of Balboa Park) and **Mission Hills** (west of Hillcrest) are feasts of Victorian mansions and Craftsman abodes. In **La Jolla,** you'll find the classic buildings created by Irving Gill (see "More Attractions," earlier in this chapter).

Downtown blends old and new with mixed results. One success is the **Martin Luther King Jr. Promende,** a 1993 walkway along Harbor Drive, between Eighth Avenue and Broadway; conceived by Max Schmidt, the slender pedestrian-friendly park parallels the trolley corridor and promotes the city's cultural heritage and features public art pieces. The older homes of **Little Italy,** the quaint business and residential district along India Street (between Ash and Laurel sts.), is both endangered by the current building craze and also thriving amid some of the city's most progressive architecture. While you're in the central business district, take a look at the sprawling scale model of the city at the Centre City Development Corporation's Downtown Information Center, 225 Broadway (© **619/235-2200**); it gives a taste of where the city is headed.

A splendid corridor of contemporary architecture has sprouted around the University of California, San Diego, including the campus's spacecraft-like **Geisel Library,** by William Pereira. Nearby is the Louis Kahn–designed **Salk Institute** and the **Neurosciences Institute,** a 1996 creation by Tod Williams-Billie Tsien. A free tour of the Salk Institute is held Monday through Friday at midday; call

---

Fun Fact **What Was That Flower?**

Balboa Park isn't the only place to see San Diego in bloom. Among the common trees and shrubs to watch for in flower:

January: Blooming aloe, agave, azalea, and camellias.

February: Acacia, angel's trumpet, gold medallion tree, strawberry snowball tree, pink trumpet tree, cup of gold vine.

March through April: Blue hibiscus, orchid tree, ceanothus, coral tree, Australian tea tree, silk oak, protea, Indian hawthorn, Mexican bush sage, bird of paradise, Chinese wisteria, roses.

May: Bougainvillea, Australian flame tree, hibiscus, southern magnolia, pink melaleuca, sausage tree, Mexican palo verde.

June through August: False heather, garden hydrangea, jacaranda, plumeria, African tulip tree, yellow oleander.

September through December: Chinese flame tree, golden raintree, Hong Kong orchid tree, weeping bottle brush, ginkgo.

© **858/453-4100,** ext. 1200, for times and to reserve a place. Not far from the Salk Institute, the Michael Graves–designed **Hyatt Regency La Jolla** garnered an "Onion" from Ann Jarmusch.

For more information on San Diego architecture, call the local branch of the **AIA** (© **619/232-0109**). And for a self-guided tour of the city's highlights, Dirk Sutro's *San Diego Architecture* (San Diego Architectural Foundation, 2002; $25) is indispensable, with maps, addresses, and descriptions of hundreds of important structures throughout the city.

FOR GARDENERS

Although most years we struggle with too little rain, San Diego is a gardener's paradise, thanks in large part to the initial efforts and inspiration of Kate Sessions, who planted the initial trees that led to today's mature landscapes in **Balboa Park** (p. 144). While in the park be sure to visit the **Japanese Friendship Garden,** the **Botanical Building and Lily Pond,** and the **rose and desert gardens** (across the road from Plaza de Balboa). And you'll notice that both the **San Diego Zoo** (p. 133) and **Wild Animal Park** (p. 134) are outstanding botanical gardens. Many visitors who admire the landscaping at the zoo don't realize that the plantings have been carefully developed over the years. The 100 acres were once scrub-covered hillsides with few trees. Today, towering eucalyptus and graceful palms, birds-of-paradise, and hibiscus are just a few of the 6,500 botanical species from all over the world that flourish here, providing a beautiful garden setting as well as dinner for some animals. In fact, the plant collection is worth more than the zoo's animal menagerie.

Garden enthusiasts will also want to stop by the 30-acre **Quail Botanical Gardens** in Encinitas (see "North County Beach Towns: Spots to Surf & Sun" in chapter 11). If you'd like to take plants home with you, visit some of the area's nurseries, starting with the charming neighborhood one started in 1910 by Kate Sessions, the **Mission Hills Nursery,** 1525 Fort Stockton Dr. (© **619/295-2808**). **Walter Andersen's Nursery,** 3642 Enterprise St. (© **619/224-8271**), is also a local favorite. See chapter 11 for information on nurseries in North County. Flower growing is big business in this area, and plant enthusiasts could spend a week just visiting the retail and wholesale purveyors of everything from pansies to palm trees.

Founded by Kate Sessions, the **San Diego Floral Association,** the oldest garden club in Southern California and based in the Casa del Prado in Balboa Park (© 619/232-5762; www.sdfloral.org), does day tours involving places of horticultural interest, and has events featuring speakers, classes, and exhibits.

FOR MILITARY BUFFS

The public is welcome to attend a **recruit graduation** at the Marine Corps Recruit Depot, off Pacific Coast Highway (near Barnett St.), held most Fridays at 10am (© 619/524-1765). **Old Town Trolley Tours** (© 619/298-TOUR) offers a "Tour of Patriots" via amphibious vehicles, on Tuesdays. You'll visit Shelter Island, tour MCRD, do a walk through the base Command Museum, and have an opportunity to purchase military memorabilia at the base gift shop. The 3-hour tour costs $24 ($12 for kids ages 4–12).

FOR WINE LOVERS

Visit **Orfila Vineyards** (© 760/738-6500; www.orfila.com), near the Wild Animal Park in Escondido. Italian-born winemaker Leon Santoro is a veteran of Napa Valley (Louis Martini and Stag's Leap). Besides producing excellent chardonnay and merlot, the winery also makes several Rhône and Italian varietals, including sangiovese. The tasting room is open daily from 10am to 6pm, and guided tours are offered at 2pm. The property includes a parklike picnic area and a shop.

Other North County wineries include the **Bernardo Winery,** just south of Escondido (© 858/487-1866), and **Fallbrook Winery** in Fallbrook (© 760/728-0156). If you have time to go farther afield, the wineries along Rancho California Road in **Temecula,** just across the San Diego County line, are open for tours and tastings; for details, see "Touring Temecula's Wineries" on p. 246.

8 Organized Tours

It's almost impossible to get a handle on the diversity of San Diego in a short visit, but one way to maximize your time is to take an organized tour that introduces you to the city. Many tours are creative, not as touristy as you might fear, and allow you a great deal of versatility in planning your day.

Centre City Development Corporation's **Downtown Information Center,** 225 Broadway, Suite 160 (© 619/235-2222; www.ccdc.com), offers free downtown bus tours the first and third Saturdays of the month at 10am and noon. Aimed at prospective home buyers in the downtown area, as well as curious locals trying to stay abreast of the developments, the 90-minute tours require reservations. Go inside the information center to see models of the Gaslamp Quarter and the downtown area. The office is open Monday through Saturday from 9am to 5pm.

BAY EXCURSIONS

The Gondola Company   This unique business operates from Loews Coronado Bay Resort, plying the calm waters between pleasure-boat docks in gondolas crafted according to centuries-old designs from Venice. It features all the trimmings, right down to the striped-shirt-clad gondolier with ribbons waving from his or her straw hat. Mediterranean music plays while you and up to five friends recline with snuggly blankets, and the company will even provide antipasto appetizers (or chocolate-dipped strawberries) and chilled wineglasses and ice for the beverage of your choice (BYOB).

4000 Coronado Bay Rd., Coronado. © 619/429-6317. Daily 11am–midnight. 1-hr. cruise $60 per couple, $15 for each additional passenger (up to 6 total).

Hornblower Cruises   This company has a fleet of seven yachts ranging from 40-passenger to a three-deck, 880-passenger behemoth. On Hornblower's 2-hour narrated harbor tour you'll see the *Star of India*, cruise under the San Diego–Coronado Bridge, visit the Hotel Del and the Submarine Base, and swing by an aircraft carrier or two; a 1-hour itinerary is also available. Guests are welcome to visit the captain's wheelhouse for a photo op, and harbor seals and sea lions on buoys and barges are a regular sighting. Whale-watching trips (mid-Dec to late Mar) are a blast, and Hornblower does special itineraries for most holidays (like a fireworks route for Fourth of July festivities). There's also a 2-hour Sunday (and Sat in summer) brunch cruise at 11am, with unlimited champagne and a plentiful buffet, and nightly dinner cruises (see "Cruises with Entertainment" in chapter 10).

1066 N. Harbor Dr. (℃ **800/ON-THE-BAY** or 619/686-8715. www.hornblower.com. Harbor tours $15–$20 adult ($2 off for seniors and military; half price for children 4–12). Brunch cruise $45; whale-watching trips $25 (both $2 off for seniors and military, half price for children 4–12). Bus: 2. Trolley: Embarcadero.

San Diego Harbor Excursions   This company also offers daily 1- and 2-hour narrated tours of the bay, using its fleet of seven boats ranging from a 1940s passenger launch to a modern, paddlewheel-style vessel. The 1-hour itinerary covers 12 miles including the *Star of India*, U.S. Navy surface fleet, the San Diego–Coronado Bridge, and shipyards; the 25-mile 2-hour route also visits the Submarine Base and North Island Naval Air Station. In winter, whale-watching excursions feature naturalists from the Birch Aquarium. The 2-hour Sunday brunch cruise aboard a sleek yacht is popular; dinner cruises sail nightly (see "Cruises with Entertainment" in chapter 10).

1050 N. Harbor Dr. (foot of Broadway). (℃ **800/44-CRUISE** or 619/234-4111. www.sdhe.com. Harbor tours $13 for 1 hr., $18 for 2 hr. ($2 off for seniors and military; half price for children 4–12). Brunch cruise $40 adults, $30 children; whale-watching trips $25 adults, $21 seniors, $15 children. Bus: 2. Trolley: Embarcadero.

BUS TOURS

Family-owned **Contact Tours** (℃ **800/235-5393** or 619/477-8687; www.contactours.com) offers city sightseeing tours, including a "Grand Tour" that covers San Diego, Tijuana, and a 1-hour harbor cruise. It also runs trips to the San Diego Zoo, SeaWorld, Disneyland, Universal Studios, Tijuana, Rosarito Beach, and Ensenada. Prices range from $26 for the 3½-hour City Tour to $52 for the full-day Grand Tour ($12–$24 for children 3–11), and include admissions. Multiple tours can be combined for discounted rates. Contact picks up passengers at most area hotels.

Tips   **San Diego by Land & Sea at the Same Time**

If you can't decide between a bus tour of San Diego's most popular neighborhoods and a cruise of the city's prettiest waterways, then opt for an amphibious tour from **Sea and Land Adventures.** Their 2-hour tours depart from Seaport Village hourly every day starting at 10am; each specially built boat holds 50 passengers. After cruising the streets of the Gaslamp Quarter, Old Town, and Coronado—and garnering the curious stares of passersby—you'll take a dip into both San Diego and Mission bays to experience the maritime and military history of San Diego from the right perspective. The trips cost $24 for adults and $12 for kids 4 to 12. For information and tickets, call ℃ **619/298-8687,** or visit www.historictours.com.

TROLLEY TOURS

Not to be confused with the public transit trolley, the narrated **Old Town Trolley Tours** (✆ **619/298-TOUR;** www.historictours.com) are an easy way to get an overview of the city, especially if you're short on time. But the open-air trolleys are also a good way to tie together visits to several of San Diego's major attractions without driving or resorting to pricey cabs. The trackless trolleys do a 30-mile circular route, and you can hop off at any one of eight stops, explore at leisure, and reboard when you please (the trolleys run every half-hour). Stops include Old Town, the Gaslamp Quarter and downtown area, Coronado, the San Diego Zoo, and Balboa Park. You can begin wherever you want, but you must purchase tickets before boarding (most stops have a ticket kiosk). The tour costs $24 for adults ($12 for kids 4–12, free for children 3 and under) for one complete loop; the route by itself takes about 2 hours. The trolleys operate daily from 9am to 4pm in winter, and from 9am to 5pm in summer.

Old Town Trolley also operates a humor-fueled **Ghosts & Gravestones** tour. The 2-hour excursion is done in conjunction with the Gaslamp Quarter Foundation and the San Diego Historical Society, and visits the Whaley House, Villa Montezuma, and the William Heath Davis House, and concludes with a walk through one of the city's oldest cemeteries. The tour departs most evenings from the Horton Grand Hotel in the Gaslamp Quarter; reservations required, and bringing a sweater or jacket is recommended. Ghosts & Gravestones costs $28 and is restricted to ages 8 and up only.

WALKING TOURS

Walkabout International, 4639 30th St., Suite C, San Diego (✆ **619/231-7463;** www.walkabout-int.org), sponsors more than 100 free walking tours every month that are led by local volunteers, listed in a monthly newsletter and on the website. Walking tours hit all parts of the county, including the Gaslamp Quarter, La Jolla, and the beaches, and there's a hike in the mountains every Wednesday and Saturday.

Coronado Touring, 1110 Isabella Ave., Coronado (✆ **619/435-5993**), provides upbeat, informative 90-minute walking tours of Coronado, including the Hotel del Coronado. Enthusiastic guide Nancy Cobb has been doing this since 1980, so she knows her subject well. Tours leave at 11am on Tuesday, Thursday, and Saturday from the Glorietta Bay Inn, 1630 Glorietta Blvd. (opposite the Hotel del Coronado). The price is $8.

The **Gaslamp Quarter Historical Foundation** offers tours of the quarter every Saturday at 11am. Tours depart from the William Heath Davis House Museum, 410 Island Ave., and cost $8. For more information, contact the foundation directly at ✆ **619/233-4692** or www.gaslampquarter.org.

Volunteers from the Canyoneer group of the **San Diego Natural History Museum** (✆ **619/255-0203;** www.sdnhm.org/canyoneers) lead free guided nature walks throughout San Diego County. The walks are held every Saturday and Sunday (except July–Aug), and usually focus on the flora and fauna of a particular area, which might be a city park or as far away as Anza-Borrego Desert. The hikes are great fun.

At the **Cabrillo National Monument** on the tip of Point Loma (p. 151), rangers often lead free walking tours. Docents at **Torrey Pines State Reserve** in La Jolla (p. 160) lead interpretive nature walks at 10am and 2pm on weekends and holidays. And guided walks are often scheduled at **Mission Trails Regional Park** (p. 155).

Also see "Outdoor Pursuits," below, for more unguided trail options.

WHALE-WATCHING

Along the California coast, whale-watching is an eagerly anticipated wintertime activity, particularly in San Diego—the Pacific gray whale passes close by Point Loma on its annual migratory trek. Local whaling in the 1870s greatly reduced their numbers, but federal protection has allowed the species to re-populate and current estimates number about 27,000 grays in the ocean today. If you've ever been lucky enough to spot one of these gentle behemoths swimming gracefully and resolutely through the ocean, you'll understand the thrill. When they approach San Diego, the 40- to 50-foot gray whales are more than three-quarters of the way along their nearly 6,000-mile journey from Alaska to breeding lagoons near the southern tip of Baja California, for mating and calving—or just beginning the trip home to the rich Alaskan feeding grounds (with calves in tow). The epic journey for these cetaceans is one of the longest migrations of any mammal. From mid-December to mid-March is the best time to see the migration, and there are several ways to view their parade.

The easiest (and cheapest) is to grab a pair of binoculars and head to a good landbound vantage point. The best is **Cabrillo National Monument,** at the tip of Point Loma, where you'll find a glassed-in observatory and educational whale exhibits, 400 feet above sea level. When the weather cooperates, you can often spot the whales as they surface for breathing—as many as eight grays per hour at peak commute (mid-Jan). Each January the rangers conduct a special "Whale Watch Weekend" featuring presentations by whale experts, children's programs, and entertainment. For more information on Cabrillo National Monument, see p. 151.

If you want to get a closer look, head out to sea on one of the excursions that locate and follow gray whales, taking care not to disturb their journey. **Classic Sailing Adventures** (© 800/659-0141 or 619/224-0800; www.classicsailing adventures.com) offers two trips per day (8:30am and 1pm); each lasts 4 hours and carries a maximum of six passengers. Sailboats are less distracting to the whales than cruises, but more expensive; tickets are $60 per person (minimum two passengers), including beverages and snacks.

Companies that offer traditional, engine-driven expeditions include **Hornblower Cruises** and **San Diego Harbor Excursions** (see "Bay Excursions," above). Excursions are 3 or 3½ hours, and fares run $25 for adults, with discounts for kids.

In La Jolla, the **Birch Aquarium at Scripps** celebrates gray whale season with classes, educational activities, and exhibits, and the outdoor terrace offers another vantage point for spotting the mammals from shore. Multi-day trips to San Ignacio in Baja California, where the whales mate and calve are offered in February and March, and Birch provides naturalists to accompany the whale watching done by San Diego Harbor Excursions (see "Bay Excursions," above). Call © 858/534-7336 for more information.

The **San Diego Natural History Museum** also offers multi-day, naturalist-led whale-watching trips to Baja. For a schedule and preregistration, call © 619/255-0203 or check www.sdnhm.org/education.

9 Outdoor Pursuits

See section 2 of this chapter for a complete rundown of San Diego's beaches, and section 8 for details on whale-watching excursions.

Outdoor Pursuits in the San Diego Area

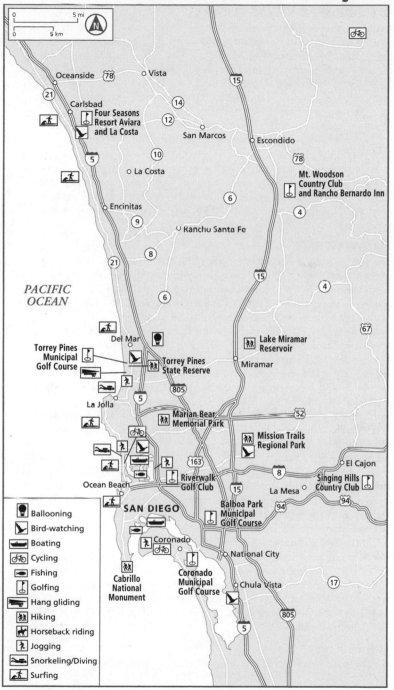

BALLOONING & SCENIC FLIGHTS

A peaceful dawn or dusk balloon ride reveals sweeping vistas of the Southern California coast, wine country, rambling estates, and golf courses. For a champagne-fueled glimpse of the county at sunrise or sunset, followed by an hors d'oeuvres party, contact **Skysurfer Balloon Company** (© 800/660-6809 or 858/481-6800; www.sandiegohotairballoons.com). The rate for a 40- to 60-minute flight is $135 per person weekdays, $145 Saturday and Sunday; sunrise flights leave from Temecula (70 min. north of downtown) and sunset flights are from Del Mar (25 min. from downtown). Or call **California Dreamin'** (© 800/373-3359 or 760/438-3344; www.californiadreamin.com). They charge $138 for 1-hour sunrise breakfast flight in Temecula, $148 for sunset flights in Del Mar that last up to 1 hour; both include champagne and a personalized flight photo. California Dreamin' also offers a **biplane adventure** over Temecula's wine country starting at $138 for two people. You may also be interested in the **Temecula Balloon & Wine Festival** held in early June; call © 909/676-4713 or visit www.tvbwf.com for information.

BIRD-WATCHING

The birding scene is huge: More than 480 species have been observed in San Diego County, more than any other county in the United States. The area is a haven along the Pacific Flyway—the migratory route along the Pacific Coast—and the diverse range of ecosystems also helps to lure a wide range of winged creatures. It's possible for birders to enjoy four distinct bird habitats in a single day.

Among the best places for bird-watching is the **Chula Vista Nature Center** at Sweetwater Marsh National Wildlife Refuge (© 619/409-5900; www.chulavista naturecenter.org), where you may spot rare residents like the light-footed clapper rail and the western snowy plover, as well as predatory species like the American peregrine falcon and northern harrier. The nature center also has aquariums for sharks and rays, aviaries featuring raptors and shorebirds, and a garden featuring native plants (p. 161). Also worth visiting along the coast are the 25-acre **Kendall Frost Marsh** on the east side of Crown Point, in Mission Bay, which draws skimmers, shorebirds, brant and, in winter, the large-billed savannah sparrow; and the **Torrey Pines State Reserve** (p. 160), north of La Jolla, a protected habitat for swifts, thrashers, woodpeckers, and wrentits. Inland, **Mission Trails Regional Park** (p. 155) is a 5,800-acre urban park that is visited by orange-crowned warblers, swallows, raptors, and numerous riparian species; and the **Anza-Borrego Desert State Park** (see chapter 11) makes an excellent day trip from San Diego—268 species of birds have been recorded here.

Birders coming to the area should obtain a copy of the free brochure **"Birding Hot Spots of San Diego,"** available at the Port Administration Building, 3165 Pacific Hwy., and at the San Diego Zoo, Wild Animal Park, San Diego Natural History Museum, and Birch Aquarium. It is also posted online at www.portof sandiego.org/sandiego_environment/bird_brochure.asp. The **San Diego Audubon Society** is another source of birding information (© 619/682-7200; www.sandiegoaudubon.org.)

BIKING

San Diego is on the verge of becoming the nation's preeminent bicycling destination, with millions of dollars earmarked for bicycle paths throughout the city and county, including one which will parallel the rail line as far as Oceanside. But already, San Diego is cyclist friendly, and was named "one of the top 10 cities in the

U.S. to bicycle" by *Bicycling* magazine. Most major thoroughfares offer bike lancs. To obtain a detailed map by mail of San Diego County's hike lanes and routes, call **Ride Link Bicycle Information** (© **619/231-BIKE** or 800/COMMUTE). You might also want to talk to the **City of San Diego Bicycle Coordinator** (© **619/533-3110**) or the **San Diego County Bicycle Coalition** (© **858/487-6063**). For more practical information on biking on city streets, turn to "Getting Around: By Bicycle," in chapter 4. Always remember to wear a helmet; it's the law.

The paths around Mission Bay, in particular, are great for leisurely rides. The oceanfront boardwalk between Pacific Beach and Mission Beach can get very crowded, especially on weekends (but that's half the fun). Coronado has a 16-mile round-trip bike trail that starts at the Ferry Landing Marketplace and follows a well-marked route around Coronado to Imperial Beach, along the Silver Strand. The road out to Point Loma (Catalina Dr.) offers moderate hills and wonderful scenery. Traveling old State Route 101 (aka the Pacific Coast Hwy.) from La Jolla north to Oceanside offers terrific coastal views, along with plenty of places to refuel with coffee, a snack, or a swim. The 13-mile climb up steep switchbacks to the summit of 6,140-foot Mt. Palomar is perhaps the county's most invigorating challenge, and offers its most gleeful descent.

Bikes are allowed on the San Diego–Coronado ferry, the San Diego Trolley, and most city buses, at no charge. *Cycling San Diego* by Nelson Copp and Jerry Schad (Sunbelt Publications) is a good resource for bicyclists and is available at most local bike shops.

RENTALS, ORGANIZED BIKE TOURS & OTHER TWO-WHEEL ADVENTURES

Downtown, call **Bike Tours San Diego,** 509 Fifth Ave. (© **619/238-2444**), which offers free delivery as far north as Del Mar. Rates for a city/hybrid bike start at $18 for a day, and include helmets, locks, maps, and roadside assistance.

In Mission Bay, there's **Mission Beach Club,** 704 Ventura Place, off Mission Boulevard at Ocean Front Walk (© **858/488-8889**), for 1-speed beach cruisers; **Cheap Rentals,** 3685 and 3221 Mission Blvd. (© **858/488-9070**), for mountain bikes and more; and **Hilton San Diego Resort,** 1775 E. Mission Bay Dr. (© 619/276-4010), for multispeed bikes. In La Jolla, try **California Bicycle,** 7462 La Jolla Blvd. (© **858/454-0316**), for front-suspended mountain bikes. In Coronado, check out **Bikes and Beyond,** 1201 First St. at the Ferry Landing Marketplace (© **619/435-7180**), for beach cruisers and mountain bikes; they also offer surrey and skate rentals. Expect to pay $6 and up per hour for bicycles, $30 for 24 hours.

Adventurous cyclists might like to participate in the **Rosarito-Ensenada 50-Mile Fun Bicycle Ride,** held every April and September just across the border in Mexico. This event attracts more than 8,000 riders of all ages and abilities. It starts at the Rosarito Beach Hotel and finishes in Ensenada and rides along paved highway. For information, contact **Bicycling West, Inc.** (© **619/424-6084;** www.rosaritoensenada.com).

BOATING

Sailors have a choice of the calm waters of 4,600-acre **Mission Bay,** with its 26 miles of shoreline; the exciting **San Diego Bay,** which is one of the most beautiful natural harbors in the world; or the **Pacific Ocean,** where you can sail south to the Islas los Coronados (that is, the trio of uninhabited islets on the Mexico side of the border). There are more than 55,000 registered water craft docked at 26 marinas throughout the county.

Seaforth Boat Rental, 1641 Quivira Rd., Mission Bay (© **888/834-2628** or 619/223-1681; www.seaforthboatrental.com), has a wide variety of boats for bay and ocean. It rents 15- to 240-horsepower powerboats ranging from $55 to $115 an hour, 14- to 25-foot sailboats for $20 to $40 an hour, and ski boats and jet skis starting at $70 an hour. Half- and full-day rates are available. Canoes, kayaks, and pedal boats also available, as well as fishing boats and equipment. Seaforth has locations downtown at the Marriott San Diego Hotel & Marina, 333 W. Harbor Dr. (© **619/239-2628**) and in Coronado at 1715 Strand Way (© **619/437-1514**).

Mission Bay Sportcenter, 1010 Santa Clara Place (© **858/488-1004;** www.missionbaysportcenter.com), rents sailboats, catamarans, sailboards, kayaks, jet skis, and motorboats. Prices range from $18 to $95 an hour, with discounts for 4-hour and full-day rentals. Private instruction is available for $30 per hour.

The Harbor Vacations Club, 1880 Harbor Island Dr. (© **619/298-6623**), rents 55-foot Bluewater yachts, a 41-troller, a 32-foot catamaran, and a houseboat. Half-day, full-day, and overnight rentals are available.

Sail USA (© **619/298-6822**) offers custom-tailored skippered cruises on a 34-foot Catalina sloop. A half-day bay cruise costs $275 for six passengers. Full-day and overnight trips are also available, as are trips to Ensenada and to Catalina.

Based at Shelter Island Marina, **Classic Sailing Adventures** (© **800/659-0141** or 619/224-0800; www.classicsailingadventures.com) offers two 4-hour sailing trips daily aboard *Soul Diversion,* a 38-foot Ericson. The afternoon cruise leaves at 1pm and a Champagne sunset sail departs at 5pm. The yacht carries a maximum of six passengers (minimum 2), and the $60-per-person price includes beverages and snacks.

FISHING

In the late 1940s, the waters off San Diego supplied as much as two-thirds of the nation's supply of tuna, so it's no wonder that San Diego offers exhilaration to sportfishers. The sportfishing fleet consists of more than 75 large commercial vessels and several dozen private charter yachts, and a variety of half-, full-, and multi-day trips are available. The saltwater fishing season kicks off each spring with the traditional **Port of San Diego Day at the Docks,** held the last weekend in April or at the beginning of May at Sportfishing Landing, near Shelter Island; for more information, call © **619/234-8791** or see www.sportfishing.org. Anglers of any age can fish free of charge without a license off any municipal pier in California. Public fishing piers are on Shelter Island (where there's a statue dedicated to anglers), Ocean Beach, and Imperial Beach.

Summer and fall are ideal for fishing, when the waters around Point Loma are brimming with bass, bonito, and barracuda; the Islas los Coronados, which belong to Mexico but are only about 18 miles from San Diego, are popular for abalone, yellowtail, yellowfin, and big-eyed tuna. Some outfitters will take you farther into Baja California waters on multi-day trips. Fishing charters depart from Harbor and Shelter Islands, Point Loma, the Imperial Beach pier, and Quivira Basin in Mission Bay (near the Hyatt Islandia Hotel). Participants over 16 need a California fishing license.

Rates for trips on a large boat average $35 for a half-day trip or $70 for a ¾-day trip, or you can spring $90 for a 20-hour overnight trip to the Islas los Coronados—call around and compare prices. Prices are reduced for kids, and discounts are often available for twilight sailings; charters or "limited load" rates are also available. The following outfitters offer short or extended outings with daily departures: **H & M Landing**, 2803 Emerson (© **619/222-1144;** www.hmlanding.com); **Lee Palm Sportfishers**, 2801 Emerson (© **619/224-3857;** www.redrooster3.com); **Point Loma Sportfishing**, 1403 Scott St. (© **619/223-1627;** www.pointlomasport fishing.com); and **Seaforth Sportfishing**, 1717 Quivira Rd. (© **619/224-3383;** www.seaforthlanding.com). All of these shops rent tackle.

For freshwater fishing, San Diego's lakes and rivers are home to bass, channel and bullhead catfish, bluegill, trout, crappie, and sunfish. Most lakes have rental facilities for boats, tackle, and bait, and they also provide picnic and (usually) camping areas. A 1-day California State Fishing License costs $11; a 1-year license is $30. For information on lake fishing, call the city's **Lakes Line** © **619/465-3474.**

For information on fishing at **Lake Cuyamaca,** 1 hour from San Diego near Julian, see "Julian: Apple Pies & More" in chapter 11. For more information on fishing in California, contact the **California Department of Fish and Game** (© **858/467-4200;** www.dfg.ca.gov). For fishing in Mexican waters, including the area off the Coronado Islands, angling permits are required. Most charter companies will take of the details, but if not, contact the **Mexican Department of Fisheries,** 2550 Fifth Ave., Suite 101, San Diego, CA 92103-6622 (© **619/ 233-6956**).

GOLF

With 90-plus courses, more than 50 of them open to the public, San Diego County offers golf enthusiasts innumerable opportunities to play their game. Courses are diverse: Some have vistas of the Pacific, others views of country hillsides or desert landscapes. I've listed the favorites below; for a full listing of area courses, including fees, stats, and complete scorecards, visit **www.golfsd.com**, or request the *Golf Guide* from the San Diego Convention and Visitors Bureau (© **619/236-1212;** www.sandiego.org). In addition to the well-established courses listed below, other acclaimed, newer links include **The Meadows Del Mar** (© **858/792-6200;** www.meadowsdelmar.com), **Maderas Golf Club** (© **858/726-4653;** www. troongolf.com), **Barona Creek** (© **619/387-7018;** www.barona.com), **The Auld Course** (© **619/482-4666;** www.theauldcourse.com), and **La Costa Resort and Spa** (p. 239).

San Diego Golf Reservations (© **800/905-0230** or 858/964-5980; www. sandiegogolfreservations.com) can arrange tee times for you at San Diego's premiere golf courses. They will consult with you on the courses you are interested in, and charge a $10 per person/per tee time coordination fee. And when you just want to practice your swing, head to **Stadium Golf Center,** 2990 Murphy Canyon Rd., in Mission Valley (© **858/277-6667;** www.stadiumgolfcenter.com). They're open daily from 7am to 10pm, with 72 artificial turf and natural grass hitting stations, plus greens and bunkers to practice your short game. A complete pro shop offers club rentals at $1 each (free for youths 17 and under); a bucket of balls costs $6 to $11. Golf instruction and clinics are also available.

Balboa Park Municipal Golf Course Everybody has a humble municipal course like this at home, with a bare-bones 1940s clubhouse where old guys hold down lunch counter stools for hours after the game—and players take a few more mulligans than they would elsewhere. Surrounded by the beauty of Balboa Park, this 18-hole course features mature, full trees; fairways sprinkled with eucalyptus leaves; and distractingly nice views of the San Diego skyline. It's so convenient and affordable that it's the perfect choice for visitors who want to work some golf into their vacation rather than the other way around. The course even rents clubs. Nonresident greens fees are $32 weekdays, $37 weekends; cart rental is $20, pull carts $5. Reservations are suggested at least a week in advance.

2600 Golf Course Dr. (off Pershing Dr. or 26th St. in southeast corner of the park), San Diego. © 619/239-1660.

Coronado Municipal Golf Course This is the first sight that welcomes you as you cross the San Diego–Coronado Bridge (the course is to the left), but it's really more for people who are vacationing in Coronado and just can't bear to leave the "island." It is an 18-hole, par-72 course overlooking Glorietta Bay, and there's a coffee shop, pro shop, and driving range. It's tough to get a tee time here, so 2-day prior reservations are strongly recommended; call anytime after 7am. Greens fees are $20 to walk and $34 to ride for 18 holes; after 4pm, it's $10 to walk and $18 to ride. Club rental is $15, and pull-cart rental is $4.

2000 Visalia Row, Coronado. © 619/435-3121.

Four Seasons Resort Aviara Golf Club 🏌🏌 Uniquely landscaped to incorporate natural elements compatible with the protected Batiquitos Lagoon nearby, Aviara doesn't infringe on the wetlands bird habitat. The course is 7,007 yards from the championship tees, laid out over rolling hillsides with plenty of bunker and water challenges. Casual duffers may be frustrated here. Greens fees are $175 (including mandatory cart) during the week, and $195 Friday through Sunday; an afternoon rate ($105–$110) starts at 1pm in winter, 3pm in summer. There are practice areas for putting, chipping, sand play, and driving, and the pro shop and clubhouse are fully equipped. Golf packages are available for guests of the Four Seasons.

7447 Batiquitos Dr., Carlsbad. © 760/603-6900. www.fourseasons.com. From I-5 north, take the Aviara Pkwy. exit east to Batiquitos Dr. Turn right and continue 2 miles to the clubhouse.

Mt. Woodson Golf Club 🏌 One of San Diego County's dramatic golf courses, Mount Woodson is a par-70, 6,180-yard course on 150 beautiful acres. The award-winning 18-hole course, which opened in 1991, meanders up and down hills, across bridges, and around granite boulders. Elevated tees provide striking views of Ramona and Mount Palomar, and on a clear day you can see for almost 100 miles. It's easy to combine a game of golf with a weekend getaway to Julian (see chapter 11). Greens fees for 18 holes (including mandatory cart) are $65 Monday through Thursday, $85 Friday and Sunday, $90 on Saturday. Early-bird, afternoon, and twilight rates are available, and seniors get a discount. Mount Woodson is about 40 minutes north of San Diego.

16422 N. Woodson Dr., Ramona. © 760/788-3555. www.mtwoodson.com. Take I-15 north to Poway Rd. exit; at the end of Poway Rd., turn left (north) onto Rte. 67 and drive 3¾ miles to Archie Moore Rd.; turn left. Entrance is on the left.

Rancho Bernardo Inn 🏌 Rancho Bernardo has a mature 18-hole, 72-par championship course with different terrains, water hazards, sand traps, lakes, and waterfalls. Lessons or 1-hour clinics with a pro, 2- to 4-day schools through the Golf University with meals and lodging included, and a standard golf package are available. Greens fees are $85 during the week and $115 Saturday and Sunday, including a cart. Twilight rates (after 1pm winter, 2pm summer) are $39 weekdays and $49 weekends.

17550 Bernardo Oaks Dr., Rancho Bernardo. © 858/675-8470; www.ranchobernardoinn.com. From I-15 north, exit at Rancho Bernardo Rd. Head east to Bernardo Oaks Dr., turn left, and continue to the resort entrance.

Riverwalk Golf Club 🏌 Completely redesigned by Ted Robinson and Ted Robinson, Jr., these links wander along the Mission Valley floor and are the most convenient courses for anyone staying downtown or near the beaches. Replacing the private Stardust Golf Club, the course reopened in 1998, sporting a slick, upscale new clubhouse, four lakes with waterfalls (in play on 13 of the 27 holes), open, undulating fairways, and one peculiar feature: trolley tracks! The bright red trolley speeds through now and then, but doesn't prove too distracting. Nonresident greens fees, including cart, are $78 Monday through Thursday, $88 Friday, and $98 Saturday and Sunday; twilight and bargain evening rates are available.

1150 Fashion Valley Rd., Mission Valley. © **619/296-4653**. Take I-8 to Hotel Circle south, turn on Fashion Valley Rd.

Singing Hills Country Club at Sycuan   The only resort in Southern California offering 54 holes of golf (2 championship courses and a 3,000-yard par-54 executive course), Singing Hills has taken advantage of the area's natural terrain. Mountains, natural rock outcroppings, and aged oaks and sycamores add character to individual holes. The golf courses are part of the Sycuan Casino & Resort. Greens fees are $39 Monday through Thursday, $45 Friday, and $53 Saturday and Sunday for the two par-72 courses, and $16 to $18 on the shorter course. Cart rental costs $12. The resort offers a variety of good-value packages.

3007 Dehesa Rd., El Cajon. © **800/457-5568** or 619/442-3425. www.singinghills.com. Take Calif. 94 to the Willow Glen exit. Turn right and continue to the entrance.

Torrey Pines Golf Course ★★   These two gorgeous, municipal 18-hole championship courses are on the coast between La Jolla and Del Mar, only 20 minutes from downtown San Diego. Home of the Buick Invitational Tournament, and the setting for the 2008 U.S. Open, Torrey Pines is second only to Pebble Beach as California's top golf destination. Situated on a bluff overlooking the ocean, the north course is picturesque and has the signature hole (no. 6), but the south course is more challenging, has more sea-facing play, and benefits from a $3.5 million overhaul in 2002 (the north course will get a similar facelift some time before 2008).

In summer, course conditions can be less than ideal due to the sheer number of people lined up to play, and "tee scalpers" aren't uncommon. Tee times are taken by computer, starting at 7pm, up to 7 days in advance and by automated telephone only—it takes only 20 to 30 minutes for all tee times for a given day to sell out. Confirmation numbers are issued, and you must have the number and photo identification with you when you check in with the starter 15 minutes ahead of time. If you're late, your time may be forfeited. Golf packages double the cost, but give you much better odds of actually getting onto the course. Golf professionals are available for lessons, and the pro shop rents clubs. Greens fees on the south course are $95 Monday through Friday, $115 Saturday and Sunday; the north course is $65 and $70, respectively. Cart rentals are $30, and twilight rates are available.

Tip: Single golfers stand a good chance of getting on the course if they just turn up and get on the waiting list for a threesome. The locals also sometimes circumvent the reservation system by spending Friday or Saturday night in a camper in the parking lot. The starter lets these diehards on before the reservations made by the computer go into effect at 7:30am.

11480 Torrey Pines Rd., La Jolla. © **858/570-1234** or 858/452-3226 for the pro shop and packages. www.torreypinesgolfcourse.com.

HANG GLIDING & PARAGLIDING

The windy cliffs at the **Torrey Pines Gliderport,** 2800 Torrey Pines Scenic Dr., La Jolla (© **877/359-8326;** www.flytorrey.com), create one of the country's top spots for hang gliding and paragliding, sports which aren't for the timid, yet deliver a bigger thrill than your average roller coaster. The difference between the two nonmotorized sports is subtle: Hang gliders are suspended from a fixed wing, while paragliders hang from a parachute. In both instances, watching the pilots control these delicate crafts for hours along the brink of the precipice is awesome. A 20- to 30-minute tandem flight with a qualified instructor costs $150. Even if you don't muster the courage to try a tandem flight, sitting at the cafe here and watching the graceful acrobatics is stirring.

If you already have experience, you can rent or buy equipment from the shop at the Gliderport—note that the conditions here are considered "P3"—or take lessons from the crew of able instructors. A 3- or 4-day beginner's package is $795, or lessons run $150 to $250 per day. Winds in December and January are slightest (that is, least conducive for the activities here), while March through June is best. The Gliderport is open daily from 9:30am to sunset.

HIKING & WALKING

San Diego's mild climate makes it a great place to walk or hike most of the year, and the options are diverse. Walking along the water is particularly rewarding. The best **beaches** for walking are Coronado, Mission Beach, La Jolla Shores, and Torrey Pines, but pretty much any shore is a good choice. You can also walk around most of Mission Bay on a series of connected footpaths. If a four-legged friend is your walking companion, head for Dog Beach in Ocean Beach or Fiesta Island in Mission Bay—two of the few areas where dogs can legally go unleashed. The **Coast Walk** in La Jolla offers supreme surf-line views (see "Hidden Attractions" on p. 157).

The **Sierra Club** sponsors regular hikes in the San Diego area, and nonmembers are welcome to participate. There's always a Wednesday mountain hike, usually in the Cuyamaca Mountains, sometimes in the Lagunas; there are evening and day hikes as well. Most are free of charge. For a recorded message about outings, call © **619/299-1744,** or call the office at © **619/299-1743** weekdays from noon to 5pm or Saturday from 10am to 4pm. Volunteers from the **Natural History Museum** (© **619/232-3821**) also lead nature walks throughout San Diego County.

Marian Bear Memorial Park, also known as San Clemente Canyon (© **619/ 581-9952** for park ranger), is a 10-mile, round-trip trail that runs directly underneath Highway 52. Most of the trail is flat, hard-packed dirt, but some areas are rocky. There are benches and places to sit and have a quiet picnic. From Highway 52 west, take the Genesee South exit; at the stop light, make a U-turn and an immediate right into the parking lot. From Highway 52 east, exit at Genesee and make a right at the light, then an immediate right into the parking lot.

Lake Miramar Reservoir has a 5-mile, paved, looped trail with a wonderful view of the lake and mountains. Take I-15 north and exit on Mira Mesa Boulevard. Turn right on Scripps Ranch Boulevard, then left on Scripps Lake Drive, and make a left at the Lake Miramar sign. Parking is free, but the lot closes at 6:30pm. There's also a pleasant path around **Lake Murray.** Take the Lake Murray Boulevard exit off I-8 and follow the signs.

Other places for scenic hikes listed earlier in this chapter include **Torrey Pines State Reserve** (p. 160), **Cabrillo National Monument** (p. 151), and **Mission Trails Regional Park** (p. 155). Guided walks are also offered at each of these parks.

JOGGING

An invigorating route downtown is along the wide sidewalks of the Embarcadero, stretching around the bay. A locals' favorite place to jog is the sidewalk that follows the east side of Mission Bay. Start at the Visitor Information Center and head south past the Hilton to Fiesta Island. A good spot for a short run is La Jolla Shores Beach, where there's hard-packed sand even when it isn't low tide. The beach at Coronado is also a good place for jogging, as is the shore at Pacific Beach and Mission Beach—just watch your tide chart to make sure you won't be there at high tide.

Safety note: When jogging alone, avoid secluded areas of Balboa Park, even in broad daylight.

SCUBA DIVING & SNORKELING

San Diego's underwater scene ranges from the magnificent giant kelp forests of Point Loma to the nautical graveyard off Mission Beach called Wreck Alley. There is an aquatic Ecological Reserve off the La Jolla Cove; fishing and boating activity has been banned in the 533-acre reserve since 1929, but diving and snorkeling is welcome, and it's a reliable place to spot the rare garibaldi, California's state fish, as well as the rare giant black sea bass. Shore diving here, or at nearby La Jolla Shores is common, and there are dive shops to help you get set up. But boat dives are the rule. Check out the Islas los Coronados, a trio of uninhabited islets off Mexico (a 90-min. boat ride from San Diego), where seals, sea lions, eels, and more cavort against a landscape of boulders (watch for swift currents); and the *Yukon,* a 366-foot Canadian destroyer that was intentionally sunk in 2000, 2 miles off the Big Dipper roller coaster at Wreck Alley, joining four other drowned vessels. Water visibility in San Diego is best in the fall, while in the spring, plankton blooms can reduce visibility to 20 feet.

The **San Diego Oceans Foundation** (© **619/523-1903;** www.sdoceans.org) is a local non-profit organization devoted to the stewardship of local marine waters. The website features good information about the local diving scene. **San Diego Divers Supply,** 4004 Sports Arena Blvd. (© **619/224-3439**) and 5701 La Jolla Blvd. (© 858/459-2691), will set you up with scuba and snorkeling equipment. **Blue Escape Dive and Charter** (© **619/223-3483**) and **Scuba San Diego** (© **800/586-3483** or 619/260-1880; www.scubasandiego.com) are other good outfits.

SKATING

Gliding around San Diego, especially the Mission Bay area, on inline skates is the quintessential Southern California experience. In Pacific Beach, rent a pair of regular or inline skates from **Resort Watersports** (© 858/488-2582), based at the Catamaran Resort, 3981 Mission Blvd.; or **Pacific Beach Sun and Sea,** 4539 Ocean Blvd. (© **858/483-6613**). In Coronado, go to **Bikes and Beyond,** 1201 First St. and at the Ferry Landing (© **619/435-7180**). Be sure to ask for protective gear.

If you'd rather ice skate, try the **Ice Capades Chalet** at University Towne Center, La Jolla Village Drive at Genesee Street (© **858/452-9110**).

SURFING

With its miles of beaches, San Diego is a popular surf destination. Some of the best spots include Windansea, La Jolla Shores, Pacific Beach, Mission Beach, Ocean Beach, and Imperial Beach. In North County, you might consider Carlsbad State

Beach and Oceanside. The best waves are in late summer and early fall; surfers visiting in winter or spring will want to bring along a wet suit. For surf reports, check out www.surfingsandiego.com or www.surfline.com.

If you didn't bring your own board, they are available for rent at stands at many popular beaches. Many local surf shops also rent equipment; they include **La Jolla Surf Systems,** 2132 Avenida de la Playa, La Jolla Shores (© **858/456-2777),** and **Emerald City–The Boarding Source,** 1118 Orange Ave., Coronado (© **619/435-6677).**

For surfing lessons, with all equipment provided, check with **Kahuna Bob's Surf School** (© **800/KAHUNAS** or 760/721-7700; www.kahunabob.com) based in Encinitas; **San Diego Surfing Academy** (© **800/447-SURF** or 760/230-1474; www.surfsdsa.com), which does lessons at Tourmaline in Pacific Beach and San Elijo State Beach in Cardiff by the Sea; and **Surf Diva** (© **858/454-8273;** www.surfdiva.com), the world's first surfing school for women and girls (with one instructor dude), based in La Jolla.

SWIMMING

Most San Diego hotels have pools, and there are plenty of other options for the visitor. Downtown, head to the **YMCA,** 500 W. Broadway, between Columbia and India streets (© **619/232-7451).** There's a $7 day-use fee for non-YMCA members staying in a local hotel; towels are supplied. It's open Monday through Friday from 5:30am to 9pm, Saturday from 8am to 1pm. In Balboa Park, you can swim in the **Kearns Memorial Swimming Pool,** 2229 Morley Field Dr. (© **619/692-4920).** The fee for using the public pool is $2 for adults; call for seasonal hours and laps-only restrictions. In Mission Bay, you'll find the fabulous indoor **Plunge,** 3115 Oceanfront Walk (© **858/488-3110),** part of Belmont Park since 1925. The huge pool has 10 lap lanes and a viewing area inside, plus full gym facility. It's open Monday through Friday from 5:30 to 8am and noon to 8pm, and Saturday and Sunday from 8am to 4pm. Admission is $3.50 for adults, $3.25 for children.

In La Jolla, you can swim at the **Jewish Community Center,** 4126 Executive Dr. (© **858/457-3030).** It has an ozone pool (kept clean by an ozone generator), instead of the typical chlorinated pool. It's open to the public Monday through Thursday from 6am to 7:30pm, Friday from 6am to 6pm, Saturday from 11am to 6pm, and Sunday from 8:30am to 6pm. Admission is $10 for adults, $5 for children under 17.

Swimmers may want to compete in (or watch) a rough-water swim. These include the **La Jolla Rough Water Swim** (© **858/456-2100),** held in early September.

TENNIS

There are 1,200 public and private tennis courts in San Diego. Public courts include the **La Jolla Tennis Club,** 7632 Draper, at Prospect Street (© **858/454-4434),** which is free and open daily from dawn until the lights go off at 9pm. At the **Balboa Tennis Club,** 2221 Morley Field Dr., in Balboa Park (© **619/295-9278),** court use is free, but reservations are required. The courts are open Monday through Friday from 8am to 8pm, Saturday and Sunday from 8am to 6pm; for lessons, call © **619/291-5248.** The ultra-modern **Barnes Tennis Center,** 4490 W. Point Loma Blvd., near Ocean Beach and SeaWorld (© **619/221-9000;** www.tennissandiego.com), has 20 lighted hard courts and four clay courts; they're open daily from 8am to 9pm. Court rental is $5 to $10 an hour, instruction an additional $12 to $14 per hour.

10 Spectator Sports

BASEBALL & SOFTBALL

The **San Diego Padres,** led to the National League championship in 1998 by stars Tony Gwynn and Trevor Hoffman, play April through September at downtown's brand-new **Petco Park,** easily accessed via San Diego Trolley. For schedules, information, and tickets, call ✆ **877/374-2784** or visit www.padres.com.

The highlight of many San Diegans' summer is the softball event known as the **World Championship Over-the-Line Tournament,** held on Fiesta Island in Mission Bay on the second and third weekends of July. For more information, see the "San Diego Calendar of Events," in chapter 2.

BOATING

San Diego has probably played host to the America's Cup for the last time, but several other boating events of interest are held here. They include the **America's Schooner Cup,** held every March or April (✆ **619/223-3138**), and the **Annual San Diego Crew Classic,** held on Mission Bay every April (✆ **619/488-0700**). The Crew Classic rowing competition draws teams from throughout the United States and Canada. The **Wooden Boat Festival** is held on Shelter Island every May ((✆ **619/574-8020**). Approximately 90 boats participate in the festival, which features nautical displays, food, music, and crafts.

FISHING TOURNAMENTS

Enthusiasts will want to attend the **Day at the Docks** event, held at the San Diego Sportfishing Landing, Harbor Drive and Scott Street, in Point Loma, every April. For more details, see the "San Diego Calendar of Events" in chapter 2; for more information, call ✆ **619/294-7912.**

FOOTBALL

Although at press time they were holding the city hostage with the threat of leaving for Los Angeles, for now, San Diego's professional football team, the **Chargers** (✆ **877/CHARGERS;** www.chargers.com), plays at **Qualcomm Stadium** ("The Q"), 9449 Friars Rd., Mission Valley. The season runs from August to December. The Chargers Express bus (✆ **619/685-4900** for information) costs $5 round-trip and picks up passengers at several locations throughout the city, beginning 2 hours before the game; the stadium is also easily reached via the San Diego Trolley.

The collegiate **Holiday Bowl,** held at Qualcomm Stadium every December, pits the Western Athletic Conference champion against a team from the Big 10. For information, call ✆ **619/283-5808.**

GOLF

San Diego is the site of some of the country's most important golf tournaments, including the **Buick Invitational,** which takes place in February at Torrey Pines Golf Course in La Jolla (✆ **800/888-BUICK** or 619/281-4653), and the **Accenture Match Play Championship** put on by World Golf Championships and held at La Costa, also in February (✆ **760/431-9110**). Now you know why February is celebrated as Golf Month by the Convention and Visitors Bureau. The **U.S. Open** will be held at Torrey Pines in 2008.

HORSE RACING & SHOWS

Live Thoroughbred racing takes place at the **Del Mar Race Track** (✆ **858/755-1141** for information and racing schedules; www.delmarracing.com) from late

July to mid-September. Post time for the nine-race program is 2pm (except for Fridays, when it's 4pm); there is no racing on Tuesdays. Admission to the clubhouse is $8, including program; stretch run seating is $5 with program and includes infield access; and reserved seats are $5. The infield area has a jungle gym where kids can play or watch exhibition shows put on by BMX riders and skateboarders. "Four O'Clock Fridays" is designed to lure the martini crowd, with a 4pm post time and live bands at 7pm.

The **Del Mar National Horse Show** takes place at the Del Mar Fairgrounds from late April to early May. Olympic-caliber and national championship riders participate. For information, call ✆ **858/792-4288** or 858/755-1161, or check www.sdfair.com.

ICE HOCKEY

The **San Diego Gulls** of the West Coast Hockey League skate at the San Diego Sports Arena from late October into March. For schedules, tickets, and information, call ✆ **619/224-4625** or 619/224-4171, or visit www.sandiegogulls.com.

MARATHONS & TRIATHLONS

San Diego is a wonderful place to run or watch a marathon because the weather is usually mild. The **San Diego Marathon** takes place in January. It's actually in Carlsbad, 35 miles north of San Diego, and stretches mostly along the coastline. For more information, call ✆ **858/792-2900,** or visit www.inmotionevents.com.

Drawing about 20,000 runners, the **Suzuki Rock 'n' Roll Marathon** is held in early June and features a route lined with rock bands, usually capped off by a headline act performing at a large venue. For additional information, call ✆ **858/450-6510,** or visit www.eliteracing.com.

Another popular event is the **La Jolla Half Marathon,** held in late April. It begins at the Del Mar Fairgrounds and finishes at La Jolla Cove. For information, call ✆ **858/454-1262,** or see www.lajollahalfmarathon.com.

The **America's Finest City Half Marathon** is held in August every year. The race begins at Cabrillo National Monument, winds through downtown, and ends in Balboa Park. For information, call ✆ **858/792-2900,** or visit www.inmotion events.com.

The **San Diego International Triathlon,** held in late June, includes an international course comprised of a 1,000m swim, a 30km bike ride, and a 10km run, plus a shorter sprint course. A kids triathlon precedes the event by one day. It starts at Spanish Landing on San Diego Bay. For information, call ✆ **858/268-1250** or check www.kozenterprises.com.

POLO

The public is invited to watch polo matches on Sundays from June to September at the **San Diego Polo Club,** 14555 El Camino Real, Rancho Santa Fe (✆ **858/481-9217;** www.sandiegopolo.com). Admission is $5.

SOCCER

The **San Diego Sockers,** members of the Continental Indoor Soccer League, play from September to March at the San Diego Sports Arena, 3500 Sports Arena Blvd. (✆ **858/836-4625;** www.sockers.com). Tickets range $10 to $35.

The WUSA's **San Diego Spirit** is the women's professional soccer team, with a season that runs April through August, played at USD's Torero Stadium. Tickets run $18 to $40 (slightly higher for walk-up). For more information call ✆ **877/4-SOCCER** or see www.sandiegospirit.com.

TENNIS

San Diego plays host to several major tennis tournaments, notably the **Acura Tennis Classic,** held at the La Costa Resort and Spa in Carlsbad. The tournament is usually held between late July and early August. For information and tickets, call © **760/438-5683** or check www.acuraclassic.com.

8

City Strolls

Wandering a city's streets and parks gives you insights that are hard to come by any other way—and the exercise can't be beat, especially under the warm (but usually not unbearably hot) Southern California sun. From the history-heavy Gaslamp Quarter to the thriving Balboa Park, San Diego easily lends itself to the long, leisurely stroll. The four walking tours in this chapter will give you a special sense of the city, as well as a look at some of its most unique and appealing sights and structures.

| WALKING TOUR 1 | THE GASLAMP QUARTER |

Start:	Fourth Avenue and E Street, at Horton Plaza.
Finish:	Fourth Avenue and F Street.
Time:	Approximately 1½ hours, not including shopping and dining.
Best Times:	During the day.
Worst Times:	Evenings, when the area's popular restaurants and nightspots attract big crowds.

A National Historic District covering 16½ city blocks, the Gaslamp Quarter contains many Victorian-style commercial buildings built between the Civil War and World War I. The quarter—set off by electric versions of old gas lamps—lies between Fourth Avenue to the west, Sixth Avenue to the east, Broadway to the north, and L Street and the waterfront to the south. The blocks are not large; developer Alonzo Horton knew corner lots were desirable to buyers, so he created more of them. This tour hits some highlights of buildings along Fourth and Fifth avenues. If it whets your appetite for more, the **Gaslamp Quarter Historic Foundation,** 410 Island Ave. (℗ **619/233-4692;** www.gaslampquarter.org), offers walking tours every Saturday at 11am ($8, including museum admission, or $6 for seniors, students, and military). The book *San Diego's Historic Gaslamp Quarter: Then and Now,* by Susan H. Carrico and Kathleen Flanagan, makes an excellent, lightweight walking companion. It has photos, illustrations, and a map.

The tour begins at:

❶ Horton Plaza

It's a colorful conglomeration of shops, eateries, and architecture—and a tourist attraction. Ernest W. Hahn, who planned and implemented the redevelopment and revitalization of downtown San Diego, built the plaza in 1985. This core project, which covers 11½ acres and 6½ blocks in the heart of downtown, represents the successful integration of public and private funding.

The ground floor at Horton Plaza is home to the 1906 Jessop Street Clock. The timepiece has 20 dials, 12 of which tell the time in places throughout the world. Designed by Joseph Jessop, Sr., and built primarily by Claude D. Ledger, the clock stood

Walking Tour: The Gaslamp Quarter

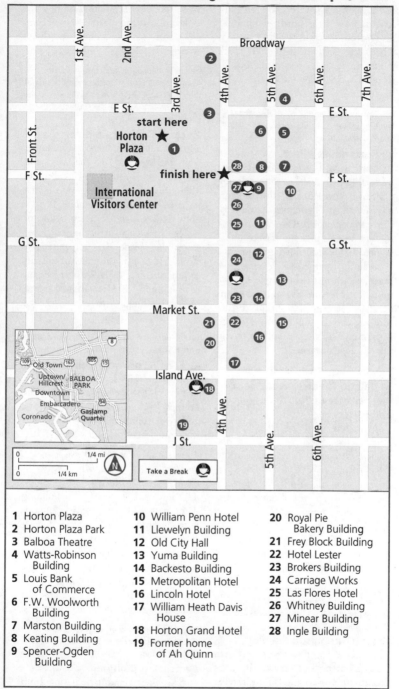

1 Horton Plaza
2 Horton Plaza Park
3 Balboa Theatre
4 Watts-Robinson Building
5 Louis Bank of Commerce
6 F.W. Woolworth Building
7 Marston Building
8 Keating Building
9 Spencer-Ogden Building
10 William Penn Hotel
11 Llewelyn Building
12 Old City Hall
13 Yuma Building
14 Backesto Building
15 Metropolitan Hotel
16 Lincoln Hotel
17 William Heath Davis House
18 Horton Grand Hotel
19 Former home of Ah Quinn
20 Royal Pie Bakery Building
21 Frey Block Building
22 Hotel Lester
23 Brokers Building
24 Carriage Works
25 Las Flores Hotel
26 Whitney Building
27 Minear Building
28 Ingle Building

outside Jessop's Jewelry Store on Fifth Avenue from 1927 until being moved to Horton Plaza in 1985. In 1935, when Mr. Ledger died, the clock stopped; it was restarted, but it stopped again 3 days later—the day of his funeral.

Exit Horton Plaza on the north side, street level, near Macy's. At the corner of Fourth and Broadway is:

② Horton Plaza Park

Its centerpiece is a fountain designed by well-known local architect Irving Gill and modeled after the choragic monument of Lysicrates in Athens. Dedicated October 15, 1910, it was the first successful attempt to combine colored lights with flowing water (the fountain is inscribed 1909, but maybe that was optimistic thinking?). On the fountain's base are bronze medallions of Juan Rodríguez Cabrillo, Father Junípero Serra, and Alonzo Horton, three men who were important to San Diego's development.

Walk south along Fourth Avenue, to the:

③ Balboa Theatre, at the southwest corner of Fourth Avenue and E Street

Constructed in 1924, the Spanish Renaissance–style building has a distinctive tile dome, striking tile work in the entry, and two 20-foot-high ornamental waterfalls inside. In the past, the waterfalls ran at full power during intermission; however, when turned off, they would drip and irritate the audience. In the theater's heyday, plays and vaudeville took top billing. It's currently closed, awaiting renovation.

Cross Fourth Avenue and proceed along E Street to Fifth Avenue. The tall, striking building to your left at the northeast corner of Fifth and E is the:

④ Watts-Robinson Building

Built in 1913, it was one of San Diego's first skyscrapers. It once housed 70 jewelers and is now a stellar boutique hotel (for complete information, see the review for Gaslamp Plaza

Suites on p. 74). Take a minute to look inside at the marble wainscoting, tile floors, ornate ceiling, and brass ornamentation.

Return to the southwest corner of Fifth Avenue and E Street. On the opposite side of the street, at 837 Fifth Ave., is the unmistakable "grand old lady of the Gaslamp," the twin-towered baroque revival:

⑤ Louis Bank of Commerce

You can admire the next few buildings from the west side of the street and then continue south from here. Built in 1888, this proud building was the first in San Diego made of granite. It once housed a 24-hour ice-cream parlor for which streetcars made unscheduled stops; an oyster bar frequented by Wyatt Earp; and, a number of upstairs rooms inhabited by ladies of the night. After a fire in 1903, the original towers of the building, with eagles perched atop them, were removed.

On the west side of Fifth Avenue, at no. 840, near E Street, you'll find the:

⑥ F. W. Woolworth Building

Built in 1910, it has housed San Diego Hardware since 1922. The original tin ceiling, wooden floors, and storefront windows remain, and the store deserves a quick browse.

Across the street, at 801 Fifth Ave., stands the two-story:

⑦ Marston Building

This Italianate Victorian-style building dates from 1881 and housed humanitarian George W. Marston's department store for 15 years. In 1885, San Diego Federal Savings' first office was here, and the Prohibition Temperance Union held its meetings here in the late 1880s. After a fire in 1903, the building was remodeled extensively.

The red brick Romanesque revival on the northwest corner of Fifth Avenue and F Street is the:

⑧ Keating Building

A San Diego landmark dating from 1890, Mrs. Keating built it as a tribute to her late husband, George, whose name can still be seen in the top cornice. Originally heralded as one of the city's most prestigious office buildings, it featured conveniences such as steam heat and a wire-cage elevator. Note the architecturally distinctive rounded corner and windows.

Continuing south on Fifth Avenue, cross F Street and stand in front of the:

9 Spencer-Ogden Building

It's located on the southwest corner at 770 Fifth Ave. Built in 1874, it was purchased by business partners Spencer and Ogden in 1881 and has been owned by the same families ever since. *San Diego's Historic Gaslamp Quarter: Then and Now* notes that a number of druggists leased space in the building over the years, including the notorious one "who tried to make firecrackers on the second floor and ended up blowing away part of the building." Other tenants included realtors, an import business, a home-furnishing business, and dentists, one of whom called himself "Painless Parker."

Directly across the street stands the:

10 William Penn Hotel

Built in 1913, in the building's former life it was the elegant Oxford Hotel, and touted itself as "no rooming house but an up-to-the-minute, first-class, downtown hotel"; a double room with private bathroom and toilet cost $1.50. It reopened in 1992 as apartments—with substantially higher prices.

On the west side of the street, at 726 Fifth Ave., you'll find the:

11 Llewelyn Building

Built in 1887 by William Llewelyn, the family shoe store was here until 1906. Of architectural note are its arched windows, molding, and cornices. Over the years, it has been home to hotels of various names with unsavory reputations. Today the Llewelyn houses a colorful hostel.

On the southwest corner of Fifth Avenue and G Street is the:

12 Old City Hall

Dating from 1874, when it was a bank, this Florentine Italianate building features 16-foot ceilings, 12 foot windows framed with brick arches, antique columns, and a wrought-iron cage elevator. Notice that the windows on each floor are different. (The top two stories were added in 1887, when it became the city's public library.) The entire city government filled this building in 1900, with the police department on the first floor and the council chambers on the fourth.

Across the street in the middle of the block, at 631–633 Fifth Ave., is the:

13 Yuma Building

The striking edifice was built in 1882—it later expanded upward two floors to feature inviting bay windows. It was one of the first brick buildings downtown.

Continue down Fifth Avenue toward Market Street, and you'll notice the three-story:

14 Backesto Building

Built in 1873, it fills most of the block. Originally a one-story structure on the corner, the classical revival and Victorian-style building expanded to its present size and height over its first 15 years.

Across Market Street, on the east side of the street, is the former:

15 Metropolitan Hotel

The building had bay windows when it was built in 1886. To the casual observer it looks decidedly contemporary, until you spot the rugged 19th-century columns still visible on the street level. The Metropolitan also features arrestingly realistic *trompe l'oeil* effects painted on the facade by artists Nonni McKinnoon and Kitty Anderson. Today the Metropolitan is another of San Diego's well-located hostels.

In the middle of the block, at 536 Fifth Ave., is the small but distinctive:

⑯ Lincoln Hotel

It dates from 1913—the date cast in a grand concrete pediment two stories up. An equally grand stone lion's head once reigned atop the parapet, but tumbled to the street during an earthquake in 1986 and was quickly snatched by a passerby. The building's unusual green-and-white ceramic tile facade is thankfully intact.

Proceed to Island Avenue and turn right. The saltbox house at the corner of Fourth Avenue is the:

⑰ William Heath Davis House

This 145-year-old New England prefabricated lumber home was shipped to San Diego around Cape Horn in 1850 and is the oldest surviving structure from Alonzo Horton's "New Town." Horton lived in the house in 1867, when it was located at the corner of Market and State (near where the *Star of India* is now docked). The most recent augmentation to the house—indoor plumbing—was added in 1911; it has never been modernized or electrified. It was located to this site in 1984, completely refurbished, and the first floor and the small park next to it are open to the public. The Gaslamp Quarter Association and Gaslamp Quarter Historical Foundation have their headquarters on the second floor. The house is open for guided tours Tuesday through Sunday from 11am to 3pm.

At the southwest corner of Island and Fourth avenues you'll see the bay windows of a building that's sure to steal your heart, the:

⑱ Horton Grand Hotel

It is two 1886 hotels that were moved here—very gently—from other sites, and then renovated and connected by an atrium; the original Horton Grand is to your left, the Brooklyn Hotel to your right. The life-size papier-mâché horse (Sunshine), in the lobby near the reception area, stood in front of the Brooklyn Hotel when it was a saddlery. The reception desk is a recycled pew from a choir loft, and old post-office boxes now hold guests' keys. By the concierge desk, to your right, is an old photo of the original and much less elegant Horton Grand Hotel. In its small museum hangs a portrait of Ida Bailey, a local madam whose establishment, the Canary Cottage, once stood on this spot. Artist Pamela Russ had been asked to retouch the somewhat austere face of her subject, but Russ's husband murdered her before she could get around to it.

☕ **TAKE A BREAK**
The **Cheese Shop,** 627 Fourth Ave. (☏ **619/232-2303**), is open for breakfast or lunch with homemade corned beef hash and tasty pork sandwiches. After 4pm, try the **Palace Bar** (☏ **619/544-1886**) in the Horton Grand Hotel, another good place to relax. The bar is part of the same choir-loft pew that has been turned into the reception desk.

Around the corner from the Horton Grand, at 433 Third Ave., stands the:

⑲ Former home of Ah Quinn

The first Chinese resident of San Diego, Ah Quinn arrived in 1879 at the age of 27 and became known as the "Mayor of Chinatown" (an area bound by Island Ave., J St., and Third and Fourth aves.). Ah Quinn helped hundreds of Chinese immigrants find work on the railroad and owned a successful general merchandise store on Fifth Avenue. He was a respected father (of 12 children), leader, and spokesperson for the city's Chinese population. When he died in 1914—he was hit by a motorcycle—his wealth included farmland, a mine, and other real estate. The modest house is not open to the public.

When you leave the An Quinn home, head north on Fourth Avenue; in the middle of the block on the west side you will come to the:

⑳ Royal Pie Bakery Building
Erected in 1911, this bakery, preceded by others, has been here since 1920; the second floor used to house the Anchor Hotel, run by "Madam Cora."

At the southwest corner of Fourth Avenue and Market Street stands the:

㉑ Frey Block Building
Built in 1911, this was first a second-hand store, then a home for Chinese restaurants. But real fame arrived in the 1950s when it became the Crossroads, San Diego's first live jazz club. It was a venue for local and touring African-American artists.

Across the street on the southeast corner, at 401–417 Market St., is the:

㉒ Hotel Lester
This hotel dates from 1906. It housed a saloon, pool hall, and hotel of ill repute when this was a red-light district. Unbelievably, it's still a scruffy hotel (not for long, if urban renewal has its way!). Café Bassam, a welcoming tearoom and espresso bar, and the cheerfully informal Wyatt Earp Museum operate at street level.

On the northeast corner of Fourth Avenue and Market Street, at 402 Market St., stands the:

㉓ Brokers Building
Constructed in 1889, it has 16-foot wood-beam ceilings and cast-iron columns. It's been recently converted to artists' lofts with the ground floor dedicated to the downtown branch of the Hooters chain.

At the north end of this block, you will find the:

㉔ Carriage Works
Established in 1890, it once served as storage for wagons and carriages. It now houses restaurants and clubs catering to the Gaslamp Quarter's bohemian residents and energetic nightlife.

Cross G Street and walk to the middle of the block to the:

㉕ Las Flores Hotel
The gray building with blue-and-red trim at 725–733 Fourth Ave. was built in 1912. It is the only Gaslamp Quarter structure completely designed by architect Irving Gill, whose work can be seen throughout San Diego and in La Jolla.

Next door, at 739–745 Fourth Ave., is the:

㉖ Whitney Building
Dating from 1906, it has striking arched windows on the second floor. The inside was once used as a union meeting hall. While you're studying details, take a look at the trim on the top of the:

㉗ Minear Building
Built in 1910, it's located at the end of the block, on the southeast corner of Fourth Avenue and F Street.

Across the street is the:

㉘ Ingle Building
It dates from 1907 and now holds the Hard Rock Cafe. The mural on the F Street side of the building depicts a group of deceased rock stars (including Hendrix and Joplin, of course) lounging at *trompe l'oeil* sidewalk tables. Original stained-glass windows from the original Golden Lion Tavern (1907–32) front Fourth Avenue. Inside, the restaurant's stained-glass ceiling was taken from the Elks Club in Stockton, California, and much of the floor is original.

WINDING DOWN
Walk to **Café Lulu**, 419 F St. (✆ **619/238-0114**), near Fourth Avenue, for casual coffeehouse fare; or try **Horton Plaza,** where you can choose from many kinds of cuisine, from California to Chinese, along with good old American fast food.

Start: The Maritime Museum, Harbor Drive and Ash Street.
Finish: The Convention Center, Harbor Drive and Fifth Avenue.
Time: 1½ hours, not including museum and shopping stops.
Best Times: Weekday mornings (when it's less crowded and easier to park).
Worst Times: Weekends, especially in the afternoon, when the Maritime Museum and Seaport Village are crowded; also when cruise ships are in port (days vary).

San Diego's colorful Embarcadero, or waterfront, cradles a bevy of seagoing vessels—frigates, ferries, paddle-wheelers, yachts, cruise ships, and even a merchant vessel. You'll also find equally colorful Seaport Village, a shopping and dining center with a nautical theme.

Start at the:

❶ Maritime Museum

It's located at Harbor Drive at Ash Street (see the review on p. 152). Making up part of the floating museum is the magnificent *Star of India*, the world's oldest merchant ship still afloat, built in 1863 as the *Euterpe*. The ship, whose billowing sails are a familiar sight along Harbor Drive, once carried cargo to India and immigrants to New Zealand, and it braved the Arctic ice in Alaska to work in the salmon industry. Another component of the Maritime Museum is the ferry *Berkeley*, built in 1898 to operate between San Francisco and Oakland. In service through 1958, it carried survivors to safety 24 hours a day for 4 days after the 1906 San Francisco earthquake. The *Medea*, the third and smallest display in the floating museum, is a steam yacht. One ticket gets you onto all three boats.

From this vantage point, you get a fine view of the:

❷ County Administration Center

This building was built in 1936 with funds from the Works Progress Administration, and was dedicated in 1938 by President Franklin D. Roosevelt. The 23-foot-high granite sculpture in front, *Guardian of Water*, was completed by Donal Hord—San Diego's most notable sculptor—in

1939. It represents a pioneer woman shouldering a water jug. The building is even more impressive from the other side because of the carefully tended gardens; it's well worth the effort and extra few minutes to walk around to Pacific Highway for a look. On weekdays the building is open from 8am to 5pm; there are restrooms and a cafeteria inside.

TAKE A BREAK
The cafeteria on the fourth floor of the **County Administration Center** (© 619/515-4258) has lovely harbor views; it's open weekdays until 3:35pm. If you can't pass up the chance to have some seafood, return to the waterfront to **Anthony's Fishette** (© 619/232-5105), the simplest entity in the Anthony's clan of seafood houses, which serves fish and chips, shrimp, and other snacks alfresco. Next door is the **Star of the Sea** restaurant (© 619/232-7408), one of the city's finest seafood restaurants; it's open for dinner only.

Continue south along the Embarcadero. The large carnival-colored building on your right is the:

❸ San Diego Cruise Ship Terminal

Located on the B Street Pier, it has a large nautical clock at the entrance.

Walking Tour: The Embarcadero

0 ___ 2 mi
0 ___ 2 km

Harbor Dr.

County Administration Center ②

Beech St.

start here
Maritime Museum ①

Ash St.

India St.

Star of India

Medea
Berkeley

Pacific Highway

Amtrak (Santa Fe) Station

A St.

B St.

B Street Pier ③

C St.

④

(Harbor Excursions)
Broadway Pier ⑤

Broadway

⑥

⑦

Navy Pier

E St.

PANTOJA PARK

G Street Pier

Harbor Dr.

Kettner Blvd.

⑧

Tuna Lane

G St.

G St.

San Diego Bay

⑨

Market St.

⑩ Seaport Village

To ⑪ ⑫

finish here →

★

EMBARCADERO MARINA PARK

109 Old Town 163 805 15

Uptown/ Hillcrest BALBOA PARK

Downtown

Embarcadero 94

Coronado Gaslamp Quarter

8

Take a Break 🍴
Trolley Line ▬ ▬ ▬

1 Maritime Museum
2 County Administration Center
3 San Diego Cruise Ship Terminal
4 Harbor cruises
5 Coronado Ferry
6 Santa Fe Depot

7 Waterfront park
8 U.S. Air Carrier Memorial
9 Tuna Harbor
10 Seaport Village
11 Marriott San Diego Hotel & Marina
12 Convention Center

Totally renovated in 1985, the flag-decorated terminal's interior is light and airy. Inside, you'll also find a snack bar and gift shop.

Farther along is the location for the:

④ Harbor cruises

They depart from sunup to sundown on tours of San Diego's harbor; ticket booths are right on the water. See "Organized Tours" in chapter 7 for more details.

A little farther south, near the Broadway Pier, is the:

⑤ Coronado Ferry

It makes hourly trips between San Diego and Coronado. Buy tickets from the Harbor Excursion booth—you can make the round-trip in about 50 minutes. See "Getting Around: By Ferry" in chapter 4 for more information.

To your left as you look up Broadway, you'll see the two gold mission-style towers of the:

⑥ Santa Fe Depot

This mosaic-draped railroad station was built in 1915, and provides one of the city's best examples of Mission Revival style. It's only 1½ blocks away, so walk up and look inside at the vaulted ceiling, wooden benches, and walls covered in striking green-and-gold tiles. A scale model of the aircraft carrier *USS Midway* is on display inside.

Continuing south on Harbor Drive, you'll stroll through a small tree- and bench-lined:

⑦ Waterfront park

South of that, at Pier 11, is the:

⑧ U.S. Air Carrier Memorial

Erected in 1993, it's a compact black granite obelisk that honors the nation's carriers and crews. It stands on the site of the old navy fleet landing, where thousands of servicemen boarded ships over the years.

Continue along the walkway to:

⑨ Tuna Harbor

This is where the commercial fishing boats congregate. San Diego's tuna fleet, with about 100 boats, is one of the world's largest.

TAKE A BREAK
The red building to your right houses the **Fish Market** (© 619/232-FISH), a market and casual restaurant, and its upscale counterpart, **Top of the Market** (© 619/234-4TOP), just upstairs. You can be assured that a meal here is fresh off the boat. Both serve lunch and dinner, and the Fish Market has a children's menu and an oyster and sushi bar. It's acceptable to drop in just for a drink and to savor the view, which is mighty. Prices are moderate to expensive. If you prefer something quick and cheap, save yourself a walk and stop in at casual **Anthony's Fishette** (© 619/232-5105). A cousin of the one you passed earlier, it's just outside Seaport Village. For dessert or coffee, go inside Seaport Village to **Upstart Crow** (© 619/232-4855), a bookstore and coffeehouse, and sip cappuccino in the company of your favorite authors.

Keep walking south, where you can meander along the winding pathways of:

⑩ Seaport Village

It contains a myriad of shops and restaurants. The Broadway Flying Horses Carousel is pure nostalgia. Charles Looff, of Coney Island, carved the animals out of poplar in 1890. The merry-go-round was originally installed at Coney Island and later moved to Salisbury, Massachusetts. Seaport Village bought it in the 1970s and spent more than 2 years restoring it to its original splendor—the horses even have real horsehair tails. If you decide to take a twirl, pick your mount from the 40 horses, 3 goats, and 3 Saint Bernard dogs. This carousel comes complete with the elusive brass ring.

As you stroll farther, you will no doubt notice the official symbol of Seaport Village. The 45-foot-high detailed replica of the famous Mukilteo Lighthouse of Everett, Washington, towers above the other buildings.

From Seaport Village, continue your waterfront walk south to the:

⑪ Marriott San Diego Hotel & Marina

Adjacent to Embarcadero Marina Park, which is well used by San Diegans for strolling and jogging, it provides a terrific view of the Coronado Bridge. A concession at the marina office rents boats by the hour at reasonable rates and arranges diving, water-skiing, and fishing outings. The impressive hotel resembles an ocean liner.

The waterfront walkway continues to the:

⑫ Convention Center

This building is another striking piece of architecture hugging the city's waterfront. When it was first completed in late 1989, its presence on the waterfront was a major factor in the revitalization of downtown San Diego. Recently, it was enlarged to an even more imposing size, to less acclaim.

WINDING DOWN
The Marriott's waterfront bar, the **Yacht Club** (① 619/234-1500), looks out onto the marina and the bay beyond. It's a choice spot for watching the sunset (you might want to plan your walking tour so the end coincides with it). You can get drinks, appetizers, and light fare here, and if you linger into the evening, there's likely to be live music and dancing.

WALKING TOUR 3   **OLD TOWN**

Start:	Old Town State Historic Park headquarters.
Finish:	Heritage Park.
Time:	Approximately 2 hours, not including shopping or dining.
Best Times:	Weekends (except the 1st one in May—Cinco de Mayo) and any day before 2pm or after 3pm. The free park tour runs from 2 to 3pm.
Worst Times:	Weekdays, when numerous school groups are touring (although it's fun to watch on-site education in action). On Cinco de Mayo weekend, the first weekend in May, Old Town is a madhouse. The holiday celebrates Mexico's defeat of the French on May 5, 1862, in the Battle of Puebla.

Old Town is the Williamsburg of the West. When you visit, you go back to a time of one-room schoolhouses and village greens, when many of the people who lived, worked, and played here spoke Spanish. Even today, life moves more slowly in this part of the city, where the buildings are old or built to look that way. The stillness inside the state park is palpable, especially at night, when you can stroll the unpaved streets and look up at the stars. You don't have to look hard or very far to see yesterday.

Begin at the park headquarters, at the eastern end of this historic district, which preserves the essence of the small Mexican and fledgling American communities that existed here from 1821 to 1872. The core of Old Town is a 6-block area with no vehicular traffic and few businesses.

The headquarters are near the intersection of Wallace and Calhoun, the location of the:

❶ McCoy House

This interpretive center and main entryway was completed in 2001, and is an historically accurate replication of the home of James McCoy, San Diego's larger-than-life lawman/legislator who lived on this site until the devastating fire of 1872. The house contains exhibits, artifacts, and visitor information.

After checking in here and getting your bearings, head to the neighboring:

❷ Robinson-Rose House

Built in 1853 as a family home, it has also served as a newspaper and railroad office; until the McCoy addition, it was also the visitor center for the park. Here you will see a large model of Old Town the way it looked prior to 1872, the year a large fire broke out (or was set). It destroyed much of the town and initiated the population exodus to New Town, now downtown San Diego. Old Town State Historic Park contains seven original buildings, including the Robinson-Rose House, and replicas of other buildings that once stood here.

From here, turn left and stroll into the colorful world of Mexican California called:

❸ Bazaar del Mundo

Located at 2754 Calhoun St., it's where international shops and restaurants spill into a flower-filled courtyard. Designer Diane Powers created the unique setting from the dilapidated Casa de Pico motel, constructed in 1936. On Saturday and Sunday afternoons, Mexican dancers perform free at the bazaar. While you're here, be sure to visit the **Guatemala Shop,** the **Design Center,** and **Libros** bookstore.

TAKE A BREAK
This is a good opportunity to sample the Mexican food in Bazaar del Mundo. In addition to the recommendations in chapter 6, try **Rancho El Nopal** (✆ 619/295-0584), **Casa de Pico** (✆ 619/296-3267), **El Fandango** (✆ 619/298-2860) or, a block away, **Casa de Bandini** (✆ 619/297-8211). All offer indoor and outdoor dining, a lively ambience, and steaming platters of enchiladas, burritos, and other familiar fare. Since the food, prices, and atmosphere are pretty comparable at all four, if the wait for a table is long at one, put your name on the list at another. Historic Casa de Bandini, completed in 1829, was the home of Peruvian-born Juan Bandini, who became a Mexican citizen; in 1869, the building, with a second story added, became the Cosmopolitan Hotel. The restaurants are open from 10 or 11am to 9 or 10pm (Fandango opens for breakfast at 8am), and Bazaar del Mundo shops are open from 10am to 9:30pm.

From Bazaar del Mundo, stroll into the grassy plaza, where you'll see a:

❹ Large rock monument

This commemorates the first U.S. flag flown in Southern California (on July 29, 1846). In the plaza's center stands a flagpole that resembles a ship's mast. There's a reason: The original flag hung from the mast of an abandoned ship.

Straight ahead, at the plaza's eastern edge, is:

❺ La Casa de Estudillo

An original adobe building dating from 1827, the U-shaped house has covered walkways and an open central patio. The patio covering is made of corraza cane, the seeds for which were brought by Father Serra in 1769. The walls are 3 to 5 feet thick, holding up the heavy beams and tiles, and they work as terrific insulators against summer heat. In those days, the thicker

Walking Tour: Old Town

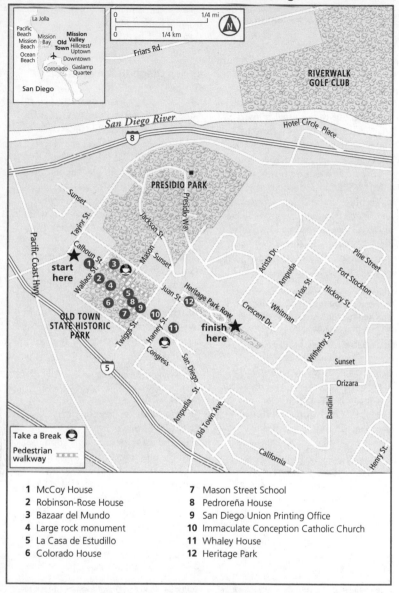

1 McCoy House
2 Robinson-Rose House
3 Bazaar del Mundo
4 Large rock monument
5 La Casa de Estudillo
6 Colorado House
7 Mason Street School
8 Pedroreña House
9 San Diego Union Printing Office
10 Immaculate Conception Catholic Church
11 Whaley House
12 Heritage Park

the walls, the wealthier the family. The furnishings in the "upper-class" house are representative of the 19th century (don't overlook the beautiful four-poster beds); the original furniture came from the East Coast and from as far away as Asia. The Estudillo family, which then numbered 12, lived in the house until 1887; today family members still live in San Diego.

After you exit La Casa de Estudillo, turn left. In front of you is the reconstruction of the three-story:

6 Colorado House

Built in 1851, it was destroyed by fire in 1872—as were most buildings on this side of the park. Today it's the home of the Wells Fargo Historical Museum, but the original housed San Diego's first two-story hotel. The museum features an original Wells Fargo stagecoach, numerous displays of the overland-express business, and a video show. Next door to the Wells Fargo museum, and cater-cornered to La Casa de Estudillo, is the small, red-brick San Diego Court House & City Hall. (A reconstruction of the three-story Franklin House is planned to the right of the Colorado House.)

From here, continue along the pedestrian walkway one short block, turn right, and walk another short block to a reddish-brown building on your right. This is the one-room:

7 Mason Street School

An original building dating from 1865, it was commissioned by Joshua Bean, uncle to the notorious "hanging judge" Roy Bean; Joshua Bean was also San Diego's first mayor and California's first governor. If you look inside, you'll notice that the boards that make up the walls don't match; they were leftovers from the construction of San Diego homes. Mary Chase Walker, the first teacher, ventured here from the East when she was 38 years old. She enjoyed the larger salary but hated the fleas, mosquitoes, and truancy; after a year, she resigned to marry the president of the school board.

When you leave the schoolhouse, retrace your steps to the walkway (which is the extension of San Diego Ave.) and turn right. On your left, you will see two buildings with brown shingle roofs. The first is the:

8 Pedroreña House

No. 2616 is an original Old Town house built in 1869, with stained glass over the doorway. The shop inside now sells fossils, minerals, and gems. The original owner, Miguel Pedroreña, also owned the house next door, which became the:

9 San Diego Union Printing Office

The newspaper was first published in 1868. This house arrived in Old Town after being prefabricated in Maine in 1851 and shipped around the Horn (it has a distinctly New England appearance). Inside you'll see the original hand press used to print the paper, which merged with the *San Diego Tribune* in 1992. The offices are now in Mission Valley, about 3 miles from here.

At the end of the pedestrian part of San Diego Avenue stands a railing; beyond it is Twiggs Street, dividing the historic park from the rest of Old Town, which is more commercial. In this part of town, you'll find interesting shops and galleries and outstanding restaurants.

At the corner of Twiggs Street and San Diego Avenue stands the Spanish mission–style:

10 Immaculate Conception Catholic Church

The cornerstone was laid in 1868, but with the movement of the community to New Town in 1872, it lost its parishioners and was not dedicated until 1919. Today the church serves about 300 families in the Old Town area. (Visitors sometimes see the little church and on a whim decide to get married here, but arrangements have to be made 9 months in advance.)

Continue along San Diego Avenue 1 block to Harney Street. On your left is the restored:

11 Whaley House

The first two-story brick structure in Southern California, it was built from 1855 to 1857. The house is said to be haunted by the ghost of a man who was executed (by hanging) out back. It's beautifully furnished with period pieces and features the life mask of Abraham Lincoln, the spinet piano used in the film *Gone With the Wind*, and the concert piano that accompanied Swedish soprano Jenny Lind on her final U.S. concert tour in 1852. The house's north room served as the county courthouse for a few years, and the courtroom looks now as it did then.

From the Whaley House, walk uphill 1½ blocks along Harney Street to a Victorian jewel called:

⑫ Heritage Park

The seven buildings on this grassy knoll were moved here from other parts of the city and are now used in a variety of ways. Among them are a winsome bed-and-breakfast inn (in the Queen Anne shingle-style Christian House, built in 1889), a doll shop, an antiques store, and offices. Toward the bottom of the hill is the classic revival Temple Beth Israel, dating from 1889. On Sunday, local art is often exhibited in the park. If you've brought picnic supplies, enjoy them under the sheltering coral tree at the top of the hill.

WINDING DOWN
At the end of your walk, wend your way back down Harney Street, and turn left at San Diego Avenue. Just ahead on the right you'll be able to stop outside the **Old Town Mexican Cafe,** 2489 San Diego Ave. (℡ **619/297-4330**), and watch corn and flour tortillas being hand-patted the old-fashioned way. Even if you thought you'd had your fill of Mexican food, this fresh spectacle—or the hungry looks from fellow patrons—might convince you to stop in for a refreshing margarita, *cerveza,* or fresh-squeezed lemonade along with a basket of warm tortillas and salsa.

WALKING TOUR 4   **BALBOA PARK**

Start:	Cabrillo Bridge, entry at Laurel Street and Sixth Avenue.
Finish:	San Diego Zoo.
Time:	2 hours, not including museum or zoo stops. If you get tired, hop on the free park tram.
Best Times:	Anytime. If you want to get especially good photographs, come in the afternoon, when the sun lends a glow to the already photogenic buildings. Most museums are open until 4 or 5pm. The zoo closes at 4pm, later in summer months.
Worst Times:	More people (especially families) visit the park on weekends. But there is a festive, rather than overcrowded spirit even then—particularly on Sunday afternoons, when you can catch a free organ concert at the outdoor Spreckels Organ Pavilion at 2pm.

Built in the late 1800s, Balboa Park is the second-oldest city park in the United States, after New York's Central Park. Much of its striking architecture was the product of the 1915–16 Panama-California Exposition and the 1935–36 California Pacific International Exposition. The structures now house outstanding museums and contribute to the park's beauty. But what makes Balboa Park truly unique is the extensive and mature botanical collection, thanks largely to Kate Sessions, a horticulturalist who devoted her life to transforming the desolate mesas and scrub-filled canyons (and other San Diego parks) into the oasis it is today. Originally called "City Park," it was renamed in 1910 when Mrs. Harriet Phillips won a contest, naming it in honor of the Spanish explorer Balboa who, in 1513, was the first European to see the Pacific Ocean.

Take bus no. 1 or 3 along Fifth Avenue or bus no. 25 along Sixth Avenue to Laurel Street, which leads into Balboa Park through its most dramatic entrance, the:

❶ Cabrillo Bridge

It has striking views of downtown San Diego and scenic, sycamore-lined Highway 163 (which John F. Kennedy proclaimed as "the most beautiful highway I've ever seen," during his 1963 visit to San Diego). Built in 1915 for the Panama-California Exposition and patterned after a bridge in Ronda, Spain, the dramatic cantilever-style bridge has seven pseudo-arches. As you cross the bridge, to your left you'll see the yellow cars of the zoo's aerial tram and, directly ahead, the distinctive California Tower of the Museum of Man. The delightful sounds of the 100-bell Symphonic Carillon can be heard every quarter-hour. Sitting atop this San Diego landmark is a weathervane shaped like the ship in which Cabrillo sailed to California in 1542. The city skyline lies to your right.

Once you've crossed the bridge, go through the:

❷ Arch

The two figures represent the Atlantic and Pacific oceans and lead into the park, where you'll find a treasure of nature and culture. For now, just view the museums from the outside (you can read more about them in chapter 7).

You have entered the park's major thoroughfare, El Prado—if you're driving a car you'll want to find a parking space (the map on p. 199 shows all public lots) and return to the:

❸ San Diego Museum of Man

An anthropological museum, it focuses on the peoples of North and South America. Architect Bertram Goodhue designed this structure, originally known as the California Building, in 1915. Goodhue, considered the world's foremost authority on Spanish-colonial architecture, was the master architect for the 1915–16

exposition. The exterior doubled as part of Kane's mansion in the 1941 Orson Welles classic *Citizen Kane*.

Just beyond and up the steps to the left is the nationally acclaimed:

❹ Old Globe Theatre

The original theatre is part of the Globe Theatres performing arts complex. The Old Globe was built for the 1935 exposition; the replica of Shakespeare's Old Globe Theatre was meant to be demolished after the exposition but survived. In 1978, an arsonist destroyed the theater, which was rebuilt into what you see today. It's California's oldest professional theater. If you have the opportunity to go inside, you can see the bronze bust of Shakespeare that miraculously survived the fire with minor damage. The summer Shakespeare series is always popular.

Beside the theater is the:

❺ Sculpture Garden of the Museum of Art

Across the street, to your right as you stroll along the Prado, is the:

❻ Alcazar Garden

It was designed in 1935 by Richard Requa and W. Allen Perry. They patterned it after the gardens surrounding the Alcazar Castle in Seville, Spain. The garden is formally laid out and trimmed with low clipped hedges; in the center walkway are two star-shaped yellow-and-blue tile fountains.

Exit to your left at the opposite end of the garden, and you'll be back on El Prado. Proceed to the corner; on your right is the:

❼ House of Charm

This is the site of the San Diego Art Institute Gallery and the Mingei International Museum of World Folk Art. The gallery is a nonprofit space that primarily exhibits works of local artists; the museum offers changing exhibitions that celebrate human creativity expressed in textiles, costumes, jewelry, toys, pottery, paintings, and sculpture.

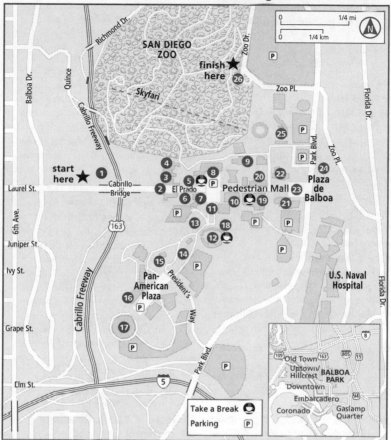

1 Cabrillo Bridge
2 Arch
3 San Diego Museum of Man
4 The Globe Theatre
5 Sculpture Garden
6 Alcazar Garden
7 House of Charm
8 San Diego Museum of Art
9 Botanical Building & Lily Pond
10 Visitors Center
11 El Cid Campeador
12 Spreckels Organ Pavilion
13 Palm Canyon
14 United Nations Building

15 House of Pacific Relations
     International Cottages
16 San Diego Automotive Museum
17 San Diego Aerospace Museum
18 Japanese Friendship Garden
19 Casa de Balboa
20 Casa del Prado
21 Reuben H. Fleet Science Center
22 Natural History Museum
23 Fountain
24 Gardens
25 Spanish Village Art Center
26 San Diego Zoo

To your left is the imposing:

8 San Diego Museum of Art

This museum holds San Diego's most extensive collection of fine art, and major touring shows swing through.

The latticework building you see beyond it to the right is the:

9 Botanical Building & Lily Pond

An open-air conservatory, this delicate wood lath structure dates to the 1915–16 Exposition, and is filled with 2,100 permanent plants, plus seasonal displays. Particularly noteworthy are the collection of cycads and ferns. Immediately in front is the Lily Pond.

Across the street is the House of Hospitality and the park's:

10 Visitors Center

Pick up maps, souvenirs, and discount tickets to the museums here. In the courtyard behind is the attractive **Prado** restaurant (see the "Winding Down" box, at the end of this tour).

Turn right toward the statue of the mounted:

11 El Cid Campeador

Created by Anna Hyatt Huntington and dedicated in 1930, this sculpture of the 11th-century Spanish hero was made from a mold of the original statue in the court of the Hispanic Society of America in New York. A third one is in Seville, Spain.

Walk downhill to the ornate:

12 Spreckels Organ Pavilion

Donated to San Diego by brothers John D. and Adolph B. Spreckels, famed contralto Ernestine Schumann-Heink sang at the December 31, 1914, dedication. A brass plaque honors her charity and patriotism. Free, lively recitals featuring the largest outdoor organ in the world (its vast structure contains 4,428 pipes) are given Sunday at 2pm, with additional concerts and events scheduled during summertime.

Exit to your right, cross the two-lane road, and follow the sidewalk down the hill. The pathway leading into the ravine to your right will take you to the:

13 Palm Canyon

Getting to this site requires some hiking. It's secluded, and probably should not be walked solo, but you can get a good sense of its beauty by venturing only a short distance along the path. Fifty species of palm, plus magnolia trees and a Moreton Bay fig tree provide a tropical canopy.

As you walk down the hill, you'll see the Hall of Nations on your left, and beside it, the:

14 United Nations Building

This building also houses the United Nations International Gift Shop, a favorite for its diverse merchandise, much of it handmade around the world. You'll recognize the shop by the United States and United Nations flags out front. Check the bulletin board, or ask inside, for the park's calendar of events. If you need to rest, there's a pleasant spot with a few benches opposite the gift shop.

You will notice a cluster of small houses with red-tile roofs. They are the:

15 House of Pacific Relations International Cottages

These charming dollhouse cottages promote ethnic and cultural awareness and are open to the public on Sunday afternoons year-round. From March to October, there are lawn programs with folk dancing.

Take a quick peek into some of the cottages, then continue on the road to the bottom of the hill to see more of the park's museums; to your right, the notable:

16 San Diego Automotive Museum

It's usually filled with exotic cars (the display changes often), and the cylindrical:

⑰ San Diego Aerospace Museum

The museums in this part of the park operate in structures built for the 1935–36 Exposition. It is not necessary to walk all the way to the Aerospace Museum (located appropriately enough in the flight path for the San Diego's airport), unless you plan to tour one or two of them now (you'll also find the Hall of Champions Sports Museum and the Marie Hitchcock Puppet Theater).

Cross the road and go back up the hill past a parking lot and the Organ Pavilion. Take a shortcut through the pavilion, exit directly opposite the stage, and follow the sidewalk to your right, leading back to El Prado. Almost immediately, you come to the:

⑱ Japanese Friendship Garden

This 11½-acre canyon has been carefully developed to include traditional Japanese elements. At the entrance is an attractive teahouse whose deck overlooks the entire ravine, with a small meditation garden beside.

TAKE A BREAK
Now is your chance to have a bite to eat, sip a cool drink, and review the tourist literature you picked up at the Visitors Center. The **Tea Pavilion** (© 619/232-2721) at the Japanese Friendship Garden serves fresh sushi, noodle soups, and Asian salads—it also carries quirky imported Japanese candies and beverages in addition to some familiar American snacks.

Return to El Prado, which is strictly a pedestrian mall to the east, and set your sights on the fountain at the end of the street and head toward it. Stroll down the middle of the street to get the full benefit of the lovely buildings on either side. On weekends you'll probably pass street musicians, artists, and clowns—one of their favorite haunts is around the fountain.

On your right, you'll see the:

⑲ Casa de Balboa

Inside you'll find the Museum of Photographic Arts, the Model Railroad Museum, and the Museum of San Diego History, with engaging exhibits that interpret past events in the city and relate them to the present. Note the realistic-looking bare-breasted figures atop the Casa de Balboa. Perhaps this was an intentional tribute to the nudist colony that temporarily sprouted in the Zoro Garden—immediately west of the building—during the 1935–36 Exposition? Today butterflies are the most frequent naturists in this nook of the park.

On the other side of El Prado, on your left, note the ornate work on the:

⑳ Casa del Prado

While it doesn't house a museum, it's one of the best—and most ornate—of the El Prado buildings, featuring almost rococo Spanish-Moorish ornamentation.

At the end of El Prado are two museums particularly popular with children; the first is the:

㉑ Reuben H. Fleet Science Center

See p. 147 for a complete review of this popular attraction.

To the left is the:

㉒ Natural History Museum

You're likely to find kids climbing on the whale statue outside. Look for the sundial that is inscribed PRESENTED BY JOSEPH JESSOP; DECEMBER 1908; I STAND AMID YE SOMMERE FLOWERS TO TELL YE PASSAGE OF YE HOURES. This sundial, which is accurate to the second, was originally presented to the San Diego Public Library, and moved here in the mid-1950s when the library relocated.

In the center of the Plaza de Balboa is the high-spouting:

㉓ Fountain

This seemingly ordinary installation, built in 1972, holds 25,000 gallons of water and spouts 50 to 60 feet into the air. What makes it unique is a wind regulator located on top of the Natural History Museum—as the wind increases, the fountain's water pressure is lowered so that the water doesn't spray over the edges. The fountain fascinates children, who giggle when it sprays them and marvel at the rainbows it creates.

From here, use the pedestrian bridge to cross the road and visit the nearly secret:

㉔ Gardens

They are tucked away on the other side of the highway: to your left, a Desert Garden for cacti and other plants at home in an arid landscape; to your right, the Inez Grant Parker Memorial Rose Gardens, home to 2,400 roses. After you've enjoyed the flowers and plants, return to the fountain.

Heading to the right and a block from El Prado on Village Place is another voluptuous Moreton Bay Fig tree, planted in 1915 for the exposition; it's now more than 62 feet tall, with a canopy 100 feet in diameter.

Farther on is the sleepy:

㉕ Spanish Village Art Center

Artists are at work here daily from 11am to 4pm. They create jewelry, paintings, and sculptures in tile-roofed studios around a courtyard. There are restrooms here, too.

Exit at the back of the Spanish Village Art Center and take the paved, palm-lined sidewalk that will take you to the world-famous:

㉖ San Diego Zoo

You can also retrace your steps and visit some of the tempting museums you just passed, saving the zoo for another day.

Bus tip: From here, you can walk out to Park Boulevard through the zoo parking lot to the bus stop (a brown-shingled kiosk), on your right. The no. 7 bus will take you back to downtown San Diego.

WINDING DOWN
Back on El Prado (in the House of Hospitality), the **Prado Restaurant** (② 619/557-9441) has a handsome view of the sloping park from oversize windows. Far from your average park concession, the Prado is run by the restaurant group responsible for some of San Diego's trendiest eateries, and boasts a zesty menu with colorful ethnic influences—plus inventive margaritas and Latin cocktails. Lunch starts at 11:30am (Sat–Sun at 11am), and a festive dinner menu takes over at 5pm (daily except Mon; reservations advisable). In between, a long list of tapas will satisfy any hunger pangs.

9

Shopping

Whether you're looking for a sou- venir, a gift, or a quick replacement for an item inadvertently left at home, you'll find no shortage of stores in San Diego. This is, after all, Southern California, where looking good is a high priority and shopping in sunny outdoor malls is a way of life.

1 The Shopping Scene

Okay, so we've embraced the suburban shopping mall with vigor. Many San Diegans do the bulk of their shopping at two massive complexes in Mission Valley where every possible need is represented. Downtown has even adopted the mall concept at whimsical Horton Plaza, and historic Old Town features textiles and color from south-of-the-border lands with great flair.

Local neighborhoods, on the other hand, offer specialty shopping that meets the needs—and mirrors the personality—of that part of town. For example, modish Hillcrest is the place to go for cutting-edge boutiques, while conservative La Jolla offers many upscale traditional shops, especially jewelers. And don't forget that Mexico is only 40 minutes away; *tiendas* (stores) in Tijuana, Rosarito Beach, and Ensenada stock colorful crafts perfectly suited to the California lifestyle. Visitors head across the border en masse each weekend in search of bargains.

Shops tend to stay open late, particularly in malls like Horton Plaza and Fashion Valley, tourist destinations like Bazaar del Mundo and Seaport Village, and areas like the Gaslamp Quarter and Hillcrest that see a lot of evening foot traffic. Places like these keep the welcome mat out until 9pm on weeknights and at least 6pm on Saturdays and Sundays. Individual stores elsewhere generally close by 5 or 6pm.

Sales tax in San Diego is 7.75%, and savvy out-of-state shoppers have larger items shipped directly home at the point of purchase, avoiding the tax.

2 The Top Shopping Neighborhoods

DOWNTOWN & THE GASLAMP QUARTER

Space is at a premium in the still-developing Gaslamp Quarter, and rents are rising as the debut of the new ballpark approaches. While only a few intrepid shops—mostly women's boutiques and vintage clothing shops—made the initial commitment to open among the area's multitudinous eateries, in the past few years a number of wonderfully individualistic stores have opened on lower Fourth and Fifth avenues. As the number of condos in the downtown area multiplies, watch for shopping to diversify. Otherwise, downtown shopping is primarily concentrated in two destination malls.

Horton Plaza *(Finds)* *(Kids)*   The Disneyland of shopping malls, Horton Plaza is the heart of the revitalized city center, bounded by Broadway, First and Fourth avenues, and G Street. Covering 6½ city blocks, the multilevel shopping center has more than 130 specialty shops, including art galleries, clothing and shoe stores, several fun shops for kids, and bookstores. There's a 14-screen cinema, three major department stores, and a variety of restaurants and short-order eateries. It's almost as much an attraction as SeaWorld or the San Diego Zoo, transcending its genre with a conglomeration of rambling paths, bridges, towers, piazzas, sculptures, fountains, and live greenery. Performers provide background entertainment throughout the year. Designed by the local Jerde Partnership and inspired by European shopping streets and districts like Athens's Plaka and London's Portobello Road, Horton Plaza opened in 1985 to rave reviews and provided an initial catalyst for the Gaslamp Quarter's redevelopment.

Parking is free with validation for the first 3 hours (4 hr. at the movie theater and the Lyceum Theatre), $1 per half-hour thereafter. The parking levels are confusing, and temporarily losing your car is part of the Horton Plaza experience. 324 Horton Plaza. ⓒ 619/238-1596. www.hortonplaza.shoppingtown.com. Mon–Fri 10am–9pm; Sat 10am–8pm; Sun 11am–7pm. Bus: 2, 7, 9, 29, 34, or 35. Trolley: City Center.

Seaport Village   This ersatz 14-acre village snuggled alongside San Diego Bay was built to resemble a small Cape Cod community, but the 75 shops are very much the Southern California cutesy variety. The atmosphere is pleasant, and there are a few gems; favorites include the **Tile Shop,** featuring handpainted tiles from Mexico and beyond; the **San Diego City Store,** with all your local signage needs; **Island Hoppers,** for resort wear; and the **Upstart Crow** bookshop and coffeehouse, with the Crow's Nest children's bookstore inside. Be sure to see the 1890 carousel imported from Coney Island, New York. Two hours free parking with purchase. 849 W. Harbor Dr. (at Kettner Blvd.). ⓒ 619/235-4014, or 619/235-4013 for events information. www.seaportvillage.com. Sept–May daily 10am–9pm; June–Aug daily 10am–10pm. Bus: 7. Trolley: Seaport Village.

HILLCREST/UPTOWN

Compact Hillcrest is an ideal shopping destination. As the hub of San Diego's gay and lesbian community, swank inspiration and chic housewares rule. There are plenty of establishments selling cool trinkets, used books, vintage clothing, and memorabilia; a couple chain stores (including **Gap**); and of course, bakeries and cafes. You'll also find a panoply of modestly priced globe-hopping dining options, too.

There's no defined zone in which shops are found within, so you may as well start at the neighborhood's axis, at the overrun intersection of University and Fifth avenues. From this corner the greatest concentration of boutiques spreads for 1 or 2 blocks in each direction, but farther east on University—between 10th Avenue and Vermont Street—you'll find good options (like the fun **Ace Hardware** store) along the south side of the street, and on the north side a small shopping complex with several choice bets. Street parking is available; most meters run 2 hours and devour quarters at a rate of one every 15 minutes, so be armed with plenty of change. You can also park in a lot—rates vary, but you'll come out ahead if you're planning to stroll for several hours.

If you're looking for postcards or provocative gifts, step into wacky **Babette Schwartz,** 421 University Ave. (ⓒ 619/220-7048), a pop-culture emporium named for a local drag queen, and located under the can't-miss "Hillcrest" street sign. You'll find books, clothing, and accessories that follow current kitsch trends. A couple of doors away, **Cathedral,** 435 University Ave. (ⓒ 619/296-4046), is dark and heady, filled with candles of all scents and shapes, plus unusual holders.

Downtown San Diego Shopping

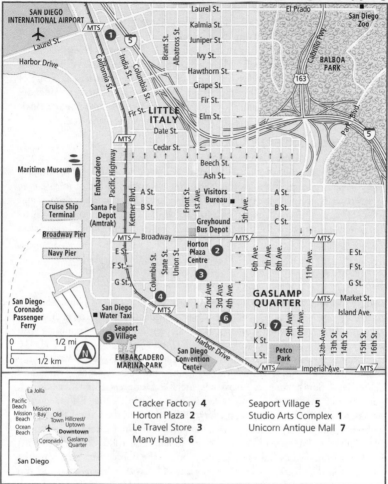

SAN DIEGO INTERNATIONAL AIRPORT

Laurel St.

Harbor Drive

Maritime Museum

Cruise Ship Terminal

Broadway Pier

Navy Pier

San Diego–Coronado Passenger Ferry

San Diego Water Taxi

Seaport Village **5**

EMBARCADERO MARINA PARK

San Diego Convention Center

Santa Fe Depot (Amtrak)

Visitors Bureau

Greyhound Bus Depot

Horton Plaza Centre **2**

3

4

6

5

7

GASLAMP QUARTER

Petco Park

Imperial Ave.

Laurel St.
Kalmia St.
Juniper St.
Ivy St.
Hawthorn St.
Grape St.
Fir St.
Elm St.
Date St.
Cedar St.
Beech St.
Ash St.

El Prado

San Diego Zoo

BALBOA PARK

LITTLE ITALY

A St.
B St.
C St.

E St.
F St.
G St.

Market St.
Island Ave.

J St.
K St.
L St.

0   1/2 mi
0   1/2 km
N

La Jolla

Pacific Beach
Mission Beach
Ocean Beach

Mission Bay

Old Town

Coronado

Hillcrest/ Uptown

Downtown

Gaslamp Quarter

San Diego

Cracker Factory **4**
Horton Plaza **2**
Le Travel Store **3**
Many Hands **6**

Seaport Village **5**
Studio Arts Complex **1**
Unicorn Antique Mall **7**

Around the corner, **Circa a.d.,** 3867 Fourth Ave. (© **619/293-3328**), is a floral design shop with splendid gift items; at holiday time it has the most extravagant Christmas ornaments in the area. Head gear from straw hats to knit caps to classy fedoras fills the **Village Hat Shop,** 3821 Fourth Ave. (© **619/683-5533;** www.villagehatshop.com), whose best feature may be its mini-museum of stylishly displayed vintage hats.

Lovers of rare and used books will want to poke around the **used bookstores** on Fifth Avenue, between University and Robinson avenues. Though their number has decreased with the advent of online shopping, you can always find something to pique your interest. This block is also home to **Off the Record,** 3865 Fifth Ave. (© **619/298-4755**), a new and used music store known for an alternative bent and the city's best vinyl selection. A few doors down is **Wear It Again Sam,** 3823 Fifth Ave., south of Robinson (© **619/299-0185;** www.wearitagain samvintage.com). It's a classy step back in time, with vintage clothing—for both females and males—in styles from the first half of the 20th century.

A half-mile east of Hillcrest is the start of San Diego's self-proclaimed **Antique Row**. It lies north of Balboa Park, along Park Boulevard (beginning at University Ave. in Hillcrest) and on Adams Avenue (extending from Park east to around 40th St. in Normal Heights). Antique and collectible stores, vintage-clothing boutiques, and dusty used book and record stores line this L-shaped district, providing many hours of happy browsing and treasure hunting. There are plenty of coffeehouses, pubs, and small restaurants to break up the excursion. For more information and an area brochure with a map, contact the **Adams Avenue Business Association** (✆ 619/282-7329; www.GoThere.com/AdamsAve).

OLD TOWN & MISSION VALLEY

Old Town Historic Park is a restoration of some of San Diego's historic sites and adobe structures, a number of which now house shops that cater to tourists. Many have a "general store" theme, and carry gourmet treats and inexpensive Mexican crafts alongside the obligatory T-shirts, baseball caps, snow domes, and other souvenirs. A reconstruction of San Diego's first tobacco shop carries cigars and smoking paraphernalia; more shops are concentrated in colorful Bazaar del Mundo (see below).

Mission Valley is the epicenter of San Diego's suburban mall explosion. There are two major and several minor shopping centers here (see "Malls," later in this chapter).

Bazaar del Mundo ✿   Take a stroll down Mexico way—and points south—through the arched passageways of this bustling corner of Old Town. A dilapidated 1930s motel-turned-world market, the central courtyard vibrates with folkloric music, mariachis, costumed dancing, and a splashing fountain. The 16 inter-connected shops—all owned by entrepreneur Diane Powers—feature one-of-a-kind folk art, home furnishings, clothing, and textiles from Mexico and Central and South America. Favorites include **Design Center Accessories,** where you'll find dinnerware and table pieces with Latin accents; **Libros,** a small but smartly chosen bookstore with a large kids' selection; the **Laurel Birch Gallerita,** featuring the namesake designer's apparel; and **The Gallery,** which showcases American Indian and contemporary jewelry and other crafts. You won't find bargains like you would on the other side of the border—it's clearly tourist central—but there isn't a more colorful place to browse in San Diego, and you won't have to deal with snoopy Customs officials. If imbibing an oversized margarita or plate of enchiladas strikes your fancy, there are a half-dozen restaurants in and around the Bazaar—12.4 million tortillas and 24 tons of avocados were served here in 2002! 2754 Calhoun St., Old Town State Historic Park. ✆ 619/296-3161. Free, but limited parking in adjacent lots. www.bazaardelmundo.com. Daily 10am–9pm. Bus: 4 or 5/105.

MISSION BAY & THE BEACHES

The beach communities offer laid-back shopping in typical California fashion, with plenty of surf shops, recreational gear, casual garb, and college-oriented music stores. If you're looking for something more distinctive than T-shirts and shorts, you'd best head east to Mission Valley.

For women in need of a new bikini, the best selection is at **Pilar's,** 3745 Mission Blvd., Pacific Beach (✆ 858/488-3056), where choices range from stylish designer suits to hot trends like suits inspired by surf- and skate-wear. There's a smaller selection of one-piece suits, too. Across the street is **Liquid Foundation Surf Shop,** 3731 Mission Blvd., Pacific Beach (✆ 858/488-3260), which specializes in board shorts for guys.

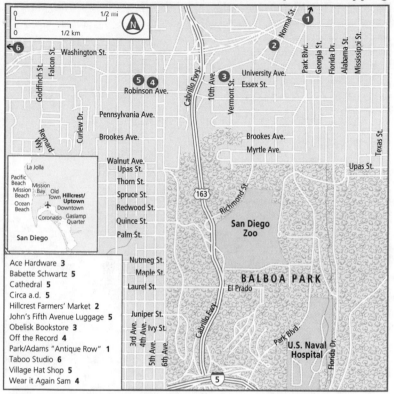

Ace Hardware **3**
Babette Schwartz **5**
Cathedral **5**
Circa a.d. **5**
Hillcrest Farmers' Market **2**
John's Fifth Avenue Luggage **5**
Obelisk Bookstore **3**
Off the Record **4**
Park/Adams "Antique Row" **1**
Taboo Studio **6**
Village Hat Shop **5**
Wear it Again Sam **4**

San Diego's greatest concentration of antiques stores is found in **Ocean Beach Antique District,** along the 4800 block of Newport Avenue, the community's main drag. Most of the stores are mall-style, featuring multiple dealers under one roof. The hundreds of individual sellers cover the gamut—everything from Asian antiquities to vintage watches to mid-20th-century collectibles. Although you won't find a horde of pricey, centuries-old European antiques, the overall quality is high enough to make it interesting for any collector. Highlights include **Newport Avenue Antiques,** 4836 Newport Ave. (© **619/224-1994**), which offers the most diversity: Its wares range from Native American crafts to Victorian furniture and delicate accessories, from Mighty Mouse collectibles to carved Asian furniture. **Ocean Beach Antique Mall,** 4847 Newport Ave. (© **619/223-6170**), has a more elegant setting and glass display cases filled with superb American art pottery and china. Names like Roseville, McCoy, and Royal Copenhagen abound, and there's a fine selection of quality majolica and Japanese tea sets. The **Newport Ave. Antique Center,** 4864 Newport Ave. (© **619/ 222-8686**), is the largest store, and has a small espresso bar. One corner is a haven for collectors of 1940s and 1950s kitchenware (Fire King, Bauer, melamine); there's also a fine selection of vintage linens. Most of the O.B. antique stores are open daily from 10am to 6pm, with somewhat reduced hours Sunday.

Shopping in Mission Bay & the Beaches

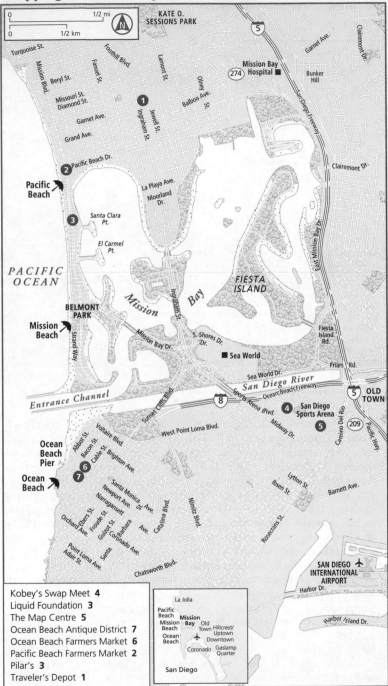

Kobey's Swap Meet **4**
Liquid Foundation **3**
The Map Centre **5**
Ocean Beach Antique District **7**
Ocean Beach Farmers Market **6**
Pacific Beach Farmers Market **2**
Pilar's **3**
Traveler's Depot **1**

LA JOLLA

It's clear from the look of La Jolla's village that shopping is a major pastime in this upscale community. Women's clothing boutiques tend to be conservative and costly, like those lining Girard and Prospect streets (**Ann Taylor, Armani Exchange, Polo Ralph Lauren, Talbots,** and **Sigi's Boutique**). But you'll also find less pricey venues like **Banana Republic, Dansk,** and **TK.**

Recommended stores include **Island Hoppers,** 7844 Girard Ave. (© **858/ 459-6055**), for colorful Hawaiian-print clothing from makers like Tommy Bahama; the venerable **Ascot Shop,** 7750 Girard Ave. (© **858/454-4222**), for conservative men's apparel and accessories; and **La Jolla Shoe Gallery,** 7852 Girard Ave. (© **858/551-9985**), for an outstanding selection of Echo, Clark's, Birkenstock, Mephisto, Josef Siebel, and other shoes built for walking.

Even if you're not in the market for furnishings and accessories, La Jolla's many home-decor boutiques make for great window shopping, as do its ubiquitous jewelers: Swiss watches, tennis bracelets, precious gems, and pearl necklaces sparkle in windows along every street.

No visit to La Jolla is complete without seeing **John Cole's Book Shop,** a local icon reviewed on p. 212.

Another unique experience awaits at the **Cave Store,** 1325 Coast Blvd., just off Prospect Street (© **858/459-0746**). This clifftop shop is equal parts art gallery and antiques store, but the main attraction is **Sunny Jim Cave,** a large and naturally occurring sea cave reached by a steep and narrow staircase through the rock (admission $3 for adults, $2 for kids 16 and under). The **Crescent Café**—not much more than a coffee cart today—is a local institution that has stood on this site for decades. Black-and-white photo enlargements line the walls, depicting this quirky corner of La Jolla through the years, and making the store well worth a stop for history buffs and collectors. The coast walk extends here along the coast into a posh neighborhood.

CORONADO

This rather insular, conservative navy community doesn't have a great many shopping opportunities; the best of the lot line Orange Avenue at the western end of the island. You'll find some scattered housewares and home-decor boutiques, several small women's boutiques, and the gift shops at Coronado's major resorts.

Coronado has an excellent independent bookshop, **Bay Books,** 1029 Orange Ave. (© **619/435-0070**). It carries a nice selection in many categories, plus volumes of local historical interest, and books on tape. **La Provençale,** 1122 Orange Ave. (© **619/437-8881**), is a little shop stocked with fabric, tablecloths, pottery, and tableware items from the French countryside; nearby **In Good Taste,** 1146 Orange Ave. (© **619/435-8356**), has a staggering selection of gourmet and food gift items—in addition to a tempting display of luscious truffles and sweets. And, if you're in pursuit of swimwear, poke your head into **Dale's Swim Shop,** 1150 Orange Ave. (© **619/435-7301**), a tiny boutique jam-packed with suits to fit all bodies, including rare European makers seldom available in this country.

The Ferry Landing Marketplace   The entrance is impressive—turreted red rooftops with jaunty blue flags that draw closer to you as the ferry pulls in. As you stroll up the pier, you'll find yourself in the midst of souvenir and other shops filled with gifts, jewelry, and crafts. You can get a quick bite to eat or have

La Jolla Shopping

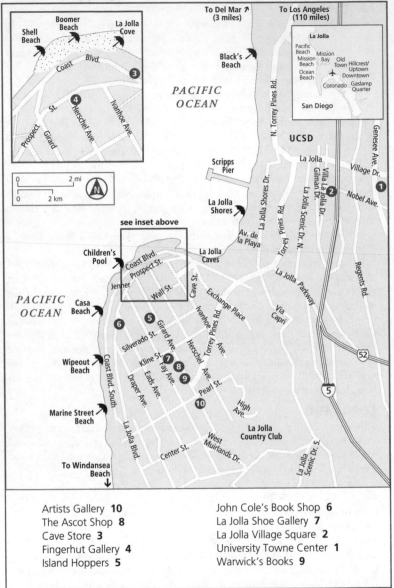

Artists Gallery **10**
The Ascot Shop **8**
Cave Store **3**
Fingerhut Gallery **4**
Island Hoppers **5**

John Cole's Book Shop **6**
La Jolla Shoe Gallery **7**
La Jolla Village Square **2**
University Towne Center **1**
Warwick's Books **9**

a leisurely dinner with a view, wander along landscaped walkways, or laze on a beach or grassy bank. There's a farmer's market every Tuesday from 2:30 to 6pm. 1201 First St. (at B Ave.), Coronado. ℭ **619/435-8895.** Daily 10am–9pm. Bus: 901. Ferry: From Broadway Pier. Take I-5 to Coronado Bay Bridge, to B Ave., and turn right.

ELSEWHERE IN SAN DIEGO COUNTY

If you're looking for San Diego's best outlet mall, head to Carlsbad, about 40 minutes north (for more information on Carlsbad, see "North County Beach

Towns" in chapter 11). The **Carlsbad Company Stores,** 5620 Paseo del Norte (© **760/804-9000**), include the usual outlet shops and upscale retailers like Barneys New York, Donna Karan, Crate & Barrel, Wilson's Leather, Dooney & Bourke, and Polo Ralph Lauren. The mall has several unique specialty shops, like **Thousand Mile Outdoor Wear** (© **760/804-1764**), which sells outerwear manufactured from recycled products, and makes the swimsuits worn by Southern California lifeguards. To get there, take the Palomar Airport Road exit off I-5; the outlet mall is open daily from 10am to 8pm.

The **Cedros Design District** ✦, along the 100 and 200 blocks of South Cedros Avenue in Solana Beach, is a outstanding place for designer interior decorating goods. Many of the shops are housed in a row of Quonset huts that were constructed for a company that made spy plane photographic equipment. Today, more than two dozen chic shops sell furniture, original art, imported goods, home decor, antiques, and clothing. There are a couple good cafes, plus **The Belly Up Tavern,** easily one of the county's top live music venues (p. 219). The strip is located just northwest of the Del Mar racetrack; reach it by taking the Via de la Valle exit off the I-5 and going right on Cedros Ave. The Coaster station is next to the district.

Garden fanciers will find North County the best hunting grounds for bulbs, seeds, and starter cuttings. **North County nurseries** are known throughout the state for rare and hard-to-find plants, notably begonias, orchids, bromeliads, succulents, ranunculus, and unusual herbs. For more information on the area's largest growers, **Flower Fields at Carlsbad Ranch** and **Weidners' Gardens,** turn to chapter 11.

3 Shopping A to Z

Large stores and shops in malls tend to stay open until about 9pm on weekdays, 6pm on weekends. Smaller businesses usually close at 5 or 6pm or may keep odd hours. When in doubt, call ahead.

ANTIQUES

See also the "Hillcrest/Uptown" and "Mission Bay & the Beaches" sections in "The Top Shopping Neighborhoods," earlier in this chapter.

The Cracker Factory Antiques Shopping Center   Prepare to spend some time here, exploring three floors of individually owned and operated shops filled with antiques and collectibles. It's across the street from the Hyatt Regency San Diego, a block north of Seaport Village. 448 W. Market St. (at Columbia St.). © **619/ 233-1669.** Bus: 7. Trolley: Seaport Village.

ART

The *Arts Down Town* guide is available at the Museum of Contemporary Art and at the David Zapf Gallery at the Studio Arts Complex (see below); it's a handy color brochure/map for exploring downtown galleries and exhibits.

The Artists Gallery   This gallery features 30 regional artists in a variety of media, primarily paintings. 7420 Girard Ave., La Jolla. © **858/459-5844.**

Fingerhut Gallery   Fingerhut is a Southern California minichain offering fine quality lithographs and etchings from masters like Picasso, Chagall, and Matisse. This branch, however, is notable for the "secret" art of La Jolla's own Theodor Geisel (aka Dr. Seuss), whose whimsical-yet-provocative unpublished works explode with the same color and exuberance of illustrations from his famous books. 1205 Prospect St., La Jolla. © **800/774-2278** or 858/456-9912. www.fingerhutart.com/lajolla.htm.

Many Hands   This cooperative gallery, in existence since 1972, has 35 members who engage in a variety of crafts, including toys, jewelry, posters, pottery, baskets, and wearable art, much of it reasonably priced. 302 Island Ave., Suite 101, Gaslamp Quarter. © 619/557-8303.

Scott White Contemporary Art   This gallery, in a grand space once occupied by the I. Magnin department store, specializes in modern and contemporary painting, sculpture, and photography. Andy Warhol, Roy Lichtenstein, and Mark Rothko are among the names. 7661 Girard Ave., Suite 200, La Jolla. © 858/551-5821.

Studio Arts Complex *(Finds*   Little Italy has been steadily gaining a reputation as San Diego's cutting-edge art and design district, and several local artists maintain studios in this industrial-style complex at the heart of the area's transformation. Some—especially the street-level galleries—maintain regular open hours. For the smaller studio/galleries upstairs, you can either call ahead for an appointment (don't be shy, the artists are eager to share their work) or take your chances with whoever is on-site working when you visit. Some recommended highlights include the **David Zapf Gallery** (no. 104, © 619/232-5004), which features painting, sculpture, drawings, photography and custom furniture. The **Pratt Gallery** (no. 106, © 619/236-0211) has a changing display space, often featuring innovative paintings, photography, or other highly individual work. Open houses are held on select Friday evenings—call David Zapf for the schedule. 2400 Kettner Blvd. (at Laurel St.), Little Italy.

Taboo Studio   This impressive shop exhibits and sells the work of jewelry designers from throughout the United States. The jewelry is made of silver, gold, platinum, and inlaid stones, in one-of-a-kind pieces, limited editions, or custom work. The gallery represents 65 artists. 1615½ W. Lewis St., Mission Hills. © 619/692-0099. www.taboostudio.com.

BOOKS

Barnes & Noble   The San Diego branch of this book discounter sits amid one of Mission Valley's smaller malls, Hazard Center. Besides a wide selection of paperback and hardcover titles, it offers a comprehensive periodicals rack. 7610 Hazard Center Dr., Mission Valley. © 619/220-0175. Daily 10am–9pm.

Borders   This full-service book and CD store just west of the Mission Valley shopping center offers discounts on many titles. Borders also stocks a stylish line of greeting cards and encourages browsing; there's an adjoining coffee lounge. 1072 Camino del Rio N., Mission Valley. © 619/295-2201. Mon–Thurs 9am–11pm; Fri–Sat 9am–midnight; Sun 10am–10pm.

John Cole's Book Shop *(Finds*   Cole's, a favorite of many locals, is in a turn-of-the-20th-century wisteria-covered cottage, the former guesthouse of philanthropist Ellen Browning Scripps. John and Barbara Cole founded the shop in 1946 and moved it into the cottage 20 years later. Barbara and her children continue to run it today. Visitors will find cookbooks in the old kitchen, paperbacks in a former classroom, and CDs and harmonicas in Zach's music corner. The children's section bulges with a diverse selection, and there are plenty of books about La Jolla and San Diego, and wonderful art books. Sitting and reading in the patio garden is acceptable, and even encouraged. 780 Prospect St., La Jolla. © 858/454-4766. Tues–Sat 9:30am–5:30pm.

Obelisk Bookstore   San Diego's main gay and lesbian bookstore is where Clive Barker and Greg Louganis do their book signings. You'll find every gay magazine there is, as well as gay-themed movies for rent on DVD and video. 1029 University Ave., Hillcrest. ℂ 619/297-4171. Mon–Thurs 10am–10pm; Fri–Sat 10am–11pm; Sun 11am–10pm.

Traveler's Depot This bookstore offers an extensive selection of travel books and maps, plus a great array of travel gear and accessories, with discounts on backpacks and luggage. The well-traveled owners, Ward and Lisl Hampton, are happy to give advice about restaurants in a given city while pointing you to the right shelf for the appropriate book or map. 1655 Garnet Ave., Pacific Beach. ℂ 858/483-1421. Mon–Fri 10am–6pm; Sat 10am–5pm; Sun noon–5pm.

Warwick's Books This popular family-run bookstore is a browser's delight, with more than 40,000 titles, a large travel section, gifts, cards, and stationery. The well-read Warwick family has been in the book and stationery business for more than 100 years, and the current owners are the third generation involved with the store. Authors come in for readings several days each week. 7812 Girard Ave., La Jolla. ℂ 858/454-0347. www.warwicks.com. Mon–Sat 9am–6pm; Sun 11am–5pm.

DEPARTMENT STORES

Macy's There are several branches of this comprehensive store, which carries clothing for women, men, and children, as well as housewares, electronics, and luggage. Macy's also has stores in the Fashion Valley (clothing only), Mission Valley Center (housewares only), University Towne Center, and North County Fair (Escondido) malls. Horton Plaza. ℂ 619/231-4747. Mon–Fri 10am–9pm; Sat 10am–8pm; Sun 11am–7pm. Bus: 2, 7, 9, 29, 34, or 35.

Nordstrom A San Diego favorite, Nordstrom is best known for its outstanding customer service and fine selection of shoes. It features a variety of stylish fashions and accessories for women, men, and children. Tailoring is done on the premises. There's a full-service restaurant on the top floor, where coffee and tea cost only 25¢. Nordstrom also has stores in the Fashion Valley, University Towne Center, and North County Fair (Escondido) malls. Horton Plaza. ℂ 619/239-1700. Mon–Fri 10am–9pm; Sat 10am–8pm; Sun 11am–7pm. Bus: 2, 7, 9, 29, 34, or 35.

FARMERS' MARKETS

We love our open-air markets. Throughout the county there are no fewer than two dozen regularly scheduled street fests stocked with the freshest fruits and vegetables from Southern California farms, augmented by crafts, fresh-cooked ethnic foods, flower stands, and other surprises. San Diego County produces more than $1 billion worth of fruits, flowers, and other crops each year. Avocados, known locally as "green gold," are the most profitable crop and have been grown here for more than 100 years. Citrus fruit follows close behind, and flowers are the area's third most important crop; ranunculus bulbs from here are sent all over the world, as are the famous Ecke poinsettias.

Here's a schedule of farmers' markets in the area:

In **Hillcrest,** the market runs Sundays from 9am to noon at the corner of Normal Street and Lincoln Avenue, several blocks north of Balboa Park. The atmosphere is festive, and exotic culinary delights reflect the eclectic neighborhood. For more information, call the **Hillcrest Association** at ℂ 619/299-3330.

In **Ocean Beach,** there's a fun-filled market Wednesday evenings between 4 and 8pm (until 7pm in fall and winter) in the 4900 block of Newport Avenue. In addition to fresh-cut flowers, produce, and exotic fruits and foods laid out for sampling, the market features llama rides and other entertainment. For more information, call the **Ocean Beach Business Improvement District** at ℂ **619/ 224-4906.**

Head to **Pacific Beach** on Saturday from 8am to noon, when Mission Boulevard between Reed Avenue and Pacific Beach Drive is transformed into a bustling marketplace.

In **Coronado,** every Tuesday afternoon The Ferry Landing Marketplace hosts a produce and crafts market from 2:30 to 6pm; see p. 209 for a full review.

FLEA MARKETS

Kobey's Swap Meet *(Value* Since 1980, this gigantic open-air market positioned at the west end of the Sports Arena parking lot has been a bargain-hunter's dream-come-true. As many as 3,000 vendors fill row after row with new and used clothing, jewelry, electronics, hardware, appliances, furniture, collectibles, crafts, antiques, auto accessories, toys, and books. There's produce, too, along with food stalls and restrooms.

Insider's tip: Although the market is open Friday through Sunday from 7am to 3pm, the weekend is when the good stuff is out—and it goes quickly, so arrive early. Sports Arena, 3500 Sports Arena Blvd. ℂ 619/226-0650 for information. Admission Fri 50¢; Sat–Sun $1; free for children under 12. Take I-8 west to Sports Arena Blvd. turnoff, or I-5 to Rosecrans St. and turn right on Sports Arena Blvd.

MALLS

See p. 203 for details on **Horton Plaza.** See "The Top Shopping Neighborhoods: Elsewhere in San Diego County," earlier in this chapter, for information on the **Carlsbad Company Stores Factory Outlet Center.**

Fashion Valley Center The Mission Valley corridor, running east-west about 2 miles north of downtown along I-8, contains San Diego's major shopping centers. Fashion Valley is the most attractive and most upscale, with four anchor stores **Neiman Marcus, Nordstrom** (which keeps longer hours), **Saks Fifth Avenue,** and **Macy's,** plus 140 specialty shops and an 18-screen AMC movie theater. Other noteworthy shops include **Z Gallerie, Smith & Hawken,** and **Bang & Olufsen.** 352 Fashion Valley Rd. ℂ 619/297-3381. Mon–Fri 10am–9pm; Sat 10am–6pm; Sun 11am–6pm. Bus: 6, 16, 25, 43, or 81. Hwy. 163 to Friars Rd. W.

Mission Valley Center This old-fashioned outdoor mall predates sleek Fashion Valley, and has found a niche with budget-minded stores like **Loehmann's, Nordstrom Rack,** and **Target;** you'll also find **Michael's, Macy's Home Furnishing,** and **TK.** There's a 20-screen AMC movie theater and about 150 other stores and places to eat. Across the streets to the north and west are other complexes that feature **Sak's Off Fifth Avenue** (an outlet store), **Borders,** and more. 1640 Camino del Rio N. ℂ 619/296-6375. Mon–Fri 10am–9pm; Sat 10am–6pm; Sun 11am–6pm. Bus: 6, 16, 25, 43, or 81. I-8 to Mission Center Rd.

University Towne Center (UTC) This outdoor shopping complex has a landscaped plaza and more than 150 stores, including some big ones like **Nordstrom, Sears,** and **Macy's.** It is also home to a year-round ice-skating rink and the popular On Tap Bistro and Brewery. 4545 La Jolla Village Dr. ℂ 858/546-8858. Mon–Fri 10am–9pm; Sat 10am–7pm; Sun 11am–6pm. Bus: 50 express, 34, or 34A. I-5 to La Jolla Village Dr. and go east, or I-805 to La Jolla Village Dr. and go west.

MUSIC

In addition to the mega chains like Tower Records and the Wherehouse, you'll find a good crop of independent outlets. Probably the best place for serious collectors is **Lou's Records,** 434 Hwy. 101 in Encinitas, about 30 minutes north of downtown (© **760/753-1382;** www.lousrecords.com). Here you'll find one building devoted to new CDs (the imports are pricey), another to used CDs and vinyl, and a new store next door catering to DVD fanatics. More central is **Off the Record,** 3849 Fifth Ave., Hillcrest (© **619/298-4755;** www.otrvinyl.com), which has a good selection of indie releases and used CDs, but I can't stand how cases are plastered with stickers and security tags, and note that the best of the store's collectable merchandise is sold online these days. Die-hard headbangers should make the trek to **Blue Meanie Records,** 916 Broadway in El Cajon, 20 minutes east of downtown (© **619/442-5034**), where a head-shop ambience adds to the selection of metal and punk albums, T-shirts, and posters. Last but not least is **Folk Arts Rare Records,** 3611 Adams Ave. in Normal Heights (© **619/282-7833**), which is nirvana for serious jazz and blues collectors. Situated in an old house, the store hasn't caught up with the CD era yet, but you'll find first-edition rarities on vinyl and 78s, most of them fairly priced.

TOYS

Freddy's Teddies & Toys   With shelves stacked literally from floor to ceiling, this Coronado shop's comprehensive inventory defies its cozy size and truly has something to interest anyone who steps inside. From vintage and antique treasures that great-granddad might remember to Hotwheels and Matchbox collections, Freddy's even has mechanized gadgets for the modern child. 930 Orange Ave. © 619/ 437-0130. www.coronadotoys.com. Daily 10am–5pm.

TRAVEL ACCESSORIES

Along with the stores listed below, try **Eddie Bauer** in Horton Plaza (© **619/ 233-0814**) or **Traveler's Depot** (p. 213) for travel gear.

John's Fifth Avenue Luggage   This San Diego institution carries just about everything you can imagine in the way of luggage, travel accessories, business cases, pens, and gifts. The on-premises luggage-repair center is an authorized airline repair facility. There is also a store in the Fashion Valley mall, with extended hours. 3833 Fourth Ave. © 619/298-0993. Mon–Fri 9am–5:30pm; Sat 9am–4pm.

Le Travel Store   In business since 1976, Le Travel Store has a good selection of soft-sided luggage, travel books, language tapes, maps, and lots of travel accessories. The long hours and central location make this spot extra handy. 745 Fourth Ave. (between F and G sts.). © 619/544-0005. www.letravelstore.com. Mon–Sat 10am–7pm; Sun noon–6pm. Bus: 2, 7, 9, 29, 34, or 35. Trolley: Gaslamp.

The Map Centre   This shop, recently relocated to this shopping plaza across I-5 from Old Town, has the whole world covered—in maps, that is. From topographical maps and nautical charts to GPS global positioning toys, the Map Centre makes for terrific browsing. Any local needs are easily met as well, with San Diego and California maps galore. 3191 Sports Arena Blvd. (west of Rosecrans). © 619/291-3830. www.mapcentre.com. Mon–Fri 10am–5:30pm; Sat 10am–5pm.

10

San Diego After Dark

San Diego's cultural scene has never been second-rate, but it's always lounged in the shadows of Los Angeles and San Francisco, content to take a back seat to the beach, the zoo, and the meteorologically inspired state of affairs. But the dot-com wave brought new blood and new money into the city, and arts organizations have felt the impact. The biggest winner was the San Diego Symphony, which in 2002 received a $120 million bequest from Joan and Irwin Jacobs—the largest single donation to a symphony anywhere, ever. The city's opera, live theaters, and other arts organizations are also thriving as new ears and eyes claim San Diego's art scene as their own.

But don't think "after dark" in this city is limited to highfalutin affairs for the Lexus crowd—it also means night *lively:* rock and pop concerts, swank martini bars and nightclubs, and dinner-and-dance cruises on the bay. You'll find fine outdoor concert venues that take advantage of our balmy weather, plus several choice indoor clubs; Dan Aykroyd and Bruce Willis have been snooping around downtown at the site of the old Woolworth building on Fifth Avenue to build a $10 million House of Blues venue. Not all of the city streets pulsate with nightlife, but you'll find late-night activity in a number of areas beyond the Gaslamp Quarter.

FINDING OUT WHAT'S ON

For a rundown of the week's performances, gallery openings, and other events, check the listings in "Night and Day," the Thursday entertainment section of the *San Diego Union-Tribune* (www.uniontrib.com), or the free *San Diego Weekly Reader* (www.sdreader.com), published on Thursday. For what's happening at the gay clubs, get the weekly *San Diego Gay & Lesbian Times.*

The local convention and visitors bureau's *Art + Sol* pamphlet is published every 6 months and provides a calendar of events and profiles of 11 member institutions; get a free copy by calling © 800/270-WAVE, or check www.sandiegoartandsol.com. The San Diego Performing Arts League produces *What's Playing?,* a performing arts guide, every 2 months. You can pick one up at the ARTS TIX booth or write to 701 B St., Suite 225, San Diego, CA 92101-8101 (© 619/238-0700; www.sandiegoperforms.com).

GETTING TICKETS

Half-price tickets to theater, music, and dance events are available at the **ARTS TIX** booth in Horton Plaza Park, at Broadway and Third Avenue. Pull into in the Horton Plaza garage (where you can validate your parking) or, if there's room, just pause at the curb. The kiosk is open Tuesday through Thursday at 11am, Friday through Sunday at 10am. The booth stays open till 6pm daily except Sunday, when it closes at 5pm. Half-price tickets are available only for same-day shows except for Monday performances, which are sold on Sunday. Only cash is accepted. For a daily listing of offerings, call © 619/497-5000 or check www.sandiegoperforms.com; the website also sells half-price tickets for some shows.

Full-price advance tickets are also available; the kiosk doubles as a Ticketmaster outlet, selling seats to concerts throughout California. As always, although Ticketmaster sells seats for a majority of local events, you'll avoid bruising "convenience" fees by purchasing directly from the venue's box office.

1 The Performing Arts

THEATER

These listings focus on the best known of San Diego's many talented theater companies. Don't hesitate to try a less prominent venue if the show appeals to you. Also, keep in mind that the **California Center for the Performing Arts** in Escondido has its own productions (see "North County Inland" in chapter 11), as does the **East County Performing Arts Center,** 210 E. Main St., El Cajon (© 619/440-2277; www.ecpac.com).

The Globe Theatres 🅐🅐   This complex of three performance venues is located inside Balboa Park, behind the Museum of Man. Though best known for the 581-seat Old Globe—fashioned after Shakespeare's—it also includes the 225-seat Cassius Carter Centre Stage and the 612-seat open-air Lowell Davies Festival Theatre. Between them, they mount 14 plays year-round, from world premieres of such subsequent Broadway hits as *Into the Woods* to the excellent summer Shakespeare San Diegans have come to expect from "their" Globe. *Dr. Seuss' How the Grinch Stole Christmas!* has been a popular family draw during the holidays since 1997. Leading performers regularly grace the stage, including Marsha Mason, John Goodman, Hal Holbrook, and Ellen Burstyn. Tours are offered Saturday and Sunday at 10:30am and cost $3 for adults, $1 for students, seniors, and military. The box office is open Tuesday through Sunday from noon to 8:30pm. Balboa Park. © 619/239-2255. Fax 619/231-5879. www.theglobetheatres.org. Tickets $19–$50. Senior, student, and military discounts available. Free parking in the park's public lots. Bus: 7 or 25.

La Jolla Playhouse 🅐🅐   Boasting a Hollywood pedigree (founded in 1947 by Gregory Peck, Dorothy McGuire, and Mel Ferrer), and a 1993 Tony Award for outstanding American regional theater, the Playhouse stages six productions each year (May–Nov) at two fine theaters on the UCSD campus. It seems like each one has something outstanding to recommend it; a nationally acclaimed director, for example, or highly touted revival (such as when Matthew Broderick starred in *How to Succeed in Business Without Really Trying,* which started out here). *The Who's Tommy* and *Big River* also premiered at the Playhouse before going on to great acclaim on Broadway. For each show, one Saturday matinee is a "pay what you can" performance, and any night, all unsold tickets are available for $12 each in a "public rush" sale 10 minutes before curtain. The box office is open Monday through Friday from noon to 6pm; extended and weekend hours apply during performance weeks. 2910 La Jolla Village Dr. (at Torrey Pines Rd.). © 858/550-1010. Fax 858/550-1025. www.lajollaplayhouse.com. Tickets $35–$55. Parking $3. Bus: 30, 34, or 34A.

Lamb's Players Theatre   The season for this professional repertory company runs from February to December. Shows take place in the 340-seat theater in Coronado's historic Spreckels Building, where no seat is more than seven rows from the stage. Recent productions include *Godspell,* Noel Coward's *Private Lives,* and Anton Chekhov's *Uncle Vanya.* The box office is open Tuesday through Saturday for noon to 7pm, Sunday from noon to 5pm. 1142 Orange Ave., Coronado. ℭ 619/437-0600. www.lambsplayers.org. Tickets $20–$40. Street parking is usually available nearby. Bus: 901, 902, or 904.

San Diego Junior Theatre   Founded in 1948, this is the country's oldest continuously producing children's theater. It provides training and performance opportunities for children and young adults. Students make up the cast and technical crew of six main-stage shows each year; recent production include *The Secret Garden* and *Footloose*. The box office is open Monday from 1 to 5pm and Tuesday through Friday from 10am to 5pm; also Saturday and Sunday from 10am to 2pm on performance days. Casa del Prado Theatre, Balboa Park. ℭ 619/239-8355. www.juniortheatre.com. Tickets $5–$10. Free parking. Bus: 7.

San Diego Repertory Theatre   The Rep mounts plays and musicals at the 550-seat Lyceum Stage and the 250-seat Lyceum Space in Horton Plaza. Situated at the entrance to Horton Plaza, the two-level subterranean theaters are tucked behind a tile obelisk. The box office is open Tuesday through Sunday from noon to showtime. 79 Broadway Circle, in Horton Plaza. ℭ 619/544-1000. www.sandiegorep.com. Tickets $23–$40. Free validated parking at Horton Plaza Shopping Center. Bus: All Broadway routes.

CLASSICAL MUSIC

La Jolla Chamber Music Society 𝕽𝕽   This well-respected organization has been bringing marquee names to San Diego since 1968. Past performers include Pinchas Zukerman, Emanuel Ax, Joshua Bell, the American Ballet Theatre, and other world-class artists. Most of the 40-plus annual shows are held October through May in the beautiful, 500-seat Sherwood Auditorium at the Museum of Contemporary Art. The annual highlight is SummerFest, a 3-week series of concerts, forums, open rehearsals, talks, and artist encounters—it's held in early August and is broadcast nationally live on NRP. At Sherwood Auditorium, 700 Prospect St., La Jolla. ℭ 858/459-3728. Fax 858/459-3727. www.ljcms.org. Tickets $15–$75. Bus: 30 or 34.

San Diego Symphony 𝕽   Like a phoenix from the ashes, San Diego's Symphony is on the verge of major triumph. The organization first took shape when a group of musicians gathered to perform at the U.S. Grant Hotel in 1910. Over time, the symphony grew and prospered with the city, but floundered for a decade starting in the late 1980s in conjunction with several years of local recession, inept management, and the malaise that gripped many fine orchestras around the country. In 1998 the symphony emerged from bankruptcy with a dedicated conductor (Jung-Ho Pak), and in 2002, enduring financial stability arrived with the announcement of a $120 million bequest by Joan and Irwin Jacobs (founder and CEO of Qualcomm). The bequest allows the organization to lure top talent, which started with the announcement of a new resident conductor, Jahja Ling (of the Blossom Music Festival). The symphony's home is the Fox Theatre, a 1929-era French rococo–style downtown landmark, restored and now known as Symphony Hall. The season runs October through May. A Summer Pops series, with programs devoted to big band, Broadway, and Tchaikovsky, is held weekends from late June to August on Navy Pier at the Embarcadero—always bring a sweater and possibly a blanket for these pleasantly brisk evenings on the water. The box office is open Monday through Thursday from 10am to 6pm, and on performance days from noon until intermission. 750 B St., at Seventh Ave. ℭ 619/235-0804. Fax 619/231-3848. www.sandiegosymphony.com. Tickets $10–$80. Bus: 1, 3, or 25. Trolley: Fifth Ave.

OPERA

San Diego Opera *★★*   Under the leadership of Ian Campbell since 1983, the San Diego Opera has grown into one of the community's most successful arts organizations. The annual season runs from late January to mid-May, with five offerings at downtown's 3,000-seat Civic Theatre, ranging from well-trod warhorses like *Madama Butterfly* to new productions such as 2003's *Thérèse Raquin*, all performed by local singers and big-name talent from around the world. The company also hosts several recitals each year at La Jolla's Sherwood Hall, featuring heavy-hitters like Marilyn Horne as well as promising new singers. The annual lineup is announced around April, and non-subscription tickets go on sale by December. The box office is at Third Avenue and B Street, open Monday through Friday from 10am to 6pm; hours vary on weekends and on the day of performance. At the Civic Theatre, 202 C St. *©* **619/570-1100** (box office) or 619/232-7636. Fax 619/231-6915. www.sdopera.com. Tickets $20–$140. Standing room, student, and senior discounts available. Bus: 2, 7, 9, 29, 34, or 35. Trolley: Civic Center.

DANCE

The **San Diego Dance Alliance** is the umbrella organization for the local dance community (*©* **619/230-8623;** www.sandiegodance.org). The alliance puts on the **Nations of San Diego International Dance Festival,** held each January and spotlighting the city's ethnic dance groups and emerging artists. The website provides links to 22 local dance outfits. Among San Diego's major dance companies are the **California Ballet** (*©* **858/560-5676;** www.californiaballet.org), a classical company that produces four shows annually at the Civic Theatre downtown, including *The Nutcracker.* **San Diego Ballet** (*©* **619/294-7378;** www.sandiego ballet.org) and **City Ballet** (*©* **858/274-6058;** www.cityballet.org) also focus on classical dance pieces.

2 The Club & Music Scene

LIVE MUSIC

SMALL VENUES

The Belly Up Tavern *★* *(Finds*   This club in Solana Beach, a 30-minute drive from downtown, has played host to critically acclaimed and international artists of all genres. The eclectic mix ranges from Duncan Sheik to Etta James to Frank Black to The Roots. A funky setting in recycled Quonset huts underscores the venue's uniqueness. Look into advance tickets, if possible, though you can avoid excessive Ticketmaster fees by purchasing your tickets at the box office. 143 S. Cedros Ave., Solana Beach (1½ blocks from the Coaster stop). *©* **858/481-9022** (recorded info) or 858/481-8140 (box office). www.bellyup.com.

The Casbah   It may have a total dive ambience (and black-walled bathrooms grimy enough to make you clench muscles you didn't even *know* you had), and passing jets overhead sometimes drown out ballads, but this blaring Little Italy club has a well-earned rep for showcasing alternative and rock bands that either are, were, or will be famous. Past headliners at the 200-capacity club have included the Yeah Yeah Yeahs, Will Oldham, White Stripes, and local act Rocket From the Crypt. Look into advance tickets if possible; live music can be counted on at least 6 nights a week. Every month or two the Casbah turns into Jivewire, with wall-to-wall bodies on the small dance floor and ear-to-ear new wave, disco, and hip-hop classics on the sound system. 2501 Kettner Blvd., at Laurel St., near the airport. *©* **619/232-HELL.** www.casbahmusic.com.

No Smoking

In 1998, California enacted legislation that banned smoking in all restaurants and bars. As a rule, don't light up in any public area indoors. If you're looking to light up in clubs, lounges, and other nightspots with outdoor terraces, check with the staff or watch to see what the locals are doing first.

Croce's Nightclubs Croce's is the cornerstone of Gaslamp Quarter nightlife: a loud, crowded, and mainstream gathering place around the corner from Horton Plaza. Two separate clubs operate a couple doors apart: You'll find traditional jazz at Croce's Jazz Bar 7 nights a week (8:30pm–12:30am), and rhythm and blues at Croce's Top Hat Friday and Saturday (9pm–1am). The music blares onto the street, making it easy to decide whether to go in or not. The clubs are named for the late Jim Croce and are owned by his widow, Ingrid, who was a vital component of the Gaslamp's revitalization. Their son, A.J., an accomplished musician, often performs. The cover charge is waived if you eat at the restaurant. 802 Fifth Ave. (at F St.). (℃ 619/233-4355. www.croces.com. Cover $5–$10.

4th & B Located in a former bank building downtown, 4th & B is a no-frills music venue made comfortable with haphazardly placed seating (balcony theater seats, cabaret tables on the main floor) and a handful of bar/lounge niches—one actually inside the old vault. The genre is barrier-free; everyone from Fishbone to Toto to They Might Be Giants to Lisa Marie Presley has shown up here, along with regular bookings of the San Diego Chamber Orchestra. Look into advance tickets; the box office is open daily from 10am to 5pm. 345 B St., downtown. (℃ 619/ 231-4343. www.4thandB.com.

LARGER VENUES

San Diego is a popular destination for major and minor recording artists. In fact, there's a worthwhile concert just about any night of the week—you just need to know where to find it. The free *San Diego Weekly Reader*, published on Thursdays, is the best source of concert information, listing dozens of shows in any given week; check the website at www.sdreader.com for an advance look. Tickets typically go on sale 4 to 10 weeks before the event—dates are usually announced in the Thursday *Reader* or the Sunday *San Diego Union-Tribune*. Depending on the popularity of a particular artist or group, last-minute seats are often available through the box office or **Ticketmaster** (℃ 619/220-8497; www.ticket master.com). You can also go through a broker like **Advance Tickets** (℃ 858/ 581-1080; www.advancetickets.com) if you're willing to pay a higher price for prime tickets at the last minute.

The city has two monster venues—hopefully an act you want to see isn't scheduled at one of them. The **San Diego Sports Arena** (℃ 619/225-9813; www.sandiegoarena.com) is located west of Old Town. Built in 1967, the 15,000- to 18,000-seat indoor venue has lousy acoustics, but many big-name concerts are held here because of the seating capacity and availability of paid parking. **Qualcomm Stadium** (℃ 619/641-3131), in Mission Valley, is a 71,000-seat outdoor stadium and is used only a few times a year for major tours like the Rolling Stones. But since the Padres have their own stadium opening in 2004, and the Chargers are thinking about abandoning San Diego for another locale, the future of "the Q" is in doubt.

The **Open Air Theater** (© 619/594-6947), on the San Diego State University campus, northeast of downtown along I-8, is a more intimate 4,000-seat outdoor amphitheater. It has great acoustics—if you can't get a ticket, you can sit outside on the grass and hear the entire show. **Cox Arena** (© 619/594-6947), also located at SDSU, has equally superb acoustics in an indoor, 12,000-seat facility that is used for bigger draws—for both of these facilities, parking is tight. **Coors Amphitheatre** (© 619/671-3600) is a slick new facility located seemingly a stone's throw north of the Mexican border, in Chula Vista. Built in 1999, the 20,000-seat venue has excellent acoustics and good sight lines, and it lures many of the summer tours. The drawbacks: overpriced snacks and drinks, and the location is 25 to 45 minutes south of downtown (depending on traffic).

Humphrey's, 2241 Shelter Island Dr. (© 619/523-1010; www.humphreys concerts.com), is a much-beloved 1,300-seat outdoor venue on the water. It has ideal acoustics, and Humphrey's seasonal lineup covers the spectrum of entertainment—rock, jazz, blues, folk, and comedy. Although there's not a bad seat in the house, you can often snag a seat in the first eight rows by buying the dinner/ concert package (usually $47 extra) for the adjoining restaurant of the same name—the food's nothing special, but if sitting up front is of value to you, it's a good deal. Concerts are held from mid-May to October only, and tickets for most shows go on sale in early April. (Seats are also available through Ticketmaster.)

The **Spreckels Theatre,** 121 Broadway (© 619/235-9500), and **Copley Symphony Hall,** 750 B St. (© 619/235-0804), are wonderful old movie houses which also are used by touring acts throughout the year; past shows have included Annie Lennox, Margaret Cho, and *Forever Tango*. For both venues, tickets are available at the box office or through Ticketmaster.

COMEDY CLUBS

The Comedy Store   Yes, it's a branch of the famous Sunset Strip club in Los Angeles, and yes, plenty of L.A. comics make the trek to headline Friday and Saturday shows here. Less prominent professional comedians perform live Wednesday and Thursday, and Sunday's open-mic night can be hilarious, horrendous—or maybe both. 916 Pearl St., La Jolla. © 858/454-9176. Cover $5–$20 (plus 2-drink minimum).

DANCE CLUBS & CABARETS

Olé Madrid   Loud and energetic, this dance club features a changing lineup of celebrated DJs spinning house, funk, techno, and hip-hop. The adjoining restaurant has terrific tapas and sangria. Open Tuesday through Saturday. 751 Fifth Ave., Gaslamp Quarter. © 619/557-0146. Cover $10 after 10pm.

Sevilla   This Latin-themed club is the spot for salsa lessons Tuesday through Thursday and Sunday at 8pm, followed by live bands at 10pm. Friday and Saturday is a Latin/Euro dance club and Monday is Rock en Español. Sevilla also has a tapas bar. 555 Fourth Ave., Gaslamp Quarter. © 619/233-5979. www.cafesevilla.com. Cover $5–$10.

CRUISES WITH ENTERTAINMENT

Bahia Belle ⟨⟩   Cruise Mission Bay and dance to live music under the moonlight aboard this stern-wheeler. Passengers are picked up from the dock of the Bahia Hotel, 998 W. Mission Bay Dr., on the half-hour from 6:30pm to 12:30am, and at the Catamaran Resort Hotel, 3999 Mission Blvd., on the hour from 7pm to midnight. 988 W. Mission Bay Dr. © 858/539-7720. www.sternwheelers.com. Tickets $6 adults, $3 children under 12. Operates nightly July–Aug; operates Fri–Sat only Sept–June. Children accompanied by an adult allowed until 9pm; after 9pm, 21 and over only (with valid ID).

Hornblower Cruises   Aboard the 151-foot antique-style yacht *Lord Horn-blower,* you'll be entertained—and encouraged to dance—by a DJ playing a variety of recorded music. The three-course meal is standard-issue banquet style, but the scenery is marvelous. Boarding is at 6:30pm, and the cruise runs from 7 to 10pm. 1066 N. Harbor Dr. (at Broadway Pier). © 619/725-8888. www.hornblower.com. Tickets Sun–Fri $55; Sat $60 adults (40% off for children ages 4–12). Price does not include sodas or alcoholic beverages. Bus: 2. Trolley: Embarcadero.

San Diego Harbor Excursion   This company offers nightly dinner on board the 150-foot, three-deck *Spirit of San Diego,* with two main courses, dessert, and cocktails. A DJ plays dance music during the 2½-hour cruise. Sometimes there's also a country-western band or even a karaoke singalong. Boarding is at 7pm, and the cruise lasts from 7:30 to 10pm. 1050 N. Harbor Dr. (at Broadway Pier). © 800/44-CRUISE or 619/234-4111. www.harborexcursion.com. Tickets $50 adults ($69 with alcoholic beverages), $30 children ages 3–12, free for children under 3; all prices $5 higher on Sat. Bus: 2. Trolley: Embarcadero.

3 The Bar & Coffeehouse Scene

BARS & COCKTAIL LOUNGES

The Beach   New and currently very "in" among trendoids, the Beach is the rooftop bar of the W hotel. What makes it truly unique is that most of the floor is sand—you can take your shoes off (drinks are served in plastic) even in winter since the sand is heated. A gas fire pit adds to the ambience, as do the cabanas lining one wall. Don't forget your flip-flops, shovel, and pail. The hotel's two other bars, the Living Room and Magnet, are also smart. 421 B St. (at State St.), downtown. © 619/231-8220. No cover.

The Bitter End   With three floors, this conceited, Brit-themed Gaslamp Quarter hot spot manages to be a sophisticated martini bar, after-hours dance club, and relaxing cocktail lounge all in one. On weekends you're subject to velvet rope/dress code nonsense. 770 Fifth Ave., Gaslamp Quarter. © 619/338-9300. www.thebitterend.com. Cover Thurs $5 after 9:30pm, Fri–Sat $10 after 8:30pm.

Cannibal Bar   Attached to the lobby of the Polynesian-themed Catamaran Hotel, the Cannibal Bar thumps to the beat of a different drum machine—though you *can* get a mean mai tai at the bar. Party central at the beach for thundering DJ-driven music, the Cannibal also books some admirable bands now and then. 3999 Mission Blvd., Pacific Beach. © 858/539-8650. Cover Wed–Sun $5–$6.

Lips   Drag review, with or without dinner. There's a different show nightly, like Bitchy Bingo on Wednesday and celebrity impersonations on Thursday. Shows start at 7 or 7:30pm Sunday through Thursday; Friday and Saturday have two seatings at 6 and 8:30pm. 2770 Fifth Ave. (at Nutmeg St.), Hillcrest. © 619/295-7900. www.lipsshow.biz. Cover $3; dinner reservations guarantee seating.

Martini Ranch   The Gaslamp Quarter's newest crowd-pleaser is this split-level bar boasting 30 kinds of martinis (or martini-inspired concoctions). Downstairs resembles an upscale sports bar playing videos, cartoons, and sports simultaneously across the room. If the sensory overload addles your brain, traipse upstairs to relax in scattered couches, love seats, and conversation pits.

528 F St. (at Sixth Ave.), Gaslamp Quarter. ℂ **619/235-6100.** www.martiniranchsd.com. Cover $10 Fri–Sat after 8:30pm.

Nunu's Cocktail Lounge   Lots of 1960s lounge style without the attitude, plus a kitchen that whips up burgers, liver-and-onions, and the like for a local Gen-X crowd. 3537 Fifth Ave., Hillcrest. ℂ **619/295-2878.** No cover.

On Broadway   This retro swanky hangout has five rooms covering the musical gamut—house, techno, hip-hop, R&B—plus a sushi bar. Open Friday and Saturday only. 615 Broadway (at Sixth Ave.), downtown. ℂ **619/231-0011.** www.obec.tv. Cover $15.

The Onyx Room   Hipsters dive into this cutting-edge underground (literally) club where the atmosphere is lounge, the drinks are up, and the music is cool. Live jazz is featured on Tuesdays. Upstairs is **Thin,** run by the same crew and open Tuesday through Friday from 4pm, Saturday and Sunday from 7pm. 852 Fifth Ave., downtown. ℂ **619/235-6699.** www.onyxroom.com. Cover Fri–Sat $10 (admission to both bars), Thurs $5 for Onyx.

Ould Sod   Irish through and through, this little gem sits in a quiet neighborhood of antiques shops northeast of Hillcrest, hosting a very local crowd. On Tuesdays the tavern features low-key folk or world-music performances; you'll find various other live bands and karaoke Wednesday through Saturday. 3373 Adams Ave., Normal Heights. ℂ **619/284-6594.** Cover Wed $3.

Princess Pub & Grille   A local haunt for Anglophiles and others thirsting for a pint o' Bass, Fuller's, Watney's, or Guinness, this slice of Britain (in Little Italy . . . go figure) also serves up overpriced bangers 'n' mash, steak-and-kidney pie, and other pub grub. The after-work crowd can be festive, and if you drink enough, the food starts to taste good. 1665 India St., Little Italy. ℂ **619/702-3021.** www.princesspub.com. No cover.

Red Fox Room   The Always Entertaining Shirley Allen tickles the ivory Wednesday through Saturday at this hipster haunt, filled with Tudor appointments that supposedly once belonged to Marion Davies. The Red Fox celebrates its 50th anniversary this year. The neighborhoody crowd of Gen-X and gay regulars has adopted it, and a late-night steak comes with all the 1954-style fixins. 2223 El Cajon Blvd., 1 mile east of Park Blvd., North Park. ℂ **619/297-1313.** No cover.

Top Of the Cove   At this intimate piano bar in one of La Jolla's most scenic restaurants, the vibe is mellow and relaxing on Fridays and Saturdays after 8:30pm. The music—mainly standards and show tunes—is piped into the outdoor patio. 1216 Prospect Ave., La Jolla. ℂ **858/454-7779.** No cover.

Turf Supper Club *(Finds*   Hidden in one of San Diego's old, obscure, and newly hip neighborhoods (about 10 min. east of downtown), the gimmick at this retro steakhouse is cheap, "grill your own" dinners. Steaks are delivered raw, but seasoned, on a paper plate—you do the rest. ***Tip:*** Don't be afraid to ask for grilling suggestions from the staff. The decor and piano bar (on Sun) are pure 1950s, and wildly popular with the cocktail crowd; the volume level other nights is not always conducive to intimate dining. 1116 25th Ave., Golden Hill. ℂ **619/234-6363.** No cover.

COFFEEHOUSES WITH PERFORMANCES

Claire de Lune Coffee Lounge *(Finds*   Every Tuesday is poetry night: It's one of the biggest in the country, drawing 200 to 300 people. The third Thursday

Late-Night Bites

Frankly, late-night meals aren't a big part of San Diego life outside downtown, but there are a few good choices. See chapter 6 for complete listings on most of the following restaurants.

DOWNTOWN   The kitchen at **Croce's** stays open till midnight all week. You can order appetizers from the eclectic menu, or opt for a full (expensive) meal. **Kansas City Barbecue,** across the street from the Hyatt, serves meals until 1am nightly. The stylish coffeehouse **Café Lulu,** a block from Horton Plaza, stays open till 1am Sunday through Thursday and 3am Friday and Saturday. It serves health-conscious vegetarian meals, and bread from Bread & Cie.

HILLCREST/UPTOWN   The relentlessly 1950s-themed **Corvette Diner** serves up terrific coffee shop–style food and a page-long menu of fountain favorites; it stays open till midnight Friday and Saturday. Or satisfy your sweet tooth with a sublime creation from **Extraordinary Desserts,** which also serves imported teas and coffees along with not-so-sweet scones and tea cakes. **Crest Café,** 425 Robinson Ave. (© 619/295-2510), is a friendly neighborhood joint for burgers, pastas, and sandwiches; it's open till midnight Sunday through Thursday, till 1am Friday and Saturday. The kitschy **Red Fox Room** in North Park serves steaks and seafood till midnight Monday through Thursday, till 1am Friday and Saturday, and till 11pm Sunday.

ELSEWHERE   In Old Town, the irrepressible **Old Town Mexican Café** stays open for basic Mexican and tasty margaritas until 11pm Sunday through Thursday, and serves until "about" midnight on Friday and Saturday. Day or night, it's hard to top the Chinese seafood delicacies found at **Emerald Restaurant** in Kearny Mesa, and it's open until midnight daily. In Pacific Beach, **Nick's at the Beach,** 809 Thomas Ave. (© 858/270-1730), is open until 1am nightly and serves laid-back seafood; nearby **Saska's,** 3768 Mission Blvd. (© 858/488-7311), stays open till 12:45am Sunday through Thursday, till 1:45am Friday and Saturday, serving steaks, fresh fish, and pasta.

of the month is live belly dancing; Friday and Saturday features varied bands. 2906 University Ave. (at Kansas), North Park. © 619/688-9845. www.clairedelune.com.

Hot Monkey Love Café   This is a new coffeehouse that draws SDSU students and residents of the up-and-coming neighborhood. In addition to local bands, poetry readings, and chess tournaments, you'll find salsa and swing dancing and lessons. 5960 El Cajon Blvd. (west of College Blvd.), SDSU area. © 619/582-5908. www.hot monkeylovecafe.com. No cover.

Twiggs Tea and Coffee Co. *Finds*   Tucked away in a peaceful neighborhood, this popular coffeehouse has an adjoining room for live music Thursday through Sunday, poetry readings every other Monday, and an open-mic night on

Wednesday. 4590 Park Blvd. (south of Adams Ave.), University Heights. Ⓒ **619/296-0616.** www.twiggs.org. Sometimes a $6–$12 cover for higher profile acts.

4 Gay & Lesbian Nightlife

Bourbon Street With an elegant piano bar and outdoor patio meant to evoke jazzy New Orleans, this relaxing spot draws mainly smartly dressed, dignified men and a good share of women. Open from 2pm on weekdays, from 11am on weekends. 4612 Park Blvd. (near Adams Ave.), University Heights. Ⓒ **619/291- 0173.** www.bourbonstreetsd.com.

The Brass Rail San Diego's oldest existing (since 1960) gay bar, this Hillcrest institution is loud and proud, with energetic dancing every night, bright lights, and a come-as-you-are attitude. Thursday and Saturday are Latino Night, hip-hop reigns on Friday and Sunday, and Wednesday is Women's Night. 3796 Fifth Ave. (at Robinson St.), Hillcrest. Ⓒ **619/298-2233.** Cover Fri–Sat $7 ($4 with gym card or military ID).

Club Montage This state-of-the-art dance club has all the bells and whistles: laser-and-light show, 12-screen video bar, pool tables, and arcade games. Three levels of dancing, four oversize bars, a video bar, and a rooftop smoking patio with views of downtown draws a mixed (gay and non-gay) crowd on Fridays. 2028 Hancock St. Ⓒ **619/294-9590.** www.clubmontage.com. Cover charge varies.

The Flame The city's top lesbian hangout has a large dance floor and two bars. It's packed on Saturdays. A mixed crowd attends Friday's Goth Night, and gender reversal takes place for Wednesday's "Drag King" contest. 3780 Park Blvd. Ⓒ **619/295-4163.** Cover Wed $3, Sat $8.

Flicks The first video bar in town, Flick's airs *Six Feet Under* and *Queer as Folk* live and offers various theme nights to supplement the rotating music and comedy clips. Tuesday is Fish Tank for lesbians. 1017 University Ave., Hillcrest. Ⓒ **619/297- 2056.** Cover Mon $2, Fri $4.

Kickers This country-western dance hall next to the ever-popular Hamburger Mary's restaurant attracts an equally male-female crowd for two-stepping and line-dancing Thursday through Saturday; free dance lessons are part of the mix. Sunday is busiest, with a high-energy tea dance and a $2 cover. Monday through Wednesday feature theme nights. 308 University Ave. (at Third Ave.), Hillcrest. Ⓒ **619/491- 0400.**

Numbers It's a predominantly male crowd at this busy dance emporium, with three bars, two dance floors, and go-go boy dancers. Friday is Ladies' Night. Open daily from 1pm. 3811 Park Blvd. (at University Ave.), Hillcrest. Ⓒ **619/294-9005.** www.numbers-sandiego.com. Cover $3–$5.

Rich's High-energy and popular with the see-and-be-seen set, Rich's offers house music and monster tribal rhythms, and a small video bar. Open Thursday through Sunday only. 1051 University Ave. (between 10th and Vermont). Ⓒ **619/497-4588.** www.richs-sandiego.com. Cover some nights.

Six Degrees Mellower than the Flame, this casual lesbian gathering place north of Little Italy has a small dance floor, occasional live entertainment, and popular Sunday barbecues. 3175 India St. (at Spruce St.). Ⓒ **619/296-6789.**

Top of the Park   The penthouse bar of this lodging, which is adjacent to Balboa Park, is a very popular social scene on Friday evenings from 5 to 10pm. 525 Spruce St. (at Fifth Ave.), Hillcrest. ✆ **619/291-0999.** www.parkmanorsuites.com.

5 More Entertainment

CINEMA

A variety of multiscreen complexes around the city show first-run films. My favorite venue, from a sheer presentation standpoint, is Pacific's **Gaslamp Stadium,** Fifth Avenue at G Street, downtown (✆ **619/232-0400**); the 15 theaters all offer stadium seating with large screens and great sound systems. The AMC chain operates swarming complexes in both the **Mission Valley** and **Fashion Valley** shopping centers (✆ **858/558-2AMC**); both have free parking but popular films sell out early on weekends. Current American independent and foreign films play at Landmark's five-screen **Hillcrest Cinema,** 3965 Fifth Ave., Hillcrest, which offers 3 hours of free parking (✆ **619/299-2100**); the **Ken Cinema,** 4061 Adams Ave., Kensington (✆ **619/283-5909**); and the four-screen **La Jolla Village,** 8879 Villa La Jolla Dr., La Jolla, also with free parking (✆ **858/453-7831**).

The **Museum of Photographic Arts** in Balboa Park (✆ **619/238-7559;** www.mopa.org) has a well-chosen revival series featuring American and foreign classics, shown Friday and Saturday and some weeknights. The **OMNIMAX** theater at the Reuben H. Fleet Science Center (✆ **619/238-1233**), also in Balboa Park, features IMAX movies in the early evening projected onto the 76-foot tilted dome screen (later screenings on weekends). Planetarium shows are held the first Wednesday of the month.

PERFORMANCE ART

Sushi is San Diego's preeminent performance art gallery, a 3,000-square-foot facility for interactive, visual art, music, dance, and other shows, attended by up to 200 people. Thought-provoking performances by Karen Finley, John Fleck, Tim Miller, and others have kept Sushi on the map. Performances are usually at 8pm, and prices range from $5 to $15. Sushi is located at 320 Eleventh Ave., between J and K streets, in the downtown warehouse district (✆ **619/235-8466;** www.sushiart.org).

CASINOS

Native American tribes operate seven casinos in east and north San Diego County. The leader is probably **Barona Valley Ranch Resort and Casino,** located at 1000 Wildcat Canyon Rd., Lakeside (✆ **888/7-BARONA** or 619/443-2300; www.barona.com). Take I-8 east to Calif. 67 north. At Willow Road, turn right and continue to Wildcat Canyon Road; turn left, and continue 5½ miles to the 7,500-acre Barona Reservation (allow 40 min. from downtown). The casino features 2,000 Vegas-style slots, 54 table games, and a 125-seat off-track betting area. The resort (which includes 397 guest rooms and an 18-hole championship golf course) is alcohol-free, but not smoke-free (Indian reservations are exempt from California's nonsmoking laws).

Sycuan Casino & Resort is outside El Cajon, at 5469 Dehesa Rd. (✆ **800/2-SYCUAN** or 619/445-6002; www.sycuan.com). Follow I-8 east for 10 miles to the El Cajon Blvd. exit. Take El Cajon to Washington Avenue, turning right and continuing on Washington as it turns into Dehesa Road; signs will direct you to the casino, about 7 miles from the freeway (allow 30 min. from downtown).

Finds Running with the Grunion

The **Grunion Run** is a wacky local tradition that few visitors experience. But if someone invites you to hustle down to the beach for a late-night fishing expedition, armed only with a sack and flashlight, do not be afraid. Grunion are 5- to 6-inch silvery fish that wriggle out of the water to lay their eggs in the sand. They make for decent eating (coated in flour and cornmeal, then fried), providing you don't mind catching them barefoot, but it's fun just to watch the action. From April to early June is peak spawning season in Southern California (which, with Baja California, is the only place you'll find grunion)—anywhere from a few dozen to thousands of grunion can appear during a run. The grunion runs happen twice a month, after the highest tides and during the full or new moon. The fish prefer wide, flat, sandy beaches (Mission Beach is usually a good spot); you'll spot more grunion if you go to a less-populated stretch of beach, with a minimum of light. You do need a valid state fishing license to catch grunion (see "Fishing" under "Outdoor Pursuits" in chapter 7). If you'd like more information, the little critters have their own website: **www.grunion.org**.

Sycuan features 1,800 slots, 65 game tables, a bingo palace, an off-track betting area, and a 450-seat theatre which features name touring acts. Sycuan acquired the neighboring Singing Hills Country Club, which includes 11 tennis courts, two 18-hole championship golf courses, and a 102-room lodge.

The **Viejas Casino** is at 5000 Willows Rd., in Alpine (© **800/84-POKER** or 619/445-5400; www.viejas.com). To get there, take I-8 east 25 miles to Willows Rd. exit; turn left to casino (allow 40 min. from downtown). Here you'll find 2,000 slots, 80 table games, an off-track betting room, a 1,500-seat Bingo pavilion, five restaurants and a showroom. Across the road is the **Viejas Outlet Center,** which features the usual suspects: Eddie Bauer, Liz Claiborne, Polo Ralph Lauren, and so on.

Other places where you'll find Las Vegas–style casino gambling, off-track betting, and bingo include **Golden Acorn Casino Travel Center** in Campo, about 1 hour east of downtown (© **866/7-WINBIG;** www.goldenacorncasino.com); **Harrah's Rincon Casino & Resort,** located in Valley Center 50 minutes north of downtown near Escondido (© **877/777-2457;** www.harrahs.com); the **Pala Casino** at the foot of Palomar Mountain, about 1 hour north of downtown (© **877/WIN-PALA;** www.palacasino.com); and the $262 million **Pechanga Resort & Casino,** located in Temecula, just north of the San Diego border in Riverside County, about 75 minutes away (© **888/PECHANGA;** www.pechanga.com).

To bet on the ponies, go to the **Del Mar** racetrack during the local racing season (July–Sept). At any time of the year, you can bet on races being run far and wide at **Del Mar Satellite Wagering,** at the Del Mar fairgrounds (© **858/755-1167**). To place a wager on **greyhound racing,** you have to cross the international border to Tijuana. It's a 40-minute ride by car or trolley from San Diego; from the border you'll need a cab to get to the racetrack. Bookmaker offices, where you can place a bet on just about any sport, are located throughout Tijuana.

6 Only in San Diego

San Diego's top three attractions—the **San Diego Zoo, Wild Animal Park,** and **SeaWorld**—keep extended summer hours. SeaWorld caps its Summer Nights off at 9pm with a **fireworks** display nightly. You can catch them from SeaWorld or anywhere around Mission Bay.

Drive-ins may be all but a thing of the past, but San Diego's most unique movie venue is experienced at **Movies Before the Mast** (© **619/234-9153**), aboard the *Star of India* at the waterfront Maritime Museum. During July and August, movies of the nautical genre (such as *The Perfect Storm* or *Twenty Thousand Leagues Under the Sea*) are shown on a special "screensail" Fridays and Saturdays at 7pm.

In summer, free concerts are offered at the Spreckels Organ Pavilion in Balboa Park on Monday (organ recitals) and Tuesday through Thursday nights (bands, dance, and vocal groups) as part of **Twilight in the Park** (© **619/239-0512**). Concerts run from mid-June to August and begin at 7:30pm. Also in the park, the **Starlight Theater** presents four Broadway musicals in the Starlight Bowl from mid-June to mid-September (© **619/544-STAR;** www.starlighttheatre. org). This venue is in the flight path to Lindbergh Field, and when planes pass overhead, singers stop in mid-note and wait for the roar to cease. The Globe's **Festival Stage** (© **619/239-2255;** www.theglobetheatres.org) in Balboa Park is a popular outdoor summer theater venue for Shakespeare.

Another Balboa Park event, **Christmas on the Prado,** has been a San Diego tradition since 1977. The weekend of evening events is held the first Friday and Saturday in December. The park's museums and walkways are decked out in holiday finery, and the museums are free and open late, from 5 to 9pm. There is entertainment galore, from bell choruses to Renaissance and baroque music to barbershop quartets. Crafts (including unusual Christmas ornaments), ethnic nibbles, hot cider, and sweets are for sale. A Christmas tree and nativity scene are displayed at the Spreckels Organ Pavilion.

11

Side Trips from San Diego

If you have time for a day trip, popular destinations include the beaches and inland towns of **"North County"** (as locals call the part of San Diego County north of the I-5/I-805 junction), as well as our south-of-the-border neighbor, **Tijuana.** All are less than an hour away.

If you have time for a longer trip, you can explore some distinct areas, all within 2 hours of the city. They include the wine country of **Temecula,** due north of San Diego; **Disneyland,** a little farther north; the gold-mining town of **Julian,** to the northeast, now known for its apple pies; and the vast **Anza-Borrego Desert,** east of Julian. Whichever direction you choose, you're in for a treat.

The following excursions are arranged geographically going north from San Diego, up to Disneyland, and then heading east toward Julian and south to Tijuana.

1 North County Beach Towns: Spots to Surf & Sun

The necklace of picturesque beach towns that dot the coast of San Diego County from Del Mar to Oceanside make great day-trip destinations for sun worshipers and surfers. Be forewarned: You'll be tempted to spend the night.

ESSENTIALS

GETTING THERE   It's a snap: **Del Mar** is only 18 miles north of downtown San Diego, **Carlsbad** about 33 miles, and **Oceanside** approximately 36 miles. If you're driving, follow I-5 north; Del Mar, Solana Beach, Encinitas, Carlsbad, and Oceanside all have freeway exits. The northernmost point, Oceanside, will take about 45 minutes. The other choice by car is to wander up the coast road, known along the way as Camino del Mar, the "PCH" (Pacific Coast Highway), Old Highway 101, and County Highway S21.

From San Diego, the **Coaster** commuter train provides service to Solana Beach, Encinitas, Carlsbad, and Oceanside, and **Amtrak** stops in Solana Beach—just a few minutes north of Del Mar—and Oceanside. The Coaster makes the trip almost hourly on weekdays, four times on Saturday; Amtrak passes through 11 times daily each way. Call © **619/685-4900** for transit information or check with Amtrak at © **800/USA-RAIL** or www.amtrak.com. United Express and America West Express fly into the **McClellan Palomar Airport,** 3 miles east of I-5 in Carlsbad.

VISITOR INFORMATION   The **San Diego North Convention & Visitors Bureau,** 360 N. Escondido Blvd. (© **800/848-3336** or 760/745-4741; www. sandiegonorth.com), is a good information source.

DEL MAR 🏵🏵

Just 18 miles up the coast lies Del Mar, a small community with just over 5,000 inhabitants in a 2-square-mile municipality. The town has adamantly maintained its independence, eschewing incorporation into the city of San Diego. It's one of the most upscale communities in the greater San Diego area, yet Del Mar somehow manages to maintain a casual, small-town ambience that radiates personality and charm. Come summer, the town swells as visitors flock in for the thoroughbred horseracing season and the county's San Diego Fair.

The history and popularity of Del Mar are inextricably linked to the **Del Mar Racetrack & Fairgrounds,** 2260 Jimmy Durante Blvd. (© **858/753-5555;** www.delmarfair.com), which still glows with the aura of Hollywood celebrity. In 1933, crooner and actor Bing Crosby owned 44 acres in Del Mar, and added a stud barn for his Thoroughbreds; in 1937 he turned the operation into the Del Mar Turf Club, enlisting the help of Pat O'Brien and other celebrity friends (like Jimmy Durante, whose eponymous street borders the racetrack grounds). Soon, Hollywood stars like Lucille Ball, Desi Arnaz, Harry James, Betty Grable, and Bob Hope were constantly seen around Del Mar, and the town experienced a resurgence in popularity. During World War II, racing was suspended. The club housed paratroopers in the horse stalls as well as marines taking amphibious training on the beach; aircraft assembly lines were even set up in the grandstand and clubhouse. Crosby sold his interest and moved out of the area just after the war, but the image of the racetrack—and the town—was set. You'll still hear the song Bing wrote and recorded to commemorate the track's opening day—"Where the Surf Meets the Turf"—played twice daily, before the first race and following the last post. A new $80 million grandstand opened in 1993, built in the Spanish mission style of the original structure; it features more seats, better race viewing, and a centrally located scenic paddock. The $1 million Pacific Classic, featuring the top horses in the country, is held in mid-August. For more information about racing here, see "Spectator Sports" in chapter 7.

Today, just as popular as racing season is the **San Diego County Fair,** more popularly known as the Del Mar Fair and held next to the racetrack. Livestock competitions, garden shows, carnival rides, and hundreds of exhibit booths draw thousands of visitors for the 3-week event, held from mid-June to early July. For more information, call © **858/793-5555** or see www.sdfair.com.

ESSENTIALS

For more information about Del Mar, contact or visit the **Del Mar Regional Chamber of Commerce Visitor Information Center,** 1104 Camino del Mar #1, Del Mar (© **858/755-4844;** www.delmarchamber.org), which also distributes a detailed folding map of the area. The hours of operation vary according to volunteer staffing, but usually approximate weekday business hours. There's also a city-run website at **www.delmar.ca.us**.

FUN ON & OFF THE BEACH

Two excellent beaches flank Del Mar: **Torrey Pines State Beach** to the south and **Del Mar State Beach.** Both are wide, well-patrolled strands popular for sunbathing, swimming, and surfing (in marked areas). Torrey Pines is accessed from I-5 via Carmel Valley Road; take a left on McGonigle Road to a large parking area. For Del Mar Beach, take 15th Street west to Seagrove Park, where college kids can always be found playing volleyball and other lawn games while older folks snooze in the shade. Just past the park is the sand, though parking spaces are in short supply on weekends and any day in summer. There are **free concerts** in the park during July and August; for information, contact the City of Del Mar (© **858/755-9313**). The sand stretches north to the mouth of the San Dieguito Lagoon, where people frequently bring their dogs for a romp in the sea. There are restrooms and showers near the park.

Beyond the surf and the turf, the hub of activities for most residents and visitors is **Del Mar Plaza,** a multi-story modern structure at the corner of Camino Del Mar and 15th Street. Though it lacks the quaint, lived-in atmosphere that most of the community shares, there are good restaurants and shops, and super views to the sea, especially at sunset.

Most evenings near dusk, brightly colored **hot-air balloons** punctuate the skies just east of the racetrack; they're easily enjoyed from the racetrack area (and by traffic-jammed drivers on I-5). If you find a balloon ride appealing, this is the place to do it, because flights are somewhat cheaper than at other California ballooning sites. See "Outdoor Pursuits" in chapter 7 for more details.

WHERE TO STAY
Very Expensive

L'Auberge Del Mar Resort & Spa ✺✺✺ Because Del Mar strives to keep a low profile, most lodgings here feel like an afterthought . . . except for prominent L'Auberge, the town's centerpiece. Sitting on the site of the historic Hotel Del

Mar (1909–69), this luxurious yet intimate inn manages to attract casual week-enders as easily as the rich-and-famous horse set, who flock here during summer racing season. Always improving, in 2002 the resort enhanced the lower-level full-service spa, polished up the poolside ambience, and completely revamped the dining room. The result is an atmosphere of complete relaxation and welcome. Guest rooms exude the elegance of a European country house, complete with marble bathrooms, architectural accents, well-placed casual seating, and the finest bed linens and appointments. Twenty-five rooms boast romantic fireplaces; all have a private balcony or terrace (several with an unadvertised view to the ocean).

The hotel is across the street from Del Mar's main shopping and dining scene, and a short jog from the sand. Overhauled in 2000, J. Taylor's, the hotel's California/Mediterranean dining room, easily stands as one of Del Mar's finest restaurants; at the very least, don't miss its legendary breakfast huevos rancheros.

1540 Camino del Mar (at 15th St.), Del Mar, CA 92014. ℭ **800/245-9757** or 858/259-1515. Fax 858/755-4940. www.laubergedelmar.com. 120 units. $290–$480 double; from $700 suite. AE, DC, MC, V. Valet parking $19. Take I-5 to Del Mar Heights Rd. west, then turn right onto Camino del Mar Rd. **Amenities:** Restaurant; bar; 2 out-door pools; tennis courts; indoor/outdoor fitness center; full-service spa; Jacuzzi; concierge; courtesy van; limited room service (6:30am–10pm); laundry service; dry cleaning. *In room:* A/C, TV w/pay movies, dataport, minibar, coffeemaker, hair dryer, iron.

Moderate

Del Mar Motel on the Beach *(Finds)*   The only property in Del Mar right on the beach, this simply furnished little white-stucco motel has been here since 1946. All rooms are of good size and are well kept (except for a number of worn-out lampshades); upstairs units have one king-size bed, downstairs rooms have two double beds. Most of them have little in the way of a view, but two ocean-front rooms sit right over the sand (and are dressed up with fake plants and larger bathrooms). This is a good choice for beach lovers because you can walk along the shore for miles, and families can be comfortable knowing a lifeguard station is right next door, as are popular seaside restaurants Poseidon and Jake's. The motel has a barbecue and picnic table for guests' use.

1702 Coast Blvd. (at 17th St.), Del Mar, CA 92014. ℭ **800/223-8449** for reservations, or 858/755-1534. www.delmarmotelonthebeach.com. 44 units (upper units with shower only). $169–$229 double. AE, DC, DISC, MC, V. Take I-5 to Via de la Valle exit. Go west, then south on Hwy. 101 (Pacific Coast Hwy.); veer west onto Coast Blvd. *In room:* A/C, TV, fridge, coffeemaker.

Les Artistes *(Finds)*   What do you get when you take a 1940s motel, put it in the hands of Sulana Sae-Onge, a Thai architect with a penchant for prominent painters, and wait while she transforms each room, one at a time? The answer is an intriguingly funky, disarmingly informal hotel, just a few blocks from down-town Del Mar, that's an art primer with European and Asian touches.

Although none of the rooms have an ocean view, and an ugly empty lot sits awkwardly between the hotel and busy Camino del Mar, there are still so many charming touches—like a lily and koi pond, Asian chimes, and climbing bougainvillea—that you feel only privacy. At last count, eight rooms had been redone as tributes to favored artists, two more were given a Japanese makeover, leaving two tastefully decorated but decidedly standard units. Artists spotlighted include Diego Rivera, whose room gives you the feeling of stepping into a warm Mexican painting (a Frida Kahlo room is in the works), while the Monet room has an almost distractingly abstract swirl of color. Other subjects include Georgia O'Keeffe, Erté, Remington, and Gauguin, while the Japanese Furo room is so authentic that a soaking tub is carved into the bathroom floor—the details are eye-filling. Though the inn is not for everyone, you really must see it to believe it. Downstairs rooms in the two-story structure have tiny private garden decks.

944 Camino del Mar, Del Mar, CA 92014. © 858/755-4646. www.lesartistesinn.com. 12 units. $115–$195 double. Rates include continental breakfast. DISC, MC, V. Free parking. From I-5 go west on Del Mar Heights Rd., the left onto Camino Del Mar Rd. Pets accepted with $50 cash deposit plus $20 cleaning fee. *In room:* TV.

Wave Crest 🏖🏖 On a bluff overlooking the Pacific, these gray-shingled bungalow condominiums are beautifully maintained and wonderfully private—from the street it looks nothing like a hotel. The studios and suites surround a lovingly landscaped courtyard; each has a queen-size bed, sofa bed, reproduced artwork, stereo, full bathroom, and fully equipped kitchen with dishwasher. The studios sleep two people; the one-bedroom accommodates up to four; two-bedroom units can sleep six. Some units face the garden or (pretty) street; rooms with ocean views are about $25 extra. In racing season (mid-June to mid-Sept), 90% of the guests are track-bound. It's a 5-minute walk to the beach, and shopping and dining spots are a few blocks away. There is an extra fee for maid service.

1400 Ocean Ave., Del Mar, CA 92014. © 858/755-0100. 31 units. $216–$246 studio summer (mid-June to mid-Sept), $174–$198 winter; $293–$415 suite summer, $214–$285 winter. Weekly rates available. MC, V. Take I-5 to Del Mar Heights Rd. west, turn right onto Camino del Mar, and drive to 15th St. Turn left and drive to Ocean Ave., and turn left. **Amenities:** Outdoor pool; Jacuzzi; coin-op laundry. *In room:* TV/VCR, kitchen.

WHERE TO DINE

Head to the upper level of the centrally located Del Mar Plaza, at Camino del Mar and 15th Street. You'll find **Il Fornaio Cucina Italiana** 🏖 (© 858/755-8876), for moderately priced and pleasing Italian cuisine and an *enoteca* (wine bar) with great ocean views; **Pacifica Del Mar** 🏖🏖 (© 858/792-0476), which serves outstanding seafood; as well as Epazote (see review below). Next to Jake's (also below) and right on the beach is **Poseidon,** 1670 Coast Blvd. (© 858/755-9345), good for modestly priced California cuisine and fabulous sunsets. The racetrack crowd congregates at **Bully's Restaurant,** 1404 Camino del Mar (© 858/755-1660), for burgers, prime rib, and crab legs; the gold-card crowd heads for special occasion meals at acclaimed **Pamplemousse Grill** 🏖🏖🏖, 514 Via de la Valle (© 858/792-9090). And if you're looking for fresh seafood—and lots of it—make a beeline to the Del Mar branch of San Diego's popular **Fish Market** 🏖, 640 Via de la Valle (© 858/755-2277), near the racetrack (and reviewed on p. 105).

Arterra 🏖🏖🏖 CALIFORNIAN   The name of this restaurant is derived from "art of the earth," and under the stewardship of a Bay Area luminary, chef Bradley Ogden (Lark Creek Inn, One Market), Arterra proves the moniker is no mere marketing gimmick. Housed in a drab, modern Marriott hotel next to the freeway and Oracle headquarters, you are excused for thinking nothing special transpires here, but take the chance. The broad dining room is impressive, cast in gold and purple tones, with accents of glass and copper; plush leather banquettes will seduce you to settle in for a long repast.

Although Ogden stops in once a month, the on-site kitchen master is Carl Shroeder, who crafts his menu based on what's on the shelves at Chino's or Be Wise, the Encinitas farms specializing in heirloom vegetables. Needless to say, the menu is regularly adapted to meet the schedule of mother earth. You'll never eat jet-lagged Chilean strawberries or rigid hot-house tomatoes—that's because Arterra doesn't serve them in winter, when tomatoes and strawberries don't grow naturally in San Diego. But come in summer and you'll feast on a plate of ravishing heirloom tomatoes lightly garnished with pickled corn and warm goat cheese. Come in December to savor the root vegetables and winter greens. The farmer's market vegetable entree is no mere sop to vegans—the plate is a trio of vivid courses. The entrees are no slouch: Wild striped bass with asparagus and garlic risotto, or chardonnay-braised pork with baby potatoes and glazed baby vegetables are recent offerings. The wine list is short but sweet—all California bottles—and wine dinners are scheduled regularly (check the website). The breakfast, by the way, is superlative, and worth the trip by itself.

11966 El Camino Real (next to I-5 in the Marriott Del Mar), Carmel Valley. © 858/369-6032. Reservations recommended. www.arterrarestaurant.com. Main courses $7–$13 breakfast, $13–$17 lunch, $19–$31 dinner. AE, DC, DISC, MC, V. Breakfast Mon–Fri 6:30–10:30am and Sat–Sun 7–11:30am; lunch Mon–Fri 11:30am–2:30pm; dinner daily 5:30–9:30pm. Free parking with validation, or $3 for valet parking.

Epazote ✿ SOUTHWESTERN/ASIAN FUSION   This splendid perch sits a couple stories above Camino del Mar, and although you're set back a few blocks from the beach, the unimpeded sea views are regal. The food is a mostly successful blend of Southwest themes with Asian accents, so fajitas are done with Hawaiian swordfish, and tamales are filled with duck and accompanied by rice and sautéed baby spinach. But some of the best items are pretty much straightforward Asian, like the shiitake mushroom/leek spring rolls, or the peanut-mint crusted sea bass. The bar has 72 different kinds of tequila, and the house margarita— made with fresh lime and lemon juice, Triple Sec, and Grand Chevalier and served in individual shakers over rocks—is one of the best in San Diego. The waitstaff look like surfers sidelined by a lull in the waves, but who's complaining?

1555 Camino del Mar (at 15th St.), Del Mar Plaza. © 858/259-9966. Reservations recommended on weekends. Main courses $8–$16 lunch, $14–$27 dinner. AE, DC, DISC, MC, V. Sun–Wed 11am–9pm; Thurs–Sat 11am–10pm. Free parking in garage with validation. Bus: 101.

Jake's Del Mar ✿ SEAFOOD/CALIFORNIAN   The spirit of Aloha permeates this Hawaiian-owned seafood-and-view outpost. Occupying a building originally constructed in 1910, Jake's has a perfect seat next to the sand so that diners on a series of terraces behind glass get straight-on views of the beach scene—sunbathers, surfers, and the occasional school of dolphins pass by (lunch here is *Endless Summer* no matter the weather). The predictable menu can't live up to the panorama, but it's prepared competently and service is swift (too swift, actually—don't let them rush you). At lunch you'll find pan-roasted Atlantic salmon in ponzu sauce, or shrimp fettuccini Provençal; sandwiches and salads round out the offerings. Dinner brings in the big boys: Maine lobster tails, giant scampi, and rack of lamb, for example. To enjoy the scene without the wallet wallop, come for happy hour (Mon–Fri 4–6pm and Sat 2:30–4:30pm), when a shorter bar/bistro menu is half-price and the mai tais are just $3.

1660 Coast Blvd. (at 15th St.), Del Mar. © 858/755-2002. Reservations recommended. Main courses $8–$14 lunch, $16–$36 dinner. AE, DC, DISC, MC, V. Tues–Sat 11:30am–2:30pm; Sun brunch 11am–2pm; daily 5–9pm. Valet parking $2–$3. Bus: 101.

SOLANA BEACH, ENCINITAS & CARLSBAD ✿

Following the shore north of Del Mar, the pretty communities of Solana Beach, Encinitas, and Carlsbad provide many reasons to linger on the California coast. They have good swimming and surfing beaches; a mile-long, two-tiered beach walk that is accessible for travelers with disabilities; lagoons perfect for walks or bird-watching; small-town atmosphere; an abundance of antiques and gift shops; and a seasonal display of the region's most beautiful flowers.

Carlsbad is the biggest of the communities and offers the most in the way of visitor attractions and amenities. The arrival of the railroad in the 1880s heralded the arrival of Carlsbad as a destination, and the historic depot, built around 1887, still stands in the heart of town. Having seen service as a Wells Fargo stagecoach station, telegraph station, post office, and general store, the depot closed in 1960; it's been reincarnated as the Visitor Information Center.

The town's name was Frazier's Station until the mineral content of its water was found to be almost identical to that of a popular resort, Karlsbad, in Czechoslovakia. During the early part of the last century, the Carlsbad Mineral Springs Hotel capitalized on the water's curative properties, and Carlsbad drew many health-minded visitors. One memorable sales pitch, employing all the hyperbole typical of that era, asked, "What more powerful inducements can be offered than Mineral Wells of Wonderful Medicinal Virtues; Magnificent Marine and Mountain Scenery; a Climate of Perpetual Summer; and Balmy Breezes from the Calm Pacific?" The European connection evoked an old-world sentiment in town, and many parts of Carlsbad still resemble a quaint village. In fact, the Danish toymaker LEGO opened a gigantic theme park in 1999; it's since become nearly as popular as the San Diego animal parks.

VISITOR INFORMATION

The **Carlsbad Visitor Information Center,** 400 Carlsbad Village Dr. (in the old Santa Fe Depot; © **800/227-5722** or 760/434-6093; www.carlsbadca.org), has lots of information on flower fields and nursery touring. The **Solana Beach Visitor Center** is near the train station at 103 N. Cedros (© **858/350-6006;** www.solanabeachchamber.com). The **Encinitas Visitors Center** is located in a small shopping mall immediately west of the I-5, at 138 Encinitas Blvd. (© **800/953-6041** or 760/753-6041; www.encinitaschamber.com). You'll find discounted LEGOLAND tickets, maps, and brochures.

FAMILY FUN

On the way to LEGOLAND is a diversion for music lovers of all ages: the **Museum of Making Music,** 5790 Armada Dr. (© **877/551-9976;** www.museum ofmakingmusic.org). It takes the visitor about an hour to journey from Tin Pan Alley to MTV, stopping along the way to learn historic anecdotes about the American music industry or to try playing drums, guitars, or a digital keyboard. It's open Tuesday through Sunday from 10am to 5pm; admission is $5 for adults, $3 for children ages 4 to 18, seniors, students, and military.

LEGOLAND California ® *Kids*   The ultimate monument to the world's most famous plastic building blocks, LEGOLAND is the third such theme park, following branches in Denmark and Britain that have proven enormously successful. Located 40 minutes north of downtown San Diego, the Carlsbad park offers a full day of entertainment for families. In addition to 5,000 LEGO models, the park is beautifully landscaped with 1,360 bonsai trees and other plants from around the world, and features more than 50 rides, shows, and attractions.

Attractions include hands-on interactive displays; a life-size menagerie of tigers, giraffes, and other animals; and scale models of international landmarks (the Eiffel Tower, Sydney Opera House, and so on), all constructed of LEGO bricks. "MiniLand" is a 1:20 scale representation of American achievement, from a New England Pilgrim village to Mount Rushmore and a new replica of Washington, D.C. There's a DUPLO building area to keep smaller children occupied, and a high-tech ride where older kids can compete in LEGO TECHNIC car races. To give the park a little more appeal for older kids, there are three relatively gentle but fun roller coasters.

The park is geared toward children ages 2 to 12; as I found with my 3-year-old nephew, there is more than enough to keep him wide-eyed and smiling for a day. There's just enough of a thrill-ride component that preteens will be amused, while teenagers will find LEGOLAND a bit of a snooze. *A touring tip:* When the park opens, many visitors hop in line for the first rides encountered (neither of which are special)—it's better to head to the back side of the park where lines are shorter for the first hour or so.

1 Legoland Dr. ✆ 877/534-6526 or 760/918-LEGO. www.legoland.com. $2 adults, $5 seniors and children 3–12, free to children under 3. AE, DISC, MC, V. Summer (late June to Aug) daily 10am–8pm; off-season Thurs–Mon 10am–5 or 6pm. Closed Tues–Wed Sept–May, but open daily during Christmas and Easter vacation periods. Parking $7. From I-5 take the Cannon Rd. exit east, following signs for Legoland Dr.

FLOWER POWER

Carlsbad and its neighbor Encinitas make up a noted commercial flower-growing region. The most colorful display can be seen each spring at **The Flower Fields at Carlsbad Ranch** ✿, 5704 Paseo del Norte, east of I-5 on Palomar Airport Road (✆ 760/431-0352; www.theflowerfields.com). The 53 acres of ranunculus fields, planted in wide stripes of contrasting hues, bloom into a breathtaking rainbow visible even from the freeway. Visitors are invited to stroll between the rows, which are primarily grown for their bulbs, from early March to early May from 9am to dusk. Admission is $7 for adults, $6 seniors, $4 for children age 3 to 10; an antique tractor ride is $2 for adults, $1 for children. Flowers, bulbs, and garden gifts are for sale.

Even if you don't visit during the spring bloom—or during December, when the nurseries are alive with holiday poinsettias—there's plenty for the avid gardener to enjoy throughout the year. North County is such a destination for horticultural pursuits, in fact, there's a **North County Nursery Hoppers Association** (✆ 800/488-6742) in Encinitas. They publish a comprehensive leaflet describing all the area growers and nurseries, including a map that shows where to find flowers; it's available at local visitor centers, or by mail from the association. Second to Carlsbad Ranch in popularity is **Weidners' Gardens,** 695 Normandy Rd., Encinitas (✆ 760/436-2194; www.weidners.com). Its field of 25,000 tuberous begonias blooms from mid-May to August; fuchsias and impatiens are colorful between March and September; and the holiday season (Nov 1–Dec 22) brings an explosion of pansies and poinsettias, and the opportunity to dig your own pansies. Touring the grounds is free; Weidners is closed Tuesdays from Labor Day to October and Christmas to February.

Shoppers' Delight

Whether you're in the market for a new-model convertible or a bargain on bed linens, Carlsbad's Paseo del Norte is for you. On one side lies the retail magnet **Carlsbad Company Stores,** Paseo del Norte via Palomar Airport Rd. (✆ **888/790-SHOP** or 760/804-9000; www.carlsbadcompanystores.com), a smart, upscale outlet mall featuring over 90 stores, including Crate & Barrel, Barney's New York, Nine West, and Harry & David; Bellefleur Winery & Restaurant anchors one end (p. 240). Across the street is Carlsbad's unofficial avenue of cars, a parade of **car dealers** from Acura to Plymouth. It's a test-driver's dream, or just plain fun for browsing the latest models and features.

Those of us with thumbs of a slightly less vibrant green are satisfied with an afternoon at **Quail Botanical Gardens** ⋒, 230 Quail Gardens Rd., off Encinitas Boulevard east of I-5, Encinitas (© **760/436-3036;** www.qbgardens.com). Boasting the country's largest bamboo collection, plus 30 acres of California natives, exotic tropicals, palms, cacti, Mediterranean, Australian, and other unusual collections, this serene compound is crisscrossed with scenic walkways, trails, and benches. Guided tours are given Saturdays at 10am, and there's a gift shop and nursery. The gardens are open daily from 9am to 5pm, the gift shop and nursery daily from 10am to 4pm. Admission is $8 for adults, $5 for seniors and military, $3 children 5 to 12, and free for children under 5. The gardens are free to everyone on the first Tuesday of the month.

MORE FUN THINGS TO SEE & DO

The hub of activity for Solana Beach is South Cedros Avenue, 1 block east of and parallel to the Pacific Coast Highway. In a 2-block stretch (from the train station south) are many of San Diego's best furniture and home design shops, antiques stores, art dealers, and boutiques selling imported goods. You'll also find **The Belly Up Tavern,** one of San Diego's most appealing concert venues (see p. 219 for a full review).

Carlsbad is a great place for antiquing. Whether you're a serious shopper or seriously window-shopping, park the car and stroll the 3 blocks of **State Street** between Oak and Beech streets. There are about 2 dozen shops in this part of town, where diagonal street parking and welcoming merchants lend a village atmosphere. Wares range from estate jewelry to country quilts, from inlaid sideboards to Depression glass. You never know what you'll find, but there's always something.

What about those therapeutic waters that put Carlsbad on the map? They're still bubbling at the **Carlsbad Mineral Water Spa,** 2802 Carlsbad Blvd. (© **760/434-1887;** www.carlsbadmineralspa.com), an ornate European-style building on the site of the original well. Step inside for mineral baths ($60 for 30 min.), massages, or body treatments in the spa's exotic theme rooms—or just pick up a refreshing bottle of this "Most Healthful Water" to drink on the go.

Carlsbad has two beaches, each with pros and cons. **Carlsbad State Beach** parallels downtown and is a fine place to stroll along a wide concrete walkway. It attracts outdoors types for walking, jogging, and in-line skating, even at night (thanks to good lighting). Although the sandy strand is narrow, the beach is popular with bodysurfers, boogie boarders, and fishermen—surfers tend to stay away. Enter on Ocean Boulevard at Tamarack Avenue; there's a $4 fee per vehicle. Four miles south of town is **South Carlsbad State Beach,** almost 3 miles of cobblestone-strewn sand. A state-run campground at the north end is immensely popular year-round, and area surfers favor the southern portion. Like many of the beaches along the county's shores, Carlsbad suffers from a high incidence of tar on the beach—you're likely to find packages of "Tar-Off" in your hotel room—but that doesn't seem to discourage many beachgoers. There's a $4 per vehicle fee at the beach entrance, along Carlsbad Boulevard at Poinsettia Lane.

In Encinitas, everyone flocks to **Moonlight Beach,** the city's long-suffering sandy playground. After overcoming a nasty sewage problem caused by a nearby treatment plant (don't ask), and receiving a much-needed replacement of eroded sand, Moonlight is back to its old, laid-back self. It offers plenty of facilities, including free parking, volleyball nets, restrooms, showers, picnic tables, and fire grates, and the company of fellow sunbathers. The beach entrance is at the end of B Street (at Encinitas Blvd.).

Also in Encinitas is the appropriately serene **Swami's Beach.** It's named for the adjacent Self Realization Fellowship (see below), whose lotus-shaped towers are emulated in the pointed wooden stairway leading to the sand from First Street. This lovely little beach is surfer central in the winter. It adjoins little-known **Boneyard Beach,** directly to the north. Here, low-tide coves provide shelter for romantics and nudists; this isolated stretch can be reached only from Swami's Beach. There's a free parking lot at Swami's, plus restrooms and a picnic area.

The **Self Realization Fellowship** was founded in 1920 by Paramahansa Yogananda, a guru born and educated in India, and the exotic-looking domes are what remain of the retreat originally built in 1937 (the rest was built too close to the cliff-edge and tumbled into the sea). Today the site serves as a spiritual sanctuary for holistic healers and their followers, with meditation gardens and a gift shop that sells Fellowship publications and distinctive arts and crafts from India. The center is located at 1105 Second St., between J and K streets, (© **760/753-2888;** www.yogananda-srf.org). The grounds are open daily from 9am to 5pm, and admission is free.

Remember the hair-raising aerial escapades in *The Great Waldo Pepper?* You can enjoy everything but wing-walking on a vintage biplane from **Biplane, Air Combat & Warbird Adventures** (© **800/SKY-LOOP** or 760/438-7680; www.barnstorming.com). Two of the six aircraft even have an open cockpit. Flights leave from McClellen-Palomar Airport in Carlsbad, taking up to two passengers per plane on scenic flights down the coast. Prices start at $149 for two-person, 20-minute biplane rides. Or, go for an Air Combat flight for a 2-hour mission which includes a 50-minute "dogfight" with another biplane "opponent" ($298 for one, or $496 if you bring your own adversary). If that's not thrilling enough, opt for a flight in a warbird, which includes loops and rolls with *you* at the helm ($325 and up)! Lastly, there's a 30-minute "sentimental journey" aboard a beautifully restored World War II V.I.P. transport followed by dinner at the Four Seasons Aviara—$400 for two including tax, tip, and parking. *Bargain-hunter's tip:* Discounts are available through the website, or ask when you call.

WHERE TO STAY
Very Expensive
Four Seasons Resort Aviara 𝒜𝒜𝒜   In 1997, the top-drawer Four Seasons chain opened their first oceanview golf and tennis resort in the continental United States, and Aviara quickly overtook nearby La Costa in the battle for chic movers-and-shakers—not to mention winning over the local residents, who head here for summer jazz concerts and an exceptional Friday night seafood buffet. The resort offers every over-the-top comfort with the ease that sets Four Seasons apart; when not wielding club or racquet, guests can lie by the dramatically perched pool, relax in a series of carefully landscaped gardens, or luxuriate in the newly expanded spa where treatments incorporate regional flowers and herbs.

The ambience here is one of both privilege and comfort; rooms are decorated with soothing neutrals and nature prints that evoke the many birds in the surrounding Batiquitos Lagoon. In fact, the name Aviara is a nod to the egrets, herons, and cranes that are among the 130 bird species nesting in the protected coastal wetlands. The hotel's Arnold Palmer–designed golf course was designed to keep the wetlands intact, and incorporates native marshlike plants throughout its 18 holes to help blend with the surroundings. The once-barren hills around the Four Seasons have since been built up with multimillion-dollar homes, but you can quickly escape to the wildness of the lagoon on a nature trail with several different access points; the hotel's staff will gladly point you in the right direction.

7100 Four Seasons Point, Carlsbad, CA 92009. ℂ **800/332-3442** or 760/603-6800. Fax 760/603-6801. www.fourseasons.com/aviara. 329 units. $395–$510 double; from $620 suite. Children 17 and under stay free in parent's room. AE, DISC, MC, V. Valet parking $18. From I-5, take Poinsettia Lane east to Aviara Pkwy. S. **Amenities:** 4 restaurants; 2 bars; 2 outdoor pools; golf course; tennis courts; health club; 15,000-sq.-ft. spa; Jacuzzi; bike rental; concierge; business center; José Eber salon; 24-hr. room service; in-room massage; babysitting; laundry service; dry cleaning. *In room:* A/C, TV w/pay movies, dataport, minibar, coffeemaker, hair dryer, iron, safe.

La Costa Resort and Spa 🏨🏨   When we last visited this famed golf, tennis, and spa resort, the property was looking tired and stodgy, particularly in comparison to the spanking new Four Seasons Aviara just a mile or so away. But in 2002 La Costa was sold to prestigious KSL Resorts, whose world-class properties include Maui's Grand Wailea Resort and the historic Arizona Biltmore in Phoenix. KSL specializes in sunny golf-and-tennis meccas, so they're a perfect fit for La Costa, which built its reputation on sports of the idle rich. It was only a matter of weeks before construction plans were unveiled and a $100 million renovation was underway.

The overall renovation redefines the resort's California ranch–style motifs in a campus-like setting, with 45-foot bell towers, white stucco walls, and red tile roofs. Already unveiled is the (Dr. Deepak) Chopra Center, which offers services and products relating to mind/body healing and transformation. The renovated rooms have been refashioned with leather headboards and beds trimmed in Egyptian cotton linens, dark walnut desks, metal accents, and bathrooms with quaint pedestal sinks; the effect is a nod to the influence of W-style big city hotels, without being a total immersion in modernist élan. The most important components of the overhaul are schedule to be completed by the time you read this; look for a relocated lobby and porte-cochere, a series of boutique-lined courtyards, a huge new spa with 42 treatment rooms and outdoor sunning areas, a second pool, and a sprawling gym. Subsequent phases will add another restaurant, a 42,000-square-foot conference facility and ballroom, and 149 villas available for shared ownership. The 400-acre property boasts two championship 18-hole golf courses (home of the annual WGC-Accenture Match Play Championship), and a 21-court racquet club (home of the WTA Toshiba Tennis Classic) with 2 grass, 4 clay, and 15 composite courts.

Costa del Mar Rd., Carlsbad, CA 92009. ℂ **800/854-5000** or 760/438-9111. Fax 760/931-7585. www.lacosta.com. 473 units. $350–$500 double; from $550 suite. Children under 18 stay free in parent's room. $15/day resort fee. Golf, spa, and tennis packages available. AE, DC, DISC, MC, V. Valet parking $16 overnight; self-parking $10. From I-5 take La Costa Ave. east; left on El Camino Real. **Amenities:** 3 restaurants; bar; 4 outdoor pools; golf course; tennis courts; spa; 6 Jacuzzis; bike rentals; concierge; business center; salon; 24-hr. room service; laundry service; dry cleaning. *In room:* A/C, TV w/pay movies, dataport, minibar, coffeemaker, hair dryer, iron.

Expensive

Tamarack Beach Resort 🏨   This resort property's rooms, in the village across the street from the beach, are restfully decorated with beachy wicker furniture. Fully equipped suites—similar to Maui-style vacation condos—have stereos, full kitchens, washers, and dryers. The pretty Tamarack has a pleasant lobby and a sunny pool courtyard with barbecue grills. Dini's by the Sea is a good restaurant that is popular with locals.

3200 Carlsbad Blvd., Carlsbad, CA 92008. ℂ **800/334-2199** or 760/729-3500. Fax 760/434-5942. www.tamarackresort.com. 77 units. $185–$215 double; from $230 suite. Children 12 and under stay free in parent's room. Rates include continental breakfast. AE, MC, V. Free underground parking. **Amenities:** Restaurant; outdoor pool; 2 Jacuzzis; exercise room. *In room:* A/C, TV/VCR, fridge, coffeemaker, hair dryer, iron.

Moderate

Beach Terrace Inn   At Carlsbad's only beachside hostelry (others are across the road or a little farther away), the rooms and the pool/Jacuzzi all have ocean views. This downtown Best Western property is tucked between rows of high-rent beach cottages and touts its scenic location as its best quality. The rooms are extra-large, and although they suffer from generic "furnished bachelor pad"–style interiors, some have balconies, fireplaces, and kitchenettes. Suites are affordable and have separate living rooms and bedrooms, making this a good choice for families. VCRs and films are available at the front desk. You can walk everywhere from here—except LEGOLAND, which is a 5-minute drive away.

2775 Ocean St., Carlsbad, CA 92008. © 800/433-5415 or 760/729-5951. Fax 760/729-1078. www.beach terraceinn.com. 49 units. $165 double; from $215 suite. Children 12 and under stay free in parent's room. Extra person $20. Rates include continental breakfast. AE, DC, DISC, MC, V. Free parking. **Amenities:** Outdoor pool; Jacuzzi; coin-op laundry; dry cleaning. *In room:* A/C, TV w/pay movies, dataport, fridge, coffeemaker, hair dryer, iron, safe.

Pelican Cove Inn ✿   Located 2 blocks from the beach, this Cape Cod–style bed-and-breakfast hideaway combines romance with luxury. Hosts Kris and Nancy Nayudu see to your every need, from furnishing guest rooms with soft feather beds and down comforters to providing beach chairs and towels or preparing a picnic basket (with 24-hr. notice). Each room features a fireplace and private entrance; some have private spa tubs. The Pacific room is most spacious, while the airy La Jolla room has bay windows and a cupola ceiling. Breakfast can be enjoyed in the garden if weather permits. Courtesy transportation from the Carlsbad or Oceanside train stations is available.

320 Walnut Ave., Carlsbad, CA 92008. © 888/PEL-COVE or 760/434-5995. www.pelican-cove.com. 10 units. $90–$210 double. Rates include full breakfast. Extra person $15. AE, MC, V. Free parking. From downtown Carlsbad, follow Carlsbad Blvd. south to Walnut Ave.; turn left and drive 2½ blocks. *In room:* TV, no phone.

WHERE TO DINE

Always crowded is **Fidel's,** known for reliably tasty Mexican food and kickin' margaritas. The restaurant has a location in Solana Beach at 607 Valley Ave. (© **858/ 755-5292**), and there's a **Fidel's Norte** branch in Carlsbad at 3003 Carlsbad Blvd. (© 760/729-0903).

The architectural centerpiece of Carlsbad is **Neiman's,** 2978 Carlsbad Blvd. (© **760/729-4131**), a restored Victorian mansion complete with turrets, cupolas, and waving flags. Inside, there's a casual cafe and bar where LeRoy Neiman lithographs hang on the walls. The menu includes rack of lamb, macadamia-crusted salmon, filet mignon, and prime rib. There are also burgers, pastas, and salads. Sunday brunch is a tremendous buffet of breakfast and lunch items, and the daily happy hour (11am–7pm) offers draft beers and well drinks for $2.

In Encinitas look for **Vigilucci's,** 505 S. Hwy. 101 (at D St.; © **760/942-7332**), where the wafting fragrance of garlic always draws a crowd in for authentic southern Italy trattoria fare served in a lively atmosphere accented with old-world touches like stained glass and a grand mahogany bar; and the nearby **Siamese Basil,** 527 S. Coast Hwy. 101 (© 760/753-3940), whose innocuous facade and bland interior belie a well-deserved reputation for fresh, zesty Thai food and a friendly attitude—you can even choose your spice quotient, from toddler-safe 1 to fire-alarm 10.

Bellefleur Winery & Restaurant ✿✿ CALIFORNIAN/MEDITERRANEAN This popular restaurant boasts the "complete wine country experience," although there's no wine country evident among the surrounding outlet mall and car dealerships. But its cavernous, semi-industrial dining room, coupled with the wood-fired and wine-enhanced aromas emanating from Bellefleur's clanging open kitchen, do somehow evoke the casual yet sophisticated ambience of California wine-producing regions like Santa Barbara and Napa. This multi-functional space includes a stylish tasting bar and open-air dining patio in addition to the main seating area and a glassed-in barrel aging room. The place can be noisy and spirited, drawing both exhausted shoppers and savvy San Diegans for a cuisine that incorporates North County's abundant produce with fresh fish and meats. Lunchtime sandwiches and salads surpass the shopping-mall standard, while dinner choices feature oak-grilled beef tenderloin or Colorado rack of lamb; mashed potatoes enhanced with garlic, horseradish, or olive tapenade; and rich reduction sauces of premium balsamic vinegar, wild mushroom demi-glace, or sweet-tart tamarind.

5610 Paseo del Norte, Carlsbad. ℂ 760/603-1919. www.bellefleur.com. Reservations recommended for Fri–Sat dinner. Lunch $9–$15; dinner $19–$29. AE, DISC, MC, V. Daily 11am–3pm and 5–9pm (till 10pm Fri–Sat).

OCEANSIDE

The northernmost community in San Diego County (actually, it's a city of 170,000), Oceanside is inextricably linked to the military. Camp Pendleton, one of the nation's largest military bases, established in 1942, is located immediately north, and the city's fortunes rise and fall with the marines. In the aftermath of September 11, 2001, and during the Gulf War, the abundant dry cleaners and barbershops downtown clung desperately to life (most of them count half of their customers as marines).

Oceanside claims almost 4 miles of beaches and has one of the West Coast's longest over-the-water wooden piers, where a tram does nothing but transport people from the street to the end of the 1,954-foot structure and back for 25¢ each way. The 1950s-style diner at the end of the pier, **Ruby's,** is a great place for a quick and inexpensive lunch over the ocean. The wide, sandy beach, pier, and well-tended recreational area with playground equipment and an outdoor amphitheater are within easy walking distance of the train station.

VISITOR INFORMATION

The **Oceanside Visitor & Tourism Center,** 928 North Coast Hwy. (ℂ **800/ 350-7873** or 760/722-1534; www.oceansidechamber.com), provides information on local attractions, dining, and accommodations.

EXPLORING OCEANSIDE

One of the nicest things to do in Oceanside is to stroll around the city's upscale **harbor.** Bustling with pleasure craft, it's lined with condominiums and boasts a Cape Cod–themed shopping village. A launch ramp, visitor boat slips, and charter fishing are here. The **Harbor Days Festival** in mid-September typically attracts 100,000 visitors for a crafts fair, entertainment, and food booths; call ℂ **760/722-1534** for more details.

Probably the area's most important attraction is **Mission San Luis Rey** ℛ (ℂ **760/757-3651;** www.sanluisrey.org), located a few miles inland at 4050 Mission Ave. Founded in 1798, it's the 18th and largest of California's 21 missions (you might recognize it as the backdrop for one of the Zorro movies). You can tour the mission, its impressive church, exhibits, grounds, and cemetery; the cost is $4 for adults and $3 for students, and hours are daily from 10am to 4pm.

For a wide selection of rental watercraft, head to **Boat Rentals of America** (ℂ **760/722-0028**), on Harbor Drive South. It rents everything from kayaks,

WaveRunners, and electric boats for relaxed harbor touring, to 14- and 22-foot sailboats, fishing skiffs, and Runabout cruisers. Even if you have no experience, there's plenty of room for exploration in the harbor. Sample rates: single kayak, $10 per hour; 15-foot fishing skiff, $60 half-day, $90 full day; and WaveRunner, $75 per hour. Substantial winter discounts are available; Boat Rentals keeps seasonal hours, so call for specific information.

Beyond Camp Pendleton, Oceanside's other main identity is with surfers, and there's no better place to learn the lore than the **California Surf Museum,** 223 North Coast Hwy. (② **760/721-6876;** www.surfmuseum.org). Founded in 1985, both surf devotees and curious onlookers will delight in the museum's unbelievably extensive collection. Boards and other relics chronicle the development of the sport. Many belonged to surfers whose names are revered by local surfers, including Hawaiian Duke Kahanamoku and local daredevil Bob Simmons. Vintage photographs, beach attire, 1960s beach graffiti, and surf music all lovingly bring the sport to life—there's even a photo display of the real-life Gidget. A gift shop offers unique items, including memorabilia of famous surfers and surf flicks, plus novelty items like a surf-lingo dictionary. The museum is open Thursday through Monday from 10am to 4pm; admission is free, but donations are requested. Oceanside's world-famous surfing spots attract competitions, including the **Longboard Surf Contest** held in August (www. oceansidelongboardsurfingclub.org).

The **Oceanside Beach** starts just outside Oceanside Harbor, where routine harbor dredging makes for a substantial amount of fluffy, clean white sand. It runs almost 4 miles south to the Carlsbad border. Along the way you can enjoy the **Strand,** a grassy park that stretches along the beach between Fifth Street and Wisconsin Avenue. Benches with scenic vistas abound, and the Strand also borders on the Oceanside Pier, which in turn is usually flanked by legions of bobbing surfers. Parking is at metered street spaces or in lots, which can fill up on nice summer days. Harbor Beach, which is separated from the rest by the San Luis River, charges $5 admission per vehicle. Farther south, there is no regulated admission, and after Witherby Street or so, parking is free (but in demand) along residential streets. Around the pier are restrooms, showers, picnic areas, and volleyball nets.

Gamblers—and fans of the swingin' Rat Pack movies—inhabit Oceanside's gaming house, **Ocean's Eleven Casino,** 121 Brooks St. (② **760/439-6988;** www.oceans11.com). It's more contemporary banquet hall than vintage Vegas, but Ocean's Eleven does its best to evoke Sin City, with murals of Frank Sinatra, Sammy Davis, Jr., Dean Martin, Joey Bishop, and Peter Lawford at the height of their hijinks, and with the retro Continental fare served up in the Rat Pack Lounge. There's nightly entertainment, and, of course, games: blackjack, poker (Hold-Em, 7-Card Stud, Omaha Hi-Lo, Pot Limit), Pai Gow, and Pan. It's open 24 hours a day, 7 days a week.

WHERE TO STAY & DINE

The inexpensive-to-moderate **Oceanside Marina Inn,** 2008 Harbor Dr. N. (② **800/252-2033** or 760/722-1561; www.omihotel.com), boasts a scenic perch way at the mouth of the harbor, and offers a quiet, nautical setting for those who want to stay overnight. Despite dingy hallways, the rooms are spacious, light, and newly refurnished in an attractive, vaguely colonial-tropical (think Bombay Company) style. An oceanview pool and spa, complimentary breakfast, and romantic gas fireplace in every room make the deal even sweeter.

Several surf-and-turf harborside restaurant stalwarts are close by, including the **Chart House** (© 760/722-1345), the **Jolly Roger** (© 760/722-1831), and the **Monterey Bay Canners** (© 760/722-3474).

Elsewhere in Oceanside, you can get a side helping of history with your burger-and-fries at the original **101 Cafe,** 631 S. Coast Hwy. (© 760/722-5220). This humble diner dates from the earliest days of the old coast highway that was the only route between Los Angeles and San Diego until 1953 brought the interstate.

2 North County Inland: From Rancho Santa Fe to Palomar Mountain

The coastal and inland sections of North County are as different as night and day. Beaches and laid-back villages, where work seems to be the curse of the surfing class, characterize the coast. Inland you'll find beautiful barren hills, citrus groves, and conservative communities where agriculture plays an important role.

Rancho Santa Fe is about 27 miles north of downtown San Diego; from there the Del Dios Highway (S6) leads to Escondido, almost 32 miles from the city. Nearly 70 miles away is Palomar Mountain in the Cleveland National Forest, which spills over the border into Riverside County. The **San Diego North Convention and Visitors Bureau,** 720 N. Broadway in Escondido (© 800/848-3336 or 760/745-4741; www.sandiegonorth.com), can answer your questions.

RANCHO SANTA FE

Exclusive Rancho Santa Fe was once the property of the Santa Fe Railroad, and the eucalyptus trees the railroad grew create a stately atmosphere. The area was "discovered" in the early 1900s by movie director Theodore Reed, who encouraged his friends Douglas Fairbanks and Mary Pickford to purchase property as an investment—they bought 800 acres in 1924. After just a few minutes in town today, it becomes apparent that Rancho Santa Fe is a playground for the über-wealthy, but not in the usual pretentious sense. Proving the adage that true breeding makes everyone feel at ease, and that it's gauche to flaunt your money, this upscale slice of North County is a friendly town that's enjoyed by everyone. Primarily residential Rancho Santa Fe has two large resort hotels that blend into the eucalyptus groves surrounding the town. The **Rancho Valencia Resort** is a premier destination and choice of at least one First Family; the more modestly priced **Inn at Rancho Santa Fe** is closer to town (see below). Shopping and dining—both quite limited—in Rancho Santa Fe revolve around a couple of understated blocks known locally as "the Village," whose curbs are usually filled with late-model Mercedes, Lexuses, and Land Rovers.

ESSENTIALS

GETTING THERE From San Diego, take I-5 north to Lomas Santa Fe (County Hwy. S8) east; it turns into Linea del Cielo and leads directly into the center of Rancho Santa Fe. If you continue through town on Paseo Delicias, you'll pick up the Del Dios Highway (County Hwy. S6), the scenic route to Escondido and the **Wild Animal Park.** This road affords views of Lake Hodges, as well as glimpses of expansive estates, some of the most expensive in the country.

SPECIAL EVENTS If you're looking for Fourth of July festivities with a small-town yet sophisticated flavor, come for the annual **Independence Day Parade.** Residents come out in droves as a marching band, equestrians, and the local fire engines wind through the tiny town center. Anyone with a vintage, classic, or just luxury car gets into the act—you might see vintage Packards, restored Model Ts, classic roadsters, or just shiny new Land Rovers strutting their stuff. Festivities continue with a barbecue and concert in the park. For more information, call © **800/848-3336** or 760/745-4741.

WHERE TO STAY
Very Expensive
Rancho Valencia Resort ♠♠♠   If you are in need of pampering and relaxation—or a seriously romantic getaway, read on. A member of Relais & Châteaux and Preferred Hotels, this sun-baked Spanish- and Mediterranean-style all-suite resort sits on 40 acres overlooking the San Dieguito Valley and the rolling hills of Rancho Santa Fe. Imagine having your own casita with cathedral ceilings, wood-burning fireplace, ceiling fans, oversize tiled bathroom, walk-in closet, and private terrace; the smallest of these suites is 850 square feet. Fresh-squeezed juice and a newspaper are left outside your door in the morning. Those who venture outside discover grounds filled with 2,000 citrus trees, bougainvillea, and air sweetened by flowers and birdsong. Friday and Saturday nights find a guitarist or cellist entertaining, and there's dancing under the stars on Thursday nights in July and August. Tea and cocktails are served in the La Sala lounge, from which there is a great view of the hot-air balloons at sunset.

5921 Valencia Circle, Rancho Santa Fe, CA 92061. © **800/548-3664** or 858/756-1123. Fax 858/756-0165. www.ranchovalencia.com. 43 units. $450–$875 suite. AE, DC, MC, V. Free valet and self-parking. Take I-5 to Del Mar Heights Rd. and go east to El Camino Real. Turn left to San Dieguito Rd., turn right, and follow signs to resort. Pets accepted with $75/night fee. **Amenities:** Acclaimed restaurant; bar; 2 outdoor pools; nearby golf; tennis courts and clinics; health club; spa; 3 Jacuzzis; complimentary bikes; concierge; 24-hr. room service; in-room massage; babysitting; laundry service; coin-op laundry; dry cleaning. In room: A/C, TV/VCR, dataport, minibar, coffeemaker, hair dryer, iron, safe.

Expensive
The Inn at Rancho Santa Fe ♠♠   Indulge your inner gentry with a surprisingly affordable stay here, where casual surroundings belie the international clientele. Like the town itself, the Inn is the epitome of cultivated, proving that those born to money needn't flaunt it, or pay unnecessarily exorbitant rates. Early California–style cottages are nestled throughout the resort's 20 acres; the decor is English country–flavored and sturdy, and many rooms have fireplaces, kitchenettes, and secluded patios. A fascinating collection of antique, hand-carved model sailing ships is on display in the lobby. Beautifully landscaped grounds contain towering eucalyptus, colorful flowers, and expansive rolling lawns (a favorite among the canine guests welcomed at the inn). Nifty extras include guest membership at Rancho Santa Fe Golf Club and use of the Inn's private Del Mar beach cottage, complete with showers and elevated deck.

5951 Linea del Cielo (P.O. Box 869), Rancho Santa Fe, CA 92067. © **800/843-4661** or 858/756-1131. Fax 858/759-1604. www.theinnatranchosantafe.com. 86 units. $185–$235 double; from $395 suite. AE, DC, MC, V. Free parking. From I-5, take the Lomas Santa Fe exit, following signs to Rancho Santa Fe. The Inn is on the right just before town. Pets accepted. **Amenities:** Restaurant; bar; outdoor pool; tennis courts; limited room service (7:30am–10pm); in-room massage; babysitting; laundry service; coin-op laundry; dry cleaning. In room: A/C, TV, hair dryer, dataport, safe.

WHERE TO DINE
If you're looking for a casual lunch, breakfast, or snack, seek out **Thyme in the Ranch,** 16905 Avenida de Acacias (© **858/759-0747**), a bakery/cafe that's open Tuesday through Saturday from 7am to 3pm. Though hidden on a small plaza

behind chic Mille Fleurs on Paseo Delicias, this tiny treasure is well known (as evidenced by constant lines at the counter). Salads, sandwiches, soup, and quiche are the menu mainstays—all delicious—but the baked treats are what keep me coming back!

Delicias 𝒦𝒦𝒦 CALIFORNIAN   Decorated in a mix of antiques and wicker, accented by flowers, woven tapestries, and floor-to-ceiling French doors, this comfortable restaurant is equally appropriate for a casual meal or special occasion. Service is attentive and personable, and the food is delicious. Intriguing— but not overly complex—flavor blends are the hallmark of a menu that ranges from the zesty Pacific Rim to the sunny Mediterranean, interpreted with a subtle French accent. Chinese duckling is slow-roasted with ginger and soy, then served with a spicy mushroom sauce; coriander-crusted salmon is sautéed with miso and ponzu, accented by papaya salsa; and rack of lamb is bathed in tamarind-plum sauce and served with cucumber-mango-mint relish. At meals like these it's not easy to leave room for dessert, but leave room—you'll kick yourself if you don't. Giant umbrellas shade a street-side outdoor patio.

6109 Paseo Delicias. © **858/756-8000.** Reservations recommended on weekends. Main courses $18–$35. AE, DC, MC, V. Sun–Thurs 5:30–9pm; Fri–Sat 5:30–10pm.

ESCONDIDO

Best known as the home of the San Diego Wild Animal Park (p. 134), Escondido is also the site of the **California Center for the Performing Arts,** an attractive 12-acre campus that includes two theaters, an art museum, a conference center, and a cafe. It's worth the 45-minute to 1-hour drive to Escondido (along I-15 north to the Escondido exits) just to see the appealing postmodern architecture of this facility, which opened in 1994. To find out what's playing and for ticket information, call © **760/738-4100.**

This city of 125,000 is in the heart of a major agricultural area, so it's not surprising that the farmers' market on Tuesday afternoons is one of the county's best. Another attraction is Orfila Vineyards, located near the Wild Animal Park (see "Special-Interest Sightseeing" in chapter 7). Grand Avenue, old Escondido's downtown main drag, is experiencing a pleasant renewal. Classy antiques stores and new restaurants are filling historic storefronts.

WHERE TO STAY & DINE
The **Welk Resort Center,** 8860 Lawrence Welk Dr. (© **800/932-9355**), is a moderate-to-expensive lodging near downtown Escondido. It offers golf, tennis, and live theatrical entertainment.

150 Grand Café 𝒦𝒦 ECLECTIC   English expatriates Cyril and Vicki Lucas run this delightful cafe on a charming stretch of historic Grand Avenue. Although Escondido is not usually associated with fine dining, this restaurant's reputation stretches to San Diego; it's definitely worth a detour. The bright, attractive decor feels like a cross between a conservatory and a library. Lunchtime favorites include roasted tomato seafood risotto and quail stuffed with fig and olive tapenade. Although the dinner menu changes nightly, it might include a lamb shank pasta, or a strawberry braised salmon, while grilled filet mignon and pecan-crusted pork tenderloin are usually represented. There's outdoor seating, or you can land in the more courtly library dining room inside.

150 W. Grand Ave. © **760/738-6868.** www.150grandcafe.com. Reservations recommended, especially for weekend nights. Main courses $11 lunch, $20–$24 dinner. AE, DC, MC, V. Mon–Fri 11:30am–3pm; Mon–Sat 5–9pm.

Finds **Touring Temecula's Wineries**

Located over the line in Riverside County, 60 miles north of San Diego via I-15, Temecula is known for its 16 wineries and the increasingly noteworthy vintages they produce. The town's very name (pronounced "ta-*meck*-you-la") provides the first clue to this valley's success in the volatile winemaking business/art. It translates (from a Native American language) as "where the sun shines through the mist," which identifies two of the three climatological factors necessary for viticulture. The third is Rainbow Gap, an opening to the south through the Agua Tibia Mountains, which allows cool afternoon sea breezes to enter the 1,500-foot elevation. Franciscan missionaries planted the first grapevines here in the early 1800s, but the land ended up being used primarily for raising cattle. The 87,000-acre Vail Ranch operated from 1904 until being sold in 1964. Grapevines began to take root in the receptive soil again in 1968, and the first Temecula wines were produced in 1971.

Most of the wineries are strung along Rancho California Road, and harvest time is generally from mid-August to September. But visitors are welcome year-round to tour, taste, and stock up. Among the more notable are **Callaway Vineyard & Winery** (© **800/472-2377** or 909/676-4001; www.callawaycoastal.com), the first winery established in the region and also the best known; Callaway's moderately priced chardonnays and other whites show up frequently on California wine lists. In-depth tours are offered throughout the day between 10:30am and 5pm (call for times), and they have a casual bistro, Allie's. Across the street from Callaway stands another old-timer, **Thornton Winery** (© **909/699-0099**), which makes a good choice if you only visit one location, for Thornton provides an all-in-one overview of Temecula's

PALOMAR MOUNTAIN ✶

At an elevation of 5,600 feet, **Palomar** is a tiny mountain community located 70 miles north of downtown San Diego. It probably wouldn't be here today but for its famous observatory. From San Diego, take I-15 north to Highway 76 east, and turn left onto County Highway S6—a serpentine road climbs to the summit. Even if you don't want to inch your way to the top, drive the 3 miles to the lookout or just beyond it to the campground, grocery store, restaurant, and post office.

For many years the largest telescope in the world, **Palomar Observatory** ✶ (© **760/742-2119**) has kept a silent vigil over the heavens since 1949. The project was proposed and funded with $1 million from the Rockefeller Foundation in 1928, but it took another 2 decades to find a suitable site, build the dome, and to perfect the massive mirror (made from the then-new glass blend Pyrex). Owned by the California Institute of Technology, the observatory's impressive dome is 135 feet high and 137 feet in diameter. The telescope's single 200-inch mirror weighs 530 tons—it took 2 days to haul the mirror up the Palomar road. Now completely computerized, the telescope has an approximate light range of more than 1 billion light years.

wine country. It has a striking setting, fragrant herb garden, extensive gift shop, and award-winning restaurant, and tours are offered weekends on the hour, from 11am to 4pm.

At **Mount Palomar Winery** (© 800/854-5177 or 909/676-5047; www. mountpalomar.com), you might see unfamiliar names on some labels. Take the informative tour to learn about the process of handcrafting Mediterranean varietals like sangiovese, cortese, and Rhône-style blends of French grapes and even cream sherry. Perhaps the most welcoming tasting room is the nouvelle yellow farmhouse of the **Maurice Car'rie Winery** (© 909/676-1711), which produces 14 varietals, and fresh bread on weekends. Farther up the road is another venture by this couple, **Van Roekel Vineyards** (© 909/699-6961)—the souvenir-minded will love Van Roekel's gift shop, filled with logo items and wine-related gifts. Each of these last two wineries is open daily from 10am to 5pm, and also has gourmet deli items for composing a picnic to enjoy in Maurice Car'rie's rose-filled front garden and patio.

For detailed information on Temecula wine touring, call the **Temecula Valley Vintners Association** (© 800/801-WINE or 909/699-2353; www.temeculawines.org) and request the *Wine Country* pamphlet, a guide with winery locations, hours, and a brief description of each. The **Temecula Valley Chamber of Commerce,** 27450 Ynez Rd. (© 909/676-5090; www.temecula.org), has a *Visitors Guide* and can provide info on accommodations, golf, fishing, and the region's famous **Temecula Valley Balloon & Wine Festival,** held in June (see "San Diego Calendar of Events" in chapter 2).

Start your visit in the museum, which is open daily from 9am to 4pm and has a continuously running informative video that makes a walk up the hill to the observatory more meaningful. Palomar is primarily a research facility, and you'll only be able to look at (not through) the mammoth telescope. Try to visit the observatory in the morning; late in the day, you'll have the sun in your eyes as you travel back down the mountain.

3 The Disneyland Resort & Knott's Berry Farm

95 miles N of San Diego

with Matthew Richard Poole

The sleepy Orange County town of Anaheim grew up around Disneyland, the most famous theme park in the West. Now, even beyond the "Happiest Place on Earth," the city and its neighboring communities are kid-central. Otherwise unspectacular, sprawling suburbs have become a playground of family-oriented hotels, restaurants, and unabashedly tourist-oriented attractions. Also nearby is Knott's Berry Farm, another family-oriented theme park, in Buena Park.

ESSENTIALS

GETTING THERE   From San Diego, take I-5 north. For the Disneyland Resort, exit at Disney Way; dedicated off ramps from both the right hand lane *and* the left-hand commuter lane lead into the attractions' parking lots and surrounding streets. The drive from downtown San Diego takes approximately 1 hour and 45 minutes in average traffic.

Eleven **Amtrak** (© **800/USA-RAIL;** www.amtrak.com) trains go to Anaheim daily from San Diego. The one-way fare is $17, and the trip takes about 2 hours; a bus shuttles you from the Anaheim train station to the Disneyland Resort. Amtrak also offers 1-day and 5-day excursion packages.

VISITOR INFORMATION   The **Anaheim/Orange County Visitor & Convention Bureau,** 1500 S. Harbor Blvd. (© **714/765-8888;** www.anaheimoc.org), can fill you in on area activities and shopping shuttles. It's across the street from the Disneyland Resort, inside the McDonald's parking lot. It's open Monday through Friday from 8:30am to 5:00pm; weekend hours vary seasonally. The **Buena Park Convention & Visitors Office,** 6601 Beach Blvd., Suite 200 (© **800/ 541-3953** or 714/562-3560; www.buenapark.com/cvo), provides specialized information on the neighboring area, including Knott's Berry Farm.

THE DISNEYLAND RESORT 🎡🎡🎡

It's not called "The Happiest Place on Earth" for nothing, you know. The theme park that originally opened in 1955 has sprouted siblings in Florida, Tokyo, and even France, but nothing compares with the original. Disneyland has always capitalized on being the original—and the world's first family-oriented mega–theme park. Nostalgia is a big part of the appeal, and despite many advancements and evolutions over the years, Disneyland remains true to the vision of founder Walt Disney.

In 2001, Disney unveiled a brand-new theme park (California Adventure), a new shopping/dining/entertainment district (Downtown Disney), and a second and third on-site hotel (Disney's Grand Californian and Disney's Paradise Pier). Though still considerably smaller than Walt Disney World Resort in Orlando, the head Mouseketeers also changed the name of the Anaheim branch to "The Disneyland Resort," reflecting a greatly expanded array of entertainment options; it's no longer a (long) day trip from San Diego. What does this all mean for you? Well, first of all, you'll probably want to think seriously about budgeting more time (and yes, more money) for your Disney visit—you'll need at least 48 hours to see it all. If you have less time, plan carefully so you don't skip what's important to you; in the pages ahead we'll describe what to expect throughout the new resort. And, most of all, get ready to have fun—there's lots of great new stuff to check out!

ADMISSION, HOURS & INFORMATION   Admission to *either* Disneyland or California Adventure, including unlimited rides and all festivities and entertainment, is $47 for adults and children age 10 and up, $45 for seniors 60 and over, $37 for children 3 to 9, and free for children under 3; parking is $8. Note that a 1-day, one-park ticket allows you into one park *only.* There are several types of multi-day tickets available—the 3-day version allows in-and-out privileges between the parks (though 3 full days is probably more time than you need to tour the two parks). The 3-day ticket costs $119, or $95 for children. In addition, some area accommodations offer lodging packages that include admission for 1 or more days. One other option worth investigating is the "Southern California Attractions

Getting Around the Disneyland Resort

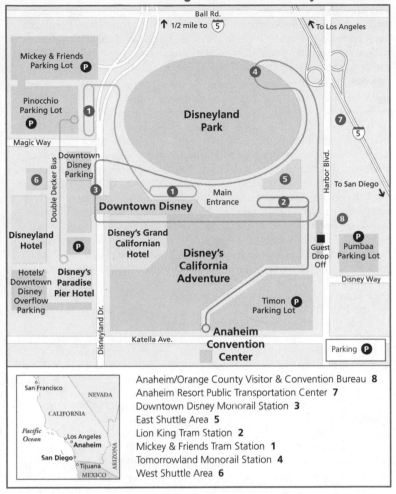

Anaheim/Orange County Visitor & Convention Bureau **8**
Anaheim Resort Public Transportation Center **7**
Downtown Disney Monorail Station **3**
East Shuttle Area **5**
Lion King Tram Station **2**
Mickey & Friends Tram Station **1**
Tomorrowland Monorail Station **4**
West Shuttle Area **6**

CityPass," which incorporates a 3-day Disneyland/California Adventure ticket, plus 1-day tickets to Knott's Berry Farm, SeaWorld, and the San Diego Zoo; the price is $166 for adults, $127 for children 3 to 9. Finally, residents of Southern California are usually offered off-season (non-summer/holiday) discounts, provided they can show a drivers license with a Southern California zip code.

Disneyland and California Adventure are open every day of the year, but operating hours vary daily, so I strongly recommend that you call for information that applies to the specific day(s) of your visit (*©* **714/781-4565**), particularly if you're doing Disneyland as a day trip from San Diego (you'll need at least 10–12 hr. to see most of this park). The same information, including ride closures and show schedules, can also be found online at **www.disneyland.com**. Generally speaking, Disneyland opens at 9am and closes around 8pm, with extended hours on weekends, holidays and during the summer; California Adventure, which requires less time to tour, is open from 10am to 6pm, and longer hours also apply many days.

If you plan to arrive when the ticket booths are most busy—from when the park gates open until about noon—purchase your tickets in advance and get a jump on the crowds. Advance tickets may be purchased through Disneyland's website (www.disneyland.com), at Disney stores in the United States, or by calling the ticket mail order line (© 714/781-4043).

DISNEY TIPS   The two theme parks are busiest from mid-June to mid-September and on weekends and school holidays year-round. Peak touring hours are from 11am to 5pm; visit the most popular rides before and after these hours, and you'll cut your waiting times substantially. Disneyland still draws the lion's share of the visitors, so by all means try to see it on a weekday (though note that shorter operating hours may negate some of the time saved waiting in lines); the whole of California Adventure is still relatively easy to conquer, even on weekends.

Many visitors tackle the parks systematically, beginning at the entrance and working their way clockwise around the park. But a better plan of attack is to arrive early and dash to the most popular rides: the Indiana Jones Adventure, Star Tours, Space Mountain, Big Thunder Mountain Railroad, Splash Mountain, the Haunted Mansion, the Many Adventures of Winnie the Pooh, and Pirates of the Caribbean in Disneyland; and, Soarin' Over California, Grizzly River Run, and California Screamin' in California Adventure. Lines for these rides can last an hour or more in the middle of the day.

However, this time-honored plan of attack is increasingly obsolete thanks to the new **FASTPASS** system. Here's how it works: Say you want to ride Splash Mountain (probably the parks' top draw), but the line is long—*so* long the wait sign indicates a 90-minute crawl! Now you can head to the automated FAST-PASS ticket dispensers, through which you swipe the magnetic strip of your entrance ticket—the machine spits out a FASTPASS which denotes a time to return later that day. When you come back you'll use the FASTPASS entrance, which bypasses most of the queue. Essentially, you're reserving a place in line, and the beauty of the system is that it evens out the flow of traffic. However, note that the most popular attractions can "sell out" of FASTPASS slots by early afternoon. Also, craft your itinerary carefully: You cannot obtain a FASTPASS for a second attraction until the window for the first ride has opened. At least 16 rides between the two parks are equipped with FASTPASS; for a complete list for each park, check your official map/guide when you enter.

Since many of the more popular rides have a set number of seats, Disney tries to fill unused single seats with a line bypass for **solo riders.** At the FASTPASS distribution area, ask the attendant for a single rider's pass—they will provide you a coupon that advances you to the front of the line to await the first single seat available.

Parents should note that a number of rides have minimum height requirements of 40 inches or more. Couples touring with someone under the height requirement can perform the **"baby pass"** at many attractions: Both parents get in line and one is allowed to wait while the other rides; then they trade the child for the other to ride (so that parents don't have to wait in the line separately). The majority of attractions favored by preteens are found in Disneyland but, following some criticism that it wasn't kid-friendly enough, A Bug's Land was added to California Adventure and seems to be keeping the moppets happy.

For much more information on touring the Disneyland Resort, pick up a copy of the candid and detailed *Unofficial Guide to Disneyland* or *Frommer's Portable Disneyland.*

⟨Value⟩ The Art of the (Package) Deal

If you intend to spend 2 or more days in Disney territory, it pays to investigate the bevy of packaged vacation options available. Start by contacting your hotel (even those in Los Angeles or San Diego), to see whether they have Disneyland admission packages. Many vacation packagers include Disneyland and/or California Adventure (and other attractions) with their inclusive packages; see "Package Deals for the Independent Traveler" in chapter 2 for contact information. Also, put a call in to the official Disney agency, **Walt Disney Travel Co.** (✆ **800/225-2024** or 714/520-5050). You can request a glossy catalog by mail, or log onto **www.disneyland.com** and click on "Book Your Vacation" to peruse package details, take a virtual tour of participating hotel properties, and get online price quotes for customized, date-specific packages. Their packages are value-packed time-savers with abundant flexibility. Hotel choices range from the official Disney hotels to one of 35 "neighbor hotels" in every price range (economy to superior) and category (from motel to all-suite); a wide range of available extras includes admission to other Southern California attractions and tours (like Universal Studios, or a Tijuana shopping spree), and behind-the-scenes Disneyland tours, all in limitless combinations. Every time I check, rates are highly competitive, considering each package includes multi-day admission, early park entry, free parking (at the Disney hotels), plus keepsake souvenirs and Southern California coupon books.

TOURING DISNEYLAND ᏧᏧᏧ

The Disneyland complex is divided into eight theme "lands," each of which has rides and attractions related to that land's theme. You'll find the practical things you might need, such as stroller and wheelchair rentals and storage lockers, just outside the park's main gate.

MAIN STREET U.S.A. At the park's entrance, Main Street U.S.A. is a cinematic version of turn-of-the-20th-century small-town America. The white-washed Rockwellian fantasy is lined with gift shops, candy stores, a soda fountain, and a silent theater that continuously runs early Mickey Mouse films.

Because there are no big-ticket rides, it's best to tour Main Street during the middle of the afternoon, when lines for popular attractions are longest, or in the evening, when you can rest your feet in the theater that features **"Great Moments with Mr. Lincoln,"** a patriotic (and AudioAnimatronic) look at America's 16th president. There's always something happening on Main Street; stop in at the information booth to the left of the main entrance for a schedule of the day's events. The **Disneyland Railroad** starts its circular journey around the park here, with stops at New Orleans Square, Mickey's Toontown, and Tomorrowland, but you can reach all of these places on foot just about as fast, so don't use it as a shortcut to the other side of the park. The railroad also passes through dioramas of the Grand Canyon and Primeval World between the Tomorrowland and Main Street stations.

ADVENTURELAND   Inspired by exotic Asia, Africa, and South America, the central icon of Adventureland is a giant tree, home to **Tarzan's Treehouse,** a stagnant attraction based on the animated film. Its safari-themed neighbor is the **Jungle Cruise,** where passengers board African Queen–style river boats and explore the animal "life" along an Amazon-like river—the quip-a-second banter of the captains is filled with groaner jokes. A spear's throw away is the **Enchanted Tiki Room,** one of the most sedate attractions in Adventureland. Inside, you can sit down and watch an 18-minute musical comedy featuring electronically animated tropical birds, flowers, and "tiki gods."

The **Indiana Jones Adventure** 🌟🌟 is Adventureland's marquee attraction. Based on the Steven Spielberg films, this ride takes you into the Temple of the Forbidden Eye, aboard joltingly realistic all-terrain vehicles. Riders follow Indy and experience the perils of bubbling lava pits, whizzing poison darts, shrieking serpents, collapsing bridges, and the familiar cinematic tumbling boulder (an effect that's very realistic!). Parents of children be warned: The volume on this ride is ear-splitting.

NEW ORLEANS SQUARE   Overlooking the "Rivers of America" and Tom Sawyer Island, New Orleans Square is a beautifully detailed re-creation of the Crescent City. There are just two rides here, but both are popular classics. The **Haunted Mansion** 🌟 is a high-tech ghost house inhabited by 999 ghouls, goblins, and other spirits; the clever events inside are as funny as they are scary.

Even more fanciful is the epic **Pirates of the Caribbean** 🌟🌟🌟, one of Disneyland's best-loved attractions. Visitors float on boats through underground caves to the Spanish Main, entering a story of swashbuckling, cannon-fire battles, and buried treasure. Even in the middle of the afternoon you can dine by the light of cool moonlight and fireflies and to the sound of crickets in the **Blue Bayou** restaurant, situated in the middle of the ride itself—other than the tasty Monte Cristo sandwich, the food nothing special but the ambience is exquisitely serene.

CRITTER COUNTRY   An ode to the backwoods, Critter Country is a corner of Frontierland without those pesky settlers. **The Many Adventures of Winnie the Pooh** 🌟 is the newest ride to be added to Disneyland—a gentle excursion through the Hundred Acre Woods (beware the heffalumps and woozles!). Everyone loves **Splash Mountain** 🌟🌟🌟, an immensely popular log flume ride. Based on the Disney movie *Song of the South,* the ride is lined with about 100 characters that won't stop singing "Zip-A-Dee-Doo-Dah." Be prepared to get wet, especially if someone sizable is in the front seat of your log. During my last visit, on a non-summer, non-holiday Friday, the line topped 2 hours, 15 minutes at 6pm! There's also **Davy Crockett's Explorer Canoes** 🌟, a perfect escape from the lines and crowds as you paddle free-floating, steady canoes around Tom Sawyer Island.

FRONTIERLAND   Inspired by 19th-century America, the centerpiece of Frontierland is the Rivers of America, sailed by the **Mark Twain Riverboat,** a detailed recreation of a Mississippi-style paddle-wheel steamer, and the **Sailing Ship Columbia,** a three-masted replica of the windjammer that first sailed the American flag around the world (both travel the same route—something that is only possible in Disney's world). The river circles **Tom Sawyer Island,** which is reached by brief raft ride; a do-it-yourself play area with balancing rocks, caves, and a rope bridge—kids love to investigate the island. The **Big Thunder Mountain Railroad** 🌟🌟 is a runaway roller coaster that races through a deserted 1870s gold mine—lots of fun here, and it's a relatively moderate coaster for those who might not be up to the more aggressive rides.

On weekends and holidays, and daily during summer, head to the Frontier-land after dark to see the **FANTASMIC! show** ☆. It mixes magic, music, live performers, and sensational special effects. Just as he did in *The Sorcerer's Apprentice,* Mickey Mouse appears and uses his magical powers to create giant water fountains, enormous flowers, and fantasy creatures. There are plenty of pyrotechnics, lasers, and fog, as well as a 45-foot-tall dragon that breathes fire and sets the water of the Rivers of America aflame. Best viewing is directly in front of Pirates of the Caribbean, but this is also the most crowded area (get there early).

MICKEY'S TOONTOWN   This is a colorful, whimsical world inspired by the film *Who Framed Roger Rabbit?*—a wacky, gag-filled land populated by 'toons. There are several rides, including **Roger Rabbit's CarToonSpin,** and a miniature roller coaster with just a 35-inch height requirement, **Gadget's GoCoaster.** But they take a back seat to Toontown itself—a trippy, smile-inducing world without a straight line or right angle in sight.

FANTASYLAND   With its storybook theme, this is the catchall land for stuff that doesn't quite fit anywhere else, much of it based on Walt Disney's animated classics. Most of the rides are geared to the under-6 set, including the **King Arthur Carousel, Dumbo the Flying Elephant,** and the **Casey Jr. Circus Train.** Some, like **Mr. Toad's Wild Ride** and **Peter Pan's Flight** ☆, appeal to grown-ups as well. You'll also find **Alice in Wonderland, Snow White's Scary Adventures, Pinocchio's Daring Journey,** and more.

The most famous lure is **It's a Small World** ☆, an indoor river ride through a Gen-Xer's saccharine nightmare of all the world's children singing the song everybody loves to hate, yet the single-digit set adores this attraction, as does the blue rinse crowd. Fantasyland's biggest thrill is the **Matterhorn Bobsleds** ☆☆, a zippy roller coaster through chilled caverns and drifting fog banks. It's one of the park's classics (and not found in Disney's sibling parks).

TOMORROWLAND   Conceived as an optimistic look at the future, Tomor-rowland employs an angular, metallic look popularized by futurists like Jules Verne.

The jet-propelled, long-time favorite **Space Mountain** ☆☆☆ offers a pitch-black indoor roller coaster that assaults your equilibrium—it's the park's hearti-est thrill ride. **Star Tours** ☆☆ is a Disney–George Lucas joint venture that spins off the Star Wars myth in a flight simulator. The 40-passenger StarSpeeders encounter a space-load of misadventures on the way to the Moon of Endor. The **Astro Orbitor** is a kid-friendly spinning spacecraft ride, while the **Autopia** offers every under-15-year-old's fantasy: driving gas-powered cars along a scenic track. The attraction **"Honey, I Shrunk the Audience"** ☆ is a eye-popping presentation by the "Imagination Institute" that rides on the characters and plot from the hit film *Honey, I Shrunk the Kids.*

The **Disneyland Monorail** ☆ stops in Tomorrowland, transporting passen-gers to and from a stop outside the park, between the Disney resorts and Down-town Disney. You don't have to get off at this stop, and the ride offers a good scenic overview of the entire resort complex.

TOURING CALIFORNIA ADVENTURE ☆☆

Despite the localized angle, California Adventure experienced a lukewarm recep-tion when it opened in 2001. Initial visitors complained that the park didn't have enough to do (yet admission was priced the same as Disneyland), that there wasn't enough for preteens, and that half the rides were dressed-up, carny-style attractions that could be found at your average county fair (rather than one-of-a-kind adventures like Pirates of the Caribbean). Disney responded quickly to the criticisms—a number of shows and attractions were added, including a half-dozen kiddie rides, and the opening of the elaborate Twilight Zone Tower of Terror in 2004 will do wonders to turn around the park's wobbly reputation.

With a grand entrance designed to resemble one of those "Wish you were here" scenic postcards, California Adventure starts out with a bang. Beneath a scale model of the Golden Gate Bridge (watch for the monorail passing overhead), handmade tiles of across-the-state scenes glimmer on either side. Just inside, an enormous gold titanium "sun" shines all day, illuminated by computerized heliostats that follow the real sun's path. From this point, visitors can head into four distinct themed areas, each containing rides, interactive attractions and live-action shows. Stroller and wheelchair rental and lockers are located just inside the main gate, on the right.

THE GOLDEN STATE   This multidimensional area represents California's history, heritage, and physical attributes. Sound boring? Actually, the park's two biggest crowd-pleasers are here. Inside a weathered corrugated test pilots' hangar is **Soarin' Over California** , the ride that immediately rose to the top on everyone's run-to-get-in-line-first list (it's equipped with FASTPASS, but often sells out by midday anyway). It uses cool technology to combine suspended, hang glider–style seats with a spectacular IMAX surround-movie—riders literally "soar" over California's scenic wonders.

Nearby, the park's iconic "Grizzly Peak" towers over the **Grizzly River Run** , a splashy gold-country ride through caverns and along craggy slopes; it culminates with a wet plunge into a bubbling geyser field. Kids can cavort nearby on the **Redwood Creek Challenge Trail,** a forest playground with smoke-jumper cable slides, net climbing, and swaying bridges.

On the back side of Grizzly Peak is the Robert Mondavi–sponsored **Golden Vine Winery,** which boasts a demonstration vineyard, Mission-style "aging room" (with a back-to-basics presentation on the art of winemaking), tastings, and the park's most upscale eatery, the **Vineyard Room** (see "Where to Dine in the Anaheim Area," later in this section). **Pacific Wharf** was inspired by Monterey's Cannery Row, and features varied food counters.

A BUG'S LAND   The Golden State blends seamlessly into this newer, pint-sized section of the park. At its entrance, and straight from the imagination of Disney CEO Michael Eisner comes the **Bountiful Valley Farm,** constructed to pay tribute to California's rich agriculture, demonstrating cultivation techniques. The 3-D attraction **"It's Tough To Be A Bug"** uses advanced film technology to expand on *A Bug's Life* characters Flik and Hopper, who lead the audience on a slap-happy underground romp with bees, termites, grasshoppers, stink bugs, spiders, and a few surprises that keep everyone hopping, ducking, and laughing along.

Just beyond is **Flik's Fun Fair,** featuring five smaller amusements that are perfect for younger visitors. The set is an amusingly detailed backyard garden, primed with a leaky spigot and towering clover, allowing visitors to view the world through a bug's perspective.

PARADISE PIER   Journey back into the glory days of California's beachfront amusement piers —remember Santa Monica, Santa Cruz, Belmont Park?—on this fantasy boardwalk. Highlights include **California Screamin'** , a classic roller coaster that replicates the whitewashed wooden white-knucklers of the past—but with state-of-the-art steel construction and a smooth, computerized ride. The zero-to-fifty takeoff packs quite a thrill. There's also the **Maliboomer,** a trio of towers (modeled after he-man sledgehammer tests) that catapult riders to the tip-top bell, then lets them down bungee-style with dangling feet; the **Orange Stinger,** a whooshing swing ride inside an enormous orange, complete with orange scent piped in; **Mulholland Madness,** a wacky wild trip along L.A.'s precarious hilltop street; and, the **Sun Wheel Carousel,** featuring unique zigzagging cars that bring new meaning to the familiar ride.

Most of the rides in Paradise Pier have minimum height requirements, but younger tikes can content themselves with the undersea-themed **King Triton's Carousel.** There are all the familiar boardwalk games (complete with stuffed prizes), and guilty-pleasure fast foods like pizza, corn dogs, and burritos.

HOLLYWOOD PICTURES BACKLOT If you've visited Disney in Florida, you'll recognize many elements of this ersatz Hollywood movie studio lot. Pass through a classic studio archway flanked by gigantic golden elephants, and you'll find yourself on a surprisingly realistic "Hollywood Boulevard." In the **Disney Animation** building, visitors can participate in six different interactive galleries: Learn how stories become animated features; watch Robin Williams become an animated character; listen to a Disney illustrator invent "Mushu" from *Mulan;* and even take a computerized personality test to see which Disney character you resemble most.

At the end of the street, the replica movie palace **Hyperion Theater** presents the live-action musical show *Disney's Aladdin,* a large-scale 40-minute musical production—the show is performed several times daily. Across the way, step aboard the **Superstar Limo,** where you're cast as a hot new star being chauffeured around Hollywood to sign a big movie deal; the wacky but tame ride winds through Malibu, Rodeo Drive, Beverly Hills, and the Sunset Strip. There's also a live version of the TV game show *Who Wants to be a Millionaire,* and guests are invited to play along, though note that the potential winnings fall well short of a million bucks.

The Backlot's main attraction is **Jim Henson's MuppetVision 3D** ⍟, an on-screen blast from the past featuring Kermit, Miss Piggy, Gonzo, Fozzie Bear—and even hecklers Waldorf and Statler. In 2004, a new adventure will open here, the **Twilight Zone Tower of Terror** ⍟⍟⍟—another import from Orlando. Guests will board a possessed elevator that travels through the bowels of a creepy hotel. You'll witness a parade of spiffy effects before making a sudden plunge down the 13-story shaft. The Tower of Terror is destined to be a monstrous hit the day it opens.

DOWNTOWN DISNEY ⍟

Borrowing another page from Central Florida's successful Disney compound, **Downtown Disney** is a district filled with restaurants, shops, and entertainment for all ages. For strolling with kids in tow, upscale dining, or just partying into the night, this colorful and sanitized "street scene" fills the bill. It's not a theme park, so you can visit admission-free, but note that this isn't a place for bargain hunting—whether it's a cup of coffee or a choice bit of Disneyana, nothing is cheap.

The promenade begins at the amusement park gates and stretches toward the Disneyland Hotel; there are 19 shops, boutiques, and snack stops, and 12 restaurants, live music venues, and entertainment options.

Highlights include **House of Blues,** the blues-jazz restaurant/club that features Delta-inspired cuisine and big-name music; **Ralph Brennan's Jazz Kitchen,** a spicy mix of New Orleans traditional foods and live jazz; **ESPN Zone,** the ultimate sports dining and entertainment experience, including an interactive game room; **Y Arriba! Y Arriba!,** where Latin cuisine combines with spicy entertainment and dancing; and, **World of Disney,** the largest Disney shopping experience in the West, with a vast and diverse range of toys, souvenirs, and collectibles. There is also a 12-screen stadium-seating movie theater, LEGO Imagination Center, Sephora cosmetics store, and much more.

Even if you're not staying at one of the Disney hotels, Downtown Disney is worth a visit. Locals and day-shoppers take advantage of the no-gate free entry and validated Downtown Disney parking lots (3 hr. free, longer with restaurant or theater validation).

KNOTT'S BERRY FARM

Cynics say that Knott's Berry Farm is for people who aren't smart enough to find Disneyland. The reality is that Knott's simply can't compete with the Disney allure, but instead focuses on newer and faster thrill rides that target Southern California youths and families instead.

Like Disneyland, Knott's Berry Farm is not without historical background. Rudolph Boysen crossed a loganberry with a raspberry, calling the resulting hybrid the boysenberry. In 1933, Buena Park farmer Walter Knott planted the boysenberry and launched Knott's berry farm on 10 acres of leased land. When things got tough during the Depression, Mrs. Knott set up a roadside stand, selling pies, preserves, and home-cooked chicken dinners. Within a year she was selling 90 meals a day. Lines became so long that Walter decided to create an Old West Ghost Town as a diversion for waiting customers.

Today the amusement park offers a whopping 165 shows, attractions, and high-tech rides that are far more thrilling than most of rides at the Disneyland Resort. Granted, it doesn't have nearly the magical appeal of Disneyland, but if you're more into fast-paced amusement rides than swirling tea cups, spend your money here.

GETTING THERE   Knott's Berry Farm is at 8039 Beach Blvd. in Buena Park. It's a 10-minute ride north on I-5 from Disneyland. From I-5 or Calif. 91, exit south onto Beach Boulevard. The park is about half a mile south of Calif. 91.

ADMISSION, HOURS & INFORMATION   Admission to the park, including unlimited access to all rides, shows, and attractions, is $42 for adults and children 12 and over, $32 for seniors over 60, kids 3 to 11, nonambulatory visitors, and expectant mothers; children under 3 are admitted free. Admission is $21 for adults and $15 kids 3 to 11 after 4pm on days when the park is open past 6pm. Parking is $8. Like Disneyland, Knott's offers discounted admission for Southern California residents during the off season, so if you're bringing local friends or family members along, be sure to take advantage of the bargain. Also like Disneyland, Knott's Berry Farm's hours vary both during the week and week to week, so call ahead. The park is generally open during the summer daily from 9am to midnight. The rest of the year, it opens at 10am and closes at 6 or 8pm, except Saturday, when it stays open till 10pm. Knott's is closed Christmas Day. Special hours and prices are in effect during Knott's Scary Farm in late October (a hugely popular event). Stage shows and special activities are scheduled throughout the day. Pick up a schedule at the ticket booth.

For more information, call ✆ **714/220-5200** or log onto **www.knotts.com.**

TOURING THE PARK

Despite all the high-tech multimillion-dollar rides, Knott's Berry Farm still maintains much of its original Old West motif, and is divided into six themed areas spread across 150 acres. The newest attraction is the **Xcelerator,** which launches you from 0 to 82 mph in 2.3 seconds. Other new attractions include the **California MarketPlace,** the farm's version of Downtown Disney, and **Knott's Soak City U.S.A.,** a 21-ride water-adventure park located right next to Knott's Berry Farm (separate admission required).

GHOST TOWN   The park's original attraction is a collection of refurbished 19th-century buildings relocated from deserted Old West towns. You can pan for gold, ride an authentic stagecoach, take rickety train cars through the Calico Mine, get held up aboard the Denver and Rio Grande Calico Railroad, and hiss at the villain during a melodrama in the Birdcage Theater. If you love wooden roller coasters, don't miss the clackity GhostRider.

FIESTA VILLAGE   Here you'll find a south-of-the-border theme. That means festive markets, strolling mariachis, and wild rides like Montezooma's Revenge and Jaguar, a roller coaster that includes two heart-in-the-mouth drops and a loop that turns you upside down.

WILD WATER WILDERNESS   This 3½-acre attraction is styled like a turn-of-the-20th-century California wilderness park. The top ride is a white-water adventure called Bigfoot Rapids, with a long stretch of artificial rapids; it's the longest ride of its kind in the world. You can also look Mystery Lodge right in the eye—it's a truly amazing high tech, trick-of-the-eye attraction based on the legends of local Native Americans. Don't miss this wonderful theater piece.

CAMP SNOOPY   This will probably be the youngsters' favorite area. It's meant to re-create a wilderness camp in the picturesque High Sierra. Its 6 rustic acres are the playgrounds of Charles Schulz's beloved beagle and his pals, Charlie Brown and Lucy, who greet guests and pose for pictures. The rides here, including the Charlie Brown Speedway and Beary Tales Playhouse, are tailor-made for the 6-and-under set.

INDIAN TRAILS   A nod to Native Americans is this Native American interpretive center on the outskirts Ghost Town. Exhibits include authentic tepees, hogans, and big houses. There's also daily educational events such as native craft making, storytelling, music, and dance.

THE BOARDWALK   This theme area is a salute to Southern California's beach culture. The main attractions are the 30-story Supreme Scream, one of the tallest (and scariest) thrill rides in the world, and a white-water adventure called Perilous Plunge, the world's tallest, steepest (think 4-story waterfall), and wettest water ride.

WHERE TO STAY IN THE ANAHEIM AREA

EXPENSIVE

The Disneyland Hotel ⭐⭐ *(Kids)*   The holy grail of Disney-goers has always been this, the "Official Hotel of the Magic Kingdom." A monorail connection via Downtown Disney means you'll be able to return to your room anytime, whether to take a much-needed nap or to change your soaked shorts after your Splash Mountain or Grizzly Peak adventure. The theme hotel is an attraction unto itself, and the best choice for families with small children. The rooms aren't fancy, but they're comfortably furnished and all have balconies. In-room amenities include movie channels (with free Disney Channel, naturally) and cute-as-a-button Disney-themed toiletries and accessories.

This all-inclusive resort offers more than 10 combined restaurants, snack bars, and cocktail lounges; every kind of service desk imaginable; the Neverland Pool Complex themed after Peter Pan and Captain Hook (complete with a white-sand beach); and video game center. The complex includes the adjoining **Paradise Pier Hotel.** Its whimsical beach boardwalk theme ties in with the Paradise Pier section of Disney's California Adventure park across the street; adults and older kids looking to escape the frenetically colorful Disney atmosphere will appreciate this option. Another bonus is the private entrance to the park via your Paradise Pier Hotel room key.

1150 Magic Way, Anaheim, CA 92802. ✆ **714/956-MICKEY.** Fax 714/956-6582. 990 units. $170–$310 double; from $265 suite. AE, MC, V. Parking $10. **Amenities:** 4 restaurants; 3 bars; 3 outdoor pools; health club; Jacuzzi; children's programs; game room; concierge; shopping arcade; room service; babysitting; laundry service; dry cleaning. *In room:* A/C, TV w/pay movies, dataport, minibar, coffeemaker, hair dryer, safe.

Disney's Grand Californian Hotel 🎿🎿 *Kids*   Disney didn't miss the details when constructing this enormous version of an Arts and Crafts–era lodge (think Yosemite's Ahwahnee or Pasadena's Gamble House), hiring craftspeople throughout the state to contribute one-of-a-kind tiles, furniture, sculptures, and artwork. Taking inspiration from California's redwood forests, mission pioneers, and plein-air painters, designers managed to create a nostalgic yet state-of-the-art high-rise hotel. Enter through subtle (where's the door?) stained-glass sliding panels to the hotel's centerpiece, a six-story "living room" with a William Morris–designed marble "carpet," angled skylight seen through exposed support beams, display cases of Craftsman treasures, and a three-story walk-in "hearth" whose fire warms Stickley-style rockers and plush leather armchairs. The hotel opens onto a landscaped area with a pair of swimming pools.

Guest rooms are spacious and smartly designed, carrying through the Arts and Crafts theme surprisingly well considering the hotel's grand scale. The best ones overlook the parks (but you'll pay for that view). Despite the sophisticated air of the Grand Californian, this is a hotel that truly caters to families, with a bevy of room configurations including one with a double bed plus bunk beds with trundle. Since the hotel provides sleeping bags (rather than rollaways) for kids, this standard-size room will sleep a family of six—but you have to share the bathroom.

Guests of the hotel can enter Disney's California Adventure through a private entrance, avoiding the crush at the main entrance, and a long roster of dining options is within a 5-minute walk.

1600 S. Disneyland Dr., Anaheim, CA 92802. ✆ **714/956-MICKEY** (central reservations) or 714/635-2300. Fax 714/956-6099. www.disneyland.com. 751 units. $205–$335 double; from $345 suite. AE, DC, DISC, MC, V. Free self-parking; valet parking $6. **Amenities:** 3 restaurants; bar; 2 outdoor pools; health club and spa; Jacuzzi; children's center; game room/arcade; concierge; business center; 24-hr. room service; laundry service; dry cleaning; concierge-level rooms. *In room:* A/C, TV w/pay movies, dataport, minibar, coffeemaker, hair dryer, iron, safe.

Sheraton Anaheim Hotel 🎿   This hotel rises to the festive theme-park occasion with its fanciful English Tudor architecture; it's a castle that lures business conventions, Disney-bound families, and local high school proms. The public areas are quiet and elegant—intimate gardens with fountains and koi ponds, plush lobby and lounges—which can be a pleasing touch after a frantic day at the amusement park. The rooms are modern and unusually spacious, but otherwise not distinctive. A large swimming pool sits in the center of the complex, surrounded by attractive landscaping. Don't be put off by the high rack rates; rooms commonly go for $100 to $130, even on busy summer weekends.

1015 W. Ball Rd. (at I-5), Anaheim, CA 92802. (C) **800/321-7251** or 714/778-1700. Fax 714/535-3889. www.sheratonanaheim.com. 489 units. $190–$225 double; $290–$360 suite. AE, DC, MC, V. Parking $10. **Amenities:** 2 restaurants; bar; outdoor pool; fitness center; Jacuzzi; concierge; courtesy Disneyland shuttle; 24-hr. room service; coin-op laundry and laundry service; dry cleaning. *In room:* A/C, TV w/pay movies, dataport, minibar, coffeemaker, hair dryer, iron.

MODERATE

Anaheim Vagabond Hotel 𝒜 *Value*   You can easily cross the street to Disneyland's main gate, or take the Anaheim Plaza's free shuttle. Once you return, you'll appreciate the way this hotel's clever design shuts out the noisy world. In fact, the seven two-story garden buildings remind me more of 1960s Waikiki than busy Anaheim. The Olympic-size heated outdoor pool and whirlpool are unfortunately surrounded by Astroturf, and the plain motel-style furnishings are beginning to look a little tired. On the plus side, nothing's changed about the light-filled modern lobby, nor the friendly rates, which often drop as low as $49.

1700 S. Harbor Blvd., Anaheim, CA 92802. (C) **800/522-1555** or 714/772-5900. Fax 714/772-8386. www.vagabondinns.com. 300 units. $79–$150 double; from $185 suite. Rates include continental breakfast. AE, DC, DISC, MC, V. Free parking. **Amenities:** Restaurant; bar; outdoor pool; Jacuzzi; courtesy Disneyland shuttle; limited room service (8am–11pm); coin-op laundry and laundry service; dry cleaning. *In room:* A/C, TV, coffeemaker.

Candy Cane Inn 𝒜𝒜 *Value*   Take your standard U-shaped motel court with outdoor corridors, spruce it up with cobblestone drives and walkways, old-time street lamps, and flowering vines engulfing the balconies of attractively painted rooms, and you have the Candy Cane. The face-lift worked, making this gem near Disneyland's main gate a treat for the stylish bargain hunter. The rooms are decorated in bright floral motifs with comfortable furnishings, including queen beds and a separate dressing and vanity area. Breakfast is served in the courtyard, where you can also splash around in a heated pool.

1747 S. Harbor Blvd., Anaheim, CA 92802. (C) **800/345-7057** or 714/774-5284. Fax 714/772-5462. www.candycaneinn.net. 173 units. $84–$129 double. Rates include expanded continental breakfast. AAA discount available. AE, DC, DISC, MC, V. Free parking. **Amenities:** Outdoor pool; Jacuzzi; courtesy Disneyland shuttle; coin-op laundry and laundry service; dry cleaning. *In room:* A/C, TV, coffeemaker, hair dryer.

Portofino Inn & Suites 𝒜 *Kids*   Emerging from the rubble of the former Jolly Roger Hotel renovation, this complex of low- and high-rise all-suite buildings sports a cheery yellow exterior and family-friendly interior—just in time for the expanded Disneyland Resort. The location couldn't be better: directly across the street from California Adventure's back side, and they'll shuttle you straight to the front gate. Designed to work as well for business travelers from the nearby Convention Center as for Disney-bound families, the Portofino offers contemporary, stylish furnishings as well as vacation-friendly rates and suites for any family configuration. Families will want a "Kid's Suite," which features bunk beds and sofa sleeper, plus TV, fridge, and microwave—and that's just in the kids' room; Mom and Dad have a separate bedroom with grown-up comforts like double vanity, shower massage, and their own TV.

1831 S. Harbor Blvd. (at Katella), Anaheim, CA 92802. (C) **800/398-3963** or 714/782-7600. Fax 714/782-7619. www.portofinoinnanaheim.com. 190 units. $94–$159 double; $109–$219 suite. Midweek, off-season, and other discounts available. AE, DC, DISC, MC, V. Free parking. **Amenities:** Restaurant; outdoor pool; fitness center; Jacuzzi; game room; tour desk; courtesy Disneyland shuttle; laundry service; coin-op laundry; dry cleaning. *In room:* A/C, TV w/pay movies, dataport, coffeemaker, hair dryer, iron.

Radisson Resort Knott's Berry Farm 🐾 *Kids*   Within easy walking distance of Knott's Berry Farm, this spit-shined Radisson (the former Buena Park Hotel) also offers a free shuttle to Disneyland, 7 miles away. The pristine lobby has the look of a business-oriented hotel, and that it is. But vacationers can also benefit from the elevated level of service. Ask about "Super Saver" rates (as low as $99—with breakfast—at press time), plus Knott's or Disneyland package deals. The rooms in the nine-story tower were tastefully redecorated when Radisson took over. Doting parents can even treat their kids to a Peanuts-themed room with Snoopy turndown service.

7675 Crescent Ave. (at Grand), Buena Park, CA 90620. © 800/333-3333 or 714/995-1111. Fax 714/828-8590. www.radisson.com/buenaparkca. 320 units. $129–$139 double; $159–$299 suite. Discounts and packages available. AE, DC, DISC, MC, V. Free parking. **Amenities:** 2 restaurants; bar; outdoor pool; outdoor tennis court (lit for night play); fitness center; Jacuzzi; video arcade; concierge; courtesy Disneyland shuttle; 24-hr. room service; coin-op laundry and laundry service; dry cleaning. *In room:* A/C, TV w/pay movies, fax, dataport, coffeemaker, hair dryer, iron, safe.

INEXPENSIVE

Best Western Anaheim Stardust   Located on the back side of Disneyland, this modest hotel appeals to the budget-conscious traveler who isn't willing to sacrifice everything. All rooms have a refrigerator and microwave; breakfast is served in a refurbished train dining car; and you can relax by the large outdoor heated pool and Jacuzzi while using the laundry room. The extra-large family rooms accommodate virtually any brood, and shuttles run regularly to the park.

1057 W. Ball Rd., Anaheim, CA 92802. © 800/222-3639 or 714/774-7600. Fax 714/535-6953. www.best western.com. 95 units. $64–$89 double; $105 family room. Rates include full breakfast. AE, DC, DISC, MC, V. Free parking. **Amenities:** Restaurant; outdoor pool; Jacuzzi; courtesy Disneyland shuttle; coin-op laundry. *In room:* A/C, TV, fridge.

Howard Johnson Hotel 🐾   This hotel occupies an enviable location, directly opposite Disneyland, and a San Francisco trolley car runs to and from the park every 30 minutes. Guest rooms were renovated in 1999. They're divided among several low-profile buildings, all with balconies opening onto a central garden with two heated pools for adults and one for children. Garden paths lead under eucalyptus and olive trees to a splashing circular fountain. During the summer you can see the nightly fireworks display at Disneyland from the upper balconies of the park-side rooms. Try to avoid the rooms in the back buildings, which get some freeway noise. Services and facilities include airport shuttle and family lodging/Disney admission packages. All in all it's pretty classy for a HoJo.

1380 S. Harbor Blvd., Anaheim, CA 92802. © 800/446-4656 or 714/776-6120. Fax 714/533-3578. www. hojoanaheim.com. 320 units. $74–$109 double. AE, DC, DISC, MC, V. Free parking. **Amenities:** Restaurant; 2 outdoor pools; Jacuzzi; concierge; game room; courtesy Disneyland shuttle; limited room service (7am–11pm); coin-op laundry and laundry service; dry cleaning. *In room:* A/C, TV w/pay movies, dataport, fridge, coffeemaker.

WHERE TO DINE IN THE ANAHEIM AREA

If you're visiting the Disneyland Resort, chances are you'll probably eat at one of the many choices inside the theme parks or at Downtown Disney; there are plenty of restaurants to choose from for all tastes and budgets. At Disneyland, in the Creole-themed **Blue Bayou,** you can sit under the stars inside the Pirates of the Caribbean ride—no matter what time of day it is. California Adventure features two sit-down options: **Ariel's Grotto,** where Disney characters serve fish and chips, lasagna, hamburgers, and such in a faux-1920s beachfront setting; and the **Vineyard Room,** which offers upscale prix-fixe wine country cuisine matched to California wines (the more casual Golden Vine Terrace is down-stairs). Make reservations early in the day for dinner, as they all fill up pretty quickly.

At Knott's Berry Farm, try the fried-chicken dinners and boysenberry pies at historic **Mrs. Knott's Chicken Dinner Restaurant** (see below for full review). Also listed are some of the best bests in the surrounding area, including nearby **Orange,** whose historic downtown is home to several of the region's best dining options—if you're willing to drive 10 to 15 minutes.

MODERATE

Anaheim White House *ᖇᖇ* ITALIAN/FRENCH   Once surrounded by orange groves, this stately 1909 colonial-style mansion now sits on a wide indus-trial street just 5 minutes from Disneyland. It's set back, though, framed by lawns and gardens, and exudes gentility and nostalgia. The home is nicely restored inside and out; the restaurant opened in 1981, named after its stylistic cousin in Washington, the White House. Owner Bruno Serato maintains this architectural treasure, serving northern Italian cuisine—with a French accent—in elegant white-on-white rooms on the main and second floors. Dinner courses are whimsically named for fashion giants (Versace whitefish, Prada rack of lamb), and sometimes arrive on oddly shaped platters that work better as art-work than dishware. Prices tend to reflect the expense account and well-heeled retiree crowd, but lunch prices (including a terrific prix fixe) deliver the same bang for fewer bucks. *Tip:* Use their website to make online reservations.

887 Anaheim Blvd. (north of Ball Rd.), Anaheim. ✆ 714/772-1381. www.anaheimwhitehouse.com. Reser-vations recommended at dinner. Main courses $10–$16 lunch, $18–$28 dinner. AE, MC, V. Mon–Fri 11:30am–2pm and 5–10pm; Sat–Sun 5–10pm.

Citrus City Grille *ᖇᖇ* CALIFORNIAN   Though housed in Orange's sec-ond-oldest brick building, this sophisticated crowd pleaser is furnished without an antique in sight, paying homage to the town's agricultural (citrus) legacy with a bold industrial chic. World-inspired appetizers range from Hawaiian-style *ahi poke* (raw tuna salad) to Southeast Asian coconut shrimp tempura accented with spiced apricots. Main courses come from the Mediterranean (pasta and risotto), Mexico (carne asada with avocado-corn relish), the American South (authentic Louisiana gumbo), and your mom's kitchen (meatloaf smothered in gravy and fried onions). Gleaming bar shelves house myriad bottles for the extensive mar-tini menu, and outdoor foyer tables are nicely protected from the street.

122 N. Glassell St. (½ block north of Chapman), Orange. ✆ 888/668-7474 or 714/639-9600. Reservations rec-ommended. Main courses $8–$13 lunch, $12–$24 dinner. AE, DC, MC, V. Mon–Sat 11:30am–3pm and 5–10pm.

INEXPENSIVE

Felix Continental Cafe *ᖇ* CUBAN/SPANISH   If you like the re-created Main Street in the Magic Kingdom, you'll love the historic 1886 town square in the city of Orange, on view from the cozy sidewalk tables outside the Felix Con-tinental Cafe. Dining on traditional Cuban specialties (such as citrus-marinated chicken, black beans and rice, and fried plantains) and watching traffic spin around the magnificent fountain and rose bushes of the plaza evokes old Havana or Madrid rather than the cookie-cutter Orange County communities just blocks away. The food is praised by restaurant reviewers and loyal locals alike.

36 Plaza Sq. (at the corner of Chapman and Glassell), Orange. ✆ 714/633-5842. Reservations recom-mended for dinner. Main courses $6–$14. AE, DC, MC, V. Mon–Thurs 7am–9pm; Fri 7am–10pm; Sat 8am–10pm; Sun 8am–9pm.

Mrs. Knott's Chicken Dinner Restaurant *(Kids* AMERICAN   Knott's Berry Farm got its start as a down-home diner in 1934, and you can still get a hearty all-American meal without even entering the theme park. The restaurant that started it all, descended from Cordelia Knott's Depression-era farmland tea room, stands just outside the park's entrance, with plenty of free parking for patrons. Looking just as you'd expect—country cute, with window shutters and paisley aplenty—the restaurant's featured attraction is the original fried chicken dinner, complete with soup, salad, buttermilk biscuits, mashed potatoes and gravy, and a slice of famous pie. Country fried steak, pot roast, roast turkey, and pork ribs are options, as well as sandwiches, salads, and a terrific chicken potpie. Boysenberries abound (of course!), from breakfast jam to traditional double-crust pies, and there's even an adjacent takeout shop that's always crowded.

8039 Beach Blvd. (near La Palma), Buena Park. (©) **714/220-5080.** Reservations not accepted. Main courses $5–$7; complete dinners $11. AE, DC, DISC, MC, V. Daily 7am–11pm.

4 Julian: Apple Pies & More

60 miles NE of San Diego; 35 miles W of Anza-Borrego Desert State Park

A trip to Julian (pop. 3,000) is a trip back in time. The old gold-mining town, now best known for its apples, has some good eateries and a handful of cute B&Bs, but its popularity is based on the fact that it provides a chance for city-weary folks to get away from it all, an asset best appreciated if you visit weekdays, when things are a little quieter here.

People first ventured into these fertile hills—elevation 4,225 feet—in search of gold in the late 1860s. They discovered it in 1870 near where the Julian Hotel stands today, and 18 mines sprang up like mushrooms. During all the excitement, four cousins—all former Confederate soldiers from Georgia, two with the last name Julian—founded the town of Julian. The mines produced up to an estimated $13 million worth of gold in their day.

Before you leave, try Julian's apple pies; whether the best pies come from Mom's Pies or the Julian Pie Company or Apple Alley Bakery or the Julian Café is a toss-up. Sample all of them and decide for yourself.

ESSENTIALS

GETTING THERE   You can make the 90-minute trip on Highway 78 or I-8 to Highway 79. I suggest taking one route going and the other on the way back. Highway 79 winds through scenic Rancho Cuyamaca State Park, while Highway 78 traverses open country and farmland.

VISITOR INFORMATION   For a brochure on what to see and do in Julian, contact the **Julian Chamber of Commerce,** at the corner of Main and Washington streets ((©) **760/765-1857;** www.julianca.com), where staffers always have enthusiastic suggestions for local activities. The office is open daily from 10am to 4pm.

Once in Julian, you'll need a car if you want to stay at a B&B outside town. However, Main Street is only 6 blocks long, and some lodgings, shops, and cafes are on it or a block away. Town maps and accommodations flyers are available from Town Hall, on Main Street at Washington Street. Public restrooms are behind the Town Hall. There's no self-service laundry (so come prepared), but you'll find a post office, a liquor store, and a few grocery stores.

SPECIAL EVENTS   Julian's popular **Arts and Crafts Show** is held every weekend between mid-September and the end of November. Local artisans display

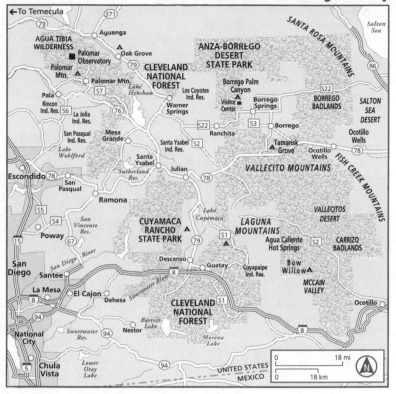

their wares; there's also plenty of cider and apple pie, plus entertainment and brilliant fall foliage.

The **Wildflower Show** is a weeklong event sponsored by the local Women's Club. Held in Julian's historic Town Hall, the event was initiated in 1926, and features displays of native plants; it takes place in early May.

One event that's better than its name is the **Julian Weed Show,** which takes place over the second half of August. Artwork and arrangements culled from the area's myriad wildflowers and indigenous plants (OK, weeds) are displayed and sold during the festival.

If you arrive on the **Fourth of July,** count on participating in a community barbecue and seeing a quilt exhibition and parade. It's also fun to visit in **December,** when activities include caroling and a living nativity pageant, and the town takes on a winter-wonderland appearance. Over the first two weekends in December, the members of the Julian Bed and Breakfast Guild hold open houses with complimentary refreshments.

The chamber of commerce has further details on these and other local events.

TOURING THE TOWN

Radiating the dusty aura of the Old West, Julian offers an abundance of early California history, quaint Victorian streets filled with apple-pie shops and antiques stores, crisp fresh air, and friendly people. While Wal-Mart and

McDonald's have invaded formerly unspoiled mountain resorts like Big Bear and Mammoth, this 1880s gold-mining town has managed to retain a rustic, woodsy sense of its historic origins.

Be forewarned, however, that downtown Julian can be exceedingly crowded during the fall harvest season. Consider making your trip during another season (or midweek) to enjoy this unspoiled relic with a little privacy. Rest assured, apple pies are baking around town year-round. But autumn is perfect: The air is crisp and bracing, and Julian sees a dusting (and often more) of snow during the winter; spring prods patches of daffodils into bloom.

The best way to experience Julian is on foot. Two or 3 blocks of Main Street offer plenty of diversions for an afternoon or longer, depending on how much pie you stop to eat. And don't worry, you'll grow accustomed to constant apple references very quickly here—the fruit has proven to be more of an economic boom than gold ever was.

After stopping in at the Chamber of Commerce in the old Town Hall—check out the vintage photos of Julian's yesteryear—cross the street to the **Julian Drug Store & Miner's Diner,** 2134 Main St. (© 760/765-3753), an old-style soda fountain serving sparkling sarsaparilla—plus burgers and sandwiches—and conjuring images of boys in buckskin and girls in bonnets. Built in 1886, the brick structure is on the National Historic Register—like many other well-preserved buildings in town—and is jam-packed with local memorabilia. It's open Monday through Thursday from 9am to 6pm, Friday and Saturday from 9am to 8pm, and Sunday from 10am to 5pm.

The **Eagle and High Peak Mines,** built around 1870, at the end of C Street (© 760/765-0036), although seemingly a tourist trap, offer an interesting and educational look at the town's one-time economic mainstay. Tours take you underground to the 1,000-foot hard-rock tunnel to see the mining and milling process; antique engines and authentic tools are on display. Tours are given between 10am and 2pm daily; admission is $8 for adults, $4 for children 6 and over, $1 for children under 6.

You'll certainly see one of Suzanne Porter's horse-drawn carriages clip-clopping around town. Some might think it touristy, while others will wax nostalgic for New York's Central Park, but a ride from **Country Carriages** (© 760/765-1471) is a quintessential Julian experience. Even the locals get into the act, snuggling under a blanket on romantic evening rides to celebrate anniversaries and birthdays. The carriages are always booked solid on Christmas Eve. A rambling drive down country roads and through town is $20 per couple; an abbreviated spin around town costs $5 per adult, $2 per child. Call for reservations, or stop by when one of the carriages is parked in front of the drugstore.

APPLE PIES

You won't be able to resist partaking of the apple pie so beloved in these parts. Stop by the aptly named **Mom's Pies,** 2119 Main St. (© 760/765-2472). Its special attraction is a sidewalk plate-glass window through which you can observe the mom-on-duty rolling crust, filling pies, and crimping edges. The shop routinely bakes several varieties of apple pie and will, with a day's notice, whip up apple-rhubarb, peach-apple crumb, or any one of a number of specialties. There's a country cafe in the store, in case a cup of coffee and a slice of fresh pie prove irresistible. Mom's is open daily from 9am to 5pm.

Another great bakery is the **Julian Pie Company,** 2225 Main St. (© 760/765-2449). This blue-and-white cottage boasts a small front patio with umbrella tables, a frilly indoor parlor, and a large patio deck in back where overhanging apple trees are literally up for grabs. The shop serves original, Dutch, apple-mountain berry, and no-sugar-added pies as well as cinnamon rolls, walnut apple muffins, and cinnamon cookies made from pie-crust dough. Light lunches (soups and sandwiches) are offered as well. It's open daily from 9am to 5pm.

SHOPPING

One of the simple pleasures of any weekend getaway is window- or souvenir-shopping in unfamiliar little shops like those lining both sides of Main Street. Keep an eye open for the old barn housing the **Warm Hearth,** 2125 Main St. (© **760/765-1022**). Country crafts, candles, and woven throws sit among the wood stoves, fireplaces, and barbecue grills that make up the shop's main business.

Nearby is the **Julian Cider Mill,** 2103 Main St. (© **760/765-1430**), where you can see cider presses at work October through March. It offers free tastes of the fresh nectar, and jugs to take home. Throughout the year, the mill also carries the area's widest selection of food products, from apple butters and jams to berry preserves, several varieties of local honey, candies, and other goodies.

A terrific browsing store is the **Bell, Book and Candle Shoppe,** 2007 Main St. (© **760/765-1377**), which specializes in only one of the above—candles, candles, and more candles. It sells pillars, tapers, hand-carved representational candles, custom personalized candles, candlesticks, and holders—plus incense, essential oils, and a few other gift items.

You'll have to step uphill 1 block to find the charming **Julian Tea & Cottage Arts,** 2124 Third St. (© **760/765-0832;** www.juliantea.com), where afternoon tea is served amid a treasure-trove of tea-brewing tools and other tea-themed paraphernalia. If that sounds too frilly for you, step next door, where a recent expansion spawned the **Culinary Cottage,** 2116 Third St. (© **760/765-0842**), home to stylish housewares, fine cookbooks, and gourmet foods (often available for tastings).

Book lovers will enjoy stopping into the **Old Julian Book House,** 2230 Main St. (© **760/765-1989**). Run by P. J. Phillips, a dedicated purveyor of new and antiquarian volumes alike, it carries a smattering of maps, sheet music, CDs, and ephemera, too. This small shop also has a comprehensive, computerized book search to help track down out-of-print or scarce material throughout the country. Most of the Main Street merchants are open daily from 10am to 5pm.

There are a number of **roadside fruit stands and orchards** in the Julian hills; during autumn they're open all day, every day, but in the off season some might open only on weekends or close entirely. Most stands sell, depending on the season, apples, pears, peaches, cider, jams, jellies, and other homemade foodstuffs. Many are along Highway 78 between Julian and Wynola (3 miles away); there are also stands along Farmers Road, a scenic country lane leading north from downtown Julian. Happy hunting!

Ask any of the San Diegans who regularly make excursions to Julian—no trip would be complete without a stop at **Dudley's Bakery,** Highway 78, Santa Ysabel (© **800/225-3348** or 760/765-0488), for a loaf or three of bread. Loaves are stacked high, and folks are often three deep at the counter clamoring for the 20 (yes, 20!) varieties of bread baked fresh daily. Varieties range from raisin-date-nut to jalapeño, with some garden-variety sourdough and multigrain in between. Dudley's is a local tradition; built in 1963, it has expanded several times to accommodate its ever-growing business. The bakery is open Wednesday through Sunday from 8am to 5pm (and may close early on Sun).

HISTORIC CEMETERIES

Finally, what's a visit to any historic hamlet without a peek at the headstones in the local cemetery? If this activity appeals to you—as it does to me—then Julian's **Pioneer Cemetery** is a must-see. Contemporary graves belie the haphazard, overgrown look of this hilly burial ground, and the eroded older tombstones tell the intriguing story of Julian's rough pioneer history and ardent patriotism. You can drive in from A Street, but I prefer climbing the steep stairway leading up from Main Street around the corner; until 1924 this ascent was the only point of entry, even for processions. As you climb, imagine carrying a coffin up these steps in the snow.

OUTDOOR PURSUITS IN & AROUND JULIAN

Within 10 miles of Julian are numerous hiking trails that traverse rolling meadows, high chaparral, and thick pine forests. The most spectacular hike is at **Volcan Mountain Preserve,** north of town along Farmers Road; the trail to the top is a moderately challenging hike of around 3½ miles round-trip, with a 1,400-foot elevation gain. From the top, hikers have a panoramic view of the desert, mountains, and sea. Free docent-led hikes are offered year-round (on Sat, about one per month); for a schedule, call ℂ **760/765-2300.**

In **William Heise County Park,** off Frisius Drive outside Pine Hills, the whole family can enjoy hikes ranging from a self-guided nature trail and a cedar-scented forest trail to moderate to vigorous trails into the mountains. A ranger kiosk at the entrance dispenses trail maps.

Cuyamaca Rancho State Park covers 30,000 acres along Highway 79 southeast of Julian, the centerpiece of which is **Lake Cuyamaca.** In addition to aquatic recreation there are several sylvan picnic areas, three campgrounds, and 110 miles of hiking trails through the Cleveland National Forest. Activities at the lake include fishing for trout (stocked year-round), plus bass, catfish, bluegill, and sturgeon, and boating. There's a general store and restaurant at the lake's edge. The fishing fee is $5 per day, $2.50 per day for kids 8 to 15, free for children under 8. A California State Fishing License is required and sold here: $11 for the day, or $30 per year. Rowboats are $14 per day, and motorboat rentals run $28 for the day ($23 after 1pm). Canoes and paddleboats can be rented by the hour for $7. For boat rental, fishing information, and RV or tent sites, call ℂ **877/581-9904** or 760/765-0515 or see www.lakecuyamaca.org. For a trail map and further information about park recreation, stop in at **park headquarters** on Highway 79 (ℂ **760/765-0755**) between 8am and 5pm Monday through Friday. An adjacent park museum is open Monday through Friday from 10am to 5pm, Saturday and Sunday from 10am to 4pm.

For a different way to tour, try **Llama Trek** (ℂ **800/LAMAPAK** or 760/765-1890; www.wikiupbnb.com). You'll lead the llama, which carries packs, for hikes to see rural neighborhoods, a historic gold mine, mountain and lake views, and apple orchards. Rates run $75 to $85 per person and include lunch. Overnight wilderness trips are available.

WHERE TO STAY

Julian is B&B country. At last count, there were more than 20 bed-and-breakfasts—and they fill up months in advance for the fall apple harvest season. Many (though not all) are affiliated with the **Julian Bed & Breakfast Guild** (ℂ **760/765-1555;** www.julianbnbguild.com), a terrific resource for personal assistance in locating accommodations. The 23 members include private cabins and other accommodations, but the agency specializes in B&Bs. There is also an assortment of country inns, hotels, and cabins for rent.

Three noteworthy choices are the **Artists' Loft** (© 760/765-0765), a peaceful hilltop retreat with two artistically decorated rooms and a cozy cabin with a wood-burning stove; the **Julian White House** (© 800/WHT-HOUS or 760/765-1764), a lovely faux-antebellum mansion 4 miles from Julian in Pine Hills, with four frilly Victorian-style guest rooms; and the romantic **Random Oaks Ranch** (© 800/BNB-4344 or 760/765-1094), which features two themed cottages, each with a wood-burning fireplace and outdoor whirlpool. To find out more about these and other member properties, call the guild between 9am and 9pm daily, or visit its website, which has links to the above-mentioned B&Bs.

EXPENSIVE

Orchard Hill Country Inn 🐾🐾   Hosts Darrell and Pat Straube offer the most upscale lodging in Julian, a two-story lodge and four Craftsman cottages on a hill overlooking the town. Ten guest rooms, a guests-only dining room, and a great room with a massive stone fireplace are in the lodge. Twelve suites are in cottages spread over 3 acres of grounds. All units feature contemporary, non-frilly country furnishings and snacks. While rooms in the main lodge feel somewhat hotel-ish, the cottage suites are secluded and luxurious, with private porches, fireplaces, whirlpool tubs, and robes. Several hiking trails lead from the lodge into adjacent woods.

2502 Washington St., at Second St. (P.O. Box 2410), Julian, CA 92036. © 800/71-ORCHARD or 760/765-1700. Fax 760/765-0290. www.orchardhill.com. 22 units. $185–$285 double. Extra person $25. 2-night minimum stay if including Sat. Rates include breakfast and hors d'oeuvres. AE, MC, V. From Calif. 79, turn left on Main St., then right on Washington St. *In room:* A/C, TV/VCR.

MODERATE

Julian Gold Rush Hotel 🐾   Built in 1897 by freed slave Albert Robinson, this frontier-style hotel is a living monument to the area's gold boom days. Centrally located at the crossroads of downtown, the Julian Gold Rush Hotel isn't as secluded or plush as the many B&Bs in town, but if you seek historically accurate lodgings to complete your weekend time warp, this is the place. The 13 rooms and two cottages have been authentically restored (with nicely designed private bathrooms added where necessary) and boast antique furnishings; some rooms are also authentically tiny, so claustrophobics should inquire when reserving! An inviting private lobby is stocked with books, games, literature on local activities, and a wood-burning stove.

2032 Main St. (at B St.), Julian, CA 92036. © 800/734-5854 or 760/765-0201. Fax 760/765-0327. www.julianhotel.com. 16 units. $135–$145 double; $165–$195 cottage. Rates include full breakfast and afternoon tea. AE, MC, V. *In room:* No phone.

WHERE TO DINE

Also consider one of Julian's many pie shops, two of which are discussed in "Touring the Town," above.

Julian Grille 🐾 AMERICAN   Set in a cozy cottage festooned with lacy draperies, flickering candles, and a warm hearth, the Grille is the nicest eatery in town. Lunch here is an anything-goes affair, ranging from soups, sandwiches, and large salads to charbroiled burgers and hearty omelets. Dinner features grilled and broiled meats, seafood, and prime rib. I'm partial to delectable appetizers like baked brie with apples and mustard sauce, Baja-style shrimp cocktail, and "Prime tickler" (chunks of prime rib served cocktail-style *au jus* with horse-radish sauce). Dinners include soup or salad, hot rolls, potatoes, and a vegetable.

2224 Main St. (at A St.). ✆ 760/765-0173. Reservations required Fri–Sun. Main courses $8–$13 lunch, $13–$28 dinner. AE, D, MC, V. Daily 11am–3pm; Tues–Sun 5–9pm.

Romano's Dodge House ✵ ITALIAN   Occupying a historic home just off Main Street (vintage photos illustrate the little farmhouse's past), Romano's is proudly the only restaurant in town not serving apple pie. It's a home-style Italian spot, with red-checked tablecloths and straw-clad Chianti bottles. Romano's offers individual lunch pizzas, pastas bathed in rich marinara sauce, veal parmigiana, chicken cacciatore, and the signature dish, pork Juliana (loin chops in a whiskey-apple cider sauce). There's seating on a narrow shaded porch, in the wood-plank dining room, and in a little saloon in back.

2718 B St. (just off Main). ✆ 760/765-1003. www.romanosjulian.com. Reservations required for dinner Fri–Sat, recommended other nights. Main courses $8–$16. No credit cards. Wed–Mon 11am–8:30pm.

JULIAN AFTER DARK

Fans of old-style dinner theater will feel right at home at **Pine Hills Dinner Theater** (✆ **760/765-1100**), one of North County's more unusual entertainment options for a Friday or Saturday night. Located at the **Pine Hills Lodge,** 2960 La Posada Way (about 2 miles from Julian off Pine Hills Rd.), the theater has staged more than 80 productions since opening in 1980 in this rustic 1912 building. Theater is usually light and comedic—past productions include *I'm Not Rappaport* and *Last of the Red Hot Lovers*—but in contrast, dinner is a filling buffet of barbecued baby back pork ribs, baked chicken, baked beans, salads, veggies, and thick sheepherder's bread. With advance notice, the kitchen will prepare a vegetarian meal or accommodate other dietary restrictions. Dinner is at 7pm, curtain is 8pm, and the combined ticket costs $29 (show only is $15).

5 Anza-Borrego Desert State Park ⟨⋆⟩

100 miles NE of San Diego; 35 miles E of Julian

The sweeping 600,000-acre Anza-Borrego Desert State Park, the nation's largest contiguous state park, lies mostly within San Diego County, and getting to it is almost as much fun as being there. From Julian, the first 20 minutes of the winding hour-long drive feel as if you're going straight downhill; in fact, it's a 7-mile-long drop called Banner Grade. A famous scene from the 1954 movie *The Long, Long Trailer* with Lucille Ball and Desi Arnaz was shot on the Banner Grade, and countless Westerns have been filmed in the Anza-Borrego Desert.

The desert is home to fossils and rocks dating from 540 million years ago; human beings arrived only 10,000 years ago. The terrain ranges in elevation from 15 to 6,100 feet above sea level. It incorporates dry lake beds, sandstone canyons, granite mountains, palm groves fed by year-round springs, and more than 600 kinds of desert plants. After the spring rains, thousands of wildflowers burst into bloom, transforming the desert into a brilliant palette of pink, lavender, red, orange, and yellow. The rare bighorn sheep can sometimes be spotted navigating rocky hillsides, and an occasional migratory bird stops off on the way to the Salton Sea. A sense of timelessness pervades this landscape; travelers tend to slow down and take a long look around.

Many people also visit the park with little interest in the desert flora and fauna. They're here to relax and sun themselves in tiny Borrego Springs, a town surrounded by the state park but exempt from regulations limiting commercial development. It is, however, somewhat remote, and its supporters proudly proclaim that Borrego Springs is and will remain what Palm Springs used to be— a small, charming resort community, with more empty lots than built ones. Yes, there are a couple country clubs, some chic fairway-view homes, a luxurious resort, and a regular influx of celebrity vacationers, but it's still plenty funky. One of the valley's unusual sights is scattered patches of tall, lush palm tree groves, perfectly square in shape: Borrego Springs' tree farms are a major source of landscaping trees for San Diego and surrounding counties.

When planning a trip here, keep in mind that temperatures rise to as high as 115°F (46°C) in summer. Winters days are very comfortable with temperatures in the low to mid-70s (21°C), but note that nighttime temps can drop to freezing—hypothermia is as big a killer out here as the heat.

ESSENTIALS

GETTING THERE   Anza-Borrego Desert State Park is about a 2-hour drive from San Diego. The fastest route is I-15 north to the Poway exit, then Highway 78 east at Ramona, continuing to Julian and on to the desert. Highway 79 to county roads S2 and S22 will also get you there. Another option is to take I-8 to Ocotillo, then Highway S2 north. Follow the Southern Overland Stage Route of 1849 (be sure to stop and notice the view at the Carrizo Badlands Overlook) to S3 east into Borrego Springs.

GETTING AROUND   You don't need a four-wheel-drive vehicle to tour the desert, but you'll probably want to get off the main highways and onto the Jeep trails. The Anza-Borrego Desert State Park Visitor Center staff (see below) can tell you which Jeep trails are in condition for two-wheel-drive vehicles. You can also call ✆ 760/767-ROAD for information on Borrego Springs road conditions. A Back Country Permit is issued free-of-charge, which is required to camp or use the Jeep trails in the park. You can also explore with Desert Jeep Tours (see below). The Ocotillo Wells area of the park has been set aside for off-road vehicles such as dune buggies and dirt bikes. To use the Jeep trails, a vehicle has to be licensed for highway use.

ORIENTATION & VISITOR INFORMATION   In Borrego Springs, the Mall is on Palm Canyon Drive, the main drag. Christmas Circle surrounds a grassy park at the entry to town. The **Anza-Borrego Desert State Park Visitor Center** (✆ 760/767-4205; www.anzaborrego.statepark.org) lies just west of the town of Borrego Springs. It supplies information, maps, and two 15-minute audiovisual presentations, one on the desert's changing faces and the other on wildflowers. The Visitor Center is open October through May daily from 9am to 5pm, June through September weekends from 9am to 5pm. You should also stop by the **Desert Natural History Association,** 652 Palm Canyon Dr. (✆ 760/767-3098; www.abdnha.org), whose sleek Borrego Desert Nature Center and Bookstore features an impressive selection of guidebooks, historical resources, educational materials for kids, native plants, and regional crafts, and a minimuseum display that includes a frighteningly real taxidermied bobcat. This is also your best source for information on the nearby Salton Sea.

For information on lodging, dining, and activities, contact the **Borrego Springs Chamber of Commerce,** 786 Palm Canyon Dr. (✆ 800/559-5524 or 760/767-5555; www.borregosprings.org).

(Moments The Desert in Bloom

From mid-March to the beginning of April, the desert wildflowers and cacti are usually in bloom—a hands-down, all-out natural special event that's not to be missed. It's so extraordinary, there's a hot line to let you know exactly when the blossoms are expected to burst forth: ℂ **760/767-4684.**

EXPLORING THE DESERT

Remember that when you're touring in this area, hydration is of paramount importance. Whether you're walking, cycling, or driving, always have a bottle of water at your side. If you will be out after dusk, or anytime during January and February, warm clothing is also essential.

You can explore the desert's stark terrain on one of its trails or on a self-guided driving tour; the Visitor Center can supply maps. For starters, the **Borrego Palm Canyon self-guided hike** (1½ miles each way) starts at the campgrounds near the Visitor Center. It is beautiful, easy to get to, and easy to do, leading to a waterfall and massive fan palms in about half an hour. It's grand for photos early in the morning.

You can also take a guided off-road tour of the desert with **San Diego Outback Tours** (ℂ **888/BY-JEEPS;** www.desertjeeptours.com). View spectacular canyons, fossil beds, ancient Native American sites, caves, and more in excursions by desert denizen Paul Ford ("Borrego Paul"), using military-style vehicles. Tours go to the awesome view point at Font's Point, where you can look out on the Badlands—named by the early settlers because it was an impossible area for moving or grazing cattle. Along the way, you'll learn about the history and geology of the area. Tours include drinks, snacks, and pickup at any Borrego Springs lodgings; prices range start at $69 for the standard 3½-hour adventure, and also enquire about Paul's nighttime tours.

Note: Whether you tour with San Diego Outback or on your own, don't miss the sunset view from Font's Point. Savvy travelers plan ahead and bring champagne and beach chairs for the nightly ritual.

If you have only 1 day to spend here, a good day trip from San Diego would include driving over on one route, going to the Visitor Center, hiking to Palm Canyon, having a picnic, and driving back to San Diego using another route.

GOLF

Golfers will find an 18-hole, par-72 championship golf course at **Ram's Hill Country Club** (ℂ **760/767-5124;** www.ramshillgolf.com), on Yaqui Pass Road just south of La Casa del Zorro. The 6,886-yard course has seven artificial lakes, and the greens fee is $35, cart included.

WHERE TO STAY

Borrego Springs is small, but there are enough accommodations to suit all travel styles and budgets. Peak season corresponds with the most temperate weather and wildflower viewing: from mid-January to mid-May. Other decent options include **Palm Canyon Resort,** 221 Palm Canyon Dr. (ℂ **800/242-0044** or 760/767-5341; www.pcresort.com), a large complex that includes a moderately priced hotel, RV park, restaurant, and recreational facilities; and, **Borrego Valley Inn,** 405 Palm Canyon Dr. (ℂ **800/333-5810** or 760/767-0311; www.borrego valleyinn.com), a newly built Southwestern complex featuring sand-colored pueblo-style rooms and upscale bed-and-breakfast amenities. Camping in the desert is a meditative experience, to be sure; but, if you truly want to splurge, you can do that too.

EXPENSIVE

La Casa del Zorro Desert Resort ★★
This pocket of heaven on earth was built in 1937, and the tamarisk trees that were planted then have grown up around it. So have the many charming tile-roofed casitas, originally neighboring homes bought by the resort's longtime owners, San Diego's Copley newspaper family. Over time the property has grown into a cohesive blend of discreetly private cottages and luxurious two-story hotel buildings—each blessed with personalized service and unwavering standards—that make La Casa del Zorro unequaled in Borrego Springs. Courtesy carts ferry you around the lushly planted grounds, and to the resort's stunning new pool area by the resurfaced tennis courts. It's easy to understand why repeat guests book their favorite casita year after year; some have a fireplace or pool, every bedroom has a separate bathroom, and they all have minifridges and microwaves (though a lack of dishes and utensils is calculated to get you into the Spanish-style main lodge's fine dining room). Outdoor diversions include horseshoes, Ping-Pong, volleyball, jogging trails, basketball, shuffleboard, and a life-size chess set. By the way, *zorro* means fox, and you'll find subtle fox motifs throughout the property.

3845 Yaqui Pass Rd., Borrego Springs, CA 92004. © **800/824-1884** or 760/767-5323. Fax 760/767-5963. www.lacasadelzorro.com. 77 units. $235–$375 double; from $250 casitas. Extra person $10. AE, DC, DISC, MC, V. **Amenities:** Restaurant (men are required to wear a jacket and a collared shirt at dinner Oct–May); bar; 5 outdoor pools; 9-hole putting green; 6 tennis courts; health club and spa; 2 Jacuzzis; bike rental; activities desk; courtesy car to golf; business center; salon; limited room service (7am–11pm); in-room massage; babysitting. *In room:* A/C, TV/VCR w/pay movies, dataport, minibar, coffeemaker, hair dryer, iron.

MODERATE

The Palms at Indian Head ★★ *Finds*
It takes a sense of nostalgia and an active imagination for most visitors to truly appreciate Borrego Springs' only bed-and-breakfast. Its fervent owners, David and Cynthia Leibert, are slowly renovating the once-chic resort. Originally opened in 1947, then rebuilt after a fire in 1958, the Art Deco–style hilltop lodge was a favorite hideaway for San Diego's and Hollywood's elite. It played host to movie stars like Bing Crosby, Clark Gable, and Marilyn Monroe. The Leiberts rescued it from extreme disrepair in 1993, clearing away some dilapidated guest bungalows and uncovering original wallpaper, light fixtures, and priceless memorabilia. As soon as they'd restored several rooms in luxurious Southwestern style, they began taking in guests to help finance the ongoing restoration.

Now up to 12 rooms, the inn also boasts a restaurant, the Krazy Coyote (see "Where to Dine," below), that's a culinary breath of fresh air in town. Also completely restored is the 42-by-109-foot pool, soon to be joined by the original subterranean grotto bar behind viewing windows at the deep end. The inn occupies the most envied site in the valley—shaded by palms, adjacent to the state park, with a panoramic view across the entire Anza-Borrego region. A hiking trail begins just steps from the hotel. If you don't mind getting an insider's view of this work-in-progress, the Palms at Indian Head rewards you with charm, comfort, and convenience.

2220 Hoberg Rd., Borrego Springs, CA 92004. © **800/519-2624** or 760/767-7788. Fax 760/767-9717. www.thepalmsatindianhead.com. 12 units. $169–$219 double. Extra person $20. DC, DISC, MC, V. Take S22 into Borrego Springs; at Palm Canyon Dr., S22 becomes Hoberg Rd. Continue north ½ mile. **Amenities:** Restaurant; bar; fantastic outdoor pool; limited room service (8am–8pm); in-room massage; laundry service. *In room:* A/C, TV, fridge, coffeemaker.

CAMPING

The park has two developed campgrounds. **Borrego Palm Canyon,** with 117 sites, is 2½ miles west of Borrego Springs, near the Visitor Center. Full hookups are available, and there's an easy hiking trail. **Tamarisk Grove,** at Highway 78 and county road S3, has 27 sites. The overnight rate at both is $10 to $19. Both have restrooms with pay showers (bring quarters!) and a campfire program; reservations are a good idea. The park allows open camping along all trail routes. For more information, check with the Visitor Center (✆ **760/767-4205;** www.anzaborrego.statepark.org).

WHERE TO DINE

Pickings are slim in Borrego Springs, but your best bet—if you're not willing to break the bank at La Casa del Zorro's classy but pricey dining room—is still the surprisingly good **Krazy Coyote,** which presents varied ingredients and gourmet preparations previously unheard of in this small town. One welcome newcomer is the **Badlands Market & Cafe,** 561 Palm Canyon Dr. in the Mall (✆ **760/767-4058**), which offers a daily board of gourmet light meals, plus a prepared foods deli and store that features imported mustards, marinated sun-dried tomatoes, delicate desserts, and other sophisticated treats; it's open Sunday through Thursday from 7:30am to 3pm, Friday and Saturday until 7pm. Or you could follow legions of locals into the downtown mainstay **Carlee's Place,** 670 Palm Canyon Dr. (✆ **760/767-3262**), a casual bar and grill with plenty of neon beer signs, a well-worn pool table, and a fuzzy-sounding jukebox. It's easy to understand why Carlee's is the watering hole of choice for motorcycle brigades that pass through town on recreational rides—and the food is tasty, hearty, and priced just right.

Kendall's Cafe COFFEE SHOP   Here's an economical little spot to grab a quick bite. Emu burgers from the local emu and ostrich farm are the specialty of the house. Buffalo burgers and Mexican dishes are also popular. Dinner choices include pork chops and chicken-fried steak. The cafe claims its apple pies are better than Julian's. Anything can be packed to go if you'd rather dine overlooking the desert.

In the Mall, Borrego Springs. ✆ 760/767-3491. Main courses $4–$8 lunch, $6–$11 dinner. MC, V. Daily 6am–8pm.

Krazy Coyote Saloon & Grille ⭐ ECLECTIC   The same style and perfectionism that pervades David and Cynthia Leibert's bed-and-breakfast is evident in this casual restaurant, which overlooks the inn's swimming pool and the vast desert beyond. An eclectic menu encompasses quesadillas, club sandwiches, burgers, grilled meats and fish, and individual gourmet pizzas. The Krazy Coyote also offers breakfast (rich and hearty for an active day, or light and healthy for diet-watchers). The evening ambience is welcoming and romantic, as the sparse lights of tiny Borrego Springs twinkle on the desert floor below.

In the Palms at Indian Head, 2220 Hoberg Rd. ✆ 760/767-7788. Main courses $6–$12 lunch, $10–$22 dinner. AE, MC, V. Open daily; call for seasonal hours.

6 Tijuana: Going South of the Border

17 miles S of San Diego

Like many large cities in developing nations, Tijuana is a mixture of new and old, rich and poor, modern and traditional. With about 2 million people—many of them transient—it's the second-largest city on the west coast of North America;

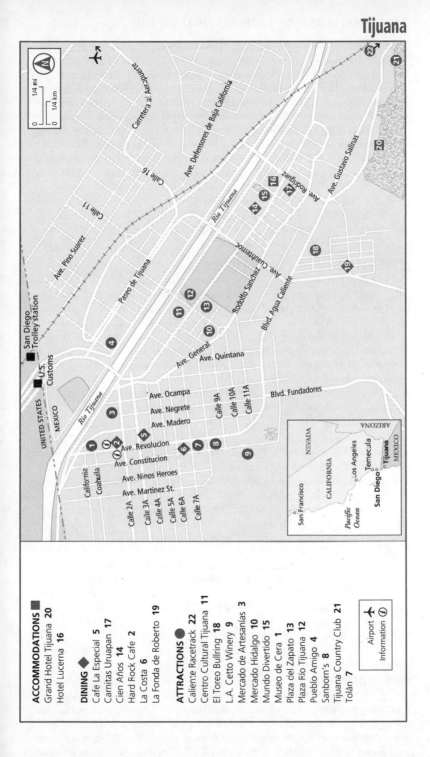

Tijuana

ACCOMMODATIONS ■
Grand Hotel Tijuana **20**
Hotel Lucerna **16**

DINING ◆
Cafe La Especial **5**
Carnitas Uruapan **17**
Cien Años **14**
Hard Rock Cafe **2**
La Costa **6**
La Fonda de Roberto **19**

ATTRACTIONS ●
Caliente Racetrack **22**
Centro Cultural Tijuana **11**
El Toreo Bullring **18**
L.A. Cetto Winery **9**
Mercado de Artesanías **3**
Mercado Hidalgo **10**
Mundo Divertido **15**
Museo de Cera **1**
Plaza del Zapato **13**
Plaza Rio Tijuana **12**
Pueblo Amigo **4**
Sanborn's **8**
Tijuana Country Club **21**
Tolán **7**

Airport ✈
Information ⓘ

only Los Angeles is larger. The maquiladoras—foreign-owned factories where appliances, furniture, and other goods are assembled by poorly paid, often under-age workers and with little environmental or labor oversight—thrives here like no other place in Mexico, providing the U.S. and other countries with bargain imports. The Mexico you may be expecting—charming town squares and churches, women in colorful embroidered skirts and blouses, bougainvillea spilling over walls—is found in a different guidebook (if you plan to spend a few days or in Baja California, pick up a copy of *Frommer's Portable Los Cabos & Baja*).

What you will find in Tijuana is poverty (begging in the streets is common), nerve-wracking sanitary conditions, and, surprisingly, a local populace that seems no more or less happy than their north-of-the-border counterparts. Much of the tourism that Tijuana generates is by under-21 types looking for a place to buy cheap liquor, as well as pharmacy traffic. Drugstores offer all manner of pills, either not conventionally or not inexpensively available in the U.S., plus Viagra, sold (seemingly) by the bucketful.

ESSENTIALS
GETTING THERE
BY TROLLEY   The easiest way to get to Tijuana from downtown San Diego is to hop aboard the bright-red **San Diego Trolley** headed for San Ysidro and get off at the last, or San Ysidro, stop (it's nicknamed the Tijuana Trolley for good reason). From there, just follow the signs to walk across the border. Tijuana's shopping and nightlife district, Avenida Revolución, is a $5 taxi ride from the border, or you can walk the mile into the tourist area. The trolley is simple, quick, and inexpensive; the one-way trolley fare is $2.50. The last trolley to San Ysidro departs downtown around midnight; the last returning trolley from San Ysidro is at 1am. On Saturday night, the trolley runs 24 hours.

BY CAR   To visit Tijuana, I recommend leaving the car behind (unless if you want to explore more of Baja California), and not just because the traffic can be challenging. But if you prefer to drive, take I-5 south to the Mexican border at San Ysidro. The drive takes about a half-hour; although the southbound border crossing rarely takes more than a few minutes, allow at least 1 hour to cross the border coming back to the U.S., or more on holiday weekends. An alternative option if you're only going to Tijuana is to drive to the border and park in one of the safe long-term parking lots on the U.S. side for about $6 to $8 a day; a shuttle takes you to Revolución Ave. for $1.50. Once you're in Tijuana, it's easier to get around by taxi than to fight the local drivers anyway.

Many car-rental companies in San Diego now allow their cars to be driven into Baja California, at least as far as Ensenada. Cars from **Avis** (© **800/230-4898**) and **Southwest Car Rental** (© **619/497-4800**) may be driven as far as Ensenada; **Bob Baker Ford** (© **619/297-5001**) allows larger rental vehicles to be driven the entire 1,000-mile stretch of the Baja Peninsula. Mexican auto insurance of $21 for 1 day or $37 for 2 days is required, and you can obtain it from your car-rental agency in San Diego; at various shops in San Ysidro, just north of the border; or from a stateside AAA office, if you're a member.

BUS TOURS   Bus tours are easy, but they only give you a few hours in Tijuana in the afternoon, so you miss evening activities. **Baja California Tours** (© **800/336-5454** or 858/454-7166; www.bajaspecials.com), based in La Jolla, offers a daily tour that visits Tijuana, Rosarito, and Ensenada, where you'll have lunch, for $59 ($44 for children 3–11). You can also use them as transportation to Tijuana ($28 round-trip) or Rosarito ($44). The buses pick up at any San

Diego hotel from La Jolla south, between 7:30am and 9am, returning to San Diego between 6:30 and 7pm. They also offer day trips to Baja's wineries, overnight trips, and other packages.

Contact Tours (© **800/235-5393** or 619/477-8687; www.contactours.com) also offers a tour of Tijuana, for $28 per person; departures from downtown San Diego are at 9am, returning from Tijuana at 3pm; and an afternoon tour leaves at 2pm, returning at 5:30pm. **Five Star Tours** (© **619/232-5049;** www.efive startours.com) offers a $50 round-trip fare into Tijuana from downtown San Diego (additional passengers are $5).

GETTING AROUND

If you've come to Tijuana on the San Diego Trolley or if you leave a car on the U.S. side of the border, you will walk through the border crossing. The first structure you'll see on your left is a Visitor Information Center, open daily from 9am to 7pm; ask for a copy of the *Baja Visitor* magazine and the *Baja Times*. From here, you can easily walk into the center of town or take a taxi.

Taxicabs are easy to find; they queue up around most of the visitor hot spots, and drivers often solicit passengers. It's customary to agree upon the rate before stepping into the cab, whether you're going a few blocks or hiring a cab for the afternoon. One-way rides within the city cost $4 to $8, and tipping is optional. Some cabs are "local" taxis, frequently stopping to take on or let off other passengers during your ride; they are less expensive than private cabs.

VISITOR INFORMATION

The **Tijuana Tourism Board** has a website that will get you started: **www.see tijuana.com**. You can request a free visitors guide by mail via the site. The cities of Baja Norte sponsor an information line that can also provide travel assistance at © **888/775-2417.** The **Baja Information Guide** is an online "newspaper" that covers Tijuana, Rosarito, and Ensenada; it's available at **www.bajatourist guide.com**. You can also request information and maps from the **Baja California Information Office** in San Diego (© **800/522-1516** in California, Arizona, or Nevada; 800/225-2786 in the rest of the U.S. and Canada; or 619/299-8518). The organization—which is not a government entity and is supported by commissions from hotel bookings—is located in Mission Valley at 6855 Friars Rd., Suite 26; it's open Monday through Friday from 9am to 5pm.

Once in Tijuana, you can pick up visitor information at the **Mexican Tourism Office,** Plaza Viva Tijuana (© **664/973-0424**), open daily from 8am to 8pm; and the **National Chamber of Commerce,** at the corner of Avenida Revolución and Calle 1 (© **664/682-8508**), open weekends only. Both are extremely helpful with maps and orientation, local events of interest, and accommodations.

The Mexican Tourism Office provides legal assistance for visitors who encounter problems while in Tijuana. The following countries have consulate offices in Tijuana: the **United States** (© **664/681-7400**), **Canada** (© **664/684-0461**), and the **United Kingdom** (© **664/681-7323**).

SOME HELPFUL TIPS The city does not take time for an afternoon siesta; you'll always find shops and restaurants open, as well as people in the streets, most of which are safe for walking—observe the same precautions you would in any large city. Most people who deal with the traveling public speak English, often very well. To maneuver around someone on a crowded street or in a shop, say *"con permiso"* ("with permission").

CLIMATE & WEATHER   Tijuana's climate is similar to San Diego's, though somehow the streets always seem a little hotter. Still, don't expect sweltering heat just because you're south of the border, and remember that the Pacific waters won't be much warmer than those off San Diego. The closest beaches you'll find are about 24km (15 miles) south of Tijuana.

CURRENCY   The Mexican currency is the peso, but you can easily visit Tijuana (or Rosarito, for that matter) without changing money—dollars are accepted just about everywhere. Many prices are posted in American (indicated with the abbreviation "dlls.") and Mexican ("m.n." *moneda nacional*) currencies—both use the "$" sign. Bring a supply of smaller-denomination ($1, $5, and $10) bills; although change is readily given in American dollars, many merchants are reluctant to break a $20 bill for small purchases. Visa and MasterCard are accepted in many places, but some places will only grudgingly take your card; don't be surprised if the clerk scrutinizes your signature and photo ID. When using credit cards at restaurants, it's a nice gesture to leave the tip in cash. At press time, the dollar was strong, worth about 10 pesos.

TAXES & TIPPING   A sales tax of 10%, called an IVA, is added to most bills, including those in restaurants. This does not represent the tip; the bill will read *IVA incluído,* but you should add about 15% for the tip if the service warrants.

EXPLORING TIJUANA

One of the first major tourist attractions below the border is also one of the strangest—the **Museo de Cera** ("Wax Museum"), Calle 1 between avenidas Revolución and Madero (© **664/688-2478**). Come to think of it, what wax museum isn't strange? But that doesn't explain the presence of Whoopi Goldberg, Laurel and Hardy, and Bill Clinton in an exhibit otherwise dominated by figures from Mexican history. If you aren't spooked by the not-so-lifelike figures of Aztec warriors, brown-robed friars, Spanish princes, and 20th-century military leaders (all posed in period dioramas), step into the Chamber of Horrors, where wax werewolves and sinister sadists lurk in the shadows. When the museum is mostly empty, which is most of the time, the dramatically lit Chamber of Horrors can be a little creepy. This side-street freak show is open daily from 10am to 7pm; admission is $1.60.

For many visitors, Tijuana's main event is bustling **Avenida Revolución,** the street whose reputation precedes it. Beginning in the 1920s, American college students, servicemen, and hedonistic tourists discovered this street as a bawdy center for illicit fun. Some of the original attraction has fallen by the wayside: Gambling was outlawed in the 1930s, back-alley cockfights are also illegal, and the same civic improvements that repaved Revolución to provide trees, benches, and wider sidewalks vanquished the girlie shows whose barkers once accosted passersby. Drinking and shopping are the main order of business these days. While youngsters from across the border knock back tequila shooters and dangle precariously at the upstairs railings of glaring neon discos, bargain hunters peruse the never-ending array of goods (and not-so-goods) for sale. You'll find

---

Telephone Tip

To call Mexico from the United States, dial **011** for an international line, then **52** (the country code), then the three-digit city code (indicated in the listings in front of the slash), followed by the seven-digit local number.

the action between calles 1 and 9; the information centers (above) are at the north end. To help make sense of the tchotchkes, see "Shopping," below.

Visitors can be easily seduced, then quickly repulsed, by tourist-trap areas like Avenida Revolución, but it's important to remember there's more to Tijuana than American tourism. Tijuana's population, currently around 2 million, makes it the fourth-largest city in Mexico. While many residents live in poverty-ridden shantytowns (you can see these *colonias* spread across the low hills surrounding the city), Tijuana has a lower unemployment rate than neighboring San Diego County, thanks to the rise in maquiladoras. High-rise office buildings testify to increased prosperity and the rise of a white-collar middle class, whose members shop at modern shopping centers away from the tourist zone. And there's tourism from elsewhere in northern Mexico; visitors are drawn by the availability of imported goods and the lure of the big city experience.

If you're looking to see a different side of Tijuana, the best place to start is the **Centro Cultural Tijuana,** Paseo de los Héroes, at Avenida Independencia (© **664/687-9600**). You'll easily spot the ultramodern Tijuana Cultural Center complex, designed by irrepressible modern architect Pedro Ramírez Vásquez. Its center-piece is a gigantic sand-colored dome that houses an OMNIMAX theater, which screens two different 45-minute films (subjects range from science to space travel). Each has one English-language show per day. Inside, the center houses the museum's permanent collection of Mexican artifacts from pre-Hispanic times through the modern political era, plus a gallery for visiting exhibits. They have included everything from the works of Diego Rivera to a disturbing, well-curated exhibit chronicling torture and human-rights violations through the ages. Music, theater, and dance performances are held in the center's concert hall and courtyard, and there's a cafe and an excellent museum bookshop. The center is open daily from 9am to 8:30pm; admission to the museum's permanent exhibits is free, there's a $2 charge for the special event gallery, and tickets for OMNIMAX films are $5 for adults and $3 for children.

Don't be discouraged if the Tijuana Cultural Center sounds like a field trip for schoolchildren; it's a must-see on my list, if only to drag you away from tourist kitsch and into the more sophisticated Zona Río (river area). While there, stop to admire the wide, European-style **Paseo de los Héroes.** The boulevard's intersections are marked by gigantic traffic circles *(glorietas),* at the center of which stand statuesque monuments to leaders ranging from Aztec Emperor Cuauhtémoc to Abraham Lincoln. Navigating the congested *glorietas* will require your undivided attention, so it's best to pull over to admire the monuments. In the Zona Río you'll find some classier shopping and a colorful local marketplace, plus the ultimate kid destination, **Mundo Divertido,** Paseo de los Héroes at Calle José Maria Velasco (© **664/634-3213**). Literally translated, it means "world of amusement," and one parent described it as the Mexican equivalent of "a Chuck E. Cheese's restaurant built inside a Malibu Grand Prix." Let kids choose from miniature golf, batting cages, a roller coaster, a kid-size train, a video game parlor, and go-carts. There's a food court with tacos and hamburgers; if you're in luck, the picnic area will be festooned with streamers and piñatas for some happy tyke's birthday party. The park is open daily, from around 11am to 10pm. Admission is free, and several booths inside sell tickets for the rides.

The fertile valleys of Baja Norte produce most of Mexico's wine, and export many high-quality vintages to Europe; most are unavailable in the United States. For an introduction to Mexican wines, stop into **L.A. Cetto Winery (Cava de**

Vinos), Av. Cañón Johnson 2108, at Avenida Constitución Sur (© 664/685-3031). Shaped like a wine barrel, the building's striking facade is made from old oak aging barrels in an inspired bit of recycling. In the entrance stand a couple of wine presses (dating from 1928) that Don Angel Cetto used in the early days of production. His family still runs the winery, which opened this impressive visitor center in 1993. L.A. Cetto bottles both red and white wines, some of them award winners, including petite sirah, nebbiolo, and cabernet sauvignon. Most bottles cost about $7; the special reserves are a little more than $10. The company also produces tequila, brandy, and olive oil, all for sale here. Admission is $2 for tour and tastings (for those 18 and over only; kids under 18 are admitted free with an adult but cannot taste the wines), $3 with souvenir wine glass. It's open Monday through Saturday from 10am to 6:30pm.

SHOPPING

Tijuana's biggest attraction is shopping—ask any of the 21 million people who cross the border each year to do it. They come to take advantage of reasonable prices on a variety of merchandise: terra-cotta and colorfully glazed pottery, woven blankets and serapes, embroidered dresses and sequined sombreros, onyx chess sets, beaded necklaces and bracelets, silver jewelry, leather bags and *huarache* sandals, "rain sticks" (bamboo branches filled with pebbles that simulate the patter of raindrops), hammered tin picture frames, thick drinking glasses, novelty swizzle sticks, Cuban cigars, and Mexican liquors like Kahlúa and tequila. You're permitted to bring $800 worth of purchases back across the border (sorry, no Cuban cigars allowed), including 1 liter of alcohol per person (for adults 21 and older). If your total purchases will come anywhere near the $800 per person limit, it's a good idea to have receipts on hand for the border crossing. Customs officers are familiar with the average cost of handcraft items.

When most people think of Tijuana, they picture **Avenida Revolución,** which appears to exist solely for the extraction of dollars from American visitors. Dedicated shoppers quickly discover most of the curios spilling out onto the sidewalk look alike, despite the determined sellers' assurances that their wares are the best in town. Browse for comparison's sake, but duck into one of the many *pasajes,* or passageway arcades, for the best souvenir shopping. There, you'll find items of a slightly better quality and merchants willing to bargain. Some of the most enjoyable *pasajes* are on the east side of the street between calles 2 and 5; they also provide a pleasant respite from the quickly irritating tumult of Avenida Revolución.

An alternative is to visit **Sanborn's,** Avenida Revolución between calles 8 and 9 (© 664/688-1462), a branch of the Mexico City department store long favored by American travelers. It sells an array of regional folk art and souvenirs, books about Mexico in Spanish and English, and candies and bakery treats. You can have breakfast in the sunny cafe.

One of the few places in Tijuana to find better-quality crafts from a variety of Mexican states is **Tolán,** Avenida Revolución between calles 7 and 8 (© 664/688-3637). In addition to the obligatory selection of standard souvenirs, you'll find blue glassware from Guadalajara, glazed pottery from Tlaquepaque, crafts from the Oaxaca countryside, and distinctive tile work from Puebla. Prices at Tolán are fixed, so you shouldn't try to bargain the way you can in some of the smaller shops and stands.

If a marketplace atmosphere and spirited bargaining are what you're looking for, head to **Mercado de Artesanías (Crafts Market),** Calle 2 and Avenida

Negrete. Vendors of pottery, clayware, clothing, and other crafts fill an entire city block.

Shopping malls are as common in Tijuana as in any big American city; you shouldn't expect to find typical souvenirs, but shopping alongside residents and other intrepid visitors is often more fun than feeling like a sitting-duck tourist. One of the biggest, and most convenient, is **Plaza Río Tijuana** (on Paseo de los Héroes at Av. Independencia). It's an outdoor plaza, anchored by several department stores, that features dozens of specialty shops and casual restaurants.

If you have a sweet tooth, seek out **Suzett** bakery, tucked in a corner behind **Comercial Mexicana,** which is kind of a Mexican Target with a full grocery store. At Suzett, grab a tray and a pair of tongs, and stroll through aisles of industrial bakery carts stacked high with fresh-baked breads, pastries, and other sweet treats. All the different shapes and patterns are irresistible; just pluck the ones you want and carry them to the register—a couple of bucks will buy enough for the whole family.

On the other side of Paseo de los Héroes from Plaza Río Tijuana is **Plaza del Zapato,** a two-story indoor mall filled with only shoe *(zapato)* stores. Though most are made with quality leather rather than synthetics, inferior workmanship ensures they'll likely last only a season or two. But with prices as low as $30, why not indulge? Men's styles include dress and casual oxfords and loafers, while women's tend toward casual sandals or traditional pumps. In general, styles tend to mimic current European trends rather than American fashion, and there are almost no athletic shoes.

For a taste of everyday Mexico, visit **Mercado Hidalgo** (1 block west at Av. Sánchez Taboada and Av. Independencia), a busy indoor-outdoor marketplace where vendors display fresh flowers and produce, sacks of dried beans and chiles by the kilo, and a few souvenir crafts, including some excellent piñatas. Morning is the best time to visit the market, and you'll be more comfortable paying with pesos, because most sellers are accustomed to a local crowd.

SPECTATOR SPORTS

If the thrill of athletic prowess and contests lure you, Tijuana is a spectator's (and bettor's) paradise.

BULLFIGHTING   While this spectacle employs the same disregard for animal rights as the now-illegal cockfights once popular in Tijuana, bullfighting does occupy a prominent place in Mexican heritage. A matador's skill and bravery is closely linked with cultural ideals regarding machismo, and some of the world's best competitors perform at Tijuana's two stadiums. **El Toreo** (© 664/686-1510) is 3km (2 miles) east of downtown on Bulevar Agua Caliente at Avenida Diego Rivera. **Plaza de Toros Monumental,** or Bullring-by-the-Sea (© 664/680-1808), is 9.5km (6 miles) west of downtown on Highway 1-D, before the first toll station. It's perched at the edge of the ocean and the California border. The season runs May through September, with events held Sunday at 4pm. Ticket prices range $18 to $50 (premium seats are on the shady side of the arena). Tickets are for sale at the bullring or in advance in San Diego from **Five Star Tours** (© 619/232-5049; www.efivestartours.com). If you want to catch the bullfights but don't want to drive, Five Star Tours offers bus trips to attend. It charges $17 round-trip, plus the cost of your bullfight ticket (prices vary). Or you can easily take a taxi from the border to El Toreo—fares are negotiable, and around $10 one-way should be fair. You can also negotiate a fare to Bullring-by-the-Sea, but fares are unpredictable.

Finds   Exploring Beyond Tijuana

Travel south of the border town and a taste of Mexico's true character is glimpsed. If you have a car, you can easily venture into Baja California for a long day trip or an overnight getaway. Rosarito is just 29km (18 miles) south of Tijuana; the lobster hamlet of Puerto Nuevo lies 12 miles farther south. Two well-maintained roads link Tijuana and Puerto Nuevo: the scenic, coast-hugging toll road (marked *cuota* or 1-D; $5 each way), and the free but slower public road (marked *libre* or 1). Start out on the toll road, but cut over to the free road at the first Rosarito Beach exit so that you can shop and enjoy the view at a leisurely pace. You can also visit Rosarito Beach and Ensenada on a tour (see "Getting There," above). *Note:* Most restaurants and even hotels along this stretch do *not* accept credit cards.

Once a tiny resort town that remained a secret despite its proximity to Tijuana, Rosarito Beach saw an explosion of development in the 1980s; it's now garish and congested beyond recognition. Why does its popularity persist? Location is one reason—it's the first beach resort town south of the border—and its reputation is another draw: For years the **Rosarito Beach Hotel** (© 866/ROSARITO or 661/612-0144; www.rosaritobeachhotel.com) was the preferred hideaway of celebrities and other fashionable Angelinos, most famously movie star Rita Hayworth and her husband, Prince Aly Khan. The hotel's entry still features the inscription *Por esta puerta pasan las mujeres mas hermosas del mundo* ("Through this doorway pass the most beautiful women in the world"). The hotel is still the most interesting place in town, and nostalgia buffs will enjoy the expert tile and woodwork, as well as the lobby's panoramic murals. Check out the colorful Aztec images in the main dining room, the magnificently tiled restrooms, and the glassed-in bar overlooking the sparkling pool and beach. Peek into the original owner's mansion, now home to a spa and gourmet restaurant.

When not too crowded, Rosarito is a good place to while away a few hours. Swim or take a horseback ride at the beach, then munch on fish tacos or tamales from any one of a number of family-run stands along **Bulevar Benito Juárez,** the town's main (and only) drag. You can wet your whistle at the local branch of Ensenada's enormously popular **Papas & Beer.** For the dozen or so blocks north of the Rosarito Beach Hotel you'll find the stores typical of Mexican border towns: **curio shops, cigar** and *licores* **(liquor) stores,** and *farmacias* (where drugs like Retin-A, Prozac, Viagra, and Zithromax—all available at low cost and without a prescription—share shelf space with unguents, liniments, and yes, even snake oil). Rosarito has also become a center for **carved furnishings,** which are plentiful downtown along Bulevar Benito Juárez, and **pottery,** which is best purchased at stands along the old highway south of town.

A few miles south of Rosarito Beach, at Km 32.8 on the free road, lies **Foxploration,** the state-of-the-art production facility used for *Titanic* and *Pearl Harbor,* and now a seaside theme park. An 800-foot-long replica was constructed for *Titanic,* and many local residents served as extras. There's also a makeshift *Titanic* "museum" with partial sets (like a first-class hallway) and numerous props, including lifeboats, furnishings, and crates from dockside scenes. There's a set replicating Canal Street (of New York City), you can explore a props and wardrobe warehouse, and learn about special effects. It ain't Universal or Disney, but for entry-level film production insight Foxploration is amusing for 2 or 3 hours. Admission fees are $12 for adults, $9 for children and seniors; Foxploration is open Saturday and Sunday from 10am to 6:30pm, and Monday, Thursday, and Friday from 9am to 5:30pm. For more information, call © **619/661-7178** or 661/614-9000, or log onto www.foxploration.com.

Leaving Rosarito, drive south on the toll highway or the local access road that parallels it. It offers a look at the curious juxtaposition of ramshackle villages and luxurious vacation homes. You'll also pass a variety of restaurants and resorts—this stretch of coastline has surpassed Rosarito in drawing the discriminating visitor. Many places are so Americanized that you feel as if you never left home. A trip down the coast isn't complete without stopping at **Puerto Nuevo,** a tiny, port-less fishing village with more than 30 restaurants—all serving the same menu! Around 1952, fishermen's wives started serving local lobsters from the kitchens of their simple shacks; many eventually built small dining rooms onto their homes or constructed restaurants. The result is a crustacean lover's paradise, where a feast of lobster, beans, rice, salsa, limes, and fresh tortillas costs $15 to $25. Drive through the arched entryway, park, and stroll the town's 3 or 4 blocks for a restaurant that suits your fancy. Not all have names; **Ortega's** is probably the oldest, and has expanded to five locations in the village, but Puerto Nuevo regulars prefer the smaller, family-run spots, where mismatched dinette sets and chipped plates underscore the earnest service and personally prepared dinners. The above-average picks include **La Casa de la Langosta** (which has a branch in Rosarito Beach), **Malecón de Puerto Nuevo, El Galleón,** and **Tony's.** Alas, overfishing means there's now a lobster season, so if you come November through February you'll probably be eating imported crustaceans.

About 16km (10 miles) farther south, roughly halfway between Rosarito and Ensenada, is **La Fonda,** a beloved hotel and restaurant (© **646/155-0307**). San Diegans make the drive on Sunday morning for La Fonda's outstanding buffet brunch, an orgy of meats, traditional Mexican stews, *chilaquiles* (a saucy egg-and-tortilla scramble), fresh fruit, and pastries (about $12 per person). Meals any day are always accompanied by a basket of Baja's best flour tortillas. The best seating is under thatched umbrellas on La Fonda's tiled terrace overlooking the breaking surf. There's a bar, and strolling mariachis entertain most of the time). Plan to walk off your heavy meal along the sandy beach below, accessible by a stone stairway. It's open daily from 9am to 10pm; Sunday's buffet brunch runs from 10am to 3:30pm.

GOLF   Once the favorite of golfing celebrities and socialites (and a very young Arnold Palmer), staying at the now-defunct Agua Caliente Resort, the **Tijuana Country Club,** Bulevar Agua Caliente at Avenida Gustavo Salinas (© **664/681-7882**), is near the Caliente Racetrack and behind the Grand Hotel Tijuana. It's about a 10-minute drive from downtown. The well-maintained course attracts mostly business travelers staying at nearby hotels, many of which offer golf packages (see Grand Hotel Tijuana in "Where to Stay," below). Weekend greens fees are $63; if you register a foursome, the group plays for $105 on weekdays. Stop by the pro shop for balls, tees, and a limited number of other accessories; the clubhouse also has two restaurants with cocktail lounges.

WHERE TO STAY

When calculating room rates, remember that hotel rates in Tijuana are subject to a 12% tax. Also note that this guide uses the term "double" when listing rates, referring to the American concept of "double occupancy." However, in Mexico a single room has one bed, a double has two, and you pay accordingly.

Grand Hotel Tijuana 🍴   This unusually high (32-story) mirrored twin tower is visible from all over the city. Modern and sleek, it opened in 1982—the height of Tijuana's prosperity—under the name "Fiesta Americana," a name locals (and many cab drivers) still use. Popular for business travelers, visiting celebrities, and society events, the hotel has the best-maintained public and guest rooms in Tijuana, which helps make up for what it lacks in regional warmth. Rooms have spectacular views of the city from the top floors.

The lobby has dark carpeting and 1980s mirrors and neon accents that feel like a Vegas hotel/casino. It gives way to several ballrooms and an airy atrium that serves elegant international cuisine at dinner and weekend brunch. Next to it is a casual Mexican restaurant; beyond there, the Vegas resemblance resumes with an indoor shopping arcade. Golf packages with the adjacent Tijuana Country Club start at $205 for two.

Agua Caliente 4500, Tijuana (P.O. Box BC, Chula Vista, CA 92012). © **866/GRAND-TJ,** or 664/681-7000. Fax 664/681-7016. www.grandhoteltijuana.com. 422 units. $135–$190 double; from $270 suite. AE, MC, V. Covered parking $2. **Amenities:** 3 restaurants; 3 bars; outdoor heated pool; tennis courts; Jacuzzi; sauna; car-rental desk; business center; shopping arcade; 24-hr. room service; in-room massage; babysitting; laundry service; dry cleaning. *In room:* A/C, TV w/pay movies, minibar.

Hotel Lucerna   Once the most chic hotel in Tijuana, the neoclassical Lucerna now offers reliable accommodations with lots of personality. The hotel is in the Zona Río, away from the noise and congestion of downtown, so a quiet night's sleep is easy. It's kept in great shape for the international visitors who enjoy Lucerna's proximity to the financial district, and the staff's friendly and attentive service reflects this clientele. The five-story hotel's rooms all have balconies or patios, but are otherwise unremarkable. Sunday brunch is served outdoors by the swimming pool.

Av. Paseo de los Héroes 10902, Zona Río, Tijuana. © **800/LUCERNA** or 664/663-3900. 167 units. $148–$153 double; from $193 suite. AE, DC, MC, V. **Amenities:** 2 restaurants; 2 bars; outdoor pool; exercise room; car-rental desk; tour desk; business center; 24-hr. room service; babysitting. *In room:* A/C, TV, dataport, hair dryer.

WHERE TO DINE

Although the irresistible aroma of street food—*carne asada* (marinated beef grilled over charcoal) tucked into corn tortillas for starters—is everywhere, less well known is that Tijuana has restaurants of real quality, despite the presence of a new Hard Rock Cafe. The following places are worth the taxi trip, and *la comida* (lunch) is the main meal of the day. Do not drink water unless it comes straight from a bottle (this includes ice, or uncooked vegetables like lettuce that have been washed) or you'll leave Tijuana with a going-away gift; restaurants listed below generally have sanitary conditions, but it doesn't hurt to be cautious.

Cafe La Especial 🍴 MEXICAN   Tucked away in a shopping *pasaje* at the bottom of some stairs (turn in at the taco stand of the same name), this restaurant is a well-known shopper's refuge. It offers home-style Mexican cooking at reasonable (though not dirt-cheap) prices. The gruff, efficient waitstaff carries out platter after platter of carne asada served with fresh tortillas, beans, and rice—it's La Especial's most popular item. Traditional dishes like tacos, enchiladas, and burritos round out the menu, augmented by frosty cold Mexican beers.

Av. Revolución 718 (between calles 3 and 4), Zona Centro. © 664/685-6654. Menu items $3–$12. No credit cards. Daily 9am–10pm.

Carnitas Uruapan 🍴 MEXICAN   *Carnitas,* a beloved dish in Mexico, consists of marinated pork roasted on a spit until it's falling-apart tender, then served in chunks with tortillas, salsa, cilantro, guacamole, and onions. It's the main attraction at Carnitas Uruapan, where the meat is served by the kilo (or portion thereof) at long, communal wooden tables to a mostly local crowd. The original is a little hard to find, but now there's a branch in the fashionable Zona Río. A half kilo of carnitas is plenty for two people, and costs around $12, including beans and that impressive array of condiments. It's a casual feast without compare, but vegetarians need not apply. Another location is on Paseo de los Héroes at Av. Rodríguez (no phone).

Bulevar Díaz Ordáz 550 (across from Plaza Pacífica), La Mesa. © 664/681-6181. Menu items under $8. No credit cards. Daily 7am–3am. Follow Bulevar Agua Caliente south toward Tecate. It turns into Bulevar Díaz Ordáz, also known as Carretera Tecate and Hwy. 2.

Cien Años 🍴🍴 MEXICAN   Perhaps Tijuana's finest restaurant, this is where *Gourmet* editor Ruth Reichl famously dined on ant roe and mexcal worms, though most of the menu is less, er, eclectic. The elegant Zona Río eatery offers artfully blended Mexican flavors you expect (tamarind, poblano chiles, and mango), but with a host of offerings that date back to traditional Mayan and Aztec preparations, all stylishly presented. Though modestly priced, Cien Años is dressy by San Diego standards, and reservations are a good idea.

José María Velazco 1407, Zona Río. © 664/634-3039. Reservations recommended. Main courses $8–$21. AE, MC, V. Daily 1–10pm.

La Costa 🍴 MEXICAN-STYLE SEAFOOD   Fish gets top billing here, starting with the hearty seafood soup. There are combination platters of half a grilled lobster, stuffed shrimp, and baked shrimp; fish filet stuffed with seafood and cheese; and, several abalone dishes. La Costa is very popular with San Diegans, and the food lives up to its reputation.

Calle 7, no. 8131 (just off Av. Revolución), Zona Centro. © 664/685-8494. Reservations recommended. Main courses $8–$20. AE, MC, V. Daily 10am–midnight.

La Fonda de Roberto 🍴🍴 MEXICAN   Though its location may appear out of the way, this modest restaurant's regular appearances on San Diego "Best Of" lists attest to its appeal. A short drive (or taxi ride) from downtown Tijuana, La Fonda's colorful dining room opens onto the courtyard of a kitschy 1960s motel, complete with retro kidney-shaped swimming pool. The festive atmosphere is perfect for enjoying a variety of regional Mexican dishes, including a decent chicken *mole* and generous portions of *milanesa* (beef, chicken, or pork pounded paper thin, then breaded and fried). A house specialty is *queso fundido*, deep-fried cheese with chiles, and mushrooms served with a basket of freshly made corn tortillas.

In the La Sierra Motel, Cuauhtémoc Sur Oeste 2800 (on the old road to Ensenada). (€ **664/686-4687.** Reservations recommended. Most dishes $5–$11. MC, V. Daily 10am–10pm.

TIJUANA AFTER DARK

Tijuana has several lively discos, and perhaps the most popular is still **Baby Rock Discoteca,** 1482 Diego Rivera, Zona Río (€ **664/634-1313**). A cousin to Acapulco's lively Baby O, it features everything from jungle rock to hard rock. It's close to La Cantina de los Remedios restaurant.

A recent addition to Tijuana's nightlife is "sports bars," cheerful watering holes that feature satellite wagering from all over the United States, as well as from Tijuana's Caliente Racetrack. The most popular bars cluster in **Pueblo Amigo,** Via Oriente, and Paseo Tijuana in the Zona Río, a new center designed to resemble a colonial Mexican village. Even if you don't bet on the horses, you can soak up the atmosphere. Two of the town's hottest discos, **Rodeo Santa Fe** (€ **664/682-4967**) and **Señor Frogs** (€ **664/682-4962**), are also in Pueblo Amigos. Pueblo Amigos is conveniently located less than 2 miles from the border, a short taxi ride or—during daylight hours—a pleasant walk.

Appendix:
San Diego in Depth

San Diego is best known for beaches and palms, pandas and orcas, soldiers and surfers, not to mention weather that is ranked as among the world's finest. But although Los Angeles and San Francisco bypassed San Diego in size and importance during the 19th and 20th centuries, a less well known fact is that (long before there was a border) San Diego is where the first European settlement took root on the west coast of America.

1 The Arrival of Spanish Mission "Style"

San Diego's first residents were probably the San Dieguitos, 8,000 to 11,000 years ago, followed by the La Jollan culture, who lived on the coastal mesas until about 1,000 to 3,000 years ago. The Dieguenos followed about 1,500 years ago, and existed in two groups: the Ipai, who lived along the San Diego River and northeast toward what is now Escondido, and the Tipai, or Kumeyaay, who lived south of the river into Baja California and east toward Imperial Valley. The men mostly went naked while the women wore a modest cover of woven fibers and animal skins. Meat was not a major part of the diet, but acorns were—the *metates* they used for grinding them into flour are sprinkled around the county—and seeds, berries, smaller prey, and shellfish rounded out their menu. Their basket-weaving and pottery talents were such that the vessels they made could hold water. The Kumeyaay were relatively peaceful, even though the individual settlements often didn't speak the same dialect as neighboring communities.

After Columbus "discovered" the New World and the Aztecs had been conquered, the myths of the fertile Pacific coast to the north started to percolate. So certain was Spain of the riches that lay ahead they had already

Dateline

- **1542** Juan Rodriguez Cabrillo sails into San Diego Bay.
- **1579** Sir Francis Drake overlooks the entrance to San Diego Bay on his way to San Francisco.
- **1602** Sebastian Vincaino arrives into the harbor and names it San Diego.
- **1769** A Spanish expedition led by Gaspar de Portolá drops off Franciscan monk Father Junípero Serra to establish Mission Basilica San Diego de Alcala, the first of 21 California missions.
- **1774** The Mission Basilica San Diego de Alcala moves inland 6 miles to its present location near Mission Gorge.
- **1821** Mexico wins independence from Spain and annexes California—the Mexican flag flies over what is now Old Town.
- **1823** Captain Francisco Maria Ruiz establishes one of the first rancheros.
- **1825** For 6 years, tiny San Diego—population 400—is the capital of the California territory.
- **1837** The population drops to 150 because of water shortages and Indian raids on the rancheros.
- **1846–48** War between the United States and Mexico.
- **1848** Gold is discovered near Sacramento; gold fever consumes Northern California.

continues

chosen a name for it: California. In 1542, Portuguese explorer Juan Rodrigues Cabrillo set out from Navidad, on the west coast of Central America, principally in search of a northwest passage that might provide an easier crossing between the Pacific Ocean and Europe. En route he landed in a place he charted as San Miguel, spending 6 days to see the sights, doing a meet-and-greet with three fearful Kumeyaay (who had heard tales of Europeans killing Indians to the east and south) before heading north along the coast. (Cabrillo died 3 months later, on the way back south, and was buried at Channel Islands off the coast of Santa Barbara.) Although Cabrillo wrote favorably about what he saw, it would be 60 years before San Miguel was visited again by Europeans, who were more concerned with the mythical northern passage, or perhaps treasure. Even Sir Francis Drake, as he looted his way from Peru to San Francisco, apparently overlooked San Miguel. When Spanish explorer Sebastian Vincaino sailed into the bay with three small ships on the feast day of San Diego de Alcala, he renamed it in honor of the saint. But again, despite Vincaino calling it "a port which must be the best to be found in all the South Sea," San Diego Bay was all but ignored by invaders for the next century-and-a-half.

In 1769 several ships finally anchored in the bay, most importantly one that carried "the sacred expedition" of Father Junípero Serra, a priest who had been charged with the task of spreading Christianity to the natives. The site for the first mission was selected just above the San Diego River, on a prominent hill offering views onto plains, mesas, marshes, and the sea. The mission at Presidio de San Diego was the first of what would be 21 missions in California; a fort was built to surround and protect the settlement. The first years were laborious and fraught with sickness and famine—by late summer the river would become an unreliable trickle and the land immediately surrounding the Presidio was infertile. The Indians were hostile to the Spanish, though eventually they were subdued

- **1850** California becomes the 31st state; San Diego is formally recognized as a city and county.
- **1867** Alonzo Horton buys 960 acres of bayfront property for $265.
- **1868** The *San Diego Union* begins publishing.
- **1869** "New Town"—what will become downtown—takes root.
- **1870** Gold is discovered in Julian, in the mountains east of San Diego—a mini–gold rush begins.
- **1885** Coronado is purchased for $110,000 and the Hotel del Coronado is built.
- **1886** The streetcar arrives.
- **1900** Population of San Diego County: 15,000.
- **1910** Marines are stationed on North Island.
- **1915–16** The Panama-California Exposition celebrates the completion of the Panama Canal; Balboa Park is created.
- **1927** *The Spirit of St. Louis* is built; Charles Lindbergh takes off from North Island.
- **1929** The Casa de Pico Motel opens in Old Town; in 1971 it becomes Bazaar del Mundo.
- **1935–36** The California-Pacific Exposition is held; Balboa Park sprouts more Spanish revival architecture.
- **1941** After the bombing of Pearl Harbor, the navy moves its headquarters for the Pacific fleet to San Diego.
- **1944** An aqueduct from the Colorado River is built to import water to the thirsty, growing city.
- **1948** Palomar Observatory opens.
- **1969** San Diego–Coronado Bridge is built.
- **1985** The Horton Plaza shopping center opens; San Diegans come downtown to shop for the first time in years.
- **2000** Population of San Diego County: 2.8 million.

by firepower. After 4 years, Father Serra requested permission to relocate the mission to Nipaguay, a site 6 miles up the valley, next to an existing Kumeyaay village.

Over the course of 3 years, delayed by a ransacking courtesy of resentful Indians from neighboring tribes, the new Mission San Diego was built, and dedicated in 1777. The new location was well chosen, and eventually a dam was built in 1817—probably the first major irrigation project in the West—which allowed the crew to grow wheat, barley, vineyards, olives, and dates, and bring in herds of cattle and sheep. Although the mission provided the Indians a more sustainable existence, it came at a price: Their culture was mostly lost; communities were shattered by foreign diseases from which they had no natural immunities; and Indians who defied the Spaniards or deserted the new settlements were punished by whipping or confinement. From 1790 to 1800, mission records noted that 1,600 Indians had been baptized—more than half of them died in the same period.

In 1798, Father Lasuen and the Franciscans founded Mission San Luis Rey on a site near what would become Oceanside, in northern San Diego County. The church, erected in 1811–15, is perhaps the finest existing example of mission style, with its composite of Spanish, Moorish, and Mexican architecture.

In 1821, as what is now known as Old Town started to take shape, Mexico declared independence from Spain. California's missions were secularized; the Mexican government lost all interest in the natives and instead focused on creating sprawling ranchos. The Mexican flag flew over the Presidio, and in 1825 San Diego became the informal capital of the California territory. Freed of Spanish restrictions, California's ports suddenly opened to trade, and for a period, the town was a hub for the hide trade: Ships brought in silks from the Orient, colognes from France, and gunpowder and clothing from Boston, and left San Diego brimming with leather. But the mission era had come to an ignominious close: The trademark roof tiles used for mission structures were taken away and recycled into new houses built in Old Town, while the adobe walls dissolved into the soil.

2 The Missions Give Way to Gold

The Mexican-American war took root in 1846, spreading from Texas west, creating brutal battles between the Californios and the Americans. By 1847 the Californios had surrendered, the treaty of Guadalupe Hidalgo was signed a year later, and Mexico was paid $15 million for what became the southwestern United States. In 1848, gold was discovered near Sacramento and the gold rush began—in 1 year, San Francisco grew from a town of less than 1,000 residents to 26,000. The road to statehood was paved with gold: In 1850, California was made the 31st state, and San Diego was established as both a city and county, formally establishing its future.

William Heath Davis, a San Francisco financier, purchased 160 acres of bayfront property with plans to develop a "new town." Residents of Old Town scoffed, and despite Davis' construction of several prefabricated houses and a wharf, the citizens stayed rooted at the base of the Presidio while San Diego soon declared bankruptcy. But in 1867, another developer, Alonzo Horton, also saw the potential of the city and bought 160 acres of bay front for $2,304. Calling it "the prettiest place for a city I ever saw," Horton laid out the grid pattern of streets, completed Davis' wharf, and built a hotel and new homes. Notably, he designated a huge 1,400-acre spread to the northeast as a city park. This time, people started moving in to the new town, and by 1869 San Diego had a population of 3,000; a devastating fire in Old Town in 1872 proved to be the final blow for the original settlement. A crucial catalyst for San Diego's development came in 1870, when gold was discovered in the mountains 60 miles northeast of town. Over the course of four swift but lucrative years, $13 million in ore was extracted and the town of Julian blossomed.

San Diego's gold rush was soon replaced by whaling as a major industry. Every winter, herds of Pacific gray whales migrated between the feeding territory of Alaska and calving grounds near the tip of Baja California. Peninsular Point Loma jutted into their course, and the easygoing whales, traveling as close as a mile from shore, were simple prey. Whalers from New England moved to the area, and by 1871, whaling was lucrative business. The mammoth carcasses were hauled ashore at Ballast Point, where the animals were butchered and their flesh rendered into oil. But like the gold rush, whaling petered out—the number of whales dwindled and they learned to avoid San Diego Bay (it wasn't until 1940s that the endangered Pacific gray whale started to make a recovery).

3 Location, Location, Location

The city endured briefs bouts of boom and bust but slowly developed, with real estate speculation providing the fuel for growth. In 1884, entrepreneurs Hampton L. Storey, who had founded a successful Chicago piano-building business, and Elisha S. Babcock Jr., the director of both a railroad and telephone company, sailed over to Coronado for a day of rabbit hunting. The desolate "island"—really a peninsular nub of sandy terra firma that protected the San Diego Bay—was uninhabited, but Babcock saw its potential as a luxury destination. The two formed a company and purchased Coronado and the land to the northwest (known as North Island, even though it, like Coronado, was connected to San Diego County by way of an isthmus of sand). They subdivided the land in 1886 and sold it for substantial profit, and then went about creating a fantastic storybook hotel, in the style of the epic beach resorts of Florida. Built in just 11 months, the $1.5 million Hotel del Coronado was the city's first link to tourism and opened to great acclaim.

Babcock and Storey also helped establish a streetcar system for San Diego; by 1888, 37 miles of trolley track canvassed the city. Around the same time, San Francisco–based sugar baron John D. Spreckels dived into San Diego's real estate market, soon owning two newspapers, downtown buildings, the streetcar network, and much of Coronado. Suburbs like La Jolla and Chula Vista began to take shape. But much of the 1880s real estate speculation was based on the prospect of a rail line linking San Diego to the rest of the country—by 1890 it was understood that San Diego would be served only by a spur line from Los Angeles. The real estate market swooned.

A pivotal moment came in 1910 when the 40,000 citizens approved a $1 million bond measure to host a world's fair, ostensibly to celebrate completion of the Panama Canal, but with a larger purpose: to promote the city to the world. The same year San Diego's Panama-California Exposition opened in 1915, a competing Panama-related event debuted in San Francisco. But San Diego's event was a fabulous success, and saw the development of 1,400-acre Balboa Park into fairgrounds of lasting beauty. Nursery owner Kate Sessions brought in and planted trees from around the world (particularly Australian eucalyptus, which remain an iconic symbol of the county today); the undulating canyons and mesas were landscaped; an outdoor organ pavilion was created; and an arched bridge was built over Cabrillo Canyon, looking much like a Roman aqueduct. Plaster workers were brought over from Italy to create the delicate flourishes on a village of Spanish colonial structures lining a graceful prado. Theodore Roosevelt, William Taft, Thomas Edison, Henry Ford, and a slew of movie stars were among the luminaries who attended the fair; Fatty Arbuckle and Mabel Normand starred in a one-reel film about their visit. The barrage of publicity from the 2-year fair touted San Diego's climate and location, and helped put the city on the map.

As the fair came to a close, a local doctor, Harry Wegeforth, was driving with his brother when he heard the far-off roar from a lion that had been brought in as a sideshow for the expo. "Wouldn't it be wonderful to have a zoo in San Diego?" said Dr. Harry. A zoological society was created and the San Diego Zoo was born. At first the zoo was a motley collection of cages that lined Park Boulevard, but in 1921 the city gave the zoo a permanent home: 100 acres in the heart of Balboa Park. (Actually, in a compromise with the private, non-profit Zoological Society, the city owns the land and the animals while the society administers its operation.) The park's canyons were ideal for containing diseases that might infect the entire menagerie, and over time proved ideal for creating naturalistic environments for the animals. Exotic species, most of them never before seen in America, came swiftly: by 1925 rare Hawaiian birds, kangaroos, and koalas had become San Diegans.

4 The Navy Builds a Home

The Hotel Del and the Exposition proved that tourism could be a successful component of San Diego's economy, but it was the military that proved to be the city's backbone. Toward the end of the 19th century, the U.S. Navy began using San Diego as a home port. In 1908 the navy sailed into the harbor with its battleship fleet and the war department laid plans to dredge the bay to accommodate even larger ships. Aviator Glenn Curtiss convinced the navy to designate $25,000 to the development of aviation, and soon after opened a flying school at North Island, the northwestern lobe of the Coronado peninsula. World War I meant construction projects and North Island was established as a marine base. The navy built a shipyard at 22nd Street in downtown, and constructed a naval training station and hospital in 1921. America's first aircraft carrier docked in San Diego in 1924.

San Diego's notable aviation history began 2 decades before the Wright Brothers, in 1883, when John Montgomery built and piloted a glider from a hillock near the Mexican border, soaring 600 feet into the air. At North Island, the first successful amphibious takeoff and landing was performed in 1911. Aviator T. Claude Ryan started Ryan Aviation to build military and civilian aircraft and equipment. In 1927 Ryan built *The Spirit of St. Louis* for Charles A. Lindbergh, a young airmail pilot; only a few weeks after taking off from North Island, Lindbergh landed in Paris and was toasted as the first to fly solo across the Atlantic. In 1928, San Diego's airport was dedicated at Lindbergh Field.

Although the Great Depression stalled growth, the military economy meant San Diego made it through the slump relatively unscathed. In 1931, the *San Diego Union* wrote that the Depression's "effects here are nothing like as severe as those reported from industrial and agricultural centers in other parts of the country." In 1935, Reuben H. Fleet moved his 400 employees at Consolidated Aircraft (later Convair) from Buffalo, New York, to San Diego. A second world's fair, the 1935–36 California-Pacific Exposition, allowed the Spanish colonial architecture in Balboa Park to be expanded, and many of the tourists became residents.

To alleviate some of the Depression's sting, the federal government created the Works Progress Administration (WPA) program in the late 1930s to provide work for artists during lean years. Local artists were supplied with funds to create public art, much of which still exists today; the mural in the La Jolla Post Office by Belle Baranceanu and Donal Hord's water fountain sculpture in front of the County Administration Center are notable examples.

But San Diego had thrown its lot in with the military, which allowed the city to prosper when World War II broke out. The attack on Pearl Harbor on December 7, 1941, mobilized the United States into a massive war machine, and San Diego was dramatically transformed. The headquarters for the Pacific Fleet were moved to the city, and the population swelled to build aircraft and ships as factories operated around the clock, employing thousands of residents. Balboa Park's ornate buildings were converted into hospitals; the bay was crisscrossed with huge nets to prevent Japanese subs from entering the harbor. In 1942, President Franklin Roosevelt signed orders authorizing the War Department to detain Japanese-Americans; almost 2,000 San Diegans were held in camps like Manzanar at the foot of the Sierra Mountains, near Death Valley.

5 An Identity Beyond the Navy & Beaches

The end of the war in 1945 didn't signal an end to San Diego's prosperity. New neighborhoods sprouted to house the thousands of military families that had been stationed here, and city leaders again cast an eye toward tourism as an economic rainmaker in times of peace. In April 1945, voters approved a $2 million plan to dredge and sculpt Mission Bay from former mud flats, allowing the communities of Mission Beach and Pacific Beach to greatly expand. By the late 1940s, the local fishing fleet comprised hundreds of boats; the catch was processed by local canneries and supplied two-thirds of the nation's tuna, a $50 million-a-year business. The Korean and Vietnam wars didn't impact San Diego like World War II, but the military link kept the city humming in the 1950s and 1960s.

In 1969, the graceful San Diego–Coronado Bridge opened and the ferries that linked downtown to the "island" were shut down. Downtown stumbled the way many urban centers did in the 1960s and 1970s, filled after dark with the homeless and inebriated. In 1974 the Gaslamp Quarter—the new name for Alonzo Horton's New Town—was designated as a historic district. Little occurred to revitalize downtown at first, but a redevelopment plan was established and the first step was to create Seaport Village, a waterside shopping complex, at the south end of the Embarcadero, in the early '80s. In 1985 a shopping center next to Horton Plaza opened to raves for its charmingly jumbled village architecture, and San Diegans responded immediately, coming downtown to shop as they hadn't in a generation. Entrepreneurs began financing the revitalization of the Gaslamp Quarter, and condos were built in the area between Horton Plaza and Seaport Village (although most sat empty for some years). A second wave of development was spurred with the opening of the new convention center between the Gaslamp and the bay in 1989, and the Quarter was cemented as a destination for restaurants and nightlife.

In 1981, the San Diego Trolley opened, providing a link between downtown and the border. By using existing rail corridors and purchasing (slightly) used trolley cars from Germany, costs were kept down and the system quickly found itself operating in the black. The lines were extended, north into Mission Valley and east to Lemon Grove and Santee. But traffic continues to be a growing obstacle, and residents look north to Los Angeles as an example of all that they don't want San Diego to become (a recurring theme you'll hear as you talk to longtime residents). Coronado plans a $369 million tunnel project that would divert the military traffic under Fourth Street to the North Island Naval Air Station, alleviating some of the street strain the community currently experiences.

In the late 1990s, a plan to build a downtown ballpark took shape, albeit with considerable opposition and delays. Backed strongly by the mayor and the local newspaper, the San Diego Padres threw a bone to the voters: a 3.8-acre public park beyond the venue's outfield. The proposal passed and the ballpark extended downtown's redevelopment area a few blocks east. Although the facility is well on its way to completion, at press time the size of the adjoining park had been scaled down by more than half, in favor of condo developments (to renewed outcry—stay tuned). No sooner had the Padres scored a new ballpark than the San Diego Chargers, the city's football team, started itching ingloriously for a new stadium of their own, to replace the recently overhauled Qualcomm Stadium in Mission Valley. As word of a "ticket guarantee" the city had quietly negotiated with the team (ostensibly to keep the Chargers in place for 20 years) was unearthed, San Diegans recoiled at the rapacity of its two home teams. By the time news of the city being billed for seats that didn't exist leaked out in late 2002, the ticket guarantee had cost the San Diegans a stinging $25 million; still, the team's ungrateful owners scrounged for an exit clause that would allow the Chargers to move to Los Angeles.

Today's San Diego owes a lot to medical and high-tech industries—biotech, pharmaceutical, and telecommunications in particular, with companies like Qualcomm, Pfizer, and Gateway being based here. The post-millennial dot-bomb fallout did not ravage the city, largely because a diversified tech economy meant jobs could be cycled from one sector to another. The infusion of talent and fresh perspective has helped the city grow beyond its beach/navy/zoo profile, as money has filtered into the arts, nourished the dining scene and, especially, empowered the real estate market, which has run red-hot since 1999. Although many of the condos built as part of the downtown redevelopment project in the 1980s and early '90s sat unoccupied, the end of the local recession allowed home-buying to take off. A one-bedroom condo in downtown's marina area sold for $225,000 in 1999; the same condo cost $400,000 in 2003. Citywide, real estate appreciated comparably: The median price for a home at the end of 2002 was $379,300 (compared to a national average of $161,600) and housing prices had increased 27% (compared to 9% nationally). Economists looked to San Diego to be one of only two bright spots for California's beleaguered economy in 2003.

In the wake of terrorism concerns, tourism in San Diego remained flat in 2002, but the city's hotels had the third-highest occupancy rate in the nation—indeed, tourism remains the city's third-biggest industry. What visitors come for is still largely focused on the beach, the zoo, and the weather, but what many discover is that there's more than meets the eye. This is a city blessed with a glorious location and climate, and San Diegans are beginning to find graceful ways to define their home beyond being "not like Los Angeles." We're happy not to have our neighbor's smog, congestion, and fast pace, and we're trying to keep a lid on growth, but we're also delighted to be nurturing some of the cultural assets we previously took for granted.

San Diego really has emerged from the shadow of LA. If we don't have a postcard icon as rich as the Golden Gate Bridge, or an industry as dominant as the military once was, our personality is starting to be defined with a smile as wide as Shamu's.

Index

See also Accommodations and Restaurant indexes, below.

GENERAL INDEX

A AA (American Automobile Association), 31, 43
AARP, 22
Accenture Match Play Championship, 181
Access Center of San Diego, 20
Accessible Journeys, 21
Accessible San Diego, 20
Accommodations. *See also* Accommodations Index
Anaheim, 257–260
best bets, 6–8
Borrego Springs, 270–272
Carlsbad, 238–240
Del Mar, 231–233
Escondido, 245
family-friendly, 80
Julian, 266–267
money-saving tips, 65–67
Oceanside, 242–243
pet-friendly, 24
Rancho Santa Fe, 244
reservation services, 66
San Diego, 65–97
shopping online for, 25–26
Tijuana (Mexico), 282
tipping, 46
what's new, 1
Accommodations Express, 66
Acura Tennis Classic, 183
Adams Avenue Business Association, 206
Adams Avenue Roots Festival, 15
Adventureland (Disneyland), 252
Aerial tours, 172
Carlsbad, 238
Aer Lingus, 42
Aeroméxico, 29, 42
Aerospace Museum, San Diego, 148, 201
African Americans, 23, 24
Ah Quinn, former home of, 188
AIDSinfo, 37

Air Canada, 29, 42
Airfares, 42
shopping online for, 25
tips for getting the best, 30–31
Airlines, 29–31
bankruptcy and, 31
foreign, 42
Air New Zealand, 42
Airport, San Diego International, 49–50
accommodations near, 97
Airport security, 30
Airport shuttles, 50
Air travel
around the United States, 42
arriving in San Diego, 49–50
Alaska Airlines, 29
Alcazar Garden, 198
American Airlines, 29
American Airlines Vacations, 32–33
American Automobile Association (AAA), 31, 43
American Eagle, 29
American Express, 62
traveler's checks, 11
American Foundation for the Blind, 21
America's Finest City Half Marathon, 182
America's Schooner Cup, 181
America West, 29
America West Express, 29
Amtrak, 32, 61, 229
Anaheim. *See also* Disneyland Resort; Knott's Berry Farm
accommodations, 257–260
restaurants, 260–262
Annual San Diego Crew Classic, 181
Antique Row, 206
Antiques, 206, 207, 211
Anza-Borrego Desert State Park, 172, 268–272
wildflowers, 14, 270
Apple pies, Julian, 264–265

Arch, Balboa Park, 198
Architectural highlights, 165–166
ARCO Olympic Training Center, 163
Area codes, 62
Art galleries, 211–212
The Artists Gallery, 211
Arts and Crafts Show (Julian), 262–263
Ascot Shop, 209
The Association of British Insurers, 39
Astro Orbitor (Disneyland), 253
ATMs (automated teller machines), 10–11
for foreign visitors, 40
Audubon Society, San Diego, 172
The Auld Course, 175
Automobile Club of Southern California, 54
Automotive Museum, San Diego, 148
Autopia (Disneyland), 253
Avenida Revolución (Tijuana), 276–278
Avis, 21

B abette Schwartz, 204
Baby Rock Discoteca (Tijuana), 284
Babysitters, 62
Backesto Building, 187
Bahia Belle, 221–222
Balboa Park
guided tours, 149
maps, 145, 199
money-saving tips, 146
organ recitals in, 4, 150, 162, 200, 228
sights and attractions, 144–151, 163
free, 162
for kids, 164
walking tour, 197–202
Balboa Park December Nights, 18

Balboa Park Municipal Golf
Course, 175–176
Balboa Park Visitors
Center, 144
Balboa Tennis Club, 180
Balboa Theatre, 186
Ballooning, 6, 15, 172, 231
Bankers Hill, 165
Barnes & Noble, 212
Barnes Tennis Center, 180
Barona Creek, 175
Barona Valley Ranch Resort
and Casino, 226
Bars and cocktail lounges,
222–223
Bay Books, 209
Bazaar del Mundo, 153, 162,
194, 206
The Beach, 222
Beaches, 138–143
Carlsbad, 237
Encinitas, 237–238
map, 139
North County, 143, 229
surfing, 179–180
for walking, 178
BearCom, 29
Bed & breakfasts (B&Bs), 67
Bell, Book and Candle
Shoppe (Julian), 265
The Belly Up Tavern, 219, 237
Bernardo Winery, 167
Best of Balboa Park
Combo, 146
Bicycling, 4, 62, 172–173
Rosarito-Ensenada 50–Mile
Fun Bicycle Ride, 14
Bicycling West, 173
BiddingForTravel, 25
Big Thunder Mountain
Railroad (Disneyland), 252
Bike-N-Ride program, 62
Bikes and Beyond, 173, 179
Bike Tours San Diego, 173
Binoculars, 18
Biplane, Air Combat &
Warbird Adventures, 238
Birch Aquarium at Scripps,
157, 158, 170
Bird-watching, 172
The Bishop's School, 157
The Bitter End, 222
Black's Beach, 143
Blue Escape Dive and
Charter, 179
Blue Meanie Records, 215
The Boardwalk (Knott's
Berry Farm), 257
Boating, 173–174
Oceanside, 241–242
San Diego Crew Classic, 14
special events, 181

Boat Rentals of America
(Oceanside), 241–242
Boat tours and cruises,
167–168, 192
with entertainment,
221–222
whale-watching, 170
Bob Davis' Camera Shop, 63
Boingo, 28
Boneyard Beach
(Encinitas), 238
Boneyards Beach, 143
Bonita Cove, 141
Books, recommended, 34–35
Bookstores, 205, 209,
212–213, 265
Borders, 212
Borrego Palm Canyon, 272
Botanical Building and Lily
Pond, 144, 146, 166, 200
Boudin Sourdough Bakery
and Cafe, 128
Bourbon Street, 225
The Brass Rail, 225
Bread & Cie., 9, 128
British Airways, 29, 42
Brokers Building, 189
Bucket shops, 31
A Bug's Land (California
Adventure), 254
Buick Invitational, 14, 181
Bullfights (Tijuana), 279
Business hours, 43, 62
Bus tours, 168
Tijuana (Mexico), 274–275
Bus travel
to/from airport, 49–50
in San Diego, 59–60
to San Diego, 32, 43, 50

Cabrillo Bridge, 144, 198
Cabrillo National Monument,
151, 169, 178
whale-watching, 170
Cabs
to/from airport, 50
in San Diego, 61
tipping, 46
Cafes and coffeehouses, 4
Internet, 27
with performances,
223–225
Calendar of events, 13–18
California Adventure, 250,
253–255
California Ballet, 219
California Bicycle, 173
California building and bell
tower, 150
California Center for
the Performing Arts
(Escondido), 245

California Dreamin', 172
California Rail Pass, 43
California Screamin' (Califor-
nia Adventure), 254–255
California Surf Museum
(Oceanside), 242
Callaway Vineyard &
Winery, 246
Camera repair, 63
Camping, Borrego
Springs, 272
Camp Snoopy (Knott's
Berry Farm), 257
Cannibal Bar, 222
Carlsbad, 229, 234–241
Carlsbad Company Stores,
211, 236
Carlsbad Fall Village
Faire, 17
Carlsbad Mineral Water
Spa, 237
Carlsbad Ranch, Flower
Fields at, 14, 236
Carlsbad State Beach, 237
Car rentals, 57
for disabled travelers, 21
insurance, 57–58
saving money on, 58
shopping online for, 26
Tijuana (Mexico), 274
Carriage Works, 189
Car travel, 31–32
to/from airport, 50
driving rules, 59
driving safety, 41
into San Diego, 50
Tijuana (Mexico), 274
Casa de Balboa, 201
Casa del Prado, 201
The Casbah, 219
Casinos, 226
Oceanside, 242
Cathedral, 204
Cave Store, 157, 209
Cedros Design District, 211
Cellphone rentals, 41
Cellphones, 28–29
Centro Cultural Tijuana, 277
Cheap Rentals, 173
The Cheese Shop, 128
Children, families with, 23
accommodations, 80
restaurants, 115
sights and attractions,
163–164
Children's Pool, 4, 142, 157
Christmas on the Prado, 228
Christmas Open House and
Parade, Coronado, 18
Chula Vista Nature Center,
161, 172
Cinco de Mayo
Celebration, 15

Cinemas, 226, 228
Circa a.d., 205
City Ballet, 219
City of San Diego Bicycle
   Coordinator, 173
Claire de Lune Coffee
   Lounge, 223–224
Classical music, 218
Classic Sailing Adventures,
   170, 174
Climate, 12–13
   Tijuana (Mexico), 276
Cloud 9 Shuttle, 21, 50
Club Montage, 225
Coastal Rail Pass, 43
Coaster, 61, 229
Coast Walk, 157, 163, 178
Coffeehouses and cafes, 4
   Internet, 27
   with performances,
      223–225
Collette Tours, 33
Collision Damage Waiver
   (CDW), 58
Colorado House, 196
Columbus Direct, 39
Comedy clubs, 221
The Comedy Store, 221
Condor Ridge, 136
Consolidators, 31
Consulates, 44
Contact Tours, 168
Continental Airlines, 29
Continental Airlines
   Vacations, 33
Convention Center, 165, 193
Coors Amphitheatre, 221
Copley Symphony Hall, 221
Coronado, 3, 54
   accommodations, 92–96
   map, 93
   brief description of, 56–57
   restaurants, 126–129
   shopping, 209–210, 214
   sights and attractions,
      160–161, 163
Coronado Bay Bridge, 51, 160
Coronado Beach, 141
Coronado Cab Company, 61
Coronado Christmas Open
   House and Parade, 18
Coronado Hospital, 63
Coronado Municipal Golf
   Course, 176
Coronado Touring, 169
Coronado Visitors Center, 51
Council Travel, 24
Country Carriages
   (Julian), 264
County Administration Center,
   165, 190
County Fair, San Diego, 15

Cox Arena, 221
The Cracker Factory Antiques
   Shopping Center, 211
Crafts Market
   (Tijuana), 278–279
Credit cards, 11
   for foreign visitors, 40
   frequent-flier, 31
Critter Country
   (Disneyland), 252
Croce's Nightclubs, 220
Culinary Cottage
   (Julian), 265
Currency and currency
   exchange, 40
   Tijuana (Mexico), 276
Customs regulations, 38–39
Cuyamaca, Lake, 266
Cuyamaca Rancho State
   Park, 266

D ale's Swim Shop, 209
Dance, 219
   Nations of San Diego
      International Dance
      Festival, 14
Dance clubs and
   cabarets, 221
David Zapf Gallery, 212
Davy Crockett's Explorer
   Canoes (Disneyland), 252
Day at the Docks, 15, 181
Daylight savings time, 46
Day Tripper pass, 59
Del Mar, 229–234
Del Mar Beach, 143
Del Mar National Horse
   Show, 15, 182
Del Mar Plaza, 231
Del Mar Racetrack & Fair-
   grounds, 16, 181, 227, 230
Del Mar Satellite
   Wagering, 227
Del Mar State Beach, 230
Delta Airlines, 29
Delta Vacations, 33
Dentists, 63
Department stores, 213
Dining. See Restaurants
Disabilities, travelers with,
   20–21
Disneyland Monorail, 253
Disneyland Railroad, 251
Disneyland Resort,
   2, 247–256
   admission, hours and
      information, 248–250
   map, 249
   sights and attractions
      California Adventure,
      253–255

Disneyland, 251–253
   Downtown Disney,
      255–256
   traveling to, 248
   visitor information, 248
Doctors, 63
Dog Beach, 24, 141
Dog Beach Dog Wash, 24
Dolphin Interaction Program
   (SeaWorld), 137
Downtown Disney, 255–256
Downtown Information
   Center, 167
Downtown San Diego, 54–55
   accommodations, 67–74
   map, 69
   restaurants, 102–107, 224
   map, 103
   shopping, 203–204
   map, 205
   sights and attractions,
      151–153, 162
Driver's licenses, 37
Drugstores, 63
Dudley's Bakery
   (Santa Ysabel), 265

E agle and High Peak
   Mines (Julian), 264
El Cid Campeador, 200
Elderhostel, 22
Electricity, 43
Ellen Browning Scripps Park,
   142, 157
El Prado, 144, 165
El Toreo (Tijuana), 279
Embassies and consulates, 44
Emerald City Surf &
   Sport, 140
Emerald City–The Boarding
   Source, 180
Emergencies, 44, 63
Emerging Horizons, 21
Encinitas, 234–241
Entry requirements, 36–37
Escondido, 245–246
Escorted tours, 33
Espresso Net, 27
Expedia, 25, 26
Eyeglass repair, 63

F allbrook Winery, 167
Fall Flower Tour (Encinitas),
   17–18
Families with children, 23
   accommodations, 80
   restaurants, 115
   sights and attractions,
      163–164
Family Travel Files, 23

Family Travel Network, 23
Family Travel Times, 23
FANTASMIC! show
    (Disneyland), 253
Fantasyland (Disneyland),
    253
Farmers markets and stands,
    4, 128, 213–214
    Julian, 265
Fashion Valley Center, 214
Fastmail, 27
FASTPASS system
    (Disneyland), 250
Fax machines, 46
Ferries, 61
    to Coronado, 3, 192
The Ferry Landing
    Marketplace, 209–210
Festival of the Bells, 16
Festivals and special events,
    13–18
Festival Stage, 228
Fiesta Island, 141
Fiesta Village (Knott's
    Berry Farm), 257
52-mile San Diego Scenic
    Drive, 162
Fingerhut Gallery, 211
Firehouse Museum, 151
Fishing, 174–175
    Day at the Docks,
        15, 174, 181
    tournaments, 181
The Flame, 225
Flea markets, 214
Fleet Science Center,
    147–148
Flicks, 225
Flights.com, 31
Flik's Fun Fair (California
    Adventure), 254
The Flower Fields at Carlsbad
    Ranch, 14, 236
Flowers, 166
FlyCheap, 31
Flying Wheels Travel, 21
Folk Arts Rare Records, 215
Font's Point, 270
Football, 181
Foreign visitors, 36–47
    customs regulations, 38–39
    entry requirements, 36–37
    health insurance, 39–40
    money matters, 40–41
    traveling to the United
        States, 42–43
Fountain, San Diego, 202
Four Points
    Communications, 29
Four Seasons Resort Aviara
    Golf Club, 176
4th & B, 220

Foxploration (near Rosarito
    Beach), 280–281
Freddy's Teddies & Toys, 215
Frequent-flier clubs, 31
Frey Block Building, 189
Frommers.com, 26
Frontier Airlines, 29
Frontierland (Disneyland),
    252–253
F. W. Woolworth Building, 186

Gardens, 166–167
    Balboa Park, 166, 202
Gaslamp Black Historical
    Society, 24
Gaslamp Quarter, 4, 54–55,
    151, 162, 165
    shopping, 203–204
    walking tour, 184–189
Gaslamp Quarter Historical
    Foundation, 169, 184
Gaslamp Stadium, 226
Gasoline, 44
Gay and lesbian travelers
    information and resources,
        21–22
    nightlife, 225–226
    San Diego Lesbian and
        Gay Pride Parade, Rally,
        and Festival, 16, 21–22
Gay Men's Health Crisis, 37
Geisel Library, 157, 165
George's Camera & Video, 63
Ghosts & Gravestones
    tour, 169
Ghost Town (Knott's
    Berry Farm), 257
Giant Dipper Roller Coaster,
    156–157
Giovanni's Room, 22
Girard Gourmet, 128
Gliderport, 163, 177–178
The Globe Theatres, 164, 217
Golden Acorn Casino Travel
    Center, 227
Golden Hill, 55
The Golden State (California
    Adventure), 254
Golden Vine Winery
    (California Adventure), 254
Golf, 175–177
    Anza-Borrego Desert State
        Park, 270
    Buick Invitational, 14
    Tijuana (Mexico), 282
    tournaments, 181
The Gondola Company, 167
GoToMyPC, 27–28
Greyhound racing, 227
Greyhound/Trailways, 32, 43
Grizzly River Run (California
    Adventure), 254

Grunion, 6
Grunion Run, 227
GSM (Global System
    for Mobiles) wireless
    network, 28

Hall of Champions Sports
    Museum, 148
H & M Landing, 175
Hang gliding, 177–178
Harbor Days Festival
    (Oceanside), 241
Harbor seals, 142, 157, 168.
    See also Seals
The Harbor Vacations
    Club, 174
Harrah's Rincon Casino &
    Resort, 227
Haunted Mansion
    (Disneyland), 252
Hawaiian Airlines, 29
Health Canada, 40
Health concerns, 19–20
Health insurance, 19
    for foreign visitors, 39–40
Heart of the Zoo project, 2
Heritage Park, 154, 197
Hertz, 21
Hiking, 178
    Anza-Borrego Desert State
        Park, 270
Hillcrest Cinema, 226
Hillcrest Cityfest Street
    Fair, 16
Hillcrest/Uptown, 54, 55–56
    accommodations, 74–77
        map, 75
    restaurants, 107–112, 224
        map, 109
    shopping, 204–206, 213
        map, 207
Hilton San Diego Resort, 173
Historical Society Museum,
    San Diego, 148
HIV-positive visitors, 37
Holiday Bowl, 181
Holidays, 44
Hollywood Pictures Backlot
    (California Adventure), 255
"Honey, I Shrunk the Audi-
    ence" (Disneyland), 253
Hornblower Cruises,
    168, 170, 222
Horse-drawn carriages,
    Julian, 264
Horse racing, 16
Horse racing and shows,
    181–182
Horton Grand Hotel, 188
Horton Plaza, 151, 184, 186,
    189, 203–204

Horton Plaza Park, 186
Hospitals, 63
Hostels, 67
Hot-air ballooning,
    6, 15, 172, 231
Hotel del Coronado, 161
Hotel Discounts, 66
HotelDiscounts.com, 26
Hotel Docs, 63
Hotel Lester, 189
Hotel Locators, 66
Hotels. *See also*
    Accommodations Index
    Anaheim, 257–260
    best bets, 6–8
    Borrego Springs, 270–272
    Carlsbad, 238–240
    Del Mar, 231–233
    Escondido, 245
    family-friendly, 80
    Julian, 266–267
    money-saving tips, 65–67
    Oceanside, 242–243
    pet-friendly, 24
    Rancho Santa Fe, 244
    reservation services, 66
    San Diego, 65–97
    shopping online for, 25–26
    Tijuana (Mexico), 282
    tipping, 46
    what's new, 1
Hotels.com, 26
Hot lines, 63
Hot Monkey Love Café, 224
Hotwire, 25
House of Charm, 198
House of Pacific Relations
    International Cottages,
    146, 200
Humphrey's, 4, 221
Hyperion Theater (California
    Adventure), 255

I Can, 21
Ice Capades Chalet, 179
Ice hockey, 182
Ice-skating, 179
Identity theft or fraud, 12
IGLTA (International
    Gay & Lesbian Travel
    Association), 22
Immaculate Conception
    Catholic Church, 196
Immigration and customs
    clearance, 42
Imperial Beach, 141
Independence Day Parade
    (Rancho Santa Fe), 243–244
Indian Fair, 15
Indian Trails (Knott's
    Berry Farm), 257

Indiana Jones Adventure,
    252
Ingle Building, 189
In Good Taste, 209
Inline skating, 179
Inspiration Point, 154
Insurance, 19
Intellicast, 29
International Ameripass, 43
International Gay &
    Lesbian Travel Association
    (IGLTA), 22
International Student
    Identity Card (ISIC), 24
International Visitor
    Information Center, 10,
    50–51, 54
International visitors, 36–47
    customs regulations,
    38–39
    entry requirements, 36–37
    health insurance, 39–40
    money matters, 40–41
    traveling to the United
    States, 42–43
International Youth Travel
    Card (IYTC), 24
Internet access, 26–28
Internet cafes, 27
Internet kiosks, 27
InTouch USA, 41
IPass network, 28
Irish Festival, 14
I2roam, 28
ISIC (International Student
    Identity Card), 24
Island Hoppers, 204, 209
It's a Small World
    (Disneyland), 253
IYTC (International Youth
    Travel Card), 24

J apan Airlines, 42
Japanese Friendship Garden,
    146, 166, 201
JetBlue Airways, 1, 29
Jewish Community
    Center, 180
Jim Henson's Muppet-
    Vision 3D (California
    Adventure), 255
Jogging, 179
John Cole's Book Shop, 212
John's Fifth Avenue
    Luggage, 215
Julian, 262–268
Julian Cider Mill, 265
Julian Drug Store & Miner's
    Diner, 264
Julian Fall Apple Harvest, 17
Julian Pie Company,
    264–265

Julian Tea & Cottage Arts, 265
Julian Weed & Craft Show,
    16, 263
June Gloom, 138
Junípero Serra Museum,
    154, 165

K ahuna Bob's Surf
    School, 180
Kayaking, 4, 174, 241–242
Kearns Memorial Swimming
    Pool, 180
Keating Building, 186–187
Ken Cinema, 226
Kendall Frost Marsh, 172
Kickers, 225
Kite Festival, Kiwanis Ocean
    Beach, 14
Kiwanis Ocean Beach Kite
    Festival, 14
Knott's Berry Farm (Buena
    Park), 256–257
Knott's Soak City U.S.A., 161
Kobey's Swap Meet, 214
Kurt's Camera Repair, 63

L a Casa de Estudillo,
    194–195
L.A. Cetto Winery (Cava de
    Vinos), 277
La Costa Resort and Spa, 175
La Jolla, 54, 165
    accommodations, 85–92
    map, 87
    brief description of, 56
    restaurants, 120–126
    map, 121
    shopping, 209
    sights and attractions,
    157–160
    free, 162–163
La Jolla Cab, 61
La Jolla Chamber Music
    Society, 218
La Jolla Cove, 142–143, 157
La Jolla Half Marathon, 182
La Jolla Playhouse, 217
La Jolla Recreation
    Center, 180
La Jolla Rough Water
    Swim, 17, 180
La Jolla Shoe Gallery, 209
La Jolla Shores, 143
La Jolla Surf Systems, 180
La Jolla Tennis Club, 180
La Jolla Village, 226
La Jolla Visitor Center, 51
La Jolla Woman's Club, 157
Lake Cuyamaca, 175
Lake Miramar Reservoir, 178

Lakes Line, 175
Lamb's Players Theatre, 217–218
La Provençale, 209
Las Flores Hotel, 189
LastMinute.com, 25
La Valencia Hotel, 157
Layout of San Diego, 51, 54
Lee Palm Sportfishers, 175
Legal aid, 44–45
LEGOLAND California (Carlsbad), 133, 235–236
Lesbian and Gay Men's Community Center, 21
Le Travel Store, 54, 215
Liberty Carousel, 157
Lincoln Hotel, 188
Lips, 222
Liquid Foundation Surf Shop, 206
Liquor laws, 45, 63
Little Italy, 55, 165
    restaurants, 102–107
Live-music clubs, 219–221
Living Room Coffeehouse, 27
Llama Trek (Julian), 266
Llewelyn Building, 187
Longboard Surf Club Competition, 17
Longboard Surf Contest (Oceanside), 242
Loss/Damage Waiver (LDW), 58
Lost-luggage insurance, 19
Lost or stolen wallet or credit card, 11–12
Louis Bank of Commerce, 186
Lou's Records, 215

Macy's, 213
Maderas Golf Club, 175
Mail, 45
Mail2web, 27
Main Street U.S.A. (Disneyland), 251
Maliboomer (California Adventure), 255
Malls, 214
The Many Adventures of Winnie the Pooh (Disneyland), 2, 252
Many Hands, 212
The Map Centre, 215
Mapquest, 29
Maps
    bike, 62
    street, 54
Marathons, 14, 182
Marian Bear Memorial Park, 178
Marie Hitchcock Puppet Theatre, 164

Mariner's Point, 141
Marion's Childcare, 62
Maritime Museum, 152, 190
Marriott San Diego Hotel & Marina, 193
Marston Building, 186
Marston House, 146–147, 165
Martini Ranch, 222–223
Martin Luther King Jr. Promenade, 165
Mary Star of the Sea, 157
Mason Street School, 196
MasterCard ATM Locator, 29
Matterhorn Bobsleds (Disneyland), 253
Maurice Car'rie Winery, 247
MayflowerTours, 33
McClellan Palomar Airport, 229
McCoy House, 194
The Meadows Del Mar, 175
MEDEX International, 19
Medic Alert Identification Tag, 20
Medical insurance, 19
    for foreign visitors, 39–40
Medical requirements for entry, 37
Mercado de Artesanías (Tijuana), 278–279
Mercado Hidalgo (Tijuana), 279
Metropolitan Hotel, 187
Metropolitan Transit System (MTS), 49
Mickey's Toontown (Disneyland), 253
Minear Building, 189
Mingei International Museum, 147
Mission Basilica San Diego de Alcala, 153, 154, 165
Mission Bay, 4, 56, 156, 173
Mission Bay and the Beaches
    accommodations, 80–85
    map, 81
    restaurants, 115–120
    map, 117
    shopping, 206–207
    map, 208
    sights and attractions, 156–157, 162
Mission Bay Boat Parade of Lights, 18
Mission Bay Park, 141
Mission Bay Sportcenter, 174
Mission Bay Visitor Information Center, 51
Mission Beach, 56, 142
Mission Beach Club, 173
Mission Hills, 165
Mission Hills Nursery, 166

Mission Point, 141
Mission San Luis Rey (Oceanside), 241
Mission Trails Regional Park, 154, 155, 162, 169, 172, 178
Mission Valley, 56
    accommodations, 77–80
    restaurants, 112–115
    shopping, 206
    sights and attractions, 153–156, 162
Mission Valley Center, 214
Model Railroad Museum, San Diego, 149
Mom's Pies (Julian), 264
Money matters, 10–12
Moonlight Beach (Encinitas), 143, 237
Moss Rehab Hospital, 21
Mount Palomar Winery, 247
Mt. Woodson Golf Club, 176
Movies, 226, 228
Movies Before the Mast, 228
Multicultural travelers, 23–24
Mundo Divertido (Tijuana), 277
Murray, Lake, 178
Museo de Cera (Tijuana), 276
Museum of Contemporary Art San Diego Downtown, 152, 162
Museum of Contemporary Art San Diego La Jolla, 157, 158–159
Museum of History and Art, 161
Museum of Making Music (Carlsbad), 235
Museum of Man, San Diego, 23, 150, 198
Museum of Photographic Arts, 147, 226
Music
    classical, 218
    live-music clubs, 219–221
Music stores, 215

Nairobi Village, 136
Nations of San Diego International Dance Festival, 14, 219
Native Americans, 15, 23, 34, 154, 156, 226, 257, 270
Natural History Museum, San Diego, 150, 170, 178, 201
Neighborhoods
    brief descriptions of, 54–57
    map, 52–53
Nelson Photo Supply, 63

Neurosciences Institute, 165–166
New Orleans Square (Disneyland), 252
Newport Ave. Antique Center, 207
Newport Avenue Antiques, 207
Newspapers and magazines, 63
Nightlife and entertainment, 216–228
    bars and cocktail lounges, 222–223
    comedy clubs, 221
    cruises with entertainment, 221–222
    current listings, 216
    dance clubs and cabarets, 221
    gay and lesbian, 225–226
    live-music clubs, 219–221
    performing arts, 217–219
    tickets, 216–217
    Tijuana (Mexico), 284
    what's new, 2
Nordstrom, 213
North County Nursery Hoppers Association, 236
Northern San Diego County
    beaches, 143, 229
    inland, 243–247
    map, 231
    nurseries, 211
Northwest Airlines, 29
Numbers, 225
Nunu's Cocktail Lounge, 223

Obelisk, 22
Obelisk Bookstore, 212–213
Ocean Beach, 56, 141
    farmers market, 213–214
Ocean Beach Antique District, 207
Ocean Beach Antique Mall, 207
Ocean Front Walk, 142
Ocean's Eleven Casino (Oceanside), 242
Oceanside, 229, 241–243
Oceanside Beach, 242
Off the Record, 205, 215
Old City Hall, 187
Old Globe Theatre, 198
Old Julian Book House, 265
Old Town Liquor and Deli, 128
Old Town State Historic Park, 56, 156
    accommodations, 77–80
    restaurants, 112–115

shopping, 206
sights and attractions, 153–156, 162
walking tour, 193–197
Old Town Trolley Tours, 167, 169
Olé Madrid, 221
OMNIMAX theater, 226
On Broadway, 223
The Onyx Room, 223
Open Air Theater, 221
Open World Magazine, 21
Opera, 219
Orange Cab, 61
Orange Stinger (California Adventure), 255
Orbitz, 25
Orfila Vineyards, 167
Organized tours, 167–170
Organ recitals in Balboa Park, 4, 150, 162, 200, 228
Ould Sod, 223
Outdoor activities, 170–180
Over the Line Tournament, 141

Pacific Beach, 54, 56, 142, 214
Pacific Beach Sun and Sea, 179
Package tours, 32–33
    Disneyland Resort, 251
Packing for your trip, 18
Pala Casino, 227
Palm Canyon, 200
Palomar, 246–247
Palomar Observatory, 246–247
Panama-California Exposition, 165
Pandas, 135
Panda Services, 62
Paradise Pier (California Adventure), 254–255
Paragliding, 177–178
Parking, 58–59
Passports, 37–38
Passport to Balboa Park, 146
Pechanga Resort & Casino, 227
Pedroreña House, 196
Performance art gallery, 226
Performing arts, 217–219
Petco Park, 2, 151, 181
Petrol, 44
Pets, traveling with, 24–25
Photo Caravans (Wild Animal Park), 136
Photographic Arts, Museum of, 147, 226
Picnic fare, 9, 107, 128

Pilar's, 206
Pine Hills Dinner Theater (Julian), 268
Pioneer Cemetery (Julian), 266
Pirate's Cove, 157
Pirates of the Caribbean (Disneyland), 252
Pizza, 110
Plaza del Zapato (Tijuana), 279
Plaza de Toros Monumental (Tijuana), 279
The Plunge, 156, 180
Poinsettia Festival Street Fair (Encinitas), 17–18
Point Loma Camera Store, 63
Point Loma Seafoods, 128
Point Loma Sportfishing, 175
Police, 64
Polo, 182
Port of San Diego Day at the Docks, 15, 174, 181
Post offices, 64
Prado of Balboa Park, 144, 165
Pratt Gallery, 212
Prescription medications, 20
Presidio Park, 154
Priceline, 25
Primavera Pastry Caffe, 128
Princess Pub & Grille, 223
Professional Photographic Repair, 63
Pueblo Amigo (Tijuana), 284
Puerto Nuevo (Mexico), 6, 281

Qantas, 42
Quail Botanical Gardens (Encinitas), 166, 237
Qualcomm Stadium, 181, 220
Quikbook, 66

Rainfall, average monthly, 13
Ram's Hill Country Club, 270
Rancho Bernardo Inn, 176
Rancho Santa Fe, 243–245
Red Fox Room, 223
Redwood Creek Challenge Trail (California Adventure), 254
Resort Watersports, 179
Restaurants, 98–129. See also Restaurants Index
    Anaheim, 260–262
    best bets, 8–9
    Borrego Springs, 272

Carlsbad area, 240–241
by cuisine, 99–101
Del Mar, 233–234
family-friendly, 115
Julian, 267–268
late-night, 224
Oceanside, 243
with ocean views, 125
off the beaten path, 129
parking near, 99
Rancho Santa Fe, 244–245
Tijuana (Mexico), 282–284
tipping, 46
what's new, 1–2
Restrooms, 47, 64
Reuben H. Fleet Science
Center, 147–148
Rich's, 225
Ride Link Bicycle
Information, 173
Rite-Aid, 63
Riverwalk Golf Club,
176–177
Roar & Snore program
(Wild Animal Park), 136
Robinson-Rose House, 194
Rodeo Santa Fe
(Tijuana), 284
Rosarito-Ensenada 50–Mile
Fun Bicycle Ride (Mexico),
14, 17, 173
Royal Pie Bakery
Building, 189

S afety, 20
for foreign visitors, 41
Sail USA, 174
St. Patrick's Day Parade, 14
*St. Peter and the Vatican:
The Legacy of the Popes*, 1
Sales tax, 64
Salk Institute for Biological
Studies, 157, 165
Sanborn's (Tijuana), 278
Sandcastle Competition, U.S.
Open, 16, 141
San Diego Aerospace
Museum, 148, 201
San Diego Art + Sol, 10, 23
San Diego Audubon
Society, 172
San Diego Automotive
Museum, 148, 200
San Diego Ballet, 219
San Diego Bay, 173
San Diego Bed & Breakfast
Guild, 67
San Diego Boat Parade of
Lights, 18
San Diego Cab, 61

San Diego Chargers, 181
San Diego City Store, 204
San Diego Convention and
Visitors Bureau, 33
San Diego Convention
Center, 165, 193
San Diego County Bicycle
Coalition, 173
San Diego County Dental
Society, 63
San Diego County Fair,
15, 230
San Diego Crew Classic,
14–15
San Diego Cruise Ship
Terminal, 190
San Diego Dance
Alliance, 219
San Diego Divers Supply,
140, 179
San Diego Floral
Association, 167
San Diego Gay & Lesbian
Chamber of Commerce, 22
*San Diego Gay and Lesbian
Times*, 22
San Diego Golf
Reservations, 175
San Diego Gulls, 182
San Diego Hall of
Champions Sports
Museum, 148
San Diego Harbor Excursions,
168, 170, 222
San Diego Historical Society
Museum, 148
*San Diego Home-Garden
Lifestyles*, 64
San Diego Hotel
Reservations, 66
San Diego International
Airport, 49–50
accommodations near, 97
San Diego International
Triathlon, 182
San Diego Junior Theatre,
164, 218
San Diego–La Jolla
Underwater Park, 157
San Diego Lesbian and Gay
Pride Parade, Rally, and
Festival, 16, 21–22
San Diego magazine, 7,
63–64
San Diego Marathon,
14, 182
San Diego Model Railroad
Museum, 149
San Diego Museum of Art,
149–150, 200
San Diego Museum of Man,
23, 150, 198

San Diego Natural History
Museum, 150, 169, 170,
178, 201
San Diego Oceans
Foundation, 179
San Diego Opera, 219
San Diego Outback
Tours, 270
San Diego Padres, 2, 181
San Diego Performing Arts
League, 10
San Diego Polo Club, 182
San Diego Region
Bike Map, 62
San Diego Repertory
Theatre, 218
San Diego Sockers, 182
San Diego Spirit, 182
San Diego Sports Arena, 220
San Diego Surfing
Academy, 180
San Diego Symphony,
16, 218
San Diego Trolley, 2, 3
San Diego Union Printing
Office, 196
San Diego Union-Tribune,
7, 51, 63
San Diego Weekly Reader,
7, 51, 63, 220
San Diego Wild Animal Park,
134–137, 164, 166
San Diego Zoo, 2, 35,
130, 132–135, 163,
166, 202, 228
Santa Fe Depot, 192
Sav-On Drugs, 63
Scenic flights, 172
Scott White Contemporary
Art, 212
Scuba diving, 179
Scuba San Diego, 179
Sculpture Garden of the
Museum of Art, 198
SDAI Museum of the Living
Artist, 150
Sea and Land
Adventures, 168
Seaforth Boat Rental, 174
Seaforth Sportfishing, 175
Seals, 4, 137, 138, 142, 157,
168, 179
Seaport Village, 151,
192–193, 204
Seasons, 13
SeaWorld San Diego, 133,
137–138, 164
Self Realization Fellowship
(Encinitas), 238
Senior travel, 22–23
Señor Frogs (Tijuana), 284

Serra Museum, 154, 165
Sevilla, 221
Shamu Adventure
  (SeaWorld), 137
Shopping, 203–215
  Julian, 265
  Tijuana (Mexico), 278–279
  top neighborhoods for,
    203–211
Side-Step, 25
Sierra Club, hikes, 178
Sights and attractions
  free, 161–163
  for kids, 163–164
  map, 131
  special-interest, 165–167
  suggested itineraries,
    130, 132
Silver Strand, 141
Singing Hills Country Club
  at Sycuan, 177
Site59.com, 25
Six Degrees, 225
Skating, 179
Skysurfer Balloon
  Company, 172
Smarter Living, 25
Smoking, 64, 220
Snorkeling, 179
Soarin' Over California
  (California Adventure), 254
Soccer, 182
Society for Accessible Travel
  and Hospitality, 21
Solana Beach, 234–241
Soledad, Mount, 158
Soul of America, 24
South Carlsbad State
  Beach, 237
Southwest Airlines, 29
Southwest Airlines
  Vacations, 33
Space Mountain
  (Disneyland), 253
Spanish Village Art
  Center, 202
Special events and festivals,
  13–18
Spectator sports, 181–183
  Tijuana (Mexico), 279–282
Spencer-Ogden Building, 187
Splash Mountain
  (Disneyland), 252
Spreckels Organ Pavilion, 4,
  150, 162, 200, 228
Spreckels Theatre, 221
Stadium Golf Center, 175
Starlight Theater, 228
Star of India, 152, 168,
  190, 228
Star Tours (Disneyland), 253
STA Travel, 24, 31

Street maps, 54
Street Scene, 17
Stuart Collection, 157,
  160, 163
Student travel, 24
Studio Arts Complex, 212
Sunglasses, 18
Sunny Jim Cave, 157, 209
Sunset-watching, 4, 162, 193
  accommodations, 84
  beaches, 4, 56
  cruises, 174
  flights, 172
  Font's Point, 270
  hikes, 136
  restaurants, 118, 119, 122
Superstar Limo (California
  Adventure), 255
Surf Diva, 180
Surfing, 179–180
  competitions, 17
  Oceanside, 242
Sushi, 226
Suzuki Rock 'n' Roll
  Marathon, 182
Swami's Beach, 143
Swami's Beach
  (Encinitas), 238
Swimming, 180
  La Jolla Rough Water
    Swim, 17
Sycuan Casino & Resort,
  226–227

T aboo Studio, 212
Taco stands at the
  beaches, 140
Tamarisk Grove (Borrego
  Springs), 272
Tauck World Discovery, 33
Taxes, 45, 64
Taxis
  to/from airport, 50
  in San Diego, 61
  tipping, 46
Telephone, 45–46
  area codes, 62
Temecula, 167, 246
Temecula Balloon & Wine
  Festival, 172
Temecula Valley Balloon &
  Wine Festival, 15
Temecula Valley Vintners
  Association, 247
Temperatures, average
  monthly, 13
Tennis, 180
  tournaments, 183
Theater, 217–218
  for kids, 164
Thin, 223

Thomas Bros. Guide, 54
Thornton Hospital, 63
Thornton Winery, 246–247
Thoroughbred racing
  season, 16
Thousand Mile Outdoor
  Wear, 211
Tide pools, 140
Tijuana (Mexico), 272–284
  accommodations, 282
  climate and weather, 276
  map, 273
  nightlife, 284
  restaurants, 282–284
  transportation, 275
  traveling to, 274–275
  visitor information, 275
Tijuana Country Club, 282
Tile Shop, 204
Time zones, 46, 64
Timken Museum of Art,
  150–151
Tipping, 46
T-Mobile Hotspot, 28
Toilets, 47
Tolán (Tijuana), 278
Tomorrowland
  (Disneyland), 253
Top Of the Cove, 223
Top of the Park, 226
Torrey Pines Gliderport, 163,
  177–178
Torrey Pines Golf
  Course, 177
Torrey Pines State Beach,
  143, 230
Torrey Pines State
  Reserve, 3–4, 157, 160,
  169, 172, 178
Torrey Pines Visitors
  Center, 165
Tourist information, 10,
  50–51
Tourmaline Surfing Park, 142
Tours
  aerial, 172, 238
  Anza-Borrego Desert State
    Park, 270
  bike, 173
  escorted, 33
  organized (guided), 149,
    167–170
  package, 32–33
    Disneyland Resort, 251
Toys, 215
Trainer for a Day program
  (SeaWorld), 137
Train travel, 32, 61
  for foreign visitors, 42–43
  to San Diego, 50
Transit information, 64
Transit Store, 50, 54, 59

Transit Travel ID, 20
Transportation, 57–62
   by bicycle, 62
   by bus, 59–60
   by car, 57–59
   for disabled travelers,
      20–21
   by ferry, 61
   by taxi, 61
   by train, 61
   by trolley, 60–61
   by water taxi, 62
Travel accessories, 215
Travel Assistance
   International, 19
TravelAxe, 26
Travel CUTS, 24
Traveler's Aid
   International, 44
Traveler's checks, 11
   for foreign visitors, 40
Traveler's Depot, 213
Travelex America, 49
Travel insurance, 19
Travelocity, 25, 26
Triathlons, 182
Trip-cancellation
   insurance, 19
Trolleys, 60–61
Trolley tours, 169
Tuna Harbor, 192
Turf Supper Club, 223
Twiggs Tea and Coffee Co.,
   224–225
Twilight in the Park, 15, 228
Twilight Zone Tower of Terror
   (California Adventure),
   2, 254, 255
Twin Peaks Press, 21

UCSD Medical
   Center–Hillcrest, 63
Underwater Pumpkin
   Carving Contest, 17
United Airlines, 29
United Express, 29
United Nations Building,
   146, 200
United Vacations, 33
University of California, San
   Diego (UCSD), 157
University Towne Center
   (UTC), 214
Upstart Crow, 204
Uptown, 55–56. See
   Hillcrest/Uptown
U.S. Air Carrier
   Memorial, 192
US Airways, 29

USA Railpass, 43
USIT, 24
U.S. Open, 181
U.S. Open Sandcastle
   Competition, 16, 141

Van Roekel Vineyards, 247
Viejas Casino, 227
Village Hat Shop, 205
Villa Montezuma, 152, 165
Visa ATM Locator, 29
Visas, 36
Visitor information, 10,
   50–51
Visit USA, 42
Volcan Mountain
   Preserve, 266

Walkabout International,
   162, 169
Walking tours
   guided, 169
   self-guided, 184–202
      Balboa Park, 197–202
      The Embarcadero,
         190–193
      Gaslamp Quarter,
         184–189
      Old Town, 193–197
Walt Disney Travel Company,
   33, 251
Walter Andersen's
   Nursery, 166
Warm Hearth (Julian), 265
Warwick's Books, 213
Waterfront park, 192
Water taxis, 62
Watts-Robinson
   Building, 186
Wayport, 28
Wear It Again Sam, 205
Weather, 13
   information, 64
   Tijuana (Mexico), 276
Weather.com, 29
Websites (online sources)
   airfares, 25
   best, 7
   traveler's toolbox, 29
Weidners' Gardens
   (Encinitas), 236
Western Union, 12
Wgasa Bush Line Railway,
   135–136
Whale-watching, 13, 18, 170
Whaley House, 156, 196–197
Wheelchair Getaways, 21
Whitney Building, 189
Whole Foods, 9, 107

Wild Animal Park, San Diego,
   132–137, 164, 166
Wildflowers, 14, 263,
   268, 270
Wildflower Show
   (Julian), 263
Wild Water Wilderness
   (Knott's Berry Farm), 257
William Heath Davis House
   Museum, 152, 188
William Heise County
   Park, 266
William Penn Hotel, 187
Windansea Beach, 142
Wines and wineries, 167
   Temecula, 246–247
   Temecula Valley Balloon &
      Wine Festival, 15
   Tijuana (Mexico), 277–278
Wireless networks, 28
Wooden Boat Festival, 181
World Bodysurfing
   Championships, 17
World Championship
   Over-the-Line Tournament,
   16, 181
World of Disney, 256

Yahoo! Mail, 27
Yard House, 2
Yellow Cab, 61
YMCA, 180
Yuma Building, 187

Zoo, San Diego, 2, 35,
   130, 132–135, 163, 166,
   202, 228

ACCOMMODATIONS
Anaheim Vagabond
   Hotel, 259
Artists' Loft (Julian), 267
Balboa Park Inn, 76
Bay Club Hotel, 97
The Beach Cottages, 84–85
Beach Haven Inn, 85
Beach Terrace Inn
   (Carlsbad), 240
The Bed & Breakfast Inn at
   La Jolla, 90–91
Best Western Anaheim
   Stardust, 260
Best Western Bayside Inn, 72
Best Western Blue Sea
   Lodge, 83
Best Western Inn by the
   Sea, 91
Best Western Seven Seas, 79

Borrego Valley Inn (Borrego Springs), 270–271
Bristol Hotel, 72
Candy Cane Inn (Anaheim), 259
Catamaran Resort Hotel, 80, 83
Comfort Inn–Downtown, 73
Coronado Inn, 95
The Cottage, 76
Crone's Cobblestone Cottage Bed & Breakfast, 75
Crystal Pier Hotel, 83
Dana Inn and Marina, 84
Del Mar Motel on the Beach, 232
The Disneyland Hotel, 257–258
Disney's Grand Californian Hotel (Anaheim), 258
El Cordova Hotel, 96
Elsbree House, 85
Embassy Suites Hotel San Diego Bay–Downtown, 68
Empress Hotel of La Jolla, 91
Four Seasons Resort Aviara (Carlsbad), 238–239
Gaslamp Plaza Suites, 7, 74
Glorietta Bay Inn, 95–96
The Grande Colonial, 88–89
Grand Hotel Tijuana (Mexico), 282
Harbor Vacations Club, 7, 72–73
Harbor View Days Inn Suites, 73
Heritage Park Bed & Breakfast Inn, 8, 78
HI Downtown Hostel, 67
Hilton San Diego Airport/Harbor Island, 97
Holiday Inn Express–Old Town, 78
Holiday Inn on the Bay, 71, 80
Horton Grand, 73
Hotel del Coronado, 6, 57, 92, 94
Hotel Lucerna (Tijuana), 282
Hotel Parisi, 8, 86
Howard Johnson Hotel (Anaheim), 260
Hyatt Regency La Jolla, 86, 166
The Inn at Rancho Santa Fe, 244
Julian Gold Rush Hotel, 267
Julian White House, 267
Keating House, 76–77
La Casa del Zorro Desert Resort (Borrego Springs), 271
La Costa Resort and Spa (Carlsbad), 239

La Jolla Beach & Tennis Club, 89
La Jolla Cove Suites, 91
La Jolla Village Lodge, 92
La Pensione Hotel, 7, 74
L'Auberge Del Mar Resort & Spa, 231–232
La Valencia Hotel, 8, 86–88
Les Artistes (Del Mar), 232–233
The Lodge at Torrey Pines, 6, 88
Loews Coronado Bay Resort, 24, 80, 93
Manchester Grand Hyatt San Diego, 8, 68
Marriott Coronado Island Resort, 94–95
Marriott Residence Inn, 86
Marriott San Diego Hotel & Marina, 6, 68–69
Mission Valley Travelodge, 79–80
Motel 6 Hotel Circle, 80
Ocean Park Inn, 84
Oceanside Marina Inn, 242
Omni San Diego Hotel, 1
Orchard Hill Country Inn (Julian), 267
Pacific Terrace Hotel, 82
Palm Canyon Resort (Borrego Springs), 270
The Palms at Indian Head (Borrego Springs), 271
Paradise Point Resort & Spa, 6–7, 80, 82
Park Manor Suites, 77
Pelican Cove Inn (Carlsbad), 240
Point Loma, 67
Portofino Inn & Suites (Anaheim), 259
Radisson Resort Knott's Berry Farm (Anaheim), 260
Ramada Plaza, 80
Rancho Valencia Resort (Rancho Santa Fe), 244
Random Oaks Ranch (Julian), 267
Red Lion Hanalei Hotel, 78
Rosarito Beach Hotel (Mexico), 280
Scripps Inn, 90
The Sea Lodge, 8, 80, 90
Sheraton Anaheim Hotel, 258–259
Sheraton San Diego Hotel & Marina, 97
Sommerset Suites Hotel, 75–76
Tamarack Beach Resort (Carlsbad), 239
USAHostels, 67

U.S. Grant Hotel, 69–70
Vagabond Inn–Hotel Circle, 80
The Village Inn, 96
Wave Crest (Del Mar), 233
Welk Resort Center (Escondido), 245
Westgate Hotel, 1, 71
W San Diego, 70–71

RESTAURANTS

Anaheim White House, 261
Anthony's Fishette, 190, 192
Arterra (Del Mar), 233–234
Atoll, 125
Azzura Point, 125, 126
Badlands Market & Cafe (Borrego Springs), 272
Baleen, 116, 118
Bay Beach Cafe, 125, 128
Bellefleur Winery & Restaurant (Carlsbad), 240–241
Berta's Latin American Restaurant, 114
Bertrand at Mr. A's, 125
Bread & Cie., 111
The Brigantine, 126–127
Brockton Villa, 8, 124, 125
Bully's Restaurant (Del Mar), 233
101 Cafe, 243
Cafe Japengo, 123
Cafe La Especial (Tijuana), 283
Café Lulu, 9, 106, 189, 224
Cafe Pacifica, 112–113
Cafe W, 107
Caffe Bella Italia, 118–119
California Cuisine, 108
Carlee's Place (Borrego Springs), 272
Carnitas Uruapan (Tijuana), 283
Casa de Bandini, 194
Casa de Pico, 194
Casa Guadalajara, 114, 115
Chart House (Oceanside), 243
Cheese Shop, 188
Chez Loma, 127
Chive, 103–104
Cien Años (Tijuana), 283
Citrus City Grille (Anaheim), 261
Clayton's Coffee Shop, 129
Corvette Diner, 111–112, 115, 224
The Cottage, 126
County Administration Center cafeteria, 190
Crescent Café, 209

Crest Café, 112, 224
Croce's, 224
Dakota Grill & Spirits, 8, 104
Delicias (Rancho
Santa Fe), 245
El Agave Tequileria, 9,
113–114
El Fandango, 194
Emerald Restaurant, 9,
129, 224
Epazote (Del Mar), 234
Extraordinary Desserts, 9,
110, 224
Fat City, 105
Felix Continental Cafe
(Anaheim), 261
Fidel's (Solana Beach), 240
Fidel's Norte (Carlsbad), 240
Fifth & Hawthorn, 111
Filippi's Pizza Grotto, 8,
9, 106, 115
Fish Market (Del Mar), 233
The Fish Market (San Diego),
105, 125, 192
Fresh, 1
Gargoyle Gallery and Café, 4
George's at the Cove,
120–121, 125
The Green Flash, 119
Hash House a Go Go, 107
High Tide Cafe, 119–120
Il Fornaio Cucina Italiana
(Del Mar), 233
Indigo Grill, 9, 104–105
Jake's Del Mar, 234
Jasmine, 129
Jolly Roger (Oceanside), 243
Julian Grille, 267–268
Jyoti Bihanga, 129
Kansas City Barbecue,
107, 224
Karl Strauss Brewery &
Grill, 106

Kendall's Cafe (Borrego
Springs), 272
Kensington Grill, 129
Kono's Surf Club Cafe, 116
Krazy Coyote Saloon & Grille
(Borrego Springs), 272
La Costa (Tijuana), 283
La Fonda (Mexico), 281
La Fonda de Roberto
(Tijuana), 283–284
Laurel, 9, 107–108
Living Room Coffeehouse, 4,
27, 114–115
Los Dos Pedros #1, 140
Los Dos Pedros #2, 140
Lou & Mickey's, 2
The Marine Room, 122, 125
Miguel's Cocina, 126
The Mission, 120
Mixx, 108
Monterey Bay Canners
(Oceanside), 243
Mrs. Burton's Tea Parlor, 112
Mrs. Knott's Chicken Dinner
Restaurant (Anaheim), 262
Neiman's (Carlsbad), 240
Nick's at the Beach, 224
Nine-Ten, 122
Ocean Terrace and George's
Bar, 125
Old Spaghetti Factory, 8,
107, 115
Old Town Mexican Café,
115, 197, 224
150 Grand Café
(Escondido), 245
Pacifica Del Mar, 233
Palace Bar, 188
Pamplemousse Grill
(Del Mar), 233
Pannikin, 4
Paquito's Mexican Food, 140
Parallel 33, 109–110
Peet's, 4

Peohe's, 125
Pizza Nova, 110
Poseidon (Del Mar), 233
Prado Restaurant, 202
Primavera Pastry Caffe, 129
Prince of Wales, 126
Qwiig's, 118, 125
Ramiro's, 140
Rancho El Nopal, 194
Red Fox Room, 224
Rhinoceros Cafe & Grill,
128–129
Roberto's Taco Shop, 140
Romano's Dodge House
(Julian), 268
Roppongi, 123–124
Rubio's, 9, 116
Ruby's (Oceanside), 241
Sammy's California
Woodfired Pizza, 9, 110
Saska's, 224
Siamese Basil
(Encinitas), 240
Spice & Rice Thai Kitchen,
125–126
Star of the Sea, 9, 102,
125, 190
Sushi Ota, 119
Taco Surf, 140
Tea Pavilion, 201
Thee Bungalow, 118
3rd Corner, 118
Thyme in the Ranch (Rancho
Santa Fe), 244–245
Top of the Cove,
122–123, 125
Top of the Market,
105, 125, 192
Trattoria Acqua, 124
Upstart Crow, 192
Vigilucci's (Encinitas), 240
Whole Foods, 107
Yacht Club, 193

Wickedly honest guides for sophisticated travelers—and those who want to be.

FROMMER'S® COMPLETE TRAVEL GUIDES

Alaska
Alaska Cruises & Ports of Call
Amsterdam
Argentina & Chile
Arizona
Atlanta
Australia
Austria
Bahamas
Barcelona, Madrid & Seville
Beijing
Belgium, Holland & Luxembourg
Bermuda
Boston
Brazil
British Columbia & the Canadian
    Rockies
Brussels & Bruges
Budapest & the Best of Hungary
California
Canada
Cancún, Cozumel & the Yucatán
Cape Cod, Nantucket & Martha's
    Vineyard
Caribbean
Caribbean Cruises & Ports of Call
Caribbean Ports of Call
Carolinas & Georgia
Chicago
China
Colorado
Costa Rica
Cuba
Denmark
Denver, Boulder & Colorado Springs
England
Europe
European Cruises & Ports of Call

Florida
France
Germany
Great Britain
Greece
Greek Islands
Hawaii
Hong Kong
Honolulu, Waikiki & Oahu
Ireland
Israel
Italy
Jamaica
Japan
Las Vegas
London
Los Angeles
Maryland & Delaware
Maui
Mexico
Montana & Wyoming
Montréal & Québec City
Munich & the Bavarian Alps
Nashville & Memphis
New England
New Mexico
New Orleans
New York City
New Zealand
Northern Italy
Norway
Nova Scotia, New Brunswick &
    Prince Edward Island
Oregon
Paris
Peru
Philadelphia & the Amish Country
Portugal

Prague & the Best of the Czech
    Republic
Provence & the Riviera
Puerto Rico
Rome
San Antonio & Austin
San Diego
San Francisco
Santa Fe, Taos & Albuquerque
Scandinavia
Scotland
Seattle & Portland
Shanghai
Sicily
Singapore & Malaysia
South Africa
South America
South Florida
South Pacific
Southeast Asia
Spain
Sweden
Switzerland
Texas
Thailand
Tokyo
Toronto
Tuscany & Umbria
USA
Utah
Vancouver & Victoria
Vermont, New Hampshire & Maine
Vienna & the Danube Valley
Virgin Islands
Virginia
Walt Disney World® & Orlando
Washington, D.C.
Washington State

FROMMER'S® DOLLAR-A-DAY GUIDES

Australia from $50 a Day
California from $70 a Day
England from $75 a Day
Europe from $70 a Day
Florida from $70 a Day
Hawaii from $80 a Day

Ireland from $60 a Day
Italy from $70 a Day
London from $85 a Day
New York from $90 a Day
Paris from $80 a Day

San Francisco from $70 a Day
Washington, D.C. from $80 a Day
Portable London from $85 a Day
Portable New York City from $90
    a Day

FROMMER'S® PORTABLE GUIDES

Acapulco, Ixtapa & Zihuatanejo
Amsterdam
Aruba
Australia's Great Barrier Reef
Bahamas
Berlin
Big Island of Hawaii
Boston
California Wine Country
Cancún
Cayman Islands
Charleston
Chicago
Disneyland®
Dublin
Florence

Frankfurt
Hong Kong
Houston
Las Vegas
Las Vegas for Non-Gamblers
London
Los Angeles
Los Cabos & Baja
Maine Coast
Maui
Miami
Nantucket & Martha's Vineyard
New Orleans
New York City
Paris
Phoenix & Scottsdale

Portland
Puerto Rico
Puerto Vallarta, Manzanillo &
    Guadalajara
Rio de Janeiro
San Diego
San Francisco
Savannah
Seattle
Sydney
Tampa & St. Petersburg
Vancouver
Venice
Virgin Islands
Washington, D.C.

FROMMER'S® NATIONAL PARK GUIDES

Banff & Jasper
Family Vacations in the National
    Parks

Grand Canyon
National Parks of the American West
Rocky Mountain

Yellowstone & Grand Teton
Yosemite & Sequoia/Kings Canyon
Zion & Bryce Canyon

FROMMER'S® MEMORABLE WALKS

Chicago
London

New York
Paris

San Francisco

FROMMER'S® WITH KIDS GUIDES

Chicago
Las Vegas
New York City

Ottawa
San Francisco
Toronto

Vancouver
Washington, D.C.

SUZY GERSHMAN'S BORN TO SHOP GUIDES

Born to Shop: France
Born to Shop: Hong Kong,
 Shanghai & Beijing

Born to Shop: Italy
Born to Shop: London

Born to Shop: New York
Born to Shop: Paris

FROMMER'S® IRREVERENT GUIDES

Amsterdam
Boston
Chicago
Las Vegas
London

Los Angeles
Manhattan
New Orleans
Paris
Rome

San Francisco
Seattle & Portland
Vancouver
Walt Disney World®
Washington, D.C.

FROMMER'S® BEST-LOVED DRIVING TOURS

Britain
California
Florida
France

Germany
Ireland
Italy
New England

Northern Italy
Scotland
Spain
Tuscany & Umbria

HANGING OUT™ GUIDES

Hanging Out in England
Hanging Out in Europe

Hanging Out in France
Hanging Out in Ireland

Hanging Out in Italy
Hanging Out in Spain

THE UNOFFICIAL GUIDES®

Bed & Breakfasts and Country
 Inns in:
 California
 Great Lakes States
 Mid-Atlantic
 New England
 Northwest
 Rockies
 Southeast
 Southwest
Best RV & Tent Campgrounds in:
 California & the West
 Florida & the Southeast
 Great Lakes States
 Mid-Atlantic
 Northeast
 Northwest & Central Plains

Southwest & South Central
 Plains
 U.S.A.
Beyond Disney
Branson, Missouri
California with Kids
Central Italy
Chicago
Cruises
Disneyland®
Florida with Kids
Golf Vacations in the Eastern U.S.
Great Smoky & Blue Ridge Region
Inside Disney
Hawaii
Las Vegas
London
Maui

Mexio's Best Beach Resorts
Mid-Atlantic with Kids
Mini Las Vegas
Mini-Mickey
New England & New York with
 Kids
New Orleans
New York City
Paris
San Francisco
Skiing & Snowboarding in the West
Southeast with Kids
Walt Disney World®
Walt Disney World® for
 Grown-ups
Walt Disney World® with Kids
Washington, D.C.
World's Best Diving Vacations

SPECIAL-INTEREST TITLES

Frommer's Adventure Guide to Australia &
 New Zealand
Frommer's Adventure Guide to Central America
Frommer's Adventure Guide to India & Pakistan
Frommer's Adventure Guide to South America
Frommer's Adventure Guide to Southeast Asia
Frommer's Adventure Guide to Southern Africa
Frommer's Britain's Best Bed & Breakfasts and
 Country Inns
Frommer's Caribbean Hideaways
Frommer's Exploring America by RV
Frommer's Fly Safe, Fly Smart

Frommer's France's Best Bed & Breakfasts and
 Country Inns
Frommer's Gay & Lesbian Europe
Frommer's Italy's Best Bed & Breakfasts and
 Country Inns
Frommer's Road Atlas Britain
Frommer's Road Atlas Europe
Frommer's Road Atlas France
The New York Times' Guide to Unforgettable
 Weekends
Places Rated Almanac
Retirement Places Rated
Rome Past & Present

Booked aisle seat.

Reserved room with a view.

With a queen – no, make that a king-size bed.